The Last Men Standing

The 8th Virginia Regiment in the American Revolution

Gabriel Neville

I0807159

Helion & Company

Helion & Company Limited
Unit 8 Amherst Business Centre
Budbrooke Road
Warwick
CV34 5WE
England
Tel. 01926 499619
Email: info@helion.co.uk
Website: www.helion.co.uk
X (formerly Twitter): @Helionbooks
Facebook: @HelionBooks
Visit our blog at http://blog.helion.co.uk/

Published by Helion & Company 2025
Designed and typeset by Mach 3 Solutions (www.mach3solutions.co.uk)
Cover designed by Paul Hewitt, Battlefield Design (www.battlefield-design.co.uk)

Text © Gabriel Neville 2025
Illustrations © as individually credited
Maps by George Anderson © Helion & Company 2025, and Gabriel Neville
Cover: Lafayette rallying troops of the 8th Virginia Regiment, by Frank Schoonover, 1921. VHS accession number: 1994 86.11 (Virginia Museum of History & Culture)

Every reasonable effort has been made to trace copyright holders and to obtain their permission for the use of copyright material. The author and publisher apologise for any errors or omissions in this work, and would be grateful if notified of any corrections that should be incorporated in future reprints or editions of this book.

ISBN 978-1-804516-72-0

British Library Cataloguing-in-Publication Data.
A catalogue record for this book is available from the British Library.

All rights reserved. No part of this publication may be reproduced, stored in a retrieval system, or transmitted, in any form, or by any means, electronic, mechanical, photocopying, recording or otherwise, without the express written consent of Helion & Company Limited.

For details of other military history titles published by Helion & Company Limited, contact the above address, or visit our website: http://www.helion.co.uk

We always welcome receiving book proposals from prospective authors.

Contents

Preface

It is almost true that this book was written on a dare. Years ago, I visited the now-closed David Library of the American Revolution to see what I could learn about the 8th Virginia Regiment. I spent two hours searching the card catalogue and browsing the stacks. When closing time came, the librarian pleasantly asked me how I had made out. I shrugged my shoulders and said, 'There doesn't seem to be much out there.' He looked at me closely, as if to discern how serious my interest was. 'There's a lot out there,' he said, 'you just have to find it.'

He was absolutely correct, but this book was nevertheless considered impossible to write for a very long time. In 1848, Pennsylvania Congressman Henry A. Muhlenberg saw his biography of his famous great uncle as a final chance to 'rescue the memory of the great and good men who achieved our independence from that oblivion into which it is fast falling.' Most Continental veterans had no such advocates, and their stories did fall into a historical void. Joseph Addison Waddell declared in a 1902 history of Augusta County, Virginia that it was 'impossible to obtain any list or particular account of troops furnished by Augusta County during the Revolutionary War.' In 1943, Shenandoah Valley historian John Walter Wayland asserted that 'no muster roll of the regiment has been preserved,' and other than a handful of officers, we 'know only a few of its members.'

In fact, we have nearly complete lists and Captain Jonathan Clark kept a diary every single day of the war. The diary has been broadly ignored because its entries are infuriatingly terse. But it is like a Rosetta Stone for a history of Clark's own regiment, as long as one knows knows how to make sense of it. Two other 8th Virginia soldiers, a sergeant and a commissioned officer, kept more colourful diaries for parts of the war. A surviving list of messes in Captain William Croghan's company tells us which soldiers brought their wives with them and reveals that an unaccompanied eight-year-old boy came along as well. The descendants of Heinrich Meier preserved what might be the only surviving letter home to Mom and Dad from an enlisted Continental soldier. There are muster rolls, pay rolls, orders, and correspondence. There are hundreds of individual data points to be found in newspapers, local histories, court records, financial records, maps, archives, museums, petitions, pension applications, and private collections. I have done my best to look at them all, though I suppose there might be more to find.

This book is the product of years of indulging in digressions and obsessing over minutia, always in pursuit of a coherent whole. In Henry A. Muhlenberg's terms, much that follows is a story rescued from oblivion. The last man capable of providing an authoritative history of the regiment from memory, Colonel Abraham Bowman, died in 1837. Recovering the story was like putting together a big jigsaw puzzle: many data points were indecipherable without their adjoining pieces. Yet, as the picture came together, it became easier to understand what

I was seeing and to know where the next pieces belonged. Mechanically, this was done by breaking pay and muster rolls into thousands of discrete data points and similarly isolating narrative elements from pension applications and other sources. Learning along the way and using the diaries and other documents as guides, I reassembled the fractured pieces. This allowed me to make connections; correct date, nomenclature, and sequence errors made by aged veterans; and understand much that what was previously unintelligible. Less mechanically, I learned as much as I could about the places the regiment's soldiers came from, the communities they established after the war, and life in eighteenth century Virginia. I think of the chapters that follow as a 'collective biography' of one regiment's men. My goal was to discover more than just their movements and actions in the war. If I have succeeded, the reader will also learn who they were, why they fought, and how their lives still matter.

My puzzle pieces produced an image of the American War for Independence that is in some ways familiar but in others grown strange. The 8th Virginia's career fills in many of the spaces left blank by the Yankee-centric version of the Revolution that has dominated American memory since its Centennial, which came in the wake of the Civil War. These men were not the great-grandchildren of Puritans or even of the Jamestown settlers. They were the sons of recent immigrants. They were Western men in a colony with a large and active western front: the Quebec Act and the Proclamation of 1763 bothered these men more than the tax on tea. Many 8th Virginia men were already fighting the Shawnee on the banks of the Ohio when the First Continental Congress convened.

Viewing the American Revolution from the perspective of one regiment brings neglected episodes to the surface and sheds new light on what is familiar. Why was Charleston's celebration of the Declaration of Independence the most spectacular in all the colonies? What were Continental skirmishers doing on the east side of the Delaware in the days before the attack on Trenton? Just how did an entire regiment, and part of another, manage to get captured at the Battle of Germantown? What exactly did George Washington say to Charles Lee at Monmouth? Did 'Light Horse Harry' Lee steal the credit for the raid on Paulus Hook? The soldiers of the 8th Virginia provide new or more specific answers to these and many other questions.

Readers should pay close attention to the 8th Virginia's captains. They represent the regiment's geography and its organisation. It was the captains' job, each with three inferior or 'subaltern' officers, to recruit the 8th Virginia's soldiers. Consequently, each company was a tight-knit collection of friends, family members, and neighbours, mostly young men between the ages of 18 and 22.

Like any complete biography, the story begins with a baby and ends with an old person. Chapters 1 and 2 serve as a prologue in which we first meet these soldiers as boys on the frontier. The war narrative runs from chapters 3 through 15. Chapters 16 and 17 are an epilogue that records our veterans' contributions to the new nation and their final years of life. Some names, like Jonathan Clark's, appear frequently. Others are mentioned only once. Together, they tell the story of 1,047 men from Virginia's west who served in nearly every theatre of the war, from Canada to Georgia, and from the Atlantic to the Mississippi. *The Last Men Standing* is written from the soldiers' perspective. No effort is made to tell both sides of the story or to analyse strategy in detail. Battles are described from the viewpoint of the men holding the weapons wherever they stood in the field. Enough context is provided for the reader to make sense of it, but not much more.

Some of the best first-hand accounts were written by barely literate men. I have limited clarifying edits to punctuation, capitalisation, and a few explanations in brackets. Edits are always disclosed in a footnote. Many accounts were also written in the third person, which will seem odd to the reader. Pension applicants verbally described their service to court clerks who did the writing. Petitions were drafted in the third person as a matter of formality.

Peter Muhlenberg, the Fighting Parson, is without question the most famous soldier of the 8th Virginia. I have not let his oft-told story overshadow the history of his regiment. The recruits Muhlenberg was appointed to lead were a particular kind of men. Most were children of north Irish and west German immigrants recently settled in Virginia's vast western territory from what is now East Tennessee all the way north to Pittsburgh. Half of the regiment's men lived in the Shenandoah Valley or the greater Valley of Virginia that runs between the Blue Ridge and the Appalachian Mountains. Most of the others were true frontiersmen who came from even farther west. Just one company formed in a county east of the Blue Ridge. Until 1777, every 8th Virginia soldier carried a rifle. He wore buckskin breeches, shoes or moccasins, and a fringed hunting shirt dyed brown with walnut husks.

Understanding history requires a certain amount of forgetting. The men of the 8th Virginia Regiment lived in a time when trees were bigger, nights were darker, and winters were colder than they are today. There was no noise pollution, and cannons could be heard almost a hundred miles away. No one had any expectation of social equality, though wartime military service offered a rare chance for a man to rise above his station. Slavery was unquestioned by those not subject to it. Native warriors were regarded as savages, and the notion that a woman or a man with no property had a right to vote was not even considered. In a continent without banks or stock markets, land was the only meaningful form of wealth. Men took great risks to acquire enough of it to achieve financial independence and the status of a gentleman. British currency was not yet decimalised. It was counted in pounds, shillings (20 to a pound), and pence (12 to a shilling). The symbols '£', 's', and 'd' were used for the three denominations, respectively, though £5 4s 2d might also be styled '£5/4/2.' When a Virginian spoke of his 'country,' he always meant the Old Dominion. Until 1781, the 'United States' was little more than an alliance.

Political geography has changed: State lines have been redrawn, new states have been created, and counties have been divided. The Virginia of 1776 is now eight different states and bits of three others. Dunmore County is now 'Shenandoah County,' and Fincastle County no longer exists. Language and culture have also changed, but I adhere to the terminology the soldiers used. Filters only make it harder to understand what time has already made distant. Though some 8th Virginia men were bilingual, Siouan and Algonquian names were unpronounceable to most English speakers. For this reason, Indians frequently took descriptive English names such as The Cornstalk, Dragging Canoe, or the Grenadier Squaw. I have seen no evidence that these names were applied disrespectfully. In some cases, they were chosen by the Indians themselves or given by their parents. The 'Big Knife' was a Shawnee term for Virginia governors that was also applied to the governors' people (Virginians), but always in the singular. Our protagonists are also called 'Whigs' (the opposite of 'Tories'), 'shirtmen' (for their fringed hunting shirts), 'Cohees' (Virginia slang, roughly equivalent to 'redneck'), 'regulars' (full-time troops), and 'Patriots' (a term more commonly used in the north).

In 1776, Virginia's regiments had 10 companies each. 'Battalion' was usually synonymous with 'regiment.' Four or five regiments made a brigade, and two or three brigades made a division. Companies were commanded by captains, regiments by colonels, brigades by brigadier generals, and divisions by major generals. George Washington's rank was simply 'general.' 'Private' was not yet a rank but rather a term that contrasted with an officer's (public) commission. Most regiments were numbered, but companies were known by their captains' names. 'Line' was a collective term for military units authorised by a particular authority. 'The Continental Line' referred only to those units organised by Congress independent of colonial or state authority. 'The Virginia Line' included units raised by Virginia generally, while 'The Virginia Continental Line' meant only those units raised by Virginia for Continental service. There was also a 'Virginia State Line' (originally 'Provincial') led by officers whose commissions were signed by the governor for in-state service. Virginians also served in militia, Minute, and volunteer organisations, each with different rules and supervising authorities. The 8th Virginia began as a provincial regiment.

Most Revolutionary War histories are about statesmen, generals, campaigns, or battles. *The Last Men Standing* is the story of regular men in irregular circumstances striving to find opportunities for themselves. In the process, they developed America's culture of westward-bound pioneers. Log cabins, lawless frontier towns, fringed shirts, Pennsylvania rifles, long migration trails, Conestoga wagons, Indian fighting, property claim disputes, duelling, and buffalo hunting were all features of life beyond the Blue Ridge that are still symbols of the American West. In this way, the men (and women) of the 8th Virginia regiment were the first generation of the America we know.

Thanks are owed to many more people than I can remember. Leon Harris and Will Graves, who have transcribed thousands of documents, deserve more praise than they will ever receive. Others who helped me in distinct but important ways include Barbara Adamson, Chris Anders, Nic Butler, Michael Cecere, Gary Ecelbarger, David Ervin, Rod Graves, Pat Hannum, Jim Holmberg, Zach Hottel, Neal Hurst, Eric Jenkins, Doug MacIntyre, Mark Maloy, April Martin, Lisa Minardi, Kristoffer Neville, Rob Orrison, Gene Procknow, Charles Reid, Jamie Rife, Jane Rissler, Robert Selig, Eric Sterner, Tim Taylor, Glenn Williams, and Patricia Zajic. Particular thanks are due to Rob Griffith for making this book much better than I could have managed on my own and to George Anderson for his patience with me and his excellent maps. Most of all, I want to thank my wife, Eileen, and my sons, Sam and Michael, for their constant encouragement and unbelievable support.

1

Boys

Enlisted Soldier Meshack Pearson. On 8 March 1754, 24-year-old Sally Pearson gave birth to triplets in Culpeper County, Virginia. The new mother and her surprised husband chose names for their boys from a story in the Book of Daniel: Three men named Shadrack, Meshack, and Abednego were ordered to bow before a golden idol created by King Nebuchadnezzar of Babylon. Though Jews, they, like Daniel, held positions of responsibility, and the king required their obedience. They stubbornly refused to kneel, and the monarch had them thrown into a fiery furnace. The young men were miraculously unharmed. 'Lo,' shouted the astounded King. 'I see four men loose, walking in the midst of the fire, and they have no hurt; and the form of the fourth is like the Son of God.'[1] Like his biblical namesake, Meshack Pearson grew up to defy a king, and prevailed.

Major Peter Helphenstine. If you called Peter Helphenstine a 'cobbler' he would have been offended. He was a *shoemaker* or a *cordwainer*, and the distinction mattered. He arrived in the New World in 1754 with a valuable skill that allowed him to succeed in his new life.[2] Shoes were as necessary then as they are today. A person who could not afford a new pair might go to a cobbler to fix an old one, but that was a different profession entirely.

Like thousands before them, Peter, his wife Catherine, and their one-year-old son Philip floated down the Rhine from contested and war-torn southwestern Germany through Cologne and Dusseldorf to the Dutch coast. They boarded the *Recovery* at Rotterdam, laid over at Cowes on the Isle of Wight, and sailed for America.[3] The little family disembarked at Wilmington, Delaware, on 23 October 1754.

The Helphenstines were not precisely 'German' because there was no such country yet. Peter, the head of the family, was identified on the passenger list at Wilmington as a 'Palatine.' This meant he was from the Electorate of the Palatinate, a Lutheran territory of the centuries-old Holy Roman Empire ruled by the Count Palatine of the Rhine. The empire was a hodgepodge of mostly German-speaking territories ruled by counts, dukes, margraves, princes, bishops, and abbots that ranged in size from the powerful Kingdom of Prussia

1 Daniel, 3:25 (KJV).

2 Ralph Beaver Strassburger (ed.), *Pennsylvanian German Pioneers: A Publication of the Original Lists of Arrivals in the Port of Philadelphia from 1727 to 1808* (Norristown: Pennsylvania German Society, 1934), vol.1, pp.659–660.

3 Strassburger, *German Pioneers*, vol.1, pp.659–660.

to small estates owned by knights. The Palatinate straddled the Rhine and had suffered greatly during the Thirty Years War (1618–1648) and later wars that pitted Catholic France against Protestant German principalities.

Many Palatines fled to England, where co-regents William III and Mary II saw their government as a bulwark of Protestant liberty locked in a contest with the arbitrary rulers of Catholic France and Spain.[4] William Penn promoted his colony to the refugees and created the borough of Germantown for them north of Philadelphia in 1683. Palatines came in increasing numbers, extending their settlements westward into central Pennsylvania and beyond. Migrants travelled on the Great Philadelphia Wagon Road, usually on foot with a packhorse. When the Helphenstines arrived in America, they took this road through Chester, Lancaster, and York Counties into the Cumberland Valley, where it turned south and continued through Maryland, across the Potomac River, and into Virginia.[5]

Curieuſe Nachricht
von
PENSYLVANIA
in
Norden=America
Welche/
Auf Begehren guter Freunde/
Uber vorgelegte 103. Fragen/ bey ſeiner Abreiß aus Teutſchland nach obigem Lande Anno 1700. ertheilet/ und nun Anno 1702 in den Druck gegeben worden.
Von
Daniel Falknern/ Profeſſore, Burgern und Pilgrim allda.

Franckfurt und Leipzig/
Zu finden bey Andreas Otto/ Buchhändlern.
Im Jahr Christi 1702.

The title page of a guidebook published in 1702 by Daniel Falckner promoting Palatine emigration to America. The book answered 103 questions about how to make the journey and settle in Pennsylvania. (Facsimile from S.W. Pennypacker, *The Settlement of Germantown*)

The Helphenstines' destination was Winchester, the county seat of Frederick County in the lower (northern) Shenandoah Valley. The rough frontier town's 60 houses were made of squared logs, many still without weatherboarding or glass windows.[6] Though exposed

4 Thomas Babington Macaulay, *The History of England from the Accession of James II* (Philadelphia: E.H. Butler & Co, 1856), vol.3, p.97; 'Coronation Oath Act 1688,' <legislation.gov.uk/aep/WillandMar/1/6/section/III>, accessed 14 Aug. 2022; John A. Lynn, *The Wars of Louis XIV: 1677-1714* (Harlow: Pearson Education, 1999), pp.308, 357.

5 Parke Rouse, Jr., *The Great Wagon Road: from Philadelphia to the South* (New York: McGraw-Hill, 1973), pp.21–42; Warren R. Hofstra, 'The Colonial Road', in Warren R. Hofstra and Karl Raitz, (eds), *The Great Valley Road of Virginia: Shenandoah Landscapes from Prehistory to the Present* (Charlottesville: University of Virginia Press, 2010), pp.79–107.

6 Adelaide Fries (trans.), 'Travel Diary of the First Company of Single Brethren Going to North Carolina, 1753,' in Newton D. Mereness (ed.), *Travels in the American Colonies* (New York: MacMillan,

and small, Winchester was strategically situated and on the cusp of a boom. About the time Peter and Catherine arrived, a stream of clattering wagons and marching soldiers came through town from lower Virginia on their way to their staging point at Fort Cumberland in western Maryland. Major General Edward Braddock had come from England to oust the French from their fort at the forks of the Ohio River. Winchester was the last settlement of any consequence on the way.[7]

Braddock's unexpected defeat on 9 July 1755 was a disaster on many levels, but it was very good for Winchester. The military road cut by Braddock's army across the Wagon Road in Frederick County created the most important intersection in frontier Virginia. George Washington, commanding the Virginia Regiment of provincial regulars, returned in 1756 to oversee the colony's northwest defences. He built Fort Loudoun on the north side of town and made it his headquarters. To the west, ranger companies patrolled along a chain of smaller forts in the wilderness.[8]

Winchester's population doubled during the years of the French and Indian War.[9] Among other things, that meant twice as many people buying shoes.[10] The Helphenstines prospered and used some of their resources to underwrite a solid stone Lutheran church building on the east side of town.[11] With Peter's status came a militia commission, and he led troops against the Shawnee with Angus McDonald at Wapatomika in 1774.[12] Then, 20 years after his arrival in Virginia, he was asked to serve as a field officer in Virginia's eighth provincial regiment.

Lieutenant Robert Higgins. Twelve-year-old Robert Higgins lived with his family 50 miles west of Winchester on the South Fork of the South Branch of the Potomac River.[13] They called the South Branch *Wappatomaka*, as the Indians did. Many of the South Branch families came from New York and New Jersey and bore Dutch names like Westfall, Vanmeter, Vanpelt, and Kuykendall. Robert's mother was a Vanzant. The long ridge of the Great North Mountain rose like a wall between the South Fork community and the Shenandoah Valley. It was sometimes called 'The Devil's Backbone.' There were no towns or roads on the South Branch, just isolated clearings, narrow horse paths, and

1916), p.334; Anon., 'The Journal of Captain Robert Cholmly's Batman' in Charles Hamilton (ed.), *Braddock's Defeat* (Norman: University of Oklahoma Press, 1959), p.36.

7 W.W. Abbot et al (eds), *The Papers of George Washington*, Colonial Series (Charlottesville: University Press of Virginia, 1983–1995), vol.1, pp.262–264; David Preston, *Braddock's Defeat: The Battle of Monongahela and the Road to Revolution* (Oxford: Oxford University Press, 2015), pp.102–103; Christopher E. Hendricks, *The Backcountry Towns of Colonial Virginia* (Knoxville: University of Tennessee Press, 2006), pp.88–95.

8 Samuel Kercheval, *A History of the Valley of Virginia*, 3rd edition (1902; reprinted Bowie, Md.: Heritage Books, 2001), p.67.

9 Hendricks, *Backcountry Towns*, p.93.

10 Library of Congress (LOC): George Washington Papers, Ser.5, Financial Papers: Virginia Military Accounts: Ledger, September 1755-December 1758; Abbot et al (eds), *Papers of Washington* (Colonial), vol.3, pp.387–391.

11 Edith Helphenstine Wayman and L. Cleo Mullins, *The Helphinstine Family in America: Major Peter Helphinstine of Winchester, Virginia, 1724–1778* (Richmond: E.H. Wayman and L.C. Mullins, 1988), pp.34–35.

12 Flora McDonald Williams, *The Glengarry McDonalds of Virginia* (Louisville: Geo. G. Fetter, 1911), p.50.

13 Kercheval, *History*, p.91.

An 1850 depiction of a frontier homestead shows a cabin surrounded by coppice and split-rail fencing with cattle, pigs, a small garden, and a clearing almost ready for agriculture. (Orsamus Turner, *Pioneer History of the Holland Purchase of Western New York*, courtesy of HathiTrust)

the creeks and rivers that ran between the ridges. Fat, centuries-old oaks and chestnuts dominated the wilderness.[14] Clearings known as 'Indian meadows' or 'old fields,' vestiges of an earlier time, occasionally interrupted the otherwise endless forest.[15] The West was a dangerous place to live, but brave people like the Higginses and Westfalls, who wanted to be self-sufficient, took the risk.

A tidal wave of violence washed over the frontier after Braddock's Defeat, but the bloodshed had begun on the upper Potomac before Braddock's army set out. Homesteads were burned by Native warriors who scalped and killed fathers, abducted mothers, and 'adopted' captured children into their own families. Nine-year-old Isaac Zane was taken in 1753 and never came home. Robert Higgins was Isaac's age and knew he might be next if he was not careful. In the spring of 1756, two 50-man war parties, reportedly accompanied by a French officer, crossed the Appalachian Mountains and attacked settlements on the Cacapon River. From there, the war parties broke up into smaller groups as they worked their way east, attacking cabins and killing settlers as they went.[16]

14 Edward K. Faison and David R. Foster, 'Did American Chestnut Really Dominate the Eastern Forest?', *Arnoldia*, 72:2 (2014), pp.18–32; Eric Rutkow, American Canopy: Trees, Forests, and the Making of a Nation (New York: Scribner, 2012), p.211.

15 David Sibray, 'Ancient West Virginia forests once a mosaic of landscapes', *West Virginia Explorer*, January 22, 2022.

16 Kercheval, *History*, pp.69–71, 84.

For safety, terrified pioneer families relied on community 'forts' that were usually just stockaded homes or cabins with strong doors and small windows. Many sought safety in numbers, giving birth to towns such as Mecklenburg (Shepherdstown), Stoverstown (Strasburg), Muellerstadt (Millerstown, Woodstock), and Romney.[17] Colonel Washington's primary mission at Fort Loudoun was to keep settlers in their homes. Their presence gave credence to Britain's and Virginia's claim to the territory. Washington first built two military posts on Patterson's Creek, south of Fort Cumberland. Then he sent Captain Andrew Waggener to the South Branch with 70 men to build two more. Robert Higgins' father likely helped build the fourth of these, Fort Pleasant, in an 'Indian old field.'[18]

Fort Pleasant was stronger than the community forts and blockhouses, but the visibility provided by the clearing had taken priority over access to fresh water. Soon after its construction in the spring of 1756, the Higginses forted up with their neighbours while Indian warriors lurked outside. When it seemed safe, Robert's mother gave him a bucket and directed him to run to the nearest spring. The stream was just a quarter of a mile away, but he knew the danger and asked a friend to come with him. They crept out of the fort, moved cautiously to the water, and filled their pail. They sprinted back, water sloshing about as they ran. Robert was the faster of the two and got 30 yards ahead of his companion. Halfway to the fort, he heard a panicked scream and knew his friend had been taken. Too young and slight for heroics, Robert just ran faster.[19]

The Indians, mostly Shawnee and Delaware, were familiar adversaries. Robert and his brother Peter probably knew the Delaware chief Bemino, who used the English name John Killbuck. Killbuck spoke English and lived among the upper Potomac settlers before the war. Any old trust or friendship was now gone. Killbuck led a band of warriors into the valley in 1756, and it was probably they who captured Robert's friend. Killbuck also used his knowledge of the community to lure 18 men from Fort Pleasant into an ambush at the river that is remembered as the Battle of the Trough. Seven settlers were killed.[20]

Thousands of pioneer children of Robert Higgins' generation spent their formative years in fear. Washington described the Western settlers as 'terrified beyond expression.'[21] Men were tortured, scalped, and dismembered. Captives were killed if they could not walk fast enough. Babies' brains were bashed out on trees, and severed heads were stuck on posts.[22] Two decades after this horror, Robert and Peter became officers in the 8th Virginia Regiment. After the war, Robert and many of his peers ventured west to Kentucky and Ohio. Their childhood experiences loomed large over the rest of their lives.

Lieutenant James Curry. Back in the Old World, James Curry boarded the *Good Return* at Belfast in 1762 with his parents, his brother, three sisters and an assortment of aunts, uncles, and cousins. They were part of a decades-long exodus of America-bound Irish Presbyterians. James was the oldest child and had begun training for the ministry. He was only 10 years old but had already been fitted for a clerical wig.[23]

17 Hendricks, *Backcountry Towns*, pp.100–101, 106, 108.
18 Abbot et al (eds), *Papers of Washington* (Colonial), vol.2, pp.263–266, vol.4, pp.10–11.
19 Kercheval, *History*, pp.91.
20 Kercheval, *History*, pp.72–74, 80–81.
21 Abbot et al (eds), *Papers of Washington* (Colonial), vol.4, pp.419–421.
22 Kercheval, *History*, pp.69–108.
23 Pliny A. Durant, *The History of Union County, Ohio* (Chicago: W.H. Beers, 1883), p.294.

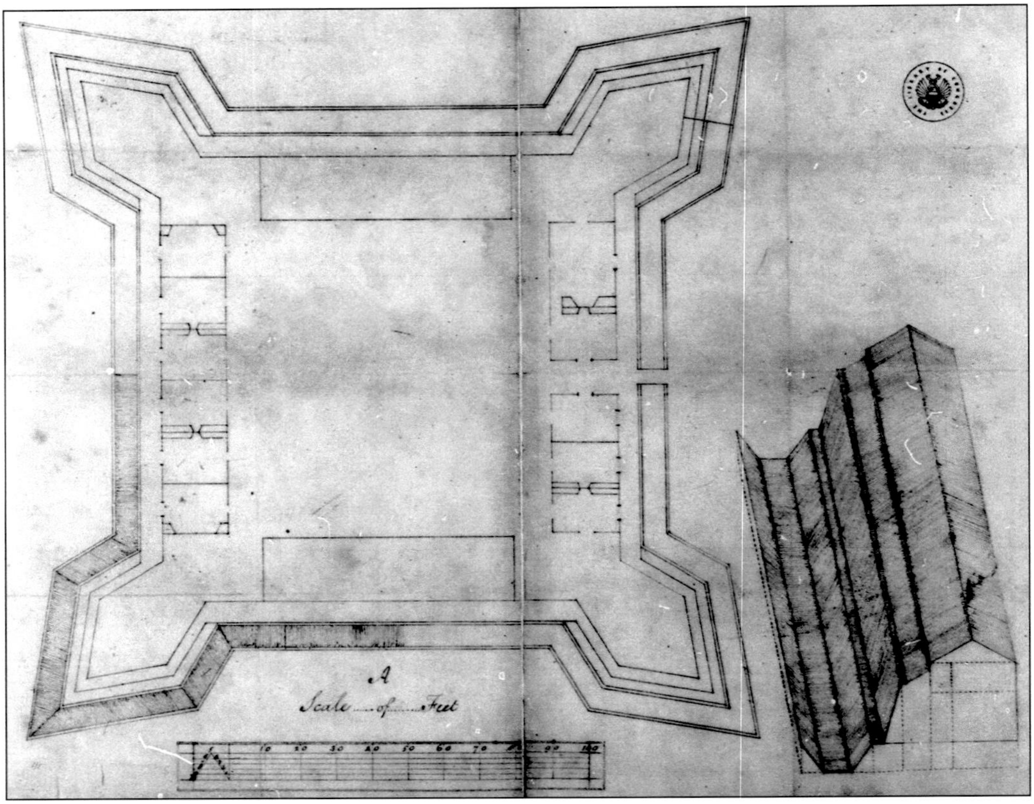

Fort Pleasant was built according to this design provided by Colonel George Washington. (Library of Congress)

The ship sailed out of Belfast Lough with the shore of County Antrim, the Currys' old home, passing by on their left. They watched from the deck as the town of Carrickfergus and its ancient Norman castle shrank into the distance behind them. Conn O'Neill's escape from that castle in 1607 marked the beginning of the Ulster Plantation.[24] Thus, the Virginia and Ulster colonies began at the same time and were overseen by many of the same men. The twin projects were strictly and pointedly Protestant, intended to counter the power of Spain.[25] Ireland's Catholics might have joined the migration, but that was not allowed.[26]

24 George Hill (ed.), *The Montgomery Manuscripts: 1603–1706 Compiled from Family Papers by William Montgomery of Rosemont, Esquire* (Belfast: Archer and Sons, 1869), pp.16–47.

25 Nicholas Canny, *Making Ireland British: 1580–1650* (Oxford: Oxford University Press, 2001), p.198; James E. Doan, '"An Island in the Virginian Sea": Native Americans and the Irish in English Discourse, 1585–1640', *New Hibernia Review* 1:1 (1997), pp.79–99; Arthur Young, *A Tour In Ireland, 1776–1779* (New York: Cassell & Company, 1887), 169–170; Rouse, *Wagon Road*, p.30.

26 Michael D. Breidenbach, *Our Dear-Bought Liberty: Catholics and Religious Toleration in Early America* (Cambridge: Harvard University Press, 2021), pp.48, 65, 162.

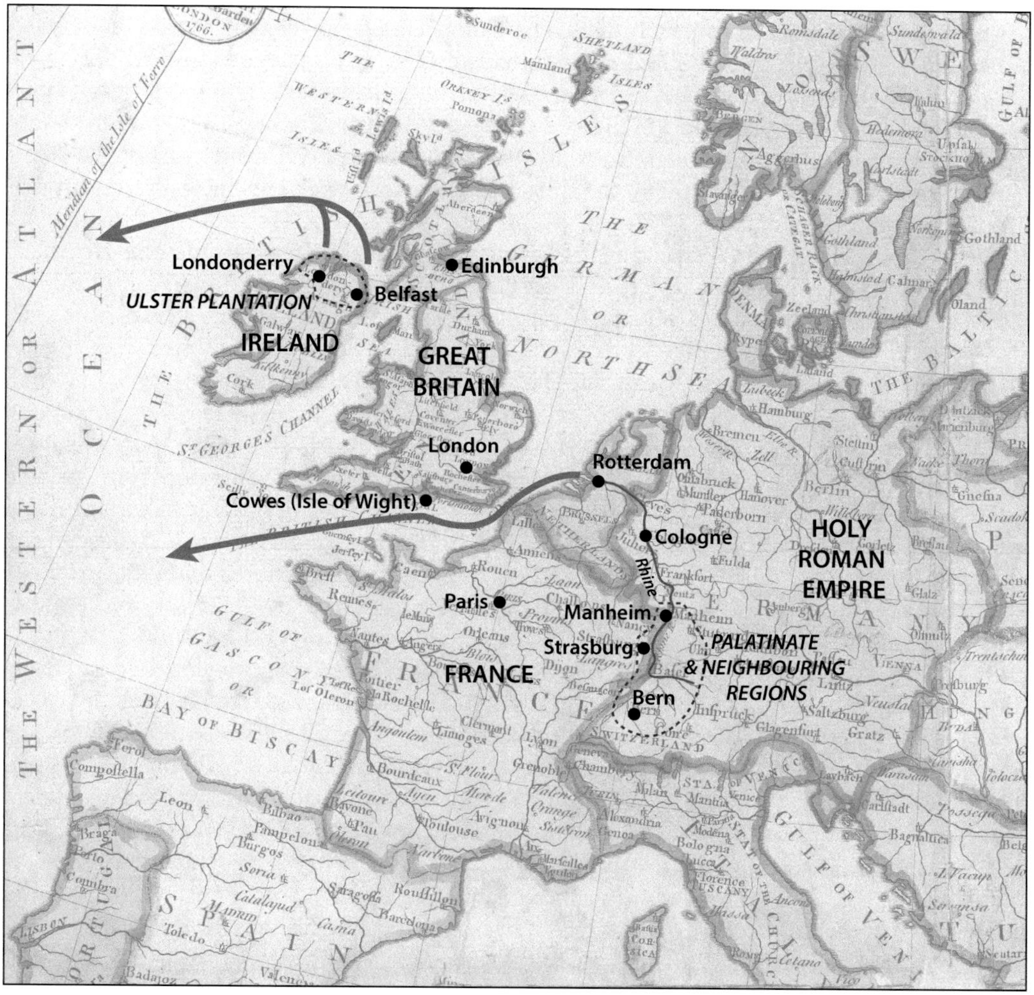

Eighteenth Century Ulster Scots & Palatine emigration to Pennsylvania, drawn on a 1766 map by J. Spillsbury.

The Scotch-Irish or 'Ulster Scots' were fiercely Protestant and fought for William and Mary during the Williamite War from 1689 to 1691. Despite exceptional service opposing ousted (and Catholic) James II at Londonderry, Presbyterians were treated poorly after the war. A ruling class of Anglicans known as the Protestant Ascendancy came to dominate Irish society. Laws enacted to suppress Catholicism hurt Protestant nonconformists as well. Like the Palatines, the unhappy Ulster Scots began to leave for America in numbers that grew larger every year.[27]

27 Kenneth W. Keller, 'The Origins of Ulster Scots Emigration to America: A Survey of Recent Research,' *American Presbyterians*, 70:2 (1992), p.75.

The *Good Return* was reputed to be a fast sailer. It had once made it from Belfast to America in five weeks, but she had no such luck this time. Overloaded and facing headwinds, the ship took 15 long weeks to cross the Atlantic. Its passengers ran out of food and drinkable water. Illness spread among the travellers, and the situation grew increasingly dire. One by one, dead bodies were tipped overboard with a prayer until most of the ship's passengers and crew were gone. Young James watched every one of his four siblings tumble limply into the water.

At last, the beleaguered vessel and its distressed occupants turned into the Delaware Bay and came to Philadelphia. James and his parents disembarked with their hopes for the family already crushed. Still, a new life lay before them.[28]

Lieutenant Colonel Abraham Bowman. The Bowman family lived on prime land on Cedar Creek, 20 miles south of Winchester.[29] They had a mill and a large house that sometimes served as a refuge and came to be known as Fort Bowman. Abraham Bowman was only six years old when the shock of Braddock's defeat swept across the frontier. Younger and safer than Robert Higgins, he was probably less aware of the French and Indian War's intense violence. As he entered his teens, he lived in relative security, surrounded by many brothers, sisters, and cousins. His grandfather, Jost Hite, had brought the first large group of Pennsylvania Germans into the Shenandoah Valley in 1732. Fort Bowman sat on the south side of a bend in the Great Wagon Road, a little north of Strasburg. Cedar Creek's wide loops found their way to the North Fork of the Shenandoah River about a mile downstream from the house. Their neighbours, the Miller family, lived beyond the road to the west.[30]

The French and Indian War ended with a European treaty in 1763, but a new Indian offensive known as Pontiac's War began the same year.[31] Abraham, his family, and their neighbours forted up one day in response to an alarm. The Millers came, as did newlyweds John and Rachel Dellinger, who lived at the edge of Strasburg. Rachel was or would soon be pregnant with their first child. Among the others present was a local scoundrel named Abraham Mitchell. He was caught in 'a petty act of theft' and tied to a post, a punishment that George Miller and John Dellinger carried out. When the alarm ended, an angry and humiliated Mitchell left the Bowman home scheming for revenge.[32]

A year later, the Millers went out to their field to sow flaxseed in the morning of what began as a normal day. Two of their children helped while a young daughter, sick in bed, watched from a window. Abraham Bowman, now 15, rode by this idyllic scene on his way back from an errand. Minutes later, Mitchell rushed out of the forest and attacked the family with a gang of eight Indians. Everyone in the field was butchered while the sick girl watched in horror from her window. Terrified, the Millers' daughter fled through a rear window

28 Durant, *Union County*, p.294.

29 John W. Wayland, *The Bowmans: A Pioneering Family of Virginia, Kentucky, and the Northwest Territory* (1943; reprinted Harrisonburg: C.J. Carrier, 1974), pp.3–4.

30 Kercheval, *History*, p.82.

31 David Dixon, *Never Come to Peace Again: Pontiac's Uprising and the Fate of the British Empire in North America* (Norman: University of Oklahoma Press, 2005), p.xiii.

32 Kercheval, *History*, pp.99–100; John Walter Wayland, *A History of Shenandoah County, Virginia*, 2nd ed. (1969; reprinted Baltimore: Genealogical Publishing, 1980), p.161.

and eventually found the teenage Bowman. Sceptical at first, he armed himself and galloped off to see what had happened. The scene he found was shocking. The Millers were writhing in pools of blood that still pulsed from their wounds. Nothing could be done for them. Approaching the house, Bowman and another neighbour found that the already gruesome scene had been diabolically festooned. The family Bible, a large, illustrated German edition, had been randomly opened to Second Samuel, placed on the door sill, and set on fire. The family's murdered cat lay on top of the burning tome.[33]

A burned page from the Miller Family Bible. (Author's photo)

Mitchell's gang also attacked John and Rachel Dellinger's house, killing John and taking Rachel captive with her infant son. The outlaws fled west across the Cacapon River, pursued by a rescue party that may have included Abraham Bowman. The baby, who was 'stout, and heavy', became a burden to the attackers, so they beat his brains out against a tree trunk and continued on. The posse caught up with them close to Fort Pleasant, opened fire, and killed one of the Indians. Mitchell and the others fled, leaving Rachel Dellinger behind, traumatised. It was she who identified the villainous Mitchell to her rescuers.[34]

These murders occurred in 1765, nearly a decade after Higgins' flight from the spring and another decade before Bowman became lieutenant colonel of the 8th Virginia Regiment. The Miller family Bible survives in the collection of a local museum. Its burned pages are a potent reminder of the lasting terrors experienced by thousands in Virginia's colonial west.

33 Kercheval, *History*, p.104.
34 Kercheval, *History*, pp.99–100.

Colonel Peter Muhlenberg. In 1766, 19-year-old Peter Muhlenberg was far from home and miserable. He was an apprentice in Lübeck, an independent city of the Holy Roman Empire on the Baltic coast near Denmark. His strict but caring father, the Reverend Heinrich (Henry) Muhlenberg, had sent him there from Pennsylvania to learn a trade and to keep him out of trouble. Peter's two younger brothers were also in the Old Country, studying for the Lutheran ministry 200 miles away at Halle. Peter was less studious than his siblings and had entered a six-year apprenticeship with a 'druggist, merchant, and tradesman' from whom he expected to learn practical business skills.[35] To his disappointment, however, he was allowed to do little more than 'pour out a glass of brandy and to sell a little tea, sugar, etc.' The shop was open to the elements, and he stood freezing at the counter through the long Baltic winters. Peter suffered quietly for two years before he began to complain. '[T]here is not much to be learned in a grocery store,' he wrote in a letter, 'and … when I had been here four weeks, I knew as much as I do now … it seems to me very hard that I must sacrifice six of the best years of my life without learning anything.'[36]

His father, the patriarch of the German Lutheran Church in America, paid Peter's master to shorten the apprenticeship.[37] But when a chance arose to go home immediately, Peter took it. During the French and Indian War, Britain formed the 60th (Royal American) Regiment, a unit intended to 'combine the characteristics of a Colonial Corps with those of a Foreign Legion.' A third of its officers were 'foreign Protestants', mostly Germans and Swiss, and most of its rank and file were German speakers recruited in America.[38] On 14 August 1766, Peter left a note for his master confessing, 'I have enlisted as cadet among the Englishmen, who are going into garrison in America.' The opportunity could not have been more perfect. A cadet was an officer-in-training. He could remain with the Royal Americans for as long as it took to reach America and then simply resign. He sailed for home a few weeks later, knowing he would have to face the music when he got there. When Peter's father learned what he had done, he declared, 'it mortifies and bows me to the ground with shame.'[39]

Captain William Croghan and Lieutenant Abraham Kirkpatrick. Like father, like son. Abraham Kirkpatrick's father fled Scotland for America in 1746, and Abraham bolted Cecil County, Maryland for the frontier in 1767. The 18-year-old fugitive travelled west across the mountains into the forbidden wilds beyond the King's Proclamation Line. Living there was illegal but so was killing a man.

Abraham's father was a Jacobite, a defender of the House of Stuart's claim to the British throne (*Jacobus* is Latin for James.) After James II's defeat in the Williamite War, his Jacobite supporters tried twice more on behalf of his son, 'James III', in 1715 and 1745. The effort reached its peak at the Battle of Culloden in 1746, when the pretender's son, 'Bonnie Prince

35 William Germann, 'The Crisis in the Early Life of General Peter Mühlenberg,' *Pennsylvania Magazine of History and Biography (PMHB)*, 37:3 (1913), p.301.
36 Germann, 'Crisis in the Early Life of Mühlenberg,' pp.307–308.
37 Germann, 'Crisis in the Early Life of Mühlenberg', pp.316–319.
38 Nesbit Willoughby Wallace, *A Regimental Chronicle and List of Officers of the 60th, or the King's Royal Rifle Corps, Formerly the 62nd, or the Royal American Regiment of Foot* (London: Harrison and Sons, 1879), p.1.
39 Germann, 'Crisis in the Early Life of Mühlenberg', pp.321, 326.

Charlie', was crushed by Prince William, the Duke of Cumberland. Reprisals followed, and the Kirkpatricks fled to Maryland. Americans, like English Whigs, celebrated Cumberland as a hero and reviled the Stuarts as agents of tyranny. In Virginia alone, the Cumberland Mountains, the Cumberland River, the Cumberland Gap, and Cumberland County were named in the Duke's honour. So was Fort Cumberland in western Maryland. Peter Helphenstine took the Great Wagon Road through Cumberland County, Pennsylvania, on his way to Winchester. Even so, America was a place for many Jacobites to make a new start. Abraham Kirkpatrick was born in Cecil County, at the top of the Chesapeake Bay, in 1749.[40]

The fight that forced Kirkpatrick to run was of far less consequence than the battle on Culloden Moor: in 1767, he found himself facing off with a belligerent drunk at a horse race.[41] The inebriated man started the fight, but Kirkpatrick finished it by giving him 'a good thrashing.' However, the vanquished sot had the gall to demand a rematch when he was sober. 'If there ever was a man who would not turn on his heel to save his life it was Major Kirkpatrick', remembered a friend who knew the champion in later years. The rematch was held, and, once again, Kirkpatrick beat the daylights out of his adversary. But the brawl had gone too far. When Kirkpatrick learned that the man was dead, he knew there would be consequences.[42]

He ran to the forks of the Ohio River, where the long arm of the law could not reach him. Though Fort Pitt had been garrisoned by Redcoats since 1761, civilian settlement west of the Alleghenies was illegal. It was Indian territory reserved for them by the Royal Proclamation of 1763. There was a small village of soldiers, traders, and friendly Indians near the fort, but its residents had approved roles supporting the Indian trade or the fort's garrison. One of the residents was George Croghan, a wily and ambitious trader and explorer who was the Crown's deputy superintendent of Indian Affairs for the region.[43] His work had taken him far across the Ohio River; he knew the territory better than any native English speaker, and his work made him an important figure in local affairs.[44]

Kirkpatrick was not the only person to ignore the King's edict. South of the fort, several illegal communities formed along the north-flowing Monongahela River and its tributaries.[45] The forks of the Ohio were 300 miles and a wilderness away from the authorities in Philadelphia, and it was not clear that the region was even in the Quaker colony. Virginia also claimed it.

Late in 1768, a treaty with the Iroquois Confederacy established the Ohio River as the new boundary between the colonies and Indian Country. After decades of war in the seventeenth century, the Six Nations of the confederacy, the *Haudenosaunee*, allowed the Shawnee and Delaware to resettle north of the river. Though the refugee tribes hunted on the south side (Kentucky) and objected to the treaty, the land on both sides was part of the Six Nations'

40 Kirk Q. Bigham, *Major Abraham Kirkpatrick and His Descendants* (Pittsburgh: J.P. Durbin, 1911), p.8.

41 George Johnston, *History of Cecil County, Maryland* (Elkton: G. Johnston, 1881), pp.387–388.

42 Bigham, *Kirkpatrick*, pp.8–10.

43 James T. Mitchell and Henry Flanders (eds), *The Statutes at Large of Pennsylvania from 1682 to 1801* (Harrisburg: Clarence M. Busch, 1896–1915), vol.7, p.153.

44 Mitchell and Flanders (eds), *Statutes of Pennsylvania*, vol.7, pp.152–155.

45 Rob Harper, *Unsettling the West: Violence and State Building in the Ohio Valley* (Philadelphia: University of Pennsylvania Press, 2018), p.16.

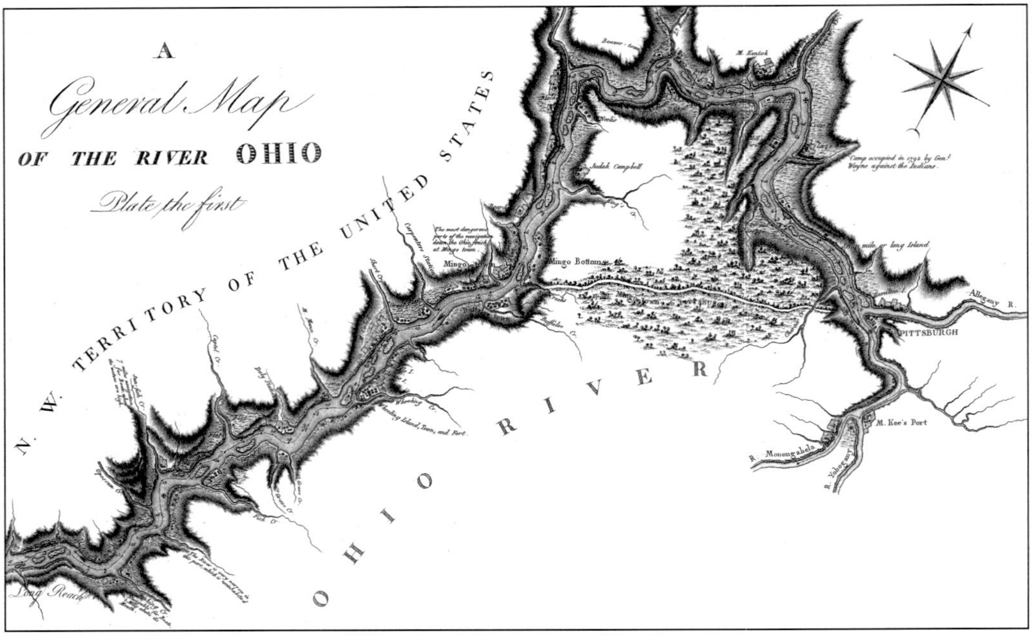

A 1796 map by French spy George Henri Victor Collot shows the junction of the Monongahela and Allegheny Rivers, the Ohio River's counterclockwise arc, Pittsburgh, and a few smaller settlements. White settlement north of the river was illegal until 1784. (David Rumsey Map Collection, David Rumsey Map Center, Stanford Libraries)

empire, and the Iroquois had a recognised right to sell it.[46] The Cherokee, who were dominant in the south, likewise approved white settlement in much of Kentucky. Thousands of Virginians appeared in the Monongahela, Youghiogheny, Redstone, and Cheat River valleys, and a few began to explore the Kentucky country.[47] Pennsylvanians came as well, bringing the territorial dispute to the fore. Pittsburgh began to grow, developing into a town with a reputation for lawlessness that grew worse after the Fort Pitt garrison withdrew in 1772. A visiting British officer described the region's people as 'a sett of lawless vagabonds.'[48] An appalled clergyman complained, 'The inhabitants of this place are very dissipated.'

> They seem to feel themselves beyond the arm of government, & freed from the restraining influence of religion. It is the resort of Indian traders, & many here have escaped from Justice & from Creditors, in the old settlements. The greater part of

46 Brady J. Crytzer, *Guyasuta and the Fall of Indian America* (Yardley: Westholme, 2013), pp.xiii–xvi, 143–146.

47 David W. Miller, *Forced Removal of American Indians from the Northeast: A History of Territorial Cessions and Relocations, 1620–1854* (Jefferson, N.C: McFarland & Co., 2011), pp.75–78; Jack M. Sosin, 'The British Indian Department and Dunmore's War', *Virginia Magazine of History and Biography (VMHB)*, 74:1 (1966), pp.39.

48 Nicholas Wainwright (ed.), 'Turmoil at Pittsburgh: Diary of Augustine Prevost, 1774', *PMHB*, 85:2 (1961), p.127.

> the Indian traders keep a squaw, & some of them a white woman, as a temporary wife.[49]

Kirkpatrick was among those who came to escape justice, and his future behaviour suggests that he yielded to more than one of the frontier's bad influences. That seems also to be true of young William Croghan, a nephew of the Indian agent, who arrived at about the same time. He was from the north of Ireland and apparently came to America as a junior officer in the British army. A Pittsburgh man named James Innes claimed later that he had 'rescued' 19-year-old William 'from beggary, drunkenness and contempt' in 1771 by giving him a job on his farm.[50] From these rough beginnings, William Croghan and Abraham Kirkpatrick rose together in just a few years to lead a company of the 8th Virginia.

49 Franklin B. Dexter (ed.), *Diary of David McClure, Doctor of Divinity, 1748–1820* (New York: Knickerbocker Press, 1899), p.53.

50 Gwynne Tuell Potts, *George Rogers Clark and William Croghan* (Lexington: University Press of Kentucky, 2020), pp.46–48, n.3.

2

Communities

The backcountry of Virginia changed dramatically after the French and Indian War. Thousands of newcomers cleared land for farming, built mills, widened paths into roads, and petitioned for the erection of new counties. Winchester's boom continued as livestock, produce, and immigrants moved up and down the Great Wagon Road.[1] By 1772, Virginia west of the Blue Ridge Mountains was organised into seven counties: Berkeley, Frederick, Hampshire, Dunmore (Shenandoah), Augusta, Botetourt, and Fincastle. Men from all these places would be united in the 8th Virginia Regiment.

Frederick County

Though Winchester was the county seat of Frederick County and the lower valley's economic hub, its commitment to civilisation still seemed half-hearted at times. On St Patrick's Day, Winchester's Germans mocked the Irish by constructing effigies of the saint 'and his wife Sheeley', which were decorated with strings of potatoes. The Irish responded in kind with effigies of St Michael the Archangel, the patron saint of the Holy Roman Empire, adorned with 'ropes' of 'sauerkraut'. A first-hand account tells us these annual demonstrations resulted in 'many a black eye, bloody nose, and broken head.'[2]

Lieutenant John Jolliffe. John Jolliffe grew up north of Winchester near Hopewell Friends Meeting, the core of a Quaker settlement established in the 1730s. The Quakers were stern folk. John's father, the clerk of the meeting, recorded the disavowal of his own brother for 'breach of Society discipline.' But John had other influences in his life. His neighbour across the road was John Neville, a veteran of the French and Indian War and a man of prominence in the coming war. Jolliffe lost both of his parents as an adolescent, and the Friends disowned him in 1772 for 'giving way to a libertine spirit.' He had 'suffred himself to be

1 Warren R. Hofstra, *The Planting of New Virginia: Settlement and Landscape in the Shenandoah Valley* (Baltimore: John Hopkins University Press, 2004), pp.2–5.

2 Kercheval, *History*, p.157; Anon. (ed.), *The Proceedings of the Convention of Delegates Held at the Capitol in the City of Williamsburg in the Colony of Virginia on Monday, the 6th of May, 1776* [5th Convention] (Richmond: Ritchie, Trueheart, & Duval, 1816), p.39.

1st Lieutenant John Jolliffe was expelled from Hopewell Friends Meeting for fighting at a horse race in 1772. (Author's photo)

guilty of fighting, and being at a horse race.' Satisfied with life outside the society, he married Mary Dragoo in a Methodist ceremony, moved into his father's house, and started a family.[3]

Captain Benjamin Berry. Ten miles east of Winchester on the road to Alexandria stood a little crossroads hamlet called 'Battletown' (Berryville). Its name came from weekly wrestling or boxing matches held at the settlement's tavern. The contests sometimes devolved into alcohol-fuelled fistfights and extended feuds. A hard-drinking, semi-literate stump-grubber and wagoner named Daniel Morgan was a frequent victor in these fights. Benjamin Berry, who operated the tavern,[4] recalled that Morgan 'was in his youth often embroiled in quarreling and engaged in fighting & bullying, with the Davis's, Stinsons, Isaac ___ & Darks (one of whom was afterwards Genl Dark) a set of the stoutest & strongest men perhaps this country ever produced.'[5] Morgan, the Stephenson brothers, and William Darke left

3 William Jolliffe, *Historical, Genealogical, and Biographical Account of the Jolliffe Family of Virginia, 1652–1893* (Philadelphia: J.B. Lippincott Co., 1893), pp.74–75, 88, 195–196.
4 James Graham, *The Life of General Daniel Morgan* (New York: Derby & Jackson, 1856), pp.36–38.
5 Virginia Museum of History & Culture (VMHC): Mss7:1 M8214:2, 'Notes, n.d., concerning Daniel Morgan,' Benjamin Berry (comp.).

the Battletown skirmishes behind and advanced to real warfare. Benjamin Berry's brother Thomas joined John Stephenson and William Darke as a captain in the 8th Virginia.[6]

Berkeley County

Captain William Darke. John Stephenson and William Darke both grew up in the northern third of Frederick that became Berkeley County in 1772. An early account tells us that Darke had a 'strong but uncultivated mind' and that he was 'active, daring, and resolute – courting danger and fearless of all consequences in his undertakings.'[7] The praise was warranted and applied equally to his friends. A Morgan biographer once mused that the perils and hardships of life in the West 'gave a dash of intrepidity and recklessness to their character, and made them regard courage and other soldier-like qualities as those entitled to the highest praise and honor.'[8]

Darke was the kind of warrior that people called an 'Indian fighter.' He served in the French and Indian War as a corporal in Captain Robert Rutherford's Rangers, probably patrolling between the forts Colonel Washington had built.[9] Otherwise unsubstantiated claims that he was with Braddock in 1755 are lent some credence by his own assertion in 1791 that he had 'been in the Service of my Country in allmost all the wars since the year 1755 in one Capossoty [capacity] or other.'[10] He was known by the early 1770s as a militia captain who led 'dangerous scouts' on the frontier.[11] His wife, Sarah, was the widow of a man who had been caught sleeping under an elm tree and scalped in 1756.[12]

The Generals. Remarkably, Berkeley County was also home to three men who became major generals in the Continental Army. All three were veterans of the Braddock Expedition, and two commanded the 8th Virginia Regiment in the war to come. Adam Stephen came from Scotland in his twenties and acquired 2,000 acres along Opequon Creek in what was then still Frederick County. He operated grist and sawmills where Martinsburg sprang up and raised cattle, a business familiar from his youth in Aberdeenshire. He had a degree in medicine and served briefly as a naval surgeon before he left for America in 1748.[13]

Stephen was an opinionated, blunt, occasionally dishonest, and ambitious self-promoter. The lure of land bounties and status attracted him to military service, and he had an impressive record from the French and Indian War. Before Braddocks' Defeat he was with Washington at Fort Necessity. The Forbes Road from Fort Loudoun (Pennsylvania) to

6 Graham, *Morgan*, pp.28–43.
7 Anon., 'Biographical Sketch of Gen. William Darke, of Virginia, by a Citizen of Frederick County, Maryland', *Military and Naval Magazine of the United States*, 6:1 (1835), pp.1–9.
8 Graham, *Morgan*, p.22.
9 Crozier, *Virginia Militia*, vol.2, p.44.
10 Jefferson County Museum (JCM): ARC140-1: William Darke to GW, 24 July 1791.
11 Library of Virginia (LVA): Legislative Petitions of the General Assembly, 1776–1865, Accession 363121, Thomas Demoss.
12 Kercheval, *History*, pp.86–88; Anon., 'Eastern West Virginia', *North American Forts*, <northamericanforts.com/East/wveast.html>, accessed 12 Sept. 2022.
13 Harry M. Ward, *Adam Stephen and the Cause of American Liberty* (Charlottesville: University Press of Virginia, 1989), pp.1–4.

Benjamin Berry's Tavern, centre right, was the site of frequent drunken battles involving William Darke, Daniel Morgan, and brothers John and Hugh Stephenson. This gave Berryville the persistent nickname 'Battletown'. James E. Taylor created this image of what was then called The Virginia House for *Frank Leslie's Illustrated Newspaper* in the 1860s. The tavern as depicted is likely altered from its eighteenth-century appearance and has since been taken down. (James E. Taylor Sketchbook, Western Reserve Historical Society, Cleveland, Ohio)

Fort Pitt was largely built under his direction. He achieved an important victory at Fort Loyalhanna (Fort Ligonier), and he reached a notable diplomatic agreement with the Cherokee during an outing to the southwest. Despite these successes, Stephen's greatest ambitions were often frustrated. Washington defeated him in a campaign for the House of Burgesses, he was passed over for the superintendency of Indian Affairs, and the clock ran out on his efforts to get a regular army commission.[14] He was, however, successful in local affairs. The governor appointed him to the Berkeley court, he served as the county's first sheriff,[15] and he successfully advocated for Martinsburg to be the county seat.[16]

14 Ward, *Stephen*, pp.48–61, 67–71, 75–79.

15 H.R. McIlwaine et al (eds), *Executive Journals of the Council of Colonial Virginia*, (Richmond: Virginia State Library, 1925–1966), vol.6, pp.456–457; Edward Ingle, 'Justices of the Peace of Colonial Virginia, 1757–1775,' *Bulletin of the Virginia State Library*, 14:2–3 (1921), pp.41–149, 78.

16 McIlwaine et al (eds), *Executive Journals*, vol.6, p.461; Ward, *Stephen*, pp.71–75; Hendricks, *Backcountry Towns*, pp.113–115.

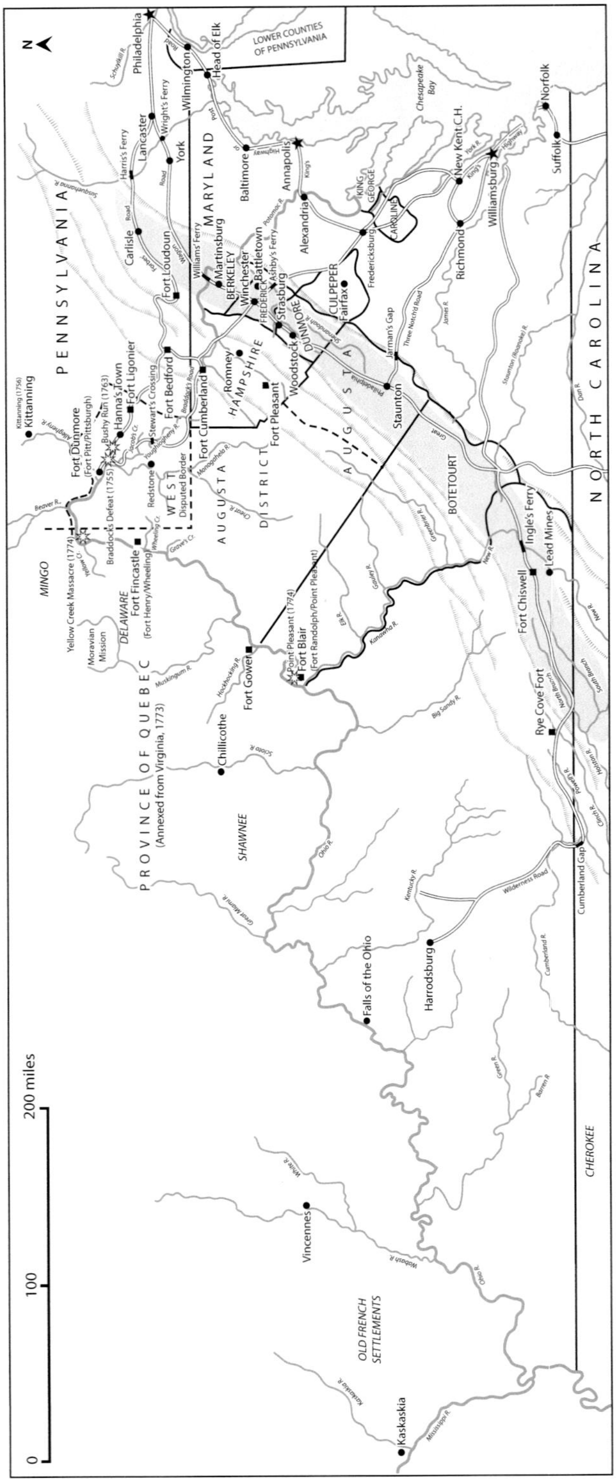

Virginia, 1774.

Horatio Gates, a major in the British Army with no prospects in England, moved to America in 1772 and settled in Berkeley.[17] Charles Lee came to America from London for similar reasons in 1773. A man of some means, he came with his dog and a small entourage just as the tea tax protests were escalating. He immediately waded into politics, travelling through the colonies and ingratiating himself with the continent's leading men.[18]

When Gates learned that Lee was in Virginia, he sent him a letter urging him to visit, buy property, and become a neighbour.[19] They knew each other from the previous war and had once dined together at a London dinner hosted by Benjamin Franklin for 'friends of America.'[20] Gates was a confirmed Whig, but Lee was a radical. He came from a wealthy family and could afford to have strong views.[21] He called French philosopher Jean-Jacques Rousseau his 'divine and incomparable master.' 'May God prosper the Americans in their resolutions,' he wrote during the Stamp Act crisis, 'that there may be one Asylum at least on the earth for men, who prefer their natural rights to the fantastical prerogative of a foolish perverted head because it wears a Crown.' Lee rarely passed on an opportunity to criticise his superiors. After Major General James Abercrombie's disastrous assault on Fort Carillon (Ticonderoga) in 1758, he asserted they could have been victorious 'if our Booby in Chief had only acted with the spirit and prudence of an old Woman.'[22]

In 1775, Lee arrived on Horatio Gates' doorstep and bought a property Gates recommended to him. The seller, who was desperately in debt, was Abraham Bowman's uncle, Jacob Hite.[23] Stephen, in his role as sheriff, had recently seized Hite's most valuable movable property (people and animals), sparking a feud that would have repercussions in the years to come. Stephen, Gates, and Lee all rose to the highest ranks they could achieve in the Continental Army. Then, one after another, they fell hard.

Hampshire County

The mountains forming the western boundary of the Shenandoah Valley were largely impenetrable, but a few passes provided access to Hampshire County on the far side. An ancient buffalo trace and Indian trail connected Winchester to settlements on the Cacapon River and the South Branch. Romney, the county seat, was described in 1772 as consisting 'of a few

17 Paul David Nelson, *General Horatio Gates: A Biography* (Baton Rouge: Louisiana State University, 1976), p.35.

18 Papas, *Renegade Revolutionary*, pp.93–103.

19 Henry Edward Bunbury (ed.), *The Lee Papers* (New York: New York Historical Society, 1871–1875), vol.1, pp.123–126; S. Allen Chambers, Jr., 'Traveller's Rest', *Society of Architectural Historians Archipedia*, <sah-archipedia.org/buildings/WV-01-JE18>, accessed 18 Sept. 2022.

20 Leonard W. Larabee et al (eds), *The Papers of Benjamin Franklin* (New Haven: Yale University Press, 1959), vol.15, p.78.

21 Phillip Papas, *Renegade Revolutionary: The Life of General Charles Lee* (New York: New York University Press, 2014), pp.2, 17–18, 25.

22 Bunbury (ed.), *Lee Papers*, vol.1, pp.6–9, 42–44, 230.

23 Papas, *Renegade Revolutionary*, pp.99, 104–105.

Prato Rio, the home of Major General Charles Lee. The ground floor of the log section was built about 1731 as a one-room dwelling by Jost Hite. Hite's son Jacob built the stone addition about 1733 and connected it to the log house with a breezeway. Lee bought the house in 1774. The upper floor of the log wing and a further stone addition on the far side of this view were built by later owners. (Author's photo)

log houses' and a jail.[24] The Cacapon River, the South Branch, Patterson's Creek, and New Creek ran north in parallel through Hampshire's mountain valleys to the Potomac River. Braddock's military road also cut northwest through the county to Fort Cumberland.[25]

Captain Abel and Sergeant Cornelius Westfall. In the county's southern end, the forks of the South Branch attracted settlers like the Higginses and the Westfalls. Abel and Cornelius Westfall were fifth-generation members of a Dutch family, born on the South Fork near Fort Pleasant during the worst years of the French and Indian War.[26] Several members of their

24 David Jones, *A Journal of Two Visits Made to Some Nations of Indians on the West Side of the River Ohio in the Years 1772 and 1773* (Burlington: Isaac Collins, 1774), p.8; Leonora W. Woods, 'The Old Northwestern Turnpike', *The Hampshire Review*, 20 Jan. 1937.

25 Hu Maxwell and H.L. Swisher, *History of Hampshire County* (Morgantown: A. Brown Boughner, 1897), p.330.

26 Dennis G. Peterson, *Juriaen Westfall Descendants in America* (place unknown: D.G. Peterson, 2016), pp.9–33. Amelia Clay Lewis Van Meter Rogers, 'The Van Meteren's of Holland and America', *Genealogies of Kentucky Families* (Baltimore: Genealogical Publishing, 1981), pp.551–562.

extended family died in that conflict, but by the 1760s, the Westfalls lived even farther west near Fort George (Petersburg, W.Va.) on the North Fork.[27]

Sergeant Ned McCarty. Ned McCarty's family settled far out near the mouth of New Creek about 1755. His parents, courageous or foolish, shared a double-pen cabin with a man named Wendell Millar. This may have been a 'dog trot' house: two cabins with a shared roof and a separating breezeway. The McCartys were from Tyrone, one of the Ulster counties. Ned (Edward) was born in the New Creek cabin in 1756 and was just five years old when Killbuck attacked as the men were stacking flax. Millar was killed. McCarty's father ran for the settlement's block house, but his assailants caught him, took him to Ohio, and burned him at the stake.[28]

Ensign Rees Pritchard and Enlisted Soldier John Chenoweth. Other Hampshire families came from Germany, Wales, and various parts of England. Rees Pritchard's Welsh family endured the Indian War at their home on the North River, a tributary of the Cacapon. Rees was about 25 years old when George Washington stayed with them for a night on his way to Fort Pitt in 1770.[29] A year or two later, a teenager named John Chenoweth came to live on the Cacapon to learn blacksmithing from his uncle. Ten-year-old Mary Pugh lived just a mile away. She watched him march off to war in 1776, welcomed him home when he was done, and married him.[30]

The Forks of the Ohio.

Captain John Stephenson, Lieutenant Edward Rice, and Enlisted Soldiers Thomas Ravenscraft and John Vance. On a spring day in 1772, John Stephenson and Edward Rice attended a clandestine wedding. Why it was secret is not known. All involved were members of a frontier community surrounding the intersection of Braddock's Road and the Youghiogheny River in what is now Fayette County, Pennsylvania. Thomas Gist, a son of explorer Christopher Gist, officiated in his capacity as a Bedford County, Pennsylvania judge.[31] It was the last time most of the attendees would recognise Pennsylvania's jurisdiction there.

Stephenson was a Battletown veteran,[32] whose name was frequently written, and evidently pronounced, 'Stinson.'[33] John and his wife Mary settled where Braddock's Road

27 Peterson, *Westfall*, pp.26–27, 32–33.
28 William W. Wolfe, *History of Keyser, West Virginia, 1737–1913* (place unknown: Keyprint, 1974), p.3.
29 Anon., 'North River Mills Historic Trace', *Historic Hampshire*, <historichampshire.org/nrm/memorials/Trace.htm>, accessed 8 Oct. 2022.
30 National Archives and Records Administration, Washington (NARA): M804, W18899, John Chenoweth pension.
31 Boyd Crumrine (ed.), 'Minute Book of Virginia Court Held for Yohogania County, First at Augusta Town (Now Washington, Pa.), and Afterwards on the Andrew Heath Farm near West Elizabeth; 1776–1780', *Annals of the Carnegie Museum*, 2:2 (1903), pp.212–222, 213.
32 VMHC: Mss7:1 M8214:2, 'Notes, n.d., concerning Daniel Morgan,' Benjamin Berry (comp.).
33 NARA: M804, S39819, John Kirk pension; S4640, William Owens pension; R8738, Bean Smallwood pension; S13939, John Milligan pension (H. Stephenson's Rifle Co.); and W6338, John Vance pension;

crossed Jacobs Creek in 1769 just a few months after the Treaty of Fort Stanwix made it legal to do so.[34] For safety, John helped a neighbour build Minter's Fort.[35] John's older half-brother, William Crawford, lived with his wife Hannah eight miles below them at 'Stewart's Crossing' (Connellsville), where the road crossed the Youghiogheny. In addition to his own children, Crawford had taken a young man named Thomas Ravenscraft under his wing.[36] Hannah's nephew, John Vance, lived across the river from them.[37] A hard future awaited the men of this new community: Vance had a bayonet thrust through his face, a tomahawk cracked Ravenscraft's skull, and Crawford burned like Ned McCarty's father.[38]

However, in 1772, they were enjoying life. Missionary David McClure's record of another wedding at Stewart's Crossing provides a glimpse of the differences between Virginia natives and the more pious German and Irish immigrant settlers.

> Attended a marriage, where the guests were all Virginians. It was a scene of wild and confused merriment … The Lady of a Mr. Stevenson, sent her husband to me, with her compliments requesting to dance a minuit with her. My declining the honor, on the principle that I was unacquainted with it, was scarcely accepted. He still politely urged, until I totally refused … The manners of the people of Virginia, who have removed into these parts, are different from those of the presbyterians and germans. They are much addicted to drinking parties, gambling, horse race and fighting. They are hospitable & prodigal. Several of them, have run through their property in the old settlements, & have sought an asylum in this wilderness.[39]

Enlisted Soldiers Henry and William Gaddis. Directly west of the Stephenson homestead, Redstone Fort was positioned at the Monongahela's southernmost navigable point.[40] From there, one could float to Pittsburgh or continue all the way to New Orleans. Brothers William and Henry Gaddis lived near Redstone on Tenmile Creek.[41] The Gaddises moved there from Hampshire County when the country opened up. According to lore, their widowed mother

---

LVA: Revolutionary War Bounty Land Claims, John Berry; Philander D. Chase et al (eds), *The Papers of George Washington*, Revolutionary War Series (Charlottesville: University Press of Virginia, 1985), vol.8, pp.428–429.

34 Mignon Larche, *Pioneers on the Bullskin: The Stephenson Story* (Eureka Spring, Ark.: Times-Echo Publishing Co., 1960), p.155; Michael J. Pauley, 'Beverley,' Jefferson Co., W.Va., National Register of Historic Places nomination, 1986, NPS ref. no. 87000486; Donald Jackson (ed.), *The Diaries of George Washington* (Charlottesville: University Press of Virginia, 1976–1979), vol.2, p.280.

35 George Dallas Albert, *The Frontier Forts of Western Pennsylvania* (Harrisburg: Clarence M. Busch, 1896), p.390.

36 Reuben Gold Thwaites and Louise Phelps Kellogg (eds), *Frontier Defense on the Upper Ohio, 1777–1778* (Madison: Wisconsin Historical Society, 1912), p.218, n.84.

37 Anon., 'Descendants of John Vance and Elizabeth Glass,' *Fort Vance Historical Society*, <http://fortvance.org/wp-content/uploads/2020/08/Vance_Descendants_of-John-Vance-and-Elizabeth-Glass.pdf>, accessed 15 Oct. 2022.

38 NARA: M804, W6338, John Vance pension, S1248, Thomas Ravenscraft pension.

39 Dexter (ed.), *Diary of David McClure*, pp.105–106.

40 H.W. Stickle, 'Monongahela River Navigation,' *Professional Memoirs, Corps of Engineers, United States Army, and Engineer Department at Large*, 11:60 (1919), p.696.

41 NARA: M804, S23652, Henry Gaddis pension.

'Fort Gaddis' was built before 1774 by an uncle of Henry and William Gaddis on Braddock's Road a few miles south of Stewart's Crossing. (Author's photo)

followed them alone on a mule carrying only her waffle iron.[42] The brothers enlisted together when the Revolution came, and one of them gave his life to the cause.

Enlisted Soldier Benjamin Biggs. The Ohio begins at Pittsburgh with the confluence of the Monongahela and Allegheny Rivers. From there, the river curls to the west, fed in its first hundred miles by the Beaver River, Yellow Creek, Short Creek, and Wheeling Creek. Under the terms of the Treaty of Fort Stanwix, the outside of this bend was Indian Country. Whether the inside, which was open for settlement, was Virginia or Pennsylvania was hotly debated. A boy named Benjamin Biggs moved with his family to Short Creek from Maryland in 1769.[43] He finished his childhood among future frontier heroes Lewis Wetzel, Samuel McColloch, and Betty Zane.[44] His own path led to the rank of brigadier general.

42 Jim Gaddis, 'William Gaddis', <findagrave.com/memorial/63481893/william-gaddis>, accessed 15 Oct. 2022.

43 Grace L. Tracy and John P. Dern, *Pioneers of Old Monocacy: Early Settlement of Frederick County, Maryland, 1721–1743* (Baltimore: Genealogical Publishing, 1987), pp.304, 307, 309–310.

44 Richard S. Klein and Alan H. Cooper, 'Biography of Samuel McCollogh', *Wheeling Intelligencer*, April 9, 1777, <ohiocountylibrary.org/history/biography-samuel-mccolloch/4298>, accessed 17 Oct.

Lieutenant James Higgins. Travelling all the way from Tidewater Virginia, James Higgins joined his friend George Rogers Clark out on the Ohio River in 1772. Clark was a surveyor, and Higgins came with Clark's father and some other men to join in some exploring.[45] There was good land to be found. They surveyed as far downriver as Graves Creek, 23 miles below Wheeling Creek, and then explored all the way to 'Point Pleasant' at the mouth of the Great Kanawha River. Higgins and Clark remained in the west to clear a claim for themselves at Graves Creek.[46] As the rest of the adventurers travelled home to Caroline County, one of them sent a note to George's older brother Jonathan: '[Y]our Brother Geo & James Higgins we left keeping house about 130 miles below Pittsburg on a Bottom of fine land on the Ohio, which would be Valuable were it not for it being so Surrounded with mountains surpassing any thing you ever saw.'[47] Now that he was settled out on the Ohio, it was just a matter of time before Higgins connected with William Croghan and Abraham Kirkpatrick.

Dunmore County

Captain Jonathan Clark. As children, Jonathan and George Rogers Clark had different gifts. They attended Donald Robertson's school in King and Queen County, and a comparison of their writing shows that Jonathan was the more studious of the two.[48] The school enjoyed a reputation as the best place in Virginia for boys (and some girls) to get an education in the 1760s.[49] Another good student, the bookish and small future president 'Jemmy' Madison, was five months older than Jonathan and attended the school for most of his teens.[50] After his schooling, Jonathan became an assistant to John Waller, the Spotsylvania County clerk.[51] It was a good first job for a young man, but there was no chance of advancement. The clerkship had been held by a member of the Waller family since the creation of the county, and it was going to stay that way.[52]

2022; Al Dickinson, 'A Leap of Faith in the Historical Record: The Legend of McColloch's Leap,' *JAR*, <allthingsliberty.com/2023/11/a-leap-of-faith-in-the-historical-record-the-legend-of-mccollochs-leap>, accessed 20 July 2024; Eric Sterner, 'Betty Zane and the Siege of Fort Henry, September 1782,' *Journal of the American Revolution (JAR)*, <allthingsliberty.com/2020/01/betty-zane-and-the-siege-of-fort-henry-september-1782/>, accessed 17 Oct. 2022.

45 Lyman Chalkley, *Chronicles of the Scotch-Irish Settlement of Virginia: Extracted from the Original Court Records of Augusta County, 1745–1800* (Rosslyn, Va.: DAR, 1912), vol.1, p.514.

46 Jones, *Journal of Two Visits*, pp.13–19; Wisconsin Historical Society (WHS): Draper Manuscript Collection, L, vol.1, pp.7–11, 18; James Alton James (ed.), *George Rogers Clark Papers*, 1771–1781 (Springfield: Illinois State Historical Society, 1912), pp.lii–liii.

47 James (ed.), *Clark Papers*, pp.1–2.

48 William Hayden English, *Conquest of the Country North-West of the River Ohio, 1778–1783 and, Life of Gen. George Rogers Clark* (Indianapolis: Bowen-Merrill, 1897), vol.1, pp.58–59.

49 Anon., 'Donald Robertson's School', *King and Queen Courthouse Tavern Museum*, <kingandqueenmuseum.org/donald-robertsons-school/>, accessed 25 Oct. 2022.

50 Anon., 'Life of James Madison', *James Madison's Montpelier*, <www.montpelier.org/learn/the-life-of-james-madison>, accessed 25 Oct. 2022; Robert E. Gatten, Jr., 'Clark Land in Virginia and the Birthplace of William Clark', *We Proceeded On* [Lewis & Clark Trail Heritage Foundation], 25:2 (1999), pp.6–10.

51 English, *Conquest of the North-West*, vol.2, p.991.

52 Frederick Johnston, *Memorials of Old Virginia Clerks* (Lynchburg: J.P. Bell, 1888), p.378; Andrew Lewis Riffe and Clayton Torrence, 'The Wallers of Endfield, King William County, Virginia', *VMHB*, 59:3–4 (1951) pp.460–463.

Clark began a diary on 1 June 1770 and rarely missed an entry until the day he died. His first entry was one word: 'Rain.' Afterward, his consistently terse entries always recorded the weather, who he visited, and where he slept if he was not at home. The diary reveals that young men in Virginia enjoyed playing 'fives', a form a handball, and 'shooting for beef', target-shooting contests offering a steer as the prize. Other entertainments included fox hunting, barbecues, dances, and singing. Though he did not enter any of his own birds, Jonathan attended cockfights a couple of times in 1771. He went to the theatre in Fredericksburg to see *Julius Caesar* and *Romeo and Juliet*. He went bee hunting with a friend and found two hives. In the winter, he went hare hunting in the snow.[53] There were court days once a month in Fredericksburg and an election of burgesses. What he loved best, however, was going fishing.[54]

He became a Baptist and attended worship services in makeshift churches and in the outdoors. Baptists were legally tolerated, but the Church of England was still the established faith of the colony and attendance at an Anglican service was required at least once a month. Jonathan complied, going to his local parish church about that often.[55]

On 23 October 1770, Clark went to a meeting to review a printed broadside from Williamsburg. Following a precedent from the Stamp Act crisis, Virginia's leaders had responded to the Townsend Acts by forming a non-importation association in 1769. The boycott was ineffective, and an enforcement mechanism was now proposed. Copies of it were printed and sent to Virginia's counties for citizens to sign.[56] The new scheme was controversial in Spotsylvania. Five men were elected to enforce the boycott, but after the meeting adjourned Clark noted there was 'much fighting in the night.'[57]

Clark travelled to Williamsburg in 1772 when the House of Burgesses was in session.[58] Three new counties were to be approved and that opened opportunities. Berkeley and Dunmore were carved out of Frederick, and Fincastle was split off from Botetourt.[59] Clark met with Thomas Marshall, a burgess from Fauquier County, and 'agreed…to keep [the] clerk's office' in Dunmore. Marshall had the clerkship, which he treated as a sinecure, and took Clark on as his deputy.[60] Clerks recorded births, deaths, real estate transactions, and the decisions of the county court, charging a fee for most tasks. Clark agreed to accept one-third of the 'profits' in exchange for doing the actual work.[61]

On 16 May, Clark set off for the Shenandoah Valley from his parents' home in Caroline.[62] It took him three days to get to his new home at Millerstown or *Muellerstadt*, the Dunmore

53 Filson Historical Society (FHS): Clark Family Papers, A C593a, Jonathan Clark Diary, 1 June 1770–11 Jan. 1772.

54 FHS: Clark Diary, passim.

55 FHS: Clark Diary, 24–26 June and 1 July 1770.

56 John Pendleton Kennedy (ed.), *Journals of the House of Burgesses of Virginia 1770–1772* (Richmond: Colonial Press, 1906), pp.xxvii–xxxi; Donald M. Sweig, 'The Virginia Nonimportation Association Broadside of 1770 and Fairfax County: A Study in Local Participation', *VMHB*, 87:3 (1979), pp.316–325.

57 FHS: Clark Diary, 23 Oct. 1770.

58 FHS: Clark Diary, 10 April 1772.

59 Kennedy, *Journals of the House*, pp.187, 197–198, 205, 221, 245, 262, 316; William Waller Hening (ed.), *The Statutes at Large, Being a Collection of All the Laws of Virginia from the First Session of the Legislature in the Year 1619* (Richmond, J. & G. Cochran, 1819–1823), vol.8, p.597–599.

60 Johnston, *Clerks*, p.360.

61 FHS: Clark Diary, 16 May 1772.

62 FHS: Clark Diary, 16 May 1772.

The house built by Lieutenant Jacob Rinker's Swiss father 10 miles west of the Wagon Road in what is now Shenandoah County ca. 1749. (Author's photo)

County seat. The legislature had renamed the town 'Woodstock', but it took years for the new name to stick.[63] On 26 May, Clark noted that 'A court [was] held for Dunmore County and the first ever held for s[ai]d county.'[64]

Monthly court sessions, often coinciding with militia musters and sometimes lasting two or three days, were the primary community events in the lives of most Virginians. Even near the coast, most people lived far from their neighbours and court days were a chance to conduct business, socialize, and catch up on news. To organise his namesake county, the governor, John Murray, 4th Earl of Dunmore, issued a 'commission of the peace', appointing 16 men to serve as justices of the peace. These were lifetime appointments. The county court was an oligarchic and functionally self-perpetuating body that governed quite independently of the superior authorities in Williamsburg. Modelled on English county governance, the court had plenary executive, legislative, electoral, and judicial power over most local matters.[65]

63 NARA: M804, S46413, Andrew Wolfe pension; S4210, James Miller pension (Shenandoah Militia).

64 FHS: Clark Diary, 26 May 1772.

65 Charles S. Sydnor, *American Revolutionaries in the Making: Political Practices in Washington's Virginia* (1952, reprinted New York: Free Press, 1965), pp.74–85.

Lieutenant Taverner Beale. Two Frederick justices transitioned to the new Dunmore court, providing continuity and experience: Burr Harrison and Taverner Beale.[66] Beale lived at the foot of the west slope of Massanutten Mountain, about 18 miles south of Woodstock, on his estate called Mount Airy.[67] He was a cousin of 'Jemmy' Madison and had married into the Hite family. One of the new justices was Abraham Bowman. Though just 22 years old, he was well-regarded.[68] The governor selected sheriffs from among the county justices for limited terms, and Beale was chosen first.[69]

Captain Richard Campbell. One of Beale's two deputies was Richard Campbell. He was about 26 years old, married, and had five children. Though he had some education and property (including two slaves),[70] his own origins are obscure. He may have been the son of Andrew Campbell, an early Frederick justice, burgess, sheriff, and vestryman who fled to the Carolinas after he was caught misappropriating funds.[71] Jonathan Clark rented a room from Richard, noting in his diary that he 'went to live with Rich[ar]d Campbell at the rate of £12.0.0 per year board.'[72]

Though Clark, Campbell, and Beale came from British families, Dunmore was thickly settled by Swiss and Rhenish people who were unfamiliar with British and Virginian civil institutions and often spoke little English.[73] This presented a challenge for the Old Dominion, even though the colony was far better than its neighbours at dispersing authority and delegating governance.[74] Bowman, a rare third-generation German, was a perfect choice to be one of four 'Dutch' members of the court.[75] 'Dutch' and *Deutsch* were linguistic variants of the same term for centuries.[76]

66 Ingle, 'Justices', pp.92, 95
67 Wayland, *Shenandoah*, p.199; Wes Allison, 'A Farm of Dreams for Sale', *Washington Post*, 31 Aug. 1996.
68 Ingle, 'Justices', pp. 114, 123.
69 Anon., 'Sheriff History', <vasheriff.org/sheriffs-resources/sheriff-history>, accessed 30 Oct. 2022.
70 LVA: Dunmore County Revolutionary War Papers, 1775–1814, Acc. 21127, 1775 census.
71 Jackson (ed.), *Diaries of Washington*, vol.1, pp.6–16; Amelia C. Gilreath (ed.), *Order Book, 1772–1774, Shenandoah County, VA* [abstracts] (Nokesville, Va.: A.C. Gilreath, 1986), p.3; Louise Phelps Kellogg (ed.), *Frontier Advance on the Upper Ohio, 1778–1779* (Madison: Wisconsin Historical Society, 1916), p.59; Michael Cecere, *A Brave, Active, and Intrepid Soldier: Lieutenant Colonel Richard Campbell of the Virginia Continental Line* (Berwyn Heights, Md.: Heritage Books, 2020), pp.1–2.
72 FHS: Clark Diary, 27 May 1772.
73 George M. Smith, 'The Reverend Peter Muhlenberg: A Symbiotic Adventure in Virginia, 1772–1783', *The Report: A Journal of German-American History*, 36 (1975), pp.51–65.
74 Emily Salmon, 'County Formation During the Colonial Period', *Encyclopedia Virginia*, < encyclopediavirginia.org/entries/county-formation-during-the-colonial-period>, accessed 20 Sept. 2024; Samuel Hazard (ed.), *Minutes of the Provincial Council of Pennsylvania* (Harrisburg: T. Fenn, 1851–1852), vol.9, pp.138–142.
75 Ingle, 'Justices', p.114.
76 Luc de Grauwe, 'Emerging Mother-Tongue Awareness: The Special Case of Dutch and German in the Middle Ages and the Early Modern Period', in Andrew R. Linn and Nicola McLelland (eds), *Standardization: Studies from the Germanic Languages* (Amsterdam: John Benjamins Publishing, 2002), pp.99–115, 101–104.

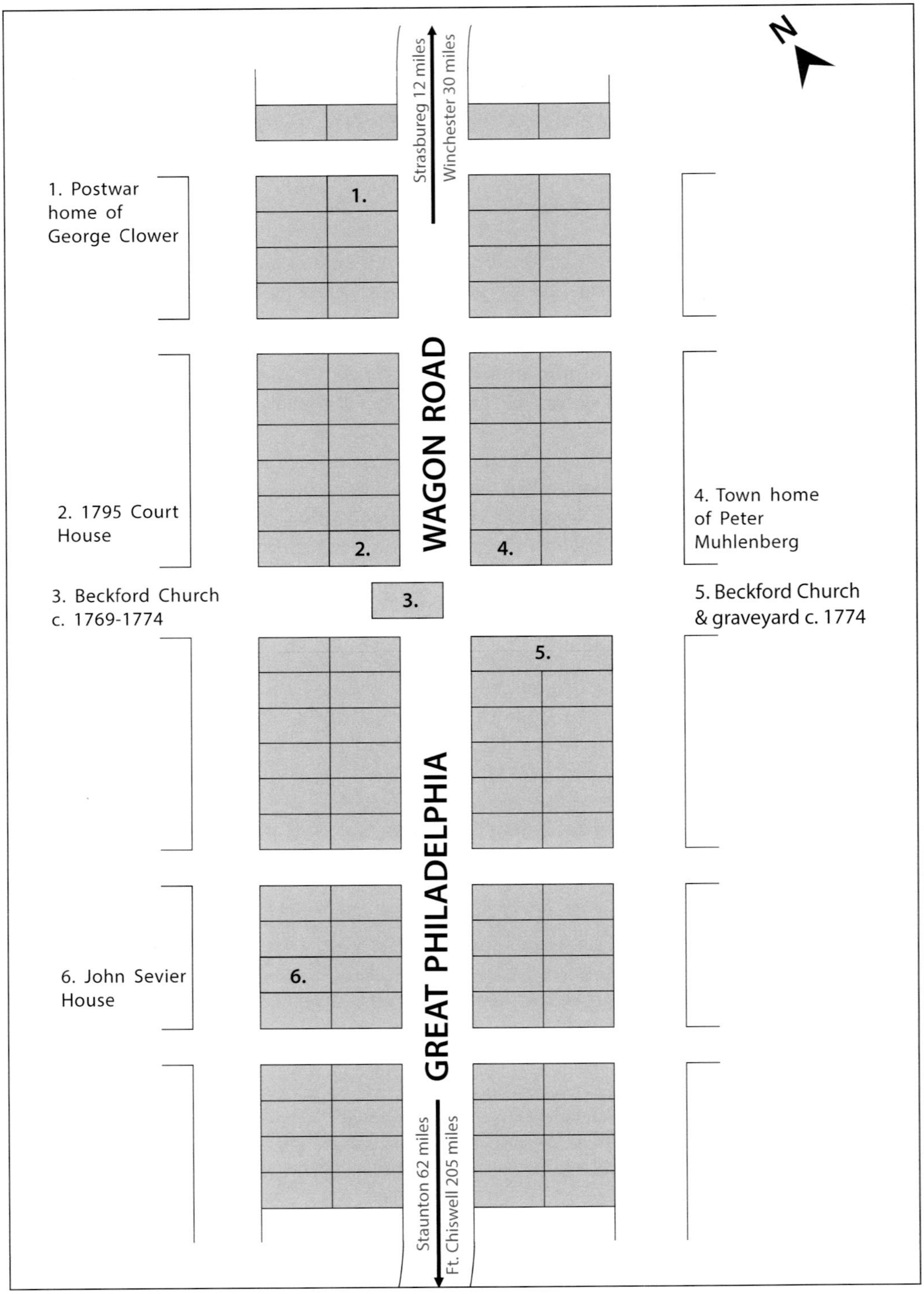

Woodstock street grid.

The Arrival of Peter Muhlenberg

Consistent with common practice, Dunmore and Berkeley counties were preceded by the creation of Beckford and Norborne parishes by two years.[77] Assembling a parish vestry for Beckford was a challenge, but finding a rector was a bigger problem. The Germans were already unhappy tithing to a church they did not really belong to.[78] Virginia had grown more comfortable making religious accommodations, especially in the West, and a practical solution was sought. It helped that relations between the Lutheran and English churches were cordial. In fact, as kings of Great Britain and electors of Hanover, any of the Hanoverian monarchs could fairly be described as both Anglican and Lutheran.[79] Even so, the Beckford rector had to be an Anglican priest.

Avoiding the unpopular Church of England commissary in Williamsburg,[80] Frederick Parish vestryman James Wood II looked to the commissary in Philadelphia for help. Soon, Peter Muhlenberg received the invitation to serve.[81] The runaway druggist's apprentice was now a 24-year-old Lutheran deacon and a lay preacher. He had studied under the provost of the Swedish Lutheran church in Philadelphia and been tutored by 'a worthy youth of poor and pious parents' named Christian Streit.[82] Swedish Lutherans were even closer to Anglicans in practice, and it was a good solution.

Anglican (and Swedish Lutheran) doctrine required ordination by a bishop, but there was no bishop in the colonies. Peter gamely sailed to England to be ordained in London. While he was there, he visited Pennsylvania's proprietors, walked in Hyde Park, and toured the Tower of London and Westminster Abbey. He attended a Methodist service and delivered a sermon at the German Chapel in the Savoy. He received his ordination on 25 April 1772 in the King's Chapel across from St James Palace.[83] Muhlenberg, the new Beckford Parish rector, arrived in Woodstock in September, beginning a career that brought him far beyond local ministry.[84]

Culpeper County

Captain George Slaughter. The Muhlenberg arrangement was the result of lessons learned in other parishes, including St Mark's, just east of the Blue Ridge. There, former settlers of the

77 McIlwaine, H.R. and John Pendleton Kennedy (eds), *Journals of the House of Burgesses of Virginia* (Richmond: Colonial Press, 1905–1915), vol.12, pp.37, 59, 78, 94, 96, 98, 108.

78 Theodore G. Tappert and John W. Doberstein (trans.), *The Journals of Henry Melchior Muhlenberg* (Philadelphia: Muhlenberg Press, 1945), vol.2, pp.367, 373–375. Typographical error corrected in translation.

79 Daniel L. Brunner, 'Anglican Perceptions of Lutheranism in Early Hanoverian England', *Lutheran Quarterly*, 20:1 (2006), pp.63–82.

80 James Terry White (ed.), *National Cyclopedia of American Biography* (New York: James T. White & Co., 1893), vol.3, p.233.

81 Smith, 'Reverend Muhlenberg', pp.55–56.

82 Paul A. Wallace, *The Muhlenbergs of Pennsylvania* (Philadelphia: University of Pennsylvania Press 1950), p.72.

83 Jacob Fry (ed.), 'Journal of the Rev. Peter Muhlenberg in London, 1772', *Lutheran Church Review*, 4:16 (1885), pp.294–300.

84 Smith, 'Reverend Muhlenberg', pp.58, 64.

Germanna Colony had organised Hebron Lutheran Church as early as 1740.[85] When Culpeper County was formed there in 1749, Anglo-Virginians came to administer it as Clark did in Dunmore. The number of Germans in Culpeper was relatively small, and no accommodations were made for them. While Beckford's vestry somewhat flagrantly included dissenting Germans, the St Mark's vestry included none, and the Lutherans had to tithe to two churches.[86]

Culpeper's leading English families (the Fields, the Slaughters, the Kirtleys, and the Greens) produced a number of capable soldiers.[87] During Pontiac's War, George Slaughter joined an independent company to support Colonel Henry Bouquet's expedition across the Ohio.[88] Bouquet forced the tribes to return more than 200 white captives, many of them children, who had disappeared over the past decade. The process was heart-rending, as many of the captives, especially those who were taken as babies and toddlers, had no desire to return. Slaughter gave up his horse for 'carrying some of those restored Captives.'[89] The future 8th Virginia captain left no record of his reaction to these events, but his later actions toward Indian combatants speak for themselves.

Augusta County

The people of Augusta County were mostly Irish Presbyterians who came from Pennsylvania to settle what was often called 'the Irish Tract.'[90] The 1738 statute authorising the creation of Frederick and Augusta counties was written to lure dissenting Protestant immigrants into the valley with promises of citizenship and, for the first time so explicitly, religious toleration.[91] Populating the valley was intended to make the interior of the colony safer from Native attacks. A Presbyterian church built by setters 50 miles south of Woodstock, now known as the Augusta Stone Church, is a veritable fortress designed for both worship and community defence. Protective earthworks were still discernible around it as late as 1856.[92] The county seat was at Staunton, a few miles to the south. Three Chop't Road (Three Notch'd Road), named for the tree blazes marking its course, ran east from the town up to Jarman's Gap on the Blue Ridge and on to Richmond.[93]

85 A.G. Roeber, *Palatines, Liberty, and Property: German Lutherans in Colonial British America* (Baltimore: Johns Hopkins University Press, 1993), p.155.

86 Philip Slaughter, *A History of St. Mark's Parish, Culpeper County, Virginia* (Baltimore: Innes & Co., 1877), pp.13, 32, 36, 38, 43.

87 Frederick Clifton Pierce, *Field Genealogy* (Chicago: Hammond Press, 1901), pp.1102–1103; McIlwaine (ed.), *Journals of Burgesses*, vol.8, pp.ix, vol.10, pp.3, 31, 45, 63, 169, 201, 225, 313; Ingle, 'Justices', p.65, 80, 121; Hening (ed.), *Statutes*, vol.7, p.214; Abbot, et al (eds), *Papers of Washington* (Colonial), vol.4, p.248; John S. Carpenter, 'Slaughter Family', *VMHB*, 21:4 (1913), p.427.

88 LVA: Virginia Land Office, Land Bounty Certificates for French and Indian War Service, George Slaughter.

89 Kennedy, *Journals of Burgesses, 1766–1769*, p.153.

90 Hofstra, *New Virginia*, pp.40–41.

91 Hening (ed.), *Statutes*, vol.5, pp.78–80.

92 William Henry Foote, *Sketches of Virginia, Historical and Biographical*, Second Series (Philadelphia: J.B. Lippincott & Co., 1855), pp.25–26, 32–33; J. Lewis Peyton, *History of Augusta County, Virginia* (Staunton: Samuel M. Yost & Son, 1882), p.81.

93 Nathaniel Mason Pawlett and Howard H. Newlon, Jr., 'The Route of the Three Notch'd Road: A Preliminary Report', *Virginia Highway & Transportation Research Council* (1976, 2003), <virginiadot.org/vtrc/main/online_reports/pdf/76-r32.pdf>, accessed 8 Jan. 2023.

Augusta Stone Church was an important centre of Scotch-Irish life in the Valley of Virginia. It was built between 1747 and 1749 by a Presbyterian congregation founded in 1740. This 1897 photograph portrays the structure before additions were built in 1922 and 1956. (Samuel M. Wilson Collection, University of Kentucky)

Captain David Stephenson. An early precedent for Peter Muhlenberg's appointment was set in Augusta when John Hindman went to London for Anglican ordination in 1747.[94] Hindman was thoroughly Presbyterian. He was first ordained in Pennsylvania by the Donegal Presbytery in 1742. Presbyterians dominated the freeholder-elected vestry, and when Hindman died, his position was left vacant for years as ministers of their own persuasion preached freely through the county. Not until 1769 did the General Assembly order the vestry dissolved and reconstituted.[95] Over time, this sort of frontier defiance looked more and more like rebellion. Many Loyalists blamed the coming war on Presbyterians and other 'Oliverian' Calvinists.[96] Among the culprits were David Stephenson, James Knox, and James Curry (the boy from County Antrim), who would serve as officers in the 8th Virginia. Stephenson's uncle likely financed Hindman's journey to London.[97] David Stephenson was not closely related to John Stephenson, but his name was also often written as 'Stinson.'

Though far away, the forks of the Ohio were in Augusta County. Because it had no statutory western boundary, Augusta extended west to the Mississippi and as far north as modern

94 Howard McKnight Wilson, *The Tinkling Spring: Headwater of Freedom* (Fishersville, Va.: Tinkling Spring and Hermitage Presbyterian Churches, 1954), p.115.

95 Hening (ed.), *Statutes*, vol.8, p.482–483.

96 Joseph Galloway, *Historical and Political Reflections on the Rise and Progress of the American Rebellion* (London: G. Wilkie, 1780), p.67; Edward H. Tatum, Jr. (ed.), *The American Journal of Ambrose Serle, Secretary to Lord Howe, 1776–1778* (San Marino: Huntington Library, 1940), pp.89–90, 115, 131, 285.

97 Wilson, *Tinkling Spring*, p.116.

Minnesota. As western populations grew, many counties (and eventually eight states) were taken from Augusta's territory. The first of these was Botetourt County in 1770.[98] Two years later, Botetourt was split to create Fincastle.

As important as the Oregon Trail of the next century, the Great Philadelphia Wagon Road carried hundreds of thousands of immigrants as far south as Georgia. This monument stands in Lewisville, North Carolina. (Photo: Keith Hall)

Fincastle County

The Valley of Virginia extended south beyond the headwaters of the Shenandoah into the James and Roanoke watersheds. From Big Lick (Roanoke), one could continue south on the Wagon Road into the Carolinas or turn west on the Warrior's Path (The Wilderness Road) through the Cumberland Gap into the Kentucky country. This route crossed the New, Holston, and Clinch Rivers. Like the Ohio's, the water in these rivers flowed west to the Mississippi and the Gulf of Mexico. Settlers living on the Western Waters were induced by nature itself to turn their backs on the political, economic, and cultural power centres of the Atlantic coast.

In 1772, the New River also became the boundary of Fincastle County, for which the governor appointed another largely Scotch-Irish court.[99] The justices met at Fort Chiswell, but the county seat was officially at nearby Chiswell's Lead Mines, which would soon supply the Continental Army.[100]

Captain James Knox. James Knox was a 'long hunter' with notable adventures in his past and an impressive career in his future. He was raised along the Cowpasture River in what

98 William C. Pendleton, *History of Tazewell County and Southwest Virginia, 748–1920* (Richmond: W.C. Hill, 1920), pp.229–230.

99 Hening (ed.), *Statutes*, vol.8, pp.600–601.

100 McIlwaine et al (eds), *Executive Journals*, vol.6, p.506.

A sign marks the beginning of Virginia's 'Western Waters' in Craig County, Virginia. (Author's photo)

A historical marker near James Knox's grave in Shelby County, Ky. (Author's photo)

is now Bath County and left home for Virginia's westernmost settlement, in the Holston River Valley.[101] 'I always heard,' remembered a neighbour, 'that in his early life he spent most of his time on the frontier.'[102] The term 'long hunter' originates from an 11-month hunting expedition he led through the Cumberland Gap, probably in 1770.[103] Daniel Boone is the most famous explorer of Kentucky, but there is evidence that Knox made it through the mountains a year before him. 'James Knox was in Kentucky in the fall of the year 1768,' wrote Robert Wickliffe in 1848, '...Boone never saw the country until 1769.'[104]

The Border Dispute with Pennsylvania

Together, the eight jurisdictions that produced the 8th Virginia Regiment stretched from the Holston River settlements 400 miles north to Pittsburgh and from the Blue Ridge roughly 700 miles west to the Mississippi. Virginia's decentralised political system made it easy for immigrant populations to organise themselves far away from eastern authorities. At the same time, the distance, the Blue Ridge, and their large numbers made it hard for the Old Dominion to assimilate Irish and German settlers into Virginia's long-established culture. The immigrants maintained close economic, familial, and ecclesiastical ties with their brethren in Pennsylvania via the Great Wagon Road. When the war came, extra measures were taken to ensure western participation in the Virginia Line. Those measures resulted in the 8th Virginia Regiment.

First, however, the early 1770s brought conflicts with Pennsylvania and the western Indians. The British garrison, two companies of the 18th (Royal Irish) Regiment, pulled out of Fort Pitt in 1772,[105] leaving a power vacuum around the forks of the Ohio. The Shawnee disputed the Iroquois cession of land below the Ohio, while Pennsylvania and Virginia argued over the territory around the river's forks. It was fair to wonder if Virginia's leaders in Williamsburg could effectively govern such faraway places as Pittsburgh and Fort Chiswell.[106] Lord Dunmore travelled to Pittsburgh to personally demonstrate the province's control.[107] He met with settlers who 'beseeched' him to organise local government institutions now that more than 10,000 people were living in the area. Adhering to law and protocol, he deferred action on this but asked some of the locals to visit him later in Williamsburg.[108]

101 Joseph Addison Waddell (ed.), *Annals of Augusta County, Virginia*, first edition (Richmond: Wm. Ellis Jones), pp.482–483.

102 John Redd, 'Reminiscences of Western Virginia, 1770–1790', *VMHB*, 7:3 (1900), p.248.

103 Humphrey Marshall, *The History of Kentucky* (Frankfort: George S. Robinson, 1824), pp.7–9; WHS: Draper Mss, C, vol.5, pp.42–45.

104 WHS: Draper Mss, C, vol.5, p.50. See also Mann Butler, *A History of the Commonwealth of Kentucky* (Louisville: J.A. James, 1834), pp.19–20.

105 G.E. Boyle, 'The 18th (or Royal Irish) Regiment of Foot in North America – 1767–75', *Journal of the Society for Army Historical Research*, 2:8 (1923), pp.63–68.

106 Warren Skidmore and Donna Kaminsky (eds), *Lord Dunmore's Little War of 1774* (Bowie, Md.: Heritage Books, 2002), pp.175–177

107 Williams, *Dunmore's War*, p.26.

108 K. G. Davies (ed.), *Documents of the American Revolution 1770–1783 (Colonial Office Series)* (Shannon: Irish University Press, 1972–1981), vol.8, pp.65–67.

To press its competing claim, Pennsylvania incorporated the territory as 'Westmoreland County.' Dunmore countered the Quaker colony by appointing the civil and military officials he had promised to consider. There was no clean way to do this. The Crown imposed a moratorium on new counties, and the Augusta County court at Staunton had no real ability to administer the disputed territory from so far away.[109] Dunmore and the Virginia Council of State decided to appoint several new Augusta County justices, resident in and around Pittsburgh, to constitute their own quorum.[110] Among them was Dr John Connolly, who had accepted the governor's invitation to visit Williamsburg. Dunmore made Connolly a captain commandant of militia and charged him with organising the region's men into companies.[111] One of Connolly's subordinate captains was John Stephenson of Jacobs Creek, who felt quite strongly about Virginia's claim.[112] In the territorial contest, there were arrests, counter-arrests, and some minor violence. But because it had no real militia, Pennsylvania was forced to stand down.[113]

Lord Dunmore's War

While the colonies bickered over boundaries, a war broke out between Virginia and two of the western tribes. The fuel was Shawnee and Mingo resentment of the Treaty of Fort Stanwix, but the spark was a massacre perpetrated by settlers at Baker's Bottom, opposite Yellow Creek on the Ohio, on 30 April. Among the dead were the wife and pregnant sister of Soyechtowa, an important Mingo warrior with the alternate given name of John Logan Shickellamy, or simply 'Logan.'[114] James Knox was deep in Kentucky guiding a surveying team when the massacre occurred and was fortunate to make it home alive.[115]

Dunmore ordered Andrew Lewis, county lieutenant of Botetourt County, to organise a southern division of Augusta, Botetourt, and Fincastle militia and approach the Indian country via the Kanawha Valley. Knox had just taken this route with the surveyors and retraced his route as a guide.[116] George Slaughter joined them with others from Culpeper. The earl returned to Fort Pitt via Winchester to lead a northern division himself. He descended the Ohio with John Stephenson and other future rebels in a flotilla of canoes, mindful of the trouble growing in the east.[117] The last 10 months had seen the Boston Tea Party and

109 Brent Tarter (ed.), 'The Orderly Book of the Second Virginia Regiment: September 27, 1775-April 15, 1776', *VMHB* 85:2 (1977), p.170, n.45.

110 McIlwaine et al (eds), *Executive Journals*, vol.6, p.543.

111 Williams, *Dunmore's War*, p.32.

112 Anon., *History of Bedford, Somerset, and Fulton Counties, Pennsylvania* (Chicago: Waterman and Watkins, 1884), pp.75, 79; LVA: State Government Records Collection, Accession 36912, Letter and depositions, 27 Nov. 1778.

113 Williams, *Dunmore's War*, pp.33–45.

114 Robert G. Parkinson, *Heart of American Darkness: Bewilderment and Horror on the Early Frontier* (New York: W.W. Norton, 2024), pp.8, 176–182.

115 Thomas Hanson, 'Thomas Hanson's Journal,' in Reuben Gold Thwaites and Louise Phelps Kellogg (eds), *Documentary History of Dunmore's War, 1774* (Madison: State Historical Society of Wisconsin, 1905), pp.110–133.

116 Thwaites and Kellogg (eds), *Dunmore's War*, pp.xvii, pp.86–87.

117 Princeton University Library (PUL): Special Collections – Manuscripts, C0938 No. 752 South 79: 'Journal of the Expedition Down the River Ohio Under the Command of his Excellency John Earl of

Witten's Fort, as reconstructed in 1926, near Tazewell, Va. The original was built in 1774 as a safe house for settlers. Small defensive structures of this kind were common on the frontier. (Author's photo)

the punitive closure of Boston Harbor. When the burgesses declared the first of June a day of fasting, humiliation, and prayer, Dunmore promptly dissolved the legislature. From the Crown's perspective, it was not a good time for the governor to be away from Williamsburg.

At Point Pleasant on 10 October, Lewis's division met an Indian army led by a Shawnee war chief known as The Cornstalk (Hokoleskwa) and engaged in an intense, hours-long battle. Several 8th Virginia men were in this fight, experiencing their first organised combat. James Curry and a small force secured high ground on the right beyond a creek to blunt an attack on the Virginians' flank. Curry was shot 'thro' the right arm at the elbow,' taking him out of the fight.[118] When the battle ended, George Slaughter sent an account of it to John Pinkney's *Virginia Gazette*. He reported that the Indians conducted a fighting retreat, maintaining sporadic fire to protect their wounded as they recrossed the river. 'They had not the satisfaction of carrying off any of our scalps,' he reported, 'save one or two stragglers, whom they killed before the engagement. Many of their dead they scalped, rather than we should have them; but our troops scalped upwards of twenty of their men, that were first killed. It

Dunmore Lieutenant and Governor General of his Majesty's Colony and Dominion of Virginia, 1774,' p.7; Wainwright, 'Turmoil at Pittsburgh,' p.140.

118 Williams, *Dunmore's War*, pp.285–286; LVA: Legislative Petitions, Accession 36121, James Curry.

is beyond doubt their loss in number far exceeds ours, which is considerable.'[119] Slaughter remained interested in scalping for years.

When he learned of the Battle of Point Pleasant, Dunmore was advancing up the Hockhocking River toward the Shawnee settlement at Chillicothe. Several days later, he met with The Cornstalk and other Shawnee leaders at Camp Charlotte to discuss peace. Though he addressed the Shawnee as 'deluded brethren', the Big Knife demanded little from them. He claimed no new territory. He only insisted that the Six Nations and Cherokee treaties be adhered to, that captives and stolen horses be returned, and that travellers on the Ohio be allowed to pass unmolested in the future. He admonished them to be at peace with their 'grandfathers', the Delaware, and not to allow 'prejudiced persons from Pennsylvania' to 'abuse their ears' with claims that the Virginians were the Shawnee's enemies. With a belt of wampum, he offered to be 'sincere and steady friends' in the future.[120] The Cornstalk agreed, but Logan and the Mingo refused to even talk.

The governor left Adam Stephen in command at a fortified magazine dubbed 'Fort Gower' and set off for Williamsburg in 'a batteau well mann'd accompanyed by the prayers of the whole Army for his safe return to his Family and Friends.'[121] While the prayers for the governor were sincere, the American dispute with Parliament could no longer be ignored. When Dunmore dismissed the Burgesses, they simply reconvened in a tavern and called for a non-importation agreement, a Continental congress, and an extra-legal Virginia Convention, which would assemble on 1 August after the delegates had time to collect 'their sense of their respective counties.'[122] Dunmore knew all of this and predicted what was coming on his way west. A man named John Struthers recalled his father's encounter with the governor in a tavern near Pittsburgh:

> I distinctly remember that when with my father, crossing the allegheny from the East, we met Lord Dunmore at Fausets tavern, on or near the Laurel Hill, and it being announced to him that a Scotch man had arrived (my father was a Scotchman) he approached my father and having asked his name, he took him aside … After extolling the Scotch for the most loyal subjects in his majestys dominions, he said, a crisis was approaching, and near at hand, when it was probable, there would be a rupture between the mother country and her american colonies, and exhorted my father to continue his alligiance to his liege sovereign, and, firmly, to withstand all attempts to seduce him.[123]

Such appeals mostly fell on deaf ears. The day after the governor's departure for Williamsburg, Adam Stephen convened a meeting of officers that resulted in the 'Fort Gower Resolves.' They expressed their loyalty to the king and their affection for Dunmore, but also declared their determination to defend their 'just Rights and Privileges.'

119 *Virginia Gazette* (Pinkney), 10 Nov.1744.
120 PUL: 'Journal of Dunmore Expedition', pp.19–20.
121 PUL: 'Journal of Dunmore Expedition', p.26.
122 William J. Van Schreeven and Robert L. Scribner (eds), *Revolutionary Virginia: The Road to Independence*, (Charlottesville: University Press of Virginia, 1973–1983), vol.1, pp.93–104.
123 NARA: M804, R18262, John Struthers pension (West Augusta Militia).

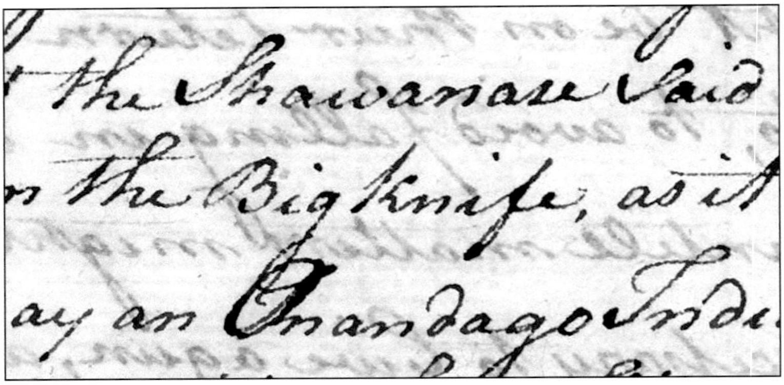

The Shawnee referred to Virginia governors as 'The Big Knife.' The name, inspired by the swords governors often wore, was also applied to Virginians collectively. (Journal of John Connelly, 1774, New York Public Library)

> We have lived about three Months in the Woods, without any intelligence from Boston, or from the Delegates at Philadelphia. ... That we are a respectable Body is certain, when it is considered that we can live Weeks without Bread or Salt, that we can sleep in the open Air without any Covering but that of the Canopy of Heaven, and that our Men can march and shoot with any in the known World. Blessed with these Talents, let us solemnly engage to one another, and our Country in particular, that we will use them to no Purpose but for the Honour and Advantage of America in general, and of Virginia in particular.

The bravado of the Fort Gower Resolves matches Adam Stephen's style. Within the swagger was a veiled threat that was the first of its kind from American men in arms: 'we will bear the most faithful Allegiance to his Majesty King George III, whilst his Majesty delights to reign over a brave and free People.'[124]

124 *Virginia Gazette* (Purdie & Dixon), 22 Dec. 1774.

3

Dissidents

An effigy of Lieutenant General Thomas Gage was hauled around Winchester in a wagon on 22 July 1774 with a noose around its neck. The real general was in Boston, where he, as the new governor, was enforcing the closure of the port. Livelihoods were lost there, and hunger threatened the whole city. When the Boston Committee of Correspondence called for a boycott of British goods, Gage issued a proclamation condemning the 'scandalous, traitorous, and seditious' plan and warned the public to think carefully about 'the high criminality and dangerous consequences' of such a course of action.[1] The proclamation was mocked throughout the colonies and converted into satirical verse. The people of Frederick County, assembling for an election, 'unanimously' agreed that Gage's effigy should 'be first hanged, and then suffer the flames, accompanied by his darling proclamation.'

> An image was fabricated like him, as he must appear to the mind's eye of every American, grim as Pluto and deformed as Vulcan. It was decorated with a soldier's coat, a soldier's cap, and a wooden sword. Thus accoutered, with a rope round his neck, in the fatal cart, supported by an African (for the general's spirits were so depressed, that it was with difficulty he could hold up his head) he was conducted through the town, attended by a rejoicing multitude, and then suspended on the highest gallows an American governor was ever yet honoured with. The proclamation was read by Mr. A. White, attorney at law, who made a very spirited and handsome speech to the people, exhorting them to be unanimous, as the certain means to preserve their liberties. The torch was then applied, and the flame, as if pleased to destroy the base destroyer of liberty, embraced him with uncommon ardour, and devoured him in an instant.[2]

The 'proclamation' published in the *Virginia Gazette* concluded with an explicit reference to the Old Dominion's Scottish governor and called out the Tory leanings of other Caledonian politicians.

1 Peter Force (ed.), *American Archives* (Washington: U.S. Congress, 1837–1846), ser.4, vol.1, pp.491–492.
2 *Virginia Gazette* (Rind), 4 Aug. 1774.

To Murray bend the humble knee;
He shall protect you under me;
His generous pen shall not be mute,
But sound your praise thro' Fox to Bute.

By Scotchmen lov'd, by Scotchmen taught,
By all your country Scotchmen thought;
Fear Bute, fear Mansfield, North and me,
And be as blest as slaves can be.

On the day of the protest, John Murray, the Earl of Dunmore, was only 12 miles away at Greenway Court, preparing for his expedition to the Ohio.[3] If anyone told the governor about the demonstration, he did nothing about it.

In preparation for the planned Virginia Convention, many counties called public meetings and put their sentiments in writing. Frederick County conducted one of the first such assemblies in Winchester,[4] moderated by parish rector and county justice Charles Mynn Thruston.[5] In an eight-point resolution, they 'most heartily and unanimously' concurred with the sentiments of their 'suffering brethren of Boston.' They called the tea tax unconstitutional and asserted that enforcing it 'by a military power will have a necessary tendency to raise a civil war.' They endorsed an 'association' to stop all commerce with Britain. The seventh point declared:

> That it is the opinion of this meeting, that Committees ought to be appointed for the purpose of effecting a general Association, that the same measures may be pursued through the whole Continent … and that when the same shall be formed and agreed to by the several Committees, we will strictly adhere thereto; and till the general sense of the Continent shall be known, we do pledge ourselves to each other and to our country, that we will inviolably adhere to the votes of this day.

The final resolve created the Frederick County Committee, which Thruston chaired. The Frederick Resolutions were 'unanimously assented to and subscribed.'[6] This unanimity was only possible, of course, because Loyalists did not attend. The resolutions did, however, represent the majority view of the county's freeholders and projected strong support for the Association and its goals.[7]

Dunmore County's citizens met eight days later in Woodstock and adopted Frederick County's language verbatim. The attendees chose Peter Muhlenberg, Francis Slaughter, Abraham Bird, Taverner Beale, John Tipton, and Abraham Bowman to form a county committee, with Muhlenberg as its chairman.[8] Culpeper County met on 7 July and pledged

3 *Virginia Gazette* (Rind), 4 Aug. 1774; Williams, *Dunmore's War*, p.182.
4 Jim Glanville, 'The Fincastle Resolutions', *The Smithfield Review*, 14 (2010), p.74.
5 Ingle, 'Justices', pp.92, 95, 114.
6 Force (ed.), *American Archives*, vol.4, pp.392–393.
7 Michael A. McDonnell, *The Politics of War: Race, Class, & Conflict in Revolutionary Virginia* (Chapel Hill: University of North Carolina Press, 2007), pp.35–36.
8 FHS: Clark Diary, 16 June 1774; *Virginia Gazette* (Rind), 4 Aug. 1774.

'at the risk of our lives and fortunes' to oppose any taxes imposed by Parliament 'unless we are legally represented.' They endorsed the Association and urged the development of domestic manufacturing. They appointed two men to represent them at the August Convention but did not yet create a local committee.[9]

The First Virginia Convention met in August and pledged to stop imports from Britain on the first of November. A cessation of exports, including tobacco, was delayed to the following year to allow the current year's crops to be sold. Farmers were urged to switch to domestically useful agriculture such as sheep raising. The Convention did not see itself as a legislature, and the Association was a pact, not a law. Participants simply pledged not to do business with any merchant who did not sign the Association and abide by its terms. The convention also urged Virginians to 'make such liberal Contributions as they can afford' to support the people of Boston.[10]

On 20 October, the 'General Congress' in Philadelphia formed a Continental Association to enforce a 12-colony trade boycott.[11] It closely mirrored the provisions of the Virginia Association and called on every county in every colony to form a committee to enforce it.[12] This produced another round of meetings and resolutions in Virginia, including an important one in Fincastle. Colonel William Christian, who had recently returned from the fight at Point Pleasant, chaired the Fincastle Committee. Its members were all militia officers, with the exception of Presbyterian minister Charles Cummings. Cummings, however, was the county's *de facto* militia chaplain, religious head, and an important local leader in the coming war.[13] The Fincastle Resolves, likely written by Cummings, reflected the Ulster origins of its signers.

> Many of us, and our forefathers, left our native land, considering it as a kingdom subjected to inordinate power, and greatly abridged of its liberties. We crossed the Atlantick, and explored this then uncultivated wilderness, bordering on many nations of savages, and surrounded by mountains almost inaccessible to any but those very savages, who have incessantly been committing barbarities and depredations on us since our first seating the country. These fatigues and dangers we patiently encountered, supported by the pleasing hope of enjoying those rights and liberties which had been granted to Virginians and were denied us in our native country, and of transmitting them inviolate to our posterity. But even to these remote regions the hand of unlimited and unconstitutional power hath pursued us, to strip us of that liberty and property with which God, nature, and the rights of humanity, have vested us.

9 Van Schreeven and Scribner (eds), *Revolutionary Virginia*, vol.1, pp.118–120.

10 *Virginia Gazette* (Purdie & Dixon), 11 Aug. 1774; *Virginia Gazette* (Rind), 4 Aug. 1774; W. F. Dunaway, 'The Virginia Conventions of the Revolution', *Virginia Law Register*, 10:7 (1904), pp.570–572.

11 Julian P. Boyd et al (eds), *Papers of Thomas Jefferson* (Princeton: Princeton University Press, 1950), vol.1, pp.149–154.

12 *Virginia Gazette* (Purdie & Dixon), 3 Nov. 1774.

13 Henry Alexander White, *Southern Presbyterian Leaders* (New York: Neale Publishing, 1911), p.102; J.G.M. Ramsay, *Annals of Tennessee* (Charleston: John Russell, 1853), pp.160, 169; Douglas Summers Brown, 'Charles Cummings: The Fighting Parson of Southwest Virginia', *Virginia Cavalcade*, 28:3 (1979), pp.138–143.

As Presbyterians in an Anglican colony, they emphasized religious freedom. 'We by no means desire to shake off our duty or allegiance to our lawful sovereign, but on the contrary shall ever glory in being loyal subjects of a Protestant prince, descended from such illustrious progenitors, so long as we can enjoy the free exercise of our religion, as Protestants, and our liberties and properties, as British subjects.' Then came the threat.

> But if no pacifick measures shall be proposed or adopted by Great Britain, and our enemies will attempt to dragoon us out of these inestimable privileges which we are entitled to as subjects, and to reduce us to a state of slavery, we declare, that we are deliberately and resolutely determined never to surrender them to any power upon earth, but at the expense of our lives.

'These,' they declared, 'are our real, though unpolished sentiments, of liberty and loyalty, and in them we are resolved to live and die.'[14]

Augusta County's freeholders met four months later under the leadership of Alexander Balmain, another Presbyterian clergyman who had travelled to London for Anglican ordination.[15] Augusta's 'resolves' were styled as written instructions to its delegates to the Second Virginia Convention. Ominously, they urged the necessity of drilling the militia throughout the colony.[16]

Kentucky

While resentment toward Parliament grew, the conclusion of Dunmore's War convinced many that it was safe to enter Kentucky. The treaties of 1768 had already made it legal. James Knox was sent back to make more surveys. Boonesborough and St Asaph's joined Harrodsburg as the original three named settlements beyond the Cumberland Gap.[17] The Cornstalk kept his promises from Camp Charlotte and delivered several captives and horses to the Virginia militia garrison at Point Pleasant.[18]

While most exploration from this period went unrecorded, Kentucky historian Lewis Collins reported in 1847 that several names carved into four beech trees on the north bank of the Barren River (near present-day Bowling Green) were still legible. They included 'J. Neaville', 'I. Hite', 'A. Bowman', 'J. Drake', 'J. Bowman', 'Tho. Slaughter', and 'I. Drake' with different dates from the middle of June 1775.[19] Two of the represented given names and

14 *Virginia Gazette* (Purdie), 10 Feb. 1775.

15 Charles Washington Coleman, 'The Virginia County Committees of Safety, 1774-'75', *William and Mary Quarterly*, 5:4 (1897), pp.245–255, 252; Bell, *Anglican Clergy*, p.111; Nelson, *Blessed Company*, p.387, n22.

16 *Virginia Gazette* (Pinckney), 16 March 1775.

17 Felix Walker, 'Felix Walker's Narrative of His Trip with Boone From Long Island to Boonesborough in March, 1775', in George W. Ranck, *Boonesborough* (Louisville: Filson Club, 1901), pp.161–168, 166; Hammon, *Floyd*, pp.13–17.

18 Force (ed.), *American Archives*, ser.4, vol.1, p.1226.

19 Lewis Collins and Richard H. Collins, *Collins' Historical Sketches of Kentucky* (Covington, Ky: Collins, 1882), vol.2, p.738.

all of the surnames are connected to the 8th Virginia Regiment. 'A. Bowman' was almost certainly the young justice from Strasburg.[20] 'I. Drake' was probably the remnant of 'E. Drake.' Ephraim Drake was a long hunter who explored with James Knox and was appointed his 1st Lieutenant in 1776.[21]

The County Committees

The county committees established to support the Virginia and Continental Associations have come to be known as 'committees of safety.' Properly, however, that name only applied to the provincewide body that filled the coming vacuum in executive authority. The local organisations often descended from committees of correspondence and were sometimes called 'committees of inspection and observation', but most often, they were simply called 'county committees'.[22] Peter Muhlenberg described the formation of Dunmore County's committee in a letter:

> The times are getting troublesome with us, and begin to wear a hostile appearance. Independent companies are forming in every county, and politics engross all conversation. I had thrown up my commission as chairman of the Committee of Correspondence, and of magistrate likewise; but last week we had a general election in the county for a Great Committee, according to the resolves of Congress, and I am again chosen chairman, so that, whether I choose or not, I am to be a politician.[23]

Muhlenberg's ecclesiastical counterpart in Frederick took an equally active role. Taverner Beale remembered that 'the most eloquent discourse he ever heard, was an address by Parson Thruston, about the commencement of the Revolutionary War, at a meeting of the people, in which the arbitrary and oppressive acts of the British government were forcibly exposed, the people urged to resistance, and the young men encouraged and excited to take up arms in defence of the country.' The impact of the speech 'was like an electric shock, causing an universal agitation of the audience.'[24]

The committees took their work seriously. Early in 1775, committee members caught a merchant named William Holliday attempting to sell tea in Frederick County and induced him to take an oath 'that he should neither sell Tea or use it.' When he was caught selling tea again in Dunmore County, he argued that 'the purport of his oath extended no further than Fred[erick] County.' While the matter was now an issue for the Dunmore Committee to consider, Reverend Thruston told the merchant that he would cease his own business

20 Wayland, *Bowmans*, pp.44–45, 64.

21 Assessed from J. [Joseph] Drake, Ephraim's brother.

22 Anon. (ed.), *Journal of Virginia Delegates, 1776*, p.19.

23 Henry A. Muhlenberg, *The Life of Major-General Peter Muhlenberg of the Revolutionary Army* (Philadelphia: Carey and Hart, 1849), pp.45–46.

24 Buckner Thruston, 'Biography of Col. Charles Mynn Thruston', *Southern Literary Messenger*, 6:3 (1840), pp.163–168, 168, n.2.

dealings with him if he did not desist. Holliday retorted that Thruston did not provide him with much business anyway and insisted that he did not really have to follow Thruston's orders because 'he was Independent of the great Men, the best part of whose Custom was to run in Debt, and let a man lay out of his Money a year & a half.'[25]

On 5 July, the Dunmore Committee 'ducked' a man named William Clark.[26] This was a punishment for 'nags' and 'scolds', but was used now to punish Clark for being a Tory. Tied to a chair at the end of a lever or a rope, he was repeatedly submerged, perhaps in the Shenandoah River. He was then compelled to sign an oath.

> I hereby declare on the holy Evangelist of Almighty God that from henceforth I will not either publickly or privately hold any correspondence with any person whatsoever who shall speak disrespectfully of the Continental Congress, or any Committee of any County, or their proceedings, and I hereby declare that the Americans are Justly entitled to those privilidges for which they are Contending and further that I will depart from the Town of Woodstock within Ten Minutes from this time, and from the County of Dunmore before tomorrow night, and not return therein for the space of one year.[27]

This may be the same William Clark, then a resident of neighbouring Hampshire County, who was drafted into the 8th Virginia in 1778.[28] Another less compliant loyalist wrote, 'so long as you remain refractory and yield no submission to the mandates of the King, I shall pay no obedience to the summons of an illegal assembly combin'd in the most unjustifiable manner and have under their Consideration [the most] treasonable proceedings.'[29] Among the purported 'treasonable proceedings' was the collection of funds to support the delegates to Congress. Jonathan Clark, who was not related to the banished Tory, raised a significant amount from the immigrant German community, including weighed silver, Spanish pistareens, and paper currency.[30]

In October, Chairman Silas Hart convened the Augusta Committee in Staunton to deal with Alexander Miller, who had called opposition to the acts of Parliament 'rebellion' and declared 'the lives and fortunes of those concerned in such opposition are forfeited, as traitors to the King.' Hart believed members of Congress, the Virginia Convention, and the Augusta Committee were using the crisis to enrich themselves. In response, the committee

> recommended to all the good people of this County and Colony, to have no farther dealings, connection, or intercourse, with the said Miller, as he appears from the whole tenour of his behavior, to be a real enemy to the general struggle of all America, now defending themselves against the tyrannical oppressions of a corrupt

25 LVA: Dunmore County Revolutionary War Papers, 1775–1814, deposition of Alexander Machir, 7 Feb. 1775.
26 FHS: Clark Diary, 5 July 1774.
27 LVA: Dunmore County Revolutionary War Papers, 1775–1814, signed oath of William Clark, 5 July 1775.
28 NARA: M881, r.973, William Clark; NARA: M804, W6683, William Clark pension.
29 LVA: Dunmore County Revolutionary War Papers, 1775–1814, undated letter from a Loyalist.
30 LVA: Dunmore County Revolutionary War Papers, 1775–1814, German donor subscriptions, 23 May 1775.

A diorama of Fort Pitt created in 1965 shows the structure's scale relative to the village of Pittsburgh. Virginia forces under John Neville occupied the outpost after the British garrison withdrew and called it 'Fort Dunmore.' (Author's photo)

> British Parliament, until he, by his future behaviour, convinces his countrymen of his sincere repentance for his past folly.[31]

When the Scottish rector of Culpeper's Bromfield Parish refused to comply with Congress's designation of 20 July 1775 as a day of public humiliation, fasting, and prayer, James Madison mused that his 'insolence' might 'abate' if he were 'ducked in a coat of Tar & surplice of feathers.'[32] Instead, the committee declared him a person 'inimical to American liberty' and expelled him from the county.[33]

In West Augusta (the forks of the Ohio), Doctor Connolly quietly 'resolved to exert every faculty in defense of the royal cause' and prevent the formation of a county committee or company of volunteers.[34] But there was no stopping it. A 'committee of observation' of 28 men,

31 Force (ed.), *American Archives*, ser.4, vol.3, pp.939–940.

32 William T. Hutchinson et al (eds), *Papers of James Madison* (Chicago: University of Chicago Press), vol.1, pp.159–162.

33 *Virginia Gazette* (Dixon & Hunter), 20 Jan. 1776; *Virginia Gazette* (Purdie), 31 Jan. 1777.

34 John Connolly, *A Narrative of the Transactions, Imprisonment, and Sufferings of John Connolly, an American Loyalist and Lieutenant-Colonel in his Majesty's Service* (London: 1788; reprinted New York: Charles L. Woodward, 1889), p.6.

chaired by George Croghan, was formed on 16 May 1775. It resolved, 'That this Committee have the highest sense of the spirited behaviour of their brethren in New-England, and do most cordially approve of their opposing the invaders of American rights and privileges to the utmost extreme, and that each member of this Committee, respectively, will animate and encourage their neighbourhood to follow the brave example.' They also expressed a rational and ultimately accurate fear that the Crown's agents would encourage the western Indian tribes to attack them.

The West Augusta Committee forced the Crown's deputy superintendent for Indian affairs at Pittsburgh (George Croghan's successor) to sign a pledge to cease his work:

> I, Alexander McKee, Deputy Agent for the Indian Affairs for the District of Fort Pitt, do hereby promise and engage that I will not transact any business with the Indians on behalf of the Crown or Ministry; that I will not, directly or indirectly, correspond with any of the Crown or Ministerial officers, nor leave the neighborhood of Fort Pitt, without the consent of the Committee of West Augusta.[35]

The Second Virginia Convention

The eight jurisdictions that raised companies for the 8th Virginia Regiment were all represented at the Second Virginia Convention when it convened in Richmond. Each county elected two men as they had previously done for the House of Burgesses. Robert Rutherford and Adam Stephen represented Berkeley. Charles Thruston and Isaac Zane represented Frederick. Peter Muhlenberg and Jonathan Clark represented Dunmore. Henry Field, Jr was paired with Henry Pendleton for Culpeper. Timely travel from the frontier was a challenge, and William Christian arrived alone from Fincastle.[36] John Harvie was the lone delegate from the West Augusta District because John Neville (John Jolliffe's former neighbour) was ill. The district was still part of Augusta County, but the Convention allowed him to be seated.[37] Hampshire County was represented by James Mercer, who was about to become a member of the Virginia Committee of Safety. Mercer lived in Spotsylvania County, but he owned property in Hampshire, which qualified him.[38] The voters may also have appreciated that Mercer's younger brother was killed in Hampshire County during the French and Indian War.[39]

The delegates who met at the Henrico Parish Church (now St John's) on 20 March included historically important figures such as Patrick Henry, Thomas Jefferson, Edmund

35 Force (ed.), *American Archives*, ser.4, vol.5, p.820.

36 Anon., *The Proceedings of the Convention of Delegates for the Counties and Corporations of Virginia in the Colony of Virginia Held at Richmond Town, in the County of Henrico on the 20th of March, 1775* [2nd Convention] (Richmond: Ritchie, Trueheart & Duval, 1816), pp.3–4.

37 Anon., *Proceedings of the 2nd Convention*, p.4; Cynthia Miller Leonard (ed.), *The General Assembly of Virginia, July 30, 1619–January 11, 1978* (Richmond: Virginia State Library, 1978), p.113.

38 Richard K. MacMaster, *The History of Hardy County, 1786–1986* (Salem, W.Va.: Hardy County Public Library, 1986), p.57.

39 Maxwell and Swisher, *Hampshire*, p.340.

Pendleton, Peyton Randolph, and George Washington.[40] They were divided over whether and how to raise troops. Professional, 'standing' or 'regular' armies had been viewed as antithetical to British liberty since the time of Oliver Cromwell. They were also expensive. Virginia only raised 'regulars' in times of true crisis. Nevertheless, Patrick Henry's famous 'Give Me Liberty or Give Me Death' speech convinced the convention to take some steps toward military readiness.[41]

Still sensitive to their extra-legal status, the Convention only offered 'recommendations' to the colony's 62 counties and three incorporated towns. The Convention resolved that 'a well regulated militia … is the natural strength, and only security, of a free government' and argued that 'such a militia in this colony would forever render it unnecessary for the mother country to keep among us, for the purpose of our defense, any standing army … and would obviate the pretext of taxing us for their support.' They urged that the militia law of 1738 (which had been allowed to expire when Dunmore dismissed the General Assembly in 1774) be put back 'in execution.'[42] They also urged each county to organise an 'independent company of volunteers' who, unlike the militia, were 'to be in constant training and readiness.'[43] A few counties had already raised volunteer companies under a precedent from the French and Indian War.[44] Like the Convention and the county committees, these companies were extra-legal, voluntary, and filled by the most ardent Whigs.

Before adjourning, the Convention selected Randolph, Washington, Henry and four others to attend the Second Continental Congress.[45] Though most of the Convention's decisions took the form of 'recommendations', its members knew the counties would treat them as law. Whether the population at large would do the same remained to be seen.

Despite receiving praise from the Convention for his conduct during the Indian war, Dunmore sent an angry report to London in December.[46] 'The steps,' he wrote, 'which have been pursued in the different Counties of Virginia to carry into execution the Resolutions of the General Congress, are of so extraordinary a nature that I am at a loss for words to express the criminality of them.'[47]

The Volunteer Companies

The First Independent Company of Dunmore was likely organised at the Dunmore Committee's fifth meeting on 18 April, soon after Muhlenberg and Clark returned from the Second Convention.[48] The company's undated organising document mirrors the language used in Richmond.

40 Anon., *Proceedings of the 2nd Convention*, pp.3–4.
41 Dunaway, 'Virginia Conventions', pp.570–578.
42 Anon., *Proceedings of the 2nd Convention*, pp.5–6; McDonnell, *Politics of War*, pp.37–40.
43 Anon., *Proceedings of the 2nd Convention*, p.6.
44 McDonnell, *Politics of War*, pp.40–43; John E. Selby, *The Revolution in Virginia, 1775–1783* (Williamsburg: Colonial Williamsburg, 1988), p.18.
45 Anon., *Proceedings of the 2nd Convention*, p.7.
46 Anon., *Proceedings of the 2nd Convention*, p.7.
47 Thomas Aspinwall et al (eds), *Collections of the Massachusetts Historical Society* (Boston: Massachusetts Historical Society, 1852–1871), ser.4, vol.10, pp.737–738.
48 FHS: Clark Diary, 18 April 1775.

> We the Subscribers, Inhabitants of the County of Dunmore and Colony of Virginia embody ourselves in one … Company, to be called the first Independent Company of Dunmore, And do bind ourselves by all ties of Honour Love to our Country, and the words of Gentlemen to adhere strictly to such resolves which shall be entered into by a Majority of the Company.[49]

Berkeley and Frederick counties also formed independent volunteer companies at this time.[50] West Augusta did the same in May or June.[51] James Higgins reported from Fish Creek on the Ohio that the West Augusta Committee decided 'it Proper that there shall be Independent Companes Raised in our side of the Mountain', and were collecting arms. 'We are Willing to Defend our Liberties', he declared.[52]

These were not militia organisations, but the distinction is easy for modern readers to miss. County militias were authorised in law and answerable to the governor. Enrolment was mandatory and officers were appointed, not elected. The opposite was true for the volunteer companies on all four points.[53]

The signatures of 88 men appear on the Dunmore Independent Company's organising document. None are identified as officers, but the first two names are Taverner Beale and Jonathan Clark. One veteran remembered Clark as the company's captain, but a contemporary letter identifies him as a lieutenant, making Beale the likely captain.[54] Six of the 14 justices of the peace, perhaps a majority of the magistrates of fighting age, signed on. Company members Taverner Beale, Abraham Bowman, Richard Campbell, Jonathan Clark, John Steed, Mathias Hite, Leonard Cooper, Philip Huffman, Jacob Parett, and Clark's younger brother John all later became officers in the 8th Virginia.[55]

Muhlenberg is not on the list, but as chairman of the committee, he was in charge. John Buskirk remembered, 'I served as a Volunteer private … in the Company commanded by Captain Jonathan Clark in a Regiment the Colonel commanding which was Colonel Mulenburgh.' Struggling 57 years later to remember how things had worked, he attested that Muhlenberg 'was not perhaps at & during their march regularly commissioned, but by common consent had charge & command. Subsequently he raised the German Regement No. 8.'[56]

The purpose of the independent companies, as envisioned by Fairfax County's George Mason, was 'to rouse the attention of the public, to introduce the use of arms and discipline, to infuse a martial spirit of emulation, and to provide a fund of officers' in case formal

49 Anon. (ed.), 'The First Independent Company of Dunmore', *VMHB* 44:2 (1936), pp.102–104.
50 *Virginia Gazette* (Purdie), 12 May 1775.
51 Force (ed.), *American Archives*, ser.4, vol.2, pp.612–615; Samuel Hazard et al (eds), *Pennsylvania Archives* (Philadelphia: Joseph Severns & Co., 1852–1856), ser.6, vol.2, p.3; Chase et al (eds), *Papers of Washington* (Revolution), vol.1, pp.28–32.
52 WHS: Draper Mss, L, vol.1, p.19, James Higgins to Jonathan Clark, 17 June 1775.
53 Selby, *Revolution in Virginia*, p.18.
54 NARA: M804, S32148, John Buskirk pension (Dunmore Volunteer Co.); WHS: Draper Mss, L, vol.1, p.21, Alexander Machir to Jonathan Clark, 3 May 1775.
55 FHS: Clark Diary, 22 May 1774; Draper Mss L, vol.1, p.27.
56 NARA: J. Buskirk pension.

The Bowman house near Strasburg. The home was built about 1771 to replace a previous log structure that had been used for defence during the French and Indian War. (Author's photo)

military organisation became necessary.[57] While Mason believed membership in the independent companies should be limited to 'gentlemen of the first fortune and character',[58] eight members of the Dunmore Independent Company joined the 8th Virginia as enlisted men: Jesse Allison, Martin Honey, John Hoy, Michael Keller, William Kennedy, Henry Maise, John White.[59] A total of 18 members of the Dunmore Independent Company served in the 8th Virginia.

The Powder Alarm

Things were quiet in the governor's namesake county after Muhlenberg and Clark returned home from the Second Virginia Convention. The spring rains of 1775 saturated farmers'

57 Robert A. Rutland (ed.), *The Papers of George Mason* (Chapel Hill: University of North Carolina Press, 1970), vol.1, p.229; Michael A. McDonnell, 'Popular Mobilization and Political Culture in Revolutionary Virginia: The Failure of the Minutemen and the Revolution from Below', *Journal of American History*, 85:3 (1998), pp.951–962.

58 Rutland, *Papers of Mason*, vol.1, p.211.

59 Anon. (ed.), 'Independent Company of Dunmore', pp.102–104. William Dennis served as a cadet, or officer in training, under Captain Richard Campbell.

fields as they considered what to plant now that exports to Britain were being halted. Clark visited Muhlenberg at the parish glebe farm and went fishing in the Shenandoah. An election was held, and Muhlenberg and Clark were selected again for the Third Convention, scheduled for July.[60]

The quiet was broken by the Williamsburg Powder Alarm. At Dunmore's direction, Royal Navy sailors from HM Schooner *Magdalen*, which was moored in the James River, slipped into town in the dead of night to remove the gunpowder from the public magazine. Word spread quickly through the colony. The Spotsylvania Independent Company heard the news as they were drilling. They sent express riders to the outer counties to summon the colony's volunteer (independent) companies to a 29 April Fredericksburg rendezvous.[61] They planned to march to Williamsburg and take the powder back. Being farther away, it was on or about the day of the rendezvous that the counties beyond the Blue Ridge learned of the purloined powder. The Dunmore Independent Company assembled under Clark's command and proceeded north toward Winchester and the gap in the Blue Ridge.[62] From there, if on foot, they could arrive in Fredericksburg in about a week. They stopped at Strasburg late on the first day, and the excited young men made camp.[63] In the morning, word arrived that their march to Williamsburg was 'countermanded.' The governor promised that he would produce the powder if it was needed.[64] The company turned around and headed to Laurence Snapp's home at Toms Brook. Since they were already together, they had a barbecue.[65] John Buskirk of the 8th Virginia remembered this as the beginning of his career in the Revolutionary War. His first service, he said, 'was when said Dunmore, robbed the magazine at Williamsburg; he was out only about one week, under Captain Jonathan Clark.'[66]

Clark received a letter after the barbecue from Alexander Machir, the Whig militia captain who caught William Holliday selling tea. Machir expressed doubts that Dunmore would ever actually return the powder and passed along the first imprecise news of bloodshed in Massachusetts:

> I Returned from Frederick Court very late last night, its believed there that the governor has passed his word and Honour in an ambiguous manner for the returning the ammunition as its thought he has fixed on no time. It is said an other action has been at Boston that one or more General officers of the regulars fell in it, but in my opinion it can be but slightly credited as it is told so many different ways.

He also reported that a fast ship from London had brought news of 'twenty men of War and Ninty five transports' coming with orders 'to block up every port except newYork and Qubeck.' 'If its so,' he commented wryly, 'there will be bloody breeches.'[67]

60 FHS: Clark Diary, 2–19, 25 April 1775.
61 *Virginia Gazette* (Purdy), 28 April 1775 (supplement) and 12 May 1775.
62 FHS: Clark Diary, 1 May 1775; NARA: J. Buskirk pension.
63 FHS: Clark Diary, 1 May 1775.
64 Edward Miles Riley (ed.), *The Journal of John Harrower: An Indentured Servant in the Colony of Virginia, 1773–1776* (Williamsburg: Colonial Williamsburg, 1963), p.94.
65 FHS: Clark Diary, 2 May 1775.
66 NARA: J. Buskirk pension.
67 WHS: Draper Mss, L, vol.1, p.17.

The Dunmore Volunteers returned to the Laurence Snapp House near Toms Brook after the Williamsburg Powder Alarm and then held a barbecue. (Author's photo)

Dunmore reconvened the General Assembly on 1 June to transmit an offer of reconciliation from London. Few of the burgesses attended, and some who did came wearing hunting shirts and tomahawks, the period equivalent of camouflage and a sidearm. They refused to consider London's offer, deferring for the sake of unity to the Continental Congress. Then, a group of young men breaking into the powder magazine were blasted by a shotgun rigged with a tripwire. The outrage was immediate. Dunmore fled to HMS *Fowey,* and though he tried to run things from the water, he ceased in any meaningful sense to be the governor of Virginia.[68]

Doctor Connolly Flees

Out west, Doctor Connolly dismissed the militia and 'secretly frustrated the machinations of the Republicans' by urging Native leaders and Loyalists to side with the Crown. But Connolly knew it was time for him to leave. 'The treaty which I had concluded with the

68 Selby, *Revolution in Virginia*, p.41–43.

Indians,' he remembered, 'gave me ostensible business to the Committee at Winchester; and the better to hide my intentions, I prevailed with three of the Indian Chiefs to accompany me thither, carrying with me a copy of the treaty, calculated for the inspection of the President of the Convention assembled at Richmond.' He got as far as Berkeley County before he was challenged. When he arrived in Winchester, he was called before Thruston and the Frederick Committee. A letter had come from the West Augusta Committee advising Thruston of Connolly's 'dangerous and Tory principles' and asserting (correctly) that he intended to join Lord Dunmore.

However, a letter also arrived from Peyton Randolph, chairman of the Convention, approving of Dunmore's Indian diplomacy and asking him to come to Williamsburg for consultation. This was enough for the committee, and Connolly was released with a 'passport' in the form of a resolution stating that he had acted 'heretofore, in a manner conducive to the liberties of America.' In Fredericksburg, Connolly dined 'with an old friend', physician and future general Hugh Mercer. Because of Connolly's silence when 'inflammatory and unconstitutional toasts' were offered, Mercer had him followed. He 'shook off' his pursuer, passed by Williamsburg at night, and joined the governor at the Gosport shipyard across the Elizabeth River from Norfolk.[69]

Volunteer companies from around the colony began to congregate in Williamsburg at the behest of Randolph, who feared an attack by British troops. Most of the volunteers were untrained, poorly disciplined, and 'led' by officers chosen for their popularity. Hundreds of young men camped on the eastern edge of the capital at Wallers Grove and things began to look like a carnival. 'We appear rather invited to feast then fight', one commented.[70] With no executive or even legislative authority in place, the encampment slid toward anarchy. The city's taverns were busy. The Governor's palace, which contained a virtual arsenal of weapons, was repeatedly invaded. The volunteers elected an unassertive Charles Scott of Cumberland County to lead them.[71] In time, Scott outgrew his caution and rose to govern a Continental brigade, the Commonwealth of Kentucky, and many bottles of whiskey.

The Third Virginia Convention

Open war had been underway for three months in the north when the Third Convention convened in Richmond in July of 1775. After Lexington and Concord, the capture of Fort Ticonderoga and the Battle of Bunker Hill washed away any thoughts of reconciliation. In Philadelphia, Congress named George Washington commander of a new 'Continental' army and called for 10 companies of frontier riflemen to support him as light infantry. Two of these companies were to come from the lower Shenandoah Valley.[72]

69 Connolly, *Narrative*, pp.6–15, 23–24.
70 Boyd (ed.), *Papers of Jefferson*, vol.1, p.237.
71 Selby, *Revolution in Virginia*, pp.45, 47–48.
72 Worthington Chauncey Ford, (ed.), *Journals of the Continental Congress, 1774–1789* (Washington: Library of Congress, 1904–1937), vol 2, p.89.

Less architecturally impressive than the original (now reconstructed) building, the 'Old Capitol' in Williamsburg was used from about 1747 to 1800. It burned in 1832. (F. Concklin, 1870, based on historic sketches, Emmet Collection, New York Public Library)

Jonathan Clark left Dunmore County for the Convention on 11 July. Muhlenberg stayed home for reasons that are not known.[73] As he always did when travelling to the Tidewater, Clark visited his parents in Caroline for a few days. From there, he continued to Hanover Court House, where he saw 'a Negro Hang.'[74] Clark's diary provides no explanation, but the episode illustrates the stark inequalities that pervaded the world at the time. The Revolutionary cause inspired many states and families to let go of slavery, but that awakening had not yet begun. Free Virginians feared political turmoil would lead to an uprising, and rumours to that effect may explain what Clark saw that day.[75] Slavery was unjust, and the danger was real. John Chapman, an 8th Virginia man who was killed by Indians late in

73 Anon (ed.), *Proceedings of the Convention of Delegates for the Counties and Corporations in the Colony of Virginia Held at Richmond Town, in the County of Henrico, on Monday the 17th of July, 1775* [3rd Convention] (Richmond: Ritchie, Trueheart & Duval, 1816), p.3; Leonard (ed.), *Assembly*, p.114; FHS: Clark Diary, 25 April 1775.

74 FHS: Clark Diary, 13–17 July 1775.

75 *Virginia Gazette* (Purdie), 16 June 1775; *Virginia Gazette* (Pinkney), 10 Aug. 1775; Robert Greenhalgh Albion and Leonidas Dodson (eds), *Philip Vickers Fithian: Journal, 1775–1776: Written on the Virginia-Pennsylvania Frontier and in the Army Around New York* (Princeton: Princeton University Press, 1934), pp.31–32.

the Revolution, had an older brother who was 'killed by his Negroes.'[76] Stories of slaves plotting to take the lives of their masters circulated frequently in Virginia's eastern counties.[77]

The Third Convention's work was considerably different from that of its predecessors. The governor was in exile, men were dying in the north, and it was only a matter of time before Redcoats marched into the province. The Convention began to act like a real legislature, and it appointed a Committee of Safety, chaired by Edmund Pendleton, to act as the Old Dominion's executive.[78]

The Convention appointed Adam Stephen, Charles Thruston, Jonathan Clark, and a few others to write an 'ordinance' for raising 'a sufficient armed force ... for the defence and protection of this colony.'[79] Then, however, a petition arrived from Berkeley County asserting that Stephen had rigged his own election to the Convention.[80] Its lead signer was Abraham Bowman's uncle Jacob Hite, who was still engaged in a nasty feud with Stephen.[81] Horatio Gates had signed it, as had Thomas Rutherford of the Berkeley Committee.[82] Other signers included William Darke and the man who would soon be his lieutenant, Isaac Israel.[83] The Convention reviewed the evidence, invalidated Berkeley's election, and sent Stephen home. Berkeley's other delegate, Thomas Rutherford's brother Robert, was also dismissed.[84]

Returning to its work, the Convention determined that having the Augusta County court adjourn back and forth between Staunton and Pittsburgh was unworkable. For now, the justices were told to 'proceed in all matters relating to keeping the peace and good behavior, and in all criminal matters, as if they were distinct counties.'[85]

The most important work was the creation of a more robust system of defence. A new militia system for the revolutionary government was created, now under the authority of the Committee of Safety and the county committees. The Old Dominion's 62 counties and three incorporated towns were grouped into 16 districts, each with a committee of deputies (three from each county committee) tasked with raising a 10-company Minute battalion and one company of full-time troops. The Minutemen were constantly armed and ready for service on a moment's notice. The regular companies were grouped into two Provincial regiments commanded by the popular but inexperienced Patrick Henry and the experienced but unpopular William Woodford. Both men were made colonels.[86] Fincastle delegate William Christian was chosen as Henry's lieutenant colonel. The regular companies raised in the four westernmost districts were to be 'expert rifle-men ... to be employed as light infantry' in the two provincial regiments. Five additional companies of regulars were raised by

76 NARA: M804, R13115, John Chapman pension.
77 Woody Holton, '"Rebel Against Rebel": Enslaved Virginians and the Coming of the American Revolution', VMHB, 105:2 (1997), pp.163.
78 Anon (ed.), *Proceedings of the 3rd Convention*, p.19.
79 Anon (ed.), *Proceedings of the 3rd Convention*, pp.5–6
80 Jacob Hite et al, 'Petition of Freeholders of Berkeley County to the Convention, 1775', in Anon. (ed), 'Virginia Legislative Papers (Continued)', *VMHB*, 13:4 (1906), pp.412–416.
81 Ward, *Stephen*, pp.104–107, 124–127.
82 VMHC: Mss1 R9339 a 10–40, Thomas Rutherford Papers.
83 Hite et al, 'Petition of Freeholders', p.415.
84 Anon (ed.), *Proceedings of the 3rd Convention*, p.7.
85 Anon (ed.), *Proceedings of the 3rd Convention*, p.21
86 Anon (ed.), *Proceedings of the 3rd Convention*, pp.11, 19, 29–39.

designated counties to act independently in defence of the frontier at Pittsburgh, Wheeling, Point Pleasant, and in Fincastle County.[87] Lord Dunmore had dismissed the militia garrisons at these places before fleeing.[88] The Convention ordered the unruly volunteer companies to disband as soon as the Minute battalions were 'fully and completely embodied.'[89]

Virginia's First Revolutionary Soldiers

Virginia's first contributions to the Continental Army were well underway when the Convention concluded in August. George Washington, Charles Lee, and Horatio Gates were generals.[90] Virginia's Continental rifle companies were raised quickly in Frederick and Berkeley under Battletown veterans Daniel Morgan and Hugh Stephenson. Nineteen-year-old Michael Tullis was one of Stephenson's recruits.[91] Seventeen-year-old Daniel Anderson was one of Morgan's men. Just across the Potomac, 26-year-old William Moody volunteered for Michael Cresap's Maryland company.[92] Tullis, Anderson, and Moody marched off for Boston, but in a year, they would belong to the 8th Virginia.

Robert Rutherford (1728–1803) was William Darke's captain in the French and Indian War, chairman of the Berkeley Committee, and a representative to Congress in the 1790s. (*Ancestral Records and Portraits*, Colonial Dames of America, 1910)

Robert Rutherford, the chairman of 'the county first named' by the Convention in his district, sent a letter to his counterparts with 'a Notification of the time I have appointed for holding the Committee of deputys to choose the officers of the regulars & the Minute Men to be raised in the district of Berkeley, Frederick, Dunmore and Hampshire.' They met in Winchester on 27 September

87 *Virginia Gazette* (Purdie), 25 Aug. 1775; Anon (ed.), *Proceedings of the 3rd Convention*, pp.11, 19, 21, 30, 36–39.
88 Force (ed.) *American Archives*, ser.4, vol.2, pp.1189–1190
89 Anon (ed.), *Proceedings of the 3rd Convention*, pp.34.
90 Robert K. Wright, Jr., *The Continental Army* (Washington: U.S. Army, 1983), p.26.
91 NARA: M804, W26558, Michael Tullis pension; Dandridge, *Shepherdstown*, p.88.
92 NARA: M804, S37677, Daniel Anderson pension, S38246, William Moody pension.

and selected Morgan Alexander to lead the Berkeley District company of regulars.[93] Philip Helphenstine, the now-grown son of Peter, was among the men who 'enlisted … in the company commanded by Captain Morgan Alexander in the 2nd Regiment Commanded by Colonel Woodford.'[94]

The Berkeley District also made at least some progress towards raising its 10 Minute companies. Leonard Cooper of Dunmore recalled that he was appointed an ensign. Abraham Moore of Berkeley remembered that he enrolled in a company led by George Washington's brother Samuel.[95] The Culpeper District was notably successful in forming its Minute battalion, but provincewide, the project was a failure.[96] Most battalions never got off the ground. The number of original 8th Virginia veterans who (erroneously) recalled that their service in the regiment began in 1775 shows that some of its companies were built on converted or incomplete Minute companies.[97]

One of the independent provincial frontier companies, led by Captain John Neville, was also a preexisting organisation, probably the Frederick volunteers.[98] Virginia sent Neville's men to West Augusta to occupy Fort Pitt, defend settlers from Indian attacks, and put force behind the colony's contested claim to the territory.[99] The West Augusta Committee chose John Stephenson to captain the second independent company of Provincial regulars ordered by the Convention. A traveller who met Stephenson at his home that year said, 'This gentleman is a great Indian Warriour, But appears to be a good natured man.'[100] After a second visit, the same diarist called him 'an honest worthy man.'[101] At the same time, 300 miles to the south, another independent company of Provincials was organised to protect Fincastle County. Point Pleasant veterans James Knox and James Craig were two of its three lieutenants.[102]

93 LVA: Dunmore County Revolutionary War Papers, 1775–1814, Robert Rutherford to Dunmore Committee, 12 Sept. 1775; E.M. Sanchez Saavedra, *A Guide to Virginia Military Organisations in the American Revolution, 1774–1787* (Richmond: Virginia State Library, 1978), pp.29–33.

94 NARA: M804, W8930, Philip Helphenstine pension.

95 NARA: M804, W6712, Leonard Cooper pension, S2856, Abraham Moore pension.

96 McDonnell, 'Popular Mobilization', pp.963–974.

97 LVA: Revolutionary War Bounty Land Claims, Zachariah Pigman and William Corbin; S38861, John Engle pension; S38747, David Great pension; S38200, Michael McKnight pension; S38246, William Moody pension; W4108, Joseph Parret pension; S35555, Meshack Pearson pension; S38316 Rees Pritchard pension; S40315, Leonard Ragar pension; S40406, Christian Shrycok pension; S4880, George Spickard pension.

98 Force (ed.), *American Archives*, ser.4, vol.3, p.370; Hening (ed.), *Statutes*, vol.9, pp.9–14.

99 *Virginia Gazette* (Pinkney), 6 July 1775; Gabriel Neville, 'Virginia's Independent Frontier Companies,' *JAR*, 17–18 March 2021, <allthingsliberty.com/2021/03/virginias-independent-frontier-companies-part-1-of-2/>, accessed 27 Feb. 2023.

100 Harold B. Gill, Jr. and George M. Curtis III (eds), *A Man Apart: The Journal of Nicholas Cresswell, 1774–1781* (Lanham, Md.: Lexington Books, 2009), p.38.

101 Gill and Curtis (eds), *Journal of Cresswell*, p.70.

102 NARA: M804, S32264, David Gamble pension (Southwest Independent Frontier Co.); Neville, 'Frontier Companies.'

The First Shots Fired

The war in Virginia began with a hurricane. Early in September, the waters of the Hampton Roadstead churned in a violent storm that smashed many boats and took several lives. Lord Dunmore 'fared but poorly in this hurricane', Pinkney's *Virginia Gazette* reported, 'his lordship fell overboard, and was severely ducked. – But, according to the old saying, *those who are born to be* h____d *will never be* drowned.'[103] Such words could not be unsaid.

The companies of the 1st and 2nd Virginia Regiments collected around Williamsburg as Dunmore's small but professional force staged raids to destroy military caches around the lower James River. There was an exchange of fire at Hampton in October, and the Committee of Safety sent Colonel Woodford's 2nd Virginia toward Tory-dominated Norfolk in November with part of the Culpeper Minute Battalion.[104]

Dunmore had no problem with slavery or indentured servitude, but he knew they were threads that could unravel the colony. He gave them a hard tug. He issued a proclamation offering liberty to male slaves and indentured servants who fled rebellious masters and fought for the Crown. The racism of American slavery roared back loudly. Richard Henry Lee derisively called Dunmore 'our African Hero.'[105] Theodorick Bland accused Dunmore of having had 'lewd and nightly orgies' with his slaves in the governor's palace.[106] A Massachusetts paper announced that 'a lusty likely negro wench was delivered of a male child, who in memory of a certain notable negro chief, is named Dunmore.'[107] Adam Stephen sneered that Dunmore wanted 'to add some more odiferous beauties to his Ethiopian seraglios.'[108] Washington, a better man, simply asserted that Dunmore 'should be instantly crushd, if it takes the force of the whole Colony to do it.'[109]

To that end, a significant engagement occurred on 9 December at Great Bridge between Woodford's provincials and Dunmore's motley force, which now included a 'Royal Ethiopian Regiment' of self-emancipated slaves. The Virginians won, were reinforced by a regiment of North Carolinians, and marched against Norfolk. Dunmore's forces burned a few buildings along the Norfolk waterfront for tactical reasons. The Whig army, happy to deny the ousted earl a base of support, burned the rest of the city to the ground.[110]

Meanwhile, the rest of Virginia was preparing. On 11 November, Reverend Muhlenberg wrote to Jonathan Clark, 'The Committee of Safety have Ordered me to send them Account of the Number of Arms within this County, and as you propose to attend the musters now Appointed, please to acquaint the Captains, that I request them to take an exact List.'[111] All of Virginia was at war.

103 *Virginia Gazette* (Pinkney), 14 Sept. 1775.
104 Unpublished research conducted by Patrick H. Hannum.
105 Boyd et al (eds), *Papers of Jefferson*, vol.1, p.471.
106 Charles Campbell (ed.), *The Bland Papers* (Petersburg: Edmund & Julian C. Ruffin, 1840), vol.1, p.43.
107 James Corbett David, *Dunmore's New World* (Charlottesville: University of Virginia Press, 2015), p.115.
108 Richard H. Lee, *Memoir of Richard Henry Lee* (Philadelphia: H.C. Carey and I. Lea, 1825), vol.1, pp.211–212.
109 Chase et al (eds), *Papers of Washington* (Revolution), vol.2, pp.551–554.
110 Selby, *Revolution in Virginia*, pp.63–85.
111 WHS: Draper Mss, L, vol.1, p.22.

4

Recruits

The Fourth Virginia Convention conceived of a German-led regiment in December 1775 and authorised it in January. The Convention assembled at the College of William and Mary two days before Woodford's victory at Great Bridge.[1] All of the colonies between Quebec and East Florida were now in open rebellion. Muhlenberg and Clark again attended the Convention for Dunmore County, and Muhlenberg was put on a committee to draft a response to the governor's November proclamation. 'We,' the resolution declared, 'as guardians of the lives and liberty of the people, our constituents, conceive it to be indispensably our duty to protect them against every species of despotism.'[2] The Convention acted accordingly.

The 'German Regiment'

The Convention came up with a detailed ordinance creating seven more provincial regiments. Recruits were to serve for two years, twice as long as before. Of the new regiments, it specified that 'one of them shall be called a German regiment, to be made up of German and other officers and soldiers, as the committees of the several counties of Augusta, West Augusta, Berkeley, Culpeper, Dunmore, Fincastle, Frederick, and Hampshire … shall judge expedient.'[3] It decided that 'the officers of the one hundred men ordered from Fort Pitt, by a late resolution of this Convention, shall be considered as part of the officers to be nominated by the committee of West Augusta, if the said officers shall incline to continue in the service of this colony'. Thus regimented, John Stephenson's West Augusta independent frontier company (which included few if any Germans) became the first and most senior company of the 8th Virginia.[4]

Next, the Convention elected Hugh Mercer colonel of the 3rd Virginia and Adam Stephen colonel of the 4th Virginia. Other appointments included William Crawford as lieutenant

1 Anon (ed.), *The Proceedings of the Convention of Delegates Held at the Town of Richmond in the Colony of Virginia on Friday, the 1st of December, 1775 and Afterward by Adjournment in the City of Williamsburg* [4th Convention] (Richmond: Ritchie, Trueheart, & Duval, 1816), p.59.

2 Anon (ed.), *Proceedings of the 4th Convention*, pp.62–63

3 Anon (ed.), *Proceedings of the 4th Convention*, pp.65. 92, 105; Hening (ed.), *Statutes*, vol.9, p.76.

4 Anon (ed.), *Proceedings of the 4th Convention*, pp.105–106; NARA: M804, S4640, William Owens pension; W6338, John Vance pension; Neville, 'Frontier Companies.'

colonel of the 5th regiment, and Thomas Marshall (the non-resident clerk of Dunmore County) as major of the 3rd.[5] The 'eighth or German Regiment' was the only one for which all field officers were elected at the same time. Peter Muhlenberg was chosen to be the colonel. The German Regiment may have been his idea, but he later insisted he 'neither wished or expected' the appointment.[6] Abraham Bowman of Strasburg was picked to be lieutenant colonel. Peter Helphenstine of Winchester was selected to be major.[7]

Perhaps because his appointment disqualified him from continuing as a delegate,[8] Muhlenberg returned to Dunmore County a week before the Convention adjourned. Jonathan Clark remained to the end but handed Muhlenberg a letter to the county committee that revealed how advanced the regiment's plans already were. Dunmore County was directed to produce two companies for the 8th Virginia and planned to raise an 'English' one and a 'German' one.

> As Mr. Muhlenberg is returning home and perhaps the Committee may be called to nominate the officers to the German Company before I can return, I beg leave to offer myself to you as a Candidate for the Captaincy of the German Company to be raised in your County. You have honored me with several important offices during the present unhappy troubles, in the civil way, but as our Disputes with Brittain are now to be determined by the sword, I am determined to try my fortune in the Military, and shall esteem it a particular favor if you will honor me with this office.[9]

The selection of field officers for the 8th Virginia was calculated to maximize German participation. Hailing from Woodstock, Strasburg, and Winchester, the three men represented different German population centres in the lower Shenandoah Valley. However, the regiment's recruits were not expected to be exclusively German. The inclusion of companies from Augusta, Fincastle, and West Augusta guaranteed a large proportion of soldiers would be Ulstermen. There was no 'Irish Regiment' because the willingness of the Scotch-Irish to fight was never in doubt. Frequent Anglicisation of names makes it impossible to calculate the regiment's ethnic proportions precisely, but it is reasonable to guess that Germans and Irish joined in roughly equal numbers, with Britons and others making up the balance. It was understood that the regiment's monicker primarily concerned the field officers. Thomas Ravenscraft recollected that the 8th was 'commonly called the German Regiment because it was commanded by Genl. Muhlenburgh.'[10] It appears, in fact, that the regiment was also designed to put the reputationally combative and unruly Scotch-Irish under more orderly and disciplined German officers.

5 Anon. (ed.), *Proceedings of the 4th Convention*, pp.93–94.
6 Lisa Minardi et al (eds), Freeman's Auction Catalogue, 2012, *Historic Muhlenberg Property: From a Private Collection Including the Grand Division Color of the 8th Virginia*, lot 4, p.25.
7 Anon. (ed.), *Proceedings of the 4th Convention*, pp.93.
8 Anon. (ed.), *Proceedings of the 3rd Convention*, pp.19, 47.
9 LVA: Dunmore County Revolutionary War Papers, 1775–1814, Jonathan Clark to Dunmore Committee.
10 NARA: M804, S1248, T. Ravenscraft pension.

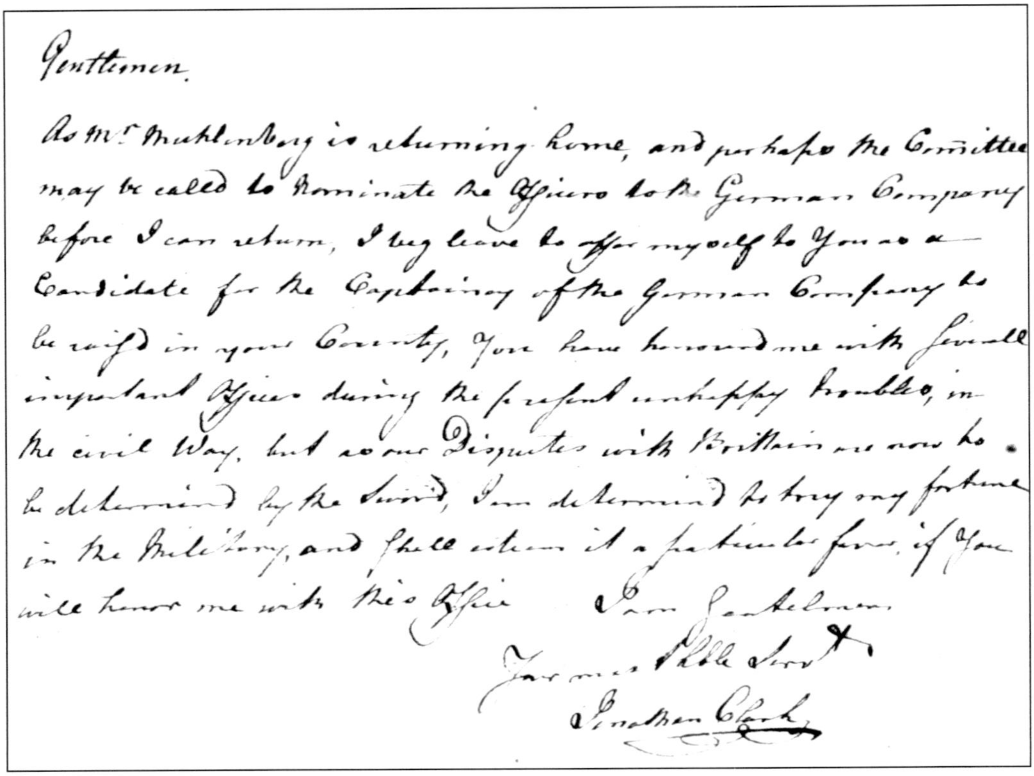

Gentlemen

As Mr Muhlenberg is returning home, and perhaps the Committee may be called to Nominate the Officers to the German Company before I can return, I beg leave to offer myself to You as a Candidate for the Captaincy of the German Company to be raisd in your County, You have honoured me with several important Offices during the present unhappy troubles, in the civil War, but as our Disputes with Brittain are now to be determined by the Sword, I am determined to try my fortune in the Military, and shall esteem it a particular favor, if You will honor me with this Office   I am Gentelmen,

Your mos Hble Servt.

Jonathan Clark

Jonathan Clark's letter to the Dunmore Committee requesting a captaincy. (Library of Virginia)

While Muhlenberg accepted his appointment in person, Bowman and Helphenstine may or may not have known of their nominations in advance. It is hard to imagine the new colonel did not stop to visit them in Winchester and Strasburg on his way home to initiate planning. The Winchester shoemaker was much older than the Woodstock pastor. Helphenstine was now 51 years old and Muhlenberg was 29. In an age when class, status, and title mattered greatly, Muhlenberg had no difficulty asserting himself over the middle-aged man. Bowman was only 26.

Muhlenberg, Bowman, and Helphenstine had many important duties before them, but recruiting was not one of them. Company officers earned their commissions by meeting enlistment quotas. Captains had to recruit 28 men, first lieutenants 21, second lieutenants 16, and ensigns nine. If quotas were not met by 29 February, the committees were empowered to replace officers at their own discretion. If a company was not complete by 25 March, the Committee of Safety would resolve the shortfall from Williamsburg. Each complete company had a total of 78 men: four officers, 68 private soldiers, four sergeants, a drummer, and a fifer. Recruits had to be between the ages of 16 and 50, 'at least five feet four inches high, healthy, strong made & well limbed, not deaf or Subject to fits.'[11]

11 Hening (ed.), *Statutes*, vol.9, pp.16–17, 76–78, 81.

Completed companies were inspected by the county committees and sworn into service at local rendezvous points. The committees then gave the officers certificates to be exchanged for commissions in Williamsburg. The date of county certification established officers' seniority relative to others of the same rank.[12] This mattered greatly. Until late in 1777, officer promotions were almost wholly determined by whose 'turn' it was. The senior officer within a rank stood a good chance of being promoted very soon.

In addition to being 'German', the 8th was also the only Virginia regiment ordered to carry rifles exclusively. The Pennsylvania Rifle was an artifact of German-American culture and its use was still largely limited to communities along the Great Philadelphia Wagon Road and the adjacent frontier.[13] Typically custom-made and sometimes ornately decorated, rifles were prized possessions that westerners relied on for food, defence, and the deer-skin trade. Men from the West consequently had a reputation for expert marksmanship, and carrying a rifle in the Revolutionary army came with some prestige. Thomas Jefferson described the counties west of the Blue Ridge, particularly those with large Scotch-Irish populations, as 'our best rifle counties' and identified western sharpshooters as the Redcoats' 'most dangerous enemies.'[14] The other Virginia regiments were armed mostly with muskets, but each had two or three companies of western riflemen to function as light infantry. Philip Helphenstine belonged to one of these companies in the 2nd Virginia. The 8th Virginia's men were asked to 'bring with them one good rifle and tomahawk, each to be approved by their captain.'[15] Most men had to be issued rifles, but those who brought their own were given 20 extra shillings a year for the weapon's use.[16]

8th Virginia Companies at Inception.

County (Committee Chairman)	Officers	Commission Date
West Augusta (George Croghan)	Capt. John Stephenson 1st Lt. Robert Beall 2nd Lt. Edward Rice Ens. Simon Morgan	10 Dec. 1775
Berkeley (Robert Rutherford)	Capt. William Darke 1st. Lt. Daniel Culp 2nd Lt. Isaac Israel Ens. John Daniel	9 Feb. 1776
Dunmore (Peter Muhlenberg)	Capt. Richard Campbell 1st Lt. Mathias Hite 2nd Lt. John Steed Ens. Leonard Cooper	19 Feb. 1776

12 Hening (ed.), *Statutes*, vol.9, p.79.
13 Steven K. Friesen, 'Martin Mylin, Gunsmith: Fact or Fancy?', *Journal of the Lancaster County Historical Society*, 93:1 (1991), pp.16–24.
14 Julian P. Boyd et al (eds), *Papers of Thomas Jefferson* (Princeton: Princeton University Press, 1950), vol.6, pp.35–38.
15 Hening (ed.), *Statutes*, vol.9, pp.81–82; Anon (ed.), *Proceedings of the 4th* Convention, p.105.
16 Anon. (ed.), *Proceedings of the 4th Convention*, p.20.

County (Committee Chairman)	Officers	Commission Date
Culpeper (Robert Green)	Capt. George Slaughter 1st. Lt. Henry Field 2nd Lt. James Kirtley Ens. John Graves	19 Feb. 1776
Dunmore (Peter Muhlenberg)	Capt. Jonathan Clark 1st Lt. Jacob Rinker 2nd Lt. Adam Dirting Ens. Jacob Parett	4 March 1776
Hampshire (Joseph Neville)[17]	Capt. Abel Westfall 1st. Lt. Robert Higgins 2nd Lt. Andrew Turk Ens. Rees Pritchard	12 March 1776
Augusta (Silas Hart)	Capt. David Stephenson 1st. Lt. Joseph Dickson 2nd Lt. John Gratton Ens. Samuel Coleman	25 March 1776
Frederick (Charles Mynn Thruston)	Capt. Thomas Berry 1st Lt. John Jolliffe 2nd Lt. Richard Eastin Ens. William Meade	27 March 1776
Fincastle (William Preston)	Capt. James Knox 1st Lt. Ephraim Drake 2nd Lt. James Craig Ens. William Ward	4 April 1776[18]
West Augusta District (Thomas Smallman)	Capt. William Croghan 1st Lt. Abraham Kirkpatrick 2nd Lt. James Higgins Ens. James Berwick	19 April 1776

John Stephenson's West Augusta Company

George Croghan and the West Augusta Committee chose John Stephenson to lead the Second West Augusta Independent Company of provincial regulars after the Third Convention. It took the officers until 10 December to finish recruiting, and they were regimented with the 8th just a month later. The locally infamous 'turncoat' Simon Girty was, if uncertain evidence is correct, one of Stephenson's three lieutenants before dropping off when the company was reduced to two lieutenants and left for Williamsburg. A West Augusta veteran remembered that Girty was 'a subaltern, but at that time chiefly engaged in intercourse with the Indians.'[19] Girty, reported Consul Willshire Butterfield in 1890, 'exerted himself in and around Pittsburgh in enlisting men for the patriot army … he was made second lieutenant in Captain John Stephenson's company of one year men … Girty did not, for some reason, go south, but remained in Pittsburgh on detached duty.'[20] The source of Butterfield's information has not been found. Girty defected to the Anglo-Native side in 1778 and watched

17 Uncertain.

18 Knox's seniority was successfully challenged.

19 NARA: M804, S2526, Francis Dunlavy pension (Pa. militia).

20 Consul Willshire Butterfield, *History of the Girtys* (Cincinnati: Robert Clarke & Co., 1890), p.41.

the torture of William Crawford in 1782.[21] He sank into infamy as the arch-villain of the northwest frontier.

No roster survives for Stephenson's Company, but an undated list of officers from early in 1776 records Stephenson's subalterns as 1st Lieutenant Robert Beall, 2nd Lieutenant Edward Rice, and Ensign Simon Morgan.[22] Beall was a frequent frontier guide who took George Washington down the Ohio in 1770.[23] Nineteen of the company's enlisted soldiers have been identified, enough to show that recruiting was conducted throughout the vast district. Thomas Ravenscraft and Zephaniah ('Seth') Bryan enlisted near Stephenson's home on Jacobs Creek.[24] Benjamin Biggs lived north of Wheeling and enlisted in November with his friend John Harrison.[25] Harrison 'left his plow standing in the furrow [and] took his father's gun' when he joined.[26] William Davis, Samuel Murphy, and John Kirk enlisted together at Fort Pitt. Murphy remembered that he and Kirk belonged to the same mess.[27]

Shortly after Stephenson's Company was certified by the West Augusta Committee, a rumour spread concerning his and William Crawford's loyalties. Both men had worked closely with Connolly in the preceding two years. They sent letters to two of the three Virginia newspapers to stop the gossip.

> Had our enemies meditated their attacks against our persons, or property, we had been silent; but they have, in violation of truth, of the duties of society, and of every principle of generosity, practiced very cruel and insidious arts to deprive us of our characters as men, and the esteem of our fellow citizens. They have depicted us to our brethren as traitors to the American cause and consequently inimical to their dearest and invaluable rights. We are accused of holding connections with the avowed enemies to this greatly injured country. It is therefore incumbent on us to challenge those wicked men into open light, that we may have the opportunity of evincing our innocence to the world in the most publick manner. In the interim, we set them at the utmost defiance...[28]

The letter had its intended effect.

William Darke's Berkeley Company

The Berkeley Committee chose William Darke to be a captain despite his signature on the petition that cost Adam Stephen his seat in the Third Convention. Stephen has been

21 Thwaites and Kellogg (eds), *Frontier Defense*, pp.249–250; Butterfield, *Girtys*, p.50; Eric Sterner, *The Battle of Upper Sandusky, 1782* (Yardley: Westholme, 2023), pp.115–123.

22 Force (ed.), *American Archives*, ser.5, vol.2, pp.321–322.

23 Ellen Eslinger, *Running Mad for Kentucky: Frontier Travel Accounts* (Lexington: University of Kentucky Press), pp.93–94; Jackson (ed.), *Diaries of Washington*, vol.2, p.294; Gill and Curtis (eds), *Journal of Cresswell*, p.91, n.5.

24 NARA: M804, W2061, Zephaniah Bryan pension.

25 LVA: Revolutionary War Bounty Land Claims, John Harrison.

26 Louise Phelps Kellogg (ed.), *Frontier Retreat on the Upper Ohio, 1779–1781* (Madison: Wisconsin Historical Society, 1917), p.335, n.1.

27 NARA: M804, S39819, John Kirk pension.

28 *Virginia Gazette* (Purdie), 26 Jan. 1776 and *Virginia Gazette* (Dixon and Hunter), 27 Jan. 1776.

mentioned as chairman of the Berkeley Committee,[29] but this is contradicted by Robert Rutherford's convening of the Berkeley District deputies in September 1775 and perhaps also by Thomas Rutherford's signatures on behalf of the committee in the new year.[30]

The Berkeley Committee certified that Darke's Company was complete on 9 February. Daniel Culp was 1st lieutenant, and Isaac Israel was 2nd lieutenant. John Daniel received the ensigncy.[31] That Darke's Company was certified within three weeks of the Fourth Convention's adjournment shows that he had a head start in recruiting. In fact, Darke, Israel, and Culp recruited most of their men before the ordinance was even written.[32]

Israel recalled that 'Dark commenced in the recruiting service some time in the fall of the year 1775 perhaps in Oct'r. or early in Nov'r.'[33] Leonard Rigar said he 'enlisted in Shepherdstown in Barclay County Virginia in the Company commanded by Captain Dark sometime in the fall of 1775 for the term of 2 years.'[34] George Hite remembered: 'I was at a muster in this County at the house of Mr. Thomas Rutherford … when I saw the late General Darke then a Captain as I understood in the American army. He was in a military dress and I understood was recruiting. This was … in Dec'r 1775.'[35] That these and other veterans all remembered enlisting so early cannot be explained as faulty memory. In fact, one soldier signed on with Darke a whole year before the 8th Virginia went into service. Christian Shryock said he

> on or about the first day of March A.D. 1775, enlisted in Shepherd's Town, Virginia, as a private Soldier in Captain William Dark's Company in the 8th Virginia Regiment commanded by Colonel … Muhlenberg for three years; That being a Gunsmith, he was detained at the United States Works, at Shepherdstown, nearly one year. That in the spring of the year 1776 his Lieutenant Daniel Kulp returned to Shepherdstown and the deponent went with his said Lieutenant Kulp to Winchester to recruit. That at Winchester he the deponent was appointed a recruiting Sergeant and continued to recruit there until after harvest in the same year.[36]

Shryock's statement glosses over some details, but it is fundamentally accurate. He misstated the duration of his provincial enlistment, but that can be explained. His account shows how Darke was able to recruit his provincial company so quickly. He had first formed his company during the period when Virginia was trying to get by with volunteer companies and Minute battalions. If Shryock's timeline is correct, Darke led Berkeley's independent volunteer company, which transitioned into a Minute company after the Third Convention and converted again into a company of provincials after the Fourth Convention. Darke was

---

29 Ward, *Stephen*, pp.119, 125, 134.
30 LVA: Dunmore County Revolutionary War Papers, 1775–1814, Robert Rutherford to Dunmore Committee, 12 Sept. 1775; VMHC: Mss1 R9339 a 10–40, Thomas Rutherford Papers.
31 Force (ed.), *American Archives*, ser.5, vol.2, p.321–322.
32 Anon. (ed.), *Journal of the House of Delegates of Virginia*, 1776 (Richmond: Samuel Shepherd & Co., 1828), p.88.
33 LVA: Revolutionary War Bounty Land Claims, William Darke.
34 NARA, M804: S40315, Leonard Ragar pension.
35 LVA: Revolutionary War Bounty Land Claims, William Darke.
36 NARA: M804, S40406, Christian Shryock pension.

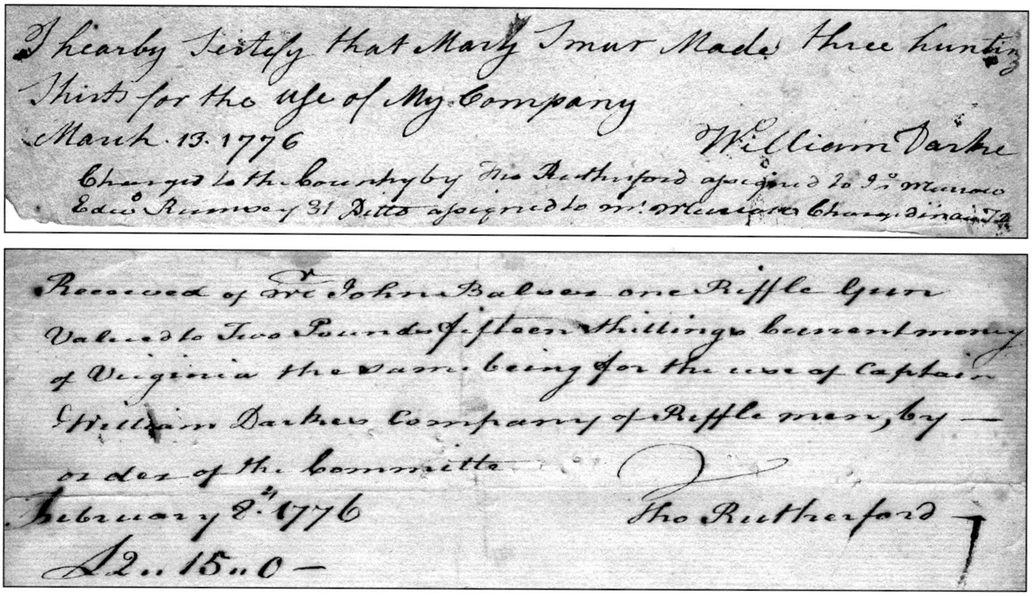

I hearby Sertefy that Mary Imur Made three hunting Shirts for the use of My Company
March 13. 1776 William Darke

Received of Mr John Balsar one Riffle Gun Valued to Two Pounds fifteen shillings current money of Virginia the same being for the use of Captain William Darkes Company of Riffle men, by order of the Committee
February 8th 1776 Tho Rutherford
£2..15..0 —

Receipts for three hunting shirts and one rifle show how used items and cottage industry were employed to clothe and equip Captain Darke's Company. (Virginia Museum of History and Culture)

recruiting almost continuously throughout this period. Abraham Moore recalled that he was in Samuel Washington's Minute company through November of 1775 and then enlisted in Darke's company of the 8th Virginia 'on the 6th day of January 1776.'[37] Darke's quick certification was not unique. Most of the new regiments had at least one company that was certified by the first half of February.[38]

The papers of Thomas Rutherford document the difficult and piecemeal process the Berkeley Committee undertook to equip the county's two companies (the second of which went to Adam Stephen's 4th Virginia). A receipt reads:

> Received of Mr. Humphrey Keyes, one Blanket valued to Twenty shillings, which he was so kind as to advance towards equiping of the two Companies of Rifflemen Raised in Berkeley County Feby 8, 1776.
> Rec[eive]d by order of Committee
> Tho[ma]s Rutherford[39]

John Balsar provided 17 pairs of shoes, seven pairs of stockings, and two hats. Michael Welch provided 35 pairs of new leather breeches, delivering them directly to Captain Darke. Mary Imur made three hunting shirts and Edward Rumsey made 31. Thomas McCune made 40 pairs

37 NARA: M804, S2856, Abraham Moore pension.

38 Force (ed.), *American Archives*, ser.5, vol.2, p.321–322; Robert C. Powell (ed.), *A Biographical Sketch of Col. Leven Powell, Including His Correspondence During the Revolutionary War* (Alexandria: G.H. Ramey & Son, 1877), pp.17–20.

39 VMHC: Mss1 R9339 a 10–40, Thomas Rutherford Papers.

of shoes. John Barns provided a 'Squar Bareled Smooth Bore gun', which cannot have been useful to the rifle company, but the three proprietors of the gunsmithing shop in Shepherdstown promised to make 24 rifles per month. Other people provided fabric and gunpowder. One of the suppliers was William Holliday, the defiant merchant who had run into trouble with the Frederick and Dunmore committees. This burst of generosity, cottage industry, and small manufacturing is recorded in a pile of receipts, now archived in Richmond.[40]

Richard Campbell's Dunmore Company

The Convention tasked the now-awkwardly named county of Dunmore with raising two companies for the 'German' regiment. Men with experience and a following competed for the commissions. Jonathan Clark was in the running, as was his landlord, Deputy Sheriff Richard Campbell. Jonathan Langdon and Benjamin Wilson also tried. Wilson, a militia or Minute company captain, wrote to Colonel Muhlenberg late in January to express his disappointment at not being chosen:[41]

> After my Complyment to you and Wishing you Much Joy and sattisfaction in your New appointment, I come to Request of you Not to propose me as Lieutenant in any of those Regular Companys Now to Be Raised, for I Will Not Serve, In any station Lower than What I am Alredy appointed. Except it Be as a soldier, What Moves me to Write in this sort Was Mr. Swains Informing me that you said if What men I had Raised Was aded to Capt Langdon Company it Would Make one Regular Company Compleat, allowing, that I should serve as first-Lieut.[42]

The impertinent Wilson ended up with nothing. Langdon was given a company in the 12th Virginia Regiment that fall. The first captaincy went to Campbell, supported by 1st Lieutenant Mathias Hite, 2nd Lieutenant John Steed, and Ensign Leonard Cooper.[43] Following the plan that had been devised earlier, Campbell's company was designated the 'English' one.[44] As still used by Amish and Old Order Mennonites, 'English' in this context simply meant 'English-speaking' or 'not German.'

Collin Mitchum's enlistment under Campbell resulted in a break with his family. It 'caused his father to disinherit him as he was not friendly towards the Struggle ... [or] The hope of that day to Shake off the yoke of oppression.' Writing in 1816, Mitchum said he was 'forced to abscond from his fathers Bed and Board in order to quench the flame of Indignation which had so willingly Incorporated Its self in the Breast of one who on Mature Deliberation had dethermined to reveng the Rongs of British oppression.'[45]

Campbell's Company was certified complete on 19 February, 10 days after Darke's.

40 VMHC: Mss1 R9339 a 10–40, Thomas Rutherford Papers.

41 Isaac Smucker, 'A Pioneer of the Alleghanies: Col. Ben. Wilson,' *American Historical Record*, 2:18 (1873), pp.263–266; Skidmore and Kaminsky (eds), *Dunmore's War*, p.51.

42 LVA: Dunmore County Revolutionary War Papers, 1775–1814, Benjamin Wilson to Peter Muhlenberg, 23 Jan. 1776.

43 Force (ed.), *American Archives,* ser.5, vol.2, p.321–322.

44 Van Schreeven and Scribner (eds), *Revolutionary Virginia*, vol.6, p.19.

45 LVA: Legislative Petitions, Accession 36121, Collin Mechem.

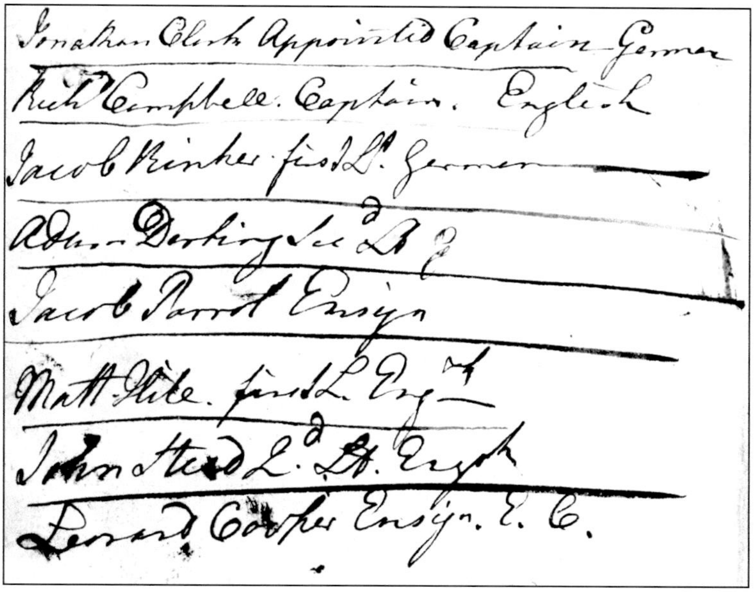

Jonathan Clark Appointed Captain German
Richd Campbell. Captain. English
Jacob Rinker first Lt. German
Adam Derting Sec Lt G
Jacob Parrot Ensign
Matt Hite. first L. Engh
John Stead 2d Lt. Engh
Lenard Cooper Ensign. E. C.

The Dunmore Committee selected two sets of officers for the county's 'English' and 'German' companies. (Library of Virginia)

George Slaughter's Culpeper Company

Culpeper's Minutemen are famous for their early service and their banner that proclaimed 'Liberty or Death' and 'Don't Tread On Me.' The Culpeper Committee, chaired by Robert Green,[46] chose George Slaughter to lead the provincial company, supported by 1st Lieutenant Henry Field, 2nd Lieutenant James Kirtley, and Ensign John Graves.[47] Lieutenant Field was one of five men with his last name in the company, all of whom were related to Slaughter by marriage.

According to an 1877 local history, George Slaughter had 'raised one of the first companies of minute-men in Culpeper.'[48] There is no evidence to support or disprove this, and he was not at Great Bridge, but it would explain his quick recruiting. William Corbin's family recalled that he 'enlisted in the year 1775' for a three-year term.[49] This inaccurate term length aligns with similar statements made by Darke's recruits and hints that Slaughter's Company had a previous incarnation. The Culpeper company was certified on the same day as Richard Campbell's.

Jonathan Clark's Dunmore Company

Jonathan Clark received the appointment he wanted and left his job as deputy clerk to his younger brother John.[50] Under Jonathan in the 'German' company were 1st Lieutenant Jacob Rinker, 2nd Lieutenant Adam Dirting, and Ensign Jacob Parett.[51] Rinker and Parett were

46 Virginia Gazette (Dixon & Hunter), 20 Jan. 1776.
47 Force (ed.), *American Archives,* ser.5, vol.2, p.321–322.
48 Slaughter, *St. Mark's Parish,* p.131.
49 LVA: Revolutionary War Bounty Land Claims, William Corbin.
50 English, *Life of General Clark,* vol.2, p.999.
51 Force (ed.), *American Archives,* ser.5, vol.2, p.321–322.

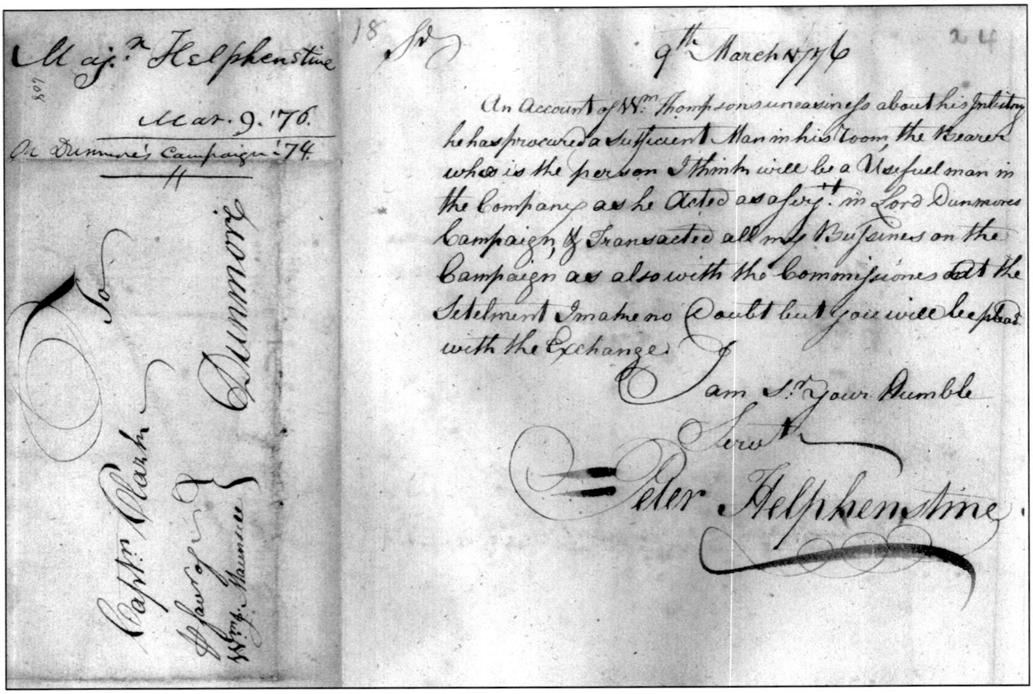
Majr. Helphenstine
Mar. 9. '76.
On Dunmore's Campaign '74

To
Captn. Clark
Dunmore

9th March 1776

An Account of Wm. Thompsons uneasiness about his Inlisting he has procured a Sufficient Man in his Room the Bearer who is the person I think will be a Usefull man in the Company as he Acted as a Serjt. in Lord Dunmores Campaign & Transacted all my Business on the Campaign as also with the Commissiones at the Setelment I make no Doubt but you will be pleas'd with the Exchange

I am Sr. your Humble Servt.
Peter Helphenstine

Major Helphenstine wrote to Captain Clark endorsing a substitute for a man who grew 'uneasy' after enlisting. (Draper Manuscripts Collection, Wisconsin Historical Society)

the sons of Swiss immigrants. Parett had served with Clark in the Dunmore Volunteers.[52] His younger brother Joseph, just 15 and still living at home, signed on as an enlisted man. This was allowed because he turned 16 before the company was certified on 4 March. The brother of enlistee Adam Cabbage was 'displeased' when he signed on because 'after that time he had all the grain to thrash himself.'[53]

Abel Westfall's Hampshire Company

Rees Pritchard recalled with rare precision that 'he was appointed an Ensign in a Company commanded by Captain Abel Westfall … in the said County of Hampshire in the fall of the year 1775' and 'having raised his quota of men entered into actual service on the 11th day of February 1776.'[54] Westfall was chosen to lead the company with 1st Lieutenant Robert Higgins, 2nd Lieutenant Andrew Turk, and Ensign Pritchard.[55] Michael Weese and many of Westfall's men enlisted 'in the spring of the year 1776 in … what was then Hampshire County Virginia on the South Branch of Potomack.'[56] The area is now Hardy County. John

52 LVA: Dunmore County Revolutionary War Papers, 1775–1814, First Independent Company of Dunmore roster.
53 NARA: M804, S2111, Adam Cabbage pension.
54 NARA: M804, S38316, Rees Pritchard pension.
55 Force (ed.), *American Archives,* ser.5, vol.2, p.321–322.
56 NARA: M804, S39121, Michael Weese pension; S41296, Robert Wadsworth pension.

Chenoweth, the young blacksmith, enlisted near what is now Capon Bridge.[57] Though not certain, Joseph Neville, who was sent £72 in recruiting money by the Committee of Safety in February, was likely the chairman of the Hampshire Committee.[58]

Lieutenant Higgins was the now-grown boy who had been chased by Indians during the French and Indian War. He still lived on the South Branch, raising cattle and periodically driving them to eastern markets. Like Richard Campbell, he was among the relatively few Westerners who owned slaves. A story recorded four decades after his death describes his purchase of an African-born man. 'While participating in his periodical drives, he chanced to stop at a hotel, where he found a Guinea negro, strangely tatooed, chained to a pillar of the front porch. The owner wanted to sell the negro, and the price asked was $40.' After examining the enslaved man, Higgins 'found him to be perfect, in regard to physical condition, and asked the negro if he would like to become a laborer on his plantation.' After 'surveying' Higgins up and down, the enslaved man replied that from his appearance he believed Higgins was 'a humane and just master.' Higgins bought the man, who we are told 'was of immense proportions' and 'rather inclined to be vicious', and removed his chains. The African, referred to as 'Old Jack', joined the cattle drive and 'became a faithful servant.'[59] If this uncomfortable story is true, Higgins' family was soon utterly dependent on Old Jack.

David Stephenson's Augusta Company

'Mr. Samuel Coleman,' David Stephenson wrote after the war, 'was very early in the year 1776 appointed an Ensign in a Company I was then to raise for the Eighth Virginia Regiment of foot.'[60] The Augusta Committee appointed Stephenson captain and certified his company on 25 March, the final deadline for recruiting. He was supported by 1st Lieutenant Joseph Dickson, 2nd Lieutenant John Grattan, and Ensign Coleman.[61] Stephenson served almost to the end of the war, but in just a few months Dickson, Gratton, and Coleman were all dead or gone. John Campbell remembered that he 'enlisted in the year 1776 in the county of Augusta State of Virginia in the Company Commanded by Capt. David Stephenson.'[62] While most of Stephenson's men came from the Shenandoah Valley, a few came from over the Great North Mountain. Adam Bible (originally 'Biebel') grew up at Henckel's Fort, an early German settlement in what is now the 'Germany Valley' area of Pendleton County, West Virginia.[63]

Thomas Berry's Frederick Company

Thomas Berry, whose older brother owned the Battletown Tavern, was a new Frederick County property owner when he was selected to lead his company. He acquired land by the

57 NARA: J. Chenoweth pension.

58 William P. Palmeret al (eds), *Calendar of Virginia State Papers and Other Manuscripts* (Richmond: James E. Good, 1875–1893), vol.8, pp.87, 90.

59 Anon. (ed.), *The History of Brown County, Ohio* (Chicago: W.H. Beers & Co., 1883), part 5, pp.21–22.

60 LVA: Revolutionary War Bounty Land Claims, Samuel Coleman.

61 Force (ed.), *American Archives,* ser.5, vol.2, pp.321–322.

62 NARA: M804, S35824, John Campbell pension.

63 Anon., Fort Henckel Militia musters for June and Sept. 1775, in 'Johann Adam Bible Senior and His Sons, Johann Christian Bible and Adam Bible, Junior,' *Greene County Genealogical Society,* <greenecountytngenealogicalsociety.org>, accessed 27 Sept. 2024; NARA: M804, W18596, Adam Bible pension.

Shenandoah River when the property of Virginia's hapless and now bankrupt Stamp Act-era stamp master was put up for auction.[64] Isaac Dunn enlisted in February and was careful to note later that 'Cap'n Berry's company was a rifle company.'[65] Berry was chosen by Charles Thruston and the Frederick Committee, along with 1st Lieutenant John Jolliffe (the former Quaker), 2nd Lieutenant Richard Eastin, and Ensign William Meade.[66] Recruiting in the county so soon after Daniel Morgan and Morgan Alexander required some effort. Berry returned to his childhood home in King George County to recruit some of his friends.[67] He also kept an eye out for men who could read and write. 'My Captain Berry gave me the appointment of Sergeant when I enlisted,' recalled Henry Wysor, 'and I believe enrolled me as such. After serving some time, I applied to be released, on the ground, I was no scholar but was refused, and I continued to do the duties of Sergeant for some time.'[68]

As they collected their men, Berry, Jolliffe, Eastin, and Meade traversed the county, enjoying their new lives as soldiers and the status that came with it. According to a Jolliffe family story, one neighbour felt the need to knock them down a peg.

> On one occasion he and two of his brother officers rode up to the house of an old woman in the mountains and asked her to get dinner for them. While they were there the old woman showed them some puppies; she went down a trap-door to the cellar and handed them up. As the first was passed they asked its name, and she replied, 'Captain,' the second the same, and when the third was passed with the same reply, 'Captain,' they exclaimed, 'Why Mrs. B., do you give all your dogs the same name?' 'Oh, any puppy dog can be a captain nowadays,' was her rejoinder.[69]

James Knox's Fincastle Company

James Knox was serving in Captain William Russell's Southwest Independent Company when he was called to form his own company. The Fincastle Committee convened at Fort Chiswell on 23 February, with William Preston presiding.[70] First, they appointed Joseph Crockett and three junior officers to lead a company destined for the 7th Virginia Regiment. Then they appointed 'James Knox Captain, Ephraim Drake first Lieutenant, James Craig second Lieutenant, William Ward Ensign' to command the company going to the 8th.[71] Drake, like Knox, was a long hunter, and all four men had served in Dunmore's War.[72]

64 Gabriel Neville, 'The Stamp Act and Captain Berry', *The 8th Virginia Regiment*, <8thvirginia.com/blog/thomas-berry-and-the-stamp-act>, accessed 4 Nov. 2024; Guerdon Groves Parry and Lee Kercheval Carr, 'Something About the Kercheval Family', *Register of the Kentucky State Historical Society*, 22:65 (1924), p.197.

65 NARA: M804, S43520, Isaac Dunn pension.

66 Force (ed.), *American Archives*, ser.5, vol.2, p.321–322.

67 NARA: M804, S31179, James Kay pension; Hening (ed.), *Statutes*, vol.9, p.78.

68 NARA: M804, S7854, Henry Wysor pension.

69 Jolliffe, *Jolliffe Family*, p.91, n.2.

70 Richard Barksdale Harwell (ed.), *The Committees of Safety of Westmoreland and Fincastle: Proceedings of the County Committees, 1774–1776* (Richmond: Virginia State Library, 1956), pp.78–82.

71 Harwell, *Westmoreland and Fincastle Committees*, pp.82–83.

72 LOC: Crockett to Jefferson, 1 Nov. 1825; Skidmore and Kaminsky (eds), *Dunmore's War*, pp.138, 144, 152–154, 157, 159, 165, 168, 176.

The site of Fort Chiswell is marked by a monument built by the Daughters of the American Revolution in 1924. (Author's photo)

None of the appointees were present for the committee's deliberations. According to Crockett, Russell's company was posted at the Long Island of the Holston River (Kingsport, Tennessee) when 'the committee of Safty wrote to Capt Russell to discharge Said company … And ordered two companies to be raised from Fincastle County.'[73] Knox enlisted Martin Maney immediately at the Long Island.[74] He picked a young man named Robert Breckenridge to be a sergeant. 'Bob' and his brother, Alexander, were from Augusta County but had moved to get away from their stepmother and learn to be carpenters. Preston was their uncle, and he hired them to build his house at Smithfield on the New River.[75] Sergeant Breckenridge was more enthusiastic about his new duties than Henry Wysor was. In time, he would preside over the Kentucky legislature.

Knox and his officers fell short of their recruiting quotas, but the Fincastle Committee nevertheless ordered on 4 April 'that Captain James Knox be ordered to march with his Company of regulars to the regement at Suffolk.'[76] It would be up to the Committee of Safety in Williamsburg to figure out how to complete the company.

William Croghan's West Augusta Company

The last company raised came from the same place as the first. George Croghan may have chosen his nephew William to be its captain, but Thomas Smallman was chairman of the West Augusta Committee when the company was certified.[77] Nepotism aside, Croghan was

73 LOC: Thomas Jefferson Papers, Ser.1, 'Joseph Crockett to Thomas Jefferson, November 1, 1825.'
74 NARA: M804, W7398, Martin Maney pension.
75 Joseph Addison Waddell (ed.), *Annals of Augusta County*, second edition (Staunton: C. R. Caldwell, 1902), p.119.
76 Harwell, *Westmoreland and Fincastle Committees*, pp.87.
77 Force (ed.), *American Archives*, ser.4., vol.5, p.820.

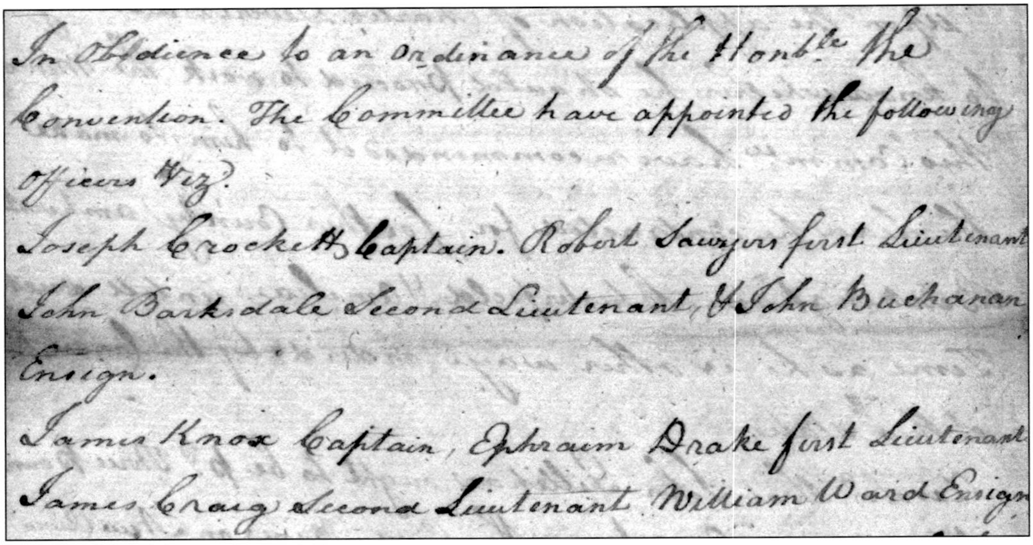
In Obedience to an Ordinance of the Honble the Convention. The Committee have appointed the following officers Viz:
Joseph Crockett Captain. Robert Sawyers first Lieutenant
John Barksdale Second Lieutenant, & John Buchanan Ensign.
James Knox Captain, Ephraim Drake first Lieutenant
James Craig Second Lieutenant William Ward Ensign

The journal of the Fincastle Committee records the appointments of James Knox and other officers on 24 February 1776. (Library of Virginia)

a good choice. Abraham Kirkpatrick, the combative son of a Jacobite, was appointed first lieutenant. James Higgins, George Rogers Clark's exploring partner,[78] was 2nd lieutenant. James Berwick, the committee's clerk,[79] became ensign.

Jonathan Grant remembered that he 'enlisted in the month of February 1776 in the town of Pittsburgh … in the Company Commanded by Captain William Croghan of the eighth Virginia Rifle Regiment.'[80] As with Knox's Company, long distances and dispersed populations caused delays. Henry and William Gaddis walked 50 miles from Tenmile Creek to the assembly point.[81] Croghan's Company was certified on 19 April, almost a month after the deadline.[82]

From Fort Pitt, the frontiersmen marched south, passing through the field where Braddock was defeated in 1755. The bodies of 600 men had been too numerous to collect or bury, and their bare skeletons still lay on the bank of the Monongahela. Some of the bones had been stacked in piles by a settler to make room for a cornfield. The rest lay in the underbrush amid rusted debris and the bones of horses. Every skull bore the mark of a scalping knife. Many had been crushed or pierced by a warclub or a tomahawk. A three-foot band of dimples covered the trees. Twenty seasons of growth had distorted the little holes, but a lead slug was still visible in most of them.[83]

78 James (ed.), *Clark Papers*, pp.1–2.
79 Anon. (ed.), 'Virginia Legislative Papers,' *VMHB*, 13:4 (1906), pp.419, 420, 423.
80 NARA: M804, S42758, Jonathan Grant pension.
81 NARA: H. Gaddis pension.
82 Hening (ed.), *Statutes*, vol.9, pp.78–79.
83 Dexter (ed.), *Diary of David McClure*, p.48; Douglas MacGregor, 'Braddock's Field: "How Brilliant the Morning, How Melancholy the Evening"', *Western Pennsylvania History*, 88:4 (2005), pp.22–29.

After passing these bleak reminders of war, Grant recalled that they 'marched to Winchester' where they 'drew their clothing & rifles.' From there, they set off for the Tidewater.[84] Suffolk, their intended destination, was almost as far from Pittsburgh as two settled places under Virginia's jurisdiction could be: over 425 miles.

The Staff and Warrant Officers

While the company officers recruited, Peter Muhlenberg looked for staff and warrant officers. The regiment's adjutant, quartermaster, quartermaster sergeant, sergeant major, and drum major appointments were entirely his to make. The chaplain and surgeon were to be chosen by the field and company officers together.[85] He appears to have held off on some appointments, perhaps planning to reward soldiers for good service. The adjutant and chaplain posts, however, he sought to fill quickly.

He chose his brother-in-law Francis Swaine to be his adjutant. Swaine was not a good pick, but family considerations overrode any doubts the colonel had. One of the first things the 22-year-old adjutant did was offend Captain Wilson.[86] That happened early enough to indicate that Swaine and his wife (Muhlenberg's sister Polly) were already in Dunmore County, probably living at Muhlenberg's glebe.[87] Swaine does not seem to have ever impressed the men of the Muhlenberg family. Frederick Muhlenberg complained in a letter to his brother Peter when 'our Poll made such a fool of herself and ran off with the drummer.'[88] The 'drummer' appears to be Swaine. Polly stayed with the colonel's wife, Hannah, during their husbands' service.

Having been parish priest for one-fifth of the regiment's men, the prospect of selecting a chaplain may have seemed an odd task to Muhlenberg. It was not technically his decision, but with the considerations involved, it makes sense that the regiment's officers looked to him for a recommendation. He knew who he wanted. He and Christian Streit had been students, catechists, and deacons together in Pennsylvania and New Jersey.[89] Streit had visited the Muhlenbergs in Woodstock and gave a sermon there in 1775.[90] He was ordained into the Lutheran clergy about the same time Muhlenberg went to London, but his start in his ministry was difficult. A congregation in New Jersey complained, 'Pastor Str[eit] was born here and grew up with the young people. He does not know much German, has no gift for catechization, is sleepy, and, as our Lord said, a prophet is not without honor, save

84 NARA: J. Grant pension; D. Williams pension; NARA: M804, R68, Abraham Atchley pension (Botetourt Militia); R4674, William Harris pension (Dunmore Militia); W3767, James Cameron pension (Crockett's Western Battalion); S6584, James Ballard pension (Crockett's Western Battalion); S9026, John Miller pension (Hampshire Militia); S8087, Joseph Britton pension (Crockett's Western Battalion). Williams remembered receiving his clothes in Williamsburg.

85 Hening (ed.), *Statutes*, vol.9, pp.10, 79.

86 LVA: Dunmore County Revolutionary War Papers, 1775–1814, Benjamin Wilson to Peter Muhlenberg, 23 Jan. 1776.

87 Theodore G. Tappert and John W. Doberstein (trans), *The Journals of Henry Melchior Muhlenberg* (Philadelphia: Muhlenberg Press, 1942), vol.2, p.356; Chase et al (eds), *Papers of Washington* (Revolution), vol.8, pp.428–429.

88 Wallace, *Muhlenbergs*, p.120. The word translated from German as 'drummer' is uncertain.

89 Tappert and Doberstein (trans), *Journals of H.M. Muhlenberg*, vol.2, pp.360, 400, 405, 451.

90 FHS: Clark Diary, 23 April 1775.

in his own country.'[91] He was settling into a new position in Easton, Pennsylvania, when he received the invitation from his old friend. Streit visited with Muhlenberg's father, who advised him that he would have to be released by the four congregations he served, and they would have to find a suitable replacement. It took until the latter half of August before Streit was ready. When he left for Virginia, the elder Muhlenberg gave him a letter 'in lieu of a pass, as it is a very critical matter to travel under present conditions.'

> Whereas Bearer of these the Revd Mr. Christian Stright has received and accepted a call to be Chaplain for the 8th Regiment of Regulars of the State of Virginia, and on his Journey to move there; these are therefore to certify, that he said Revd Gentle man is a regularly ordained Minister of the Gospel, sound in Protestant Principles and sober in life, desirous and virtuous to promote the Glory of God and Wellfare of the State, and therefore recommended to all Friends and Well-wishers of Religion and State:
> p[er] H[einrich] M[uhlen]b[erg],
> Senior Minister and P[resident] of the
> German Lutheran Ministry in
> the State of Pennsylvania.[92]

Some historians view this letter as the United States' first ecclesiastical endorsement of a military chaplain.[93]

The Fighting Parson

Peter Muhlenberg is celebrated in history for one thing his brothers could not abide: being a 'fighting parson.' If he had chosen one job and set the other aside, they might not have complained, but he continued to preach, wed, and baptise after his appointment. 'You think,' wrote his brother Frederick, 'a man can be both preacher and colonel at the same time. How different are our ways of thinking!'

'I am a Clergyman it is true,' Peter replied, 'but I am a Member of Society as well as the poorest Layman, & my Liberty is as dear to me as to any Man, shall I then sit still & enjoy myself at Home when the best blood of the Continent is spilling?'

Frederick lived in New York, which Peter suggested 'must be purged with Fire, before ever it is cleaned from Toryism; may there be none to pity it.' Frederick rightly retorted that advocating against pity was 'contrary to the teachings of Jesus.'

Not contesting that point, Peter pressed further: 'Seriously Brother, I am afraid you have imbibed bad Principles in N.Y.' Frederick countered, 'How do you make that out? Because I think it wrong for you to be both preacher and soldier in one? … I believe I have always

91 Tappert and Doberstein (trans), *Journals of H.M. Muhlenberg*, vol.2, p.539; Mark, 6:4 (KJV).

92 Tappert and Doberstein, *Journals of H.M. Muhlenberg*, vol.2, p.736.

93 Richard M. Budd, *Serving Two Masters: The Development of American Military Chaplaincy, 1860–1920* (Lincoln: University of Nebraska Press, 2002), p.24.

A clerical robe with a tradition of ownership by Peter Muhlenberg. Pennsylvania or Virginia, late eighteenth century. Silk and wool. (United Lutheran Seminary; photo courtesy of Historic Trappe)

been, and still am, as firm in our American cause as you are, even though I am not a colonel marching to the field.'

Either way, Peter insisted, Frederick had to concede that he had 'acted for the best.' 'You know that from the Beginning of these Troubles, I have been compelled by Causes to you unknown to have a Hand in public affairs. I have been Chairman of the Committee & Delegate for this County from the first, do you think then if America should be conquered I should be safe, on the contrary, & would you not sooner fight like a man than die the Death of a dog?'

'You would have acted for the best,' his brother replied, 'if you had kept out of this business from the beginning.'[94]

Peter and Frederick were both members of the House of Representatives when the first United States Congress convened in 1789. Frederick was a Federalist. Peter was an Antifederalist.

Marching Off to War

Though the recruits and officers of the 8th Virginia's companies had known their regiment from the start, Edmund Pendleton of the Committee of Safety included their county committees in his early February letter informing companies of their assignments. 'Persuant to an Ordinance of Convention,' he wrote, 'I am to inform you that the Regular Companys raised or to be raised in your county are allotted to the eighth Regiment Stationed at Suffolk to which place you'll please to direct the march of said Companys as soon as reviewed.'[95] *Rage militaire* swept the countryside. A Presbyterian minister in Winchester wrote:

94 Wallace, *Muhlenbergs*, pp.120–121.

95 LVA: Dunmore County Revolutionary War Papers, 1775–1814, Edmund Pendleton to Dunmore Committee, 9 Feb. 1776.

> Mars, the great God of Battle, is now honored in every part of this spacious colony, but here every presence is warlike – every sound is martial – drums beating, pipes and bagpipes playing and only sonorous and venic music. Every man has a hunting shirt, which is the uniform of each company. Almost all have a cockade and bucktail in their hats to represent that they are hardy, resolute and invincible natives of the woods of America.[96]

Barely a third of the adventure-seeking liberty lovers who volunteered in the winter and spring of 1776 would make it all the way through their two-year enlistments, and their replacements would come far less willingly.

Even amid the early enthusiasm, the soldiers' departures were hard on their families and disruptive to their communities. Thomas McCarty enlisted in Pittsburgh a month after losing his first child. He had married his wife, Anne, right before floating down the Ohio during Dunmore's War.[97] He returned home in time for the birth but left again with Captain Croghan just weeks after the baby died.[98]

In Frederick, Lieutenant Jolliffe wrote his will before he left his pregnant wife and young son. The Quaker-turned-Methodist gave his land to his son but provided for his wife for as long as she might live. He allotted a substantial £450 and one slave to his unborn child.[99] When it was time to leave, Rees Bowen remembered that Captain Berry's Frederick County shirtmen assembled at Ashby's Gap in the Blue Ridge, several miles east of Winchester on the main route to Williamsburg.[100]

In Culpeper, Drury and Utey Jackson invited their friends to come stay with them for a few days before marching with Captain Slaughter. On their last full day, the Jacksons congregated with several others at the home of Augustine Rucker 'to stay all night' and then set off in the morning.[101] Meshack Pearson, the triplet, remembered that he 'marched under the command of his Captain from Culpepper on 9th of March 1776 to join the Regiment.'[102]

David Stephenson's Company collected at Staunton and crossed the Blue Ridge through Jarman's Gap. They were joined in their eastward march by another Augusta company that was on its way to join the 9th Virginia Regiment.[103] At New Kent Court House, 2nd Lieutenant John Grattan discovered that his valuable rifle had been stolen.[104]

In southern Hampshire, a neighbour remembered when Abel Westfall 'enlisted a company of men in that neighbourhood to join Gen'l. Washington' and that he 'was in the town of Moorfield (now) on the day they marched from that ground to join the army.'[105] Moorefield was chartered in 1777.[106]

---

96 James R. Graham, *The Planting of the Presbyterian Church in Northern Virginia Prior to the Organisation of Winchester Presbytery, December 4, 1794* (Winchester: Geo. F. Norton, 1904), p.99
97 Skidmore and Kaminsky (eds), *Dunmore's War*, pp.33, 35.
98 NARA: M804, W8424, Thomas McCarty pension.
99 Jolliffe, *Jolliffe Family*, 90.
100 LVA: Revolutionary War Bounty Land Claims, Rees Bowen.
101 NARA: M804, S38075, Drury Jackson pension.
102 NARA: M804, S35555, Meshack Pearson pension.
103 NARA: M804, W10112, George Hooke pension (4th N.C.).
104 *Virginia Gazette* (Dixon & Hunter), 13 April 1776.
105 NARA: M804, W9883, Abraham Westfall pension.
106 Hening (ed.), *Statutes*, vol.9, p.425.

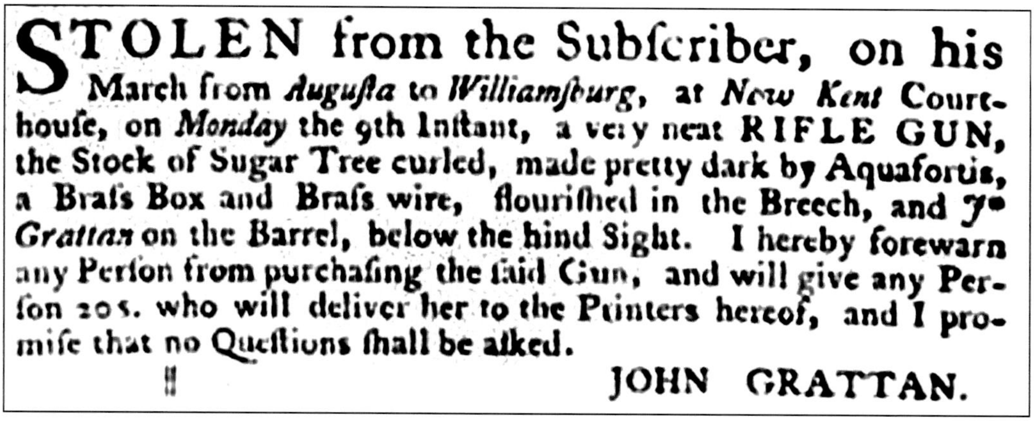

STOLEN from the Subſcriber, on his March from *Auguſta* to *Williamſburg*, at *New Kent* Court-houſe, on *Monday* the 9th Inſtant, a very neat RIFLE GUN, the Stock of Sugar Tree curled, made pretty dark by Aquafortis, a Braſs Box and Braſs wire, flouriſhed in the Breech, and *Jⁿ Grattan* on the Barrel, below the hind Sight. I hereby forewarn any Perſon from purchaſing the ſaid Gun, and will give any Perſon 20s. who will deliver her to the Printers hereof, and I promiſe that no Queſtions ſhall be aſked.

JOHN GRATTAN.

The advertisement 2nd Lieutenant John Grattan placed in the *Virginia Gazette* offering a 20-shilling reward for the return of his prized rifle. (Colonial Williamsburg)

The Sermon

The 'fighting parson' delivered his final sermon to a packed house.[107] The church was a new log structure in the centre of Woodstock, facing the Great Wagon Road.[108] He arrived dressed as an officer, wearing a sword on his hip and a cockade on his hat.[109] He threw his black clerical robe over his uniform, entered the pulpit, and preached from the third chapter of Ecclesiastes.[110]

> To every thing there is a season, and a time to every purpose under the heaven:
> A time to be born, and a time to die; a time to plant, and a time to pluck up that which is planted;
> A time to kill, and a time to heal; a time to break down, and a time to build up;
> A time to weep, and a time to laugh; a time to mourn, and a time to dance;
> A time to cast away stones, and a time to gather stones together; a time to embrace, and a time to refrain from embracing;
> A time to get, and a time to lose; a time to keep, and a time to cast away;
> A time to rend, and a time to sew; a time to keep silence, and a time to speak;
> A time to love, and a time to hate; a time of war, and a time of peace.[111]

107 James Thacher, *A Military Journal During the American Revolutionary War from 1775 to 1783* (Boston: Cottons & Barnard, 1827), p.152; Muhlenberg, *General Muhlenberg*, pp.51–55.
108 Hendricks, *Backcountry Towns*, p.109.
109 Thacher, *Military Journal*, p.152.
110 Muhlenberg, *General Muhlenberg*, pp.51–55; Michael Cecere, 'The Fighting Parson's Farewell Sermon,' *JAR*, 15 April 2020, <allthingsliberty.com/2020/04/the-fighting-parsons-farewell-sermon>, accessed 21 July 2024.
111 Ecclesiastes, 3:1–8 (KJV).

Peter Muhlenberg's farewell sermon as imagined by Stanley Arthurs ca. 1920. Like most depictions, this painting is heavily influenced by a fictionalised version in Thomas Buchanan Read's 1863 epic poem *The Wagoner of the Alleghanies.* The wig, the style of the uniform, and the 'revelation' of the uniform are all inaccurate. (Image courtesy of Seminary Archives, United Lutheran Seminary, from the Fine Art Collection)

Neither the sermon text nor any witness account of it survives, but one can see how these eight verses might serve as a rich text for the day. When he removed his robe to reveal his uniform again, many saw a poetry in the gesture that launched the event into the stratosphere of Revolutionary lore. It has been portrayed in stained glass, a statue in the United States Capitol, and epic verse.[112] Generations of children learned a version of the tale in *McGuffey's Reader,* and sceptics continue to spar with Christians over its meaning and historicity.[113] There is no reason to doubt the sermon itself occurred. Muhlenberg was scolded by his brother for blending his military and spiritual duties and the homily was reported in writing 32 months after it was delivered. 'General Muhlenberg was a minister of a parish in Virginia,' wrote Continental Army surgeon James Thacher in 1778, 'but participating in the spirit of the times, exchanged his clerical profession for that of a soldier. Having in the pulpit inculcated the principles of liberty and the cause of his country, he found no difficulty in enlisting a regiment of soldiers, and he was appointed their commander.' Making no mention of Muhlenberg's robe, Thacher confirms, 'He entered the pulpit with his sword and cockade, preached his farewell sermon, and the next day marched at the head of his regiment to join the army, and he does honor to the military profession.'[114]

112 Thomas Buchanan Read, *The Wagoner of the Alleghanies: A Poem of the Days of Seventy-Six* (Philadelphia: J.B. Lippincott, 1863), pp.87–92.

113 William Holmes McGuffey (ed.), *McGuffey's Fifth Eclectic Reader*, revised edition (New York: American Book Company, 1879), pp.200–204; Chris Rodda, '"Debunk U" Study Guide – Lesson 1', *Huffington Post*, 14 July 2010, revised 6 Dec. 2017, <huffpost.com/entry/debunk-u-study-guide-le_b_645528>, accessed 21 July 2024.

114 Thacher, *Military Journal*, p.152.

Even though he was a field officer, Muhlenberg probably wore a hunting shirt that day. Virginia provincials wore blue coats with red facings in the French and Indian War, and the Fairfax Volunteers adopted blue and buff coats in 1775.[115] Nevertheless, the suddenly ubiquitous hunting shirt really was the Virginia provincial uniform, and the shirts were also closely associated with rifles. Even eastern Fairfax County aspired to have a rifle company that distinguished itself from the others by wearing 'painted Hunting Shirts.'[116]

Late in March, Muhlenberg wrote to his brother-in-law Emanuel Schulze.

> I make no doubt you have heard long before this of my appointment to the Command of a Reg[imen]t of Regulars, an appointment I neither wished or expected. I flattered myself I should have it in my power to pay You a visit, before I should be call'd to the field, but my Regiment is compleat, & I am ordered to take the Field with all possible expedition, & to march to Suffolk, a place below Williamsburg, near to Norfolk. I expect to go myself in about 3 Weeks, at furthest. ... I shall be very glad to hear from You before I go, & should take it as a favor if You and my sister would now & then write to my Wife and Polly during my absence.'[117]

Captains Campbell and Clark led their companies out of Woodstock on 19 March, proceeding just five miles to the north on the Great Wagon Road and then camping at Muhlenberg's glebe. Another day brought them eight more miles to Strasburg. After crossing the Blue Ridge, they entered Caroline County on 30 March and camped at Clark's parents' farm. They rested for a day and then arrived in Williamsburg on 5 April.[118] They were almost fully equipped, but the Dunmore Committee was still trying to find stockings for them.[119]

The Suffolk Rendezvous

A few days before Muhlenberg arrived in Williamsburg, the arrogant, ruthless, self-serving, and capable Major General Charles Lee came to take command of the Southern Department. Though Lee owned land in Berkeley County, he had spent very little time there. He was warmly greeted but immediately critical of Virginia's preparations.[120] 'There is not a man or officer in the Army,' he complained, 'that knows the difference betwixt a *Chevaux de Frise*, and a Cabbage Garden.'[121]

Lee now ranked third in the Continental Army behind only Washington and Artemis Ward of Massachusetts. He was an odd man in every way. A relative bluntly described him as 'ugly'.[122] Benjamin Rush observed that Lee 'loved and admired public virtue, but

115 Rutland, *Papers of Mason*, vol.1, p.211
116 Rutland, *Papers of Mason*, vol.1, p.216.
117 Minardi et al. *Historic Muhlenberg Property*, lot 4, p.25.
118 FHS: Clark Diary, 19 March-5 April 1776; Bunbury (ed.), *Lee Papers*, vol.1, p.396.
119 WHS: Draper Mss, L, vol.1, p.26, Alexander Machir to Jonathan Clark, 1 May 1776.
120 Bunbury (ed.), *Lee Papers*, vol.1, p.364.
121 Bunbury (ed.), *Lee Papers*, vol.1, pp.376–378, 477–480.
122 George H. Moore, *The Treason of Charles Lee* (New York: Charles Scribner, 1859), pp.ix–x.

was addicted to many private vices. He was obscene, profane and at all times impious in his conversation ... He had many successive intimates whom he called friends, but he appeared to have no affection for anything human.' But he loved his dogs. They followed him everywhere.[123]

On the third of April, Muhlenberg, Bowman, and Helphenstine appeared before the Virginia Committee of Safety, signed their names to the Articles of War, took their oaths, and received their provincial commissions.[124] Company officers, too, had to appear before the Committee of Safety when they arrived. They presented their county certificates and assembled their companies for inspection by the commanding general (Lee).[125] They were promised their commissions, but did not receive them immediately. To determine seniority, George Slaughter drew lots with captains from Prince Edward and Caroline counties whose companies had been reviewed on the same day as his. He came in second. William Darke did the same with a captain from Loudoun County and came in first.[126]

The companies of the 8th Virginia arrived one or two at a time. Slaughter presented his certificate on 1 March. John Stephenson presented his on 13 March.[127] The next day he was issued 253 yards of Osnaburg linen for hunting shirts.[128] The Dunmore companies appeared on 5 April and Captain Westfall's men arrived two weeks later.[129] One of David Stephenson's men remembered that two Augusta companies marched together from Staunton. 'At Williamsburg our two Companies were separated,' he wrote, 'my Company put in the 8th and Hays in the 9th.'[130] Captain Berry's company marched into Williamsburg on 14 May.[131] Though this was two and a half months after Slaughter's punctual arrival, they were not the last to arrive.

He may not have said so, but Lee was impressed with the 8th Virginia companies when they lined up before him. Most of Virginia's young men had no real military experience. Militia duty was a social activity in most counties. A member of the Committee of Safety lamented, 'Our army is but an handful of raw, undisciplined troops, indifferently armed, wretchedly clothed, and without tents or Blankets.'[132] Lee was an expert and could certainly distinguish between combat veterans and eager boys. There were plenty of pimple-faced

123 Louis Alexander Biddle (ed.), *A Memorial Containing Travels Through Life or Sundry Incidents in the Life of Dr. Benjamin Rush Written by Himself* (Philadelphia: privately published, 1905), p.119
124 Palmer et al (eds), *Calendar*, vol.8, p.150.
125 Charles Campbell (ed.), *The Orderly Book of That Portion of the American Army Stationed at or Near Williamsburg, Va., Under the Command of General Andrew Lewis from March 18th, 1776, to August 28th, 1776* (Richmond: privately printed, 1860), pp.16, 20.
126 Palmer et al (eds), *Calendar*, vol.8, pp.129, 145.
127 Palmer et al (eds), *Calendar*, vol.8, pp.102, 121.
128 Gregory B. Sandor, *Journal of the Public Store at Williamsburg, 1775–1776* (place unknown: G.B. Sandor, 2015), p.103.
129 Campbell (ed.), *Lewis Orderly Book*, p.16; Palmer et al (eds), *Calendar*, vol.8, p.155; LVA: C. Mitcham petition; Robert Alonzo Brock (ed.), 'Orderly Book of the Company of Captain George Stubblefield, Fifth Virginia Regiment,' *Collections of the Virginia Historical Society*, New Series, 11 vols. (Richmond: Virginia Historical Society, 1882–1892), vol.6, p.164.
130 NARA: G. Hooke pension.
131 Palmer et al (eds), *Calendar*, vol.8, p. 175.
132 John R. Thompson (ed.), 'Selections and Excerpts from the Lee Papers,' *Southern Literary Messenger*, 27:5–6 (1858), pp.250–266, 324–332, 255.

recruits in the 8th Virginia, but there were also quite a few veterans of Dunmore's War and other conflicts. Lee could tell that officers like John Stephenson, William Darke, and George Slaughter knew what they were about.

Lee was also impressed that Muhlenberg's regiment was well-equipped and that each of the eight present companies came fully recruited. They wore linen hunting shirts and buckskin breeches that were made for them at home, acquired on the way, or sewn in Williamsburg. Each man arrived with a rifle, many of which were newly made. Soldiers in other regiments often showed up carrying old inherited weapons, fowlers, or no weapons at all. The contrast was unambiguous: 'except the Rifflers,' Lee complained, 'we are horribly armed.'[133]

A rifleman wore a powder horn and a shot pouch. His weapon was for distance shooting and could not hold a bayonet, but he carried a knife or a tomahawk for hand-to-hand combat. Like a musketeer, he had a blanket, a canteen, and a haversack. All Virginia provincials wore their equipment over fringed linen hunting shirts. The shirt was a cultural artefact of the frontier that combined European material with Native style.[134] Wearing one made a statement. 'These shirt men,' carped one Loyalist, '...are dressed with an Oznaburg shirt over their cloaths, a belt round them with a Tommyhawk or Scalping Knife. They look like a band of Assassins and it is my opinion if they fight at all, it will be in that way.'[135]

The 'Indian Shirts' (as Washington once called them) are sometimes assumed to be second-preference attire worn by those who could not afford or obtain a real uniform. This was true in the Continental Army after 1778, but it was not the case in Virginia in 1776. The shirts were standard attire for the provincial forces, and they were proud to wear them. The Second Virginia Convention initially 'recommended' that the volunteer companies, mostly members of the gentry, dress each man 'in a hunting shirt, by way of uniform.'[136] Patrick Henry was presented with a shirt during the Powder Alarm, and a witness recorded that at the Fredericksburg rendezvous, 'every Man rich and poor' came 'with their hunting shirts, belts, tomahawks fixed in the best manner.'[137] The Third Convention promised to provide 'every minute-man not already furnished, one hunting shirt and a pair of leggins.'[138] The promise was not repeated in the first authorisation of provincial regulars but, at the request of Lieutenant Colonel Christian, the Fourth Convention retroactively promised each recruit 'a hunting shirt, a pair of leggings, and binding for his hat.'[139] The commitment was made again in the second authorisation (creating the 3rd through 9th regiments) and again in the third (creating the 10th through 15th).[140] Hunting shirts were dyed (or bleached) a wide variety of colours, including dark brown, black, white, yellow-brown, pink, purple,

133 Bunbury (ed.), *Lee Papers*, vol.1, p.425.

134 Neal Thomas Hurst, *'kind of armour, being peculiar to America:' The American Hunting Shirt* (Bachelors Thesis, College of William and Mary, 2013), p.20.

135 William Abbatt (ed.), 'Letters from Virginia, 1774–1781', *The Magazine of History with Notes and Queries*, 3 (1906), p.159.

136 Anon. (ed.), *Proceedings of the 2nd Convention*, p.6; McDonnell, 'Popular Mobilization,' pp.946–981, 951–962.

137 Hurst, 'American Hunting Shirt', p.20.

138 Anon. (ed.), *Proceedings of the 3rd Convention*, p.33.

139 Anon. (ed.), *Proceedings of the 4th Convention*, p. 72.

140 Anon. (ed.), *Proceedings of the 4th Convention*, p.107; Hening (ed.), *Statutes*, vol.9, pp.82, 194.

and red.[141] According to Charles Wilson Peale, this was done 'according to the fancy of the companies.'[142] Peale's assertion that shirts were coloured for unit identification is supported by a witness account that the 8th Virginia was dressed 'in split shirts, neatly dyed in walnut, and they made a handsome appearance.'[143]

The hunting shirt was typically worn with buckskin breeches. It was a natural pairing. Hunting shirts were first worn by Western deer hunters as early as the late 1750s. Long hunters like James Knox were at the top of a robust supply chain that, before the war, shipped hundreds of thousands of skins to Britain annually. 'Buckskin' did not refer to the gender of the deer but rather to skins that had been de-haired and brain-tanned. The leather was light, porous, durable, and excellent for clothing.[144] Though buckskin was preferred, some soldiers wore fabric breeches. A waistcoat and a regular shirt were worn under the hunting shirt, and leggings (Indian-style gaiters), shoes, and a hat completed the outfit. When shoes wore out, they were replaced by buckskin moccasins or bare feet. A Virginia soldier wore the familiar tricorne cocked hat, a round hat, a cap with a leather brim, or a knitted wool hat.[145] Period images of Virginia riflemen show them wearing round black hats with fairly wide brims.

The Williamsburg army camp was in Waller's Wood on the east side of town, where measures had to be taken to stop the Western soldiers from engaging in their 'Custom of Throwing Tomahawks' at the trees.[146] From Williamsburg, Muhlenberg's riflemen marched to Virginia's original settlement at Jamestown and crossed the James River to Cobham. From there, they continued through the village of Smithfield and marched to Suffolk.[147] The village smelled of the pitch and turpentine that were made in the area's longleaf pine forests.[148] It was strategically positioned between the enormous Great Dismal Swamp and the Nansemond River estuary, making it a choke point between the Loyalist region around Norfolk and the rest of Virginia. Slaughter's, John Stephenson's, and Darke's companies arrived before Muhlenberg did.[149] Stephenson's West Augusta men were posted forward, guarding Great Bridge.[150] Clark's Company arrived on 11 April,[151] but Campbell's Company was halted at Smithfield to guard provisions.[152] Captain Berry's Company was held at Cobham when it arrived.[153]

141 Jules David Prown, *Art as Evidence: Writings on Art and Material Culture* (New Haven: Yale University Press, 2001), p.170; Hurst, 'American Hunting Shirt', p.68; Andrew Gallup, *A Sketch of the Virginia Soldier in the Revolution* (Westminster, Md.: Heritage Books, 2008), pp.29–50, 57, 73.

142 Prown, *Art as Evidence*, p.170.

143 *Columbian Herald*, 20 Jan.1794. 'Split shirt' was a South Carolina term for a hunting shirt.

144 Kathryn E. Holland Braund, *Deerskins and Duffels: The Creek Indian Trade with Anglo-America, 1685–1815* (Lincoln: University of Nebraska Press, 1993), pp.87–88.

145 Gallup, *Virginia Soldier*, p.63.

146 Brock (ed.), 'Stubblefield Orderly Book', p.162.

147 FHS: Clark Diary, 5–11 April 1776.

148 Hugh Buckner Johnston (ed.), 'The Journal of Ebenezer Hazard in North Carolina, 1777 and 1778', *North Carolina Historical Review*, 36:3 (1959), pp.360–361.

149 Palmer et al (eds), *Calendar*, vol.8, p.145; HSP: 2nd Va. Orderly Book, 4–5 April 1776.

150 Palmer et al (eds), *Calendar*, vol.8, p.121; NARA: M804, W2061, Zephaniah Bryan pension; S22413, Samuel Murphy pension; S4740, William Owens pension.

151 FHS: Clark Diary, 11 April 1776.

152 Bunbury (ed.), *Lee Papers*, vol.1, p.396; HSP: 2nd Va. Orderly Book, 4–8, 12–14 April 1776.

153 NARA: J. Morrison pension.

Suffolk was also the rendezvous point for Adam Stephen's 4th Virginia and parts of Colonel Woodford's 2nd Virginia were also still there.[154] Colonel Muhlenberg, however, was the senior officer on site and took command when he arrived on 6 April.[155] Stephen had spent the preceding months in Pittsburgh formalizing the terms of the Camp Charlotte armistice and was now at home complaining about the less experienced colonels who outranked him: Woodford and Mercer of the 2nd and 3rd regiments. He wisely kept his mouth shut about the 1st Virginia's Patrick Henry, who had no military experience at all.[156]

The 8th Virginia's arrival reunited Major Helphenstine with his son. Philip was still in Morgan Alexander's Berkeley District rifle company of the 2nd Virginia. His protective father pulled him out of enlisted service and hired a substitute. Philip then attached himself to Captain Clark as an unenrolled volunteer.[157] The care Major Helphenstine showed for his son may reflect a role he filled more generally. As the oldest field officer, twice Lieutenant Colonel Bowman's age, he was well-positioned to be a father figure for the enlisted men, about half of whom were teenagers.

Heinrich Meier, an adolescent soldier in Captain Clark's 'German' company, wrote home to his family from Suffolk on his first full day there. The letter, written in a sort of pidgin German, was addressed to his father 'fasst an der nerrow besen 3 meil von wutstak in donmor' (near the Narrow Passage [Creek], 3 miles from Woodstock in Dunmore).

> God greet you, father and mother, brothers and sisters. I hope this letter will find you all healthy. And I am also healthy and God be thanked a thousand fold and we are in sof vuck [Suffolk] and because of the war I have, most unusually for me, written you a letter. And when you can, send a letter on down as quickly as you can. And we were three weeks and two days on the journey. So much from me.[158]

Continental Musical Chairs

The 8th Virginia was a provincial regiment when it came together, and it appeared it was going to stay that way. Just before the new year, Congress approved six Virginia regiments for Continental status.[159] The one-year enlistments of the Old Dominion's 1st and 2nd regiments were about to expire, but the colony had just authorised six new full-sized regiments (the 3rd through 8th). The small 9th Regiment was created specifically for local service on Virginia's eastern shore (the lower Delmarva Peninsula). Congress may have initially

154 LVA: Dunmore County Revolutionary War Papers, 1775–1814, Edmund Pendleton to Dunmore Committee, 9 Feb. 1776; Ward, *Stephen*, p.135.

155 HSP: Ferdinand J. Dreer Collection, 1492–1925 (Collection 175), General Muhlenberg orderly book, 1775 [orderly book of the 2nd Virginia Regiment], 5 April 1776.

156 Ward, *Stephen*, pp.133–134.

157 NARA: M804, W8930, Philip Helphinstine pension; John H. Gwathmey (ed.), *Historical Register of Virginians in the Revolution: Soldiers, Sailors, Marines* (1938, reprinted Baltimore: Genealogical Publishing Co., 1973), p.368; Erna Risch, Supplying Washington's Army (Washington: U.S. Army, 1981), pp.44, 56, 62, 68, 90.

158 Collection of Deborah M.S. Brown. Translated from German.

159 Ford (ed.), *Journals of Congress*, vol.3, p.463.

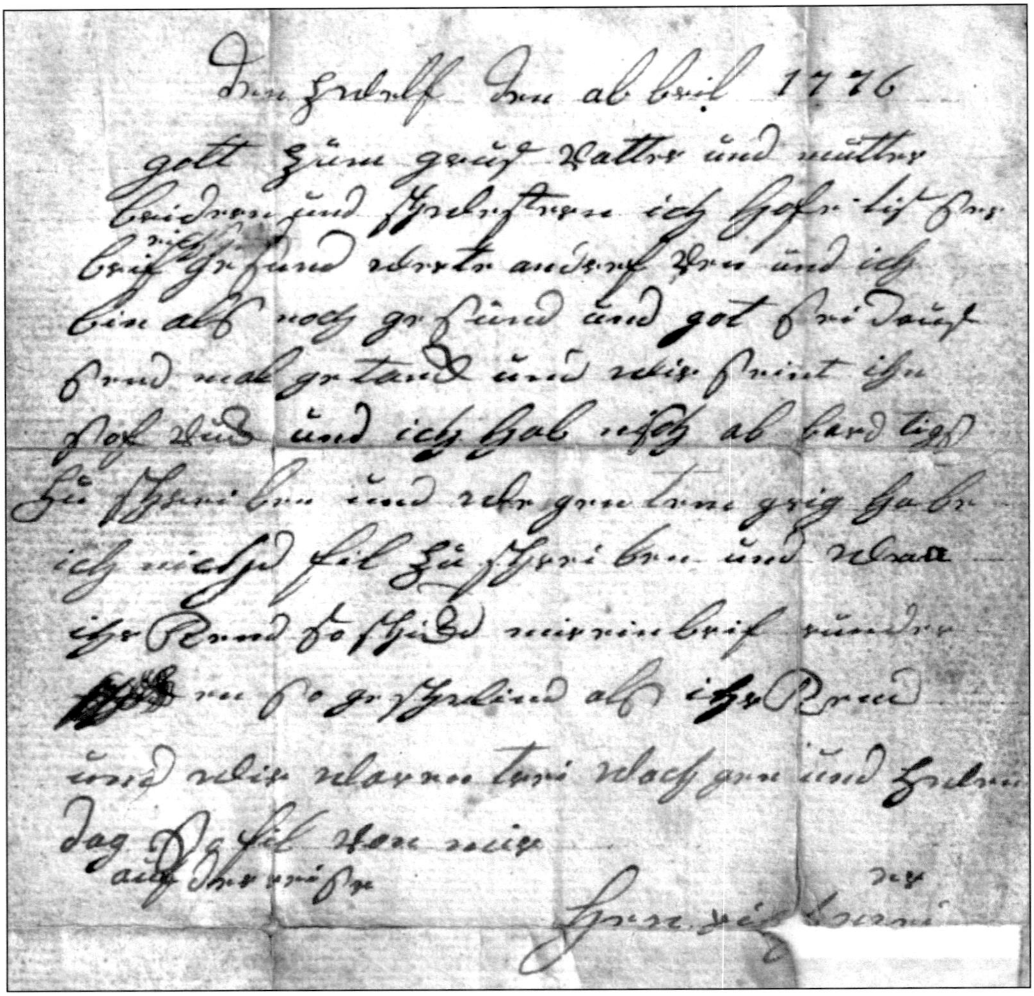

Heinrich Meier's letter home to his family. (Collection of Deborah M.S. Brown)

understood the net of these changes to be six regiments. Though the officers of the 1st and 2nd wanted to reenlist their men and remain in service, a report came that Congress 'would not agree to take the other two,' and that created a serious problem. Continental officers always outranked provincial ones, so Congress's plan would have meant a relative demotion for the officers of the first two regiments despite their longer service. The Committee of Safety quietly instructed Virginia's delegates, if the six-regiment limit was 'unalterably fixed', to see that the Continental commissions went to 'the first six' regiments, and the 7th, 8th, and 9th were left out.[160]

160 *Virginia Gazette* (Dixon and Hunter), 16 March 1776.

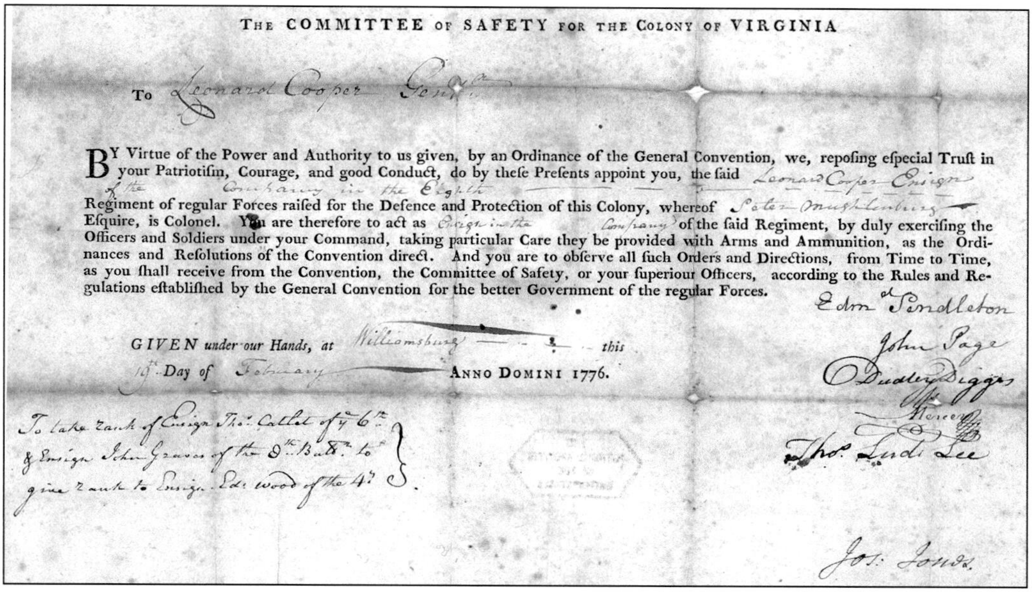

THE COMMITTEE OF SAFETY FOR THE COLONY OF VIRGINIA

To Leonard Cooper Gent.

BY Virtue of the Power and Authority to us given, by an Ordinance of the General Convention, we, repoſing eſpecial Truſt in your Patriotiſm, Courage, and good Conduct, do by theſe Preſents appoint you, the ſaid Leonard Cooper Ensign of the Company in the Eighth Regiment of regular Forces raiſed for the Defence and Protection of this Colony, whereof Peter Muhlenberg Eſquire, is Colonel. You are therefore to act as Ensign in the Company of the ſaid Regiment, by duly exerciſing the Officers and Soldiers under your Command, taking particular Care they be provided with Arms and Ammunition, as the Ordinances and Reſolutions of the Convention direct. And you are to obſerve all ſuch Orders and Directions, from Time to Time, as you ſhall receive from the Convention, the Committee of Safety, or your ſuperiour Officers, according to the Rules and Regulations eſtabliſhed by the General Convention for the better Government of the regular Forces.

GIVEN under our Hands, at Williamsburg this 15th Day of February ANNO DOMINI 1776.

To take rank of Ensign Thos. Catlet of ye 6th & Ensign John Graves of the 8th Batt. to give rank to Ensign Edw. Wood of the 4th.

Edmd Pendleton
John Page
Dudley Digges
Ja. Mercer
Thos. Lud. Lee
Jos. Jones

Ensign Leonard Cooper's provincial commission, signed by Virginia Committee of Safety members Edmund Pendleton, John Page, Dudley Diggs, James Mercer, and Thomas Ludwell Lee. (National Archives)

Though most of this was explained in the *Virginia Gazette* in March, the Committee of Safety acted as though Continental commissions were on the way for Muhlenberg's officers. 'The Committee of Safety have determined,' Jonathan Clark was informed, 'that until the Continental Commissions come, some [provincial] com[issions] ought to be granted the officers of the three last Regiments. They have therefore enclosed yours.' The letter also reveals that Captain Campbell failed for some reason to finish his business when he was in Williamsburg. 'The other Captain from Dunmore did not return a Certificate of the service of the Company. Youl please to be kind enough to desire him to send up his Certificate. His Commission will be sent him. We do not know his name or should have wrote to him.'[161]

161 WHS: Draper Mss, L, vol.1, p.25.

5

Soldiers

Remembering the regiment's first assignment, Adam Cabbage said he 'Assisted in driving Lord Dunmore from Virginia.'[1] The earl was now living on a ship in the Hampton Roadstead, where he had attracted a 'floating town' of nearly 200 vessels. As many as 3,000 people may have lived in this flotilla of Loyalists, soldiers, prisoners, runaway servants, and Africans fleeing bondage. Increasingly desperate for food and eager to punish Virginia's rebels, Dunmore authorised raids on coastal plantations. The Whigs accused him of piracy.[2]

Dunmore received support from the 44-gun HMS *Roebuck* shortly before the first of Muhlenberg's riflemen appeared in Suffolk. Under the ship's protection, the governor fortified Tucker's Point, a small peninsula near Portsmouth on the Elizabeth River. This provided the desperate Loyalists with a place to build ovens, isolate the sick, dig wells, and bury their dead.[3] Dunmore's boats, meanwhile, continually raided up the James River. Captain Berry's Company experienced one of these raids at Jamestown. As related by John Morrison:

> Two English vessels came up the river in the night. Owing to the darkness of the night the vessels were not discovered til break of day. The vessels passed up the River and took a vessel loaded with flour from the Americans. Next night, the vessels attempted to land down the river, when a cannonade commenced between the troops on shore and the vessels, but none of the men on shore were hurt.[4]

Near the same place on another day, one of the gazettes reported, several black men mistook an armed Virginia boat for a British tender. Seeking freedom, they called out to the vessel, declaring their desire to serve the ousted governor. Two of the men were executed by local authorities 'as an example to others.'[5]

Downriver, the regiment's complicated and sometimes ugly mission involved recapturing servants and enslaved people, stopping Tories from supplying the governor's floating town,

1 NARA: M804, S36431, Henry Brock pension; W8926, Reuben Harrell pension; A. Cabbage pension.
2 *Virginia Gazette* (Purdie), 9 August 1776; David, *Dunmore's New World*, p.101.
3 Muhlenberg, *General Muhlenberg*, p.55; Selby, *Revolution in Virginia*, 86; Elizabeth A. Fenn, *Pox Americana: The Great Smallpox Epidemic of 1775–1782* (New York: Hill and Wang, 2002), pp.58–59. Tucker's Point is now the site of Portsmouth Naval Medical Center.
4 NARA: M804, S45874, John Morrison pension. Edited for clarity.
5 *Virginia Gazette* (Dixon & Hunter), 13 April 1776.

and directly skirmishing with the governor's forces. Dunmore had the advantage of mobility, but hunger and spreading disease made his flotilla's situation increasingly desperate. The bodies of smallpox and typhus victims were tossed into the bay with alarming frequency.[6]

The Virginia regulars had problems of their own. A doctor in Suffolk complained about the 'filth and nastiness' of the huts sick soldiers were housed in.[7] Some junior officers had not yet learned to take orders. A court-martial found Lieutenant Thomas Hughes of the 2nd Virginia guilty of refusing to participate in parade duty. Hughes was from Augusta County and third in command of one of Woodford's two rifle companies.[8] He had concluded that the light infantry companies were exempt from parade duty and appealed the verdict. His men were elite troops, in his view, and had better things to do. Colonel Muhlenberg, still the senior officer on site, knew that if Hughes were to prevail, the entire 8th Virginia would also be exempt. He elevated the matter to Major General Lee, who complimented the German colonel for his 'very judicious' halting of the appeal. If Hughes had his way, Lee scoffed, the musketeers might also be made to 'black the former's shoes, and wash their shirts.'[9]

Meanwhile, the 4th Virginia's Lieutenant Colonel Isaac Read was instructed to withdraw his companies from Suffolk to Smithfield, one at a time, as more of Muhlenberg's companies arrived. This allowed Richard Campbell's Company to advance and join the regiment.[10] The 8th Virginia was strategically situated, but most of Virginia's nine regiments were positioned to satisfy political, not military, considerations. They were sent, generally in pairs, to the colony's coastal peninsulas, where they were further split into detachments to guard multiple points. Everyone wanted protection, and the politicians tried to oblige.

Lee was appalled when he arrived to find that Virginia's troops were dispersed all over the Chesapeake. The distribution of the troops was 'a master piece', he wrote, snidely. 'I wonder they did not carry it still further, and post one or two men by way of general security in every individual Gentleman's house.' He ordered most of Virginia's regular forces to consolidate on the Virginia Peninsula, between the James and York rivers, assessing that 'if the enemy arrive with considerable force, the possession of Williamsburg and York will be their first object.' He also wanted to forcibly relocate Tories from the coast. At a minimum, he argued, 'their Wives & Children should be carried into a place of security, as hostages for the good behavior of the Husbands and Fathers.' The Committee of Safety and a council of officers were reticent to do this.[11] Lee, however, did not believe in half measures, and the threat of a near-term attack was quite real. In February, Lieutenant General Henry Clinton had arrived in the Chesapeake with three transports full of British troops, met with Dunmore, and (to the governor's 'mortification') sailed on.[12] Intelligence suggested their destination was the Carolinas, but one could not be sure.[13]

6 *Virginia Gazette* (Purdie), 8 March 1776, pp.2–3; David, *Dunmore's New World*, pp.123–124.
7 Bunbury (ed.), *Lee Papers*, vol.1, pp.413–415.
8 Force (ed.), *American Archives*, ser.5, vol.2, pp.321–322; LVA: Revolutionary War Bounty Land Claims, William Fontaine (2nd Virginia).
9 Bunbury (ed.), *Lee Papers*, vol.1, pp.422–423.
10 Bunbury (ed.), *Lee Papers*, vol.1, pp.390–391, 396, 403. 422–423.
11 Bunbury (ed.), *Lee Papers*, vol.1, pp.369, 393–394, 375–376, 387, 403–405.
12 Selby, *Revolution in Virginia*, p.86.
13 Powell (ed.), *Biographical Sketch*, pp.17–20.

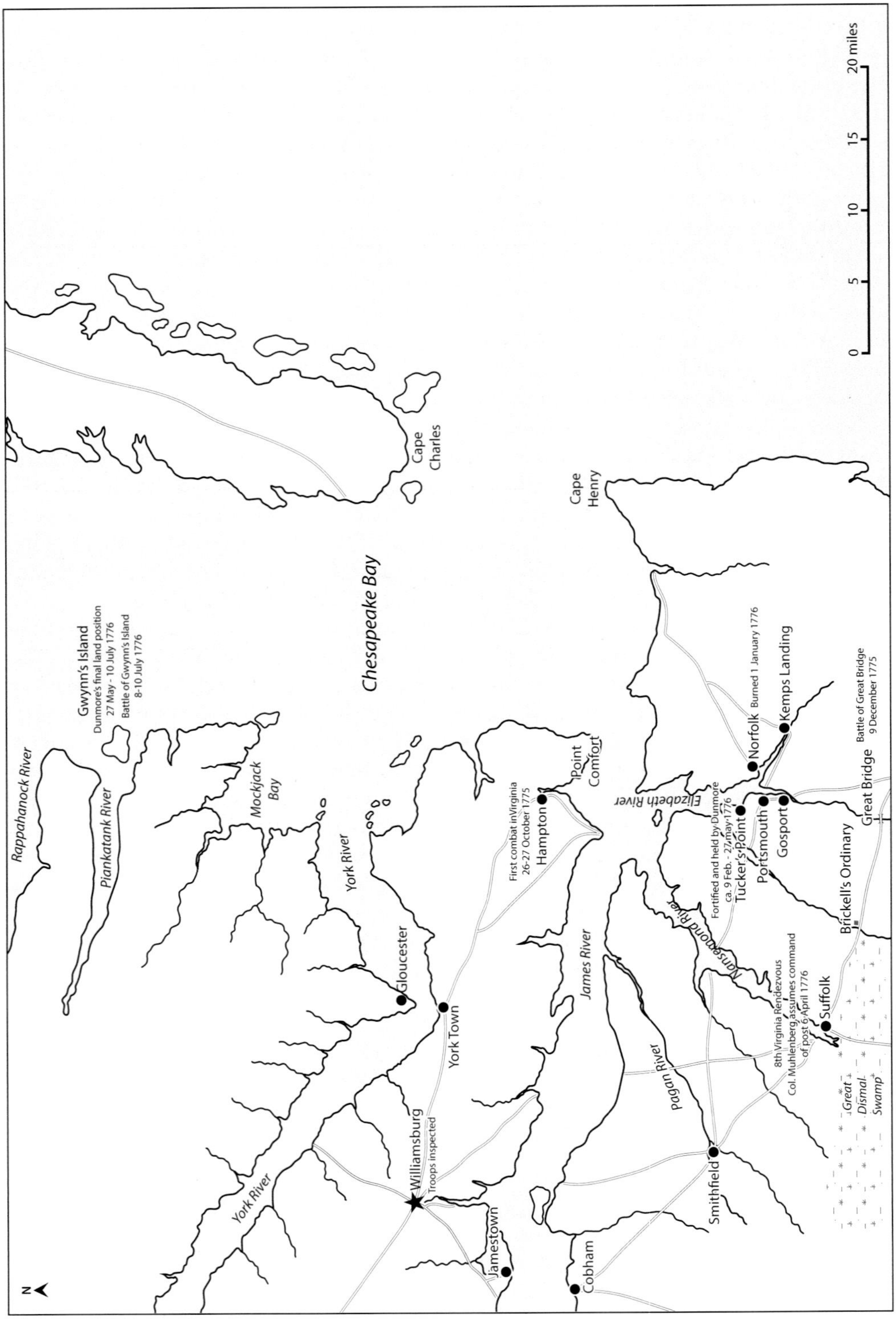

The Tidewater theatre.

With the 4th Virginia withdrawn to Smithfield, the 8th Virginia began to coordinate with the 1st. Patrick Henry had just resigned this regiment's colonelcy in a huff after Congress passed him over and made Andrew Lewis Virginia's first Continental brigadier general.[14] Fincastle's William Christian was promoted to take Henry's place and was tasked by Lee with surveying the 'bays or landing places' along the James River to identify likely British approaches to Williamsburg.[15] A detachment of the 1st under Lieutenant Colonel Francis ('Frank') Eppes was tasked with conducting a detailed reconnaissance of Dunmore's position at Tucker's Point. Near the mouth of the north-flowing Elizabeth River, the position could be supplied by Loyalists using the river's east, south, and west branches. Kemp's Landing, Great Bridge, and Brickell's Ordinary were the controlling points on these tributaries, and the Virginians needed to cover all three.

Lee received a letter from North Carolina's Brigadier General Robert Howe telling him that Clinton was now at Cape Fear training 700 men and expecting reinforcements.[16] Purdie's *Gazette* published captured correspondence indicating that a force 'of seven regiments, with a fleet of frigates and small ships' was on its way to attack North Carolina, and 'from thence either to South Carolina or Virginia.'[17] This news convinced the Committee of Safety to approve Lee's plan for Tory evacuation. The general urged North Carolina's leaders to do the same.[18]

Lee quickly began organising his troops to tighten the circle around Tucker's Point and nearby Portsmouth. The Virginians would then clear out Tories and enslaved men of military age. 'I intend in a very few days to visit your post,' the Southern Department commander wrote to Muhlenberg. 'I desire, Sir, you will contrive to make room for as many troops in and about Suffolk as possible.'[19] Eppes, too, was directed to quietly identify a place 'for the cantonment of a considerable body of troops, for instance two thousand men, in as compact a circle as possible.'[20]

Additional troops were moved to each branch of the Elizabeth. Captain Westfall's Hampshire men marched to Kemp's Landing and engaged in minor combat there.[21] They joined Eppes' soldiers in rounding up Tories and livestock and sending them back to Muhlenberg at Suffolk.[22] Great Bridge was guarded by Minutemen.[23] Lee ordered Muhlenberg to 'detach two hundred men to post themselves near Brickels at the head of the Western Branch, to prevent the Enemies procuring any supplies from that quarter.'[24]

The two Dunmore County companies left Suffolk with the latter detachment on 15 April and pressed in on Tucker's Point the next day. One of Clark's sergeants, Joseph Parett,

14 Selby, *Revolution in Virginia*, pp.88–89.
15 Bunbury (ed.), *Lee Papers*, vol.1, pp.369–370; Sanchez-Saavedra, *Virginia Military Organisations*, p.29.
16 Bunbury (ed.), *Lee Papers*, vol.1, pp.398–400.
17 *Virginia Gazette* (Purdie), 12 April 1776
18 Bunbury (ed.), *Lee Papers*, vol.1, pp.417–418, 488.
19 Bunbury (ed.), *Lee Papers*, vol.1, pp.410–411.
20 Bunbury (ed.), *Lee Papers*, vol.1, pp.411–412.
21 NARA: M804, W4603, William Taylor pension; M. Weese pension; R. Pritchard pension.
22 Bunbury (ed.), *Lee Papers*, vol.1, pp.364–365, 373–386, 411–412.
23 NARA: M804, S6204, Samuel Templeman Pension (Princess Anne Minute Battalion).
24 Bunbury (ed.), *Lee Papers*, vol.1, pp.410–412.

reported being close enough to see the burnt ruins of Norfolk.[25] According to Clark, it 'rain[ed] very hard at Portsmouth' on the 16th, where a 'few shots [were] exchanged.'[26] Anjer Price said 'he was in a scouting party near Norfolk Virginia under Captain Campbell and received in a skirmish which took place a wound in his thigh the impression of which he still wears.' Price's wound was severe enough that he was sent home for six months, a break that may have saved his life.[27] To further effect Dunmore's isolation, Clark's men returned to Suffolk and spent two days collecting boats in the Nansemond River and its tributaries.

Then, the operation moved into high gear. Lee ordered most of the 8th Virginia to advance from Suffolk to Brickell's Ordinary on the Elizabeth's west branch. Muhlenberg advanced with the remainder to Portsmouth, at the mouth of the middle branch, just south of Dunmore's 'fort' at Tucker's Mill. His men began rounding up Loyalists and sending them to Suffolk. Following orders, they burned the houses of the most 'dangerous' Tories. Portsmouth's population was given five days to leave, and Lee floated the idea of destroying the town entirely.[28] Similarly, 'All the Negroes capable of bearing Arms' were 'secured immediately, & sent up to Suffolk.'[29] On a rainy Monday, 29 April, Muhlenberg joined Colonel Woodford at Kemp's Landing on the east branch to continue the operation there.[30] A May 2nd order from Woodford, lacking a salutation but in Jonathan Clark's papers, reads:

> I am informed by Mr. Calvert that several Negros have escaped from his neighborhood & he thinks if some of your men were posted at Mr. Towhim's Warf, & Mr. Godfrey's, it would be impossible for more to escape. You'll Please to inform yourself of this particular & act accordingly. If you think your party will be insufficient for the purposes they was intended, inform me & they shall be further reinforced. Please send me up word to night.[31]

It was ugly work. Woodford reported, 'The distress of these unfortunate people is hardly to be described, its the most disagreeable service I have ever been engaged in'. It was also a massive logistical challenge. Twenty thousand people had to be moved. 'I pitty you most sincerely for your damn'd employment,' Lee replied to the colonel, but he insisted that his soldiers continue the operation 'with vigor.'[32]

The Loyalists fought back. Captain Clark recorded being 'attacked by a Tender without Loss' on 7 May and being attacked again the next day 'by a small party who some made their escape.'[33]

A week later, he received a confidential letter from Woodford about a plan to rescue some captured comrades. He intended 'to take the prisoner vessel this evening by boats sent from Kemp's Landing.' Two men who had escaped on their own would be guides. 'You'll keep a

25 LVA: Revolutionary War Rejected Claims, Joseph Parret.
26 FHS: Clark Diary, 15–16 April 1776.
27 NARA: M804, W21073, Anjer Price pension.
28 Bunbury (ed.), *Lee Papers*, vol.1, p.468.
29 Bunbury (ed.), *Lee Papers*, vol.1, pp.444–445.
30 FHS: Clark Diary, 25–28 April 1776.
31 WHS: Draper Mss, L, vol.1, p.28.
32 Bunbury (ed.), *Lee Papers*, vol.1, pp.462–463, vol.2, pp.23–24.
33 FHS: Clark Diary, 8–9 May 1776.

good look out, and afford them any assistance in your power, but do not communicate this affair to any person, lest it should take wind.'[34]

Back in Suffolk, meanwhile, Lieutenant Rinker wrote to Clark to complain that Lee had authorised Virginia's incipient navy to poach their company's men.

> I must acquaint you that there are a parcel [of] our men that Have entered into the Marine service since you left this place, and are going on board the Row Galleys, & as I do not know but what some of them are in your Debt I don't know how to manage the affair with them. Would be very glad you were here present or give me instruction how to manage them. The Names of them that have entered to my knowledge are these: Patrick Duffy, Henry Hamilton, Wm Mansel, James Grant, Henry Crafton & John Rinn.
>
> The officer that inlisted them, it seems, has orders from General Lee, but I don't believe he has a right to take them away untill you have settled with them. All our men here are yet well. 50 men are this day gone up to Williamsburg to Cary up the prisoners from here.[35]

The Committee of Safety ordered Lee to wind down his aggressive operation after it received a petition outlining the 'distresses and ruin' the operation was causing.[36] The order turned out to be unnecessary. Colonel Woodford organised a plan to send fire ships into the Loyalist flotilla at Tucker's Point, and intelligence of this induced Dunmore to abandon his position. 'Dunmore evacuated the Fort, and with all his Ships, Troops, Tories & Slaves,' a Minuteman recalled, and 'took post up the Bay on Gwin's Island below the mouth of Piankitank River.'[37]

Ordered South

As predicted, Commodore Sir Peter Parker's fleet and more than 3,000 Redcoats from Ireland joined Henry Clinton's small force from Boston at Cape Fear, North Carolina.[38] The Loyalist army they planned to join had already been defeated at Moore's Creek Bridge at the end of February, so they were now looking for a new target. Lee prepared to counter the threat by travelling south with Muhlenberg's riflemen.[39] Halifax, Lee decided, was the best place to initiate operations in North Carolina. The North Carolina Provincial Congress was in session there, and Lee was advised that 'Halifax and the neighbouring Counties abound in good horses and men.'[40] It also had a powder magazine and a supply depot.[41] Lee

34 WHS: Draper Mss, L, vol.1, p.29.
35 WHS: Draper Mss, L, vol.1, p.28; Bunbury (ed.), *Lee Papers*, vol.1, p.403.
36 Palmer et al (eds), *Calendar*, vol.8, p.166.
37 *Virginia Gazette* (Dixon and Hunter), 25 May 1776; Thompson (ed.), 'Lee Papers,' pp.325–326.
38 William Bell Clark et al (eds), *Naval Documents of the Revolution* (Washington, United States Navy, 1964), vol.5, p.325; Robert Beatson (ed.), *Naval and Military Memoirs of Great Britain from 1727 to 1783* (London: Longman, Hurst, Rees, and Orme, 1804), vol.6, p.45.
39 Thompson (ed.), 'Lee Papers,' p.330.
40 Bunbury (ed.), *Lee Papers*, vol.1, pp.449–450.
41 Anon., 'Halifax and the Revolution,' *North Carolina Historic Sites*, <historicsites.nc.gov/all-sites/historic-halifax/history/halifax-historic-district-importance/halifax-and-revolution>, accessed 8 April 2023.

brought the 8th Virginia with him because it was 'the most compleat, the best arm'd, and in all respects the best furnish'd for service.' 'I cannot avoid detaching the strongest Battalion we have to [North Carolina's] assistance,' he said, 'but I own, I tremble at the same time, at the thoughts of stripping [Virginia] of any part of its inadequate force.' Virginia theoretically had 5,000 regulars, but no more than 3,000 were properly armed even after the Minute battalions were stripped of their weapons. Knox's and Croghan's companies still had not arrived, but Lee nevertheless chose the 8th because it was 'the most complete ... of the whole Continent.'[42]

Lee ordered all furloughs cancelled and handed military command in Virginia to Brigadier General Lewis.[43] He ordered Woodford, the senior officer in the Norfolk area, to send the 8th Virginia directly to Halifax. Lee informed Woodford that 'Captn Knox will follow the Regiment, so the Colonel must not wait for him.' On May 11, Lee impatiently prodded Woodford:

> ... have you order'd Muhlenberg's Regiment to march to Halifax? I hope to God you have, for no time is to be lost, as we have certain news of the Enemy's arrival in the River Cape Fear ... Let Muhlenberg have the waggons & provisions necessary as far as Halifax ...You may inform him that I have also order'd stores of all kinds for his Regiment to Halifax – once more, I entreat he may march immediately.[44]

Though Knox's Fincastle company was close, Captain Croghan's West Augusta company was still a month from arriving. Thomas Berry's Company was at Cobham, having just arrived from Frederick County.[45] Consequently, Berry took his men on a different route to Halifax. Weak evidence suggests they were joined by William Darke's Company.[46] In his final report to Congress before leaving,[47] Lee informed President John Hancock that he had 'detached a Battalion of Riflemen to Halifax for which place I intend to set out myself.'[48] The general rode with Robert Howe. When he got to Halifax, he made a lasting impression by refusing to let his dog Spado eat bacon. He was afraid it would make the animal stupid.[49]

'Disorderly and Mutinous'

Muhlenberg's shirtmen marched on 16 May with rifles on their shoulders and tomahawks in their belts.[50] They were also given pikes, which were carried in a wagon. These were weapons

42 Bunbury (ed.), *Lee Papers*, vol.1, pp.477–480, vol.2, pp.185–186, 191.
43 Brock (ed.), 'Stubblefield Orderly Book,' p.171; Bunbury (ed.), *Lee Papers*, vol.2, pp.23–24.
44 Bunbury (ed.), *Lee Papers*, vol.2, pp.23–24; FHS: Clark Diary, 21 May 1776.
45 Palmer et al (eds), *Calendar*, vol.8, p.175.
46 NARA: M804, S8019, George Alban pension; I. Dunn pension; J. Kay pension; H. Wysor pension.
47 Thompson (ed.), 'Lee Papers,' p.330.
48 Bunbury (ed.), *Lee Papers*, vol.2, p.17.
49 Griffith J. McRee (ed.) *Life and Correspondence of James Iredell* (New York: D. Appleton and Co., 1857), vol.1, p.282
50 FHS: Clark Diary, 16 May 1776; LVA: C. Mitcham petition.

from a previous age, issued to them for defensive use and in lieu of bayonets.[51] The soldiers began to grumble almost immediately. They had already marched as far as 450 miles to get to Suffolk, and the trek they were now beginning promised to be just as long. They had few, if any, tents and had to sleep in the open each night.[52] Muhlenberg did acquire 79 yards of ravens duck canvass from the Williamsburg public store before the march, but there was no time to make tents with it. He also acquired a few blankets and 2,654 yards of osnaburg, drilling, and other fabrics for clothing and other needs.[53]

Muhlenberg's men had a larger complaint. They had enlisted in a *provincial* regiment which had, furthermore, been explicitly passed over for Continental status. Defending the Carolinas was not their job. Moreover, some of their own communities, Fincastle in particular, were under threat in the west. Six men from Captain Knox's company, which was still trying to catch up, deserted on 20 May.[54] Muhlenberg arrived in Halifax on 21 May. Two days later, five of Captain Westfall's men ran off, followed a day later by several of Captain Clark's recruits.[55]

Halifax sat on the west bank of the Roanoke River, 16 miles below the Virginia line. North Carolina's fourth Provincial Congress had just adjourned after passing its strongly worded Halifax Resolves. Among the military stores in town was a large collection of guns taken from Loyalists at Moore's Creek Bridge in February. A North Carolina soldier named Henry Guthrie had the repetitive, months-long task of repairing the weapons one by one. 'I very well recollect,' he said, 'that I was at that work when General Lee with his Army marched through.'[56] Darke's and Berry's companies arrived four or five days after Muhlenberg.[57] There was still no sight of Knox and no word on Captain Croghan.

'A few days after our arrival here,' wrote Brigadier General Howe in a letter, 'we were joined by Colo. Mulenberg, with his Battalion. Many of his people seem'd discontented at marching farther, and about 20, or thirty have deserted.' He also noted that 'every possible step has been taken to regain them.'[58] The deserters went home, where it was up to local authorities to do something about it. Jonathan Clark's brother (the new deputy clerk) reported from Dunmore County that there was considerable sympathy for the runaways. Many people asserted that 'they would do the same, for they were not oblidgd to go out of the Colony.' The deserters themselves explained that they 'were starved, for want of provisions for they were allowed only one pint of Indian meale per Day, and further was not obliged to go out of the Colony.' Joseph Pugh, the new Dunmore committee chair or county lieutenant,[59] was determined to find the deserters and return them to the regiment.

51 Bunbury (ed.), *Lee Papers*, vol.2, pp.18–20; Brock (ed.), 'Stubblefield Orderly Book,' p.172; Campbell (ed.), *Lewis Orderly Book*, p.17.

52 George Bancroft, *History of the United States from the Discovery of the American Continent* (New York: Little, Brown & Company, 1860), vol.8, p.400.

53 Gallup, *Virginia Soldier*, pp.29–31, 45; Bunbury (ed.), *Lee Papers*, vol.2, pp.23–24.

54 NARA: M246, f.216, p.8.

55 NARA: M246, f.210, p.2, f.219, p.27; Bunbury (ed.), *Lee Papers*, vol.2, p.30.

56 NARA: M804, W4975, Henry Guthrie pension (N.C. Militia).

57 NARA: M804, S8019, George Alban pension; I. Dunn pension; J. Kay pension; H. Wysor pension.

58 Anon. (ed.), 'The Letters of Col. William Woodford, Col. Robert Howe, and Gen. Charles Lee to Edmund Pendleton,' *Richmond College Historical Papers*, 1:1 (1915), pp.158.

59 NARA: M804, S16672, Thomas Buck pension (Dunmore Militia); Wayland, *Shenandoah*, p.629.

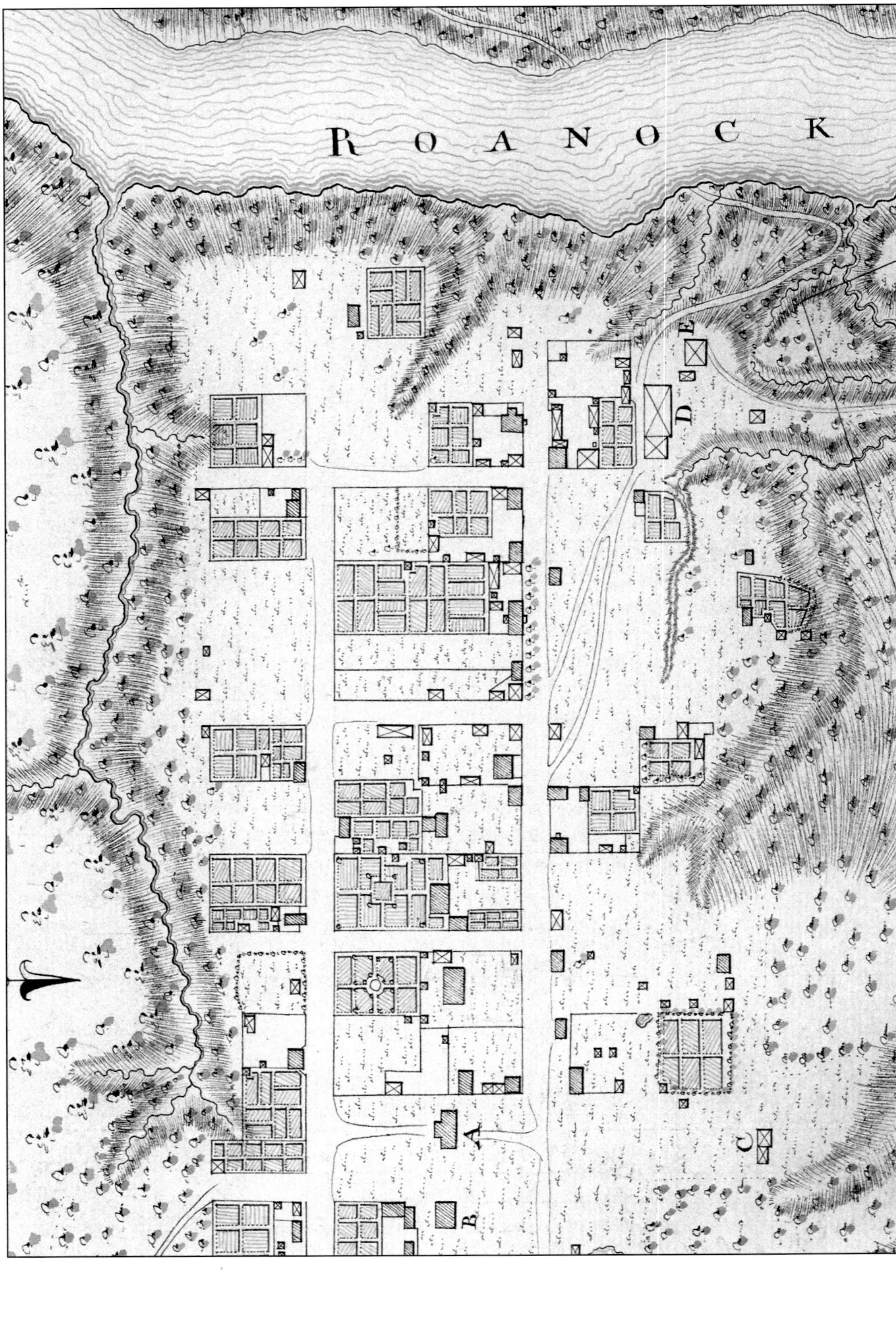

Halifax, North Carolina in 1769. Detail from a map by Claude Joseph Sauthier. (Norman B. Leventhal Map & Education Center, Boston Public Library)

Sometimes, this was accomplished by talking to a soldier's parents. Heinrich Meier, who had written home from Suffolk, was brought back this way. 'Mr. Moyer has promised to Deliver his son up without further Trouble,' John Clark reported. A seven- or eight-year-old fifer named Philip Kibler was another. 'Mr. Cibler,' Clark wrote, 'came to town and told Colo Pugh, that his son should be delivered up any moment, and was much displeased with his son for his bad Conduct.' The German boy confessed that he was one of a group of enlistees who had run off together under the influence of Christopher Coffelt, Martin Honey, and John Bley – all men in Captain Clark's Company.[60]

Richard Campbell sent 1st Lieutenant Mathias Hite home to collect deserters and recruit some more men. Thomas Harding, a sergeant from Clark's Company, went with him. When they were done, John Clark sent several items with them for his brother, including fabric, clothing, shoes, and two quires of paper. Hite promised to help fulfil a request for sealing wafers, John said later, but 'Hite not being a man of his word' the matter 'was neglected.' The younger Clark also learned that the gossipy lieutenant spread some nasty rumours while at home. Hite had a penchant for drama that surfaced repeatedly.[61]

The German boys from Dunmore were brought back to Williamsburg and their desertions were not recorded. Conversely, 15 Fincastle men who walked away from Captain Knox never returned. Applying for a pension many years later, Greenberry Choat tried to claim 'a term of one month' under Knox that included the march to Williamsburg. He thought better of it and asked the court scribe to cross that part out and limit his claim to the role he had in William Christian's 1776 campaign against the Cherokee.[62]

By July, at least 56 men had deserted from the regiment. Lee was a martinet, which did not help. He did not hesitate to have soldiers flogged.[63] He disliked the Irish and wanted them purged from the Virginia Line. He complained that 'the old Countrymen, particularly the Irish whom the officers have injudiciously inlisted in order to fill up their Companies, have much contaminated the Troops.'[64] To get rid of them, he urged Virginia to allow South Carolina to recruit out of the regiment. Even with an extra bounty, he did not believe that many 'native Virginians' would accept the offer. 'The Irish I am persuaded will,' he predicted, 'in crowds.' Lest Virginia believe he was trying to 'purge your army of bad subjects, at the expense of another province,' he argued that,

> … the ordinances of S Carolina, are much better calculated to keep those sort of refractory spirits in order, than the Continental ordinances. There laws are more severe – and severity is necessary for an Irish soldiery. – I am well acquainted with thei[r] dispositions, and know that the lenient measures, and familiar manners adopted to the genius of your people; only tend to Inspire the Irish with the spirit of stubbornness and mutiny.[65]

60 WHS: Draper Mss L, vol.1, p.30. 'Moyer' and 'Meyer' are an Anglicizations of 'Meier.'
61 WHS: Draper Mss, L, vol.1, p.31.
62 NARA: M804, S32176, Greenberry Choat pension.
63 Papas, *Renegade Revolutionary*, p.28; Selby, *Revolution in Virginia*, p.91.
64 Bunbury (ed.), *Lee Papers*, vol.2, p.35.
65 Anon. (ed.), 'Letters of Woodford, Howe, and Lee', p.160.

On his way out of Halifax, Lee testily reported, 'The disorderly, mutinous, and dangerous disposition of the soldiers of the 8th Regt have detain'd me longer in this place than I cou'd have wish'd... We have at length after infinite trouble got this Banditti out of the Town.'[66]

Virginia Defines the Future

Henry Brock of Captain Clark's Company stayed back in Virginia, where he had been sick since the Suffolk rendezvous. Communicable diseases tore through military encampments like wildfire. It may have been any illness, but mumps and smallpox were swirling about at the time.[67] Because he was in Williamsburg, he witnessed a world-changing transformation of government.[68]

On 15 May, England's oldest and largest North American colony, the King's Fourth Dominion, the 'Old' Dominion, and the namesake of Queen Elizabeth I that had refused to submit to Cromwell, separated from the Crown and declared itself a Commonwealth. The fifth and final Virginia Convention decided that attempts at reconciliation had only brought 'an imperious and vindictive Administration, increased insult, oppression, and a vigorous attempt to effect our total destruction.' Thus, they determined, 'In this state of extreme danger we have no alternative left but an abject submission to the will of those overbearing tyrants, or a total separation from the Crown and the Government of Great Britain.'[69]

Two resolutions were adopted unanimously. The first instructed Virginia's Congressional delegation to propose declaring 'the United Colonies free and independent States.' The second resolution appointed a committee of the Convention to prepare a Declaration of Rights and a written plan of government.[70] A witness wrote that 'the exultation here was extreme. The British Flag was immediately struck on the Capitol, and a Continental hoisted in its room. The troops were drawn out, and we had a discharge of Artillery and small arms.' A day was set aside for prayer and fasting.[71] Virginia's fate was in the hands of the Almighty.

The pressure had been building for some time. The committee of Augusta County, where Presbyterians had absurdly dominated the Anglican vestry for decades, sent a resolution to the Convention in May calling for independence and 'abolishing the established church.'[72] Major General Lee pushed hard for independence during his weeks in Virginia. Without it, he believed, there would be no foreign military support.[73]

Captain Croghan's Company finally arrived in Williamsburg as Virginia's transformation was underway. They were reviewed on 19 June.[74] The Convention adopted the Declaration

66 Bunbury (ed.), *Lee Papers*, vol.2, pp.34–35.
67 Bunbury (ed.), *Lee Papers*, vol.1, pp.392, 432.
68 NARA: H. Brock pension. Benjamin Carter, Philip Faint, Peter Jordan, Meredith Price, and James Taffe were also left behind.
69 Anon (ed.), *Proceedings of the 5th Convention*, p.16.
70 Force (ed.), *American Archives*, ser.4, vol.6, p.1524.
71 Thompson (ed.), 'Lee Papers,' pp.324–325.
72 Chase et al (eds), *Papers of Washington* (Revolution), vol.9, pp.622–624.
73 Bunbury (ed.), *Lee Papers*, vol.2, p.20; Papas, *Renegade Revolutionary*, p.159.
74 Palmer et al (eds), *Calendar*, vol.8, p.214.

of Rights on 12 June and the new state constitution on 29 June.[75] These documents, more than any others, formed the basis of American constitutionalism. George Mason's draft of the Declaration of Rights appeared in a Philadelphia newspaper the day before Virginia's Richard Henry Lee proposed independence in Congress.[76] Three weeks and five days later, the Declaration of Independence was adopted. Its text was closely modelled on the Virginia document. The United States Constitution and the Bill of Rights would also draw heavily from Mason's work. Then, on its last day, the 5th Virginia Convention ordered prayers for the King removed from the liturgy in Virginia's churches and chose Patrick Henry to be the governor. The printed announcement concluded with the words: 'GOD Save the Commonwealth.'[77]

More 8th Virginia soldiers arrived in Williamsburg after the July wheat harvest wrapped up.[78] First Lieutenant Daniel Culp came with Sergeant Christian Shryock and some new recruits. Shryock was the Berkeley gunsmith who signed up for William Darke's Minute or volunteer company in 1775. Culp reenlisted him that winter and put him to work processing new men at Winchester. Lieutenant Hite and Sergeant Harding returned with Heinrich Meier, the other runaways, and some new recruits from Dunmore County.[79]

Shryock reported the 'two parties of recruits under Lieutenants Kulp & Hyde remained for some time to guard the Tories at Williamsburg.'[80] These were the Loyalists who had been forcibly relocated. After an engagement with Andrew Lewis at Gwynn's Island, Dunmore sailed away in August, never to return.[81] His 'Ethiopian Regiment' suffered horribly from smallpox on Gwynn's Island. Lewis's men were 'struck with horrour at the number of dead bodies, in a state of putrefaction, strewen from their battery to Cherry-Point, about two miles in length, without a shovelful of earth upon them; others gasping for life; and some had crawled to the water's edge, who could only make known their distress by beckoning to us.'[82] It was a grisly end for men who had risked everything in their own way for freedom.

A Forced March

Lee and Howe spurred their horses from Halifax to Wilmington, North Carolina as Muhlenberg's surly men trudged along behind. Lee ordered them to abandon the tent fabric and other supplies so they could move faster.[83] Clinton's Redcoats were camped on Battery Island at the mouth of the Cape Fear River. Commodore Parker's fleet was in the process of arriving with 3,397 infantrymen from Ireland under Lieutenant General Charles, Earl Cornwallis.[84] The Virginians marched toward Wilmington, upriver from the island, from

75 *Virginia Gazette* (Purdie), 14 June 1776 (supplement).
76 *Pennsylvania Evening Post,* 6 June 1776.
77 *Virginia Gazette* (Purdie), 5 July 1776 (supplement).
78 Harold B. Gill, Jr., 'Wheat Culture in Virginia', *Agricultural History* 52:3 (1978), pp.380–393, 386–387
79 NARA: C. Shryock pension.
80 NARA: C. Shryock pension.
81 Force (ed.), *American Archives*, ser.5, vol.1, p.151; *Virginia Gazette* (Purdie), 19 July 1776.
82 *Virginia Gazette* (Purdie), 19 July 1776.
83 McIlwaine et al (eds), *Council of the State of Virginia*, vol.1, p.340.
84 Beatson (ed.), *Naval and Military Memoirs*, vol.6, p.45.

where Lee hoped to direct an assault. Captain Knox's Company finally caught up near Tarboro.[85]

'[W]e marched toward Wilmington,' One of Captain Darke's men remembered, 'but did not reach it, an express having met us, informing us that the British had gone to Charlestown.'[86] Lee was not sure the report was accurate. 'However, as South Carolina is weaker in numbers than Virginia,' he reported, 'I have ordered Muhlenberg's regiment, at a venture, to Charleston immediately.'[87] He took North Carolina's 1st and 2nd Continental regiments with him as well and hurried straight to the southern capital.[88] A Carolina man remembered, 'We had a hard march to get to Charleston' before it was attacked.[89]

The British fleet appeared outside Charles Town (Charleston) on 1 June, and the city was not prepared to defend itself.[90] South Carolina's anxious new revolutionary president, John Rutledge, wrote urgently to Lee. 'For God's sake,' he pleaded, 'lose not a moment. There are fifty sail at anchor off the bar, within sight of the town.'[91] Lee made it there in three days and relayed orders to Muhlenberg to increase his pace. The regiment was bogged down in the rain at Duplin Court House, 55 miles north of Wilmington, when the new orders arrived. They waited five days for the rain to stop,[92] and then turned directly west to Cross Creek (Fayetteville).[93] John Chenoweth remembered, 'Part of our march was a force march as the brittish waire exppected every day.'[94] Major Helphenstine reported that his horse 'died through hard service' on the way.[95] They paused briefly at Cross Creek, continued southwest into South Carolina, and then crossed the Peedee River at the Cheraws on 14 June. Four more days brought them to Camden, from where they continued in boats down the Wateree and Santee rivers.[96]

The Route from Suffolk to Charles Town

16 May: Depart Suffolk, Va.
17 May: Somerton, Va.
18 May: Chowan River at Winton, N.C.
20 May: Roanoke River
21 May: Halifax, N.C.
23 May: Depart Halifax, N.C.
26 May: Tarboro, N.C.
30 May: Neuse River

85 NARA: M804, S38421, John Taylor pension.
86 NARA: A. Moore pension.
87 Bunbury (ed.), *Lee Papers*, vol.2, p. 51.
88 Hugh F. Rankin, *The North Carolina Continentals* (Chapel Hill: University of North Carolina Press, 1971), pp.71–72; Force (ed.), *American Archives*, ser.6, vol.1, pp.631–632.
89 NARA: M804, S30570, James McCoullough pension (2nd N.C.)
90 William Moultrie, *Memoirs of the American Revolution So Far as It Related to North and South-Carolina, and Georgia*, (New York: David Longworth, 1802), vol.1, p.140.
91 Bunbury (ed.), *Lee Papers*, vol.2, p.53.
92 FHS: Clark Diary, 31 May-5 June 1776.
93 NARA: J. Chenoweth pension.
94 NARA: J. Chenoweth pension; *Virginia Gazette* (Purdy), 21 June 1776.
95 Anon. (ed.), *Journal of the House of Delegates*, 1776, p.35.
96 FHS: Clark Diary, 5–21 June 1776.

31 May: Duplin Court House, N.C.
5 June: Depart Duplin Court House, N.C.
7 June: Johnston County, N.C.
8 June: Cumberland County, N.C.
9 June: Cross Creek, N.C.
11 June: Depart Cross Creek, N.C.
13 June: Anson County, N.C.
14 June: Peedee River and Cheraw, S.C.
18 June: Camden, S.C.
19 June: Wateree River by boat
20 June: Santee River by boat
21 June: Santee River to Cook's Landing, S.C.
22 June: Monk's Corner, S.C.
24 June: Arrive Charles Town, S.C.[97]
(Approximately 510 miles)

The Virginia riflemen rode the Santee's current into the Carolina low country, where rivers wound their way through forests and swamps before turning into estuaries among tidal flats at the coast. One planter complained that his island farm in the Santee was exposed to 'aguish vapours and infever'd air' and that only five of his island's 3,000 acres were habitable. The rest was submerged half of each day by the tide. The terrain was perfect for rice cultivation and an ideal habitat for mosquitos, which the planter called 'devils in Miniature.'[98] The farming was done by enslaved Africans who made the 'rice kings' of Charles Town wealthy. Muhlenberg's men climbed out of their boats at Cook's Landing and proceed to Charles Town on foot. They arrived in the rain on 24 June.[99] The Virginia shirtmen made a lasting impression. Eighteen years later, a suggestion was made to model South Carolina militia uniforms after the 8th Virginia's garb. 'In 1776, General Muhlenburgh's regiment, of 700 men, from Virginia, came to our assistance,' wrote a contributor to the *Columbian Herald*, 'they were all in split shirts, neatly dyed in walnut, and they made a handsome appearance.'[100]

Preparing for Battle

Brigadier General John Armstrong of Pennsylvania was supposed to be in charge in South Carolina, but he was not. He was an experienced military man and a trained civil engineer. He was an Ulster immigrant and a veteran of the French and Indian War.[101] Congress gave him a commission in March 1776 and sent him to take command of forces in and around

97 FHS: Clark Diary.
98 S. Max Edelson, *Plantation Enterprise in Colonial South Carolina* (Cambridge: Harvard University Press, 2006), pp.144–145.
99 FHS: Clark Diary, 21–24 June 1776.
100 *Columbian Herald*, 20 Jan.1794.
101 J.W. King, 'Colonel John Armstrong: His Place in the History of Southwestern Pennsylvania', *Western Pennsylvania Historical Magazine*, 10:3 (1927), pp.132–143.

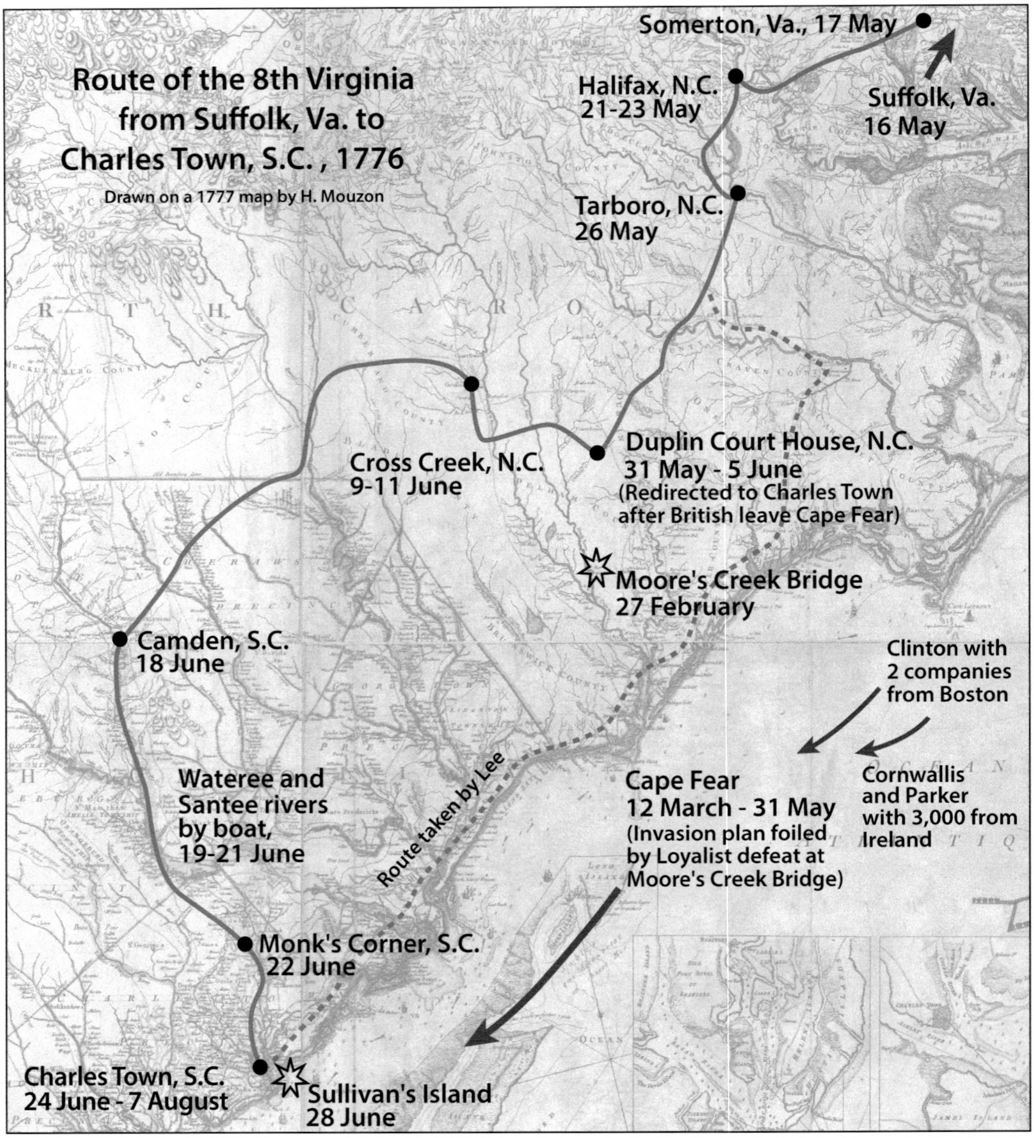

Route to Charles Town.

Charles Town.[102] He was surprised when he arrived to find there was 'not a single soldier on the Continental Establishment' because the colony's officers had unanimously turned down Continental commissions. Among their quibbles were the limits Congress placed on punishment. Charles Lee said they believed Continental Army rules were 'too mild for the perverse Soldiery of this meridian, to whom 39 lashes wou'd prove but a light breakfast.'[103]

102 Ford (ed.), *Journals of Congress*, vol.4, p.181.
103 Bunbury (ed.), *Lee Papers*, vol.2, pp.10–11.

When Lee arrived, he found the city still unprepared despite its natural advantages. Charles Town sat on a peninsula between the Ashley and Cooper Rivers. Its harbour was in a protected channel between James Island on the south and a section of the mainland now called Mount Pleasant on the north. The roadstead had been known as 'Rebellion Road' since 1692,[104] and the name was newly fitting. Morris Island and Sullivan's Island bracketed the entrance to the roadstead. The entrance itself was traversed by a shifting collection of shoals known as the Charles Town Bar. The right winds, the right tide, and the aid of a pilot were all needed for large ships to enter.[105] Locals were busy building a wooden fort on Sullivan's Island that Lee was sure could not last 30 minutes under cannon fire. He called it a 'slaughter pen.'[106] The real fight, he was sure, would be in the city.

Given the immediate danger, Rutledge reluctantly instructed the colony's troops to obey Lee's (and Howe's and Armstrong's) commands.[107] The Southern Department commander ordered the construction of a pontoon escape bridge for the Fort Sullivan garrison. A fascine battery had been built about where the bridge began at Haddrell's Point on the mainland.[108] In the city, he put everyone to work. 'True soldiers and magnanimous citizens,' he announced grandly, 'must brandish the pick-axe and spade as well as the sword, in defence of their country.'[109] 'Charles Town was in a very short time inclosed by Lines, Trenches, and Redoutes', South Carolina Vice President Henry Laurens reported. 'Wharves were cleared of all encumbrances, Streets strongly barricaded, retrenchments within, Batteries erected for defence at practicable Landings above the town.'[110]

The Whigs needed time, and nature gave it to them. Commodore Parker spent days waiting for the winds and tides to align so his ships could cross the bar. Clinton, meanwhile, offloaded more than 3,000 soldiers onto Long Island (Isle of Palms), a barrier island north of Sullivan's Island. The channel between the two islands was known as 'the breach.' Today, it is called the Breach Inlet. The British plan seemed clear: naval gunnery would pummel the fort while Cornwallis's infantry crossed the channel and assaulted it from the northeast. Charles Town would be next.

---

104 A. S. Salley, Jr. (ed.), *Journal of the Grand Council of South Carolina, April 11, 1692–September 26, 1692* (Columbia: The State Company for the Historical Commission of South Carolina, 1907), pp.5, 8, 9, 14, 16, 18.

105 Nic Butler, 'Navigating the Bar of Charleston Harbor: Gateway to the Atlantic', *Charleston Time Machine*, Charleston County Public Library, 17 June 2022, <www.ccpl.org/charleston-time-machine/navigating-bar-charleston-harbor-gateway-atlantic>, accessed 23 April 2023.

106 Moultrie, *Memoirs*, vol.1, p.141.

107 Bernard Elliott, 'Diary of Captain Bernard Elliott,' in *Charleston Year Book, 1889* (Charleston: Walker, Evens & Cogswell: 1890), p.210.

108 Edward McCrady, *History of South Carolina in the Revolution, 1775–1780* (New York: MacMillan Company, 1902), p.137; Anon., 'Revolutionary War in Mount Pleasant', *Mount Pleasant, South Carolina*, <tompsc.com/740/Revolutionary-War-in-Mount-Pleasant>, accessed 29 Nov. 2024. In the context of these events, 'Haddrell's Point' refers to the corner of land facing the fort at Cove Inlet. Later in the war, the name was used to describe the east shore of Charleston Harbor between Shem Creek and Cove Inlet. Today, this area is called 'Mount Pleasant,' and 'Haddrell's Point' is applied only to the north portion at the mouth of Shem Creek.

109 Elliott, 'Diary', p.217.

110 Bunbury (ed.), *Lee Papers*, vol.2, pp.220–221.

Charles Town as seen from HMS *Bristol* the day after the Battle of Sullivan's Island. (New York Public Library)

A miniature portrait of William Thomson by Edward Savage, ca. 1790. (Image Courtesy of The Gibbes Museum of Art/Carolina Art Association)

Colonel William Moultrie commanded the fort, which was garrisoned by his regiment of provincial regulars and a detachment of artillery. At the northeast end of the island, Lieutenant Colonel William Thomson's 3rd South Carolina mounted ranger regiment prepared to fend off the crossing (without their horses). Thomson's men, like Muhlenberg's, carried rifles. The colonel and many of his men had more than that in common with the Virginians. Thomson was the Pennsylvania-born, Protestant Irish sheriff of Orangeburg, which was an originally German, Swiss, and Dutch frontier settlement.[111] His rangers had been skirmishing with the British for a week.[112] They built a small barricade of sabal palm ('palmetto') logs near the water and were now building a larger entrenchment 500 yards behind it.[113]

Armstrong was put in command at Haddrell's Point and Howe commanded the troops in Charles Town. Lee positioned a reserve force in Lynch's Pasture, a field near the Cooper just outside of town. On the far side of the pasture stood a large southern live oak, the sort of tree that is associated today with plantations, often draped with Spanish moss. This was Charles Town's Liberty Tree and had been known as such since the Stamp Act Crisis. In 1766, Christopher Gadsden and more than two dozen others stood around it, hand-in-hand, and pledged to always defend American liberty.[114]

Lee ordered Muhlenberg's regiment to Haddrell's Point. From there they could provide cover for Moultrie's men in a retreat or, if things went well, cross over and join the battle. The general's intentions, however, were not properly communicated to Virginian Thomas

111 Johnson, *Traditions*, pp.90–91.

112 Doug MacIntyre, 'Danger at the Breach,' *JAR*, 11 May 2023, <allthingsliberty.com/2023/05/danger-at-the-beach>, accessed 3 March 2024.

113 William B. Willcock (ed.), *The American Rebellion: Sir Henry Clinton's Narrative of His Campaigns, 1775–1782, With an Appendix of Original Documents* (New Haven: Yale University Press, 1954), p.32; Clark et al (eds), *Naval Documents*, vol.6, pp.983–984.

114 Joseph Johnson, *Traditions and Reminiscenses Chiefly of the American Revolution in the South* (Charleston: Walker & James, 1851), pp.27–29.

Bullitt, a member of Lee's entourage and deputy adjutant general for the Continental Army's Southern Department. Armstrong received a note from Lee informing him that because Bullitt 'had contrary to my intentions & order put a great part of Muhlenberg's Regiment on duty, it is impossible to send 'em as I proposed.' A battalion of rifle-bearing militiamen were directed to reinforce Thomson at the breach, but once again Lee found himself having to make other arrangements. 'I have ordered General Armstrong to send a hundred volunteers to ease Colonel Thompson's Regiment of their heavy duty,' he fumed, 'for I find that a part of Colonel Horry's Regiment had most magnanimously refused to take this duty on them. We shall live I hope to thank them.'[115] Commodore Parker, meanwhile, got the first of his warships over the bar by ordering its heavy guns removed. The guns were put back, and the next ship repeated the manoeuvre.[116]

Clinton's foot soldiers planned to wade across the breach, but he learned within hours of his arrival that it was too deep.[117] He then planned a flatboat crossing covered by two warships and guns set on Green Island and behind an oyster reef on a tidal flat facing the inlet.[118] When Lee directed Thomson to reposition 500 yards from the water,[119] this plan, too, became unworkable. Thomson's new breastwork was outside the effective range of the guns on Green Island and nearly out of range for the guns on the tidal flat. Pension accounts show that several 8th Virginia men helped Thomson dig into his new position, which had a more extended front, a salt marsh on one side, a gun battery on the other, and abatis in front. James Johnston of Captain Slaughter's Company remembered that he, 'together with the detachment then commanded by Maj'r Helverson threw up small breast works for the purpose of preventing the British from Landing at that point.'[120] Clinton watched these improvements for 10 days and knew his task was 'rendered more difficult every hour.'[121]

Weeks of digging, building, and shifting men and supplies wrapped up in the night of 27 June. The warships were across the bar and their big guns were back on their naval four-truck carriages. The dreaded attack was coming. Lee confessed he was 'in pain' from the 'little confidence I reposed in our troops, the officers being all boys, and the men raw recruits.'[122]

The Battle of Sullivan's Island, 28 June 1776

The battle began mid-morning. Three ships of the line 'came boldly up to the attack', while a bomb vessel fired shells in a high arc from farther away. Though half-finished and made of wood, the fort was tougher than Lee or the British expected. Its double walls, made of

115 Bunbury (ed.), *Lee Papers*, vol.2, pp.60, 68, 80, 89, 90.
116 Clark et al (eds), *Naval Documents*, vol.6, p.803.
117 Willcox (ed.), *American Rebellion*, pp.30–31, 374–375.
118 Clark et al (eds), *Naval Documents*, vol.6, p.983.
119 Willcox (ed.), *American Rebellion*, p.32; Clark et al (eds), *Naval Documents*, vol.6, p.984.
120 NARA: M804, S5640, James Johnston pension.
121 Clark et al (eds), *Naval Documents*, vol.6, p.760.
122 Bunbury (ed.), *Lee Papers*, vol.2, p.100.

sabal palm and filled with sand, absorbed the shock of each iron ball almost like a cushion pounded by marbles. The fort's sandy interior yard swallowed most of the bombs. Only the luckiest and best-aimed of the British projectiles were dangerous to Moultrie's men inside.[123]

More warships sailed around their engaged cohorts, seeking to enfilade the fort on its unfinished west side. They got stuck on a shoal known as the 'Middle Ground' and became stationary targets. The bomb vessel's mortars, meanwhile, shook loose from their mountings and had to stop firing. Parker's other ships continued to fire, but a British victory now depended entirely on a successful crossing by Clinton's infantry.[124]

Lee stood with four or five companies of the 8th Virginia at Haddrell's Point,[125] where they had a clear view of the fort. He was encouraged to see Moultrie's men were holding their own, so he sent more men across. Perhaps because they could see so much from their position, veterans' accounts lack specificity about their own movements. One of Captain Campbell's men said he 'was there when the first attack was Commenced on Sullivan's Island.' John Vance of John Stephenson's Company said, 'the Company I belonged to, with two more Companies, was sent to assist at the Battle of Sullivan's Island.' Men from more than three of Muhlenberg's companies were present at the breach that afternoon. Some may have crossed the day before when Horry's men refused to go. This was the recollection of a North Carolina man who attested they 'remained encamped on Hardwell point untill the fleet came in when the Volunteers were ordered to the upper end of Sullivan's Island.'[126]

When ordered to go, Helphenstine led his detachment across the wobbly pontoon bridge. James Johnston of Captain Slaughter's Company remembered, 'at the time and on the day the attack was made on Fort Sullivan' he was marched from Haddrell's Point 'to the lower point of Sullivans island.'[127] The bridge connected to the island's narrow tail and a path to the unfinished rear of the fort.[128] The edifice left a deep impression in their memories.[129] The trail continued along the island's contours to the left and led straight to Colonel Thomson, three miles away.

Joseph Parett claimed that 'he was in an active engagement of about 8 hours in the fort on Sullivan's Island at that place, in the heat of battle, in which the British were defeated.' This may be a reference to Thomson's entrenchments, but the statement notably fails to clarify. Similarly, Isaac Dunn of Captain Berry's Company asserted that he was 'at the attack made on the fort on Sullivans Island.' Philip Helphenstine specifically claimed he was 'at the attack on Fort Moultrie.'[130]

Early in the day, a British sloop and an armed schooner approached the north end of the island to cover Clinton's soldiers as they prepared to cross. Facing them, according to the official report, were 'Colonel Thompson with his Rangers, some companies of Militia, and a

---

123 Force (ed.), *American Archives*, ser.5, vol.1, p.438; Bunbury (ed.), *Lee Papers*, vol.2, p.92.
124 Force (ed.), *American Archives*, ser.5, vol.1, p.438.
125 Force (ed.), *American Archives*, ser.5, vol.1, pp.438–439.
126 NARA: M804, S35859, William Combs pension, W6338, John Vance pension, S41446, John Boyd pension (1st N.C.)
127 NARA: M804, S5640, James Johnston pension.
128 McCrady, *South Carolina 1775–1780*, p.146.
129 NARA: M804, S39819, John Kirk pension; R14599, Duncan Graham pension; J. Parret pension; P. Helphenstine pension; I. Dunn pension; H. Wysor pension; W. Owens pension; M. Weese pension.
130 NARA: J. Parret pension, I. Dunn pension, P. Helphenstine pension.

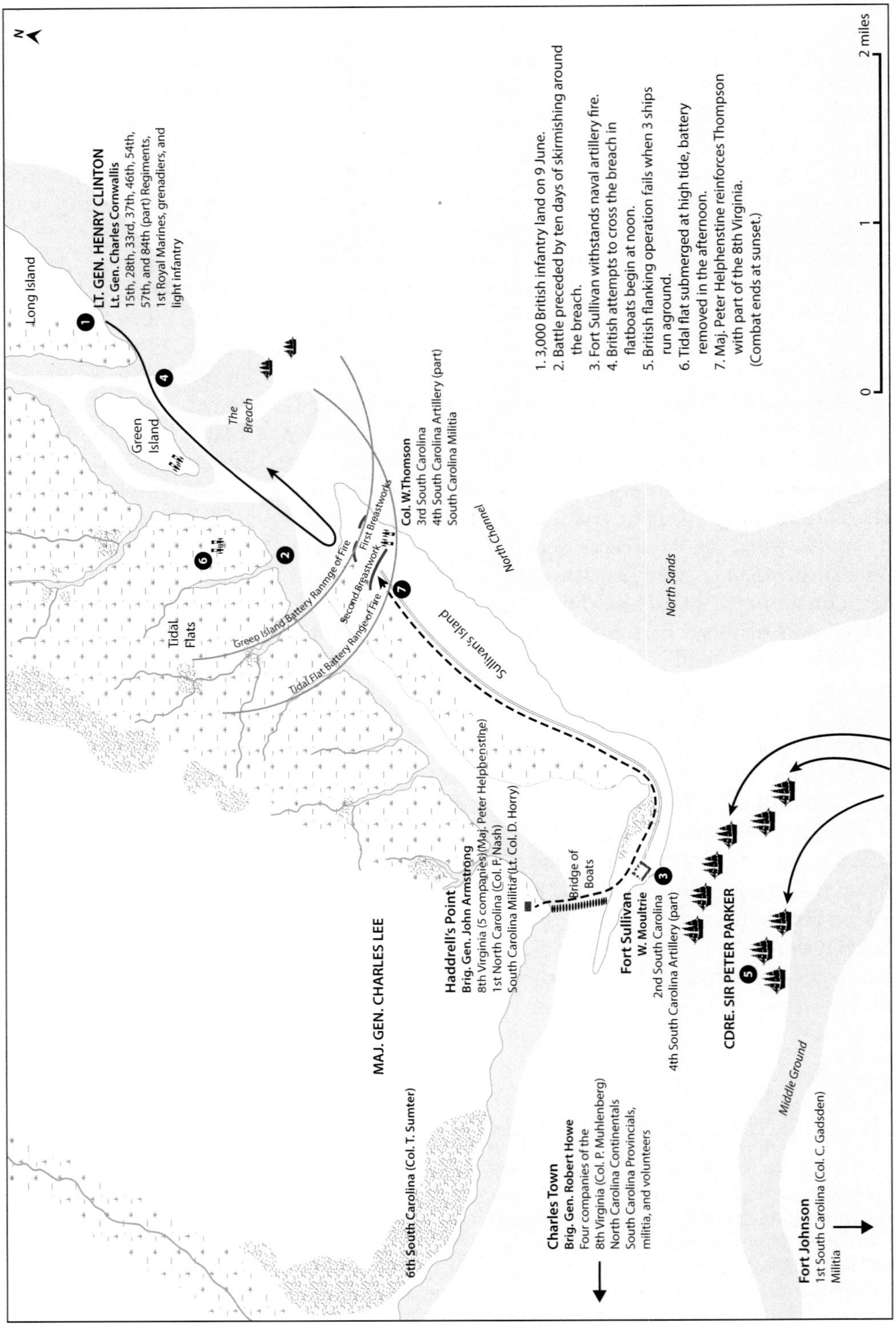

Sullivan's Island.

The waters of the Breach Inlet remain dangerous today. (Author's photo)

detachment of Artillery,' or about 780 men.[131] The 100 volunteers ordered the day before are not mentioned.[132] At three o'clock, Lee wrote Moultrie, 'I have sent for more ammunition for you, and ordered a large corps of Riflemen to reinforce Col Thompson.'[133]

Rising water forced the British to remove their artillery from the tidal flat. Johnston remembered that 'a small skirmish then ensued between us and we prevented the greater part of the British from Landing. Some of them However, succeeded but were soon driven back to their boats.'[134] Thomson's men, reinforced by about half of the 8th Virginia Regiment, also successfully fended off the two Royal Navy vessels. Historian Joseph Johnson preserved a first-hand account from Alexander Forrester, a Charles Town Loyalist, that casts doubt on Clinton's official report.

> He said, in my presence, that he was in the schooner, and that it was impossible for any set of men to sustain so destructive a fire as the Americans poured in upon them on this occasion; that it was the destructive fire from Colonel Thomson's fort which prevented the flotilla from advancing, and not the shoals and sand bars, as

131 Force (ed.), *American Archives*, ser.5, vol.1, p.439; MacIntyre, 'Danger at the Breach.'
132 NARA: John Boyd pension; S32378, Savage Littleton pension (S.C. Militia); W11223, James Harris pension (N.C. Militia); R8301, Charles Polk pension (N.C. Volunteers); S32297, John Hargrave pension (S.C. Militia).
133 Bunbury (ed.), *Lee Papers*, vol.2, pp.91–92.
134 NARA: J. Johnston pension. Edited for clarity.

> was alleged; that it was the repulse of the flotilla which prevented General Clinton from fording the inlet, and not the depth of the water.[135]

The British warships continued to batter Fort Sullivan for the rest of the day. Colonel Moultrie, shepherding limited resources, returned fire at intervals, inflicting substantial damage. One of the ships exploded into flames, another lost its bowsprit, and two more lost their mizzenmasts.[136] A North Carolina Continental said the ships 'looked like canoes when they had lost their masts.'[137] A militiaman in Colonel Horry's reluctant South Carolina regiment reported that they crossed on the pontoon bridge to the island 'just about the conclusion of the engagement.'[138] The final cannonball was fired at 9:30 p.m. The American victory was unambiguous.

The location of the 8th Virginia's senior officers and companies during the Battle of Sullivan's Island were:

Colonel Muhlenberg	Charles Town or Haddrell's Point
Lieutenant Colonel Bowman	Charles Town or Haddrell's Point
Major Helphenstine	Haddrell's Point and Breach Inlet
John Stephenson's Company	Haddrell's Point and Breach Inlet
Darke's Company	Charles Town
Slaughter's Company	Haddrell's Point and Breach Inlet
Campbell's Company	Haddrell's Point and Breach Inlet
Clark's Company	Charles Town
Westfall's Company	Haddrell's Point and Breach Inlet
David Stephenson's Company	Charles Town
Berry's Company	Haddrell's Point and Breach Inlet
Croghan's Company	Virginia
Knox's Company	Charles Town[139]

The day after the battle, general orders included a notice that 'Gen. Lee thinks it his duty in the most public manner to return his thanks to Col. Moultrie and his garrison for their brave defence of the fort in the late attack. As likewise Col. Thompson and the corps under him, for their spirited and gallant behavior in preventing the enemy from making good their landing on the east end of Sullivan's Island.'[140] In his report to the Virginia Convention Lee changed his tune about the 'banditti' he had criticized before. 'I know not which Corps I have the greatest reason to be pleased with, Muhlenberg's Virginians, or the North Carolina troops – they are both equally alert, zealous and spirited.'[141]

135 Johnson, *Traditions*, pp.93–94.
136 Bunbury (ed.), *Lee Papers*, p.93.
137 NARA: M804, S7773, Nicholas Tyner pension (3rd N.C.).
138 NARA: M804, S21123, Edward Conner pension (S.C. Militia).
139 Assessed from pension statements and Clark diary.
140 Elliott, 'Diary', p.220
141 Bunbury (ed.), *Lee Papers*, vol.2, p. 93.

Only five of the 8th Virginia's 10 companies, under Major Helphenstine's command, participated in the battle. Croghan's Company was in Virginia and Clark's, Knox's, and David Stephenson's companies were in the city because of Bullitt's error.[142] Delayed for some reason, Captain Darke's Berkeley men marched into town as the battle was underway.[143]

The fighting at the breach has been overshadowed by the remarkable events at Fort Sullivan, but it was memorable enough for those who were there. 'By satisfactory evidence and accurate examination,' a physician later determined after a visit with Bryant Sloane of Culpeper, 'at or near a place called Fort Moultrie on Sullivan's Island … he received a wound in his left hand from a leaden bullitt as is supposed, discharged from a muskett or Rifle, and he is … One half disabled from obtaining his subsistence from manual labour.'[144]

After the Battle

Captain Clark was ordered to Haddrell's Point on 1 July. He dutifully marched his men to the wharf but found the boat was not ready for them. Back at Gadsden's house that evening, perhaps because he had given up his bed, Clark tried to sleep in the garden. The sky was clear after two days of rain, promising a pleasant evening for sleeping in the open. He wrote, however, that upon the 'arr[ival] of [the] Moschetto,' he got up and moved into the house.[145] Enlisted men, of course, did not have the option of going indoors.

Clark's Company made it to Haddrell's Point the next morning, crossed the bridge, and marched out to the breach where some of their comrades were still posted. Then, one of Captain Slaughter's men remembered, 'after lying several days on the lower end of Sullivans island we returned to Hattens point and joined the remainder of our Regiment'.[146] The British warships were still floating outside the bar, and the soldiers were put back to work building defences. Fascines and gabions were made in the city and transported across the harbour.[147] John Stephenson's Company remained in Charles Town, working on the supply end of the train or on other duties.[148] On the island, some men were detailed to collect expended cannon balls.[149] Others were issued fishing nets.[150]

Parker's fleet sailed away on 18 July, and, once again, there was no way to know where it was going. Lee ordered two dozen horsemen down the coast to see if they could assess British intentions. The reconnaissance party was directed to come back with the 8th Virginia's wagons, which had been used to send supplies to the Port Royal militia.[151]

Colonel Muhlenberg, meanwhile, presided over a court martial. A soldier from the 1st North Carolina was found guilty of sleeping at his post. Much more seriously, Duncan

142 NARA: M804, S35824, John Campbell pension; C. Mitchum pension.
143 NARA: A. Moore pension.
144 NARA: M804, S11406, Bryant Sloane pension.
145 FHS: Clark Diary, 26 June–1 July 1776.
146 NARA: J. Johnston pension.
147 Elliott, 'Diary', p.232.
148 FHS: Clark Diary, 7 July 1776.
149 NARA: M804, R995, Spencer Boulton pension (S.C. Militia).
150 Elliott, 'Diary,' p.231.
151 Elliott, 'Diary,' p.233.

Fletcher of the same regiment was found guilty of trying to desert to the enemy. Brigadier General Howe approved the court's recommended sentences: 39 lashes for the sleeper, and the death penalty for the traitor. It was announced that 'Monday is appointed for the day of execution … He is immediately to be apprized of his sentence, that he may prepare himself for the awful event.'[152] Off-duty soldiers were assembled at Charles Town's Horn Work to watch the man die.[153]

The Declaration of Independence

Late in the morning of Monday, the 5th of August, South Carolina's leaders congregated outside the State House at Broad and Meeting streets to hear important news from Philadelphia. President Rutledge and Major General Lee presided over the assembled dignitaries, including the city's diverse clergy, generals Howe and Armstrong, members of the Privy Council, and members of the General Assembly.[154] Peter Muhlenberg and Abraham Bowman were likely there, but Major Helphenstine was now terribly sick.[155]

Three days prior, an express rider from the colony's congressional delegation in Philadelphia had arrived in Charles Town after a three-week journey carrying a bundle of documents for Rutledge. The covering letter summarised the packet's contents, noting first some important Congressional decisions regarding the status South Carolina's troops. The delegates also included 'some other occasional Resolutions of Congress and a very important Declaration which the King of Great Britain has, at last, reduced us to the necessity of making.'[156]

Though Whig morale in Charles Town was already sky-high and the city's dissenters were quiet, Rutledge and Lee wanted the reading of the Declaration of Independence to be 'as imposing and impressive as possible.'[157] The printing presses had been removed from the city during the battle preparations, but the document had to be read aloud anyway. Charles Town, like other cities, had a long tradition of public readings. The city sheriff routinely paraded through the streets with a drummer to read laws and proclamations to the people. For this occasion, however, Rutledge and Lee rolled out the full ceremony reserved for coronations and declarations of war.[158]

152 Elliott, 'Diary,' p.231.

153 Elliott, 'Diary,' p.234; Nic Butler, 'The Horn Work: Marion Square's Tabby Fortress', *Charleston Time Machine*, Charleston County Public Library, 29 May 2020, <ccpl.org/charleston-time-machine/horn-work-marion-squares-tabby-fortress>, accessed 6 May 2023.

154 South Caroliniana Library, University of South Carolina (SCL): William Tennent Papers, Travel Journal and Album of Collected Papers of William Tennent III, 1740–1777, p.62; Johnson, *Traditions*, p.189.

155 LVA: Revolutionary War Bounty Land Claims, Peter Helphenstine.

156 William Edwin Hemphill et al (eds), *State Records of South Carolina: Journals of the General Assembly and House of Representatives 1776–1780* (Columbia: University of South Carolina Press, 1970), p.69.

157 Joseph Johnson, *Traditions*, p.189.

158 Nic Butler, 'Wielding the Sword of State in Early South Carolina', *Charleston Time Machine*, Charleston County Public Library, November 5, 2021, <ccpl.org/charleston-time-machine/wielding-sword-state-early-south-carolina>, accessed 21 July 2022.

Broad Street and the Exchange Building in 1906. (Library of Congress)

At noon, the 700-man Charles Town Militia paraded under arms, halting to form a line along the length of Broad Street, west to east, from the State House to the Exchange Building, while drums rolled and sergeants shouted. The assembled civil, military, and religious leaders walked to the west end of the line to listen. An informed reconstruction of the thinly documented event proposes the text was read by the colony's secretary of state, Captain John Huger, with each line repeated loudly through a conical megaphone by the clerk of the Legislative Council. Reading the Declaration of Independence in this fashion took perhaps 20 minutes, after which Sheriff Thomas Grimball performed an ancient and stirring ritual laden with unmistakable meaning: he unsheathed the Sword of State.[159]

The 50-inch, double-edged sword with an undulating *flamberge* blade had been acquired in the earliest days of the colony to represent the Crown's authority, much like the sword in the King's regalia.[160] The ceremonial weapon had been used for decades to precede processions

159 Nic Butler, 'Declaring Independence in 1776 Charleston', *Charleston Time Machine*, Charleston County Public Library, July 5, 2019, <ccpl.org/charleston-time-machine/declaring-independence-1776-charleston>, accessed 21 July 2022.

160 Jeffrey Collins, 'S.C.'s Sword of State missing for more than 70 years', *Post and Courier*, 1 Jan. 2014 (updated 2 Nov. 2016), <postandcourier.com/archives/s-c-s-sword-of-state-missing-for-more-than/article_03e6ddab-656c-504b-b0e1–2c0f42c64496.html>, accessed 21 July 2022.

in state ceremonies, including the recent inauguration of President Rutledge.[161] American leaders had, until now, continued to profess loyalty to the King. Use of the sheathed sword at Rutledge's inauguration had not by itself communicated disloyalty. Unsheathing it now was another matter entirely.

Grimball extracted the sword from its scabbard and held it high for the crowd to see. He brandished it three times as the people cheered. Older citizens had seen this before, but only rarely and not for many years. The sword was only drawn from its scabbard for declarations of war. Henry Laurens could remember seeing it done four times during the reigns of George I and George II. It was done during the War of Jenkin's Ear, King George's War, and twice during the French and Indian War. Laurens gushed to his son, 'There I saw that Sword of State which I had before seen four several Times unsheathed in Declarations of War against France & Spain by the Georges now unsheathed & borne in a Declaration of War against George the third.' He was enthralled. The 'scene,' he said, 'was Serious Important & Awful.'[162]

Then, South Carolina's leaders paraded in front of the militia line to the Exchange Building. There, the ceremony was repeated before a growing crowd of people that filled the streets and windows. A witness remembered the Declaration was 'read a second time, with the acclamations of the People & discharge of cannon at Granville's & Broughton's Bastions.'[163] The procession then turned north up East Bay Street 'amidst loud acclamations of Thousands' along the Cooper River to the open fields north of town.[164] There, on the far side of Lynch's Pasture, Muhlenberg's men and the rest of the army waited by the Liberty Tree. The soldiers had received their orders from Major General Lee the day before: 'The whole troops, Continental and Provincial, that are off of duty are to parade to-morrow afternoon at 3 o'clock, near Liberty Tree, where they are to hear the Declaration of Independence read and a sermon on the occasion by Dr. Percy.'[165]

'Thither the procession moved from the city,' wrote Joseph Johnson, '...embracing all the young and old, of both sexes, who could be moved so far. Aided by bands of music, and uniting all the military of the country and city, in and near Charleston, the ceremony was the most splendid and solemn that ever had been witnessed in South-Carolina.'[166] The reading was reported in Dixon and Hunter's *Virginia Gazette* as occurring 'amidst the acclamations of a vast concourse of people.'[167]

The Virginia riflemen stood in their walnut-dyed shirts and watched the Sword of State precede the train of dignitaries, noting their own field officers as they arrived. There was an invocation by the Reverend William Percy, a minister in the Church of England who had

161 Terry W. Lipscomb, 'The South Carolina Constitution of 1776', *South Carolina Historical Magazine,* 77:2 (1976), pp.138–141.

162 Philip M. Hamer et al (eds), *The Papers of Henry Laurens* (Columbia: University of South Carolina Press, 1968–2003), vol.11, pp.222–236, 228.

163 SCL: Tennent Journal, p.62; Laurens, 'To John Laurens', p.228.

164 SCL: Tennant Journal, p.62; John Drayton, *Memoirs of the American Revolution From Its Commencement to the Year 1776, Inclusive; As Relating to the State of South-Carolina: And Occasionally Referring to the States of North-Carolina and Georgia* (Charleston: A.E. Miller, 1821), vol.2, p.315.

165 Elliott, 'Diary', p.235.

166 Johnson, *Traditions*, pp.27–29, 189.

167 *Virginia Gazette* (Dixon and Hunter), 27 Sept. 1776.

A mature southern live oak. Charles Town's Liberty Tree was cut down by the British in 1780. (Photo: Dawna Moore)

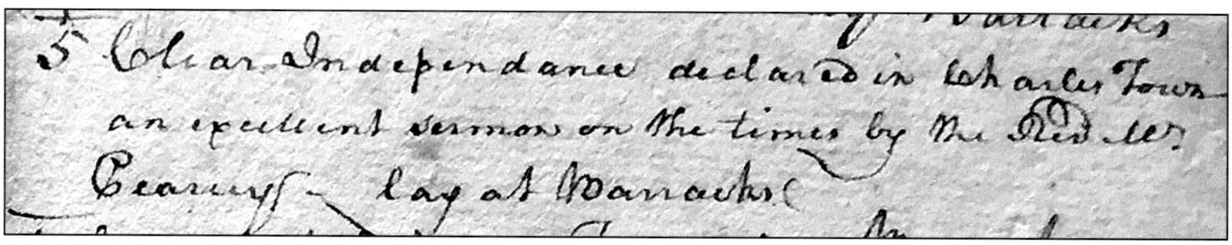

5 Clear Independance declared in Charles Town
an excellent sermon on the times by the Revd Mr
Pearcey – lay at Barracks

Captain Clark's account of the 5 August 1776 reading of the Declaration of Independence in Charles Town. (The Filson Historical Society, Louisville, KY)

preached before to rebel soldiers.[168] Major Bernard Elliot of the 4th South Carolina read the Declaration 'in the most impressive manner.' Reverend Percy rose again to deliver what Captain Clark called 'an excellent sermon on the times.'[169] Joseph Johnson said the address inspired 'the crowded audience with piety and patriotism.' When Percy finished, the audience erupted in cheers. The city's cannons thundered, and the soldiers fired their weapons in a *feu de joie*.[170] Every man triggered a blank charge after the man next to him, creating an extended rolling celebratory fire that ran through the entire army.

168 Frederich Dalcho, *Historical Account of the Protestant Episcopal Church in South Carolina* (Charleston: E. Thayer, 1820), pp.236–241.
169 FHS: Clark Diary, 5 August 1776.
170 Johnson, *Traditions*, pp.189–190.

Percy delivered his sermon in the hot summer sun, shaded by a parasol held by an African. As Percy's face flushed in the heat, the enslaved man fanned him with his other hand. A Tory or two in the audience reported the scene to friends in England, where the press mocked the event with a racist ditty:

> Good Mr. Parson, it is not quite civil
> To be preaching rebellion, thus fanned by the devil.[171]

No one in eighteenth-century Charles Town seems to have noted the incongruity of a preacher fanned by a slave as he expounded on liberty. It took a long time for the Declaration's assertion that 'all men are created equal' to penetrate American minds. One symbol of this halting progress, Charles Town's Liberty Tree, was cut down by the British in 1780. Another artefact of the day, the Sword of State, was stolen from the state capitol building in 1941 and has not been seen since.[172]

A plaque on Alexander Street marks the approximate location of Charles Town's Liberty Tree. (Author's photo)

171 Johnson, *Traditions*, p.190.
172 Federal Bureau of Investigation, National Stolen Art File, Ref. No. 00622.

This photograph of the original South Carolina Sword of State was discovered in the basement of the State House by House Clerk Charles Reid in 2021. Only two low-quality images were previously known to exist. (Courtesy of Charles Reid)

6

Georgia

Summertime in the coastal south was deadly for men from the mountains of Virginia. Reuben Hollaway, one of Captain Slaughter's first recruits, died on Saturday, 3 August. Cornelius Mershon, a corporal, died on Sunday. William Weekly died on Monday. Abraham Field died on Tuesday.[1] They were all members of the same company, and the deaths kept coming.

Captain Clark first felt ill at Haddrell's Point on 11 July. Lieutenant Colonel Bowman allowed him to sleep in his tent. His first symptoms were chills, a high fever, body pains, and lethargy. After a week of this, Clark allowed a surgeon to perform a bloodletting, after which he felt good enough to go to church at the city's Baptist meeting house.[2] The bloodletting did no good, of course, but the fever did come and go.[3]

Lee attributed the illness to working in the summer sun, sleeping on damp ground, and drinking bad water. He ordered Armstrong to move the men at Haddrell's Point into the woods. He asked President Rutledge for boards for them to sleep on and dispensed rum as an antidote to the suspect water.[4] None of this worked. It was not the sun, earth, air, or water that made the men sick.

Mosquito-borne diseases have killed more people than any other cause in human history, and they killed far more 8th Virginia men than the British did. They were the conquistadors' greatest allies and are still a top killer in the developing world. Mosquitos may have even contributed to the extinction of the dinosaurs.[5] The diseases they carried, malaria and yellow fever, were brought to the New World from Europe and Africa. Their symptoms are similar, but only malaria was endemic and featured the telltale 'intermittent fever.' The untreated malaria that killed Reuben Holloway and his comrades brought vomiting, convulsions, haemorrhaging, and kidney failure. It was a bad way to die.[6]

Survivors were not immune, but locals did acquire resistance over time. There were two varieties: *Plasmodium vivax* and *Plasmodium falciparum*. *Vivax* peaked earlier in the

1 NARA: M246: f.217, p.2.
2 FHS: Clark Diary, 11–28 July 1776.
3 McNeill, *Mosquito Empires*, pp.52–53.
4 Bunbury (ed.), *Lee Papers*, vol.2, pp.139–140.
5 Timothy Winegard, *The Mosquito: A Human History of Our Deadliest Predator* (New York: Dutton, 2019), pp.2, 16–17, 151–155.
6 Peter McCandless, *Slavery, Disease, and Suffering in the Southern Lowcountry* (Cambridge University Press, 2011, Kindle e-book), chapter 3.

summer and was less deadly, but it could also remain in a person's liver for decades and cause relapses at any time. *Falciparum* peaked later in the summer and was more likely to kill.[7] Mosquitos did not live long and did not fly far. The two bites necessary to transmit the disease required two people to be close to each other. Spreading the disease at scale required a large and concentrated population. An army of men living in the open near swamps and rice paddies was all the bugs needed to create an epidemic.

The men of the 8th Virginia Regiment were far more susceptible to getting seriously ill than were natives of the Carolina low country. 'The Virginians especially,' wrote Muhlenberg's great-nephew, adhering to the bad air (*mal aria*) theory, 'accustomed to the pure air of the mountains of the northern part of their state, suffered severely.'[8] Indeed, a soldier born and raised in the cooler and less populated regions of Virginia had no resistance. The mosquitos also did not care about rank. John Armstrong complained to Lee that he 'had a disagreeable swiming' in his brain.[9] Colonel Muhlenberg got sick, and so did Major Helphenstine.[10]

The 8th Virginia Regiment, July 1776

Field Officers: Col. Peter Muhlenberg, Lt. Col. Abraham Bowman, Maj. Peter Helphenstine (sick)
Captains: John Stephenson, Darke (sick), Campbell, Slaughter, Clark, Westfall, David Stephenson, Berry, Croghan,[11] Knox
Lieutenants: 13
Ensigns: 5
Staff and Warrant Officers: Adj. Francis Swaine, Chap. Christian Streit,[12] Surgeon, Surg. Mate, Quartermaster, Sgt. Maj. John Hoy
NCOs: Sergeants: 31, **Drum and Fife:** 5
Rank & File: fit for duty: 310, sick: 150, furlough: 4.
Total: 464
1 recruited, 4 dead, 45 discharged, 56 deserted since last return.
Surgeon, surgeon's mate, and quartermaster present but not identified.[13]

Seniority

There were other blood-suckers in Charles Town. 'The Inhabitants of this Town ... fleece the Army most unmercifully,' Lee complained to President Rutledge. 'Six pounds one & three-pence is demanded for burying a Soldier of Muhlenberg's,' Lee wrote to Benjamin Harrison VI, deputy paymaster general for the Southern Department, begging for money. 'The Army here and in North Carolina are in the greatest distress from want of Continental currency,' he continued, adding, 'I am inform'd that the Troops in Virginia have been on the brink of mutiny and general desertion from a discontent from not being regularly paid.'[14]

7 McCandless, *Southern Lowcountry*, chapter 3; Winegard, *Mosquito*, pp.27, 266
8 Muhlenberg, *General Muhlenberg*, p.69.
9 Bunbury (ed.), *Lee Papers*, vol.2, p.198.
10 Muhlenberg, *General Muhlenberg*, p.69; LVA: P. Helphenstine bounty claim.
11 Detached and subalterns not counted.
12 Not yet joined. Formally appointed 1 Aug. 1776.
13 Force, *American Archives*, ser.5, vol. 1, pp.631-632; NARA: M246, f.208, p.4; NARA: J. Vance pension.
14 Bunbury (ed.), *Lee Papers*, vol.2, pp.156, 175.

It was also now obvious that the 8th Virginia had been intentionally excluded from Continental status. Ironically, it was Congress's decision to start paying them anyway that removed any doubt. On 25 March, aware of Clinton's movements and having few Continentals in the south, Congress resolved that Virginia's 7th, 8th, and 9th provincial regiments would be 'on the pay and at the expense of the continent.' If they were Continentals, no such decision would have been necessary.[15] The Virginians' service alongside North Carolina's Continentals made it impossible to ignore the problem any longer. Muhlenberg went to Lee on 31 July to politely insist that the issue be 'settled some way or other, before We leave this place.' He memorialised his protest in writing: 'All the Continental Troops in this place have hitherto taken rank of my officers,' he wrote, 'because they have no commissions to produce & suffer them to Rank only as Provincials.' He had learned that Congress was avoiding a resolution.

> I have received another letter from Williamsburg, which mentions that the Convention had apply'd to the General Congress to take the 7th 8th & 9th Regiments on the Continental Establishment – That the answer was, it could not be done immediately, but when those Regiments were completely mann'd & arm'd they might be taken. That the Convention had retained those three Regiments in their Service, & in consequence of this, the 7th & 9th Regts had receiv'd Provincial Pay to the 25th of June. As this is the Case, I must beg leave to say, that I should use myself ill, were I to accept a Continental Commission after this date, when other Regiments, raised long after mine, would take rank before me. I should prefer being oldest Provincial Officer before the youngest Continental. I can assure your Excellency nothing should have prompted me to mention this, did I not conceive that my Regiment had been slighted in some respects.[16]

The 'completeness' of the regiment was not the problem. Lee made this clear in his written response:

> What the Continental Congress can mean by not taking your Regiment and the others on their establishment until they are compleat, is above my conception – if they mean that it was to have its full complement to a man, or that it shou'd be compleat enough for service, I am at a loss – if they meant the former, it was almost impossible that these Regiments shou'd ever be on their establishment – if they meant the latter, your Regiment certainly must have the precedency over all the Regiments on the Continent ... on every principle your Regiment must be considered as Continental, at least from the time you were ordered to march out of the Province.

He promised to get it fixed.

15 Ford (ed.), *Journals of Congress*, vol.4, p.235.
16 Bunbury (ed.), *Lee Papers*, vol.2, pp.183–184.

> You may depend therefore when the Congress is inform'd of the Circumstances, your Rank will not be disputed – the fact is that the Congress having no military Men in their Body are continually confounding themselves and every body else in military matters. However, to do 'em justice they will bear being corrected with candour & patience. There is now a Board of War establish'd, so we have reason to flatter ourselves that things will go on with somewhat less confusion. I shall write immediately on the subject if it is necessary for your satisfaction and that of your Officers but think you need be in no pain about it.[17]

Even Lee, the commander of the Southern Department, was oblivious to the real reason for the lack of Continental commissions. Many of the Provincial commissions had been awarded on the bases of cronyism and popularity.[18] The very first colonelcy had gone to Patrick Henry, who was the most popular man in Virginia but clearly unqualified. Not counting the small Eastern Shore regiment, Muhlenberg had been given the last-numbered colonelcy. He commanded a regiment composed of valley men and backwoodsmen who were ethnically, religiously, and culturally second-class. 'Perhaps of all the Virginia Colos my Connexions, and Fortune are smallest,' Muhlenberg protested to Lee, 'but according to my abilities I have sacrificed perhaps as much as they.'[19] In the contest for a limited number of Continental commissions, Muhlenberg, Bowman, and Helphenstine had been boxed out by more popular and well-connected men.

Lee's response to Muhlenberg was flattering and reassuring. The victory at Charles Town had cemented Lee's reputation as the most brilliant military mind in the American army. He used some of that political capital to help the young German-American colonel attain fair treatment. He wrote to the Board of War: 'I have ventured to assure him, and his officers, who are equally uneasy, that there must be some mistake in this affair. In fact, the hardship would be so great, that I cannot believe their apprehensions are well founded.' When he took them south, he said,

> Muhlenberg's regiment was not only the most complete of the Province, but I believe of the whole Continent ... Muhlenberg's regiment wanted only forty at most. It was the strength and good condition of the regiment that induced me to order it out of its own Province in preference to any other. I certainly considered them at that time as Continental troops; otherwise, I could have had no authority to order them out of the Province.
>
> I must now submit it to the consideration of the Congress, if it would not really be the greatest cruelty that their strength and good condition should be turned against them. It was their strength and good condition which carried them out of their Province, where, had they remained and known that it was a necessary condition of their establishment to be complete to a man, they certainly could have accomplished it in three days. I do, therefore, most sincerely hope, and confidently persuade myself, that Muhlenberg's regiment will at least date their rank from the

17 Bunbury (ed.), *Lee Papers*, vol.2, pp.185–186.
18 Powell (ed.), *Biographical Sketch*, pp.21–23.
19 Bunbury (ed.), *Lee Papers*, vol.2, pp.183–184.

> day I ordered them to march out of their Province. Not only justice, but policy requires it, for you will otherwise lose a most excellent regiment.[20]

Lee's entreaty had an immediate effect. On 13 August, Congress ordered, 'That the 8th Virginia battalion be taken into pay from the 27th day of May last.'[21] In the meantime, however, the 8th Virginia's seniority relative to the North Carolina Continentals had to be litigated. Specifically at issue was whether Colonel Jethro Sumner of the 3rd North Carolina was senior to Peter Muhlenberg. Continentals always outranked Provincials, but Lee knew better than to resolve the question that way. A court of officers was assembled, chaired by Brigadier General Armstrong, to work something out.[22] They recommended that the two colonels cast lots.[23] Muhlenberg, provisionally, took the senior spot when Sumner failed to appear for the exercise.[24]

Bold and Lucky Fellows

Including Bermuda, Great Britain had 20 North American colonies, of which 13 were in open rebellion. To the north, Newfoundland, Nova Scotia, St John's (Prince Edward Island), and Quebec remained loyal. To the south, the colonies of East and West Florida did as well. Unlike Bermuda, which was as old as Virginia, the two Florida colonies had come into British possession with Quebec at the end of the French and Indian War. East Florida was controlled from St Augustine by a British governor and a garrison of soldiers primarily from the 60th (Royal American) Regiment housed in the century-old Castillo de San Marcos.[25] An influx of Loyalists from the rebelling colonies had transformed East Florida into a significant threat to neighbouring Georgia. The colony built a fort on the south bank of the St Mary's River and called it Fort Tonyn, after the colony's governor. Using this stronghold as a base, a Loyalist unit known as the East Florida Rangers conducted raids across the river into Georgia.[26]

Jonathan Bryan, a Patriot leader from Savannah, travelled to Charles Town to ask Lee for help. The British military presence in St Augustine was small, he reported, and Lee could easily take the town if he acted quickly.[27] Lee did not need much convincing. Parker and Clinton were gone, as were the royal governors of Virginia, the Carolinas, and Georgia. The East Florida Rangers were the only active threat in the Southern Department, and a successful campaign might have the added benefit of dissuading the nearby Creek Indians from allying with the British. Lee might even add a fourteenth colony to the union.[28]

20 Force (ed.), *American Archives*, ser.5, vol.1, p.721.
21 Ford (ed.), *Journals of Congress*, vol.5, p.649. Pay rolls show Continental service beginning May 25th.
22 University of Michigan, William L. Clements Library (WLCL): William Howe Orderly Book, p.16; Bunbury (ed.), *Lee Papers*, vol.2, pp.197–198.
23 WLCL: Howe Orderly Book, p.19.
24 Rankin, *North Carolina Continentals*, p.76.
25 Charles Loch Mowat, *East Florida as a British province, 1763–1784* (Berkeley and Los Angeles: University of California Press, 1943), pp.107–108.
26 Drayton, *Memoirs*, vol.2, pp.333–334.
27 Moultrie, *Memoirs*, vol.1, p.184; Drayton, *Memoirs*, vol.2, p.334.
28 Force (ed.), *American Archives*, ser.5, vol.1, pp.719–722.

Lee did contemplate dispatching the 8th to support the coordinated multi-state response to frontier attacks by the Cherokee that William Christian was leading for Virginia, but he decided against it.[29] At the same time, the general knew that convincing the Virginia and North Carolina troops to go even farther south was going to be hard. To encourage them, he did something South Carolina's John Drayton said, 'manifestly tended to debauch the minds of our patriotic soldiers, and to divert them from the cause of freedom.'[30] Lee lured them by appealing to vanity and greed. He lined the men up and praised them for their service. He told them he had planned a secret mission for them as a reward. He said it would be easy, that there would be no danger, and that 'a very large booty, of which he would resign his share to them, attended their steps.' He did not mean to force anyone to become rich with the plunder that awaited them, of course. This mission was only for volunteers.[31]

Abraham Moore of Captain Darke's Company remembered, 'Genl Lee made a speech to us in which he told us, we had come a great way, and that our wages were low. That there were a good many Tories in St Augustine, who had plunder and that we were at Liberty to go there if we choose.'[32] They were, reported a *Virginia Gazette* correspondent, setting off 'to make reprisals, for the emolument of each lucky and bold fellow.'[33]

South Carolina's Legislative Council, however, declined to let its soldiers go. Lee was furious. '[I]s it reasonable?' he demanded to know, 'is it just that the other Colonies shou'd be oblig'd to march to their assistance, and refuse in their turn to assist others?' He demanded that South Carolina provide troops 'equal to a compleat Battalion' for the expedition. If, he said, 'the Council cannot comply with this requisition I should be glad to be inform'd of the reasons that I may lay 'em before Congress, and be able to exculpate myself if any calamities fall upon that, at present, defenceless country.'[34] When Rutledge refused to budge, Lee executed a power play. He assembled a council of officers composed of generals Howe and Armstrong and the field officers of the 1st, 2nd, 4th, and 5th South Carolina regiments. He asked them to give their opinions on whether an 18 June Resolution of Congress 'allowing' and 'permitting' South Carolina to elevate its troops to Continental status could be construed to mean they were already in Continental service. The generals said yes, as did five of the nine South Carolina officers.[35] With this majority, he leveraged a provision in the same resolution of Congress that allowed him to take up to one third of South Carolina's 'Continentals' out of the state without Rutledge's permission.[36] He got his troops. About 460 men were pulled out of the 1st through 4th South Carolina regiments and put under the command of Colonel Moultrie.[37]

29 Bunbury (ed.), *Lee Papers*, vol.2, p.187.
30 Drayton, *Memoirs*, vol.2, p.335.
31 Drayton, *Memoirs*, vol.2, p.334; *Virginia Gazette* (Purdie), 13 Sept. 1776. See also Bunbury (ed.), *Lee Papers*, vol.2, p.187.
32 NARA: A. Moore pension.
33 *Virginia Gazette* (Dixon and Hunter), 27 Sept. 1776.
34 Bunbury (ed.), *Lee Papers*, vol.2, p.156.
35 Bunbury (ed.), *Lee Papers*, vol.2, p.202; Ford (ed.), *Journals of Congress*, vol.5, pp.461–462.
36 Bunbury (ed.), *Lee Papers*, vol.2., pp.200–205; Ford (ed.), *Journals of Congress*, vol.5, pp.462–463.
37 Bunbury (ed.), *Lee Papers*, vol.2, p.200; WLCL: Howe Orderly Book, p.19; Drayton, *Memoirs*, vol.2, p.335.

Major Dick Campbell

Lee had intimated that cowards and fools could remain behind, but most or all of the 150 8th Virginia enlisted men who stayed in Charles Town were simply too sick to move.[38] John Chenoweth remembered, 'what ware able to march ware marched to Sunsburey.'[39] Major Helphenstine, in the words of Colonel Muhlenberg, was 'taken with a painful & lingering disorder which rendered him incapable of performing his Duty.' He received permission from Lee to return home to Winchester to recover. James Wood of Frederick, who had recruited Muhlenberg to be rector of Beckford Parish, recalled, 'Major Helphinston … returned home in a low state of Health of which he never recovered.'[40]

Lee wanted to elevate a new major, even if just provisionally. Protocol dictated that the job should go to the senior captain, John Stephenson. Stephenson may in fact have performed the job for a brief time, as three veterans attested. He too, however, fell ill and returned home.[41] The men of his once-independent company also left when their one-year 1775 enlistments ended. A return of forces for July, likely taken in sometime in August, records the discharge of 45 men.[42]

Next in line was Captain Darke, but he did not get the job either. The reason is not recorded, but two 8th Virginia captains were reported as too sick to head for St Augustine. The fact that he was passed over completely may indicate that he was not only sick but also not expected to recover. It could also be that Lee simply did not like him. Darke had a strong personality. He was 'a stoutly built man of brusque address.'[43] The job went to Richard Campbell.[44] The senior captain from Dunmore County was a good officer,[45] affectionately called 'Dick Campbell' by his men.[46] One veteran remembered that the former sheriff's deputy had a 'stentorian voice.'[47]

Lee marched his little army of 1,500 men out of Charles Town on 7 August. A week into the march, he sent a note to Armstrong:

> One hundred and forty seven of Colonel Mughlenburghs Regiment with two Captain and three subalterns are left sick at Charlestown; as fast as they recover I must request you to order 'em back to Williamsburg where they are to aggregate themselves with Capt. Cochrane's Company of that Regiment – it will be politick

38 Force (ed.), *American Archives*, ser.5, vol.1, pp.631–632; Bunbury (ed.), *Lee Papers*, vol.2, p.230. Lee reported 147 men sick.

39 NARA: J. Chenoweth pension.

40 LVA: P. Helphenstine bounty claim.

41 LVA: Revolutionary War Bounty Land Claims, John Stephenson; Larche, *Pioneers on the Bullskin*, p.156.

42 Force (ed.), *American Archives*, ser.5, vol.1, pp.631–632; Abbot, et al (eds), *Papers of Washington* (Colonial), vol.4, p.248; LVA: J. Stephenson bounty claim.

43 George M. Beltzhoover, *James Rumsey, the Inventor of the Steamboat* (West Virginia Historical and Antiquarian Society, 1900), p.17.

44 Ford (ed.), *Journals of Congress*, vol.7, p.52; LOC: George Washington Papers, Ser.4, General Correspondence: George Johnston to Peter Muhlenberg, March 9, 1777.

45 NARA: M804, W1912, Zackquil Morgan pension (Va. militia).

46 NARA: M804, R8522, George H. Puntenney pension (13th Va.).

47 NARA: F. Dunlavy pension.

> to apprize them of their destination, for as I have reason to think that the Devil of Desertion has in some measure possess'd 'em, their being acquaint'd that they are to return home, will be the means of casting out the Dæmon.[48]

Captain Croghan's Detachment

Captain 'Cochrane's' company was still in Williamsburg, guarding Loyalists and waiting for the regiment to return. That union would not occur for nearly a year. While the other nine companies suffered pointlessly in Georgia, Croghan's men made history.

The Irish captain from Pittsburgh was suddenly in charge of a substantial body of men. In addition to his own company, men like Henry Brock, who had been left behind by their captains, were now under his command.[49] Croghan was also responsible for the men under Edward Moody, a second lieutenant who had been appointed to recruit men around Williamsburg to complete Captain Knox's Company.[50] Then, 1st Lieutenant Culp, 1st Lieutenant Hite, and Sergeant Harding from Darke's, Campbell's, and Clark's companies arrived with recruits and collected deserters.[51] Altogether, Croghan had nearly enough men to fill two full companies or one-fifth of the regiment.

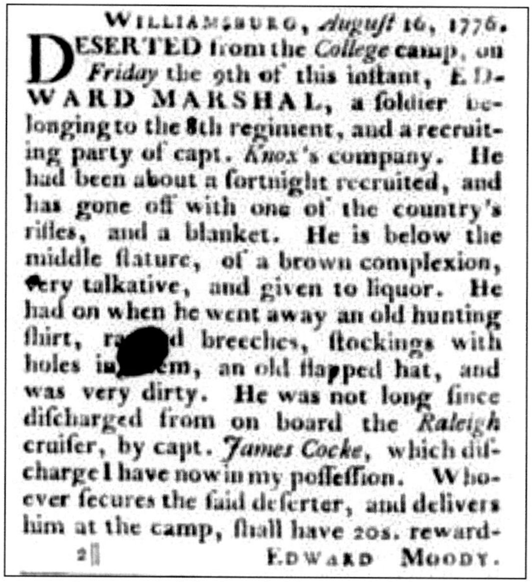
WILLIAMSBURG, *Auguſt* 16, 1776.
DESERTED from the *College* camp, on *Friday* the 9th of this inſtant, EDWARD MARSHAL, a ſoldier belonging to the 8th regiment, and a recruiting party of capt. *Knox*'s company. He had been about a fortnight recruited, and has gone off with one of the country's rifles, and a blanket. He is below the middle ſtature, of a brown complexion, very talkative, and given to liquor. He had on when he went away an old hunting ſhirt, r[illegible]d breeches, ſtockings with holes in[illegible]em, an old flapped hat, and was very dirty. He was not long ſince diſcharged from on board the *Raleigh* cruiſer, by capt. *James Cocke*, which diſcharge I have now in my poſſeſſion. Whoever ſecures the ſaid deſerter, and delivers him at the camp, ſhall have 20s. reward.
2 EDWARD MOODY.

The Virginia Committee of Safety tasked First Lieutenant Edward Moody with recruiting in Virginia to bolster Captain Knox's understrength company. When Edward Marshal deserted two weeks after enlisting, Moody placed this advertisement in the *Virginia Gazette*. (Colonial Williamsburg)

Andrew Lewis received orders from Congress to send two regiments north to meet the Flying Camp. This was a mobile reserve force of mid-Atlantic men in short-term Continental service posted opposite Staten Island in New Jersey.[52] Hugh Mercer, now a newly promoted brigadier general, was in command there. The 1st and 2nd Virginia regiments were chosen to go but, like John Stephenson's men, the men in these units were on one-year 1775 enlistments that were about to expire. The decision was made to immediately reenlist the regiments, this time for three-year terms. Any men who were

48 Bunbury (ed.), *Lee Papers*, vol.2, p.230.
49 WHS: Draper Mss, N, vol.2, p.89.
50 *Virginia Gazette* (Purdie), 16 Aug. 1776.
51 WHS: John Clark to J. Clark, 12 Aug. 1776; NARA: C. Shryock pension.
52 Ford (ed.), *Journals of Congress*, vol.4, p.412, vol.5, pp.597–598.

unwilling to rejoin were discharged without pay for the balance of their time to make room for men who would serve.[53]

The 1st Virginia, commanded by Fincastle's William Christian, reenlisted 'almost to a man.' However, when the unpopular Colonel Woodford gave the men of the 2nd Virginia an 'eloquent harangue', he found to his 'great mortification' that they refused to rejoin. They were willing to follow their lieutenant colonel, Charles Scott, but Scott had already been elevated to lead the 5th Virginia.[54] Consequently, the 2nd Virginia, which had won the Battle of Great Bridge, disintegrated, and George Weedon's 3rd Virginia went north instead.

Colonel Weedon's men were posted on the Potomac River when the orders came, and were quickly on their way. The 1st Virginia, despite willing reenlistments, was still short more than 100 soldiers. Lewis fixed the problem by attaching Croghan's men. 'I have succeeded so well,' he was delighted to report, 'that with the addition of 120 of the Eighth Battalion they will be compleat.'[55]

Henry Brock remembered that 'upon his recovery [he] was transfered or ordered to join Captain William Croghan's Company.'[56] Elihu Chilcott recorded that he served 'in the company commanded by Captain Croghan (but was enlisted by Capt. Hite).' David Fulke, one of Culp's recruits, recalled that 'Capt. Dark with his Com'y. had previously march'd. to South Carolina', so he 'was put into ... Croghans Company.'[57] Lieutenants Moody and Culp joined joined Croghan's detachment, but Hite remained behind with the Dunmore County deserters and others not detached.[58] Hite may or may not have known at this time that he had a claim to a captaincy following Richard Campbell's promotion.

Before the 1st Virginia marched, Colonel Christian resigned to lead Virginia's western forces in the expedition against the Cherokee.[59] Isaac Read was promoted from the 4th Virginia to take command.[60] He was a tall, blue-eyed, patrician planter from Charlotte County who had been deeply involved in revolutionary activities.[61] Frank Eppes, Thomas Jefferson's brother-in-law, was still the lieutenant colonel.[62] Both of these officers had coordinated with Muhlenberg in and around Suffolk. It appears Read did not physically join the regiment for some time.[63] Eppes was sick and never left Virginia.[64] Next in rank was Major John Green, a child of Culpeper County and a veteran of the Culpeper Minute Battalion.[65]

53 H.R. McIlwaine et al (eds), *Journals of the Council of the State of Virginia* (Richmond: Virginia State Library, 1931–1982), vol.1, p.97.
54 Powell (ed.), *Biographical Sketch*, pp.37–38.
55 Bunbury (ed.), *Lee Papers*, vol.2, p.212; Powell (ed.), *Biographical Sketch*, pp.37–38.
56 NARA: H. Brock pension. See also S21701, Harmon Commins pension.
57 NARA: M804, W6665, Elihu Chilcott pension, S39554, David Fulke pension.
58 WHS: Draper Mss, N, vol.1, p.90.
59 *Virginia Gazette* (Purdie), 9 Aug. 1776.
60 Sanchez-Saavedra, *Virginia Military Organisations*, p.29.
61 Alice Read, *The Reads and Their Relatives* (Cincinnati: Johnson & Hardin Press, 1930), pp.310–329; Calder Loth (ed.), *Virginia Landmarks* Register (Charlottesville: University Press of Virginia, 1999), p.102; *Virginia Gazette* (Dixon and Hunter), 11 March 1775.
62 *Virginia Gazette* (Dixon and Hunter), 6 July 1776.
63 WHS: McCarty Notebook, 22 Sept. 1776; NARA: T. McCarty pension.
64 Force (ed.), *American Archives*, ser.5, vol.2, p.901; *Virginia Gazette* (Dixon and Hunter), 27 Dec. 1776.
65 The farm, but not the original home, survives between Rixeyville and Brandy Station.

Thomas McCarty kept a list of the six-person messes in Croghan's Detachment, some of which included soldiers' wives and other camp followers. (Draper Manuscripts Collection, Wisconsin Historical Society)

Henry Lee ('Light Horse Harry') called Green 'one of the bravest of brave soldiers.'[66] Sergeant Thomas McCarty recalled, 'about this time the 8th Regiment was broke and the different Companies Joined Croghan and was called a detachment and went under the name of the 1st Virginia Regiment and was Commanded by Maj'r John Green.'[67]

Before their departure, Croghan had his men mustered and counted. While his official report no longer exists, a preparatory list compiled in a notebook by Sergeant McCarty does survive. This unique document lists 111 private soldiers (the last of which is crossed out) and nine non-commissioned officers – a number precisely equal to the headcount reported by Andrew Lewis. Another 28 sick men are listed as 'Left with Lt. Higgins,' who was himself ill.[68] The names of three deserters are also crossed out. McCarty's notebook includes lists of sick men from later dates and a complete list of six-person messes. The sextets include

66 Henry Lee, *Memoirs of the War in the Southern Department of the United States* (Philadelphia: Bradford and Inskeep, 1812), vol.1, p.350.

67 NARA: T. McCarty pension.

68 WHS: McCarty Notebook, p.19.

non-soldiers such as the wives of Sergeant Edward McGinn, Corporal William Penny, and Nicholas Doran, two other women, and a boy named Adam Dietz.[69]

Sergeant McCarty's notebook also contains a diary covering the detachment's activities over most of the next few months, beginning shortly after their march out of Williamsburg.[70] His diary begins just north of Fredericksburg on 23 August.

> Friday, August 23 – We lay at Potomack Creek and I was very sick with fevers, a sort of ague.
>
> Saturday, August 24 – We lay there and I had some beef killed, and our officers had a barbycue, and the Captain passed the day very sick. Likewise the Doctor was sick, and his mate, and our First Lieutenant.[71]

Captain Croghan, 1st Lieutenant Abraham Kirkpatrick, and Sergeant McCarty had all spent the last several weeks in the Tidewater and may have had malaria. They were moving away from the malarial zone, however, and were less likely to have gotten the deadlier *Falciparum* variant than their unmet comrades to the south.[72]

Georgia

'Gen. Lee hastily marched off the Virginia and North-Carolina troops,' South Carolina's William Moultrie wrote in his memoirs, 'at this inclement season of the year ... without one necessary article, nor a field piece, nor even a medicine chest.'[73] Moultrie and Howe followed a few days later with the South Carolina detachment.[74] What the army desperately needed but did not have was Peruvian cinchona bark. It contained quinine, which was the only effective treatment for malaria. The Virginians marched with Lee through the gate in Charles Town's tabby Horn Work, proceeded about nine miles on the Broad Path (Dorchester Road) to an inn called the Quarter House, and camped in the woods.[75] From there, they tramped 10 miles south, crossed the Ashley River, and camped near a bridge that crossed Wallace Creek. They continued west and south for a few days, crossing the Ponpon (Edisto) River to Jacksonborough. They passed through the village of Ashepoo, ferried across the Combahee River, and marched to Pocotaligo, where they camped near Van Bibber's Tavern.[76] On the way, Lee took the opportunity to visit Whig leader Stephen Bull at Sheldon Plantation.[77]

69 WHS: Draper Mss, N, vol.2, pp.25–55, 89–108, Thomas McCarty Diary.
70 *Virginia Gazette* (Dixon and Hunter), 17 Aug. 1776.
71 WHS: Draper Mss, N, vol.2, p.108
72 McNeill, *Mosquito Empires*, pp.3, 43–44, 54–55, 204–205; Winegard, *Mosquito*, pp.27, 266.
73 Moultrie, *Memoirs*, vol.1, p.184
74 Bunbury (ed.), *Lee Papers*, vol.2, pp.207–208.
75 FHS: Clark Diary, 7 Aug. 1776; Harriette Kershaw Leiding, *Historic Houses of South Carolina* (Philadelphia: J.B. Lippincott, 1921), pp.20–21.
76 FHS: Clark Diary, 8–12 Aug. 1776; John R. Todd and Francis M. Sutton, *Prince William's Parish and Plantations* (Richmond: Garrett and Massie, 1935), p.53; W. Jackson Greene, 'Few Traces of Gowen Family Remain at Combahee Ferry', *Gowen Research Foundation Newsletter*, 6:8 (1995).
77 Bunbury (ed.), *Lee Papers*, vol.2, p.211.

From Pocotaligo, they continued south across the Tulifiny and Coosawhatchie rivers. Two more days brought them to Purrysburg.[78]

Purrysburg was a village on the Savannah River that was, like the Lower Shenandoah, settled in the 1730s by Swiss and Palatine immigrants.[79] Captain Clark camped on the riverbank 'on a small round hill very high, said to be an Indian Grave.'[80] The Virginians watched the South Carolina troops climb into boats and float down the river. Horses and wagons followed on the riverbank. Muhlenberg's men and the North Carolinians marched a few miles downstream to Jonathan Bryan's rice plantation at Monmouth Point and nursed their sore feet while they waited for the boats to return.[81]

The Route from Charles Town to Savannah
7 Aug: Depart Charles Town, S.C.
8 Aug: Wallace Bridge, S.C.
9 Aug: Jacksonborough, S.C.
10 Aug: Ashepoo, S.C.
11 Aug: Combahee Ferry, S.C.
12 Aug: Pocotaligo, S.C.
13 Aug: Coosawhatchie, S.C.
15 Aug: Purrysburg, S.C.
17 Aug: Monmouth Point, S.C.
19 Aug: Savannah River by boat
20 Aug: Arrive Savannah, Ga.[82]
(Approximately 115 miles)

When the boats came back, the Virginians crowded into them, spent a day and a half on the water, and marched into Savannah on the 20th. Captain Clark described the Georgia capital as a town of 'two or three hundred houses on a high bank of Savana River.'[83] The newest of the 13 united colonies, Georgia was lightly populated and politically divided. Patriots fought with Loyalists, Savannah had disputes with the countryside, and elected leaders argued with the military. In 1777, Lachlan McIntosh, colonel of Georgia's only Continental regiment,[84] killed one of the Peach State's delegates to Congress in a duel.[85]

78 FHS: Clark Diary, 13–15 Aug. 1776.
79 Lawrence S. Rowland et al, *The History of Beaufort County, South Carolina* (Columbia: University of South Carolina Press, 1996–2015), vol.1, pp.118–121; Anon., 'A History of Purrysburg, South Carolina,' *Carolana*, <carolana.com/SC/Towns/Purrysburg_SC.html>, accessed 7 March 2024.
80 FHS: Clark Diary, 15–16 Aug. 1776.
81 Bunbury (ed.), *Lee Papers*, vol.2, p.252; FHS: Clark Diary, 17–18 Aug. 1776; Allan Gallay, 'Jonathan Bryan's Plantation Empire: Land, Politics, and the Formation of a Ruling Class in Colonial Georgia,' *William and Mary Quarterly* 45:2 (1988), pp.262–263.
82 FHS: Clark Diary.
83 FHS: Clark Diary, 19–20 Aug. 1776.
84 Ford (ed.), *Journals of Congress*, vol.3, p.325; Bunbury (ed.), *Lee Papers*, vol.2, p.242.
85 Charles E. Bennett and Donald R. Lennon, *A Quest for Glory: Major General Robert Howe and the American Revolution* (Chapel Hill: University of North Carolina Press, 1991), pp.45–46.

Lachlan McIntosh commanded forces in Georgia in 1776. He killed a signer of the Declaration of Independence in a 1777 duel and commanded 8th Virginia veterans at Fort Pitt in 1778. (Library of Congress)

Lee learned from the locals that there were no roads beyond 50 miles of Savannah. He bluntly asked the Georgia Council if the expedition still made sense given that there was 'no possibility of transporting cannon, ammunition, provisions, or collecting a sufficient number of men for the siege and reduction of Augustine.' The invasion of Florida, the Georgians insisted, could be done on foot with pack horses, with boats supplying them with rice on the way.[86] Lee was flabbergasted. He mocked the 'harum skarum' Georgians in a letter to Armstrong.

> They have propos'd securing their Frontiers by constant patroles of horse Rangers, when the scheme is approv'd of they scratch their heads for some days, and at length inform you that there is some small difficulty in the way; that of the impossibility to procure a single horse – their next project is to keep their inland Navigation clear of Tenders by a numerous fleet of Guarda Costa arm'd boats, when this is agreed to, they recollect that they have not a single boat – Upon the whole I shou'd not be supris'd if they were to propose mounting a body of Mermaids on Alligators.[87]

Taking St Augustine was out of the question. Having come this far, however, and with the Georgians insisting, Lee opted to stage an 'incursion of insult' across the St Mary's River but declined to lead it himself.[88] The Virginians and one company of South Carolinians were sent onward as Lee spoke with Colonel Moultrie about commanding the expedition.[89] The general ordered:

86 Bunbury (ed.), *Lee Papers*, vol.2, pp.233–234.
87 Bunbury (ed.), *Lee Papers*, vol.2, p.246.
88 Bunbury (ed.), *Lee Papers*, vol.2, p.236.
89 Moultrie, *Memoirs*, vol.1, p.186; FHS: Clark Diary, 21 Aug. 1776.

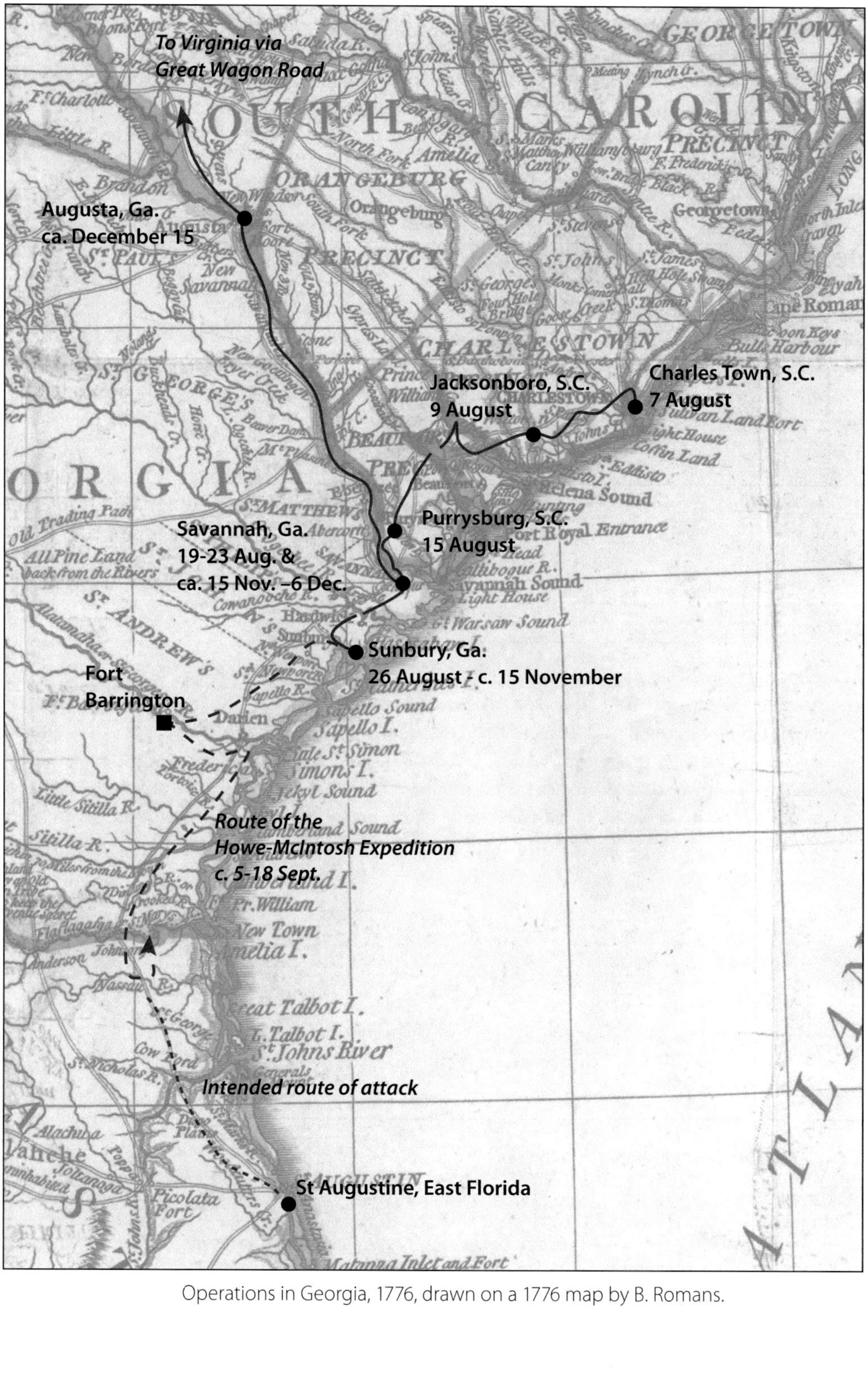

Operations in Georgia, 1776, drawn on a 1776 map by B. Romans.

> Colonel Mughlenburg's Regiment to be supplied with two flints per man from the Stores – Capt. Harden's Company to furnish themselves immediately with skins for Monkeshins [moccasins] and leggings – powder horns and shot bags. Those who have not arms shall be furnish'd at Sunbury to which place they and Muhlenburg's are to march to-morrow morning.[90]

The leather was easy to come by in Savannah, which was a leading centre for the export of deerskins.[91] The Virginians, too, must have been desperate for footwear after marching 600 miles. William Harden, mentioned in the order, was a South Carolina artillery captain whose men were there without their cannons. Lee 'accidentally' took the whole company, in violation of the limit set by Congress.[92]

Muhlenberg and Harden were ordered to parade their men 'at half past five in the rear of the Garden Battery.'[93] As ordered, they lined up at the site of the former Trustees Garden, where the unimpressive walls of Fort Halifax remained from the French and Indian War.[94] The men were reviewed by Lee and Howe, but it began to rain and they waited a day for the sky to clear.[95] Lee stayed in Savannah until 9 September, doing his best to organise Georgia's defences. He was then recalled by Congress to support the defence of New York City, where the British had just arrived with a huge force.[96] Captain Croghan and the 1st Virginia were marching north to respond to the same emergency.

Sunbury

When the skies cleared on 23 August, Muhlenberg's men 'marched from Savana for Florada' and made camp the first night just five miles from the Georgia capital. The next day, they crossed the Ogeechee River and camped in the woods after an 11-mile march. They made good time the next day, covering 25 miles. On 26 August, the moccasin-shod force reached the southernmost town of any importance in the rebellious colonies.[97] Sunbury sat on the peninsula between the Newport and Medway rivers, facing the latter. It had a harbour and a population almost as large as Savannah's.[98] Rice plantations extended beyond it for about

90 Bunbury (ed.), *Lee Papers*, vol.2, pp.252–253.
91 Braund, *Deerskins and Duffels*, pp.97–98.
92 Bunbury (ed.), *Lee Papers*, vol.2, pp.232–233, 254.
93 Bunbury (ed.), *Lee Papers*, vol.2, p.253.
94 Allen D. Candler and Clement A. Evans (eds), *Georgia: Comprising Sketches of Counties, Towns, Events, Institutions, and Persons, Arranged in Cyclopedic Form* (Atlanta: State Historical Association, 1906), vol.2, p.60.
95 FHS: Clark Diary, 21–23 Aug. 1776.
96 Bunbury (ed.), *Lee Papers*, vol.2, pp.205–206, 241–250, 258–259.
97 FHS: Clark Diary, 23–26 Aug. 1776; Hugh McCall, *The History of Georgia, Containing Brief Sketches of the Most Remarkable Events, Up To the Present Day* (Savannah: William T. Williams,1816), vol.1, p.96.
98 William Bartram, *Travels Through North and South Carolina, Georgia, East and West Florida, the Cherokee Country, the Extensive Territory of the Muscogulges or Creek Confederacy, and the Country of the Choctaws* (1791; reprinted London: J. Johnson, 1792), p.5; Daniel T. Elliott, *Sunbury Battlefield Survey*, LAMAR Institute Publication Series, Report Number 64 (Box Springs, Ga.: The LAMAR Institute, 2005), p.2.

40 miles to the Altamaha River. After that, there was nothing but unsettled wilderness all the way to Florida.[99]

The officers found accommodations for themselves while the enlisted men bivouacked in the open for the time being.[100] On the first of September, Major Campbell and Adjutant Swaine got into a fight with Major John White of the 2nd North Carolina. The settlement between Colonels Muhlenberg and Sumner over seniority had apparently left Sumner's subordinates unhappy.[101] Lee had scolded White for a similar argument in Charles Town.[102] 'Majr. White, Cap. Campbell & Mr. Swaine had a dispute,' Jonathan Clark wrote in his diary, and they were 'all arrested.'[103] There is no record of a resolution.

Brigadier General Howe arrived two days after the fight and was unhappy to see soldiers dismantling fences and other structures for firewood. 'Every soldier to consider himself as ordained to protect the Inhabitants of every American state,' he ordered, 'and if, contrary to this Intention, he should offer Insult to the persons or injure the property of any individual he may depend upon being punished with the greatest severity.'[104]

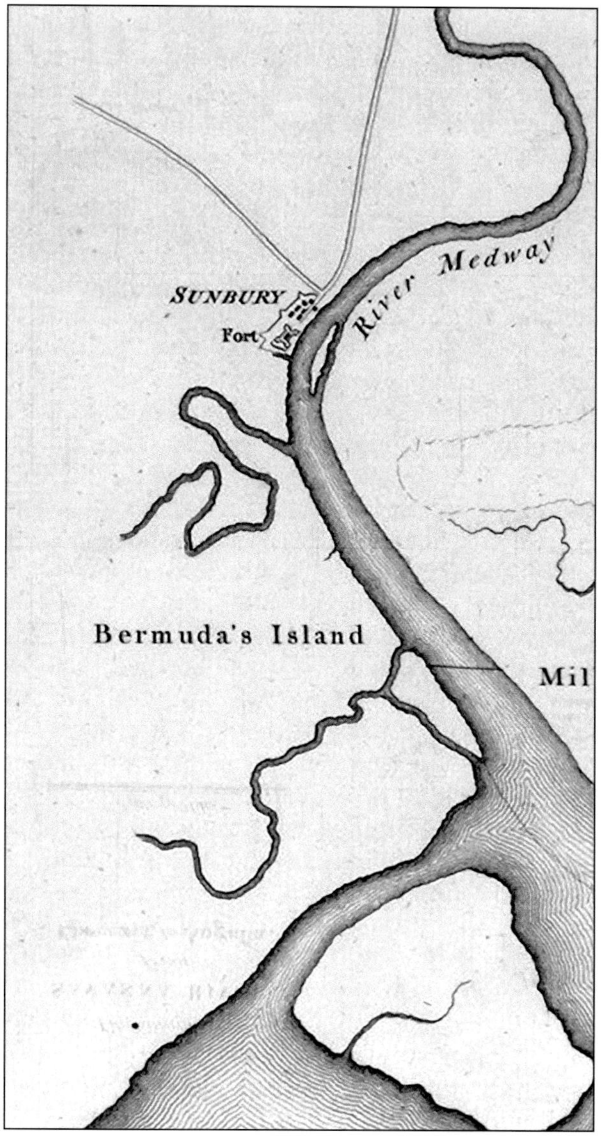

Detail from a 1780 British map of Georgia shows the location of Sunbury on the Medway River. Fort Morris, which is depicted, was not yet built when the 8th Virginia was posted there. (Library of Congress)

99 Bartram, *Travels Through North and South Carolina*, pp.16–17.
100 FHS: Clark Diary, 26 Aug.–4 Sept. 1776; WLCL: Howe Orderly Book, pp.23–24.
101 WLCL: Howe Orderly Book, p.19.
102 Bunbury (ed.), *Lee Papers*, vol.2, p.196.
103 FHS, Clark Diary, 1 Sept. 1776.
104 WLCL: Howe Orderly Book, pp.22–23.

The 8th Virginia was now divided in three: 120 men were with Captain Croghan in the north, 150 were sick in Charles Town, and about 300 were in Sunbury. The balance of the roster formed an uneven trail of sick men stretching almost a thousand miles from Sunbury to New York. The Sunbury contingent had been the healthier ones when they left South Carolina, but now illness began to overcome them as well. When Clark's symptoms returned on 3 September, he fell into 'a violent fever.' He recorded himself sick every day for the next three months and barely moved until November.[105] Henry Wysor of Captain Berry's Company had marched south with a broken arm and was now likewise 'taken sick and lay near three months.'[106] Sergeant Rees Bowen of the same company was the first man at Sunbury to die. Another of Berry's men, Isaac Dunn, remembered that he 'frequently visited' Bowen during his illness 'and after his death assisted in burying him.'[107] Many more sick men followed Bowen into the ground. Robert Howe, insisting that 'cleanliness is essential to the Health of the soldiers' ordered that the barracks be swept and cleaned out every day.[108] It made no difference. According to Colonel Moultrie, 'The troops that went to Georgia, suffered exceedingly by sickness; at Sunberry, 14 or 15 were buried every day.'[109]

A 15-day silence in Howe's orderly book is preceded by a 4 September order: 'The detachment of Volunteers under the command of Major White are immediately to get in readiness to go on command.' During those two weeks, a force composed mostly or entirely of North Carolinians headed for Florida, led by Brigadier General Howe and Major White.[110] One of White's men recalled that the Patriots marched to Fort Barrington on the Altamaha, where they joined up with the 1st Georgia Regiment. Howe evidently stayed at the fort while Colonel McIntosh took command of the expedition.[111] A North Carolinian remembered that when they reached Florida, 'the British had already landed and were receiving reinforcements dayly from the Indians, and the Americans thought it inexpedient to attack the enemy and therefore concluded it would be better to retreat back to Savannah.'[112] There is no evidence of 8th Virginia men participating in this foray. The reason is clear in McIntosh's description of the Virginians in a 7 October report. 'Colo. Muhlenburgh and his Corps,' he wrote, 'are ... very uneasy to return home as they have so few men left and are all sick.'[113]

Purging the Irish

After leaving Savannah, Lee stopped in Charles Town and implemented a plan he had first called for in the spring. He allowed the officers of the South Carolina and Georgia battalions

105 FHS: Clark Diary, 3 Sept.–28 Dec. 1776
106 NARA: H. Wysor pension.
107 LVA: Revolutionary War Bounty Land Claims, Rees Bowen.
108 WLCL: Howe Orderly Book, pp.23–24.
109 Moultrie, *Memoirs*, vol.1, p.186.
110 Chase et al (eds), *Papers of Washington* (Revolution), vol.10, pp.190–191
111 NARA: M804, W4502, Thomas Ragains pension (2nd N.C.)
112 NARA: M804, W11223, James Harris pension. See also S10748, Thomas Glaze pension (6th S.C.) and W10589 Absalom Candel pension (1st N.C.)
113 Lilla M. Hawes (ed.), *The Papers of Lachlan McIntosh, 1774–1779* (Savannah: Georgia Historical Society, 1957), p.14.

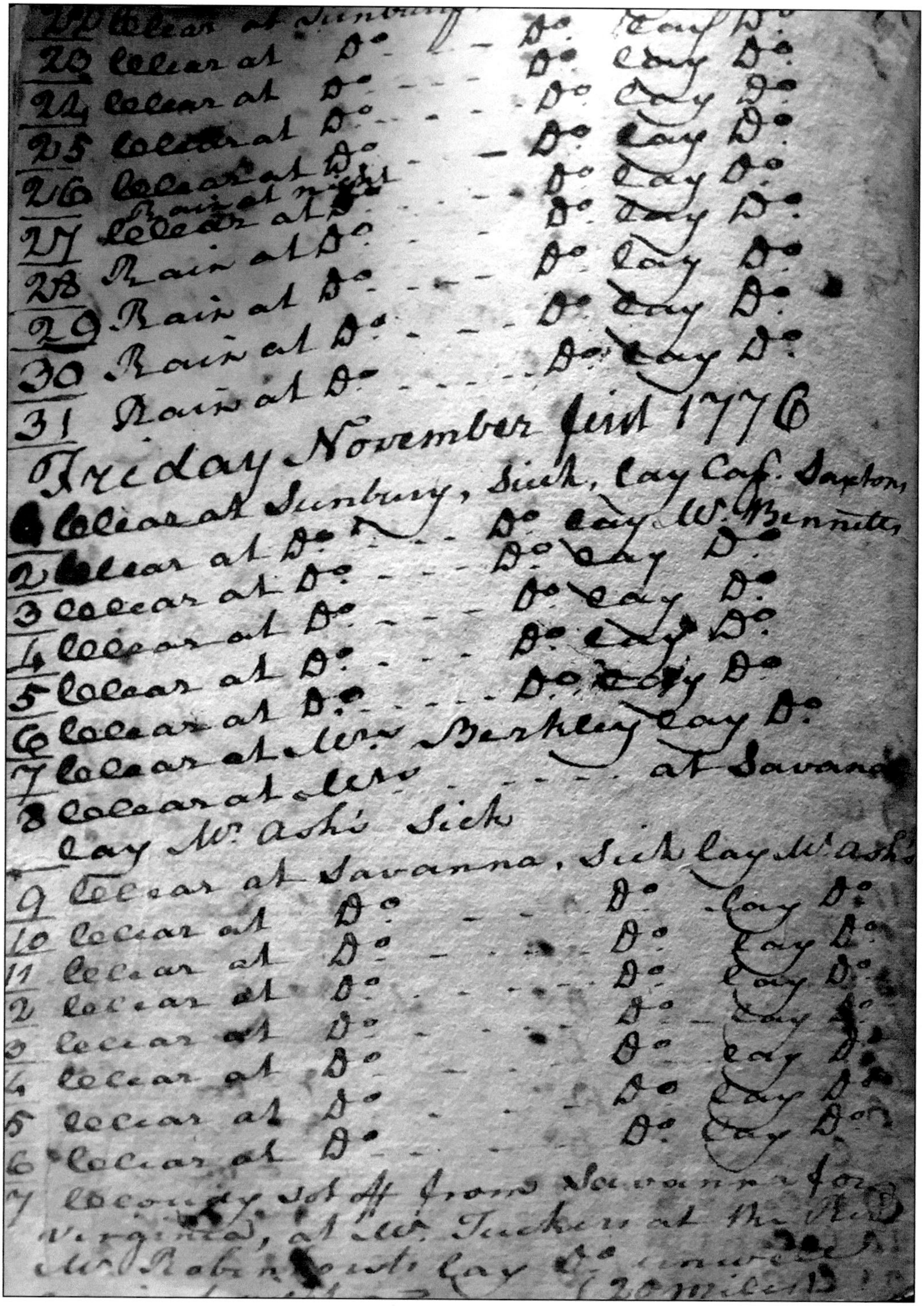

22 Clear at Sunbury - - Do lay Do
23 Clear at Do - - - Do lay Do
24 Clear at Do - - - Do lay Do
25 Clear at Do - - - Do lay Do
26 Clear at Do Rain at night - - Do lay Do
27 Clear at Do - - - Do lay Do
28 Rain at Do - - - Do lay Do
29 Rain at Do - - - Do lay Do
30 Rain at Do - - - Do lay Do
31 Rain at Do
Friday November first 1776
Clear at Sunbury, Sick, lay Capt. Saxton
1 Clear at Do - - Do lay Mr. Bennetts
2 Clear at Do - - - Do lay Do
3 Clear at Do - - - Do lay Do
4 Clear at Do - - - Do lay Do
5 Clear at Do - - - Do lay Do
6 Clear at Do - - - Do lay Do
7 Clear at Mrs. Berkley lay Do
8 Clear at Mrs - - - at Savanna
lay Mr. Ash's Sick
Clear at Savanna, Sick lay Mr. Ash's
9 Clear at Do - - - Do lay Do
10 Clear at Do - - - Do lay Do
11 Clear at Do - - - Do lay Do
12 Clear at Do - - - Do lay Do
13 Clear at Do - - - Do lay Do
14 Clear at Do - - - Do lay Do
15 Clear at Do - - - Do lay Do
16 Clear at Do
17 Cloudy set off from Savanna for Virginia, at Mr. Tucker's at the [illegible] Mr. Robinson's lay Do [illegible] (20 miles)

Jonathan Clark recorded himself sick every day for three months. (The Filson Historical Society, Louisville, KY) 'to engage into the service of their respective regiments, any soldiers or non-commissioned officers of the regiments of Virginia and North Carolina' as long as accounts were settled first.[114] As 1st Lieutenant Rinker remembered, 'the officers of some of the regiments which were to be raised in the Southern States got permission to enlist men of the said Eighth Regiment.'[115]

Lee had predicted Irish soldiers would accept the offer 'in crowds', but from September to November, only 30 of the 150 8th Virginia men in Charles Town took the offer. Isaac and Elias Bridgewater left Captain Darke's Company to join William Thomson's 3rd South Carolina Rangers.[116] Thomson's regiment was familiar from Sullivan's Island. Collin Mitchum left Captain Campbell's Company 'on the information being given to the Soldiers that they might return home [for continued service in the 8th Virginia] or enlist in the South Carolina service under Captain Thomas Jarvey of the 5th Regiment of riflemen.'[117] Duncan Graham likewise left Captain Westfall's Company for 'Colo Isaac Hugers Redgiment under Capt Thomas Jarvey for during the war.' His service in South Carolina continued until 1782 when, while out in the backcountry with the 'Swamp Fox' (Brigadier General Francis Marion), he 'was surprised by the enemy and he received a large wound on the back of the left hand and two on the head.' He lost three of his fingers, and he was discharged.[118]

Robert Howe. (Benson J. Lossing, *Pictorial Field Book of the Revolution* (New York: Harper & Bros, 1855))

114 Elliott, 'Diary', p.243
115 LVA: C. Mitcham petition.
116 NARA: M881, r.882, Elias Bridgewater, Isaac Bridgwater, r.1040, Elias Bridgwater, Isaac Bridgwater
117 NARA: M804, S38215, Collin Mitchum pension.
118 NARA: D. Graham pension.

Transfers to South Carolina Line, Autumn, 1776[119]

Elias Bridgewater (Darke)	3rd South Carolina
Isaac Bridgewater (Darke)	3rd South Carolina
John Casa (Darke)	'South Service'
John Connely (Darke)	'South Service'
Isaac Colton (Berry)	South Carolina
William Elice (Darke)	'South Service'
William Gillihan (Knox)	5th South Carolina
Duncan Grimes (Westfall)	5th South Carolina
John Graham (Westfall)	5th South Carolina
Stephen Hacket (Darke)	'South Service'
James Hagin (Darke)	'South Service'
John Hogg (Westfall)	South Carolina
David Jackson (Darke)	'South Service'
William Kelsey (Darke)	'South Service'
Herman Keyser (Darke)	'South Service'
William Lard (Westfall)	5th South Carolina
Mich Mahoney (Darke)	'South Service'
Collin Mitchum (Campbell)	South Carolina
Daniel Norris (Clark)	5th South Carolina
Gilbert Norris (Berry)	5th South Carolina
William Price (Westfall)	South Carolina
Joseph Sever (Darke)	'South Service'
James Staunton (Knox)	South Carolina
John Smith (Darke)	'South Service'
George Walker (Clark)	South Carolina
William Wells (Darke)	'South Service'
Joshua Williams (Clark)	South Carolina
Andrew Winebranor (Clark)	South Carolina
James Work (Westfall)	South Carolina
William Wright (Knox)	South Carolina

'South Service' transfers may include transfers to Georgia Line.

Lee departed for New York and left Brigadier General Armstrong in command at Charles Town. Armstrong was sick, however, and returned home to Pennsylvania as soon as he heard Robert Howe was coming back from Georgia.[120] The day before Howe's arrival, the South Carolina General Assembly finally 'acquiesced' to Congress's resolution taking its six provincial regiments into the Continental Army.[121]

119 NARA: Revolutionary War Rolls.
120 Bennett and Lennon, *Quest for Glory*, pp.49–50.
121 Moultrie, *Memoirs*, vol.2, p.187; WLCL: Howe Orderly Book, pp.26–27.

The malarial season continued into October, and in Charles Town, Howe once again tried to combat it with cleanliness. Lack of food was the primary complaint of the sick soldiers, and the cause of their hunger was simple callousness. Howe ordered, 'Compassion and Public Good exact of all persons the greatest attention to sick soldiers, who devote their Lives to the service of the Common Cause.' Distressed that a cold-hearted attitude persisted, he reiterated his order a few days later: 'Complaint having again been made from the Hospital that the sick are not serv'd as they ought to be with Bread, Gen'l Howe positively orders the Commissary to inspect into this matter and prevent any farther Cause of complaint.' He took the unusual step of having the order written out and carried to the commissary so the men responsible could not plead ignorance.[122]

Captain David Stephenson's second lieutenant was one of several sick soldiers at Charles Town who never made it home. John Grattan, the officer who lost his fancy rifle on the way to Williamsburg, was born in Ireland and came to America with his parents in the late 1750s. His parents had money, and his father built mills in the Shenandoah Valley that employed many of their 'Dutch' neighbours. John ran his father's general store in Botetourt County until he returned to Augusta County to earn his commission.[123] A generation later, a nephew confessed he knew little about him. 'He died in Charleston, S.C. before I was born. My dear mother loved him with all a sister's heart, and ever spoke of him as her dear brother and friend, whose affection, advice and support she so much missed and needed.'[124]

122 WLCL: Howe Orderly Book, pp.26, 28.

123 John T. Foster and Sarah Whitmer Foster, *Contentment and the Pursuit of Ambition: the Grattans and Their Remarkable Women* (Tallahassee: Rose Digital Publishing, 2011), p.7.

124 VMHC: Rare Books Collection, CT275.G77 G14, John G. Gamble, 'Reminiscences of Major John Grattan as compiled from brief notes found among the papers of his grand-son, Col. John G. Gamble.'

7

Winter

Croghan's detachment was pounded by rain as they marched from Dumfries, Virginia to the crossing of the Occoquan River at Colchester. It was almost September, and the men may already have begun to wonder what winter was like in the northern states. Sergeant McCarty spent much of the journey tending to wagons and sick soldiers.[1] The column reached Alexandria, Virginia, on the kind of 'fine and cool' morning that often follows a day of hard rain. They were making good time but losing men along the way. Twenty-eight sick men were left with James Higgins in Williamsburg at the start,[2] two more were left in Fredericksburg, and 22 were about to be left in Alexandria.[3] Illness and injury continued to whittle away at their numbers until only seven remained on a critical day in January.[4]

McCarty was ordered to go from camp to Alexandria to retrieve a soldier who had been put in jail. After a court-martial, the men were assembled to watch the offender receive the maximum 39 lashes permitted under the Articles of War.[5] Though harsh to modern sensibilities, Congress actually increased what Charles Lee described as 'but a light breakfast' to 100 lashes just a few weeks later.[6]

After several days camped outside Alexandria, the men struck their tents and marched to the Belhaven docks south of town. From there, they took boats up the Potomac River to George Town, Maryland. Most of the journey from Williamsburg followed the King's Highway, a 1,300-mile postal road Charles II ordered cut to connect Charles Town to Boston. They continued on the century-old route, camping next at Bladensburg, Maryland where they spent an extra day taking a size roll of the men and watching another flogging.[7]

From Baltimore most of the men took boats up the Chesapeake Bay to Head of Elk (Elkton) near the mouth of the Susquehanna River. Sergeant McCarty was ill but took a dozen men and drove the detachment's wagons by land.[8] They continued to Wilmington, Delaware and

1 WHS: Draper Mss, N, vol.2, p.89.
2 NARA: M246, f.364, p.61, Return of the Virginia Brigade, 14 Oct. 1776.
3 WHS: Draper Mss, N, vol.2, pp.19, 20, 21, 23.
4 Robert A. Selig, Matthew Harris and Wade P. Catts, *Battle of Princeton Mapping Project: Report of Military Terrain Analysis and Battle Narrative* (West Chester, Pa.: John Milner Associates, 2010), sec.4, p.39
5 WHS: McCarty Notebook, 28 Aug. 1776; Ford (ed.), *Journals of Congress*, vol.2, p.119.
6 Bunbury (ed.), *Lee Papers*, vol.2, pp.10–11; Ford (ed.), *Journals of Congress*, vol.5, p.806.
7 WHS: McCarty Notebook, 3 Sept. 1776.
8 WHS: McCarty Notebook, 3–10 Sept. 1776.

An abandoned stretch of the King's Highway at Colchester Va., where Croghan's men crossed the Occoquan River. (Author's photo)

took a ship up the Delaware River to Philadelphia. As they approached America's largest city, they saw several merchant ships and a fort under construction on the aptly-named Mud Island.[9] They stopped for the night, but the men were required to stay on board. Instead, Sergeant McCarty made several beer runs for them. In the morning, they sailed for Trenton, New Jersey 'happy in liquor.'[10]

The Route from Williamsburg to Fort Constitution

16 Aug: Depart Williamsburg, Va.
ca. 21 Aug: Fredericksburg, Va.
23 Aug: Falmouth, Va.
26 Aug: Dumfries and Colchester, Va.
27 Aug to 2 Sept: Alexandria, Va.
2 Sept: Georgetown, Md.
3 Sept: Bladensburg, Md.

9 WHS: McCarty Notebook, 11–13 Sept. 1776; G. D. Scull (ed.), *The Montresor Journals* (New York: New York Historical Society, 1882), pp.414–417.

10 WHS: McCarty Notebook, 13–14 Sept. 1776.

4 Sept: Snowden's Furnace, Md.
5 Sept: Baltimore, Md.
6 Sept: Chesapeake Bay to Head of Elk, Md.
7 Sept: Wagons to Lawson Works, Md.
9 Sept: Wagons cross Susquehanna River
10 Sept: Wagons to Head of Elk, Md.
11 Sept: Newport and Wilmington, Del.
12 Sept: Delaware River to Philadelphia, Pa.
13 Sept: Delaware River to Trenton, N.J.
17 Sept: Depart Trenton to Princeton and Brunswick, N.J.
18 Sept: Raritan River
19 Sept: Elizabethtown and Newark, N.J.
21 Sept: Passaic River
22 Sept: Arrive Fort Constitution, N.J.[11]
(Approximately 510 miles)

They took a three-day break at Trenton, during which they heard the faint sound of cannons far off to the north. Colonel Weedon's 3rd Virginia Regiment participated in the Battle of Harlem Heights that day, approximately 70 miles away. 'We heard the English guns to play,' McCarty jotted optimistically into his notebook, 'but they might expect no success from their play.'

Croghan's men continued marching on the King's Highway through Princeton to Brunswick (New Brunswick), where four more men were flogged. As they approached the place of their intended rendezvous with Hugh Mercer and the Flying Camp, new orders came to proceed directly to the main camps on the Hudson River. They passed through Elizabethtown (Elizabeth) to Newark, where they spent two days preparing to join General Washington. They bought camp kettles. The detachment was divided by lots into musketeers and riflemen. 'They drew lots and mine was for to be a musqueteer,' wrote McCarty, 'but I kept my rifle.' One of the men who had been whipped two days earlier was flogged again for drunkenness.[12]

The Situation at New York

American confidence was riding high. The southern states had won important victories at Moore's Creek Bridge, Great Bridge, Sullivan's Island, and Gwynn's Island. In the north, following Lexington and Concord, Bunker Hill, and the capture of Fort Ticonderoga, British troops were forced to evacuate Boston when cannons taken from the latter fort appeared on Dorchester Heights. Thomas Gage was gone, and Britain had a new commander in chief for its North American forces: General William Howe. He was not related to North Carolina's Robert Howe. Washington correctly predicted that New York was Howe's first target.

11 WHS: McCarty Notebook.
12 WHS: McCarty Notebook, 16–20 Sept. 1776.

Charles Lee had spent a month preparing the city's defences before his journey south.[13] William Alexander, a general from New Jersey recognised in Scotland but not in London as the Earl of Stirling,[14] took over the project.[15] Forts were built at Brooklyn Heights (Fort Stirling), at Harlem Heights (Fort Washington), and atop the Hudson Palisades in New Jersey (Fort Constitution). Despite the prior victories and the time spent fortifying New York, the following months went badly for the Americans.

The massive British fleet that began arriving in New York's harbour on 1 July brought a stunning 33,000 British and German soldiers to crush the rebellion.[16] Most of these red- and blue-coated men landed on Staten Island. It was then that the 1st and 3rd Virginia regiments were called north in response, with more Virginians to follow. Before either regiment arrived, Howe sent his men across the bay to Long Island, flanked the Americans, captured Lord Stirling, and cornered the rebel army on Brooklyn Heights. Under the cover of a providential fog, the Americans escaped by water to Manhattan. It was quickly apparent that despite months of preparation, Manhattan simply could not be defended. The Royal Navy sailed up the East River and began blasting iron balls into the city. Washington's men ran from an amphibious landing at Kip's Bay but regrouped on Harlem Heights and succeeded in fending off a British advance by land. In this first action for the 3rd Virginia, Weedon lost his senior captain and acting major.[17] Facing grave danger, the American generals were discussing a complete evacuation of Manhattan when Croghan's frontiersmen arrived at Fort Constitution.

George Washington and the Main Army

The junction with Washington's army was not something a Virginia officer wanted to miss. Colonel Read and Captain Croghan were present and reported healthy when the 1st Virginia arrived.[18] In the morning of Sunday, 22 September, the 1st Virginia and its attached men from the 8th Virginia broke camp, took a ferry over the Hackensack River, and marched to the American camp on the Palisades. The tents and campfires of nearly 1,600 men covered the high ground along the Hudson River overlooking upper Manhattan.[19] Fort Constitution sat just beyond the camp and about 1,500 feet from the cliffs. Colonel Read halted his wide-eyed boys short of the fort and went to find the man in charge, Major General Nathanael Greene. The sun was dipping low when he returned, and they marched back to the encampment and pitched their tents.[20]

13 Bunbury (ed.), *Lee Papers*, vol.1, pp.271–272, 308–310, 350, 354–357; Paul David Nelson, *The Life of William Alexander, Lord Stirling* (Tuscaloosa: University of Alabama Press, 1987), p.71.

14 Nelson, *Stirling*, pp.38–40.

15 Nelson, *Lord Stirling*, p.73.

16 David Hackett Fischer, *Washington's Crossing* (Oxford: Oxford University Press, 2004), p.33.

17 *Virginia Gazette* (Purdie) 4 Oct. 1776, 18 Oct. 1776.

18 NARA: M246, f.1, p.93, muster of 1st Va. Rgt, 30 Sept. 1776.

19 Charles H. Lesser (ed.), *The Sinews of Independence: Monthly Strength Reports of the Continental Army* (Chicago: University of Chicago Press, 1976), p.33.

20 WHS: McCarty Notebook, 22 Sept. 1776.

They enjoyed themselves for a couple of days. Each man received a gill of rum, a pound of flour, a pound of beef, and his pay. Sergeant McCarty walked up to see the fort on Monday. He noted on Tuesday that 'our men drunk very hard as they had plenty of money.' The fun ended on Wednesday when they heard the boom of British cannons in the river below. 'The force,' McCarty wrote, 'heard the cannon fire very brisk from the shipping of the English, and we could see them land. We could easy see their camps and every turn they would make.'[21] It was not the start of a battle they were watching, but it was a sign that the lull following the success at Harlem Heights was ending.

The bulk of Washington's army was on the other side of the river, some at Fort Washington near the northern end of Manhattan and many more above the south slope of Harlem Heights, where the American line stretched across the narrow northern part of the island. Croghan's men and the 1st Virginia crossed the river to Fort Washington and were put together with Colonel Weedon's 3rd Virginia as an ad hoc brigade under Weedon's command as the senior colonel.[22]

The 1st Virginia Regiment, 14 October 1776[23]

<table>
<tr><td colspan="3">Field Officers:
Col. Isaac Read
Lt. Col. Frank Eppes*
Maj. John Green</td><td colspan="2">Staff Officers:
Adjutant Joseph Scott
Surgeon
Surgeon's Mate
Quartermaster</td></tr>
<tr><td>Captains</td><td>1st Lieutenants</td><td>2nd Lieutenants</td><td>Ensigns</td><td>Enlisted Men</td></tr>
<tr><td>John Sayres
William Davies*
John Fleming
Robert Ballard
George Gibson§
Thomas Nelson*
Edmund Dickinson
Richard Taylor
William Croghan*
William Cunningham</td><td>Goodrich Crump
William Lewis
Edward Garland*
Alexander Cummings*
William Lynn*
John Moss
Abraham Kirkpatrick
Daniel Culp</td><td>John Eustace*
Joseph Scott†
John Clayton*
Matthew Smith
John Pettus
Joseph Godwin
David Thompson
James Higgins*
Edward Moody
Claiborne Lawson*</td><td>Tarlton Woodson
Nathaniel Burwell
Tarlton Payne*
Ballard Smith
James Berwick
Thomas Blackwell*
(3 more not identified)</td><td>30 sergeants
13 drum and fife
274 fit for duty
76 sick, present
87 sick, absent
22 on command
32 on furlough
Total rank and file: 516</td></tr>
<tr><td colspan="5">Based on 14 October muster roll with additional information added. Seniority within ranks is uncertain in some cases. Previous captains include John Green and John Markham. †Adjutant and brother of Brig. Gen. Charles Scott. §Company raised in West Augusta, on mission to New Orleans for gunpowder.</td></tr>
</table>

The Evacuation of Manhattan

Over the next two weeks, the British methodically encircled Manhattan. Their ships passed through the narrow, treacherous Hell Gate channel in the East River into Long Island Sound.[24]

21 WHS: McCarty Notebook, 23–25 Sept. 1776.
22 Chase et al (eds), *Papers of Washington* (Revolution), vol.6, pp.469–471.
23 NARA: M246, f.1, p.91, f.6, p. 2, f.9, p.2., f.18, p.2; f.364, p.61; M. Lee Minnis, *The First Virginia Regiment of Foot: 1775-1783* (Westminster: Willow Bend Books, 1998), pp.133–147, 173, 241, 295, 391.
24 Clark et al (eds), *Naval Documents*, vol.6, pp.1199–1200.

Warships in the lower Hudson peppered the American encampments with grapeshot and a few high-arcing bombs.[25] Forts Washington and Constitution were built to keep the British out of the Hudson, but they had yet to be tested. Jonathan Grant remembered that on 9 October, 'two of the British Vessels came up the river [and] got past our Shivaurdefreeses.'[26] The *chevaux de frise* were spiked obstructions placed in the water between the forts. An American deserter told the British how to get past them. American cannons pounded away, killing 27 British sailors, but the ships made it through.[27] On 12 October, 2,000 British soldiers in flatboats made their way through Hell Gate to Throg's Neck on the mainland below the border of Connecticut. Washington's 30,000-man army, the largest he would ever command, was on the verge of being trapped on the island.[28] 'Immediately,' remembered Grant, 'our ragement (first ragement) [and] some others was ordered to Martch to the white plains.'[29]

Then Superman came to save the day. 'Gen. Lee arrived to the universal Satisfaction of the Camp,' wrote a New Jersey chaplain.[30] Fort Constitution was rechristened in his honour. Before Sullivan's Island, Lee was regarded as a very competent, professionally trained officer. Now, he was an absolute celebrity.

Lee struggled to rise to the rank of lieutenant colonel in the British Army, but the King of Poland and the Continental Congress both made him a major general. After Sullivan's Island, his reputation grew to oddly quantifiable superhuman proportions. In June, William Moultrie and others at Charles Town had thought Lee's mere appearance 'equal to a reinforcement of 1000 men.'[31] When he travelled through Philadelphia four months later, his presence was declared to be equal to *ten thousand* men.[32] When he passed through Perth Amboy, the Hessians on Staten Island packed up and disappeared in the night, 'perhaps occasioned,' mused Colonel Samuel Patterson, 'by General Lee's arrival here last evening.' Realising he was ascribing almost supernatural powers to the man, Patterson added, 'This I leave to the world's wise conjectures, as many such prophecies have lately been.'[33]

While Lee had presided over an important victory in South Carolina, General Washington had lost a much larger battle on Long Island and was about to retreat once more. Both Congress and the officer corps were fully aware of their contrasting records.

When Washington convened his 15 generals, all but one said they should evacuate the island.[34] At the same time, a complete withdrawal meant abandoning Fort Washington, which they were loath to do. Intense effort had gone into its construction and leaving it

25 Henry Hobart Bellas (ed.), *Personal Recollections of Captain Enoch Anderson, an Officer of the Delaware Regiments in the Revolutionary War* (Wilmington: Historical Society of Delaware, 1896), p.24.

26 NARA: J. Grant pension.

27 Clark et al (eds), *Naval Documents*, vol.6, pp.1182–1183.

28 Force (ed.), *American Archives*, ser.5, vol.3, pp.921–922; Lesser (ed.), *Sinews*, p.33.

29 NARA: J. Grant pension.

30 Liz Tait (ed.), 'The Revolutionary War Diary of Chaplain Andrew Hunter, New Jersey Brigade, Continental Army,' *RevWar '75*, <revwar75.com/library/bob/Hunter17762.htm>, 14 Oct. 1776, accessed 3 June 2023.

31 Moultrie, *Memoirs*, p.141.

32 John Richard Alden, *General Charles Lee: Traitor or Patriot?* (Baton Rouge: Louisiana State University Press, 1951), p.138. Emphasis added.

33 William Thompson Read (ed.), *Life and Correspondence of George Read, A Signer of the Declaration of Independence with Notices of Some of His Contemporaries* (Philadelphia: J.B. Lippincott, 1870), pp.202.

34 Force (ed.), *American Archives*, ser.5, vol.2, pp.1117–1118, vol.3, pp. 471.

would permit British warships unfettered access to the Hudson, which was navigable as far north as Albany. At Nathanael Greene's urging, Washington instructed the fort's commander to hold his post 'as long as a good Officer ought to do.'[35] Greene was 'positive' that if Fort Washington could not be held, American guns at Fort Lee could cover an evacuation across the Hudson.[36] He was wrong.

Stirling's Brigade

On paper, there was a full chain of command above Captain Croghan's detached men. Over the coming months, however, only Major Green, a captain named John Fleming, and their own 1st Lieutenant Abraham Kirkpatrick provided any real continuity of command. The 1st Virginia's Colonel Read was with them only briefly, Lieutenant Colonel Eppes never joined, and Captain Croghan's illness took him out of service for the rest of the year.[37]

When Lord Stirling was released in a prisoner exchange, Washington put the Virginians under his command. The Scottish earl's brigade included the Virginians, Colonel John Haslet's Delaware Regiment, the two battalions of Colonel Samuel Miles' Pennsylvania State Rifle Regiment (commanded by Major Ennion Williams and Major John Patton), and two Pennsylvania Flying Camp battalions (from Berks and Lancaster counties).[38] The Pennsylvania riflemen were state regulars who had fought on Long Island. Miles was a prisoner and Lieutenant Colonel Daniel Brodhead, nominally in command, was sick.[39] Except for the Flying Camp men, this brigade stayed together into January and shared some of the most important service of the war.

Stirling marched his new brigade, supported by New Jersey militia, across King's Bridge as far as Mile Square, a settlement on the west bank of the Bronx River. From there, they followed the river north toward White Plains. They stayed on the river's west side for protection, but it was fordable in many places.[40] Two or three days into the march, Lieutenant Kirkpatrick bedded down with a blanket on the high ground overlooking a little village called Tuckahoe. He may have smiled for a moment when he heard its name. In Virginia, 'Tuckahoe' was slang for a member of the wealthy, eastern elite. His men were definitely 'Cohees', men who might today be called 'rednecks.'[41]

Kirkpatrick had command of Croghan's detachment. Second Lieutenant James Higgins was sick in Williamsburg, but Kirkpatrick had the company's well-educated ensign, James

35 Chase et al (eds), *Papers of Washington* (Revolution), vol.7, pp.3–5.
36 Force (ed.), *American Archives*, ser.5, vol.3, p.740.
37 NARA: M246, f.364, p.61 and f.1, pp.82, 85, 87, 89, 91, 93, 98, 99.
38 Chase et al (eds), *Papers of Washington* (Revolution), vol.6, pp.582–584; Lesser (ed.), *Sinews*, p.37; Francis E. Devine, 'The Pennsylvania Flying Camp, July–November, 1776', *Pennsylvania History*, 46:1 (1979), pp.59–78, 63. The Flying Camp was an attempt at a highly mobile reserve force recruited in the mid-Atlantic states. Their enlistments expired on 1 December.
39 John. B. B. Trussell, Jr., *The Pennsylvania Line: Regimental Organisation and Operations, 1776–1783* (Harrisburg: Pennsylvania Historical and Museum Commission, 1977), p.165.
40 Abbatt (ed.), *Heath Memoirs*, p.83.
41 Catherine Hawes Coleman Seaman, *Tuckahoe and Cohee: The Settlers and Cultures of Amherst and Nelson Counties, 1607–1807* (Sweet Briar, Va.: Sweet Briar College, 1992), pp.1, 135–152.

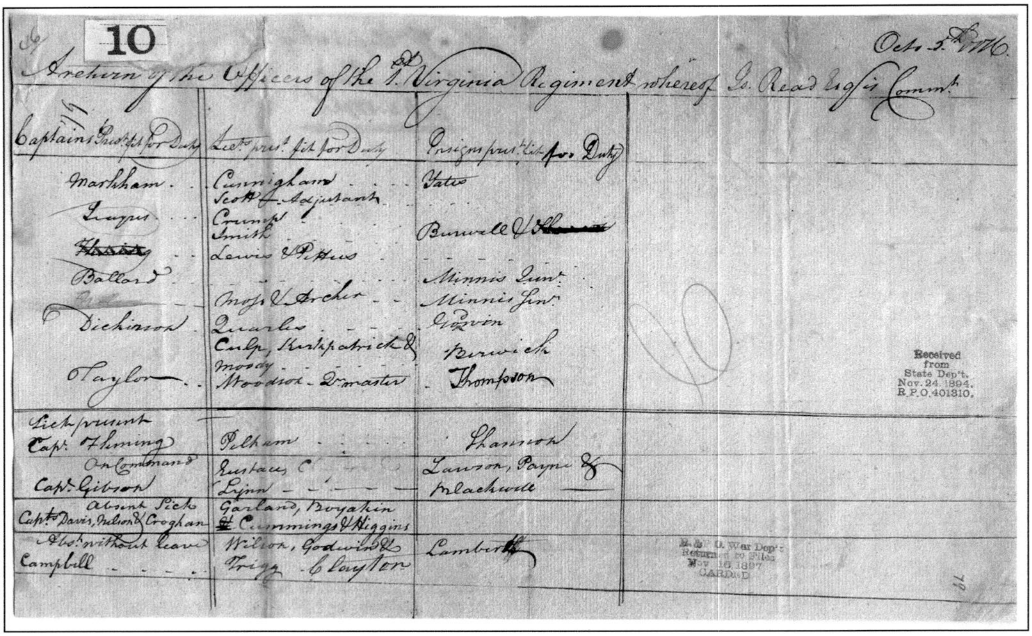

A 5 October 1776 return of 1st Virginia officers shows Captain Croghan and 2nd Lieutenant Higgins sick and absent. First Lieutenant Kirkpatrick and Ensign Berwick are present, as are 1st Lieutenants Culp and Moody of Darke's and Knox's companies. (National Archives)

Berwick, to support him. Stirling's Brigade and the New Jersey militia made up a 2,000-man advance force sent to protect the Army's supply base at White Plains. There was little safety in the number because the bulk of Howe's 33,000 men were coming across West Chester County from Long Island Sound. There was no way to know when or where they would appear, and Kirkpatrick's men were terrified. 'March'd to Tookahoe where we encamped,' wrote a soldier, 'we were obliged to place a large number of out Centries, expecting the Enemy to attack us in the Night – The Anxiety attending such a state is only known to those who experienced it.'[42]

Their orders were to move quickly without their tents and baggage.[43] During the restless night, Colonel Rufus Putnam of Massachusetts rode into camp after conducting a solo reconnaissance mission in disguise. The situation, he reported, was dire. The British were proceeding on the east side of the Bronx River in parallel to Stirling's command. They were only nine miles from White Plains, which was clearly their destination. An advanced body was even closer, at Mamaroneck, where American stores were guarded by just 300 militiamen. Putnam gave his report to Stirling, accepted some food and drink, and galloped off again into the dark.[44]

42 Hunter, *Diary*, 19 Oct. 1776.

43 Chase et al (eds), *Papers of Washington* (Revolution), vol.6, pp.594–595.

44 Rowena Buell (ed.), *The Memoirs of Rufus Putnam and Certain Official Papers and Correspondence* (Boston: Houghton, Mifflin and Co., 1903), pp.61–63.

Stirling's Brigade reached White Plains on 21 October.[45] Behind them, men guarded the fords of the Bronx. These manoeuvres and William Howe's 'stupidity' allowed the rest of Washington's army to reach White Plains in time to dig in on the high ground beyond the village. Colonel Putnam credited the arrival in White Plains to 'an interposing providence,' noting that God's protection was also manifested in the 'Stupidity of the British General' who could have taken the depot the day before with little effort.[46] Had the British taken White Plains before Stirling arrived, the war might have been over.

The Mamaroneck Raid, 22 October 1776

The once-vaunted Robert Rogers, now commanding a Loyalist ranger regiment, captured the small supply depot at Mamaroneck. The village sat on the King's Highway (known locally as the Boston Post Road) near the Connecticut line, facing the Long Island Sound. The experienced partisan pitched camp on Heathcote Hill below the mouth of the Mamaroneck River and took a nearby schoolhouse for his headquarters.[47]

Major Rogers was a hero of the French and Indian War, during which he led a ranger unit on the northern frontier. Bells rang for him when he arrived in Philadelphia in 1760 to recognise his accomplishments. He enjoyed a royal audience during a visit to London. A strong proponent and pioneer of British ranger tactics, he authored two top-selling books about his frontier exploits. Though they were suspicious of his motives, the British command elevated him to lieutenant colonel, and he raised a Loyalist force dubbed the Queen's American Rangers in a few short weeks.[48] In 1776, neither Rogers nor his rangers lived up to the reputation earned 20 years before. However, the Queen's American Rangers did go on to perform important service under Lieutenant Colonel John Graves Simcoe.

Lord Stirling knew the local geography and probably knew Rogers. They had both served under Major General (and Massachusetts governor) William Shirley in the old war.[49] Rogers and his reputation were real threats, and Stirling devised a plan to capture him. He explained the plan to John Haslet and sent him off to execute it with his Delaware Regiment and 150 Virginians. These Virginians included men from Croghan's detachment and the rifle companies of the 1st and 3rd. The Virginians went first, acting as light infantry during the raid.[50]

---

45 Tait (ed.), *Hunter Diary*, 20–21 Oct. 1776; Chase et al (eds), *Papers of Washington* (Revolution), vol.7, pp.3–5; Joseph Lee Boyle (ed.) 'The James McMichael Journal, May 27, 1776-Ocotber 29, 1776', *JAR*, <allthingsliberty.com/2018/02/james-mcmichael-journal-may-27–1776-october-29–1776/>, accessed 7 Oct. 2024, 21 Oct. 1776.; Buell (ed.), *Memoirs of Putnam*, p.63.

46 Buell (ed.), *Memoirs of Putnam*, pp.63–64.

47 William S. Hadaway (ed.), *The McDonald Papers* (White Plains: Westchester County Historical Society, 1926), vol.1, pp.21–22.

48 Scott M. Smith, 'Major Robert Rogers and the America Revolution', *JAR*, 23 Nov. 2021 <allthingsliberty.com/2021/11/major-robert-rogers-and-the-american-revolution>, accessed 18 June 2023.

49 Nelson, *Lord Stirling*, pp.28, 92.

50 NARA: M804, W9625, William B. Rice pension (1st Va.); S16450, Paul Leathers pension (3rd Va.); J. Grant pension; D. Williams pension; Sanchez-Saavedra, *Virginia Military Organisations*, pp.31, 39.

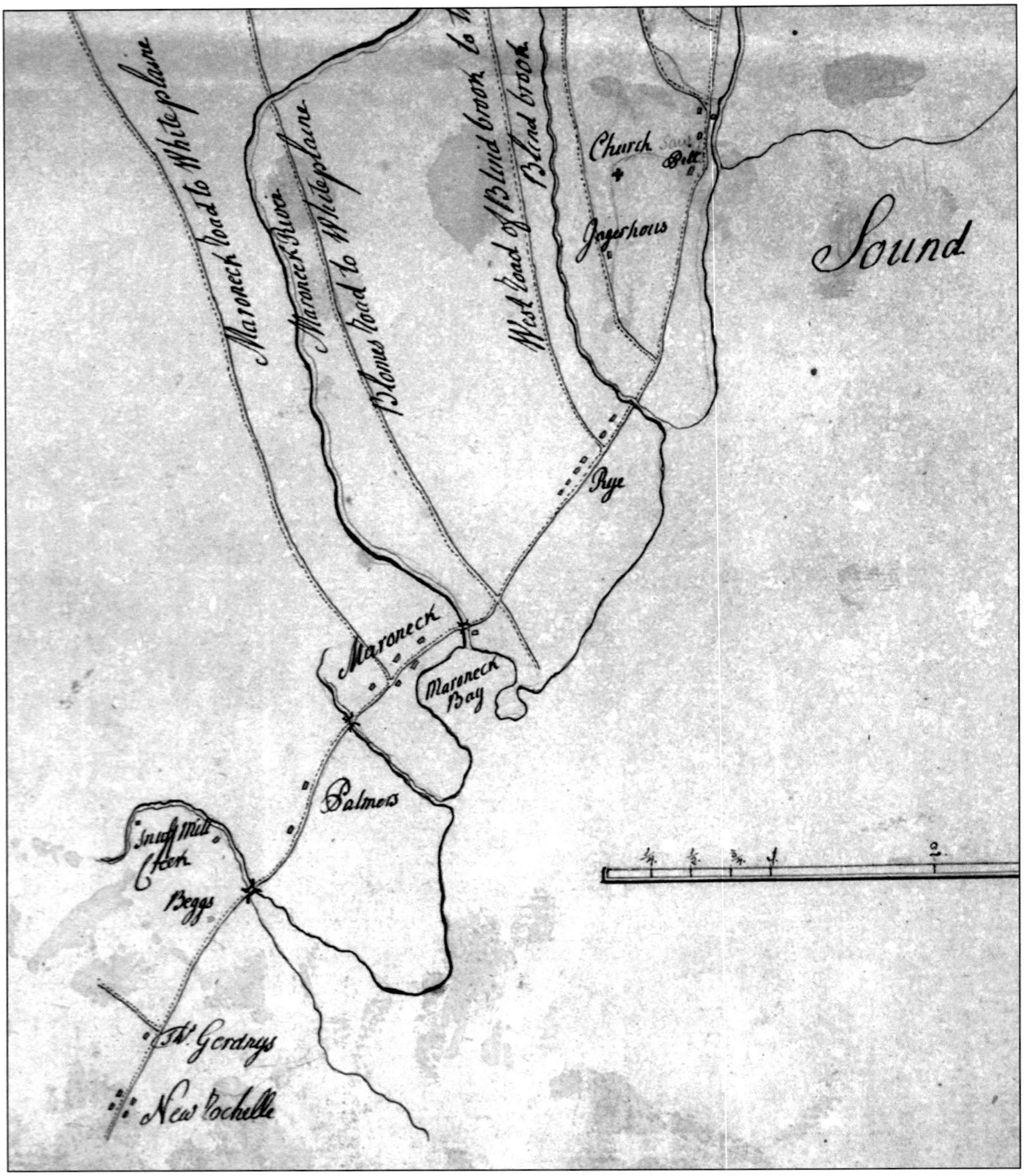

This detail of a 1770 map shows Mamaroneck on the King's Highway between New Rochelle and Rye, N.Y. Two other roads lead to White Plains. (Library of Congress)

Rogers had placed pickets on the roads north and west of Mamaroneck. Haslet and Green, travelling in the dark with guides, carefully approached Heathcote Hill from the south. Intelligence told them that a single Indian warrior was posted as a sentry on that side. The Virginians went forward undetected, with the waters of Mamaroneck Harbor lapping the shore beyond the road to their right. After some searching, they located the Native sentinel

A historical marker in Westchester County, N.Y. marks the site of the Skirmish at Mamaroneck. (Photo: M.A. Kleen)

at about four o'clock. They crept up on him, intent on keeping him from firing his weapon. He fought hard, kicking and struggling until one of the officers silenced him with the thrust of a sword.[51]

Haslet and Green were told to expect no more guards between the Indian and the crest of the hill, but Rogers had decided in the night to move 60 men down the slope toward the sentry's position. The Virginians stumbled on the sleeping Loyalists in the dark. A melee ensued that was made more confusing by the lack of uniforms on Rogers' recently-recruited men. The fight ended when Haslet's Delawareans came up. Thirty-six of Rogers' men were captured; the rest were killed or ran off. Major Green and about 14 other Whigs were wounded. Roberts' camp atop the hill was now up and in arms, so Haslet wisely decided to retreat with what he had in hand: his prisoners, a pair of Rogers' colours, 60 stand of arms, and some blankets.[52]

The raiders' muzzle flashes were visible in the night from the hills at White Plains, seven miles away.[53] When Haslet's party returned to camp, Stirling was delighted with the

51 Hadaway (ed.), *McDonald Papers*, vol.1, p.22.

52 Anon. (ed.), *Delaware Archives: Military and Naval Records* (Wilmington: Public Archives Commission of Delaware, 1911–1916), vol.2, p.1030; *Virginia Gazette* (Purdie), 15 Nov. 1776.

53 Abbatt (ed.), *Heath Memoirs*, pp.84–85.

mission's outcome. The Delaware colonel reported that 'the late worthless Major', Robert Rogers, had 'skulked off in the dark' on the first fire.[54] Some who were in the fight were less effusive. 'Though we were successful, I must confess this the most terrible instance of War I have seen,' wrote one soldier, 'so much is the horror of this terrible business increased by darkness.'[55] Major Green had two holes in him. Balls had pierced his right shoulder and shoulder blade.[56] He returned to duty the following year but could not put on his own coat even a decade later. This meant that all three 1st Virginia field officers were now unfit for duty. The senior captain, John Fleming from Goochland County, took command. Jonathan Grant, identifying Fleming by a rank he never held in life, remembered, 'Major Green was wounded & did not [thereafter] command the s'd ragement while we remained in it. Magor Fleming Commanded in his place.'[57]

The Battle of White Plains, 28 October 1776

Grant also remembered that 'a short time after this engagement' on Heathcote Hill 'we had another in the Plains.'[58] The White Plains straddled the Bronx River below the foothills of the Hudson Highlands. An attractive village of the same name sat near the plains' northern edge, beyond which a cluster of hills offered an imperfect defensive position for the Americans. Washington had no intention of holding the position for long, but he needed to buy time to remove supplies, so they dug in. Evacuating the army from Manhattan was a frustratingly difficult process. Wagons moved slowly and, since there were not enough of them, soldiers were forced to carry heavy gear and 'almost fainted under their Burdens.'[59] The dearth of wagons also meant that large numbers of sick men had to make their way on foot, including more than a dozen 8th Virginia men.[60] Orders came, one Virginian recalled, 'for all the sick, that were able to walk, to make the best of their way in the direction that the baggage went.' The battle was already underway when they got there.

> [He] kept on with the sick, until he arrived at the White Plains, but could not keep so far ahead … The shot from the enemy's artillery frequently passed over his head. When he arrived at the White Plains, he found a few loads of baggage; no provision, or any kind of convenience for the sick: – of consequence, the sick straggled out to the farm houses, and begged.[61]

54 Anon. (ed.), *Delaware Archives*, vol.2, p.1030.

55 Christopher L. Ward, *The Delaware Continentals* (Wilmington: Delaware Historical Society, 1941), p.81.

56 LVA: Revolutionary War Bounty Land Claims, John Green.

57 NARA: J. Grant pension; LVA: Revolutionary War Bounty Land Claims, Thomas Fleming (1st Va.)

58 NARA: J. Grant pension.

59 Benjamin Trumbull, 'Journal of the Campaign at New York, 1776–1777', Anon. (ed.), *Collections of the Connecticut Historical Society* (Hartford: Connecticut Historical Society, 1860–1967), vol.7, pp.175–218, 202.

60 NARA: M246, f.1, pp.82, 85, musters of 1st Va. Rgt, 22 Oct and 5 Nov. 1776.

61 NARA: M804, W1531, John Almy pension (3rd Va.).

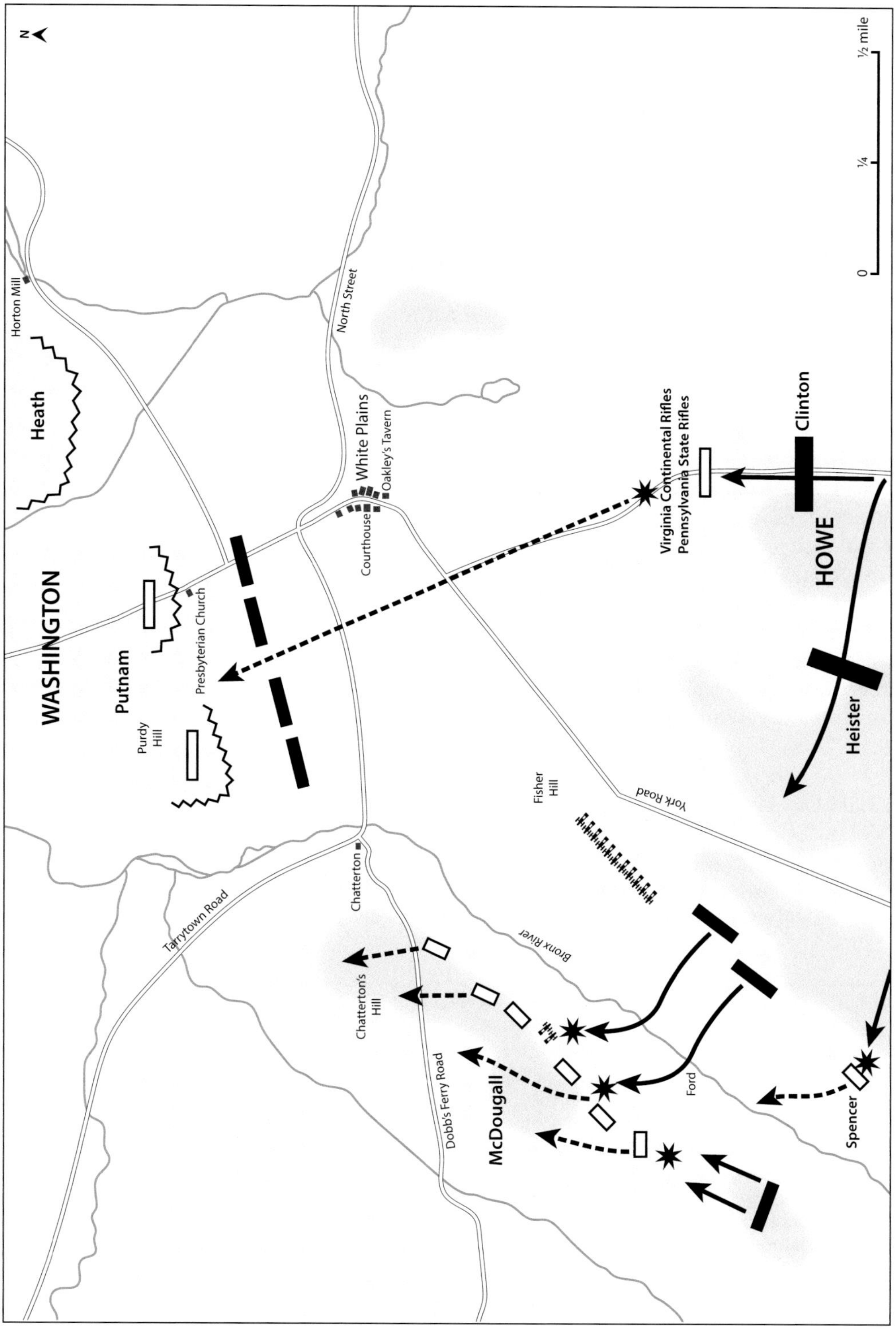

The Battle of White Plains, 28 October 1776.

The 8th Virginia men were positioned on a low rise in the centre of the line between two hills.[62] The Delaware Regiment was pulled from the brigade to help defend Chatterton's Hill on the other side of the river. The generals decided at the last minute that this hill, higher and farther forward than the others, had to be held to secure the American flank and a bridge below.[63]

Jonathan Grant remembered fighting 'in the Plains', rather than the usual construction 'at White Plains' because the riflemen were sent out front into the actual flatland. Henry Gaddis, one of the brothers from Tenmile Creek, likewise referenced the natural geography rather than the village when he remembered that he 'march'd to the White plains where we fought against the Lite horsemen.'[64] The Crown forces advanced in the morning of 28 October in two columns, red-coated British soldiers on the Mamaroneck Road and blue-coated Hessians to their left. As the Crown forces advanced,[65] Lord Stirling sent out the riflemen, including half of Kirkpatrick's men, as skirmishers. 'My regiment was sent to the front to bring on the action,' recalled a Pennsylvania rifleman, 'but not to endanger ourselves to be taken prisoners.' They marched south on the Mamaroneck Road for nearly two miles and engaged in an hour-long exchange of fire. Then, 'we were informed by our flanking party, that their light horse was surrounding us when we retreated to the lines.'[66] This was what riflemen were best suited for: delaying, harassing, and skirmishing. Their accuracy allowed engagement from the distance their slow-loading weapons required.

With their path now clear, the British focused on Chatterton's Hill, captured it after a hard-fought contest, and halted. The Americans retreated to prepared positions to the north. Still short of wagons, the full retreat from White Plains took days to complete, and Kirkpatrick's men remained separated from their gear. They made camp with Stirling's brigade in the woods near Tarrytown to keep watch on their enemy.[67] They slept in the open in freezing nighttime temperatures with their feet pointed at their fires.[68] Sergeant McCarty, meanwhile, was 10 miles north with a wagon full of tents and blankets.

The Last Days in Georgia

Almost a thousand road miles away, the rest of the regiment was still sick and dying. They were also out of supplies and money, so Georgia lent them £500 from the state treasury.[69] On

62 Charles Stedman, *The History of the Origin, Progress, and Termination of the American War* (London: P. Wogan, P. Byrne, J Moore, and W. Jones, 1794), vol.1, pp.213.

63 Abbatt (ed.), *Heath Memoirs*, pp.87–88

64 NARA: M804, S23652, Henry Gaddis pension.

65 Force (ed.), *American Archives*, ser.5, vol.3, pp.921–925.

66 Boyle (ed.) 'McMichael Journal, May-October, 1776', 28 Oct. 1776. See also Stedman, *American War*, vol.1, pp.213–214.

67 Read (ed.), *George Read*, p.211

68 Force (ed.), *American Archives*, Ser.5, vol.2, pp.1311–1312; Joseph Lee Boyle (ed.) 'The James McMichael Journal, November 1, 1776-June 3, 1777', *JAR*, <allthingsliberty.com/2018/02/james-mcmichael-journal-november-1-1776-june-3-1777/>, accessed 7 Oct. 2024, 1–8 Nov. 1776; Bellas (ed.), *Enoch Anderson*, pp.24–25.

69 Allen D. Candler (ed.), *The Revolutionary Records of the State of Georgia* (Atlanta: Franklin-Turner Company, 1908), vol.1, p.208.

29 October, Lachlan McIntosh – recently promoted to brigadier general and in command at Savannah – reported to Howe on the dire situation at Sunbury.

> Coll Mughlenbourgh who has only about 100 Sick Men left now altogether, none of whom are fit for duty and the North Carolinians are become so very uneasy that I was obliged t[o] promise them leave to return home if I did not hear from you – post. they say they will soon loose the recruiting season and eve[ry] chance of filling their Regiments if they are not allowed to go without delay and in their present state they are not fit for any duty here…[70]

Two days later, Abraham Bowman wrote to McIntosh from Sunbury explaining his inability to help defend the thirteenth colony. The Georgia Council of Safety believed an attack was coming and ordered McIntosh to move two armed boats 40 miles south to 'the dividings of Saint Simon's Island' and to move available infantry closer to the coast.[71] McIntosh relayed the order to Bowman, asking him to provide the vessels. The soldier from Strasburg could only provide one.

> I received yours of yesterday a few minutes ago by express, and have endeavoured to render the Inhabitants of St. Simons Island, and the other Islands to the Southward, all the assistance in my power, by ordering Lt. Bacon down imdeatily in an armed boat, which is the only armed vessel at this place; … it is with reluctance I inform you that was their more armed vessells here, it would not be in our power to man them, as almost all our men are sick and unfit for duty.[72]

Below his signature, he wrote, 'Lt. Col., 8 Virga. Regt. & Com[mandin]g. officer at Sunbury,' which, with McIntosh's letter, reveals that Colonel Muhlenberg was at Savannah, not Sunbury. Captain Clark, despite having written 'sick', 'very sick', or 'ditto' in his diary every day since early September, also made his way to Savannah in November. Bowman wrote to him, addressing him as the 'Commanding Officer at Savannah', which shows that Muhlenberg had by then left Georgia entirely. The rest of the men were preparing to follow. Bowman's letter was carried by Captain Knox and recommended that at least two companies be transferred to the Georgia capital immediately. Bowman informed Clark that 2nd Lieutenant Leonard Cooper was bringing him his horse and that his other possessions would follow soon. He let Clark know that he had paid for a coffin for a 'Mr. Ray' who does not appear to be one of his soldiers. 'However I shant be in want of that,' he wrote, 'if we are not Detained at this Infernall place Sunbury too Long.' In closing, he wished Clark 'a speedy jurney from Georgia.'[73]

---

70 Hawes (ed.), *Papers of McIntosh*, pp.17–18.
71 Candler (ed.), *Records of Georgia*, vol.1, pp.204–206.
72 HSP: Gratz Mss, case 4, box 17, Abraham Bowman to 'Colonele,' 31 Oct. 1776. Possibly Lieutenant Nathanael Bacon, South Carolina Militia. Though only addressed to 'Colonele,' McIntosh was the likely recipient.
73 WHS: Draper Mss, L, vol.1, p.32.

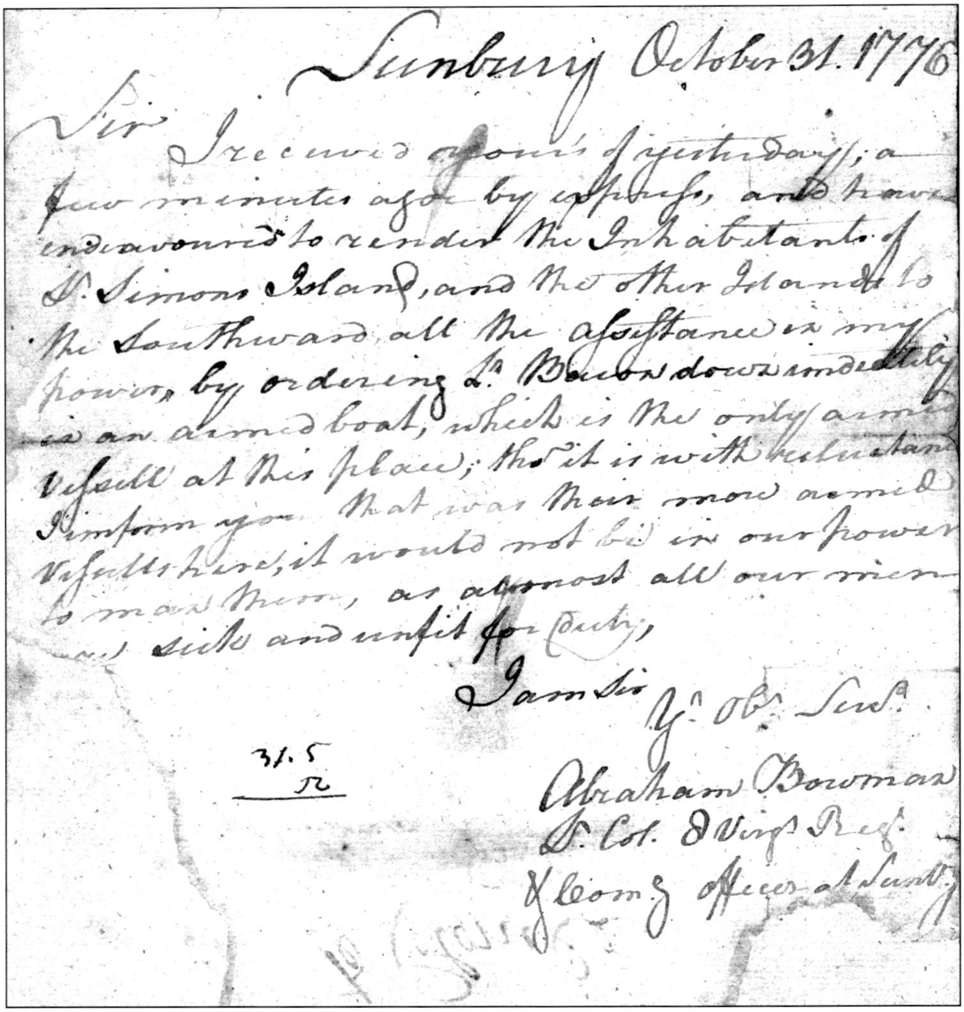

Sunbury October 31. 1776

Sir

I received yours of yesterday; a few minutes ago by express, and have endeavoured to render the Inhabitants of St. Simons Island, and the other Islands to the southward all the assistance in my power, by ordering Lt. Bacon down immediately in an armed boat, which is the only armed vessell at this place; tho' it is with reluctance I inform you that was there more armed vessells here, it would not be in our power to man them, as almost all our men are sick and unfit for Duty,

I am Sir
Yr. Obt. Servt.
Abraham Bowman
Lt. Col. 8 Virg Regt.
& Comg. Officer at Sunbury

A letter from Abraham Bowman bluntly describes the state of the regiment at Sunbury. (Letter from Abraham Bowman to 'Colonele', 31 October 1776. Simon Gratz autograph collection (collection #250B), Historical Society of Pennsylvania)

Clark set off for home two days later with a letter from Woodstock in his pocket.[74] His brother John informed him that Joseph Bowman (the lieutenant colonel's brother) was back from Kentucky with news that the Indian 'Nations are turned, and are Killing, scalping, and Dragging our people from their plantations.' John also reported on Mathias Hite's 'scandalous' conduct while in Woodstock the previous spring. He promised a full account of Hite's 'proceedings,' but shared that Hite had told friends 'that you got Drunk every Day and neglect your Business.'[75] Everything we know of Jonathan Clark tells us this charge was false.

74 FHS: Clark Diary, 17 Nov. 1776.
75 WHS: Draper Mss, L, vol.1, p.31, John Clark to J. Clark, 12 Aug. 1776.

John Morrison of Captain Berry's Company remembered that in Sunbury, 'nearly all the troops sickened and many died.' In his case, he 'was taken sick and removed three miles out of Town and lay sick a long time.' Eventually, 'when the weather became cool he recruited and he returned to his Colonel in Savanah being still weak and feeble.'[76] Isaac Dunn similarly recalled that the sick men were 'stationed round in the neighbourhood fo[u]r or five at each house in the country and at length they were commanded when they had a little recovered, to rendevouz at Savannah.'[77]

Robert Howe, meanwhile, returned to Savannah from Charles Town. He was not pleased with what he found. 'It is with concern,' he warned in his orders for 30 November, 'the General observes the great Decline of Discipline since his Departure from Camp.' He directed the officers to drill the miserable soldiers two times each day to 'reestablish the men in that Discipline they have lost.' The roll was to be called twice a day, and anyone absent would be tried by a court martial. Drunkenness was to be punished 'with utmost severity.'[78] Finally, on 6 December, Howe ordered Bowman to march his men home.

> You are to proceed with the Detachment now under your Command by way of Augusta [Georgia] to Virginia there to join your Regimt. You are also to take under your Command the detachment of Col: Sumner's [3rd North Carolina] Regimt. now here who are to march with you till they arrive at North Carolina where they are to join the Battalion to which they belong. If in your March you should fall in with any Posts where Officers superior to you in Command should happen to be you will obey such Orders as they from the Necessity of Service many have Occasion to issue. you are to be particularly careful that the Men observe the strictest Discipline and that they do not injure the Property or offer any Insult to the Person of the Inhabitants as they pass along. Any misdemeanour of this sort will be punished with the utmost Severity.[79]

Howe liked to threaten 'the utmost severity.' On 7 December, before leaving, Bowman paid for two more coffins. They were for Samuel Watson of Captain Darke's Company and for Henry Wallis of Captain Knox's Company. Watson is recorded as having died the next day.[80]

Captain Westfall's brother Cornelius, then a sergeant, remembered that 'After remaining in Georgia some time the remains of the Regiment returned to the state of Virginia.'[81] 'Utmost severity' aside, the journey north looked nothing like what Howe ordered. The first frost had come, and the mosquito season was over, but many of the men were still not healthy enough to march.[82] Morrison was quite weak, 'only being able to travel three miles the first day.' Others, like Mannaseh Bramen and Alexander McDonald of Captain

76 NARA: J. Morrison pension.
77 NARA: I. Dunn pension.
78 WLCL: Howe Orderly Book, p.34.
79 WLCL: Howe Orderly Book, p.35. See also NARA: I. Dunn pension and J. Johnston pension.
80 NARA: M246, f.208, p.51.
81 NARA: M804, S36842, Cornelius Westfall pension.
82 NARA: J. Morrison pension.

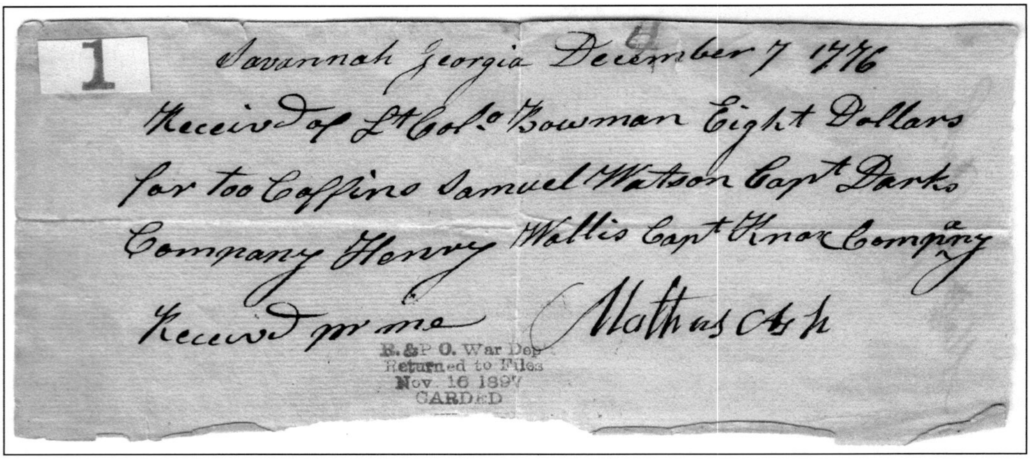
1
Savannah Georgia December 7 1776
Receivd of Lt Colo Bowman Eight Dollars
for too Coffins Samuel Watson Capt Darks
Company Henry Wallis Capt Knox Company
Receivd pr me Mathias Ash
R.&P.O. War Dep. Returned to Files Nov 16 1897 CARDED

Abraham Bowman paid Mathias Ash to make coffins for two dead soldiers as he prepared to leave Georgia. (National Archives)

Darke's Company, had to be left behind.[83] The fate of most of those who remained is unknown, but reports of some deaths eventually reached Virginia.[84] '[F]ew of my old company lived to return,' Henry Wysor remembered.[85] Nearly 300 men were discharged early, left behind, or simply dropped from the rolls over the regiment's career – almost all during this period of time.

Bowman realised immediately that keeping his detachment together required travelling at the pace of the most infirm man. That was not going to work, so he put the men on furlough and told them to find their own way home. Adam Cabbage said that while 'many of them died' in Georgia, 'those that were well was fulowed to go home.'[86] Getting home was difficult. Morrison said, 'the Colonel Furlowed the soldiers and he then had neither money or clothes.' The one item of value in Morrison's position was the rifle he brought from home.[87] He sold it and used the money to get back to Frederick County. He dissembled in his 1832 pension application, claiming he enlisted for one year and that 'when he got home his year was up and Term of service ended.'[88] Like everyone in Captain Berry's Company, he had signed up for two years. He was listed as sick in 'Carolina' until October of 1777 and then dropped from the rolls.[89]

Back in April, Lee had informed Congress, 'We want medicines (bark in particular) most cruelly.' In August, he wrote a letter to the governor of Cape Francois (Haiti) proposing to barter rice, corn, and lumber for cinchona bark and military supplies.[90] In September,

83 NARA: M246, f.212, p.2.
84 NARA: R. Bowen bounty claim; LVA: Revolutionary War Rejected Claims, Thomas Newman.
85 NARA: H. Wysor pension.
86 NARA: A. Cabbage pension.
87 NARA: M247: r.54, p.136, George Lyne to Board of War.
88 NARA: J. Morrison pension.
89 NARA: M881, f.1049, John Morrison.
90 Bunbury (ed.), *Lee Papers*, vol.1, p.449, vol.2, pp.255–258.

Congress finally ordered its Medical Committee to 'forward 300 lb. of Peruvian bark to the Southern department, for the use of the troops.'[91] If the bark ever arrived, it came too late.

The Retreat Through New Jersey

By November, there were just 57 rank-and-file 8th Virginia soldiers left of the 120 Andrew Lewis put under Colonel Read in Williamsburg. Among those absent (including commissioned and non-commissioned officers) were Captain Croghan, Lieutenant Higgins, and 60 more men who were sick. Four were 'on command' performing separate tasks. One man had deserted.[92]

Kirkpatrick led his 8th Virginia men across the Hudson to Haverstraw with Stirling's 2,000-man brigade during the night of 9 and 10 November. A scouting party was sent forward, and a hundred men took control of a pass in the mountains above the river.[93] Intelligence suggested the British had 'designs upon the Jerseys', but the generals decided to hedge their bets for the time being. Washington followed Stirling with another 3,700 men while Major General William Heath took 4,000 soldiers to Peekskill to guard the upper Hudson. Lee remained at North Castle with 7,500, and Greene oversaw about 5,000 men who were divided between the twin forts on the lower Hudson.[94]

Wasting no time, Stirling's advanced brigade turned south and marched for two days. 'It was about dusk when the head of the troops entered Hackensack,' recalled a resident of that town. 'I had a fair view of them from the light of the windows as they passed on our side of the street. They marched two abreast, looked ragged, some without a shoe to their feet, and most of them wrapped in their blankets.'[95] It was not a look that inspired confidence. After a two-day rest in Hackensack, they continued south across the Passaic River and marched through Newark, Elizabethtown, and Bonhamtown. On the evening of 16 November, they heard the booming of cannons again.[96] Still in the lead, Stirling's men trudged into Brunswick the next day and immediately sought out the village's stores of liquor. The rest of Washington's diminished command was 40 miles behind.[97]

Hugh Green ran off the day after they got to Brunswick. He had enlisted in Captain Croghan's Company when it was on the road to Williamsburg,[98] but the adventure he signed up for had turned into an ordeal. Croghan's West Augusta men had now marched nearly 1,000 miles. Half of the army from September was gone, the enlistments of the Flying Camp were about to expire on 1 December, and most of the Main Army's enlistments would end with the new year. Winter was coming, but tents and supplies that could not be hauled

91 Ford (ed.), *Journals of Congress*, vol.5, p.788.
92 NARA: M246, f.1, pp.82.
93 Chase et al (eds), *Papers of Washington* (Revolution), vol.7, pp.136–137.
94 Chase et al (eds), *Papers of Washington* (Revolution), vol.7, pp.133–135; Tait (ed.), *Hunter Diary*, 9–10 Nov. 1776; Lesser (ed.), *Sinews*, pp.36–42.
95 John W. Barber and Henry Howe (eds), *Historical Collections of New Jersey* (New Haven: J.W. Barber, 1868), p.81. See also Bellas (ed.), *Enoch Anderson*, p.26.
96 Boyle (ed.) 'McMichael Journal, Nov. 1776-June 1777,' 14–16 Nov. 1776; Force (ed.), *American Archives*, Ser.5, vol.3, p.789.
97 Force (ed.), *American Archives*, Ser.5, vol.3, p.750.
98 NARA: M246, f.211, p.3.

were burned.[99] Worst of all, Stirling's Brigade had no idea what their enemy was up to. The cannons in the distance could be a Guy Fawkes Day celebration or an attack. Conflicting rumours circled that the British had retaken Fort Ticonderoga, were being called home to stop a French invasion, and were going into winter quarters.[100]

The Route from White Plains to Brunswick
28 Oct: Depart White Plains, N.Y.
28 Oct–7 Nov: Near Tarrytown, N.Y.
7 Nov: North Castle, N.Y.
8 Nov: Peekskill, N.Y.
9 Nov: Hudson River by ferry
10 Nov: Haverstraw and Clarkstown, N.Y.
11 Nov: Tappan, N.Y.
12 Nov: Hackensack, N.J.
14 Nov: Newark, N.J.
15 Nov: Elizabethtown, N.J.
16 Nov: Bonhamtown, N.J.
17–23 Nov: Arrive Brunswick, N.J.[101]
(Approximately 125 miles)

The rumbles they heard were not a celebration. They were a disaster. Nearly 2,900 soldiers were captured or killed when the garrison at Fort Washington surrendered on 16 November.[102] Four days later, the British crossed the Hudson and took Fort Lee, capturing tents, cannons, and supplies.[103] After taking the Hudson River defences, the British turned their attention to General Washington, who decided to make a stand at Newark. Instructions were sent to Lord Stirling to backtrack.[104] 'We were ordered,' Sergeant McCarty noted, 'to march back to stop the enemy.'[105]

Stirling turned his men around, leaving only Miles' Pennsylvania Rifles behind.[106] Haslet's 'Delaware Blues' took the lead, followed by the 1st and 3rd Virginia musketeers. The Virginia riflemen formed a rear guard behind the baggage wagons. They trod 14 miles the first day and tried to sleep by the road while 'it rained excessive hard all night.' Sixteen miles 'through mud and myre' brought them back to Elizabethtown.[107] They were still six miles from Newark but held there to prevent an encirclement from Staten Island.[108]

99 Tait (ed.), *Hunter Diary*, 31 Oct. 1776; Chase et al (eds), *Papers of Washington* (Revolution), vol.7, pp.106–107.
100 Tait (ed.), *Hunter Diary*, 4–6 Nov. 1776.
101 Boyle (ed.), 'McMichael Journal, May 27, 1776–October 29, 1776;' WHS: McCarty Notebook
102 Boyle (ed.) 'McMichael Journal, Nov. 1776-June 1777,' 16 Nov. 1776; Force (ed.), *American Archives*, Ser.5, vol.3, p.789.
103 Force (ed.), *American Archives*, ser.5, vol.3 pp.1058–1059; Tait (ed.), *Hunter Diary*, 20 Nov. 1776.
104 WHS: McCarty Notebook, 23 Nov. 1776; Boyle (ed.) 'McMichael Journal, Nov. 1776-June 1777,' 24 Nov. 1776.
105 WHS: McCarty Notebook, 23 Nov. 1776
106 Boyle (ed.) 'McMichael Journal, Nov. 1776–June 1777,' 24 Nov. 1776.
107 WHS: McCarty Notebook, 23–24 Nov. 1776
108 Chase et al (eds), *Papers of Washington*, vol.7, pp.262–264.

They waited there anxiously for a week in the cold rain while the army's situation grew more desperate. A witness said they were 'almost naked and hardly able to walk or rather wade through the mud' when they moved. 'I shudder to tell you,' he reported, 'that they fall dead on the road with their packs on their backs or are found accidentally perishing in hay lofts.'[109] Sergeant McCarty was fortunate to get a billet in the home of a 'Mr. Taylor,' whom he described as 'a very moral like man.'[110] He stuck to his billet when he could, 'tired of wading the mud', but also pursued his ambition to become 1st Virginia quartermaster. He visited with the incumbent 'to see the form of the returns, etc.' and, at the instruction of 1st Virginia Adjutant Joseph Scott, filled in as sergeant major for a while.[111]

They heard cannons again on 26 November, much closer than before. 'At evening roll call,' McCarty wrote, 'there was several stories concerning the English, and there came in about twenty or thirty wagons.'[112] Washington, preparing to fight at Newark, had sent his wagons to his rear. In the morning, his generals advised him a retreat was more prudent, so the Virginians returned to Brunswick, this time with Washington's entire division. When they arrived, they found Adam Stephen, a general now, with three more regiments of Virginians: a reconstituted 2nd, the 4th, and the 5th.[113] Their arrival offset the 1 December departure of the Flying Camp and the New Jersey militia.[114] Virginians now constituted a fifth of the Continental soldiers under Washington's immediate command. Even the reinforcements, however, were weakened by disease. 'We were unlucky during the Fall,' remembered one Virginia officer, 'beaten allmost everywhere, driven through the Jerseys – had the Small Pox among our Troops – lost a great number of our Men as but few of the Virginians had ever had the disease.'[115] This attrition was reflected in the 1st Virginia's shrinking roster.

'Early in the morning, I drank some stewed rum and walked out to the parade,' McCarty wrote on the day he got his promotion to quartermaster.[116] Perhaps because of the Flying Camp's departure, they were once again short on wagons. Captain Fleming flatly told McCarty, 'wagons must be had', so the new quartermaster 'set out and got one.' The King's forces came closer, and the Americans got ready to move. 'The enemy began to cannonade us,' McCarty wrote, 'The first shot they fired killed one man, wounded a lieutenant in the thigh, a Captain in the foot.'[117] One of Haslet's men reported several more killed.[118] The American artillery fired back as the infantry withdrew toward Princeton. The single wagon McCarty found did not come close to filling the need, so the retreating soldiers burned a hundred more tents. Stirling's brigade held back as the rear guard.[119]

109 Paul H. Smith (ed.), *Letters of Delegates to Congress, 1774–1789* (Washington: Library of Congress), vol.5, p.547.
110 WHS: McCarty Notebook, 24–27 Nov. 1776.
111 WHS: McCarty Notebook, 25 Nov. 1776.
112 WHS: McCarty Notebook, 26 Nov. 1776; S.S. Bradford (ed.), 'A British Officer's Revolutionary War Journal', *Maryland History Magazine*, 56:1 (1961), p. 165.
113 Ward, *Stephen*, p.147.
114 Devine, 'Pennsylvania Flying Camp', p.78; Lesser (ed.), *Sinews*, pp.37, 43.
115 LVA: Revolutionary War Bounty Land Claims, John Curle (6th Va.).
116 NARA: M246, f.211, p.2; T. McCarty pension.
117 WHS: McCarty Notebook, 25 Nov., 1 Dec. 1776.
118 Bellas (ed.), *Enoch Anderson*, p.27.
119 Bellas (ed.), *Enoch Anderson*, p.27; David Price, *John Haslet's World: An Ardent Patriot, The Delaware Blues, and the Spirit of 1776* (New York: Knox Press, 2020), p.134.

The Route from Brunswick to Bowman's Hill
22 Nov: Depart Brunswick, N.J.
23 Nov: Near Metuchen, N.J.
24–28 Nov: Elizabethtown, N.J.
28 Nov–1 Dec: New Brunswick, N.J.
2–7 Dec: Princeton, N.J.
7 Dec: Trenton
8 Dec: Across Delaware River
9 Dec: Arrive Bowman's Hill[120]
(Approximately 37 miles)

The Virginians camped in Princeton for nearly a week as the slow-moving British crept closer. On 6 December, the distraught new quartermaster wrote just three words in his diary: 'Sick. Bad finger.' Washington's division retreated further to Trenton and crossed the Delaware to Pennsylvania on the 8th. They fired a few cannon volleys over the water to cover the last of their men and then spread out along the river. 'We drew some ammunition,' McCarty wrote, 'then started and marched up Delaware River 12 miles. Halted late in the night.' Then on the 10th of December: 'We lay in the woods all day and I had great pain with my finger as the nail came clean off.'[121] He had frostbite.

John Stephenson's Men Join the 13th Virginia Regiment

Back at the forks of the Ohio, Captain John Stephenson's discharged men returned to their homes after an 800-mile march from South Carolina. Stephenson, like Major Helphenstine, 'was taken sick & went home to his family.' The status of the two officers during this period had to be investigated later to calculate the veterans' and survivors' benefits. For that purpose, two former comrades asserted in 1820 that Stephenson held his Continental commission until 'some time in the commencement of the year 1779.'[122] This is contradicted by a militia commission he received from Governor Henry in 1778.[123] Stephenson was also appointed to the Yohogania County Court in May of 1778.[124]

Stephenson's first lieutenant, Robert Beall, continued in Continental service by accepting a promotion to captain and forming a company for Virginia's new 13th Regiment. Ensign Simon Morgan joined him as the company's 1st lieutenant. Private soldiers John Berry, John Harrison, Thomas Ravenscraft, Samuel Murphy, William Owens, John Vance, and an unknown number of other veterans of Stephenson's Company also followed Beall into the 13th.[125] Sergeant Benjamin Biggs received a lieutenancy in another company.[126] Beall,

120 Boyle (ed.), 'McMichael Journal, 27 May 27, 1776-October 29, 1776;' WHS: McCarty Notebook.
121 WHS: McCarty Notebook, 6–10 Dec. 1776.
122 LVA: J. Stephenson bounty claim.
123 Boyd Crumrine, *History of Washington County, Pennsylvania* (Philadelphia: L.H. Everts, 1882), p.217.
124 Crumrine (ed.), 'Minute Book of Yohogania,' pp.78, 123.
125 NARA: M246, f.309, p.2; S. Murphy pension; W. Owens pension; J. Vance pension.
126 NARA: M246, f.312, p.2; NARA: M881, r.1020, Benjamin Biggs.

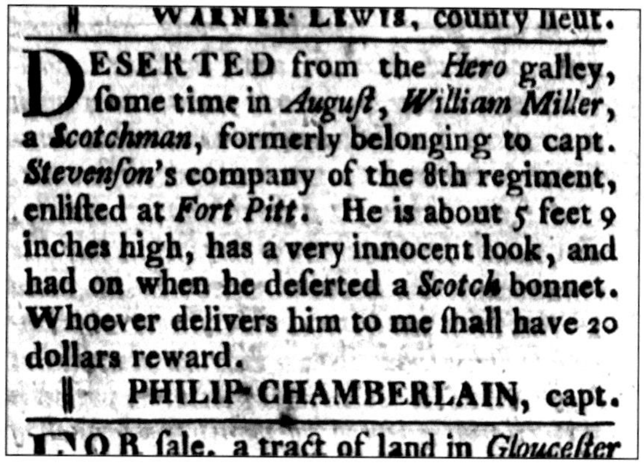
WARNER LEWIS, county lieut.

DESERTED from the *Hero* galley, ſome time in *Auguſt*, *William Miller*, a *Scotchman*, formerly belonging to capt. *Stevenſon*'s company of the 8th regiment, enliſted at *Fort Pitt*. He is about 5 feet 9 inches high, has a very innocent look, and had on when he deſerted a *Scotch* bonnet. Whoever delivers him to me ſhall have 20 dollars reward.

PHILIP CHAMBERLAIN, capt.

FOR ſale, a tract of land in *Glouceſter*

A newspaper advertisement offering a reward for deserter William Miller. (Colonial Williamsburg)

Biggs, Harrison, and Morgan all eventually commanded companies of this regiment, which was sometimes called the West Augusta Battalion.[127] The 13th was commanded by Colonel William Russell, James Knox's captain from the Southwest Independent Frontier Company of 1775.[128] Alexander Balmain, the lead author of the Augusta Resolves, was its chaplain.[129] Though a Continental Regiment, enlistees were told they would be tasked only with defending the frontier close to home.[130]

Another veteran of John Stephenson's Company, William Miller, enlisted in the Virginia Navy instead of walking all the way home. He was assigned to the crew of the galley *Hero*. A galley was a low, almost raft-like boat with a cannon fixed to a sliding carriage on its deck. Galleys combined sails and oars to outmanoeuvre large British vessels in rivers and bays. The *Hero* was a big, 90-foot version that carried two guns, an 18-pounder and a 24-pounder.[131] It was hard work and Miller did not like it, so he deserted.[132]

'The Cold Camps'

As the temperature dropped, the 8th Virginia's other West Augusta company huddled in the woods on the west bank of the Delaware River. The American army was stretched out for miles, living in barns and brush huts.[133] Kirkpatrick's detached Cohees camped at the Thompson-Neely farm on the east side of Bowman's Hill, near the mouth of Pidcock Creek.[134] Despite a few days that were 'more like spring than winter',[135] the temperature

127 Sanchez-Saavedra, *Virginia Military Organisations*, pp.61, 69.
128 Sanchez-Saavedra, *Virginia Military Organisations*, pp.68; Neville, 'Frontier Companies.'
129 William Meade, *Old Churches, Ministers and Families of Virginia* (Philadelphia: J.B. Lippincott & Co., 1861), vol.2, pp.285–286, 317.
130 Chase, et al (eds), *Papers of Washington* (Revolution), vol.13, pp.656–657.
131 Sanchez-Saavedra, *Virginia Military Organisations*, pp.157, 175.
132 *Virginia Gazette* (Purdie), 19 Sept. 1777.
133 WHS: McCarty Notebook, 13 Dec. 1776; Hazard et al (eds), *Pennsylvania Archives*, ser.1, vol.5, p.128; Horace Wells Sellers (ed.), 'Charles Willson Peale, Artist-Soldier', *PMHB*, 38:3 (1914), pp. 271–286; Bellas (ed.), *Enoch Anderson*, p.28.
134 David Price, 'When War Came to the Thompson-Neely Farmstead', *JAR*, <allthingsliberty.com/2021/06/when-war-came-to-the-thompson-neely-farmstead>, accessed 23 July 2023; Colin Zimmerman, 'A Study in Sustainability: The Continental Encampment in Bucks County, December 1776', *JAR*, 20 July 2023, <allthingsliberty.com/2023/07/a-study-in-sustainability-the-continental-encampment-in-bucks-county-december-1776>, accessed 23 July 2023; Anon., 'Bowman's Hill Tower', *Washington Crossing Historic Park*, <washingtoncrossingpark.org/park/bowmans-hill-tower/>, accessed 21 Dec. 2014.
135 Sellers, 'Charles Willson Peale', p.272.

A Boy Scout leader demonstrates how to keep warm in a brush hut insulated with dry leaves. (Author's photo)

often fell below freezing.[136] Soldiers sorely missed their tents. Worried officers wrote home, begging state officials for blankets and clothing.[137] In Virginia, Governor Henry led a statewide effort to collect blankets and rugs for the Old Dominion's suffering men.[138]

British soldiers stared at them from across the water. Boats had been pulled from the eastern bank, but the Americans feared the river might freeze solid.[139] Muskets were useless over the river's breadth, but the riflemen took occasional shots. They toyed with some Redcoats by firing at a sheep carcass whenever the hungry soldiers tried to collect their mutton.[140] McCarty spent these weeks in 'the cold camps' managing stores, distributing rations, and finding shelter for men sick with smallpox. 'I drew some stores for the Regiment,' the quartermaster wrote, 'and Colonel Weedon made me answerable for 17 pair more than what I received.' A week later, he still had 'a great deal of trouble on my hands to get the returned rations.'[141]

136 Tait (ed.), *Hunter Diary*, 1 Nov. 1776.
137 Hazard et al (eds), *Pennsylvania Archives*, ser 1, vol.5, p.105.
138 Anon. (ed.), *Journal of Virginia Delegates, 1776*, p.84; Boyd et al (eds), *Papers of Jefferson*, vol.1, pp.658–59.
139 Chase et al (eds), *Papers of Washington* (Revolution), vol.7, pp.248–249.
140 Sellers, 'Charles Willson Peale', p.272.
141 WHS: McCarty Notebook, 11, 15, 22–23, 25 Dec. 1776.

McCarty never forgot his three weeks on the west bank of the Delaware River with 'no Tents nor Blankets nor shoes nor stockings but very hard service.' He also remembered that a concerned 'Gen'l Washington passed and repassed at times' to check on the men.[142] The diary McCarty kept is surprisingly matter-of-fact, as if he lived at a time when words still had their own power and emphasis was not needed. The night was 'somewhat colder than usual', he wrote on 12 December. The next day, while eating supper with Captain Fleming, he 'had the misfortune to have my hut burned and most everything I had, a pair of new leather breeches, two shirts, stocks, and several things.' He began to use more adjectives on the 14th when he wrote, 'I lay in camp and the excessive cold weather made me very unwell.' On the 17th, he complained, 'I was very unwell with a terrible cold I had got', and on the 18th, 'I got to a house, which was of great service to me.' Yet, on the 20th: 'It was snowing, which was the 1st for the season this winter, and very cold weather. We had at this time no house to cover us, and I had no blanket.'[143]

While McCarty was freezing in the snow, many of his comrades were on the other side of the Delaware doing what riflemen were supposed to do: skirmish, harass, and reconnoitre. It was a dangerous duty with no possibility of support or quick retreat. Captain Kirkpatrick led this ad hoc light infantry, which was probably another all-rifle force. 'I was detached with others under Lieut. Kilpatrick,' remembered a Berkeley County man from the 1st Virginia, 'to protect the people of Trenton from the roberies of the Hessians.'[144] A 6th Virginia man remembered, 'a detachment of 200 men was sent across the Delaware … for the purpose of reconnoitering about Trenton' and continued there until Christmas.[145] The New Jersey militia were also stepping up their efforts. McCarty recorded the taking of enemy prisoners four times between 13 and 21 December. On the latter day he wrote, 'Lieutenant Kirkpatrick's party killed one light horseman of the English, wounded another and the two horses. Daily we are getting prisoners.'[146]

The German Auxiliary garrison in Trenton, *Oberst* Johann von Rall's Brigade and a few others, found their pickets and patrols so hard to maintain that von Rall began sending his dispatches to Princeton with escorts of a hundred men.[147] 'We have not slept one night in peace since we came to this place,' wrote a Hessian officer. 'The troops have lain on their arms every night and they can endure it no longer.'[148]

The Battle of Trenton, 26 December 1776

The weather was terrible on the road to Trenton. Two men froze to death, and the operation was so far behind schedule that there was little chance now of surprising the German Auxiliaries posted there. Impelled by desperation, the Americans continued the operation anyway.

142 NARA: T. McCarty pension.
143 WHS: McCarty Notebook, 12–20 Dec. 1776.
144 NARA: M804, S18490, Benjamin Lemasters pension (1st Va.).
145 NARA: M804, S9269, Benjamin Alsop pension (6th Va.).
146 WHS: McCarty Notebook, 13, 16, 19, and 21 Dec. 1776.
147 Fischer, *Washington's Crossing*, p.193. Many of the German Auxiliaries were not from the Hessian states, but the Americans nevertheless called them all 'Hessians.'
148 William M. Dwyer, *The Day Is Ours! November 1776-January 1777: An Inside View of the Battles of Trenton and Princeton* (New York: Viking Press, 1983), p.222.

By all indications, the Revolution had failed. General William Howe had been batting the Americans about like a cat with a wounded mouse since August. Lee and Gates both avoided joining Washington's perilous winter offensive. Lee was taken captive after foolishly staying at a tavern away from his division. The spectacle of the army fleeing across New Jersey had crushed the spirit of nearly every Patriot who saw it. One of New Jersey's signers of the Declaration accepted British amnesty and, under duress, pledged his loyalty to the Crown.[149] The government of New Jersey went into hiding and Congress fled Philadelphia for Baltimore. Even after Gates' and Lee's Divisions (the latter now under Major General John Sullivan) rejoined Washington, the army was just a third of its earlier size, and most of the Continental Army's enlistments expired in a week. Yet, Washington could not leave the entirety of New Jersey in British hands. It could mean the end of the war.[150] He had to do something dramatic, and he had to do it immediately.

That imperative is what brought 30 or 40 8th Virginia soldiers back into New Jersey in the middle of a blizzard just before dawn. It took hours and intense effort to recross the river 10 miles north of Trenton.[151] The operation began on Christmas Day and continued overnight. Stirling's brigade was among the last to cross.[152] Kirkpatrick's skirmishers met them on the east bank and returned to their companies.[153] The plan was to execute a synchronised attack in four divisions. Sullivan would take a division of mostly New England soldiers straight down the River Road to Trenton. Nathanael Greene would take another division, primarily the Virginians in Stirling's and Stephens' brigades, on a parallel road. Miles to the south, two other divisions, mostly of militia, were instructed to approach Trenton from the south and directly east across the river.[154] Both of them failed to get across.

As the exhausted Continentals plodded through the storm, they were surprised to find a company of their own soldiers wandering back from the vicinity of Trenton. These were not Kirkpatrick's men, but rather George Walls' Company from the 4th Virginia. Walls was a Berkeley County man who had recruited a lieutenant's quota alongside the 8th Virginia's Captain Darke and Lieutenant Israel. Walls' first colonel was Adam Stephen.[155] Stephen was now a general and Walls had become a captain.[156] Though unequal in rank, Walls and Stephen were close enough to connive. After a Hessian soldier picked off one of Walls' men in a boat, Stephen permitted the angry captain to go to seek revenge. The foray was foolish and ill-timed. The Berkeley company took their shots, were chased by the Hessians, and stumbled, exhausted, into their advancing compatriots. 'You, sir,' Washington reportedly growled at Stephen, 'may have ruined all my plans.'[157]

149 Christian McBurney, 'Was Richard Stockton a Hero?', *JAR*, 18 July 2016, <allthingsliberty.com/2016/07/was-richard-stockton-a-hero>, accessed 28 July 2023.
150 Michael Troy, 'American Revolution' [podcast], interview with William L. Kidder, 18 Feb. 2021, <blog.amrevpodcast.com/2021/02/ar-sp07-larry-kidder-revolutionary.html>, accessed 28 July 2023.
151 William S. Stryker, *The Battles of Trenton and Princeton* (Boston and New York: Houghton, Mifflin and Company, 1898), pp.371–372.
152 WHS: McCarty Notebook, 25 Dec. 1776.
153 NARA: B. Alsop pension.
154 Fischer, *Washington's Crossing*, pp.208–209.
155 NARA: M804: R18785, George Walls pension.
156 NARA: M246, f.106, p.50.
157 LOC: Adam Stephen Papers, Adam Stephen to Jonathan Seaman, 5 Jan. 1777; Ward, *Stephen*, pp.150–151.

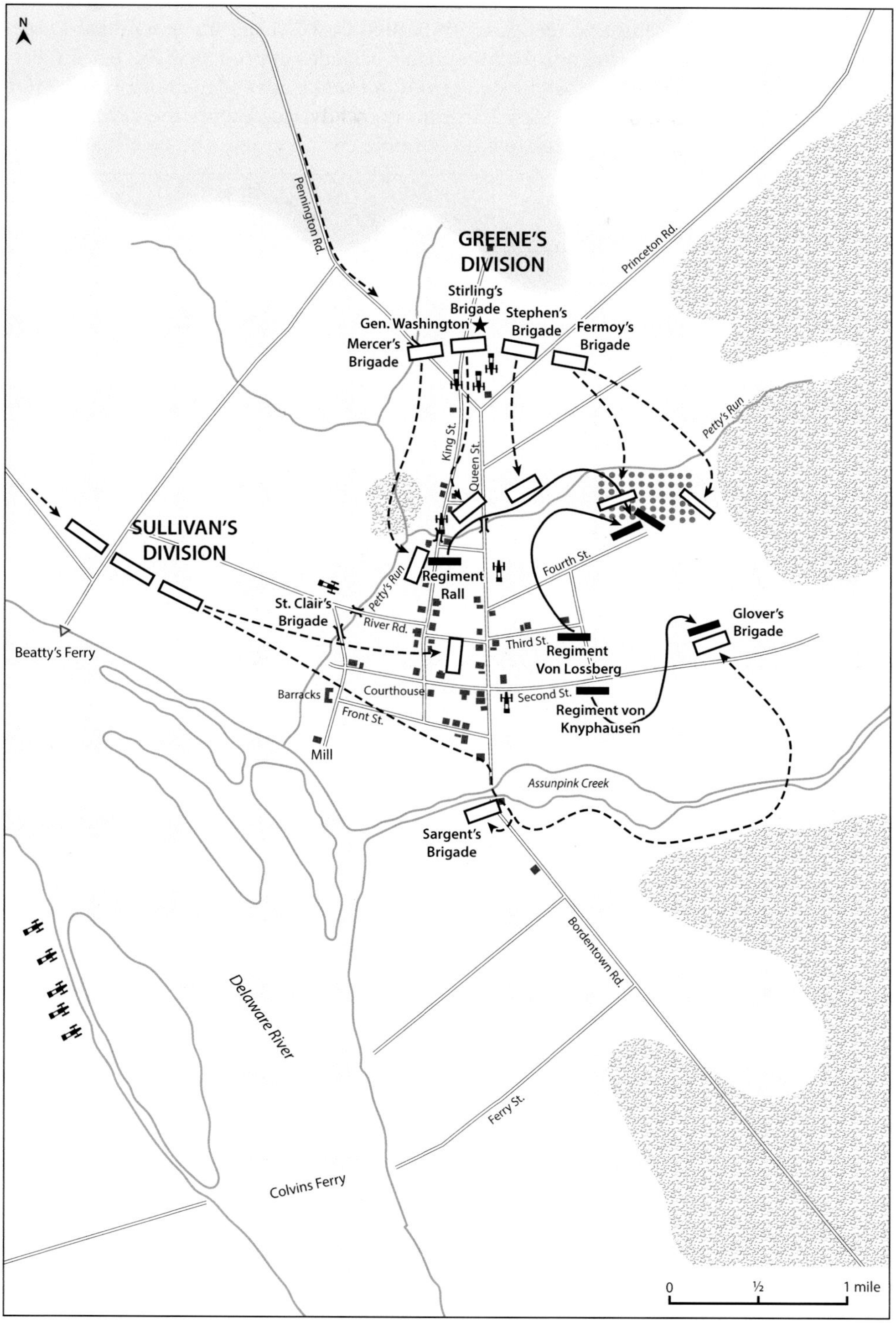

The Battle of Trenton, 26 December 1776.

As they approached Trenton, Greene, accompanied by Washington, assembled his division behind a row of trees. Stirling's and Stephen's brigades approached the town directly while brigadiers Matthias Alexis Roche de Fermoy, a French adventurer, and Hugh Mercer took the left and right flanks. The 8th Virginia men advanced with the commander in chief. One of Washington's aides related, 'Our noble countryman, the Gen'l, at the head of the Virginia Brigades, exposed to the utmost danger, bid us follow. We cheerfully did so in a long trot.'[158] As they approached, they could hear the guns of Sullivan's division firing, a happy sign that the plan was working.[159] The Virginians easily dislodged a Hessian picket and marched on the town. Stirling reported:

> Their guard gave our advanced party several smart fires, as we drove them; but we soon got two field-pieces at play, and several others in a short time; and one of our Colonels pushing down on the right while the others advanced on the left, into town. The enemy, consisting of about fifteen hundred Hessians, under Col. Rohl, formed and made smart fires from the musketry and six field-pieces, but our people pressed from every quarter, and drove them from their cannon.[160]

Most of the Hessians surrendered in an orchard, but a few escaped. Colonel Haslet wrote that 'a party of Virginians formed the van Guard & did most of the fighting – Lord Stirling's Brigade had the honor of fighting 1000 Hessians to a surrender.'[161] Quartermaster

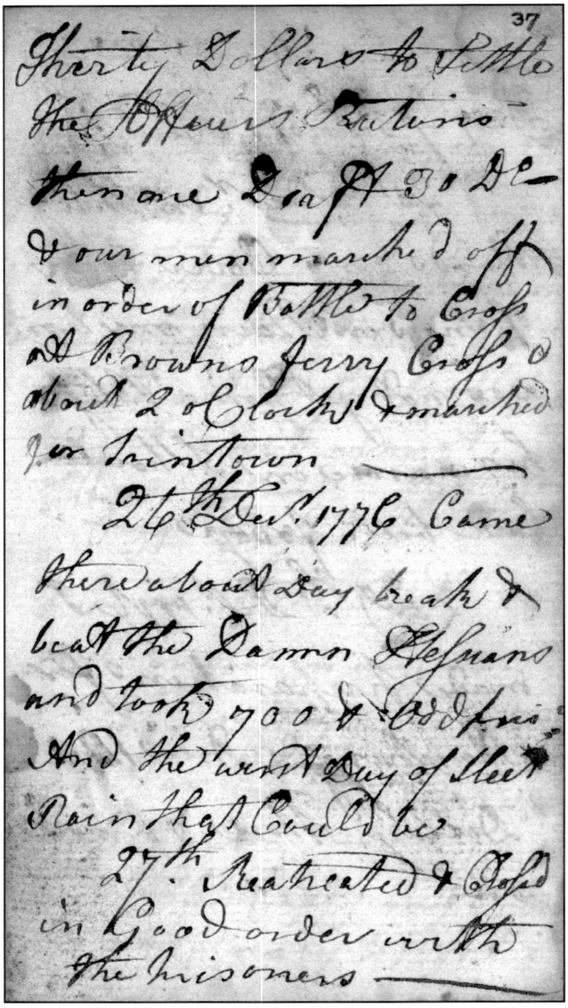
37
Thirty Dollars to Settle
the Affairs Rations
then one Draft 30 De-
& our men marched off
in order of Battle to Cross
At Browns ferry Cross'd
about 2 oClock & marched
for Trintown
26th Decr 1776 Came
there about Day break &
beat the Damn Hessians
and took 700 & odd pris-
And the worst Day of Sleet
Rain that Could be
27th Reatreated & Cross'd
in Good order with
the Prisoners

Sergeant McCarty recorded the American victory at Trenton in his diary. (Draper Manuscripts Collection, Wisconsin Historical Society)

158 Powell (ed.), *Biographical Sketch*, pp.41–43.
159 Fischer, *Washington's Crossing*, p.235
160 Stryker, *Trenton and Princeton*, pp.367–368.
161 George Herbert Ryden (ed.), *Letters To and From Caesar Rodney* (Philadelphia: University of Pennsylvania Press, 1933), pp.152–153.

Thomas McCarty was more succinct: 'beat the damn Hessians and took 700 and odd prisoners.'[162]

The return from Trenton to the 'cold camps' was even more difficult than the approach, and the men suffered severely. Stirling was incapacitated for weeks.[163] Colonel Haslet fell into the freezing river.[164] Thomas McCarty managed to conjure up another adjective and called it 'an excessive bad day.'[165] One of Kirkpatrick's Pittsburgh men, Corporal James Tucker, died. Another, Patrick Hall, died a few days later. A third, Adam Duck, had reached his limit and ran away.[166]

The Battle of Princeton, 3 January 1777

The moon glowed weakly as a waning crescent, leaving the night almost as dark as it could be.[167] The little remnant of Lord Stirling's Brigade huddled by the side of the road, breathing on their hands and rubbing their arms to stay warm. Though it was intensely cold, the first hints of sunlight in the east promised only danger.[168] The third dawn of the new year was about to rob them of the cover of darkness.

There had been more than 3,000 men in Stirling's brigade two months before, but barely 200 of those men were left. The Pennsylvania state rifles remained, but the Flying Camp was long gone. All but Colonel Haslet and five men from the Delaware Regiment were gone, and the 3rd Virginia had taken the Hessian prisoners to Philadelphia. Prolonged hardship had cut deeply into the remaining ranks. Of the 120 detached 8th Virginia men, only Lieutenant Kirkpatrick and a few enlisted men were left: Henry Brock, Harmon Commins, David Foulke, Jonathan Grant, David Williams, and perhaps Meredith Price.[169] Quartermaster McCarty was still on his feet, but he was in Burlington with the wagons.[170] Colonel Read lay dying at the Bethlehem army hospital.[171] Lieutenant Colonel Eppes was dead in Virginia.[172] Major Green was recovering from the wounds he received at Mamaroneck, and Captain

162 WHS: McCarty Notebook, 26 Dec. 1776
163 Hazard et al (eds), *Pennsylvania Archives*, ser.1, vol.5, p.157.
164 Ryden (ed.), *Rodney Letters*, p.153
165 WHS: McCarty Notebook, 27 Dec. 1776
166 NARA: M246, f.211, pp.2–3.
167 James Wilkinson, *Memoirs of My Own Times*, 3 vols (Philadelphia: Abraham Small, 1816), vol.1, p.140; 'Phases of the Moon, 1701 to 1800,' <astropixels.com/ephemeris/phasescat/phases1701.html>, accessed June 27, 2022.
168 Wilkinson, *Memoirs*, vol.1, pp.140–141.
169 NARA: H. Brock pension; H. Commins pension; J. Grant pension; S39554, David Foulke pension; S4729, David Williams pension; S8194, Robert Chambers pension; William L. Kidder, *Ten Crucial Days: Washington's Vision for Victory Unfolds* (Lawrence Twp., NJ: Knox Press, 2018), p.302. Additional undocumented 8th Virginia men may have been present, but this number is proportional to the detachment's number in the 1st Virginia.
170 WHS: Draper Mss, N, vol.2, pp.40–41.
171 John W. Jordan, 'The Military Hospitals at Bethlehem and Lititz During the Revolution', *PMHB*, 22:2 (1889), pp.137–157, 143–144; Foote, *Sketches of Virginia*, p.574.
172 'Return of Field Officers of the First Virginia Regiment', 5 October 1776, *American Archives*, Ser.5, vol.2, p.901; LVA: Legislative Petitions, Accession 36121, Thomas Woodlief.

Croghan was also still sick.[173] Of the commanders who had been above Kirkpatrick in the autumn, only George Washington and Nathanael Greene were still in the field. Captain Fleming, who was just 21 years old, took command of the 1st Virginia Regiment. Including Kirkpatrick's five or six men, it was now a regiment with just 20 soldiers fit for duty.[174]

Kirkpatrick's hardy few were near the ends of their own ropes, freezing in the darkness somewhere in New Jersey. Their march began after sunset following an hours-long battle across the Assunpink Creek at Trenton. The British expected combat to resume in the morning, but Washington had silently marched his men around them and headed north.

The Route from Bowman's Hill to Morristown
25 Dec: Depart Thompson-Neely Farm, Pa.
26 Dec: Across Delaware to Battle of Trenton, N.J.
27–28 Dec: West bank of Delaware
29 Dec: Across Delaware to Trenton, N.J.
2 Jan: Battle of Assunpink Creek, N.J.
3 Jan: To Battle of Princeton and Somerset Court House, N.J.
4–5 Jan: Pluckemin, N.J.
6 Jan: Arrive Morristown, N.J.[175]
(Approximately 75 miles)

'It was now dead winter,' a Virginian recalled, 'and the soldiers suffered severely, for they were badly clothed.'[176] A thermometer near Philadelphia showed 21° F (-6°C).[177] The plummeting temperatures froze the previous day's mud into hard, rough ice, which was good for the wagons but bad for bare feet.[178] Kirkpatrick's remnant walked through the night and were now waiting by a creek for army engineers to get cannons across.[179] The bridge, built by Quakers for hay wagons and churchgoing, was not sturdy enough. The men could see General Washington in a huddle, giving verbal instructions to the field officers. When the meeting ended, word came back that they were going to attack Princeton. The plan had been a closely guarded secret known only to general officers.[180]

173 *Virginia Gazette* (Purdie), 15 Nov. 1776; Chase et al (eds), *Papers of Washington* (Revolution), vol.7, pp. 27–31; Anon. (ed.), *Delaware Archives*, vol.2, p.1030; Franklin B. Hough (ed.), *Journals of Major Robert Rogers*, (Albany: Joel Munell's Sons, 1883), pp.275–277; Read (ed.), *George Read*, pp.209–211; LVA: J. Green bounty claim; WHS: McCarty Notebook, 23 Aug. 1776; NARA: M246, f.1, pp.61, 82, 85, 87, 93, 98–99, and f.364, p.61.

174 Boyle (ed.) 'McMichael Journal, Nov. 1776-June 1777', 3 Jan. 1777; Selig et al, *Princeton Mapping Project*, sec.4, p.39; Stryker, *Trenton and Princeton*, p.455. Selig et al. estimate Stirling's brigade at between 50 and 75 men on 3 Jan. 1777.

175 WHS: McCarty Notebook; Boyle (ed.) 'McMichael Journal, Nov. 1776-June 1777.'

176 NARA: M804, S31035: Jesse Ford pension (3rd Va.).

177 Fischer, *Washington's Crossing*, p.400.

178 [Sergeant] R., 'The Battle of Princeton,' *PMHB*, 20:4 (1896), pp.515.

179 Franklin Bowditch Dexter (ed.), *The Literary Diary of Ezra Stiles* (New York: Scribner, 1901), vol.2, p.119.

180 Caesar A. Rodney (ed.), *Diary of Captain Thomas Rodney, 1776–1777* (Wilmington: Historical Society of Delaware, 1888), p.32; Richard K. Showman et al (eds.), *The Papers of General Nathanael Greene* (Chapel Hill, 1976–2005), vol.2, pp.6–7; Kidder, *Ten Crucial Days*, pp.249–250.

The remainder of Stirling's leaderless brigade was attached to Brigadier General Hugh Mercer's even more depleted brigade. Mercer was a passionate soldier who had just declared his willingness to lay down his life for the cause.[181] Like Kirkpatrick's father, Mercer was a Jacobite. After fleeing Scotland, he lived in Pennsylvania for a decade and commanded men in the French and Indian War. Wounded and left behind at the Battle of Kittanning in 1756, he walked for two weeks through the wilderness subsisting on wild plums and the uncooked flesh of a rattlesnake. In 1758, he served with Washington in the Forbes Expedition and was the first commandant of Fort Pitt. Then, encouraged by his new Virginia friends, he moved to Fredericksburg. When the Revolution began, he was passed over for a colonelcy because he was a 'North Briton', but he was given command of the 3rd Regiment that winter and rose to brigadier.[182]

It was time to go. Colonel Hausseger's Germans from Pennsylvania and Maryland were already heading out. The Virginians watched Sullivan's division form up and march over the creek.[183] The two brigades of Greene's division followed: Mercer's and an associator (Pennsylvania quasi-militia) brigade under Brigadier General John Cadwalader. Even combined, the Mercer-Stirling brigade had only about 300 soldiers.[184] Its largest unit was the 200-man Pennsylvania State Rifle Regiment, which was itself a fifth of its original size.[185] John Haslet supported Mercer in command. 'If I return it will be to salute you,' the Delaware colonel wrote to a friend, 'if not we shall meet in Heaven.'[186] Captain Fleming performed the battlefield duties of a major. Cadwalader had over 1,000 men, but they were inexperienced, slow to get going, and Mercer was unwilling to wait for them. The sun was coming up, and they had to move.[187]

Mercer's tired warriors marched up the road from the bridge toward a Society of Friends meeting house. The sun cleared the horizon to reveal a beautiful morning. The quickly-falling temperatures of the night had turned the air's moisture into a feathery hoarfrost that covered fence rails and tree branches like a billion tiny, sparkling swords. Short of the meeting house, Sullivan's and Mercer's Divisions turned right, one after the other, onto a little-used road that ran along the edge of the frozen woods. At a farm belonging to a man named Thomas Clarke, the road turned sharply to the right to parallel the King's Highway, which now ran less than half a mile to their left.[188] Both roads led to Princeton. It was here, on elevated ground just past the farm, that they saw a single mounted Britisher looking straight at them from the northwest, squinting as the morning sun shone in his face. 'Pick him off!' Mercer ordered the nearest riflemen, but the rider was already charging away.[189]

181 Wilkinson, *Memoirs*, vol.1, p.146.

182 Michael Cecere, *Second to No Man But the Commander in Chief, Hugh Mercer* (Berwyn Heights, Md.: Heritage Books, 2015), pp.1–76.

183 Selig et al, *Princeton Mapping Project*, Sec. 4, p.50.

184 Rodney, *Rodney Diary*, pp.33–37; Wilkinson, *Memoirs*, vol.1, p.141; Boyle (ed.) 'McMichael Journal, Nov. 1776-June 1777', 3 Jan. 1777; Selig et al, *Princeton Mapping Project*, pp.39–46, 50.

185 Trussell, *Pennsylvania Line*, p.165; Selig et al, *Princeton Mapping Project*, sec. 4, p.39.

186 Ryden (ed.), *Rodney Letters*, p.153

187 Selig et al, *Princeton Mapping Project*, sec.4, p.52.

188 Harvard University Library (HUL): MS Sparks 53, Miscellaneous Papers Related to the Revolution, 1752–1779, item 4, pp.11–19; Selig et al, *Princeton Mapping* Project, sec.3, p.20.

189 Wilkinson, *Memoirs*, vol.1, pp.141–142; Rodney (ed.), *Rodney Diary*, pp.33–37; Sergeant R, 'Princeton', p.517; Selig et al, *Princeton Mapping Project*, sec.4, pp.52, 58–61.

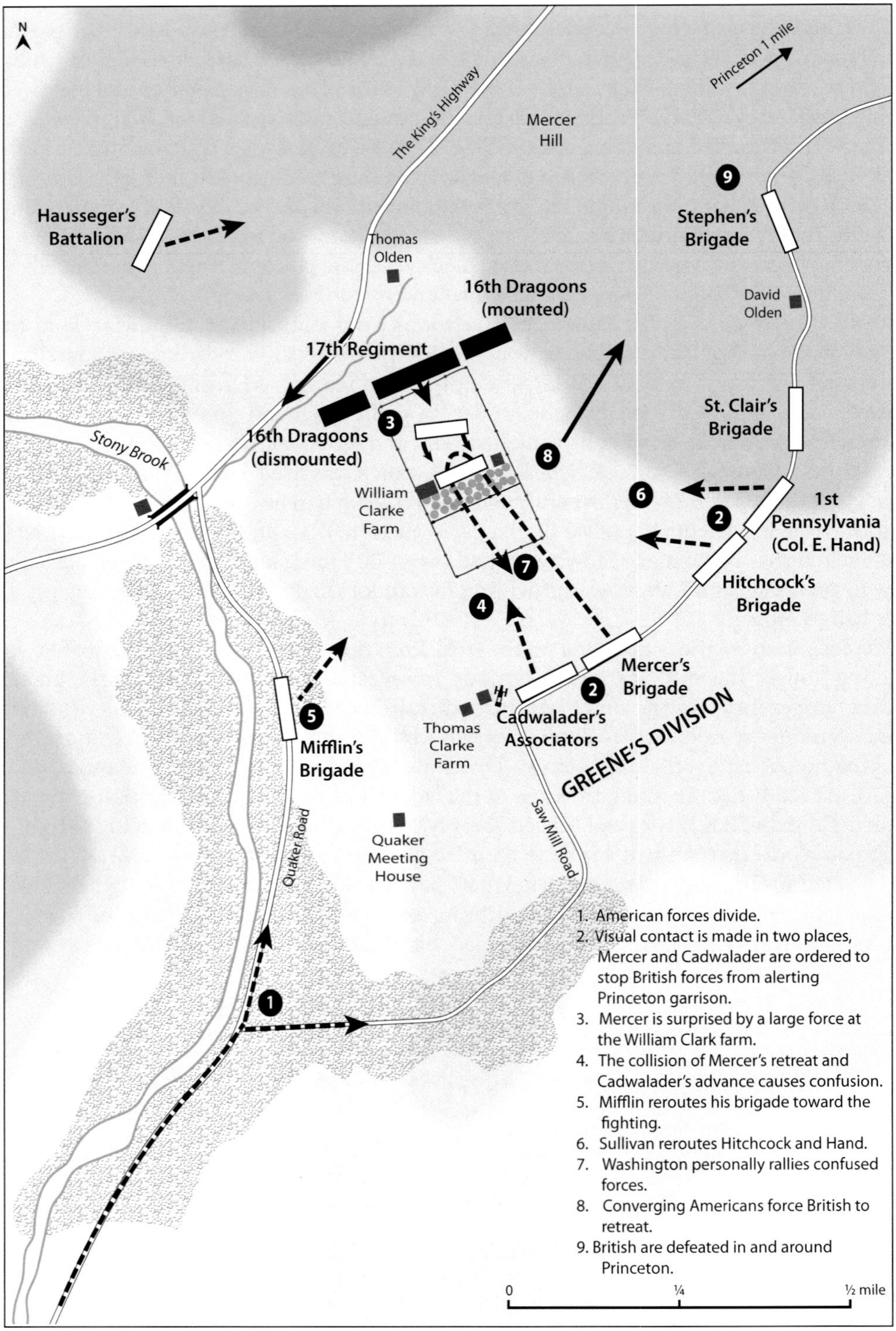

The Battle of Princeton, 3 January 1777.

Riding farther ahead on the road with Sullivan's Division, General Washington had a similar encounter. His plan endangered, the commander-in-chief ordered Mercer to intercept the patrol while he and Sullivan pressed ahead.[190] The old Jacobite took the Virginians and the Pennsylvania Rifles and rushed overland after the Redcoats. Mercer commanded in the saddle while Colonel Haslet proceeded on foot with the men. From Jonathan Grant's perspective, they were 'the advance guard & that day commanded by Colonel Hazlet & Major Fleming.'[191] Unshod artillery horses pulled the two rattling New Jersey 3-pounders along as quickly as they could.[192] Cadwalader's associator brigade lagged behind.[193] The goal was the highway, where they could stop the British soldiers from rushing back to Princeton to alert the garrison there.[194] To do it, they had to move quickly.

They rushed 450 yards up a gradual incline to another farm.[195] A densely planted orchard and a fence running between a house and a barn slowed them down as they approached. They filed through a gate and began spreading out again into a line as they navigated their way through the trees. With the highway still some distance off, they resumed their pace over the crest of the hill. They were stunned coming out of the orchard to find themselves looking at a line of Redcoats. Three companies from the 17th Regiment of Foot were arrayed behind another fence 50 yards ahead, flanked by companies of mounted and dismounted dragoons.[196] This was not a patrol; it was part of a significant reinforcement that had set out for Trenton.[197]

Someone broke discipline and fired.[198] Mercer's men began forming at about 25 yards and the British fired a volley. As often happened when firing uphill, the volley went high, splitting the branches of the fruit trees.[199] With few exceptions, the men coming out of the orchard carried rifles and this was precisely the kind of engagement they were supposed to avoid. They emerged from the trees, approaching the Redcoats at an oblique angle that exposed their left flank, so the officers wheeled the line counterclockwise before firing a volley into the British line. '[T]he enemy screamed as if many devils had got hold of them,' reported one soldier. Several of their targets dropped to the ground, a few dead and others twisting in pain.[200]

---

190 NARA: M804, S9006, Cary McClellan pension (Pa. Rifles); Dexter (ed.), *Diary of Ezra Stiles,* 2:119.

191 Selig et al, *Princeton Mapping Project*, sec.4, pp. 54–61; NARA: J. Grant pension; Selig et al, *Princeton Mapping Project*, appendix I, no.7.

192 Fischer, *Washington's Crossing* p.321.

193 William Henry Smith (ed.), *The St. Clair Papers: The Life and Public Services of Arthur St. Clair.* 2 vols. (Cincinnati, 1882), vol.1, pp.36–42; Selig et al, *Princeton Mapping Project*, sec.4, p.52.

194 Boyle (ed.) 'McMichael Journal, Nov. 1776-June 1777,' 3 Jan. 1777; Armstrong, 'Mercer.'

195 Selig et al, *Princeton Mapping Project*, sec.4, p.61.

196 Appollos Morris cited in Princeton Mapping Project, sec.4, p.62–64.

197 Selig et al, *Princeton Mapping Project*, sec.3, p.20 and sec.4, p.64. The British force was primarily from the 17th Regiment supported by mounted and dismounted elements of the 16th Light Dragoons.

198 Selig et al, *Princeton Mapping Project*, sec.4, p.62.

199 Varnum Lansing Collins (ed.), *A Brief Narrative of the Ravages of the British and Hessians at Princeton in 1776–1777* (Princeton: Princeton University Library, 1906), p.36; Sergeant R, 'Princeton,' p.517; Selig et al, *Princeton Mapping Project*, sec.4, pp.61–63.

200 Sergeant R, 'Princeton,' p.517; *Virginia Gazette* (Dixon & Hunter), 31 January 1777; Collins, *Narrative,* 36.

The British retreated several yards from the fence to reload.[201] A slight embankment in front of the railing offered some cover for the Americans if they advanced, but Mercer and Haslet decided it was more important to protect their flanks.[202] They moved their men back towards the orchard and began shifting them to anchor the ends of the line on the house and the barn. The British came at them, leaping over the fence and following them up the slope.[203] The men were eager to defend themselves, but their officers knew it was essential to finish dressing the line before firing. 'Gentlemen,' Captain Fleming shouted as the British soldiers came within 10 yards, 'dress before you make ready!' Now within easy earshot, a British soldier taunted back, '*We* will dress you!' It was a macabre play on words: a promise to gut them as a cook dresses a turkey or a pig.[204] The Redcoats fired a volley, more effective than the first, and rushed forward with their bayonets menacingly lowered. Expended rifles were now useless.

The assault was angry and brutal, and the American line broke quickly. Mercer desperately shouted, 'Retreat!' just as his horse was shot out from under him.[205] The attackers mercilessly clubbed and bayonetted the fallen general. Some may have thought he was General Washington.[206] Captain Fleming was killed.[207] His lieutenant, 18-year-old Bartholomew Yeates, was shot, beaten, and bayoneted 13 times.[208] Lieutenant Kirkpatrick was wounded, but not fatally.[209] Colonel Haslet attempted to rally the men behind one of the buildings but was shot through the head and 'dropt dead on the spot.'[210] The British turned a captured cannon on the Americans as they ran.[211]

The fleeing soldiers collided with Cadwalader's associator brigade, which was just now catching up. This briefly turned confusion into chaos. However, Major General Greene had wisely directed Cadwalader to detach his cannons and 100 men to his left by Thomas Clark's farm.[212] A volley from these guns was enough to check the Redcoats' advance. This gave momentary cover to Mercer's frantic men, but it did not reverse the tide of the battle.[213] But the tide did turn. Sullivan's division turned away from Princeton and closed in on the British left. Other Americans tasked with holding the King's Highway bridge beyond the Quaker meeting house closed in on the British right. Washington personally rallied Mercer's and

201 Sergeant R, 'Princeton', p.517.
202 Appollos Morris cited in Princeton Mapping Project, sec.4, pp.62–64.
203 Selig et al, *Princeton Mapping Project*, appendix II, sec.18.
204 *Virginia Gazette* (Dixon & Hunter), 31 Jan. 1777.
205 Sergeant R, 'Princeton', p.517.
206 Anon. (ed.), 'The Diary of Captain John Chilton, 3d Virginia Regt', *Tyler's Quarterly Magazine* 12:4 (1931), p.283; Charles Chauncey Haven, *Thirty Days in New Jersey Ninety Years Ago, An Essay revealing new Facts in Connection with Washington and his Army in 1776 and 1777* (Trenton: State Gazette, 1867), pp.40–43; NARA: M804, S22134, John Borrows pension (Pa. Militia).
207 Chase et al (eds), *Papers of Washington* (Revolution), vol.7, pp.519–530; *Virginia Gazette* (Purdie), 24 Jan. 1777; *Virginia Gazette* (Dixon & Hunter), 24 January 1777.
208 William S. Stryker (ed.), *Documents Relating to the Revolutionary History of the State of New Jersey* (Trenton: J.L. Murphy, 1901–1917), vol.1, p.363.
209 NARA: J. Grant pension.
210 Rodney (ed.), *Rodney Diary*, pp.33–37.
211 Selig et al, *Princeton Mapping Project*, appendix 4, no.19.
212 Stryker, *Trenton and Princeton*, p.447; Sellers, 'Charles Willson Peale,' p.271.
213 Selig et al, *Princeton Mapping Project*, pp.63–67.

A mortally wounded Hugh Mercer is supported by a square-jawed Virginia rifleman in sculptor Frederick MacMonnies' 1922 Princeton Battle Monument. (Author's photo)

Cadwalader's men, riding the length of the line in clear view of the enemy and cheerfully calling, 'Parade with us, my brave fellows, there is but a handful of the enemy, and [we] will have them directly!'[214]

In minutes, disaster was transformed into a triumph. While Kirkpatrick bled on the field, the army pushed the Crown forces back toward Princeton. The Redcoats retreated in disarray, and though many escaped, those who took refuge at the college soon surrendered. But the jubilant Americans had little time to celebrate. The main British force was sure to be on its way back from Trenton and could appear at any time. The rebels seized the British stores and prepared to head for the mountain safety of Morristown.

Back between the two farms, men attended to their fallen comrades. Though still alive, it was clear that Lieutenant Yeates was not long for this world.[215] A wounded 1st Virginia man was taken from the battleground on Captain Fleming's horse.[216] Jonathan Grant carried Lieutenant Kirkpatrick from the field.[217] Grant, Brock, Commins, Foulke, and Williams were fortunate to be unharmed. Meredith Price, detached from Jonathan Clark's Dunmore County company, died on the day of battle. Following the ordeal of Trenton, however, that might be a coincidence.[218] Like Yeates, Mercer was a bloody mess but still alive. As he was carted down the hill to Thomas Clark's house, the Scotsman called weakly to his worried men, 'Cheer up my boys, the day is ours.'[219] He lived a few more days.

214 Wilkinson, *Memoirs*, vol.1, p.143; Sergeant R–, 'Princeton', p.517.
215 Stryker (ed.), *Documents*, vol.1, p.363.
216 NARA: B. Lemasters pension.
217 NARA: J. Grant pension.
218 NARA: M246, f.210, p.2.
219 NARA: M804, S13381, John Hendy pension (Northampton Militia).

The Forage War

Thomas McCarty spent his first two days in Morristown drunk. 'That night I lay in the wagon after having bar with General Stephen and General Mifflin and with the doctors', he wrote in his diary. The following day he noted, 'I was in the same capacity remarked.'[220] The word that looks like 'bar' in the manuscript is uncertain, but Stephen and Mifflin were both heavy drinkers.[221] On another day, Stephen was reportedly 'seen in open view of all soldiers very drunk taking snuff out of the Boxes of strumpets.'[222]

After sobering up, the quartermaster spent two days organising and distributing supplies to the men. He was, he wrote, 'sick, most excessive bad.' After a couple of days of rest, he felt the lure of alcohol again. He 'took a walk through the country … and bought a barrel of cyder.' On Wednesday, 22 January, he received orders to ready the men to march with three days' provisions. They marched to Springfield, New Jersey, where McCarty acquired a supply of new shoes, stockings, and breeches. The men, some of them barefoot, lined up in the snow for the desperately needed clothing. On Saturday evening, his tasks complete, McCarty once again 'took a walk to the country, where I got some cyder and a very good supper.' Quartermastering definitely came with privileges. Again, on Sunday, he went 'into the country', took some lodgings and 'stayed all day.'[223]

The main winter encampment was at Morristown, but forward posts were maintained to guard the gaps in the Watchung Mountains and conduct raids on British foragers. Croghan recruit David Williams attested, 'the main body of their Regiment went into winter quarters at Morristown New Jersey, but this deponent, with some others were sent to Chatham New Jersey where they wintered.'[224] A 6th Virginia man recalled, 'This duty was extremely severe, by night as well as by day, constant patroling, frequent skirmishes, some of them very bloody, nocternal surprises, the cuting off of pickets &c, allways attended with loss of men and great fatigue.'[225]

On 27 January, the Virginia troops headed out to find the enemy. McCarty followed behind, responsible for the wagons. 'Our Virginia troops had marched,' he noted, 'and I got orders from General Stephen to follow on, and I marched to Westfield, and then to Scotch Plains, it being in the night and very muddy. I got lodgings at one Mr. Halsey's.'[226] There was a regiment of Connecticut men in the field as well, commanded by Colonel Andrew Ward.[227] The Yankees' enlistments ended in May, but they had been

220 WHS: Draper Mss, N. vol.1, pp.43.

221 Kenneth R. Rossman, *Thomas Mifflin and the Politics of the American Revolution* (Chapel Hill: University of North Carolina Press, 1952), pp.265, 300–302; Ward, *Stephen*, pp.177, 182, 189, 191–195, 200–206, 210, 245.

222 Showman et al (eds), *Papers of Greene*, vol.2, pp.188–189.

223 WHS: Draper Mss, N. vol.1, pp.43–47.

224 NARA: D. Williams pension.

225 NARA: M804, W7403 Thomas Massie pension (6th Va.).

226 WHS: Draper Mss, N, vol.2, p.48.

227 Henry P. Johnston (ed.), *The Record of Connecticut Men in the Military and Naval Service During the War of the Revolution, 1775–1783* (Hartford: Adjutant General's Office, 1889), p.109.

begging to go home since December and were beginning to run off.[228] McCarty caught up with the Virginians, commanded in the field by the popular and aggressive Colonel Charles Scott, and joined them in taking quarters at Quibbletown (New Market). The next couple of days were spent scouting for Cornwallis's foraging parties. Part of the Americans' winter strategy was to prevent the British from collecting hay for their horses or food for themselves.

On Saturday, 1 February, they spotted five light horsemen. They captured one of them, but several dozen balls of lead failed to stop the others as they rode away. Scott and his 90 men were walking into a trap set by an enemy that was tired of American ambushes. The Virginians pursued them to Drake's Farm, near Metuchen, where they 'discovered their main body where they were loading hay.'[229] The riders who got away had done their job. The Virginians were approaching a much larger force.

Colonel Ward's grouchy Connecticuters were nearby but not answerable to Scott. The Virginians attacked immediately, not realising they faced two brigades of British and Hessian troops supported by eight artillery pieces. They were heavily outnumbered but still drove back a battalion of grenadiers, counting on Ward's men to back them up.[230] 'We attacked the body, and bullets flew like hail,' McCarty wrote. Artillery checked their momentum, but they kept fighting. 'We stayed about 15 minutes, when we retreated with loss. We drove them first, but at our retreat the balls flew faster than ever.'[231]

The Virginians were furious that Ward's men had failed support them.[232] 'There was a body of above 400 men that never came up to our assistance till we retreated', McCarty complained. 'Then they came up, but too late, and only some.'[233] His anger, however, was soon directed back at the Crown forces. Several British soldiers (officers, according to McCarty), 'went to the field where we retreated from, and the men that was wounded in the thigh or leg, they dash out their brains with their muskets and run them through with their bayonets, made them like sieves. This was barbarity to the utmost.'[234]

The Redcoats in New Jersey had a reason to be angry. The Forage War was an important success for the Americans. Denying their adversaries forage and forcing them to live in close quarters for several months took a serious toll. Howe had 33,000 troops in August 1776. When spring came, several thousand of them were dead.[235]

---

228 Chase et al (eds), *Papers of Washington* (Revolution), vol.8, pp.70–71, 249–253; Harold C. Syrett (ed.), *The Papers of Alexander Hamilton*, 27 vols (New York: Columbia University Press, 1962–1987), pp.204–205; George K. Ward (ed.), *Andrew Warde and His Descendants, 1597–1910* (New York: A.T. De La Mare, 1910), p.490.

229 WHS: Draper Mss, N, vol.2, pp.50–52.

230 Chase et al (eds), *Papers of Washington* (Revolution), vol.8, pp.70–71, 249–253

231 WHS: Draper Mss, N, vol.2, pp.50–52.

232 Chase et al (eds), *Papers of Washington* (Revolution), vol.8, pp.234–236.

233 WHS: Draper Mss, N, vol.2, pp.50–52; Lee, *Memoir of Richard Henry Lee,* vol.2, pp.163–165.

234 WHS: Draper Mss, N, vol.2, pp.50–52.

235 Showman et al (eds), *Papers of Greene*, vol.2, p.3; Chase et al (eds), *Papers of Washington* (Revolution), vol.8, pp.113–114; Fischer, *Washington's Crossing*, 536, n.51; Harris, *Brandywine,* pp.33–34.

8

Home

Far away in western Pennsylvania, Matthew Hennen was doing exactly what he signed up for. Hennen and his company of the 8th Pennsylvania Regiment were posted on the Allegheny River at Kittanning, north of the zone that was contested by Virginia, guarding Fort Pitt and the West Augusta settlements from downriver Indian attacks.[1] Twenty years after Hugh Mercer was wounded there, it was still wild country.[2] It was also 100 miles from Hennen's home on the Monongahela.[3] He was promised that his regiment would remain in the west to protect his neighbourhood and, though far from his family, Hennen's company was in a good place to do that.[4]

The same commitment was made to the 13th Virginia Regiment and its 8th Virginia veterans. Many of the married men in the two regiments would not otherwise have agreed to serve.[5] The 8th Pennsylvania and the 13th Virginia shared more than that in common: Hennen might easily have enlisted in the other regiment, which recruited from the same disputed geography. As one officer described it, the two regiments 'ware raised in adjoining neighbourhoods, though in different states, the one in Virginia and the other in Pennsylvania, with only an amaginary line between them.'[6] Most of the enlisted men in these regiments were Irish immigrants with no particular stake in the boundary fight.

An express rider arrived at Kittanning on 4 December (three weeks before the Battle of Trenton) with orders for the 8th Pennsylvania to join Washington's desperate army in the east. The field officers dutifully led their resentful men across the mountains, sending word ahead that they were not equipped for winter service.[7] Supplies of any kind were hard to get in the far West. They left on 6 January and arrived in Philadelphia five weeks later, having suffered terribly on the way. Hennen's colonel, lieutenant colonel, and dozens

1 NARA: M804: S22828, Matthew Hennen pension; S41594, John Guthery pension (8th Pa.); W3270, Gideon Long pension (8th Pa.); Trussell, *Pennsylvania Line*, pp.102–110. Wilson's captaincy is not acknowledged in Trussell but is corroborated by the Guthery and Long pensions.

2 Cecere, *Hugh Mercer*, pp.11–16.

3 William Hanna, *History of Greene County, Pa.* (place unknown: W. Hanna, 1882), p.121.

4 Hazard et al (eds), *Pennsylvania Archives*, ser.5, vol.3, pp.305–306.

5 Chase et al (eds), *Papers of Washington* (Revolution), vol.13, pp.656–657.

6 LVA: Revolutionary War Rejected Claims, James Sullivan.

7 Hazard et al (eds), *Pennsylvania Archives*, ser.5, vol.3, pp.305–306.

of other men died. While 151 men and several officers deserted,[8] Hennen found a legitimate way to get home sooner. He 'exchanged from the 8th Penna. regiment to the 8th Virginia regiment' by trading places with George Askins of Captain Croghan's Company. Croghan's men, of course, were from the same disputed 'neighbourhood.' Hennen attested that he 'had nearly three years to serve in the Penna. line & said Askins had fifteen months to serve in the Virginia line.' Askins agreed to switch places and take the longer enlistment in exchange for £10.[9]

Much to the alarm of their families, John Stephenson's veterans in the 13th Virginia were also called east early in 1777.[10] Taking time to recruit and perhaps to contest their orders, they did not arrive until July.[11]

Back in the Old Dominion

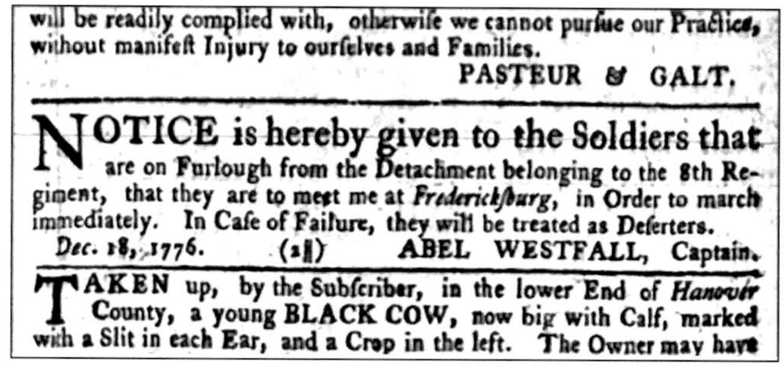
will be readily complied with, otherwife we cannot purfue our Practice, without manifeft Injury to ourfelves and Families.
PASTEUR & GALT.

NOTICE is hereby given to the Soldiers that are on Furlough from the Detachment belonging to the 8th Regiment, that they are to meet me at *Fredericksburg*, in Order to march immediately. In Cafe of Failure, they will be treated as Deferters.
Dec. 18, 1776. (2f) ABEL WESTFALL, Captain.

TAKEN up, by the Subfcriber, in the lower End of *Hanover* County, a young BLACK COW, now big with Calf, marked with a Slit in each Ear, and a Crop in the left. The Owner may have

Virginia Gazette notice for Westfall's men on furlough to report to Fredericksburg. (Colonial Williamsburg)

Just 12 days after Lieutenant Colonel Bowman received his marching orders in Savannah, Captain Abel Westfall placed a notice in the *Virginia Gazette*. The advertisement ordered returning soldiers, technically on furlough, to report to Fredericksburg as they arrived.[12] Leonard Rigar of Captain Darke's Company remembered the Sunbury survivors 'returned to Virginia sometime in December 1776 and took winter quarters at Fredericksburg.'[13]

Though he clearly left Savannah before Bowman did, Westfall was not the first officer to return. Adjutant Francis Swaine received his pre-Continental service pay at Williamsburg on 10 December,[14] which probably indicates that Colonel Muhlenberg stopped there at that time to confer with the state's leaders. Captain Westfall received a similar reimbursement on 17 December.[15] Muhlenberg wrote to his family in Pennsylvania to let them know that he 'had just returned from a strenuous campaign, that his reg[iment] had suffered a great deal from disease in Georgia, that not all had returned as yet, that they had orders to march to

8 Hazard et al (eds), *Pennsylvania Archives*, ser.5, vol.3, pp.306–308; Trussell, *Pennsylvania Line*, p.107.
9 NARA: M. Hennen pension.
10 Ford (ed.), *Journals of Congress*, vol.8, p.21; McIlwaine et al (eds), *Council of the State of Virginia*, vol.1, p.368; Chase et al (eds), *Papers of Washington* (Revolution), vol.8, pp.314–316.
11 NARA: M247, i.78, pp.227–229, William Russell to Congress, not dated.
12 *Virginia Gazette* (Dixon & Hunter), 20, 27 Dec. 1776.
13 NARA: L. Rigar pension.
14 McIlwaine et al (eds), *Council of the State of Virginia*, vol.1, p.273.
15 McIlwaine et al (eds), *Council of the State of Virginia*, vol.1, p.285.

Philadelphia, etc.'[16] Muhlenberg sent Swaine 'Express to his Excellency Genl Washington' in New Jersey to report and receive instructions.[17]

After a month on the road, Captain Clark went to his parents in Caroline County and scarcely stirred for two weeks.[18] Richard Campbell was also sick when he got to Fredericksburg and went home to Woodstock to recover. Though ailing, Campbell was happy when he learned about the victories at Trenton and Princeton. 'We have glorious News from the N. ward,' he wrote to Clark, 'altho' we have lost our Old Friend Gen. Lee.' If 'Old Friend' communicated sarcasm, as it seems to have, Clark must have grinned as he read it.[19]

Still eager for reinforcements, Washington wanted the 8th Virginia to join him as soon as possible.[20] Campbell headed north in mid-January, perhaps primarily to defend his promotion.[21] Most of the ambulatory men in Bowman's detachment were back in Virginia by the end of the year. The soldiers left behind in Charles Town, however, remained there until 21 January, when Congress ordered them to go north.[22] Lieutenant John Steed brought the last group from Georgia in April.[23] Colonel Muhlenberg was directed to recruit his companies 'to their full complement of men, and to march the companies, as fast as compleat, to join General Washington.' Congress confirmed Lee's promotion of Richard Campbell and ordered that '300 dollars be advanced to Major Campbell, to enable him to discharge wagons, and furnish the troops he has now on the way to camp, with shoes, and other necessaries they may want.'[24]

Orders notwithstanding, the regiment simply was not in a condition to rush to New Jersey. They remained in Fredericksburg for two months while the officers did their best to bring the organisation back into fighting condition. Captain Slaughter sent Corporal Abner Newman back south to find a couple of his men.[25]

Among the other issues facing them was the fact that the soldiers had not been paid. Governor Henry and the Council of State addressed this on 3 February.

> It appearing to the Board that the eighth Virginia Regiment is in great distress for want of their pay it is therefore Ordered that it be recommended to mr Harrison the paymaster to advance to Colo Muhlenberg by the hands of Captain Dark the sum of two thousand five hundred pounds … and give the necessary notice for making the proper stopages.[26]

16 Tappert and Doberstein (trans), *Journals of H.M. Muhlenberg*, vol.3, p.3.
17 NARA: M881, r.1053, Francis Swaine.
18 FHS: Clark Diary, 17 Nov.–29 Dec. 1776.
19 WHS: Draper Mss, L, vol.1, p.33, Richard Campbell to Jonathan Clark, 11 Jan. 1777.
20 Chase et al (eds), *Papers of Washington* (Revolution), vol.8, pp.540.
21 WHS: Draper Mss, L, vol.1, p.33, Richard Campbell to Jonathan Clark, 11 Jan. 1777.
22 Ford (ed.), *Journals of Congress*, vol.7, p.52.
23 LVA: State Government Records Collection, Accession 44269, Return of the 8th Virginia Regiment, 11 April 1777.
24 Ford (ed.), *Journals of Congress*, vol.7, p.52.
25 Anon. (ed.), *Journal of Delegates*, 1778, p.15.
26 McIlwaine et al (eds), *Council of the State of Virginia*, vol.1, p.321.

While the money helped with morale, the men also wanted to see their families. The governor and the council were informed of this as well, perhaps in a message communicated by Captain Clark, who was in Williamsburg on 12 February.[27]

> Colo Muchlenburg having informed the Board that the Business of recruiting men to fill up his Regiment, and of furnishing them with necessaries, woud be greatly forwarded by marching from Fredericksburg to Winchester as many of the men already enlisted have Relations there and express a desire of seeing them before they go to the Northward. It is Ordered that he be permitted to do so.[28]

Most of the soldiers from Charles Town returned about the time the regiment moved to Winchester.[29] But the regiment was still not whole: Captain Croghan's detachment, led for the last few months by Lieutenant Kirkpatrick, remained in New Jersey.

The Situation in Virginia

Though far from major military operations, the regiment's home communities were significantly impacted by the war. Barely two years after the Battle of Point Pleasant, there were renewed reports of Shawnee warriors taking scalps and captives around the forks of the Ohio.[30] Fear grew that the British garrison at Detroit would provide the Indians with weapons and ammunition.[31] That was why Matthew Hennen was so impatient to get home.[32] Fincastle, attacked by British-supported Cherokee, was the staging ground for William Christian's 1776 counteroffensive. Berkeley, Frederick, and Culpeper were asked to house early British prisoners of war with local families ('thus to become the Citizens of America instead of its enemies').[33] Virginia abandoned this high-minded plan and kept Hessians captured at Trenton together in a barracks outside of Winchester.[34] In Hampshire, antiwar and antitax sentiments grew among immigrant settlers living in the county's isolated valleys.[35]

With a new constitution, Virginia's era of conventions and committees was over. The fifth and last Convention turned itself into the first House of Delegates and selected Governor Henry and his Council of State. Then the voters elected the state's first Senate.[36] Benjamin

27 FHS: Clark Diary, 12 Feb. 1777.

28 McIlwaine et al (eds), *Council of the State of Virginia*, vol.1, p.339. See also NARA: J. Johnston pension.

29 Chase et al (eds), *Papers of Washington*, vol.8, pp.428–429.

30 Herman Wellenreuther and Carola Wessel (eds), *The Moravian Missionary Diaries of David Zeisberger, 1772–1781* (University Park: Pennsylvania State University Press, 2005), pp.307, 328, 340, 353, 360.

31 Wellenreuther and Wessel (eds), *Diaries of Zeisberger*, p.358.

32 NARA: M247, i.78, pp.227–229, William Russell to Congress, not dated.

33 Bunbury (ed.), *Lee Papers*, vol.2, p.98; Force (ed.), *American Archives*, ser.4, vol.6., p.1587; Palmer et al (eds), *Calendar*, vol.8, pp.218–221.

34 NARA: M804, S6114, John Smith pension (Frederick Militia).

35 Klaus Wust, 'Disaffection in the Rear: German Tories in the West Virginia Mountains', *The Report: A Journal of German-American History*, 36 (1975), pp.67–68.

36 Francis Newton Thorpe (ed.), *The Federal and State Constitutions Colonial Charters, and Other Organic Laws of the States, Territories, and Colonies Now or Heretofore Forming the United States of America* (Washington, D.C.: Government Printing Office, 1909), vol.2, pp.3812–3819; William Wirt

Biggs, John Chenoweth, William Darke, Robert Breckenridge, James Knox, and George Slaughter all served in future assemblies.[37] The county courts and militia operated as before, but parish vestries lost the power to tax. One of the new regime's earliest decisions was to formally divide Augusta County and split its western district into not one but three new jurisdictions: Ohio, Monongalia, and Yohogania.[38] The assembly likewise replaced Fincastle with the counties of Montgomery, Washington, and Kentucky.[39]

Many soldiers returned home still desperately ill. They received treatment from a pair of Continental Army doctors named David Gould and Robert Macky, one of whom may have been the regiment's first surgeon.[40] Peter Helphenstine had been home for months, and his health seems to have stabilised for a while.[41] There is no record of visits from his former comrades, but they must have occurred. Muhlenberg remembered that Helphenstine 'lingered for a considerable period, & then Died.'[42] The date of his death is unclear. A pair of the major's descendants deduced that he died between 4 June 1778 and 4 May 1779.[43] A modern cenotaph gives the date of his death as 11 May 1779.[44]

New Officers and New Orders

Colonel Muhlenberg rode to Dunmore County to see his family. His wife Hannah, his infant son Henry, and his sister, Mary ('Polly') Swaine, lived together at the glebe, for which he now had to pay rent.[45] Polly enjoyed Hannah's company, but she was otherwise homesick and lonely. The colonel knew that he and Francis Swaine might not be home again for months or even years and thought the best solution might be for his parents and youngest sister to relocate from Pennsylvania. Virginia would be safer for them, too. Polly was insistent: if no family from Pennsylvania wanted to come, then she wanted to go home to them. Peter wrote to his father, offering to send a wagon, and urged him to decide quickly.[46] He also wrote to General Washington to report that recruiting was slow and to ask for guidance on filling officer vacancies.

Swaine rode off with the letters, travelling 218 miles in five days to the Muhlenberg home in Trappe, Pennsylvania. Then he continued to Continental Army headquarters in New Jersey.[47] Muhlenberg's letter to Washington covered four issues. First, he reported that he

Henry (ed.), *Patrick Henry: Life, Correspondence, and Speeches* (New York: Charles Scribner's Sons, 1891), vol.1, p.490.

37 Leonard (ed.), *Assembly*, pp.154, 169, 180, 183, 184, 192, 196, 205.

38 Anon. (ed.), *Journal of Virginia Delegates*, 1776, p.35; Hening (ed.), *Statutes*, vol.9, pp.262–266.

39 Anon. (ed.), *Journal of Virginia Delegates*, 1776, p.87.

40 NARA: M881, r.1044, David Gould, r.1047, R. Macky, r.1070, Robert Macky; W1041, Robert Macky pension; LVA: Revolutionary War Bounty Land Claims, David Gould.

41 Anon. (ed.), *Journal of Virginia Delegates*, 1776, p.35.

42 LVA: P. Helphenstine bounty claim.

43 Wayman and Mullins, *Helphinstine*, pp.63–64.

44 Mount Hebron Cemetery, Winchester, Va.

45 Muhlenberg, *General Muhlenberg*, p.165.

46 Tappert and Doberstein (trans), *Journals of H.M. Muhlenberg*, vol.3, p.20.

47 Tappert and Doberstein (trans), *Journals of H.M. Muhlenberg*, vol.3, pp.17–18.

could not quickly comply with a congressional directive to fill his 10 companies with new recruits and forward them on to New Jersey. 'The Detachment from the Southward Arrivd here this Week,' he wrote, 'in a Shattred Condition, with only Seventy Men fit for duty.' It would, consequently, 'be Allmost impossible to March the Men as soon as I could wish, if the Companies are to be wholly Compleat.' He had enough recruits to fill the three senior companies present and hoped to send them in about 10 days.

Second, Muhlenberg asked about replacing more than a dozen officers who had died, resigned, or become incapacitated. The regiment was going to need company officers for command duties, but they were needed immediately for recruiting. He had asked Patrick Henry about it, but the governor had no power to give commissions now that the 8th was in Continental service.

Third, Muhlenberg reported, 'There is at present one entire Company wanting in my Regiment in the room of Captn Stinson's from Pittsburg, whose Time of Enlistment expird in September last.' Looking out for family, he made a recommendation. 'Mr Swain who waits on Your Excellency with this Letter has Servd as Adjutant in my Regt since it was raisd. He bears the Character of a Good Officer, & would willingly undertake to raise this Company with Your Excellencys Approbation.'

Fourth, he asked to get rid of the regiment's rifles, which were harder to maintain than muskets. 'The whole Regt at present consists of Riflemen, & The Campaign we made to the Southward last Summer fully convinces me, that on a march where Soldiers are without Tents, & their Arms continually exposd to the Weather; Rifles are of little use, I would therefore request Your Excellency to Convert my Regt into Musketry.'[48]

Muhlenberg's fifth query was too sensitive to put in writing. Richard Campbell's promotion was out of order, and the other captains resented it. The job properly belonged to William Darke, who was not one to mince words when wronged. The Berkeley captain's 'heart and purse were open to his friends', wrote an early biographer, 'but, despising hypocrisy, he was, toward his personal enemies, sometimes harsh and imperious.'[49] Muhlenberg could not ignore the problem. It appears Swaine delivered the colonel's message on this delicate point verbally.

With Washington's orders in his pocket, the adjutant returned to Trappe to pick up the elder Muhlenberg's response. Fearing criticism, the family patriarch had decided to stay in Pennsylvania. Henry watched as Swaine rode away and was concerned for his safety. 'He has a young, wild horse, and is not an experienced rider,' he wrote in his journal. 'The horse tried to throw him. Unless the lord affords him special protection, it is a question whether he will reach home, two hundred miles from here, without an accident.'[50]

General Washington's responses to Colonel Muhlenberg's questions came from the pen of his aide de camp, Major George Johnston. The letter also included instructions for colonels Daniel Morgan and James Wood of the new 11th and 12th Virginia Regiments. Johnston wrote:

48 Chase et al (eds), *Papers of Washington* (Revolution), vol.8, pp.428–429.

49 Anon., *Sketch of Darke*, p.2.

50 Tappert and Doberstein (trans), *Journals of H.M. Muhlenberg*, vol.3, p.23.

Peter Muhlenberg's parents moved into this house in Trappe, Pa. in 1776 and lived in it throughout the war. Peter bought the house from his father in 1787. (Author's photo)

> You will use your utmost Industry & Diligence in collecting together all the parts of the Virga Continental Battalions within your reach, & send them off to Philada as they assemble, where they will receive Orders from the Commanding Officer stationed in that City. We have already wrote to Colo. Morgan on this subject, & Mr Swain has Orders similar, to Colo. Wood – These, being immediately under your Eye, You can dispatch. Let a sufficient number of proper Officers from each Battalion be left behind for the purpose of recruiting, with Orders to follow as soon as any of them has completed the quota allotted to him. Much, very much indeed, depends upon our being reinforced immediately. The least tardiness in the recruiting Officers must produce Effects, which they may repent.

'I am desired to inform You,' Johnston continued, 'That his Excelly wishes You would nominate Ten Ensigns, to whom he will give Commissions immediately on the Regiments joining the Army, provided they are such Gentlemen as will not disgrace the Appointment & Commission. This however he does not suspect, convinced that You will not take into service any Person whom his Excelly can with propriety discharge.'

The rank and succession issues were more complicated. 'Congress having confirmed Majr Campbell in his Office,' Johnston wrote, 'leaves his Excellency no power to remove him,

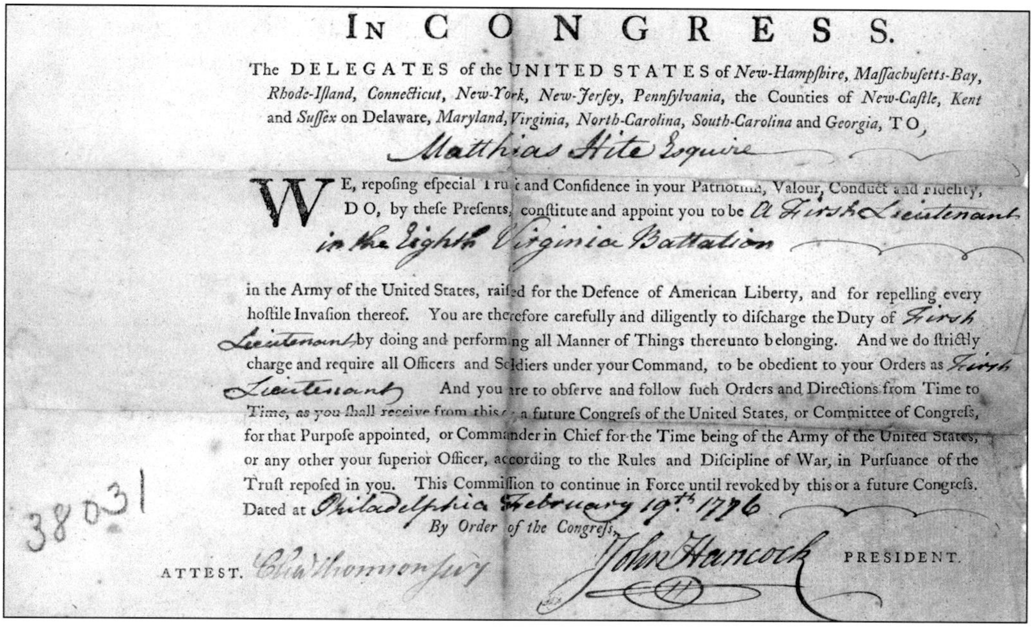
IN CONGRESS.

The DELEGATES of the UNITED STATES of *New-Hampſhire, Maſſachuſetts-Bay, Rhode-Iſland, Connecticut, New-York, New-Jerſey, Pennſylvania,* the Counties of *New-Caſtle, Kent* and *Suſſex* on Delaware, *Maryland, Virginia, North-Carolina, South-Carolina* and *Georgia,* TO,

Matthias Hite Esquire

WE, repoſing eſpecial Truſt and Confidence in your Patriotiſm, Valour, Conduct and Fidelity, DO, by theſe Preſents, conſtitute and appoint you to be a First Lieutenant in the Eighth Virginia Battalion

in the Army of the United States, raiſed for the Defence of American Liberty, and for repelling every hoſtile Invaſion thereof. You are therefore carefully and diligently to diſcharge the Duty of First Lieutenant by doing and performing all Manner of Things thereunto belonging. And we do ſtrictly charge and require all Officers and Soldiers under your Command, to be obedient to your Orders as First Lieutenant And you are to obſerve and follow ſuch Orders and Directions from Time to Time, as you ſhall receive from this or a future Congreſs of the United States, or Committee of Congreſs, for that Purpoſe appointed, or Commander in Chief for the Time being of the Army of the United States, or any other your ſuperior Officer, according to the Rules and Diſcipline of War, in Purſuance of the Truſt repoſed in you. This Commiſſion to continue in Force until revoked by this or a future Congreſs.

Dated at Philadelphia February 19th 1776

By Order of the Congreſs,

John Hancock PRESIDENT.

ATTEST. Cha Thomson secy

38031

Mathias Hite's Continental commission, signed by John Hancock. Though it bears the date of his company's certification by the Dunmore Committee on 19 February 1776, the 8th Virginia was not then in Continental service. It is unlikely that he received the document before December. (National Archives)

but for the Commission of some Offence.' With regard to Swaine, Washington knew and trusted John Stephenson and preferred that he remain in service. 'You will apply to Capt. Stephenson to raise his Company. Till he determines, His Excelly inclines not to interfere.' Swaine was allowed to raise a company, but it would be assigned to one of the 'additional' Continental regiments unless Stephenson declined to continue.

On the question of arms, Johnston wrote, 'His Excellency satisfied of the Justice of your Observations about Rifles, has determined to have as few used as possible. He will put Musketts into the hands of all that Battalion that is not very well acquainted with Rifles.' It had been a mistake for the Convention to assume that every recruit from the western counties would be a rifle expert, but Washington still wanted rifles in the hands of the regiment's real sharpshooters.[51]

The meaning and import of these instructions are best understood with the knowledge that Congress promoted Muhlenberg to brigadier general on 21 February.[52] Accordingly, the Fighting Parson was directed not only to ensure the 8th Virginia refilled its ranks, but also to collect 'all the parts of the Virga Continental Battalions' within his reach. 'His Excellency expects to see you here in a few days,' Johnston concluded, 'there being at present not a sufficient Number of Genl Officers with the Army.[53]

51 LOC: George Washington Papers, Ser.4, General Correspondence: George Johnston to Peter Muhlenberg, March 9, 1777.

52 Ford (ed.), *Journals of Congress*, vol.7, p.141.

53 LOC: George Washington Papers, Ser.4, General Correspondence: George Johnston to Peter Muhlenberg, March 9, 1777

Abraham Bowman, now 27 years old, was promoted and became the regiment's new colonel. One of his first actions was making room for all 10 new ensigns by promoting the few existing ones. He took more than one approach in helping Muhlenberg select the new junior officers. He pulled Sergeants Robert Breckenridge and John Kay out of Knox's and Berry's companies. Reuben Field and Jonathan Smith were cadets (officers in training) in Slaughter's and Croghan's companies and now received their hoped-for appointments. Peter Higgins and Cornelius Westfall were brothers of existing officers. Bowman had served with Philip Huffman in the Dunmore Volunteers and now invited him to join. Thomas Miller, uniquely, came from Maryland and joined the regiment based on a recommendation. He was 16 years old.[54] James Hook of Augusta came from a fervently Whiggish family. A close family friend, John Campbell of David Stephenson's company, stayed with the Hooks for two or three months in 1778. He remembered, 'The males of the family of Hooks being true Whigs were generally from home in the service & I staid with their women.'[55]

The Ten New Ensigns

Peter Higgins (Higgins' Co., March 9th)
Reuben Field (Slaughter's Co., March 11th)
Robert Breckenridge (Hite's Co., March 16th)
Philip Eastin (Clark's Co., March 16th)
James Hook (D. Stephenson's Co., March 16th)
Cornelius Westfall (Westfall's Co., March 16th)
John Kay (Berry's Co., March 16th)
Philip Huffman (Slaughter's Co., March 16th)
Jonathan Smith (Croghan's Co., March 17th)
Thomas Miller (Darke's Co., March 18th)[56]

Washington's promise to issue muskets to the regiment's soldiers 'not very well acquainted with Rifles' explains much that is otherwise confusing about the regiment's next year. Virginia regiments under the province's first and second force authorisations had two or more companies of riflemen each, all recruited in the western counties.[57] Virginia and Congress both specified in 1775 that riflemen were to serve 'as light infantry.'[58] This mimicked the British practice of having one company of grenadiers and one company of light infantry per regiment, which were often detached to serve together as elite independent corps.[59] Of Virginia's regiments, only the 8th was raised with 10 rifle companies. Going forward, an unknown proportion of the regiment carried muskets while their rifle-bearing comrades were occasionally detached to serve as light infantry under Daniel Morgan, William Maxwell, and their own William Darke.

54 NARA: M804, W7454, Thomas Miller pension.
55 NARA: M804, W10112, George Hooke pension (Augusta Militia).
56 NARA: Revolutionary War Rolls.
57 Anon (ed.), *Proceedings of the 4th Convention*, p.105.
58 Ford (ed.), *Journals of Congress*, vol.2, p.89; Anon (ed.), *Proceedings of the 3rd Convention*, pp.30; Anon (ed.), *Proceedings of the 4th Convention*, p.105.
59 Don N. Hagist, *These Distinguished Corps: British Grenadier and Light Infantry Battalions in the American Revolution* (Warwick: Helion & Company, 2021), pp.14–16.

Recruiting

Company officers, old and new, got busy recruiting. The old provincial county-based system no longer applied,[60] but that did not make it any easier. A sergeant from Augusta reported that recruiting was 'very difficult, as the major part of the youth who were zealous for the cause, were already in service against the King's troops.'[61] Consequently, recruiters had to be less selective. A prominent resident of Augusta harshly asserted that 'Convicts, Servants & Vagrants are what the majority is composed of.' As for propertied men, he said, 'their excuse is an Indian war threatens them, their harvest is coming on, and there is men enough much nigher the camp than they to afford assistance.' Governor Henry calculated that there were too many regiments competing for too few men. 'Add to all this,' he continued, 'our Indian Wars & marine Service, almost total Want of Necessarys; The false Accounts of Deserters, many of whom lurk here; The Terrors of the small pox, & the many Deaths occasion'd by it.'[62]

Arrenah Redman, a daughter of Fifer Henry Redman, became an honorary member of the Daughters of the American Revolution as an old woman in 1896. Illiterate, penniless, childless, and blind, she posed for this photograph holding her father's empty fife case shortly before she died. (Peaks of Otter Chapter, Daughters of the American Revolution)

But the recruiters did their best. They concentrated their efforts around Winchester and the lower Shenandoah Valley and were able to top off three companies.[63] One of the first to sign up was 16-year-old William Eagle of Dunmore. In Frederick County, Henry Redman enlisted with his sons William, Henry, Jr., and John.[64] Eagle was assigned to Campbell's (Lieutenant Hite's) Company and the Redmans joined Captain Clark's Company. Henry Redman, Jr. was made a fifer.

Three other recruits were veterans of the 1775 Continental rifle companies. Daniel Anderson, who joined Captain Berry's Company as a sergeant, had served in Daniel Morgan's

60 Chase et al (eds), *Papers of Washington* (Revolution), vol.8, pp.44–45; Ford (ed.), *Journals of Congress*, vol.7, p.133.

61 Wiliam Grant, 'Narrative of Sergeant William Grant' in John Romeyn Brodhead and E.B. O'Callaghan (eds), *Documents Relative to the Colonial History of the State of New York Procured in Holland, England and France* (Albany: Weed, Parsons and Co., 1856–1883), vol.8, pp.728–734, 728.

62 Chase et al (eds), *Papers of Washington* (Revolution), vol.9, pp.12–13, 622–624.

63 Chase et al (eds), *Papers of Washington* (Revolution), vol.8, pp.438–429.

64 NARA: M804, W5690, Henry Redman pension.

Company. Like Morgan, he was wounded and captured at Quebec and then exchanged. Michael Tullis joined Captain Darke's Company after a year with Hugh Stephenson. William Moody came across the river from Maryland to join Captain Darke's Company after a year in Michael Cresap's Company.[65] Many recruits were friends or brothers of soldiers already in service. There was a small bump in the headcount when, in mid-March, John Steed (Campbell's junior lieutenant) arrived with the last of the sick men from Georgia, but few of these soldiers returned to active service.[66]

The regiment's seniormost company, Darke's, drew only a handful of new men after experiencing significant attrition.[67] This might be because Darke believed himself entitled to be a major and thus not required to recruit. Or, because he did not return from Charles Town until February, he may simply have missed out on the first recruits.[68]

A friend of Drury Jackson's in Culpeper remembered that, 'Jackson returned home with a furlough in the fall or winter of the year 1776 or 1777 and in the spring following said Jackson set out towards Culpeper Court house to join his Regiment and marched towards the North.'[69] Mary Chenoweth in Hampshire County remembered that her husband 'was at home a very short time on furlow' at Capon Bridge '& then returned to the army.'[70] Colonel Bowman marched out of Winchester on 21 March 1777 with 177 soldiers, including most of his 10 new ensigns and 58 new enlisted men. He left a few officers behind to follow with a 'second division' of hoped-for recruits and men recovered from illness.[71] Captain Croghan and his men were waiting for him in New Jersey.

Smallpox

In New Jersey, meanwhile, Sergeant McCarty recorded, the soldiers in Captain Croghan's detachment 'Marched for Whippany, where our men was to be inoculated for the smallpox.'[72] Following many deaths under his own command and reports of tragedy in Canada, Washington decided there was no other way of protecting his men from the deadly disease. The operation was kept strictly secret because it put the army in a vulnerable state. The eight weak Continental regiments Washington had with him, five of them Virginians, were reduced to mere 'handfuls' of already immune soldiers while the others went through the procedure.[73]

Americans were terrified of smallpox. A continent-wide epidemic coincided with the war years and killed perhaps 100,000 people from Canada to Mexico.[74] The disease trav-

65 NARA: D. Anderson pension, M. Tullis pension, W. Moody pension.
66 LVA: Return of the 8th Virginia Regiment, 11 April 1777.
67 NARA: M246, f.212, p.2.
68 Ford (ed.), *Journals of Congress*, vol.7, p.52; McIlwaine et al (eds), *Council of the State of Virginia*, vol.1, p.321.
69 NARA: D. Jackson pension.
70 NARA: J. Chenoweth pension.
71 LVA: Return of the 8th Virginia Regiment, 11 April 1777.
72 WHS: Draper Mss, N, vol.2, p.54.
73 Chase et al (eds), *Papers of Washington* (Revolution), vol.8, pp.102–104, 264.
74 Fenn, *Pox Americana*, p.3.

elled from person to person or through blankets and clothing. If an individual survived its horrid symptoms, they were immune to smallpox for life. Inoculation with live virus was first done in America in the 1720s and was still controversial but growing in acceptance. 'If you obe[y] Orders to March to the Northward,' Campbell wrote to Clark before heading to New Jersey in January, 'I would strongly recommend to you to get inoculated for the small pox.'[75] Brigadier General Muhlenberg gave Clark the same advice from Woodstock or Winchester in March: 'I have waited for you all this Week with anxiety and now begin to despair of seeing you before I set out for Camp. Should this be the case I would advise you to get inoculated before you go ... and come with the next Detachment that marches of[f].'[76]

Clark arrived back in the valley on 19 March, taking the road through Chester's Gap to Colonel Bowman's house near Strasburg. He spent the night at Traveler's Hall, the nearby home of Bowman's uncle, Isaac Hite.[77] Clark was a frequent visitor there and was perhaps already interested in Hite's 16-year-old daughter, Sarah, whom he married in 1782. He had a good reason to see her father, too. Hite was one of a few men in the lower valley who received permission to perform smallpox inoculations in 1771, and Clark must have had questions.[78] In the morning of 21 March, the 26-year-old captain rode north to Winchester and arrived just in time to see Muhlenberg, Bowman, and the regiment march away.[79]

First Lieutenant John Jolliffe, the former Quaker in Captain Berry's Company, remained behind as well. He was under the care of John McDonald, a local doctor who, like Isaac Hite, had gotten permission to conduct smallpox inoculations in 1771 and was now at it again.[80] The doctor was a Loyalist but avoided political arguments and was professional in his work.[81] Jolliffe was sick with the disease, but it is unclear whether McDonald gave it to him.[82] Inoculation involved putting pustule fluid from a sick person into an incision in a healthy person's arm. This produced an illness that was usually less severe but still gave immunity. Sometimes, however, it was fatal.

Having been urged to do it and having consulted with Isaac Hite, Clark went to Dr McDonald and requested the procedure. It did not take long. When it was done, Clark went to Thomas Edmondson's tavern. He felt sick, but not because of the inoculation. He had felt that way for months.[83]

In the morning, Clark rode his horse back to Traveler's Hall and stayed there again for a couple of nights. He rode through falling snow on 25 March to attend a county court meeting in Woodstock. He spent three more days with the Campbell family and then rode back to Edmondson's in Winchester.[84] He had live virus in him the whole time, but he was not yet symptomatic or contagious. McDonald surely told him that it took about 11 days

---

75 WHS: Draper Mss, L, vol.1, p.33, Richard Campbell to Jonathan Clark, 11 Jan. 1777.
76 WHS: Draper Mss, L, vol.1, p.34, Peter Muhlenberg to Jonathan Clark, 15 March 1777.
77 FHS: Clark Diary, 19 March 1777. Hite's estate is now Long Meadow Farm.
78 J.E. Norris (ed.), *History of the Lower Shenandoah Valley* (Chicago: A. Warner & Co., 1890), pp.123–124.
79 FHS: Clark Diary, 21 March 1777.
80 FHS: Clark Diary, 30 March–6 April 1777. The onset of Jolliffe's illness is calculated from usual disease progression.
81 Williams, *Glengarry McDonalds*, p.47.
82 See NARA: M804, W6355, John Vandeman pension (12th Va.).
83 FHS: Clark Diary, 22 March 1777.
84 FHS: Clark Diary, 23–29 March 1777.

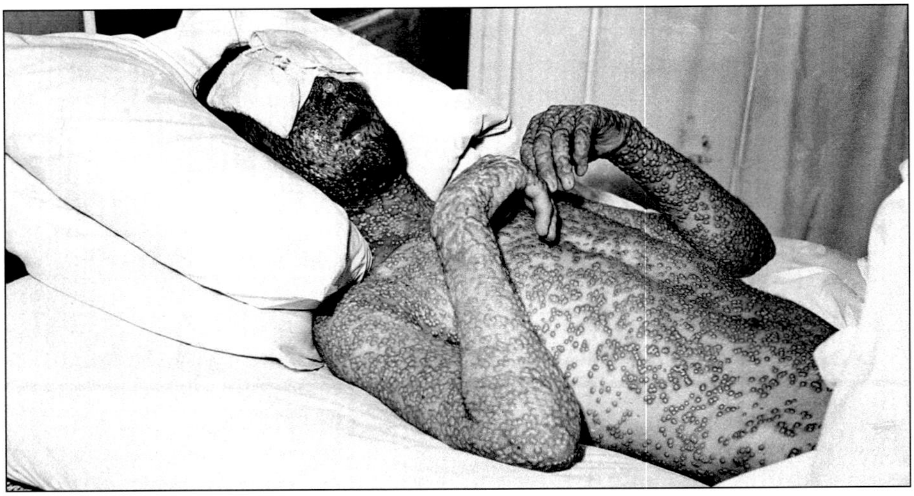

An early twentieth-century patient with advanced smallpox. (State of New York)

for the illness to start, and Clark was back in eight.[85] He visited with Jolliffe, who was at his own home, and took a walk to George Washington's old French and Indian War fort north of town.[86]

Jolliffe, meanwhile, was in bad shape. He was covered with pustules that concentrated on the most sensitive parts of his body. He may have been blind and haemorrhaging internally. Oozing sores converged to form patches of diseased skin that fused to his bedsheets as they scabbed over. He was in terrible pain.[87] The lieutenant died on 6 April, apparently with his wife Mary, Captain Clark, and the doctor all by his side.[88]

Clark visited with Mary Jolliffe and her young children twice more before his own symptoms took hold.[89] When it was time, he stayed with McDonald day and night until the last sore fell off on 16 April.[90] Then the doctor scrubbed him down to make sure no potentially infectious scabs remained and sent him on his way.[91]

Brigadier General Muhlenberg

Muhlenberg followed Washington's order to collect the 8th, 11th, and 12th Virginia regiments and march them to New Jersey. Daniel Morgan's 11th was built on the remains of one-year rifle companies.[92] It was one of six new regiments authorised by the young

85 Fenn, *Pox Americana*, p.19.
86 FHS: Clark Diary, 30 March-3 April 1777.
87 Fenn, *Pox Americana*, pp.16–20.
88 FHS: Clark Diary, 4–6 April 1777.
89 Jolliffe, *Jolliffe Family*, pp.91–92.
90 FHS: Clark Diary, 30 March-6 April 1777.
91 FHS: Clark Diary, 7–16 April 1777.
92 Wright, *Continental Army*, p.108

A 1788 illustration of the countryside near York, Pennsylvania. The Bushong Tavern, in the foreground, was five miles below the Great Wagon Road on the Baltimore-York Road. Etching by James Trenchard. (New York Public Library)

Commonwealth for the 1777 campaign. All its field officers were veterans of the expedition against Quebec. The 12th Virginia was a virtual sister regiment to the 8th, raised in Augusta, Dunmore, Hampshire, and other western counties.[93] Also like the 8th, two of its companies were originally independent frontier companies.[94] It was commanded by James Wood of Frederick. All three regiments congregated in Winchester before marching in detachments to Philadelphia. Washington had also been authorised to raise several 'additional' Continental regiments, independent of state authority. Charles Thruston was appointed to raise one of them (sometimes called the '16th Virginia') and some of his recruits may have marched at this time as well.[95] Muhlenberg made one important stop on the way. On 31 March, his proud father recorded in Trappe: 'When I arrived at home I found a brigadier general of the American army, from Virginia ... He was on his way to the American camp in Jersey.'[96]

Muhlenberg apparently rode with the column part of the way to Philadelphia. His days with the 8th Virginia were over, the regiment was not in his brigade, but he did take two of its men with him. One was John Elsey, a private soldier from Richard Campbell's Company. Elsey served as the general's personal assistant or 'waiter.'[97] Muhlenberg also brought Francis Swaine with him to serve as his brigade major.[98] This was a great opportunity for Swaine, but he botched it. His equestrian skills were not the only thing lacking.[99]

93 Sanchez-Saavedra, *Virginia Military Organisations*, pp.64–68.
94 Neville, 'Frontier Companies.'
95 Chase et al (eds), *Papers of Washington* (Revolution), vol.8, pp.520–522, 574–575.
96 Tappert and Doberstein (trans), *Journals of H.M. Muhlenberg*, vol.3, p.27.
97 NARA: M881, r.1043, John Elsey.
98 Chase et al (eds), *Papers of Washington* (Revolution), vol.9, p.437.
99 Chase et al (eds), *Papers of Washington* (Revolution), vol.11, pp.30–36.

9

United

The route from Winchester to Philadelphia traced the path of Palatine and Ulster migration in reverse. Places with names such as Germantown, Bern, Heidelberg, Manheim, and Strasburg alternated with names like Antrim, Colerain, Donegal, Londonderry, Rapho, and Tyrone to reveal the history of settlement. The Great Philadelphia Wagon Road led Abraham Bowman and his 8th Virginia men all the way from Winchester to the Pennsylvania capital. Philadelphia was home to about 34,000 people in the 1770s, making it larger than Boston and New York put together.[1] It was, before American independence, the third most important commercial centre in the British Empire.[2]

General Washington, meanwhile, announced that John Markham, major of the 2nd Virginia, was going to be the 8th Virginia's new lieutenant colonel.[3] Markham's lack of history with the regiment and Major Campbell's disputed rank made the continuity provided by Colonel Bowman's leadership especially important. Bowman was a capable horseman, physically large, and from the heart of the Shenandoah Valley.[4] The credibility those traits earned him was magnified by his descent from Jost Hite. The new colonel had proved his courage as a boy, explored Kentucky, helped adopt the Dunmore Resolves in 1774, joined Peter Helphenstine in a raid against the Shawnee village of Wapatomika early in Dunmore's War,[5] and cut ties with a Loyalist older brother.[6] No one possessed more Shenandoah Valley frontier-warrior credibility than he.

Markham, on the other hand, had little in common with the men. His family moved from New York to the fall-line county of Chesterfield in about 1750.[7] He captained a company of the Amelia District Minute Battalion that became a company of the 1st Virginia Regiment in 1775, and the early date of his rank assured quick promotions. Despite the early start of

1 W.S. Rossiter, *A Century of Population Growth* (Washington: Bureau of the Census, 1909), p.11.

2 Anon., 'History of Philadelphia', <britannica.com/place/Philadelphia/History>, accessed 20 Aug. 2023.

3 Chase et al (eds), *Papers of Washington* (Revolution), vol.8, pp.614–616.

4 Wayland, *Bowmans*, pp.9, 108.

5 Williams, *Glengarry McDonalds*, p.50.

6 Lucien Beckner (ed.), 'Reverend John D. Shane's Notes on an Interview with Elijah Foley of Fayette County,' *Filson Club History Quarterly* 11:4 (1937), pp.252–259, 255.

7 Pamela Hutchison Garrett, 'Bio: John Markham', *Markham of Chesterfield*, <markhamchesterfield.com/biographies/markjohn005_bio.pdf>, pp.1–2, accessed 30 December 2023.

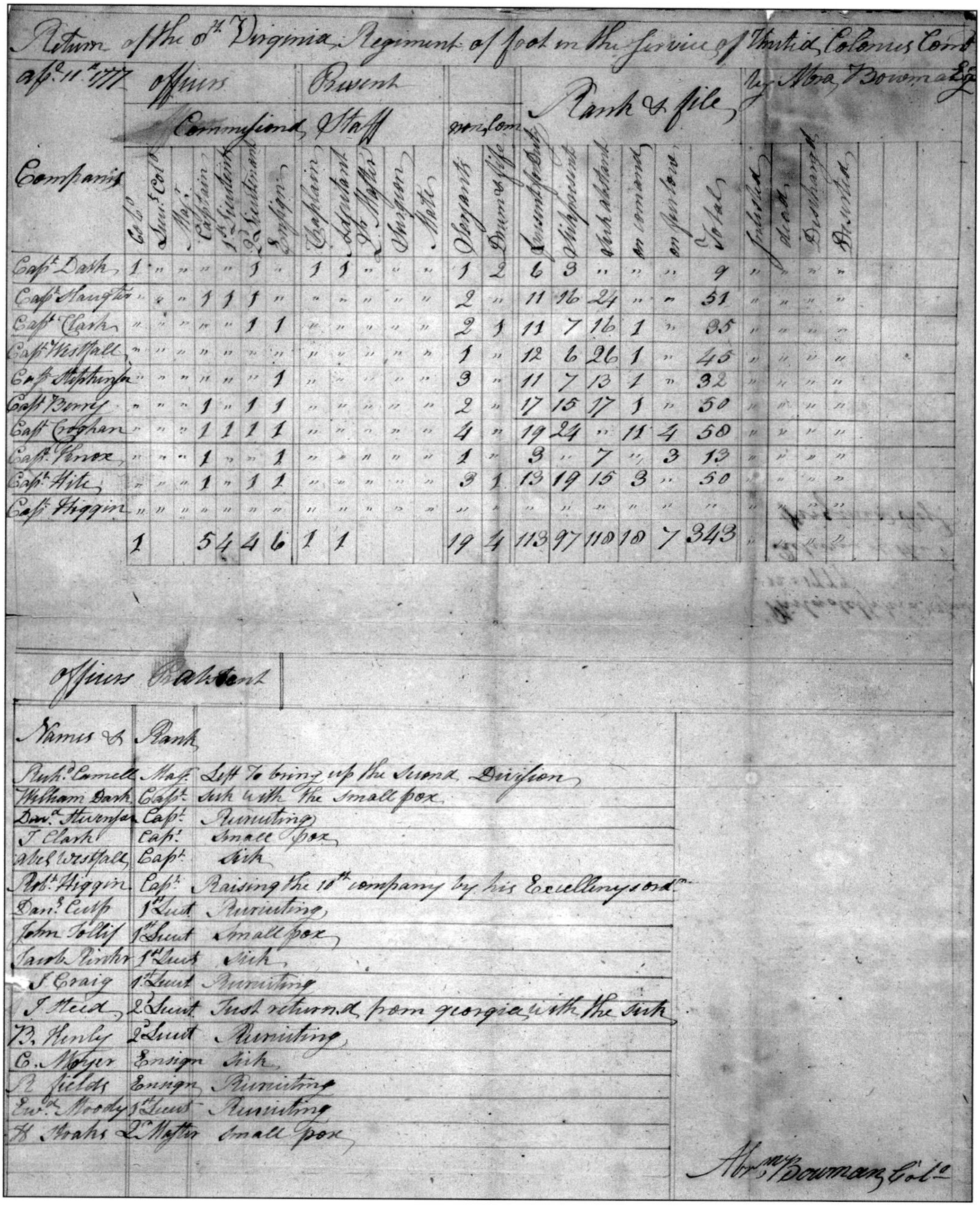
Return of the 8th Virginia Regiment of foot in the Service of United Colonies Comd by Abra Bowman Esq

Apl. 11th 1777

Companies	Col.	Lieut. Col.	Maj.	Captain	1st Lieutenant	2d Lieutenant	Ensign	Chaplain	Adjutant	Qr Master	Surgeon	Mate	Serjeants	Drum & fife	Present fit for Duty	Sick present	Sick absent	On command	On furlough	Total	Enlisted	Dead	Discharged	Deserted
	Officers Present														Rank & file									
	Commissiond							Staff					Non Com											
Capt. Dark	1	"	"	"	"	1	"	1	1	"	"	"	1	2	6	3	"	"	"	9	"	"	"	"
Capt. Slaughter	"	"	"	1	1	1	"	"	"	"	"	"	2	"	11	16	24	"	"	51	"	"	"	"
Capt. Clark	"	"	"	"	"	1	1	"	"	"	"	"	2	1	11	7	16	1	"	35	"	"	"	"
Capt. Westfall	"	"	"	"	"	"	"	"	"	"	"	"	1	"	12	6	26	1	"	45	"	"	"	"
Capt. Stephenson	"	"	"	"	"	"	1	"	"	"	"	"	3	"	11	7	13	1	"	32	"	"	"	"
Capt. Berry	"	"	"	1	"	1	1	"	"	"	"	"	2	"	17	15	17	1	"	50	"	"	"	"
Capt. Croghan	"	"	"	1	1	1	1	"	"	"	"	"	4	"	19	24	"	11	4	58	"	"	"	"
Capt. Knox	"	"	"	1	"	"	1	"	"	"	"	"	1	"	3	"	7	"	3	13	"	"	"	"
Capt. Hite	"	"	"	1	"	1	1	"	"	"	"	"	3	1	13	19	15	3	"	50	"	"	"	"
Capt. Higgin	"	"	"	"	"	"	"	"	"	"	"	"	"	"	"	"	"	"	"	"	"	"	"	"
	1			5	4	4	6	1	1				19	4	113	97	118	10	7	343	"		"	

Officers Absent

Names &	Rank	
Richd. Campbell	Majr.	Left to bring up the second Division
William Dark	Capt.	Sick with the Small pox
David Stevenson	Capt.	Recruiting
J. Clark	Capt.	Small pox
Abel Westfall	Capt.	Sick
Robt. Higgin	Capt.	Raising the 10th company by his Excellency's ordrs.
Danl. Cutts	1st Lieut	Recruiting
John Tollis	1st Lieut	Small pox
Jacob Pinker	1st Lieut	Sick
J. Craig	1st Lieut	Recruiting
J. Heid	2d Lieut	Just returnd from georgia with the sick
B. Henly	2d Lieut	Recruiting
C. Moyer	Ensign	Sick
R. fields	Ensign	Recruiting
Edwd. Moody	1st Lieut	Recruiting
H. Strahs	Qr. Master	Small pox

Abrm. Bowman Colo.

The first return of the united regiment, recorded in Philadelphia on 11 April 1777. (Library of Virginia)

his service, it appears Markham had no actual combat experience, and he did not physically join the regiment until late May or June.[8]

Soldiers arriving in Philadelphia were inoculated and quarantined before they continued on to the army in New Jersey.[9] The lethality of smallpox and other diseases was plain to see in a potter's field just a block from the Pennsylvania State House (Independence Hall). More than 2,000 dead soldiers were buried there, side-by-side in trenches. The place is now Washington Square, the site of the Tomb of the Unknown Revolutionary War Soldier.[10] Isaac Dunn of Captain Berry's Company said they 'were ordered to meet on the common,' the undeveloped western side of the city, 'and all that had not taken the small pox, were taken into the city again and innoculated.'[11] Like Captain Clark, many of these men had barely recovered from malaria. One of Captain Slaughter's soldiers remembered that 'as soon as he recovered from said sickness he went into the North and joined the Army a[t] Philadelphia when he took the small pox.'[12] Sergeant Parett said he 'marched to Philadelphia, where he remained about two months in and about the City, suffering greatly from Small Pox and other diseases incident to the services.'[13]

It was at Philadelphia that Captain Croghan joined the regiment for the first time. After missing much of the fall and winter campaign, he had gone home to Pittsburgh for a while. Matthew Hennen, the man who transferred from the 8th Pennsylvania and was eager to be home, had gone with him. Hennen remembered, 'Capt Crochan and himself came out to Pittsburg in search of deserters.' Croghan then let him have 'a permit to stay with his family (who then lived about fifty miles South West of Pittsburg) for three weeks.'[14]

An 11 April roster shows that Chaplain Christian Streit was finally with the regiment. He remained with the regiment only through June, when regimental chaplaincies were eliminated,[15] but he continued as an army chaplain to the end of the war. The April roster also reveals the regiment was at about half of its original manpower.[16] Richard Campbell was in Virginia preparing to 'bring up the second division'. Captains Slaughter, Berry, Croghan, Knox, and Mathias Hite were present, but Darke, Clark, Lieutenant Jolliffe, and Quartermaster Hezekiah Stoakes were recovering (or dead, in Jolliffe's case) from smallpox. Abel Westfall was simply 'sick'. Captain David Stephenson, Lieutenant Edward Moody (now serving in Captain Westfall's Company), Lieutenant Benjamin Kinley of Stephenson's Company, and Ensign Field of Slaughter's Company were home recruiting. Robert Higgins, likewise, was home 'Raising the 10th company by his Excellency's ordr.' Though disputed, Campbell was still listed as major, and Hite was listed as a captain.[17]

8 Sanchez-Saavedra, *Virginia Military Organisations,* pp.13, 30, 35, 54; NARA: M246, f208, p.2, Muster Roll of Field and Staff Officers, 20 May 1777.
9 NARA: I. Dunn pension; J. Johnston pension; W. Smith pension; LVA: J. Parret rejected claim.
10 Butterfield et al (eds), *Adams Papers* (Family Correspondence), vol.2, pp.209–210.
11 NARA: I. Dunn pension.
12 NARA: M804: S7548, William Smith pension.
13 LVA: J. Parret rejected claim.
14 NARA: J. Grant pension, M. Hennen pension.
15 Ford, *Journals of Congress*, vol.8., pp.390–391; Chase et al (eds), *Papers of Washington* (Revolution), vol.9, pp.540–541, 644–645, vol.10, pp.338–339.
16 LVA: Return of the 8th Virginia Regiment, 11 April 1777; NARA: M246, f.208, p.2, Muster Roll of Field and Staff Officers, 20 May 1777.
17 LVA: Return of the 8th Virginia Regiment, 11 April 1777.

Speaking of men under inoculation, Isaac Dunn remembered that later in April the 'army left the sick and marched into Jersey.'[18] They went to Bound Brook, a forward post just nine miles from the British garrison at Brunswick. The post was commanded by a kind man named Benjamin Lincoln, who had been plucked out of the Massachusetts militia to become a Continental major general. Like Washington, Lincoln's lack of formal military training was counterbalanced by his sterling character.[19] Washington held 'a very high opinion' of the Yankee general, who owed his unconventional appointment entirely to the Virginian's recommendation. The exposed garrison at Bound Brook was Lincoln's first Continental command,[20] and it was under his eye that the 1776 stragglers attached to Croghan began to return to their own companies. Henry Brock, for example, said it was there that 'he joined his company commanded by Capt. Clark who had returned from the Southward with the eighth Virginia Regiment.'[21]

Since Francis Swaine and John Stephenson were both gone, the captaincy of the replacement company would normally have gone to the regiment's senior lieutenant. However, many of the original 1st lieutenants were gone. Robert Beall was now a captain in the 13th Virginia. Henry Field of Captain Slaughter's Culpeper company quit with a bad case of malaria as did Joseph Dickson of David Stephenson's Augusta company. Jacob Rinker resigned to be deputy clerk of Dunmore, John Jolliffe was dead, and Ephraim Drake of James Knox's Fincastle

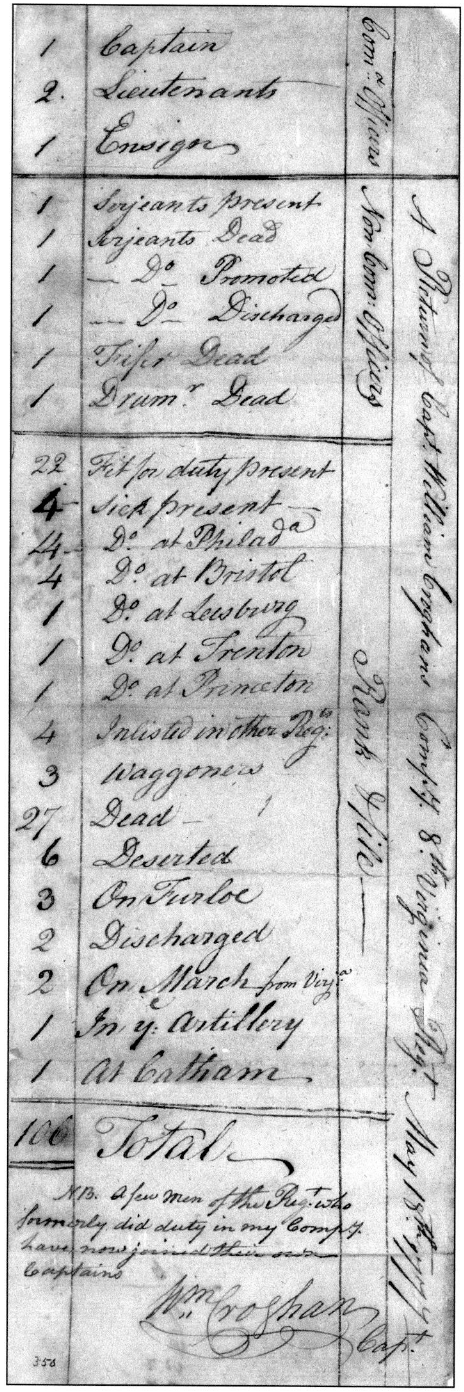

A Return of Capt William Croghan's Compy 8th Virginia Regt May 13th 1777

1	Captain	Comm.d Officers
2	Lieutenants	
1	Ensign	
1	Serjeants present	Non Comm. Officers
1	Serjeants Dead	
1	Do Promoted	
1	Do Discharged	
1	Fifer Dead	
1	Drumr Dead	
22	Fit for duty present	Rank & File
4	Sick present	
4	Do at Philada	
4	Do at Bristol	
1	Do at Leesburg	
1	Do at Trenton	
1	Do at Princeton	
4	Inlisted in other Regts	
3	Waggoners	
27	Dead	
6	Deserted	
3	On Furloe	
2	Discharged	
2	On March from Virga	
1	In ye Artillery	
1	At Catham	
106	Total	

N.B. A few men of the Regt who formerly did duty in my Compy have now joined their own Captains

Wm Croghan Capt.

350

A May return for Croghan's Company notes that men detached under him in 1776 have begun returning to their captains. (Draper Manuscripts Collection, Wisconsin Historical Society)

18 NARA: I. Dunn pension.

19 John T.S. Sullivan, *The Public Men of the Revolution* (Philadelphia: Carey and Hart, 1847), pp.128–129.

20 David B. Mattern, *Benjamin Lincoln and the American Revolution* (Columbia: University of South Carolina Press, 1995), pp.33, 36–37; Chase et al (eds), *Papers of Washington* (Revolution), vol.9, p.157.

21 NARA: H. Brock pension.

company either turned down his appointment or resigned to protect his home in the militia. Daniel Culp of Captain Darke's Company and Abraham Kirkpatrick of Captain Croghan's Company were still in service but had both been detached with the 1st Virginia since the previous summer.

Culp was the senior 1st lieutenant, but he was passed over, evidently for cause. Mathias Hite was next in line, but he was already acting as the captain of Richard Campbell's Company.[22] That left Robert Higgins of Abel Westfall's Company. It was understood, however, that Culp was certain to object and that the challenge to Campbell's promotion might also leave Hite in a bad place. In an unusual move, General Washington personally made the decision to put Higgins at the head of the new company. A note reading, 'by order of Genl. Washington' was put next to Higgins' date of rank on lists of officers.[23]

As it struggled to organise in Virginia, Higgins' new company needed subaltern officers and recruits. James Curry, the now-grown boy from County Antrim, entered Continental service as Higgins' 1st lieutenant. John Clark let Jacob Rinker have his job as deputy clerk of Dunmore and took an appointment as 2nd lieutenant.[24] Captain Higgins' younger brother Peter joined as an ensign.

The 8th Virginia Regiment, April 1777

Field Officers: Col. Abraham Bowman Maj. Richard Campbell*†			**Staff Officers:** Chap. Christian Streit Adj. Abraham Kirkpatrick Qtr. Master Hezekiah Stoakes		
Company	**Captain**	**1st Lieut.**	**2nd Lieut.**	**Ensign**	**Enlisted Men**
Darke's	William Darke*	Daniel Culp*	Isaac Israel	Christopher Moyer*	12/12 Present
Slaughter's	George Slaughter	James Kirtley	John Graves	Reuben Field*	13/53 Present
Clark's	Jonathan Clark*	Jacob Rinker*	Jacob Parett	Philip Eastin	14/38 present
Westfall's	Abel Westfall*	Edward Moody*		Cornelius Westfall*	13/46 present
Stephenson's	David Stephenson*			Benjamin Kinley	14/35 present
Berry's	Thomas Berry	John Jolliffe*	Richard Eastin	Francis Baldwin	19/52 present.
Croghan's	William Croghan	Abraham Kirkpatrick	James Higgins	Jonathan Smith	23/62 present
Knox's	James Knox	James Craig*		William Lewis Lovely	4/14 present
Hite's (Campbell's)	Mathias Hite†		John Steed	Leonard Cooper	17/54 present
Higgins'	Robert Higgins			Peter Higgins	Not formed
136/366 enlisted men present/fit for duty. 97 sick/present. 118 sick/absent. 7 on furlough.					

*Sick/absent. †Rank disputed. Return does not report absent NCOs. (LVA: Return of the 8th Virginia Regiment, 11 April 1777)

22 NARA: M804, f.214, r.106, Capt. Hite Payroll 31 July 1776–30 April 1777.

23 NARA: M804, f.364, p.118, Arrangement of 8th Va. Officers, Sept. 1777.

24 Wayland, *Shenandoah County*, pp.114, 117.

Colonel Bowman received a letter from Washington, directing him to identify four 'sober, young, active & well made' soldiers for the commander-in-chief's life guard. The Great Virginian wanted men of good character and of a particular height who possessed 'the pride of appearing clean & soldierlike.' To ensure their fidelity, he asked for 'Natives, & Men of some property, if You have them.'[25] The men Bowman selected were George Albin and Jonathan Chenoweth of Thomas Berry's Company, Michael Tullis of William Darke's Company, and Robert Wadsworth of Abel Westfall's Company. Chenoweth was a cousin of blacksmith John Chenoweth of Westfall's Company. Tullis was the veteran of Hugh Stephenson's one-year rifle company. All four were transferred immediately.[26]

A court martial was held on 2 May, presided over by Colonel Alexander McClanahan of the 7th Virginia. McClanahan was Ensign Robert Breckenridge's uncle by marriage. The court decided that Breckenridge's acting captain, Mathias Hite, was 'to be reprimanded by the commanding Officer of the regiment, in presence of Lieutenant Culp and other officers of the regiment.'[27] Though not recorded, the nature of the issue between the two officers is easy to deduce. The dispute between Darke and Campbell was on ice with both men absent, but their lieutenants (Culp and Hite) were in camp. Culp had been with Croghan's detachment for months while Hite, paid and addressed as a captain, commanded Campbell's Company. Culp was not wrong to object to Hite's presumed promotion. However, he had also been passed over for command of Higgins' company, which suggests there were concerns about his performance. Culp resigned from the army on 20 May.[28]

The court martial also tried Jacob Parett of Captain Clark's Company. Though recently promoted to 2nd lieutenant, Parett was 'discharged from the service, and his pay stop'd from the time he left his detachment, until he did duty in his regiment again.' The charge indicates he failed to report timely to Fredericksburg after returning from the south in December. Washington approved Hite's and Parett's sentences.[29]

Reverend Thruston Picks Up the Sword

Virginia did everything it could to reinforce Washington's dwindling army during its desperate days in December 1776. The General Assembly authorised Governor Henry and the Council of State to take extraordinary measures.[30] Three companies of quickly recruited volunteers were raised on six-month enlistments,[31] one of which was led by Frederick County's 'fighting parson' Charles Mynn Thruston. Finding that Virginia was, as he said later, 'culled' of fighting men,[32] Thruston relied partly on teenage boys to fill his ranks. Sixteen was the minimum age for regular service,[33] but that did not apply to volunteers.

25 Chase et al (eds), *Papers of Washington* (Revolution), vol.9, p.315.
26 NARA: M246, f.209, p.2; f.212, p.2; f.219, p.27; M804, S41296, Robert Wadsworth pension.
27 Chase et al (eds), *Papers of Washington* (Revolution), vol.9, pp.361–362.
28 NARA: M881, r.1041, Daniel Culp.
29 Chase et al (eds), *Papers of Washington* (Revolution), vol.9, pp.361–362.
30 Anon. (ed.), *Journal of Virginia Delegates*, 1776, p.107.
31 McIlwaine et al (eds), *Council of the State of Virginia*, vol.1, p.300, 350.
32 Chase et al (eds), *Papers of Washington* (Revolution), vol.8, pp.500–502, 574–575.
33 Hening (ed.), *Statutes*, vol.9, pp.16–17.

John Kercheval, Henry Bush, William McGuire, and Thruston's son Charles were 'all boys nearly of an age.' A classmate said that when Kercheval left school to join the army he 'was a boy and called a very young soldier.' He was 14 years old.[34]

Oddly, Thruston's recruits left Winchester on the same day the legislature authorised the volunteers,[35] which presumably means the priest was told his company would be authorised if he could raise it. After crossing into Maryland, Kercheval 'distinctly' recollected that 'they arrived at Frederick Town on Christmas day about 12 o'clock 1776.' Washington's ragged little army was preparing to cross the Delaware towards Trenton at that very hour. Thruston's volunteers crossed the frozen Susquehanna River, passed through Philadelphia and Trenton, and arrived in Morristown on 10 January.[36] Despite their best efforts, they arrived too late to support the critical offensives of the Ten Crucial Days (25 December 1776–3 January 1777). They arrived at headquarters the day before Thomas McCarty rolled into town with his supply wagon looking for liquor.[37]

Washington appointed Thruston captain commandant of the three six-month volunteer companies.[38] They were posted under Lord Stirling at Basking Ridge and served alongside Captain Van Swearingen's company of riflemen from what Kercheval called the 'Catannian' (Kittanning) Regiment (the 8th Pennsylvania) and some cavalry. On 1 March, Thruston's left humerus was shattered, and 14 of the volunteers were killed during an engagement at Piscataway.[39] Thruston's 12-year-old son was next to him when he was shot.[40] The survivors of the volunteer company were discharged in May, but the one-time Frederick Committee chair, despite his wound, was promoted by Washington to colonel and empowered to form one of the 'additional' Continental regiments authorised by Congress.[41]

Still not healed and unable to support recruiting, Thruston never organised his new command. One of his boy soldiers, however, attached himself to the 8th Virginia when it arrived in New Jersey. Still too young to enlist, John Kercheval continued to identify himself as a 'volunteer.' He later explained, 'the Reason of his joining Captain Berry's Company in preference to any other was that Captain Berry was a near neighbor to his Father in Frederick County Virginia.'[42] He stayed with the army until after Yorktown.

Kercheval was not the only child volunteer. Adam Dietz is clearly listed in Sergeant McCarty's August 1776 roster of Croghan's men but had no mess assignment and appears nowhere else in the records of the Virginia Line.[43] In 1818 and 1820, he made his mark on affidavits claiming six years of service under 'Captain Kilpatrick' that began when he was eight years old. He claimed, falsely it seems, that he was a musician.[44]

34 NARA: M804, W3023, John Kercheval pension.
35 Anon. (ed.), *Journal of Virginia Delegates*, 1776, p.107.
36 NARA: J. Kercheval pension.
37 WHS: Draper Mss, N, vol.2, p.43.
38 Chase et al (eds), *Papers of Washington* (Revolution), vol.8, pp.574–575.
39 Chase et al (eds), *Papers of Washington* (Revolution), vol.8, pp.500–502; NARA: J. Kercheval pension; X806, Charles M. Thruston pension; Thruston, 'Biography of Thruston,' p.166.
40 NARA: C.M. Thruston pension.
41 Chase et al (eds), *Papers of Washington* (Revolution), vol.8, pp.574–575.
42 NARA: J. Kercheval pension.
43 WHS: McCarty Notebook, p.19.
44 NARA: M804, W98, Adam Deets pension.

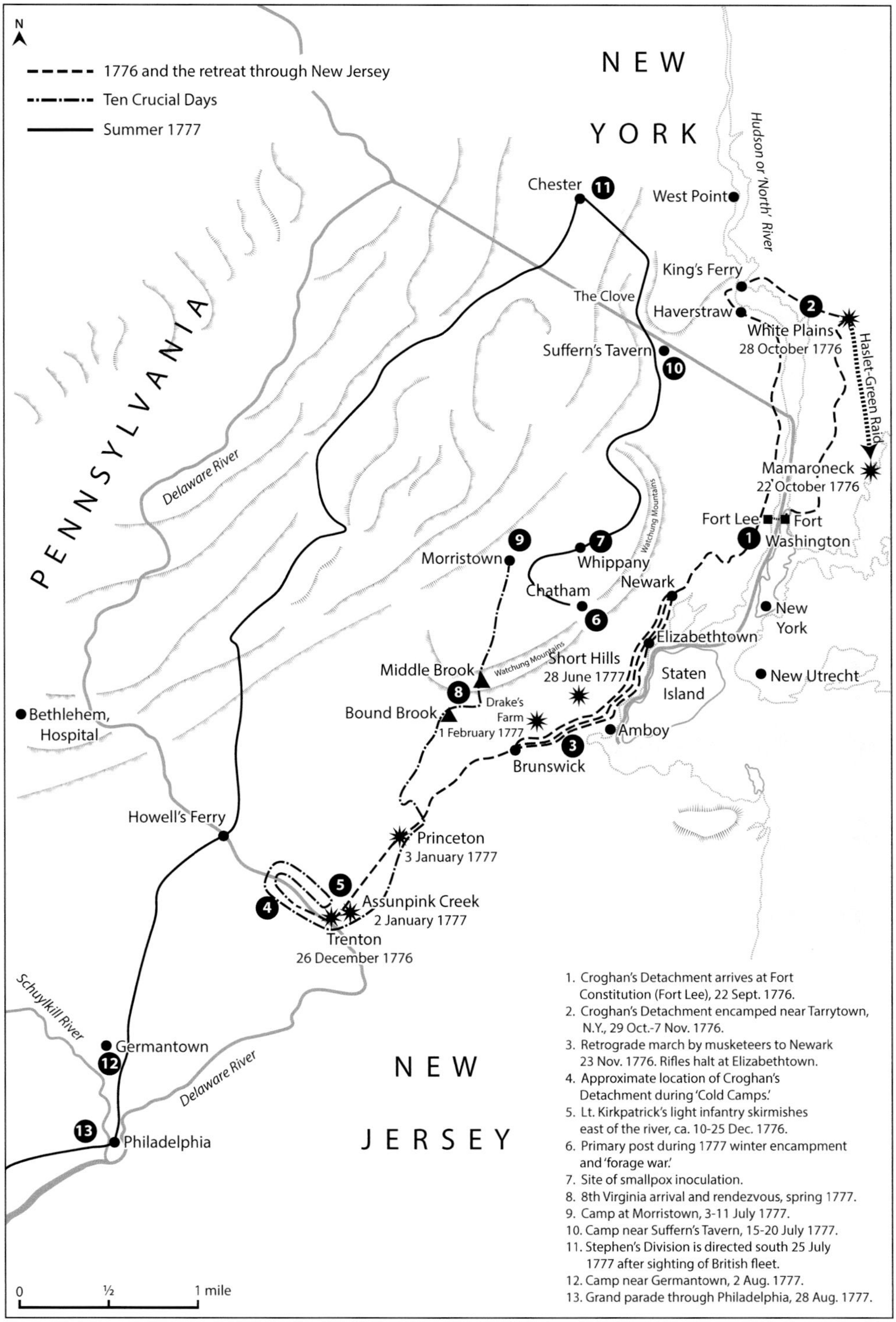

The campaign in New Jersey, 1776–1777.

Adam Stephen's Division

On 11 May, the regiment was assigned to a brigade commanded by recently promoted Brigadier General Charles Scott.[45] Over the winter, brigades (made of four or five regiments) had replaced regiments as the basic combat units of the Main Army. The change was born of necessity at Trenton when regiments were significantly understrength. Washington also began assigning artillery units to support each of the brigades directly. These innovations resulted in a lower officer-to-soldier ratio, better command and control, and greater intensity of fire.[46]

'Charley Scott' was not elite or well-educated.[47] He typified a second generation of Continental officers that was beginning to replace socially prominent but less competent men. An officer in the 3rd Virginia referred to him in 1777 as 'the gallant and not enough to be esteemed Col. Scott.'[48] The new general had enlisted in the Virginia Regiment in 1755 as a 16-year-old orphan. He was described as 'Dark and swarthy with blk Hair and slim made.' A neighbour remembered hearing that he was part Indian. He rose through the ranks because of his courage, leadership abilities, and performance in the field. In 1775 he was a lieutenant colonel in William Woodford's 2nd Virginia. He ranked as a colonel at Assunpink Creek, where he successfully defended the bridge with humour and determination. 'Well boys,' he said to his men, 'you know the *old boss* has put us here to defend this bridge; and by God it must be done.'[49] He counselled his men that 'one man Wounded in the leg is better [than] a dead one for it takes two more to carry them off and there is three gone. Leg them dam 'em I say leg them.'[50] Now he and Woodford were peers, each commanding a brigade.

Adam Stephen had also been promoted again; he was now a major general. Scott's and Woodford's brigades were paired together to make his division. Stephen had significant military experience, but he was a problematic officer. His career tracked closely with Washington's, and that was not a good thing for him. He was always a step behind the future president and seems to have resented it. Stephen was a shameless self-promoter, and his feud with Jacob Hite leaves little doubt that many 8th Virginia men did not like him. Colonel Bowman was Jacob Hite's nephew and Mathias Hite was probably his son. Taverner Beale was his son-in-law, and Jonathan Clark was (or would soon be) courting his niece.[51] William Darke, Cornelius Baldwin, and Philip Eastin were later tied to the family by marriage. The trouble between Stephen and the financially distressed Jacob Hite peaked in 1774 when Stephen, as Berkeley sheriff, seized Hite's slaves and horses to satisfy a debt. Daniel Hendricks, now one of Darke's sergeants, organised a gang to take the human and equine chattels back. Hendricks, who was

45 Chase et al (eds), *Papers of Washington* (Revolution), vol.9, p.384.
46 Wright, *Continental Army*, pp.97–98, 104.
47 Harry M. Ward, *Charles Scott and the 'Spirit of '76'* (Charlottesville: University Press of Virginia, 1988), p.2.
48 John Chilton to Leven Powell, 11 Feb. 1777, in Anon. (ed.), 'The Old Virginia Line in the Middle States During the American Revolution', *Tyler's Quarterly*, 12:2 (1930), pp.111–114.
49 Ward, *Scott*, pp.ix, 2–12, 27.
50 William S. Powell (ed.), 'A Connecticut Soldier Under Washington: Elisha Bostwick's Memoirs of the First Years of the Revolution', *William and Mary* Quarterly 6:1 (1949), p.106. Edited for clarity.
51 Frances Smith Beale Hodges, *The Genealogy of the Beale Family, 1399–1956* (Ann Arbor: Edwards Brothers,1956), p.85.

purportedly seven feet tall,[52] chopped open the doors of the jail and the stable with an axe.[53] The following year, Hite initiated the successful petition to have Stephen unseated from the 3rd Virginia Convention in 1775.[54] Hite was killed by a Cherokee war party in 1776,[55] but hard feelings persisted. Sergeant Hendricks left the regiment about the time it was assigned to Stephen's Division. No explanation was given on the rolls.[56]

At the start of 1777, Major General Adam Stephen's Division consisted of:

William Woodford's Brigade
3rd Virginia Regiment, Colonel Thomas Marshall
7th Virginia Regiment, Colonel Alexander McClanachan
11th Virginia Regiment, Lieutenant Colonel Christian Febiger[57]
15th Virginia Regiment, Colonel David Mason

Charles Scott's Brigade
4th Virginia Regiment, Colonel Thomas Elliott
8th Virginia Regiment, Colonel Abraham Bowman
12th Virginia Regiment, Colonel James Wood
Grayson's Additional Regiment, Colonel William Grayson
Patton's Additional Regiment, Colonel John Patton

Colonel Grayson's men were from Virginia and Maryland.[58] Colonel Patton, previously a major in the Pennsylvania State Rifle Regiment, raised his companies in Pennsylvania, Delaware, and New Jersey.[59]

For the first time, the regiment had a full roster of staff and warrant officers. Cornelius Baldwin of New Jersey became its surgeon on 20 May. Frederick Heimberger, a German man of obscure origins, was Baldwin's surgeon's mate. Hezekiah Stoakes served briefly as quartermaster before switching to paymaster. Martin Carney joined as quartermaster sergeant on 3 May and followed Stoakes as quartermaster early in June. Ashkenaz Shappee replaced him as quartermaster sergeant. 'Shappee' is believed to be an Anglicization of a French name, perhaps *Chapuis*. His name was usually recorded as 'Askin Shippy' on the regiment's rolls. Nicholas Neal was drum major, and William Palmer was sergeant major. With Francis Swaine gone, Abraham Kirkpatrick served as adjutant while retaining his lieutenancy under Captain Croghan.[60]

---

52 Florence Hendricks Moore, *Descendants of Albert(us) Hendricks(on), 1673–1984* (Charleston, W.Va.: F.H. Moore, 1985), p.37.
53 Ward, *Adam Stephen*, pp.104–106; Woody Holton, *Forced Founders: Indians, Debtors, Slaves, and the Making of the American Revolution in Virginia* (Chapel Hill: University of North Carolina Press, 1999), pp.xiii-xv.
54 Hite et al, 'Petition of Freeholders, *VMHB*, 13:4 (1906), pp.412–416.
55 Wayland, *Bowmans*, pp.116–117.
56 NARA: M246, f.212, pp.2, 21.
57 Colonel Daniel Morgan was detached to the Provisional Rifle Corps.
58 Sanchez-Saavedra, *Virginia Military Organisations*, pp.73–74.
59 Trussell, *Pennsylvania Line*, pp.147–151.
60 NARA: M246, f208, pp.2, 4.

Another Court Martial and More Rank Disputes

Jonathan Clark left the Shenandoah Valley with Richard Campbell and the regiment's 'second division' on 11 May,[61] riding a second-rate horse. Clark's father wrote to him earlier from Caroline, 'I cannot heare of a horse to sell in thes parts that I think would sute you.' Knowing this might mean his son would not visit again soon, the elder Clark added a blessing.

> Should you go to the North before you come down we expect it will be a long long time before we see you again. Perhaps never in this life. So hope it is please God to spare your life and your Business will admit you will come & see us before you go to the Army. But should your affairs be so as to oblige you out before we see you – our Blessing atend you – and we shall pray by the help of God to that same & grate God almighty to guide covering & protect you in all your undertakings so that when your Task is finishd we may the[n] receive you safe & sound. These I say will be the prayers of your affectionate Parrants as your mother joins me in what I write.[62]

Campbell and Clark led their men up the Wagon Road to the Potomac and followed its curve to the east. After a week on the road, Clark stayed for three days in Philadelphia at the home of 'Mr. Lee,' perhaps one of the Lee brothers representing Virginia in Congress. He arrived in Bound Brook two days before the regiment decamped for a new post between the First and Second Ridges of the Watchung Mountains. 'Camp struck,' he wrote on 25 May, 'and moved over Mountain and encamped between two mountains call'd middle brook.' The east and west branches of Middle Brook (a creek) ran through the valley, joining to flow south through Bound Brook Gap to the Raritan River. Headquarters also relocated there from Morristown and General Washington reviewed the troops when he arrived. Most of the 8th Virginia men had never seen him before.

Clark's Company was assigned to picket duty close to New Brunswick for a couple of days while the rest of the army stayed close to the Watchung Mountains, organising, drilling, and receiving supplies. Captain Clark then visited several farms looking for a better horse.[63] Washington scolded the troops over gambling, uncleanliness, and wasting ammunition. He encouraged them to eat salad made from the sorrel and water cress that grew near the camp.[64] The 8th Virginia received new tents and was, for the first time in a year, well-equipped.[65]

Another court martial convened. James Kirtley, Captain Slaughter's new 1st lieutenant, was arrested and accused of 'Disobedience of orders, and absenting himself three months, beyond the time allotted him to join his regiment.'[66] It appears Kirtley, like Jacob Parett, took an inor-

61 FHS: Clark Diary, 11 May 1777.
62 WHS: Draper Mss, L, vol.1, p.35, John Clark to Jonathan Clark, April 1777.
63 FHS: Clark Diary, 18, 23–29 May, 20 June 1777.
64 Chase et al (eds), *Papers of Washington* (Revolution), vol.9, pp. 551–552, 588–590, 597–599, 651–652.
65 Chase et al (eds), *Papers of Washington* (Revolution), vol.9, pp.543–544; Harry M. Ward, *Duty, Honor or Country: General George Weedon and the American Revolution* (Philadelphia: American Philosophical Society, 1979), p.89.
66 NARA: M246, f.217, p.5.

dinately long time returning to duty in Virginia. He was acquitted of being away without leave but found guilty of disobeying orders and 'sentenced to be discharged from the service.'[67] John Graves, Slaughter's capable 2nd lieutenant and former ensign, took Kirtley's place.[68]

In May, Congress empowered Washington to resolve the question of Richard Campbell's rank.

> Resolved, That General Washington be requested to enquire into the case of Major Campbell, of the 8 Virginia regiment, and if his commission, which was ordered him by the resolution of Congress ... was out of course, that the General be empowered to settle all disputes between the said Major Campbell, and all the other officers belonging to the State of Virginia, concerning rank; and, if the General shall so determine, that the said commission be rendered null and void.[69]

Washington promised President John Hancock, 'The inquiry directed, respecting Major Campbell, shall be made and that be done, which shall appear right.'[70] The commander in chief directed Brigadier General Scott to appoint a board of officers to investigate the dispute and another between James Knox and William Croghan. Though Croghan's Company was the last of the original companies to be approved by its committee, Knox's Company had failed to fill its quota at formation. Followed rules established by the Convention, the Fincastle Committee sent Knox's recruits east anyway, counting on the Committee of Safety to address the shortfall.[71] (This was done by appointing Edward Moody to continue recruiting.)[72] Croghan objected to having a date of rank later than Knox's, and the board ruled in his favour.[73]

Knox and Croghan may not have known there was an issue between them until they met in Philadelphia in April. The matter of Campbell's majority, on the other hand, had dragged on for months. After reviewing the facts, the board found that 'Captain Richard Campbell has a Majors Commission dated the 10th August 1776 which appears to be out of Turn.' Captain Darke was senior to Campbell by 10 days. Not only was he due a promotion, but justice demanded that it should be retroactive to ensure his seniority relative to other majors in the army. It was not possible, however, for it to date from Helphenstine's resignation. Instead, Darke was 'entitled to a Majority on the death of Major Fleming' at the Battle of Princeton. A copy of the board's report kept by Jonathan Clark is undated but appears to have been written in the middle of June. Abraham Bowman is the only field officer named on it, which reflects the dispute over the majority and shows that Lieutenant Colonel Markham still had not joined the regiment.[74]

67 Chase et al (eds), *Papers of Washington* (Revolution), vol.9, pp.657–660.
68 NARA: M246, f.217, p.8.
69 Ford (ed.), *Journals of Congress*, vol.7, pp.351–252.
70 Chase et al (eds), *Papers of Washington* (Revolution), vol.9, pp.438–440.
71 NARA: M246, f.364, p.16; Harwell (ed.), *Westmoreland and Fincastle Committees*, pp.87; Hening (ed.), *Statutes*, vol.9, pp.76–78.
72 *Virginia Gazette* (Purdie), 16 Aug. 1776.
73 FHS: Clark Family Papers, Mss. A C592c, 'Rank of officers & Col. Abraham Bowman's regiment as settled by the Board of officers appointed by the Hon Brig. Gen. Scott.'
74 FHS: 'Rank of Officers.'

If Washington did nothing but accept the board's assessment, Campbell's promotion would have been 'null and void.' Instead, he worked with his subordinate generals to smooth the transition. To buy time, Scott put Darke in charge of the brigade's riflemen and sent Campbell back to Virginia to supervise recruiting and report back 'once a Month.'[75] Campbell's malcontent lieutenant, Mathias Hite, was sent with him, along with 2nd Lieutenant Leonard Cooper of Clark's Company, and others.[76]

Morgan's Rifles

On 1 June, Scott ordered Colonel Bowman to count the number of riflemen under his command. He was specifically instructed to 'include none but such as are known to be perfectly skilled in the use of these guns, and who are known to be active and orderly in their behaviour.' Scott and the other brigadiers passed the reported names on to Adjutant General Timothy Pickering.[77] There were companies of western riflemen in most or all of the Old Dominion's regiments. Pennsylvania also had significant numbers of riflemen, and Maryland had some. Virginia's original regiments, the 1st and 2nd, were raised with two each.[78] The 3rd, 4th, 5th, 6th, and 7th each had three. The 9th, originally formed for service on Virginia's eastern shore, had two.[79] Virginia does not seem to have specifically ordered rifle companies for the six newest regiments, but the 11th,[80] 12th, and 13th certainly included riflemen, and the 10th, 14th, and 15th may have as well.[81]

The Virginia Conventions intended the Old Dominion's regimented rifle companies 'to act as light infantry', often in detached and semidetached roles.[82] The independent 1775 rifle companies raised in western Virginia, Maryland, and Pennsylvania for Continental service were not regimented with musketeers, but a rifle corps was authorised under John Stephenson's brother, Hugh, in 1776. Hugh died that summer, and most of his men were captured when Fort Washington fell in November.[83] A less successful combined-arms light infantry unit was authorised by Congress in December under the command of Major Nicholas Dietrich, Baron von Ottendorf, a foreign adventurer.[84]

75 Chase et al (eds), *Papers of Washington* (Revolution), vol.10, pp.382–383.

76 NARA: M881, r.1045, Mathias Hite.

77 Chase et al (eds), *Papers of Washington* (Revolution), vol.9, pp.577–578.

78 Anon (ed.), *Proceedings of the 3rd Convention*, p.30; NARA: M804, S8312, William Dews pension (9th Va.).

79 Anon (ed.), *Proceedings of the 4th Convention*, p.105.

80 McIlwaine et al (eds), *Council of the State of Virginia*, vol.1, p.339; Anon. (ed.), *Journal of Virginia Delegates*, 1776, p.50.

81 NARA: M804, S37779, John Neal Blair pension (12th Va.), S4719, Moses Waller pension (13th Va.), S40538, William Subbuth pension (10th Va.)

82 Anon (ed.), *Proceedings of the 3rd Convention,* p.30; Anon (ed.), *Proceedings of the 4th Convention,* p.105.

83 LVA: Revolutionary War Bounty Land Claims, Hugh Stephenson; Sanchez-Saavedra, *Virginia Military Organisations*, pp.86–88.

84 Ford (ed.), *Journals of Congress*, vol.6, pp.1007, 1013, 1022; John U. Rees, *Capt. John Paul Schott's Independent Rifle Company, Ottendorff's Corps, Battle of Short Hills, 26 June 1777*, <scribd.com/document/347250413/Capt-John-Paul-Schott-s-Independent-Rifle-Company-Ottendorff-s-Corps-Battle-of-Short-Hills-26-June-1777>, accessed 30 August 2023; Wright, *Continental Army*, pp.133–134.

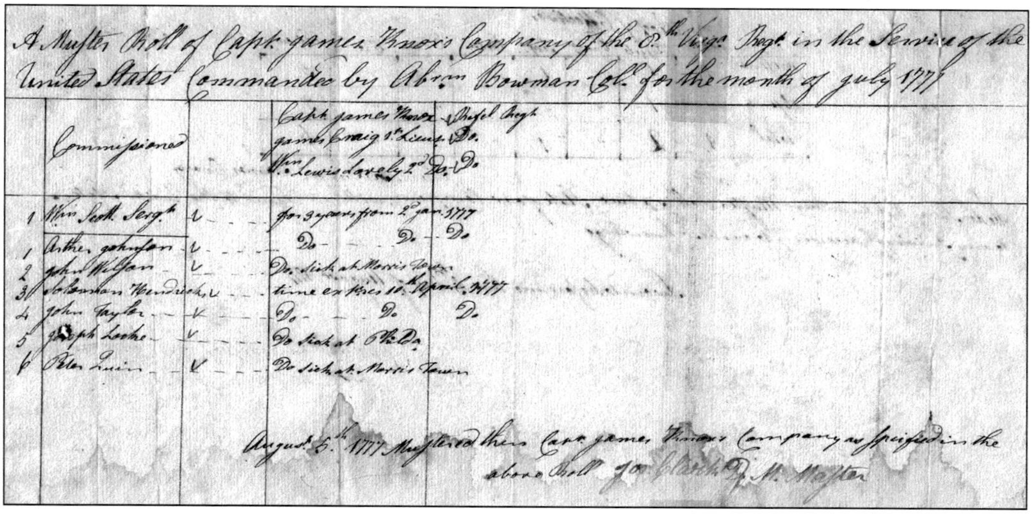
A Muster Roll of Capt. James Knox's Company of the 8th Virga Regt. in the Service of the United States Commanded by Abram Bowman Col. for the month of July 1777

August 5th 1777 Mustered then Capt. James Knox's Company as specified in the above Roll

The last muster for Knox's Company shows just one sergeant and three soldiers fit for duty, and all officers detached to Morgan's Rifles. (National Archives)

When the army's marksmen had been identified at Middle Brook, 500 of them were organised into a Provisional Rifle Corps. They were mostly from Virginia and Pennsylvania, selected individually or as whole companies,[85] and were detached for temporary service with Colonel Daniel Morgan commanding.[86] Captain Knox led one of the 10 companies with his lieutenants, James Craig and William Lewis Lovely.[87] Of the four enlisted men remaining in his 8th Virginia company, Knox took Sergeant William Scott and Solomon Hendricks with him.[88] The two not chosen were put in Captain Berry's Company, marking the end of the Fincastle company. All told, a dozen 8th Virginia enlisted men followed

Daniel Morgan ca. 1780. (National Portrait Gallery, Smithsonian Institution)

85 Sanchez-Saavedra, *Virginia Military Organisations*, pp.88–89; Trussell, *Pennsylvania Line*, pp.27, 24, 104,107, 134, 136.
86 Albert Louis Zambone, *Daniel Morgan: A Revolutionary Life* (Yardley: Westholme, 2018), pp.120–124.
87 NARA: M246, f.226, pp.82–104.
88 M246, f.216, p.5, f.226, pp.82–103; NARA: M804, S4352, Solomon Hendricks pension.

Knox into Morgan's Rifles.[89] Henry Wysor, the reluctant sergeant from Captain Berry's Company, remembered that 'when I joined the main army in the Jerseys I was attached to a strange company, in a few days I joined General Morgan's rifle regiment … I was again appointed Sergeant and served as such.'[90] Most of Knox's men came from the 3rd Virginia.[91] A few came from the 8th Pennsylvania,[92] the 11th Virginia,[93] and other regiments.

8th Virginia Men Detached to Morgan's Rifles

Captain James Knox
1st Lieutenant James Craig
2nd Lieutenant William Lewis Lovely
Sergeant William Scott (Knox's Company)
Sergeant Henry Wysor (Berry's Company)
William Courtney (Slaughter's Company)
Osborn Flyn (Westfall's Company)
Solomon Hendricks (Knox's Company)
John Hicks (Westfall's Company)
Abraham Hornback (Westfall's Company)
Patrick Johnston (Westfall's Company)
Benjamin Kercheval (Berry's Company)
Henry Miller (Westfall's Company)
Joseph Pancake (Westfall's Company)
James Taff (Westfall's Company)[94]

Other 8th Virginia men gave up their rifles for muskets as Muhlenberg had requested, even though some of the rifles were personal property. Benjamin Crow of David Stephenson's Company went to court in 1782 to get reimbursed for 'a Rifle gun, powder horn, shot pouch and knife taken from Him When a continental soldier in the year 1777.'[95] A complete account of Captain Croghan's original recruits, which may not be typical, shows only four men (John Brown, William Gaddis, Lewis Greenstaff, and James Smith) brought their own arms in 1776.[96] At Middlebrook, Crow's new weapon was a French Charleville musket, one of 11,000 that arrived in Philadelphia in March.[97]

89 NARA: M246, f.209, pp.13, 16, f.226, pp.82–103.
90 NARA: H. Wysor pension.
91 NARA: M804, S41462, Reuben Bryan pension (3rd Va.); W5553, Benjamin Powell pension (3rd Va.); M246, f.226, pp.82–104, pay rolls of Capt. Knox's company.
92 NARA: M804, W7408, Abijah McClain pension (8th Pa.); M246, f.226, pp.82–104, pay rolls of Capt. Knox's company.
93 NARA: M804, S40351, John Robinson pension (11th Va.); M246, f.226, pp.82–104, pay rolls of Capt. Knox's company.
94 NARA: M246, f.226, pp.83, 85, 87, 89, 91, 93, 99, 101, 103.
95 Rockingham County: Minute Book 1 (1778–1792), p.174.
96 WHS: Draper Mss, N, vol.1, p.90.
97 George D. Moller, *American Shoulder Arms* (Albuquerque: University of New Mexico Press, 2011), vol.1, p.484.

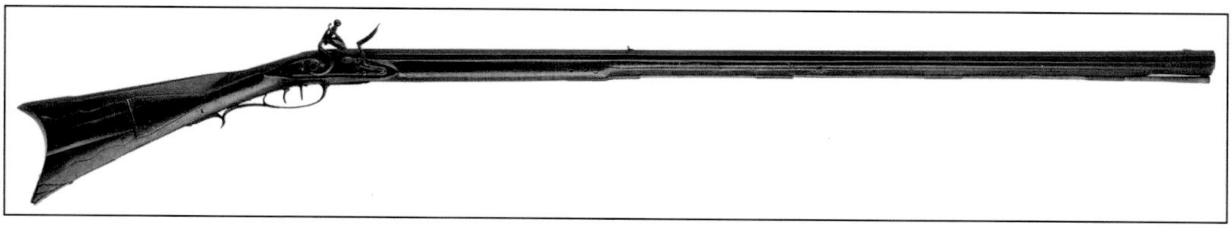

An unornamented long rifle made by John Sheets of Staunton, Va. The undated weapon is stylistically representative of the rifles made by his kinsmen Philip and Henry Sheetz in Shepherdstown for Captain Darke's Company. (Courtesy of Tim Hodges. Photo: Ric Lambert)

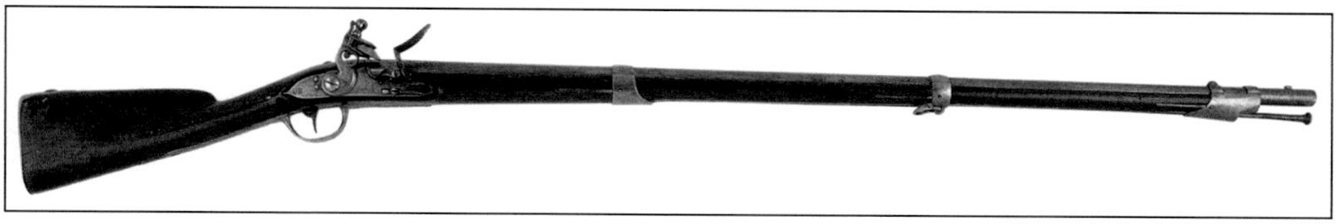

8th Virginia men who gave up their rifles in 1777 were issued French Charleville Model 1763 muskets. (Division of Military and Society, National Museum of American History, Smithsonian Institution)

That only 15 men and officers from a previously all-rifle regiment went with Morgan begs explanation. Abraham Kirkpatrick led three weeks of successful cross-river skirmishing before Trenton, yet not even one of his men went with Morgan. Sticking with Virginia's early plan, Scott retained most of his brigade's riflemen so he could detach his own light infantry in the field.[98] William Darke led 150 detached Virginia marksmen in the army's next engagement, a number exactly equal to the size of John Haslet's light infantry advance at Mamaroneck and (if a single reference is correct) 50 shy of the 200 skirmishers Kirkpatrick's led in the lead-up to Trenton.[99] Elihu Chilcott, one of Kirkpatrick's men from the winter of 1776, remembered that detachments were frequent during his service through 1779: 'he being a rifle man was from time to time attached to other Regiments and Corps' which, by 1820, he could no longer list.[100]

Darke's Riflemen at the Battle of Short Hills, 28 June 1776

The British sought to draw the Americans out of the mountains so they could fight them in the open. On 14 June, Redcoats advanced to Somerset Court House (Somerville), near the Watchungs' southwestern end, where they plundered and burned houses, barns, and churches.[101] The Americans did not take the bait, but Scott did move his brigade west to Pluckemin to counter further advances in that direction.[102] Here, where the two sides tested each other, Joachim Fetzer of Woodstock remembered being in 'a scrimmage with the

98 Chase et al (eds), *Papers of Washington* (Revolution), vol.10, pp.137–138.
99 NARA: B. Alsop pension.
100 NARA: E. Chilcott pension.
101 Grant, 'Narrative', p.731.
102 Grant, 'Narrative', p.731; FHS: Clark Diary, 14 June 1777.

Enemy.'[103] After a few days of fruitless skirmishing, the British returned to New Brunswick while Morgan's riflemen dogged their rear. Scott took his brigade to a gap in the mountains.[104] The British continued east through Bonhamtown towards Staten Island, where transports waited for them. Washington cautiously moved his army down from the mountains to Quibbletown and dispatched more skirmishers after his foe.[105]

According to a contemporary account from a 12th Virginia man, 'there was a detachment of 150 Riflemen chosen from among the Virginia regiments, dispatched under the command of Capt. James Dark a Dutchman, belonging to the eighth Virginia Regt to watch the enemy's motions.' Captain Darke was neither 'James' nor German, but the regiment still carried the 'Dutch' association in the mind of an Ulsterman from the middle valley. 'The same day this party, of which I was one, marched to Quibbleton, and from thence proceeded towards Amboy.'[106] Another 12th Virginia man recalled that 'he went as a Scout under Captain Darke to Amboy.'[107] A New Jersey officer's report concurs that early in the morning of 26 June, '150 Virginians went Down to or near Woodbridge as Did a small scout from our Brigade.'[108]

Howe unexpectedly turned his army around in the earliest hours of 26 June and approached the Americans in two divisions. He pushed Morgan's men aside near Woodbridge and marched directly at Darke's riflemen, who were posted on a hill with Ottendorf's 300 men and some other skirmishers, adding up to a force the British estimated to be 600 strong.[109] Ottendorf's men were now under the command of Colonel Charles Armand.[110] What transpired that morning was recorded by William Grant of the 12th Virginia.

> ...that night we posted ourselves within a little of their camp and sent an officer with 50 men further on the road as a picquet guard, to prevent our being surprised in the night. Next morning a little before sun rise the British army before we suspected them, were upon pretty close on our picquet before they were discovered, and fired

103 NARA: M804, S39518, Joachim Fetzer pension.

104 Grant, 'Narrative', p.731; FHS: Clark Diary, 15–19 June 1777.

105 Chase et al (eds), *Papers of Washington* (Revolution), vol.10, pp.123–125, 145–147.

106 Grant, 'Narrative', p.731.

107 NARA: M804, W6481, Jacob Wheat pension (12th Va.).

108 LOC: Geography and Map Division, G3814.N4S3 1777 .W3, Friedrich Adam Julius von Wangenheim, 'Plan de notre camp à New Brunswick le 12e. juin, notre marche le 14 à Middlebush, la situation du camp le 15e juin, et cette du Genl. Washington à Boundbrook, le poste que le Genl. Sulivan occupoit le 15 dans la nuit pour courir Philadelphia, se postant sur la route de Pennington'; John U. Rees, *'We ... wheeled to the Right to form the Line of Battle': Colonel Israel Shreve's Journal, 23 November 1776 to 14 August 1777 (Including Accounts of the Action at the Short Hills)*, <scribd.com/document/153790118/We-wheeled-to-the-Right-to-form-the-Line-of-Battle-Colonel-Israel-Shreve-Cars-Journal-23-November-1776-to-14-August-1777-Including-Accounts-of#>, accessed 2 Sept. 2023, p.65.

109 Charles F. Heartman (ed.), *Narrative of Johan Carl Buettner in the American Revolution* (New York: C.F. Heartman, 1915), p.42; LOC: Geography and Map Division, G3813.E7S3 1777 .W3, Friedrich Adam Julius von Wangenheim, 'Plan de l'affaire de Westfield & du camp de Raway.'

110 Wright, *Continental Army*, pp.133–134; Sanchez-Saavedra, *Virginia Military Organisations*, pp.93–94; Brook Blades and Wade Catts, *'...The Musket Balls Flew Like Hail Stones... The Short Hills Battlefield Study'*, John Milner Associates, December 2011, <metuchen-edisonhistsoc.org/resources/The+Short+Hills+Battlefield+Study+12-2011+FINAL.pdf>, accessed 23 April 2025.

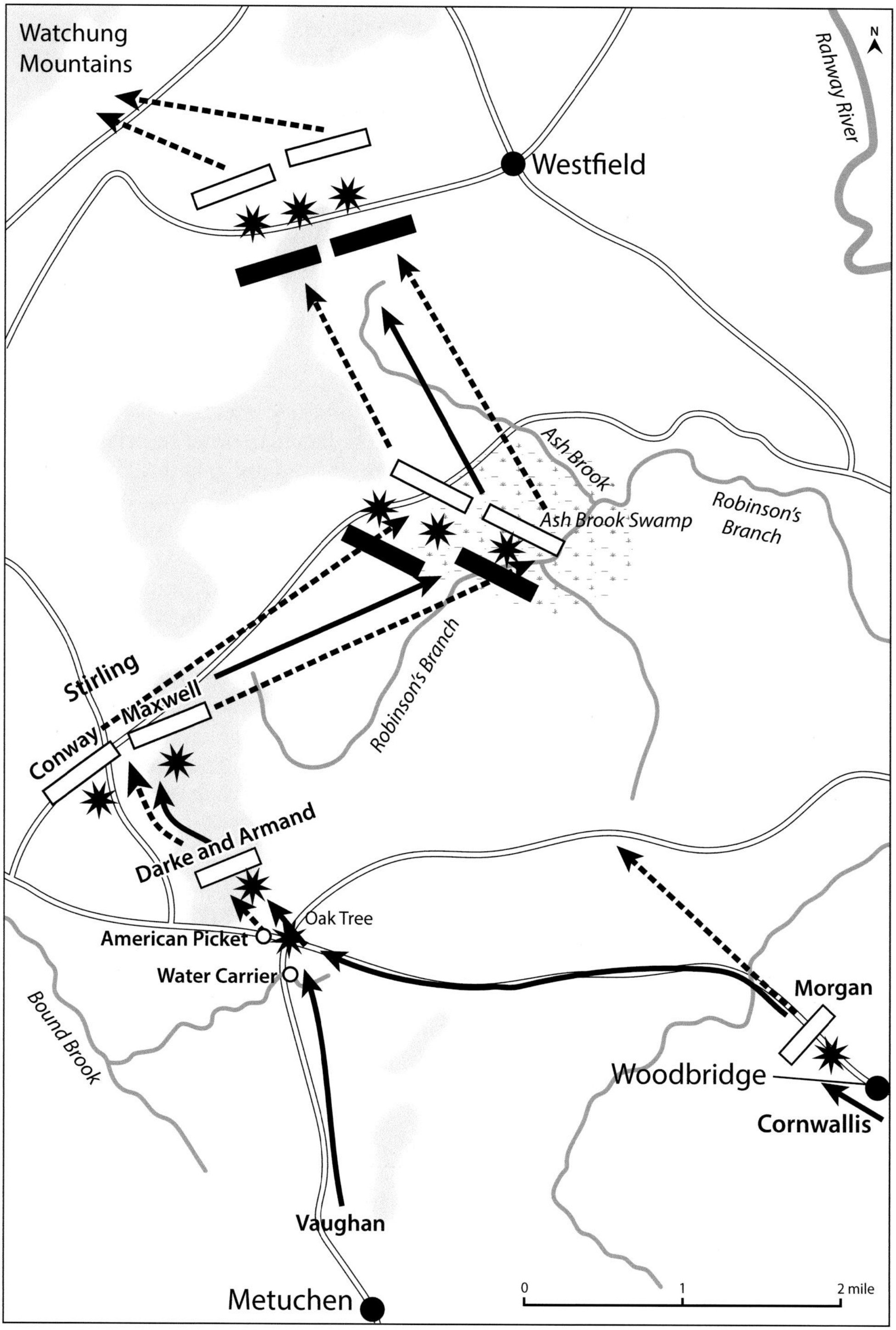

The Battle of Short Hills, 26 June 1777.

> at a negroe lad that was fetching some water for the officer of sd guard, and broke his arm. Upon which he ran to the picquet and alarmed them, affirming at the same time that there was not upwards of sixty men in the party that fired at him.

The warning was relayed to Darke and Armand, who 'prepared as quick as possible to receive them and assist our picquet who was then engaged.' The officers lined their men up on the hill and were soon the targets of the advancing army's field artillery. 'We immediately retreated into the woods,' Grant wrote, 'from whence we returned them a very brisk fire with our rifles, so continued firing and retreating without any reinforcement till about 10 oClock, they plying us very warmly both with their artillery and small arms all the time.'[111] William Grant took Armand's German-speaking troops to be Hessian defectors, and indeed some of them were.[112]

> ...we were reinforced with about 400 Hessians ... and three brass field pieces under the command of Lord Stirling. They drew up immediately in order to defend their field pieces and cover our retreat, and in less than an hour and a half were entirely cut off; scarce sixty of them returned safe out of the field; those who did escape were so scattered over the country that a great number of them could not rejoin the Army for five or six days...[113]

One of Armand's men reported, 'When we saw that we were outnumbered and resistance was hopeless, we abandoned our cannon and baggage and fled down the other side of the [hill]. Many threw away their rifles and knapsacks, and ran like hares into the forest. I fell into a ditch and my comrades, leaving me for dead, jumped over me.'[114]

Morgan's riflemen were not engaged on the hill, though one nonparticipant report says they were.[115] Sergeant Grant does not mention Morgan. Washington's correspondence indicates that Morgan was close to Amboy when the British made their 'sudden and rapid' reversal and were almost cut off at Woodbridge. Washington referred to the units on the hill as 'some of our Light parties', which is clearly distinct from 'Colo Morgans Corps of Riflemen', mentioned in his preceding sentence.[116]

Thomas Conway's Pennsylvania brigade covered the light infantry retreat and then fell back to join William Maxwell's New Jersey brigade at Ash Swamp. These brigades belonged to Stirling's Division (Lord Stirling was now a major general). Significant numbers of men engaged on both sides and there was fighting for some time. The battle ended when Stirling's outnumbered men retreated into the mountains just in time to avoid capture. Today this

111 Grant, 'Narrative', pp.731–732.

112 Joseph P. Tustin (ed.), *Diary of the American War: A Hessian Journal, Johann Ewald, Field Jäger Corps* (New Haven: Yale University Press, 1979), p.55; Ford (ed.), Journals of Congress, vol.11, pp.642–645.

113 Grant, 'Narrative', p.732. See also Ernst Kipping and Samuel Smith (trans. and ed.), *At General Howe's Side, 1776*–1778 [diary of Capt. Friedrich von Muenchhausen] (Monmouth Beach, N.J.: Philip Freneau Press, 1974), p.19.

114 Heartman (ed.), *Narrative of Buettner*, p.44. Translated from German.

115 Anon. (ed.), 'The Old Virginia Line in the Middle States During the American Revolution', *Tyler's Quarterly Historical and Genealogical Magazine*, 12:2 (1931), p.118.

116 Chase et al (eds), *Papers of Washington* (Revolution), vol.10, pp.137–138, 147–148.

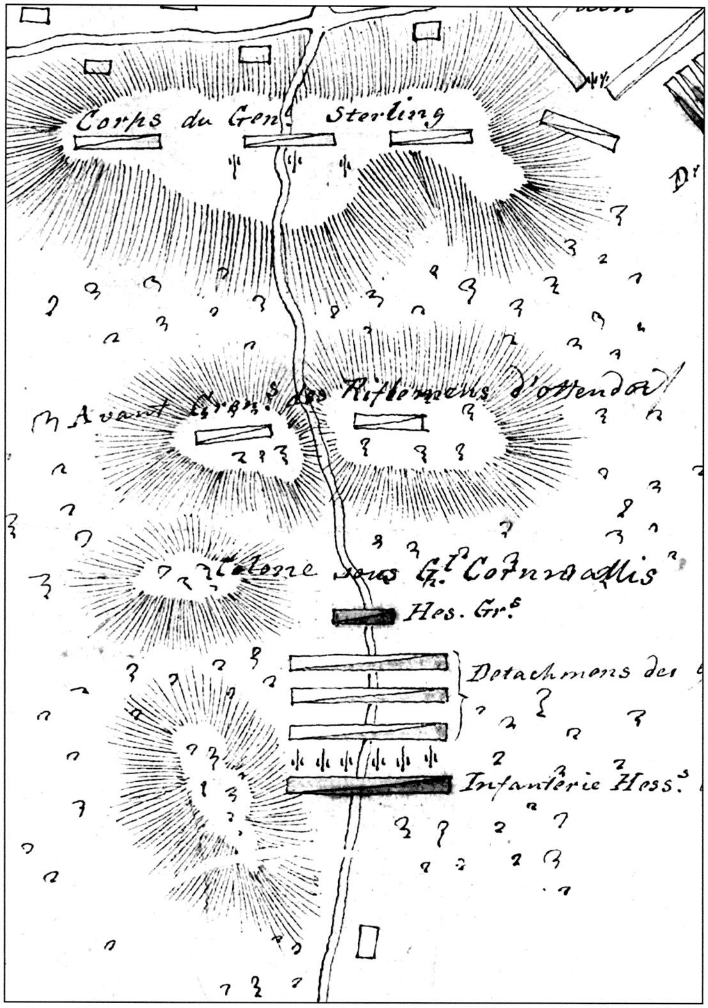

Detail of a contemporary map of the Crown forces' approach at Short Hills. The 'riflemens d'Ottendorf' were actually under the command of Charles Armand and paired with William Darke's detachment of riflemen from Scott's Brigade. Friedrich Adam Julius von Wangenheim. (Library of Congress)

engagement is called the Battle at Short Hills, but many soldiers remembered it as the battle 'at Ash Swamp.'[117] William Moody, the veteran of Michael Cresap's 1775 Maryland rifle company, said he 'was wounded at ash Swamp near Amboy … in the left knee.'[118] William Forsyth of Campbell's Company was taken prisoner.[119] The main body of the 8th Virginia remained in the mountains throughout the battle and did not participate.[120] Afterward, William Howe took his forces to Staten Island and sailed away.

117 NARA: M804, W23093, William Galbreath pension (6th Pa.); S16916, Robert Lemon pension (6th Pa.); J. Wheat pension; W. Moody pension; Hazard et al (eds), *Pennsylvania Archives*, ser.5, vol.3, p.761

118 NARA: W. Moody pension.

119 NARA: M246, f.214, p.4.

120 FHS: Clark Diary, 26 June 1777.

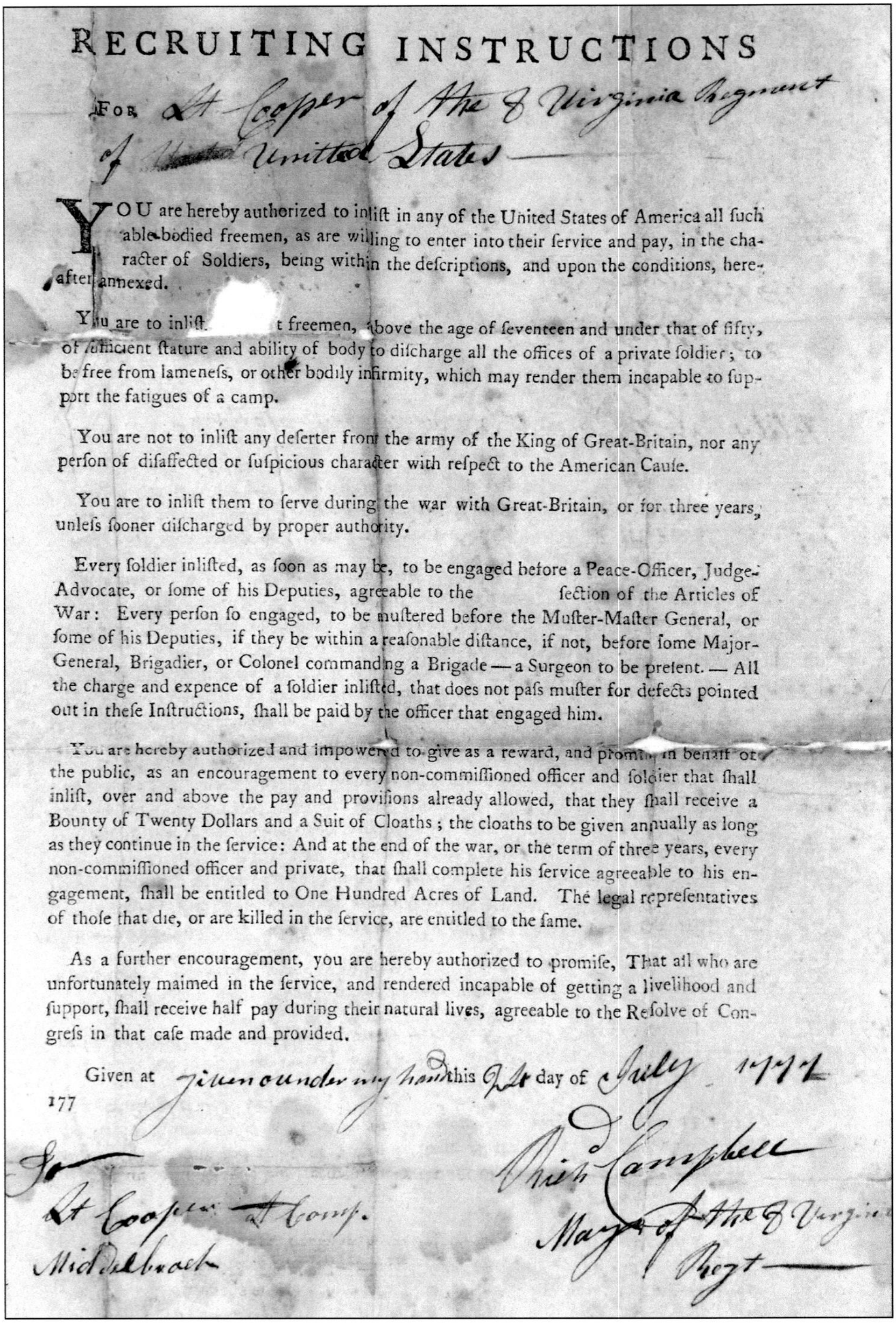

RECRUITING INSTRUCTIONS

FOR Lt Cooper of the 8 Virginia Regiment of United States

YOU are hereby authorized to inliſt in any of the United States of America all ſuch able-bodied freemen, as are willing to enter into their ſervice and pay, in the character of Soldiers, being within the deſcriptions, and upon the conditions, hereafter annexed.

You are to inliſt … t freemen, above the age of ſeventeen and under that of fifty, of ſufficient ſtature and ability of body to diſcharge all the offices of a private ſoldier; to be free from lameneſs, or other bodily infirmity, which may render them incapable to ſupport the fatigues of a camp.

You are not to inliſt any deſerter from the army of the King of Great-Britain, nor any perſon of diſaffected or ſuſpicious character with reſpect to the American Cauſe.

You are to inliſt them to ſerve during the war with Great-Britain, or for three years, unleſs ſooner diſcharged by proper authority.

Every ſoldier inliſted, as ſoon as may be, to be engaged before a Peace-Officer, Judge-Advocate, or ſome of his Deputies, agreeable to the ſection of the Articles of War: Every perſon ſo engaged, to be muſtered before the Muſter-Maſter General, or ſome of his Deputies, if they be within a reaſonable diſtance, if not, before ſome Major-General, Brigadier, or Colonel commanding a Brigade — a Surgeon to be preſent. — All the charge and expence of a ſoldier inliſted, that does not paſs muſter for defects pointed out in theſe Inſtructions, ſhall be paid by the officer that engaged him.

You are hereby authorized and impowered to give as a reward, and promiſe in behalf of the public, as an encouragement to every non-commiſſioned officer and ſoldier that ſhall inliſt, over and above the pay and proviſions already allowed, that they ſhall receive a Bounty of Twenty Dollars and a Suit of Cloaths; the cloaths to be given annually as long as they continue in the ſervice: And at the end of the war, or the term of three years, every non-commiſſioned officer and private, that ſhall complete his ſervice agreeable to his engagement, ſhall be entitled to One Hundred Acres of Land. The legal repreſentatives of thoſe that die, or are killed in the ſervice, are entitled to the ſame.

As a further encouragement, you are hereby authorized to promiſe, That all who are unfortunately maimed in the ſervice, and rendered incapable of getting a livelihood and ſupport, ſhall receive half pay during their natural lives, agreeable to the Reſolve of Congreſs in that caſe made and provided.

Given at given under my hand this 24 day of July 1777
177

To Lt Cooper at Camp Middlebrook

Richd Campbell Major of the 8 Virginia Regt

Formal recruiting instructions given to 1st Lieutenant Leonard Cooper by Richard Campbell at Middle Brook on 24 July 1777. Both men returned to Virginia at this time to enlist more soldiers. (National Archives)

10

Fire

The war had grown ugly over the winter and spring. Combatants destroyed wells,[1] burned farms, and desecrated churches.[2] Women were 'ravished', and a man's head was cut off.[3] A Loyalist sleeping outdoors at Bonhamtown in June reported being 'poisoned with the stink of some Rebels who have been buryed about three weeks in such a slighty manner that Waggons have cut up part of the half corrupted carcasses and made them stink most horrible.'[4]

Darke's riflemen kept skirmishing with Howe's army until it left. 'Capt. Dark,' William Grant remembered, 'collected the remains of his shattered party in the best manner he possibly could and continued to execute his orders in reconnoitring and sending intelligence to the Camp, untill Generall Howe crossed over in Strattan Island [Staten Island], at which time we returned to the Camp with scarce two thirds of the men we took away'.[5] The rest of Scott's brigade also came forward to Amboy for a short time.[6] Captain Clark spent a few days looking for deserters.[7]

On 1 July, Ensign Lawrence Greenholm asked for permission to resign. The subaltern, whose real name was Lars Grönholm, was a foreign adventurer who had received a commission in Captain Westfall's Company after Rees Pritchard's resignation 'on account of certain family misfortunes.'[8] The timing shows Greenholm joined the regiment at Charles Town. Now, he was sick and desperate to get home to Sweden. He petitioned Congress for help, telling them that he had 'applied to several able Physicians for relief, without the least Success, & that after defraying his Expenses for Lodging & paying his Physicians Bills, he is left almost destitute of Cash & what is still more deplorable, hath not a Friend to afford him the least Assistance in his present calamitous Situation.' If he could just get home, where he had 'Parents of good Estate & likewise many Friends,' he would be fine. The only way to get home,

1 Scull (ed.), *Montresor Journals*, pp.424–425.
2 Grant, 'Narrative', p.731.
3 Thomas J. McGuire, *The Philadelphia Campaign*, (Mechanicsburg, Pa.: Stackpole Books, 2006), vol.1, p.59; Tappert and Doberstein (trans), *Journals of H.M. Muhlenberg*, vol.3, p.51, McGuire, *Philadelphia Campaign*, vol.1, p.29.
4 Gill and Curtis (eds), *Journal of Cresswell*, p.170.
5 Grant, 'Narrative', p.732.
6 FHS: Clark Diary, 30 June-1 July 1777; Ward, *Scott*, pp.32–33.
7 FHS: Clark Diary, 3–6 July 1777.
8 NARA: R. Pritchard pension.

however, was via New York, which was in British hands. He asked Congress for a passport to travel that way or, 'if that request should be disagreeable', money to subsist on.[9] His plea was referred to the Board of War, which took no action on it. Greenholm's fate is not known.

Racing British Sails

When Howe's army sailed off, there was no way for the Americans to know its destination. Speculation focused on two scenarios. An attack on Philadelphia had been Howe's obvious goal for some time. However, news came that Lieutenant General John Burgoyne and a second British army were coming south from Canada via the Lake Champlain-Hudson Valley corridor.[10] Smart minds believed Howe would sail up the Hudson River and link up with Burgoyne to isolate New England from the other colonies. The Americans marched north.

'The Clove,' called the Ramapo Pass today, was a valley with narrow defiles near each end that ran through the Ramapo Mountains and across the New Jersey–New York boundary. It was described as 'extremely wild and … scarcely known before the war.'[11] The eponymous Clove Road followed the Ramapo River through the pass, providing a land-based route for travel and commerce after the British took control of the lower Hudson. The army marched through Pompton Plains and camped outside the Clove's southern pass near Suffern's Tavern, waiting for further intelligence.[12]

The Route from Morristown to Germantown
11 July: Morristown to Pompton Plains, N.J.
14 July: The Ponds (Oakland), N.J.
15 July: Suffern's Clove, N.J.
20 July: East of Tuxedo Lake, N.Y.
23 July: Smith's Clove and Chester, N.Y.
25 July: Warwick, N.Y.
26 July: Andover Furnace, N.J.
27 July: Hackettstown, N.J.
28 July: Quakertown, N.J.
29 July: Vicinity of Sand Brook, N.J.
30 July: Howell's Ferry, N.J.
31July: West side of Delaware River, Pa.
1 Aug: Crooked Billet Tavern, Pa.
2 Aug: Germantown, Pa.[13]
(Approximately 183 miles)

9 NARA: M247, Papers of the Continental Congress, Petitions, pp.193–194, Lawrence Greenholm, 13 Aug. 1777.
10 FHS: Clark Diary, 6 July 1777.
11 François-Jean de Chastellux, *Travels in North-America in the Years 1780–81–82* (New York: White, Gallagher, & White, 1827), p.160.
12 FHS: Clark Diary, 10–15 July 1777.
13 FHS: Clark Diary.

An early twentieth-century photograph shows the narrow road inside the clove at Ramapo. (New York Public Library)

Here, Charles Scott placed several 8th Virginia officers under arrest: Captains Clark, Berry, and Westfall; Lieutenants James Higgins, Benjamin Kinley, and Christopher Moyer; and Ensign Cornelius Westfall. The charge was the same in every case: 'Neglect of duty, in not having their men's arms in good order.'[14] A court martial was delayed, however, when Howe's transports were reported to be in the Hudson. The Continentals marched 13 miles into the unnerving pass. 'It was an infringement on the rights of the wild Beasts for man ever to enter this Clove,' wrote an American, 'it ought to have remained as Nature certainly intended for it for the sole use of snakes, adders, & Beasts of prey.'[15] Delayed by rain, it took them four days to reach 'Smith's Clove', the northern defile, just 11 miles from the defences at the Hudson Highlands. Hedging due to questionable intelligence, Washington sent Stephen's and Lincoln's Divisions west to Chester, New York, from where they could rush east to the Hudson or south to Philadelphia as events might dictate.[16]

Solid intelligence then arrived that the British were, in fact, headed south, and the army had to turn around. Washington told Stephen to take his division to Philadelphia 'by the shortest route and in the most expeditious manner you can, without injuring the Troops.'[17]

14 FHS: Clark Diary, 16, 19 July 1777; Chase et al (eds), *Papers of Washington* (Revolution), vol.10, pp.539–542.

15 J. Watson Webb (ed.), *Reminiscences of Gen'l Samuel B. Webb of the Revolutionary Army* (New York: Globe Stationery and Printing, 1882), p.309.

16 FHS: Clark Diary, 23 July 1777; Anon (ed.), 'Diary of Joseph Clark', *Proceedings of the New Jersey Historical Society*, original ser., 7:3 (1854), pp.97; Chase et al (eds), *Papers of Washington* (Revolution), vol.10, pp.410–412.

17 Chase et al (eds), *Papers of Washington* (Revolution), vol.10, p.399.

This put the 8th Virginia in another footrace with British sails. According to Clark's diary, they marched 16 miles south, past the village of Warwick, on 25 July and, on the following days, 20 miles and across the New Jersey line to Andover Furnace, 23 miles to Hacketts Town, 17 miles to Pittstown, and so on until they crossed the Delaware River at Howell's Ferry on the 30th.[18] One soldier called it a 'very hard and fatiguing march.' Exhausted, they set up camp near Germantown at the Schuylkill River falls, north of Philadelphia, on 2 August.[19]

Until Washington knew his enemy's intentions, Captain Knox was kept in constant movement with Morgan's Rifles in New Jersey. As intelligence changed, new orders were given to halt, go, or proceed to Hackensack, Philadelphia, Brunswick, Trenton, and Maidenhead.[20] According to a civilian account, they joined the army outside Philadelphia for at least a day. They pitched their tents at Stenton, one of the area's finest estates. 'They do but little damage to the garden, & not any to the house except making it extremely dirty,' wrote the owner's daughter. 'One company dine in the large back room, & another company upstairs in the large empty room that is there. They find their own provisions & have their own cook but make use of all our kitchen furniture & cook in the kitchen'.[21] They left again with orders to go and help oppose Burgoyne's march down the Hudson River Valley.[22]

Broken Promises

While the generals were wondering which way to turn out of the Clove, a few 8th Virginia men remained at Morristown, sick or otherwise detained. James Berwick, one of Captain Westfall's lieutenants, convinced George Carthey and John White to reenlist there. Carthey had signed on with Captain Clark in February 1776 and was more than halfway through his two-year enlistment.[23] White had just joined in January. The army was eager for experienced soldiers to commit to longer terms and offered a 20-dollar incentive. White and Carthey appeared before a justice of the peace to 'swear on the Holy Evangelists of Almighty God that We will honorably and faithfully serve the united States of America against all their Enemies and Opposers whatsoever.' Carthey received his 20 dollars, signing a predated receipt. White's receipt is unsigned, perhaps because he was lame in one arm and only six months into his first enlistment. Neither man kept his oath.[24]

Matthew Hennen, however, kept a promise to Captain Croghan when he returned from Wheeling after his three-week furlough. There were 380 miles between his home and his expected destination at Morristown, but the erstwhile Pennsylvania Continental's journey was shortened by 70 miles when he met the 8th Virginia on their way to Germantown.[25]

18 FHS: Clark Diary, 25–30 July 1777.
19 Grant, 'Narrative', p.732. The falls are now submerged.
20 Chase et al (eds), *Papers of Washington* (Revolution), vol.10, pp.247–248, 338, 377, 390, 435–437, 443, 455–456, 473–474, 566, 557, 641.
21 Nicholas B. Wainwright (ed.), 'A Diary of Trifling Occurrences: Philadelphia, 1776–1778 [Sarah Logan Fischer Diary]', *PMHB*, 82:4 (1958), pp.439–440.
22 Chase et al (eds), *Papers of Washington* (Revolution), vol.10, p.641.
23 NARA: M881, r.1040, George Carthey.
24 NARA: M246, f.208, p.55, f.210, p.19.
25 NARA: M. Hennen pension.

Traveling the same way, despite promises they would stay in the west, Captain Robert Beall and most of the 13th Virginia arrived from Fort Pitt a week or two later.[26] As with the 8th Pennsylvania, a portion of the regiment was left behind. Captain Beall, 1st Lieutenant Simon Morgan, and Ensign John Harrison, all 8th Virginia veterans, trekked east.[27] Benjamin Biggs, now a lieutenant in another company, did as well.[28] Other former members of John Stephenson's company, like Thomas Ravenscraft and Isaac Sissel, remained behind to guard the frontier.[29]

Recruiting Comes to a Halt

Lieutenant John Clark rode into camp on 3 August with a letter from Richard Campbell, written in Woodstock on 24 July. It was the first of Campbell's monthly recruiting reports, and he hoped it would also be the last. Citing lack of progress and Virginia's new draft law,[30] he asked to return to camp.

> There is a great number of Officers of our Regimt from Camp in this State, & no probability of raising Men by that Means – Capt. Higgins & the Officers of his Company (who was appointed in the Room of Capt. John Stinson of the 8th Regimt) have not raised more than 20 Men in the course of five months. Tho' the greatest Industry has been used by them. The other Officers ordered from Camp has met with less success, Our Assembly have fallen on ways to fill up our Battalions, which I hope will render it unnecessary to keep so many Officers on the Recruiting Service, as are now absent from the 8th Regimt – Things thus circumstanced make me wish to return to my post, will thank your Excellency for orders to do so. the draughts will take place the 10th of next Month, which I hope will answer the purpose intended – 'Till I receive your Orders, shall continue to use my endeavours to forward the recruiting Business, tho' have no prospect of being successfull – The bearer Lieut. Clark is to return immediately, by him expect your Excellencys order

Washington's aide-de-camp John Fitzgerald handed the younger Clark brother Washington's reply the next day: 'Your Letter of 24th of July was handed to his Excelly yesterday, in Answer to which I am direct'd to Inform you that you are immediately to return to Camp with the other Officers of your Corps & Join your Regiment … the Men already inlisted you will put under proper officers & send on to the Army as soon as possible.'[31]

---

26 Chase et al (eds), *Papers of Washington* (Revolution), vol.13, pp.656–657.
27 NARA: M246, f.309 pp.203, Muster Roll of Capt. Beall's Company, Sept. 1777; Grant, 'Narrative', p.732.
28 NARA: M246, f.312, p.2, Muster Roll of Capt. Lemon's Company, Sept. 1777.
29 NARA: M246, f.309 pp.203, Muster Roll of Capt. Beall's Company, Sept. 1777; Grant, 'Narrative', p.732; NARA: M804, W2974, Elisha Thomas pension (13th Va.).
30 Hening (ed.), *Statutes*, vol.9, pp.275–280.
31 Chase et al (eds), *Papers of Washington* (Revolution), vol.10, pp.382–383.

The 8th Virginia Regiment, August 1777.[32]

<table>
<tr><td colspan="2">Field Officers:
Col. Abraham Bowman
Lt. Col. John Markham
Maj. William Darke†</td><td colspan="2">Staff Officers:
Adj. Abraham Kirkpatrick
Chap. Christian Streit
Surg. Francis Baldwin
Surg. Mate Frederick Heimberger
Paymstr. Hezekiah Stoakes
Qtr. Master Martin Carney</td><td colspan="2">Warrant Officers:
Qtr. Mst. Sgt. Ashkenaz Shappee
Sgt. Maj. William Palmer
Drum Maj. Nicholas Neal</td></tr>
<tr><td>Company</td><td>Captain</td><td>1st Lieut.</td><td>2nd Lieut.</td><td>Ensign</td><td>Enlisted Men</td></tr>
<tr><td>Darke's</td><td></td><td>Isaac Israel</td><td>Christopher Moyer</td><td>Thomas Miller</td><td>22/43 present</td></tr>
<tr><td>Campbell's</td><td>Richard Campbell†</td><td>Mathias Hite</td><td>John Steed</td><td>Robert Breckenridge</td><td>44/65 present</td></tr>
<tr><td>Slaughter's</td><td>George Slaughter</td><td>John Graves</td><td>Reuben Field</td><td>Philip Huffman</td><td>29/38 present</td></tr>
<tr><td>Clark's</td><td>Jonathan Clark</td><td></td><td>Leonard Cooper</td><td>Philip Eastin</td><td>22/36 present</td></tr>
<tr><td>Westfall's</td><td>Abel Westfall</td><td>Edward Moody*</td><td>James Berwick</td><td>Cornelius Westfall</td><td>21/49 present</td></tr>
<tr><td>Stephenson's</td><td>David Stephenson</td><td></td><td>Benjamin Kinley</td><td>James Hooke</td><td>18/36 present</td></tr>
<tr><td>Berry's</td><td>Thomas Berry</td><td>Richard Eastin</td><td>Francis Baldwin</td><td>John Kay</td><td>28/49 present</td></tr>
<tr><td>Croghan's</td><td>William Croghan</td><td>Abraham Kirkpatrick‡</td><td>James Higgins</td><td>Jonathan Smith*</td><td>37/56 present</td></tr>
<tr><td>Higgins'</td><td>Robert Higgins*</td><td>James Curry*</td><td>John Clark*</td><td>Peter Higgins*</td><td>Not joined</td></tr>
</table>

225/379 enlisted men present. 154 absent. Musters for May and June recorded early August. *Absent. †Rank disputed. ‡Adjutant.

When they received these orders, Campbell, Higgins, and Hite rode straight to camp, and their men followed on behind. On his arrival, Campbell was subjected to the humiliation of being listed again with his old company as a captain, with a muster roll note that he was 'supp[ose]d pro[moted].'[33] Hite went back to being a lieutenant. First Lieutenant James Curry, meanwhile, followed with Higgins' small number of recruits, taking them directly to Philadelphia to be inoculated and equipped.[34]

On 7 August, Washington approved the court martial verdicts for the officers whose soldiers had neglected their weapons on the way to the Clove. Jonathan Clark, James Higgins, and Benjamin Kinley were acquitted. Thomas Berry and Cornelius Westfall were found guilty and reprimanded in general orders. Lieutenant Moyer was 'severely' reprimanded. At the same time, George Fant, a recent recruit in Captain Westfall's Company, was one of several enlisted men found guilty of 'various crimes' but pardoned by the commander in chief.[35]

32 NARA: M246, f.208, p.4; f.209, pp.8-9, f.210, pp.5–6; f.211, pp.6–7; f.212, pp.2–3; f.214, pp.4–5; f.216, pp.2–3; f.217, pp.8–9; f.218, pp.2–3; f.219, pp.8–9

33 NARA: M246, f.214, p.10, Muster Roll of Capt. Richd. Campbell's Co., Aug. 1777.

34 NARA: M246, f.208, p.61; M804, S6181, Michael Sword pension; R. Chambers pension.

35 Chase et al (eds), *Papers of Washington* (Revolution), vol.10, pp.539–542.

A sketch from life of a wagon belonging to the North Carolina Brigade as it passed through Philadelphia in August 1777. The Continental Army marched through the city on 24 August in a carefully choreographed parade, prior to which Washington ordered, 'Not a woman belonging to the army is to be seen.' The North Carolinians did not put on a show when they followed behind a day later, giving the artist a better look at what life on the road was actually like for the 8th Virginia and the rest of the army. Among the nine people depicted are a barefoot soldier in a hunting shirt, a man taking a nap, two women, and a baby. Pierre Eugène du Simitière. (Museum of the American Revolution, Gift of Judith F. Hernstadt; Conserved with support from the North Carolina Society of the Cincinnati, 2023.16.01)

Maxwell's Light Infantry

After a definite sighting of Howe's fleet entering Chesapeake Bay, the 8th Virginia followed Washington in a grand parade through Philadelphia, crossed the Schuylkill, and camped outside Wilmington, Delaware. William Penn's city was manifestly the British target and, if he took the King's Highway, Wilmington would be in Howe's way. Both sides had learned from the last two years of war: Howe avoided frontal assaults on entrenched positions and Washington avoided set-piece battles in open fields. The Americans consistently looked for elevated ground behind rivers while Howe sought ways to get around them. Wilmington sat between the junction of Brandywine Creek and the Christina River, which poured into the Delaware River 30 miles below Philadelphia. The revolutionary army camped west of town, remaining behind the Christina's next tributary, Red Clay Creek.[36] After a couple of days, the 8th Virginia was sent farther out to White Clay Creek, where Stephen's and Greene's Divisions prepared to blunt an expected enemy advance.[37] Captain Clark recorded that the 8th Virginia marched 'through Wilmington, thro Newport, over Ridley [Red Clay] Creek & to Whiteclay Creek and remained there all night.' American skirmishers were already starting to pick up deserters from the British Army.[38]

36 FHS: Clark Diary 28 Aug.-2 Sept. 1777; Chase et al (eds), *Papers of Washington* (Revolution), vol.11, pp.73–74; Anon. (ed.), 'Diary of Joseph Clark', p.97.

37 Chase et al (eds), *Papers of Washington* (Revolution), vol.11, pp.73–74; Anon. (ed.), 'Diary of Joseph Clark', p.97.

38 FHS: Clark Diary, 26–28 Aug. 1777; Anon. (ed.), 'Diary of Joseph Clark', p.97. Clark confused the name with Ridley Creek nearby in Pennsylvania.

The Route from Germantown to Wilmington
8 Aug: Depart Germantown, Pa.
9 Aug: Hatboro, Pa.
10–23 Aug: Neshaminy Creek Camp
23 Aug: 6 miles north of Philadelphia, Pa.
24 Aug: Parade through Philadelphia to Derby, Pa.
25 Aug: Marcus Hook, Pa.
26 Aug: Arrive Wilmington, Del.[39]
(Approximately 70 miles)

On the 28th, Washington created a unified corps of light infantry 'to consist of one Field Officer, two Captains, six Subalterns, eight Serjeants and 100 Rank & File from each brigade.'[40] Brigadier General William Maxwell,[41] who had performed well during the Forage War, commanded the formation. Captain Darke was again detached from Scott's brigade.[42] Stephen's and Greene's Divisions were pulled back behind Red Clay Creek, and the light infantry corps went forward.[43] Most of the men in the Light Infantry volunteered for the assignment. 'Patriotism and love of Country prompted us to the act,' said one. 'I was one of those turnout Boys: we immediately under the command of General Maxfield [Maxwell] found & hovered upon the lines of the Enemy … In this service, which was severe, we had many tolerable affairs of fighting.'[44]

Sergeant Parett recalled that he was selected 'on account of his skill as a rifleman' and, after the British landing in the Chesapeake 'was constantly engaged in skirmishes with the enemy, using his rifle effectually.'[45] Another soldier from Scott's brigade remembered the light infantry as '8 hundred men chiefly volunteers' and listed some of the other senior officers: '[Lieutenant Colonel] Rich[ard] Parker, [Lieutenant] Colonel [William] Heath [Heth] with a glass eye, Colonel [William] Crawford with his leather hunting shirt, pantaloons and Rifle, Colonel [Alexander] Martin from North Carolina.'[46] Another soldier said the brigades each 'detached a party of 100 light armed men, as scouts, under the command of Col. Crawford',[47] who was often in active command. Virginia had specifically designated its rifle companies as 'light infantry' in 1775 and 1776, but the term was also applied to musketeers in other contexts and at other times. Maxwell's Light Infantry may have been a mix, but there is reason to believe it was all rifles. A battle witness and an aged veteran both confused Maxwell's Light Infantry with Morgan's Rifles, and a Hessian opponent called them 'nothing but sharpshooters.'[48]

39 FHS: Clark Diary.
40 Chase et al (eds), *Papers of Washington* (Revolution), vol.11, pp.81–82.
41 Chase et al (eds), *Papers of Washington* (Revolution), vol.11, p.91.
42 Grant, 'Narrative', p.733.
43 FHS: Clark Diary, 29 Aug. 1777.
44 NARA: M804, S5832, Jesse Nicholson pension (15th Va.).
45 LVA: J. Parret rejected claim.
46 NARA: M804, S6340, William Walker pension (4th Va.).
47 Grant, 'Narrative', p.733.
48 John C. Dann (ed.), *The Nagle Journal: A Diary of the Life of Jacob Nagle, Sailor, From the Year 1775 to 1841* (New York: Weidenfeld & Nicolson, 1988), p.10; LVA: J. Parret rejected claim; Harris, *Brandywine*, p.257.

Portrait miniature of Peter Muhlenberg, probably Pennsylvania, watercolour on ivory, c. 1785. Collection of a descendant. (Image courtesy of Historic Trappe)

Portrait of Francis Swaine, oil on canvas. (Collection of Historic Trappe, gift of Jeremy Cooper, descendant of Henry Melchoir Muhlenberg, 2014.002.0001)

Major William Croghan. Miniature, artist unknown. (Courtesy of Historic Locust Grove)

Lucy Croghan (née Clark). Miniature, artist unknown. (Courtesy of Historic Locust Grove)

Lieutenant Colonel William Darke. A portrait depicting his participation in St Clair's Defeat in 1791. Frederick Kemmelmeyer, ca. 1792–1800. (Collection of the Museum of Early Southern Decorative Arts (MESDA))

Chaplain Christian Streit, attributed to Francis Cezeron, ca. 1808–1810.
(Grace Evangelical Lutheran Church, Winchester)

Charles Scott was the 8th Virginia's brigade commander in 1777 and 1778 and governor of Kentucky from 1808 to 1812. Paul Sawyer, 1907. Copied from an undated miniature by Matthew Harris Jouett. (Author's photo)

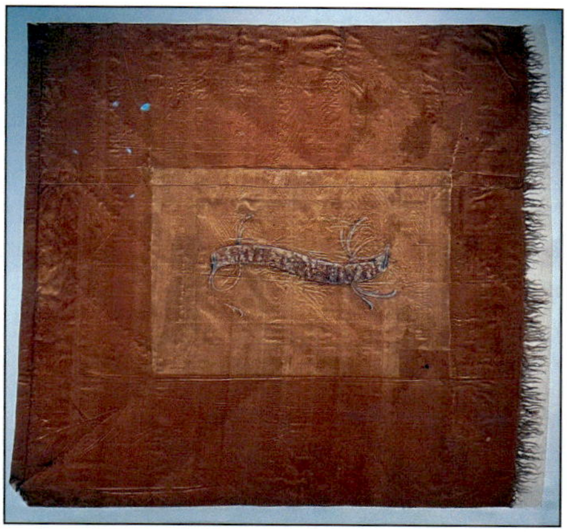

A 'grand division' banner of the 8th Virginia, once owned by Peter Muhlenberg's descendants. It was not the regimental standard, but one of two banners used for battlefield direction. Private collection. (Author's photo)

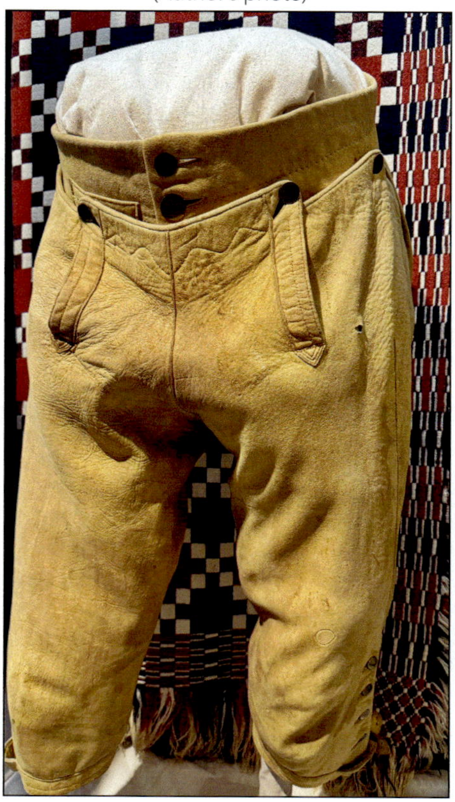

Buckskin (sometimes fabric) breeches were standard military attire for Virginians in 1775 and 1776. Full-length 'overalls' (trousers) were preferred later in the war. (Luray Valley Museum, Cullers collections)

Hunting shirts were standard uniform items for Virginia troops from 1775 through 1777. The shirts of the 8th Virginia were dyed brown. (Museum of the American Revolution, 2013.05.0001)

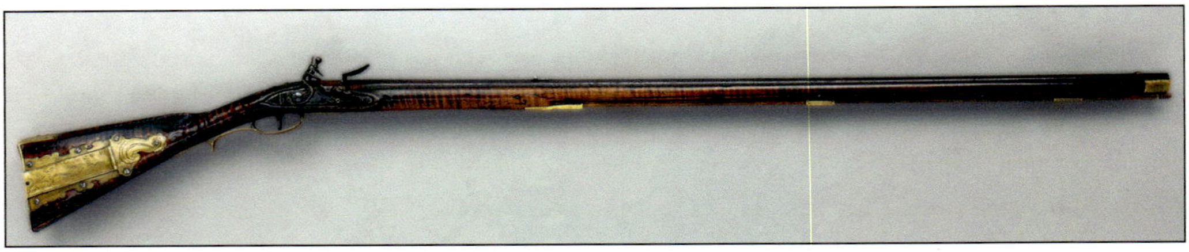

An ornate rifle representative of those carried by soldiers who provided their own weapons. Probably made by George Schreyer, Sr. ca. 1770 in York County, Pennsylvania. (Metropolitan Museum of Art)

A double-edged boat guard smallsword given to George Washington by William Darke and worn by the president at his first inauguration. James Perry, London, 1770. (Morristown National Historical Park)

Holster pistols carried by Peter Muhlenberg during the war. London, ca. 1750–1760. (Museum of the American Revolution, 2003.00.0017, 2003.00.0018)

The grave of Swiss soldier and surveyor Jacob Rinker in Shenandoah County. (Author's photo)

The log house built by Colonel Abraham Bowman near Lexington, Ky. ca. 1784. (Author's photo)

Pittsburgh in 1790, looking north across the Monongahela River. Drawn by S. Eastman in 1853 from a 1790 watercolour by Lewis Brantz. (Archives & Special Collections, University of Pittsburgh Library System)

The barouche Abraham Bowman rode in with Lafayette in 1825. (Collection of the Studebaker National Museum. Conserved by B.R. Howard & Associates)

Though some 3rd Virginia soldiers were recorded as detached 'with Colo Crawford',[49] men who served in Maxwell's Light Infantry are generally hard to identify. There is no way to know from musters which, if any, men from Clark's and Darke's companies were detached with Captain Darke. The August musters for the other companies, however, record the presence of 41 men 'at the lines' or 'on the lines.'[50] These musters were taken on 2 September, the day before the Battle of Cooch's Bridge, and a pension record supports the correlation.[51]

Men Detached to Maxwell's Light Infantry[52]

Darke's	Campbell's	Slaughter's	Clark's	Westfall's	Stephenson's	Berry's	Croghan's
Capt. William Darke	George Ashby, Abraham Hogman, George Lair, Daniel Nichols, William Shovel, Barton Whitehorn	William Campbell, Joseph Delaney, William Fincham, James Johnston, William Robert, Richard Roberts, John Rosson, Elzaphan Rucker, James Vowels	Sgt. Joseph Parett†	Sgt. Edward McCarty, Richard Cain, Zachariah Pigman, John Williams	Cornelius Cain, William Donavan, George McVey, Charles Sanders, James Young	Sgt. John Chapman, Sgt. Arthur Johnson, Charles Love, Robert McGill, Bryan Mooney, Solomon Redman, John Taylor	Ezekiel Abel, Moses Crawford, Jesse Davis, Jonathan Grant, Aneas Lany, Thomas Owens, John Reed, Sr., John Reed, Jr., David Williams

†From pension application.

Maxwell and Crawford took their men forward to the spot where the King's Highway crossed the Christina River, near the home of Thomas Cooch. Another road came north from Aiken's Tavern (Glasgow), intersected the highway, and also shared a bridge with it via a dogleg. Iron Hill, the only high ground, rose in the northwest quadrant of the intersection. Maxwell's men joined the Militia that were already posted there.[53] A soldier recorded:

> On Saturday August 30th we received intelligence by some prisoners that General Howe intended to make an attack on Ironhill next day. Accordingly next morning

49 NARA: M246, f.74, p.7, Muster Roll of Capt. William Croghan's Co., Aug. 1777; NARA: M246, f.214, p.10, Muster Roll of Capt. Richd. Campbell's Co., Aug. 1777; NARA: M246, f.217, p.14, Muster Roll of Capt. George Slaughter's Co., Aug 1777; NARA: M246, f. 218, p.8, Muster Roll of Capt. David Stephenson's Co., Aug. 1777; NARA: M246, F.219, P.14, Muster Rolls of Capt. Abel Westfall's Co., Aug. 1777

50 NARA: M246, f.211, p.12.

51 NARA: J. Grant pension.

52 The data is incomplete. NARA: Revolutionary War Rolls; LVA: J. Parret rejected claim.

53 Michael C. Harris, *Brandywine: A Military History of the Battle that Lost Philadelphia but Saved America, September 11, 1777* (El Dorado Hills, Ca.: Savas Beatie, 2014), pp.134–135.

> between two and three o'Clock, we marched over the hill, and formed our selves into an ambuscade, in which position we continued till five, when being persuaded that no attack would be made, a party of 150 men was immediately chosen and sent under the command of the aforesd Capt. Dark, to reconnoitre.[54]

According to this contemporary account, Darke's skirmishers 'took several by roads, until we had got past several of the Hessians posts undiscovered, and proceeding toward an ironwork where they had another post.'[55] This was Elk Forge, a little north of Head of Elk, Maryland where a couple of British battalions were positioned.[56] Fifty men from the 23rd Regiment of Foot (the Royal Welsh Fuzileers) were posted as a picket two miles from the forge.[57] With a tip from a resident, Darke's men 'discovered a few of the 23rd cooking at a barn in the middle of a large field of Indian Corn.' Darke attempted a Native tactic quite different from standard light infantry practice. He divided his force into six parties of 25 men, each under a lieutenant and two sergeants. They spread out to surround the fusiliers. They were, however, 'discovered by those whom we thought to surprise.' The fusiliers in the cornfield 'were only a few of a party consisting of fifty ... They drew up immediately and marched out of the field.'[58] One of the fusiliers recorded that the larger British force at the Elk Forge heard gunfire and 'marched immediately towards them, but the Rebels kept firing and retreated' in order.[59]

If Darke's men were exclusively carrying rifles, and they probably were, they were at a disadvantage as soon the 50 fusiliers came together. Even with a numerical advantage, slow-loading rifles were no match for muskets and bayonets at short range. The best Darke could do was cover the retreat of his most exposed men. 'The party I belonged to,' wrote William Grant, 'upon the approach of the rest, retreated' and he 'saw severall of the rebells lying dead.' Grant himself was taken or, as he claimed to his captors, defected.[60] His account was written at the direction of the British but seems generally accurate from an enlisted man's perspective, except for some exaggerated descriptions of the Americans' weakness.

Cooch's Bridge, 3 September 1777

Maxwell's position at Iron Hill was not a perfect one. The Christina was just a creek this far upstream, and the high ground was on its southwest side. Iron Hill would have provided an advantage facing an eastward approach up the King's Highway with the creek as a fall-back, but on 3 September Howe's army smartly detoured and approached from the south via Aiken's Tavern. The Americans could still use the hill and creek for defence, but the water

54 Grant, 'Narrative', p.733.
55 Grant, 'Narrative', p.733.
56 HSP: Forges and Furnaces collection (Collection 212), finding aid, p.22.
57 Joseph Lee Boyle (ed.), *From Redcoat to Rebel: The Thomas Sullivan Journal* (Bowie, Md.: Heritage Books, 1997), p.127.
58 Grant, 'Narrative', p.733.
59 Boyle (ed.), *Sullivan Journal*, p.127.
60 Grant, 'Narrative', p.733.

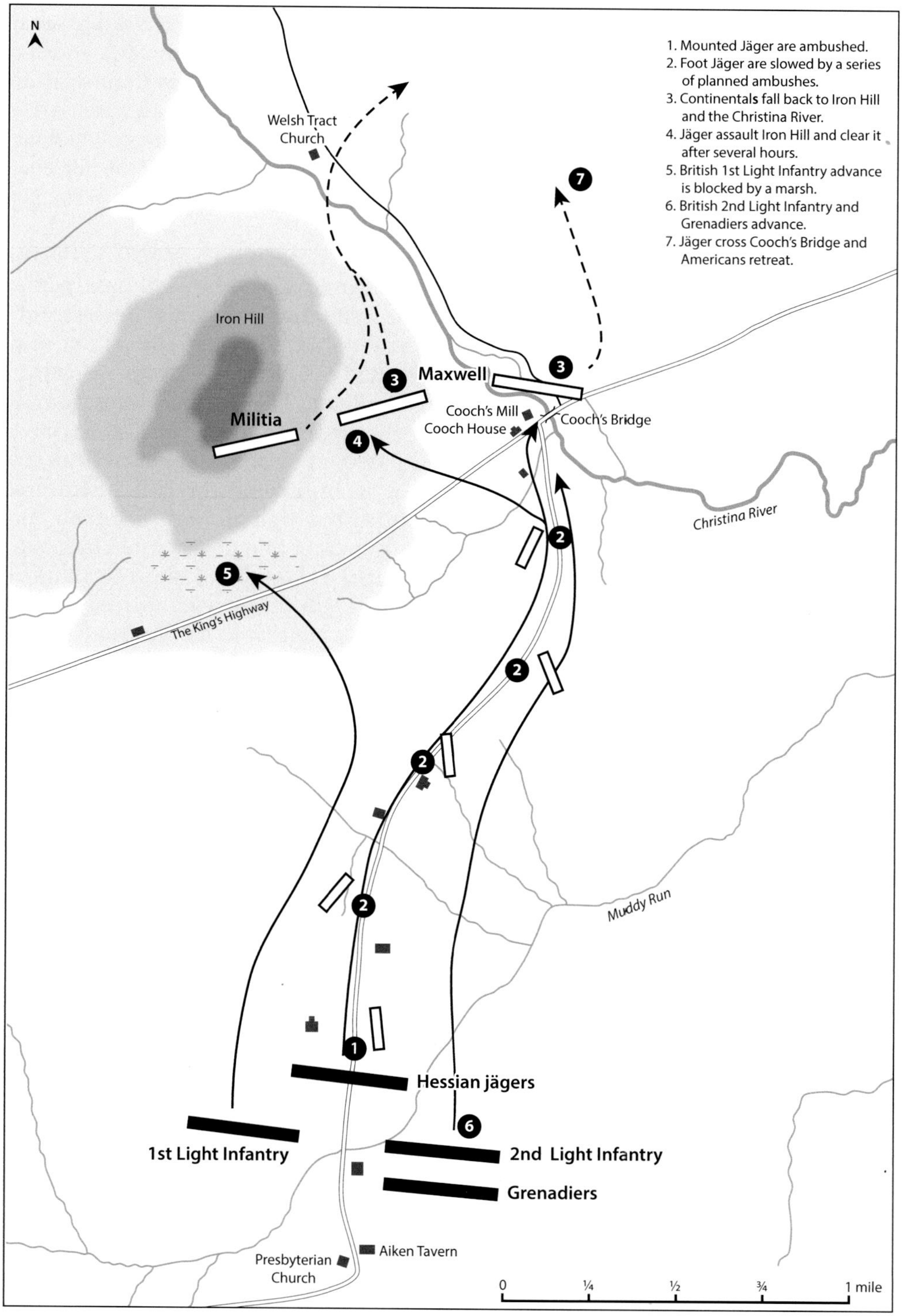

The Battle of Cooch's Bridge, 3 September 1777.

would divide them. The British general sent his jäger ('hunters') from Hesse-Kassel and Aspach-Bayreuth first. These green-jacketed skirmishers carried German rifles and short swords instead of muskets and bayonets and were in that way like the western shirtmen. Some of Maxwell's prepared men hid behind a hedgerow along the road from Aiken's Tavern. Seven mounted jäger, taking 'the greatest caution', approached with 400 foot jäger following behind. On a cue, the Americans fired, instantly neutralising six of the horsemen. The seventh, a captain on the back of a mortally wounded horse, shouted, 'Vorwärts, Jäger zu fuss!' (Foot Jäger forward!) and resumed the advance.[61]

The American skirmishers retreated, as they were supposed to. Their goal on the road was to harass, delay, and exhaust their foe. The jäger advanced in a column, perhaps with some flankers on the sides. When they came under fire, only those in the front of the column could shoot back. Standard doctrine required that they spread out into a line to avoid falling like dominos under concentrated fire. The Americans retreated to join some of their comrades in another prepared ambush. The Hessians went from line to column to line again as they 'became heavily engaged' in a second attack. Maxwell's men retreated again.[62] This continued for nearly two miles before the American light infantry took positions behind the creek and with the militia on Iron Hill.[63] Reinforced by the rest of the Jägerkorps, the Germans assaulted the high ground with their short rifles and swords and cleared it after a long and nasty fight that deteriorated into hand-to-hand combat.[64] An effort by the British 1st Light Infantry Battalion to flank the Americans' left was foiled by a swamp,[65] but the 2nd Light Infantry reinforced the jäger after the Americans abandoned the hill.[66] Maxwell's men fired across the Christina for a while, but with their ammunition dwindling and the opposing force growing, they withdrew.[67] No detailed record of the 8th Virginia contingent's role in the battle survives, but a 4th Virginia man who was there under Darke's command called it 'a very bloody conflict.' 'For myself,' he said, 'I can say that this detachment on that day deserved well of their country.'[68]

Back Into Pennsylvania

With the Crown forces now on the north side of the Christina, Colonel Bowman prepared the regiment for another fight closer to Wilmington by helping build defences behind Red Clay Creek. It was a better position than Iron Hill. The lower Christina was on their left, the 'heights of Wilmington' and the Brandywine River were to their right, and Red Clay

61 Tustin (ed.), *Ewald Journal*, p.77.
62 Tustin (ed.), *Ewald Journal*, pp.77–78; Lee, *Memoirs of the War*, vol.1, pp.15–16.
63 Scull (ed.), *Montresor Journals*, p.445; NARA: M804, W911, Andrew Cummings pension (Pa. Militia).
64 Tustin (ed.), *Ewald Journal*, p.78; McGuire, *Philadelphia Campaign*, vol.1, pp.152–154.
65 Tustin (ed.), *Ewald Journal*, p.78.
66 McGuire, *Philadelphia Campaign*, vol.1, p.154.
67 Wade Catts, 'The Battle of Cooch's Bridge', Cooch's Bridge Chapter, Daughters of the American Revolution, <coochsbridge.wildapricot.org/Battlefield-History>, accessed 23 Sept. 2023.
68 NARA: W. Walker pension.

Creek was in front of them.[69] This time, the entire army was prepared to engage. A member of Adam Stephen's staff wrote: 'On Saturday night all the heavy baggage was sent off to Brandywine, expecting next morning to make the attack, but the enemy did not come on, so nothing was done but fortifying; parapet walls were thrown up to a great extent, trees felled to secure the flanks and important passes.'

They kept working in the morning. If Howe wanted to approach on the King's Highway, the most direct route to Philadelphia, he was going to have to fight. 'By Monday morning everything was in readiness for an engagement; the troops marched down and took post in the entrenchments and went through the exercise. The reserved corps took their station at a proper distance and performed several manœuvres.' Again, the British did not come. 'After waiting till about 10 o'clock, the troops from the lines marched to their old camping ground.'[70]

Jonathan Clark wrote that the 'Enemy advanced' and the troops 'lay on arms,'[71] meaning they went to sleep that night prepared for a sudden fight. Then the American alarm guns fired, and word spread that 'the enemy were advancing very fast.' Bowman's men steeled themselves for combat. Stephen's Division formed a second line behind Stirling's Division on the American left. Darke, however, took his riflemen forward with Maxwell to bring on the attack. Though they 'fired several times upon the enemy',[72] Maxwell discovered too late that the 'very fast' approach was a feint.[73] Not until 1:00 or 2:00 a.m. did they realise that their opponents 'by a by road, with good guides' had 'got privately round our right wing of encampment and was advancing towards Philadelphia.'[74] Once again, Howe had simply walked around the American line.

The next natural barrier was the Brandywine River, which flowed southeasterly through the lower Pennsylvania piedmont to Wilmington. Though usually called a 'creek' at the time, it carried enough water to be useful for defence if combined with high ground and prepared fortifications. The two armies marched north in parallel. The British travelled in three columns, following the course of the White Clay Creek for a time, to the Pennsylvania village of Kennett Square.[75] The Americans stayed east of Red Clay Creek before crossing the lower Brandywine and following it north to Chads' Ford (Chadds Ford).[76]

As they left the coastal plain of Delaware and entered the hills of Pennsylvania's Chester County, the sentiments of the people changed with the geography. The farms and villages of Delaware and Maryland had been mostly abandoned. Pennsylvania's Quakers, believing that 'wars and fightings proceed from the lusts of men',[77] remained stoically in their homes, trusting in the Lord for their safety.

69 McGuire, *Philadelphia Campaign*, vol.1, p.159.
70 Anon. (ed.), 'Diary of Joseph Clark', pp.97–98.
71 FHS: Clark Diary, 8 Sept. 1777.
72 Anon. (ed.), 'Diary of Joseph Clark', p.98.
73 Chase et al (eds), *Papers of Washington* (Revolution), vol.11, pp.179–180.
74 Anon. (ed.), 'Diary of Joseph Clark', p.98.
75 Kipping and Smith (trans. and ed.), *Muenchhausen Diary*, p.30; Boyle (ed.), *Sullivan Journal*, p.129.
76 FHS: Clark Diary, 9 Sept. 1777.
77 James, 4:1–3 (KJV); John L. Nickalls (ed.), *The Journal of George Fox* (Cambridge: Cambridge University Press, 1952), p.399.

Like most roads of the time, the thoroughfare that connected Kennett Square and Chads' Ford went by different names.[78] Eastbound travellers called it 'the Chester Road' and Westbound travellers called it 'the Great Nottingham Road,' or 'the Baltimore Road' (it turned south). Travellers could wade or ride through the Brandywine Creek at Chads' Ford, but a causeway and a ferry provided a drier crossing half a mile downstream.[79] The river has been made to flow neatly between two defined banks today, replacing the marshy forests that paralleled the channel in 1777.[80] Several creeks ran to the river through ravines and hollows. Soldiers were posted, mostly by division, on the hills between them on the east side of the river. The militia guarded two minor fords about a mile south of the road. The crossing at Chads' Ford was just north of Harvey Run. Washington posted detachments at other fords to the north, but only for a few miles. About two miles back from the Brandywine and about the same distance directly north of Chads' Ford, a Quaker meeting house sat atop Birmingham Hill. To the hill's north, Street Road paralleled the course of Renwick Run. On the southern side of the hill, Wylie Run coursed through Sandy Hollow to the river. Jonathan Clark wrote on 9 September that they 'march'd to Benningham in Chester County on Brandywine,' where they 'lay on arms' at night ready for an engagement.[81]

The Battle of Brandywine, 11 September 1777

Three booms from the alarm guns broke the morning quiet on 11 September.[82] As the drummers beat 'To Arms,' Colonel Bowman's Virginians assembled and took their place in Scott's Brigade behind Chads' Ford. Woodford's Brigade assembled next to them and the two brigadiers looked to Major General Stephen for direction. Brigadier General Anthony Wayne's Pennsylvania division assembled in front of them. Somewhere in those lines was George Askins, the man from Captain Croghan's Company who had traded places with Matthew Hennen.[83] To their right, Lord Stirling's Pennsylvania and New Jersey division stood behind John Sullivan's mostly Maryland division. To Scott's left was the North Carolina Brigade, which included veterans of Sullivan's Island and Sunbury. Nathanael Greene's Virginia division, which included Muhlenberg's brigade and Captain Kirkpatrick's friends in the 1st Virginia Regiment, stood in front of the Carolinians.

Though the men surrounding the 8th Virginia were now familiar, the manoeuvres ahead of them were not. They knew how to stand their ground and they knew how to retreat, but the choreography involved in moving five divisions, an independent brigade, dragoons, artillery, and militia in battle required training they simply did not have.

78 John T. Faris, *Old Roads Out of Philadelphia* (Philadelphia: J.B. Lippincott, 1917), pp.77–95; J. Smith Futhey and Gilbert Cope, *History of Chester County Pennsylvania* (Philadelphia: Louis H. Everts, 1881), p.354; Henry Graham Ashmead, *History of Delaware County, Pennsylvania* (Philadelphia: Louis H. Everts, 1884), p.324.

79 Harris, *Brandywine*, p.327.

80 Tustin (ed.), *Ewald Journal*, pp.81.

81 FHS: Clark Diary, 9 Sept. 1777. Land east of the river lay in Birmingham Township.

82 NARA: M804, W3395, Robert Devin pension (14th Virginia); Chase et al (eds), *Papers of Washington* (Revolution), vol.8, p.111, vol.12, p.494.

83 NARA: M. Hennen pension.

'A Virginia Rifleman,' drawn by Richard Mansergh St George, a British officer in the 52nd Regiment's light company. The artist was engaged in close combat with Maxwell's Light Infantry at Cooch's Bridge and Brandywine. The rifleman is dressed in a hunting shirt and similarly fringed 'overalls' (trousers). (Harlan Crow Library)

Two years into the war, many officers, Lieutenant Colonel John Markham for instance, remained untested in combat and most of the 1777 recruits were still green. Drill manuals still varied among the states, so soldiers marched at different paces and manoeuvered to different commands.[84]

The light infantry's movements were less complicated. Including picked, rifle-bearing militia, Maxwell had about 1,000 men.[85] As they had at Cooch's Bridge, his men prepared a collapsing defence to delay, exhaust, and bloody the Crown troops as they came on. 'At Brandywine,' a Virginian remembered, 'it was our set to bring on the Battle'.[86] Captain Charles Porterfield of the 11th Virginia and Woodford's Brigade was posted far out front near Welch's Tavern on both sides of the road.[87] Porterfield's superior, Lieutenant Colonel William Heth of the 3rd Virginia and the same brigade, was positioned less than a mile behind him near Kennett Friends Meeting. Farther back, in unclear sequence, Major Charles Simms of the 13th Virginia and Scott's Brigade and Lieutenant Colonel Richard Parker of the 2nd Virginia and Weedon's Brigade prepared additional ambush points. Finally, near the river, Maxwell's men had built a large barricade of loose timber. The balance of the light infantry, perhaps including William Darke and his 8th Virginia men, waited there.[88]

Porterfield's men first engaged the British at about six o'clock in the morning, fell back to join Heth, and fired again. The first to come were the jäger and a small corps of men carrying experimental breech-loading rifles under Major Patrick Ferguson. At least four ambushes were set. The Americans prayed for an outright victory, but buying time and surviving until sunset were more realistic goals.[89] Either way, delaying the British advance was important. Porterfield's ambush did better than expected, killing or wounding about half of the British vanguard.[90] Colonel Heth praised the courage of a 12th Virginia captain from Scott's brigade with whom Darke's men may have been paired (if they were not behind the barricade).[91] A member of Washington's Life Guard, posted directly above the ford, wrote two days later that he was 'a witness to the havock which general Maxwell made among' the British forces as they approached.[92]

Indeed, the Light Infantry fended off the British from behind their log barricade for an extended time. A witness said they 'repulsed the advanced party in three several attempts,

84 Robert M. Dunkerly, *Decision at Brandywine: The Battle on Birmingham Hill* (Yardley: Westholme, 2021), pp.xiv, 2–9, 22.

85 Samuel S. Smith, *The Battle of Brandywine* (Monmouth Beach, N.J.: Philip Freneau Press, 1976), p.9; Harris, *Brandywine*, p.171; NARA: A. Cummings pension.

86 NARA: J. Nicholson pension. See also W4723, John Matlock pension (4th N.C.) and LVA: Revolutionary War Bounty Land Claims, Charles Porterfield.

87 Lee, *Memoirs of the War*, vol.1, p.15; B. Floyd Flickinger (ed.), 'The Diary of Lieutenant William Heth while a Prisoner in Quebec, 1776', *Annual Papers of Winchester Virginia Historical Society*, 1 (1933), pp.33; Tustin (ed.), *Ewald Journal*, pp.81; Lee, *Memoirs of the War*, vol.1, p.15; Harris, *Brandywine*, pp.223–225.

88 Lee, *Memoirs of the War*, vol.1, p.15; Harris, *Brandywine*, pp.228–231.

89 Harris, *Brandywine*, p.226.

90 Tustin (ed.), *Ewald Journal*, pp.81.

91 Flickinger (ed.), 'Diary of Heth', p.33.

92 Stryker (ed.), *Documents*, vol.1, p.483.

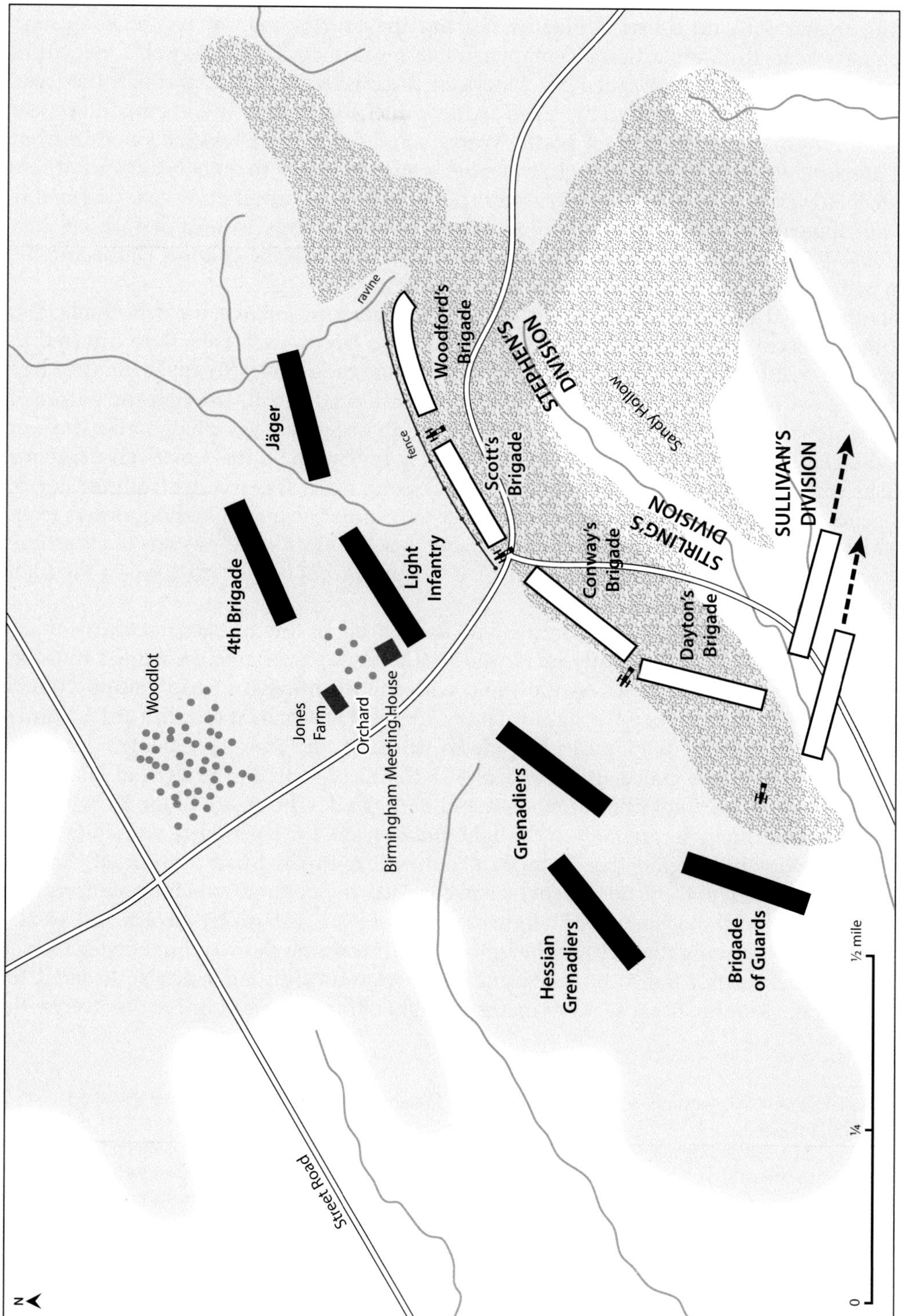

The Battle of Brandywine, 11 September 1777.

killing many, with little loss.'[93] Finally, nearing the fourth hour of battle, Ferguson's riflemen waded through 'an almost impenetrable morass' to flank Maxwell's men from the north side of their barricade. The American skirmishers retreated through the river, and heavier projectiles began to fly.[94] The artillery duel continued while the main body of the 8th Virginia readied itself for battle. Wayne's and Sullivan's Divisions stood in front and prepared to take the first hits while Stephen's men got ready to quickly advance where needed. However, to the Continentals' surprise, as a Maryland officer observed, 'The enemy did not appear very numerous, and began to intrench themselves' instead of pushing their way across the water.[95] The implication was chillingly obvious: the column Darke and his men had been fighting all morning was just a diversion.

Continental dragoons galloped north, looking for a flanking force on the American right, and new orders were given to Stephen's and Sterling's Divisions.[96] They were directed to march to Birmingham Hill and oppose whatever came their way.[97] To get there, they had to march east on the Chester Road and then take back roads north through the village of Dilworthtown. They hiked a mile and a half before an order came to a halt a mile short of the village.[98] They idled in the hot sun for two long hours. Then, the American dragoons rode by with confirmation that a second British column really was coming from the north. The generals got into an argument over whether to resume the march without orders from Washington. Scott was reticent but yielded to Stephen's seniority.[99] It was not the last time they would disagree. The divisions marched at 'a trott' through Dilworthtown to the high ground at the Quaker meeting house.[100]

Events unfolded quickly. The Continentals formed up in line of battle at the military crest of Birmingham Hill (slightly forward of the topographical crest). Stirling's division stood on the left and Stephen's on the right, with the Birmingham Road running down the hill between them. Since the light infantry was still at Chads' Ford, the 3rd Virginia was sent forward from Woodford's brigade to skirmish and slow the enemy's advance. This regiment was now commanded by Colonel Thomas Marshall, the clerk of Dunmore County and previous employer of Jonathan and John Clark. The cream of the King's army appeared before them: the grenadiers, the light infantry, and the Jägerkorps, with thousands more were following behind. The American commander-in-chief had committed Colonel Bowman's shirtmen to the kind of fight he had consistently sought to avoid: whole divisions of men engaged in the open against a larger enemy force on unfamiliar terrain. The weakness of the Americans' situation and the limits of their training showed immediately.

Major General John Sullivan's Maryland and Delaware division was also ordered to Birmingham. However, because it was on the far right of the American line at the river, with

93 Daniel Agnew, 'A Biographical Sketch of Governor Richard Howell, of New Jersey', *PMHB*, 22:2 (1898), pp.224.
94 Tustin (ed.), *Ewald Journal*, pp.81; Agnew, 'Sketch of Howell', p.224; Harris, *Brandywine*, p.248.
95 J. Thomas Scharf (ed), *The Chronicles of Baltimore; Being a Complete History of 'Baltimore Town' and Baltimore City From the Earliest Period to the Present Time* (Baltimore: Turnbull Brothers, 1874), p.166.
96 Campbell (ed.), *Bland Papers*, vol.1, p.67.
97 Agnew, 'Sketch of Howell', p.224.
98 Chicago Historical Society (CHS): George Weedon Letters, George Weedon to John Page, 11 Sept. 1777.
99 Chase et al (eds), *Papers of Washington* (Revolution), vol.11, pp.468–470, 602.
100 CHS: Weedon to John Page, 11 Sept. 1777.

detachments covering the upper fords, it came by a different route and had to find the other divisions. When it arrived on the left, it was too far forward and had insufficient space for an alignment. Sullivan, who was senior, took command, riding back and forth and ordering the other divisions to move to the right. Woodford's Brigade on the far right was squeezed against a ravine while Sullivans's Division botched its alignment manoeuvre on the left.[101]

Marshall's men skirmished with the British advance at the bottom of the hill and then fell back to the Birmingham Meeting House. There, behind a graveyard wall, they held out as long as they could. American cannons on Scott's right and left opened fire when the Old-World forces came into range, switching from solid shot to grape and canister as the distance narrowed. Marshall's courageous men moved back to rejoin Woodford's already squeezed brigade as Sullivan's Division, under the temporary command of an incompetent French general, fell into chaos on the left. The Guards battalions bore down on them, and the disorganised Marylanders fled, leaving Stirling's left unprotected.

Stephen's division was well-positioned, despite the squeeze on the right. His men had a clear field of fire, a strong fence before them, a ravine to their right, and partial cover from trees.[102] The troops opposing them, the British light infantry and the Jägerkorps, had to cross ground that had recently been ploughed.[103] As any farm boy knows, upturned clods of soft soil are a challenge to traverse. Seven captains and one lieutenant (Campbell, Slaughter, Clark, Westfall, David Stephenson, Berry, Croghan, and Lieutenant Israel for Captain Darke) encouraged the 8th Virginia's men and kept them steady in line. The thunder of the cannons mixed with the sounds of splintering trees and the jarring screams of the wounded. Since the rifles were at the river, the infantry had to stand and take it until the Anglo-German army came into musket range.

When small arms fire began, the British light infantry periodically dropped to their bellies but returned fire and kept coming.[104] Bowman's men fired as rapidly as they could until muskets began to foul or become too hot to handle.[105] One man in Scott's brigade claimed he fired 'upwards of eighty rounds' in the battle, a very high number.[106] All along the line, cries were heard as bones were crushed and fingers were blown off.[107] Henry Gaddis of Croghan's Company described the fight as a 'severe contest.' David Great of Campbell's Company was shot through the knee.[108] So was William Jones of Darke's Company.[109] James Kay of Berry's Company was 'wounded badly in one hand.'[110] Another man said it was 'the heaviest firing I

101 CHS: Weedon to John Page, 11 Sept. 1777.
102 Kipping and Smith (trans. and ed.), *Muenchhausen Diary*, p.31; W.H. Wilkin, *Some British Soldiers in America* (London: Hugh Rees, 1914), p.230; Ira D. Gruber (ed.), *John Peebles' American War* (Mechanicsburg, Pa.: Stackpole Books, 1998), p.133; Anne Hunter and Elizabeth Bell (eds), *The Journal of Gen. Sir Martin Hunter* (Edinburgh: Edinburgh Press, 1894), p.29.
103 Scull (ed.), *Montresor Journals*, pp, p.450; Dunkerly, *Brandywine*, p.84.
104 Harris, *Brandywine*, pp.303, 314.
105 Dunkerly, *Brandywine*, p.79.
106 NARA: M804, S38072, Isaac Jackson pension (12th Va.).
107 NARA: M804, S39148, John Alverson pension (11th Va.); LVA: Revolutionary War Bounty Land Claims, Levi Grooms (7th Va.).
108 NARA: H. Gaddis pension, D. Great pension.
109 LVA: Revolutionary War Pension Applications, pen. 224, William Jones; Revolutionary War Bounty Land Claims, David Jones; Anon. (ed.), *Journal of Delegates*, 1778, p.15.
110 NARA: J. Kay pension.

ever heard.'[111] Enough of Stephen's men were wounded in the head, knees, hands, and feet to suggest their torsos were protected by the fence rails.[112] As the Redcoats closed in, thrusting steel replaced propelled lead. Though the Marylanders had collapsed quickly, one British officer credited the rest of the American line at Birmingham with holding out until they heard the battle at the river coming nearer.[113]

Whether motivated by what they heard in the distance or the grenadier battalions coming at them with bayonets, Stirling's division began to give way.[114] Among them and immediately to the left of Scott's Brigade was the brigade led by Thomas Conway, an Irish-born French general. As Conway's men came under pressure, another Frenchman, Gilbert du Motier, Marquis de Lafayette, rushed forward to assist his countryman. In his battlefield debut, the 19-year-old major general 'dismounted and did his utmost to make the men charge with fixed bayonets.' The Gallic officers 'personally attached their bayonets for them, and Lafayette pushed them in the back to make them charge.' It was futile. Stirling's Division retreated into Sandy Hollow and Lafayette himself was wounded in the left calf.[115] One British soldier, reaching the top of Birmingham Hill, tossed his hat in the air and shouted, 'Victory!'[116]

But the battle was not over. Stephen's Division, alone now, continued to fight. Woodford's Brigade was hard up against the ravine, which was a defensible position as long as the 8th Virginia and Scott's Brigade held out on their left. Scott's men could not do that for long, however, with their own left hanging open. The commanders had no choice but to order a withdrawal into Sandy Hollow. Peter McDonald, a soldier in Abel Westfall's Company, was so focused on maintaining fire on the advancing light infantry battalions that he was oblivious to the retreat. Colonel Bowman had to grab him and turn him around.[117] Woodford was shot in the hand before his got his brigade over the hill.[118]

Back at the Brandywine River, the King's forces were instructed to push across the water once they heard gunfire from the north. Because Greene's Division and the North Carolina Brigade were sent to back up Sullivan's wing, only Anthony Wayne's Division, Maxwell's Light Infantry, some Pennsylvania militia, and some Pennsylvania state artillery were left to defend the crossings. There was little chance of holding the enemy off for long. Still, felled trees and effective artillery fire forced the men under Hessian *Generallieutenant* Wilhelm von Knyphausen to cross farther south at Chads' Ferry. They waded chest-deep through

111 Agnew, 'Sketch of Howell', p.224
112 NARA: M804, S39148, John Alverson pension (11th Va.), S10351, Glover Baker pension (4th Va.), S37758, William Beale pension (12th Va.), S42627, Francis Boyd pension (7th Va.), S6110, John Slaven pension (12th Va.); LVA: Revolutionary War Bounty Land Claims, Thomas Galford (12th Va.), Legislative Petitions of the General Assembly, 1776–1865, George Black (12th Va.), James Davenport (7th Va.), Banks Dudley (7th Va.). However, torso wounds were also likely to be fatal.
113 Kipping and Smith (trans. and ed.), *Muenchhausen Diary*, p.31.
114 Anon. (ed.), 'Diary of Joseph Clark', pp.98–99.
115 Stanley J. Idzerda et al (eds), *Lafayette in the Age of the American Revolution: Selected Letters and Papers, 1776–1790* (Ithaca: Cornell University Press, 1977–1983), vol.1, p.84; Laura Auricchio, *The Marquis: Lafayette Reconsidered* (New York: Alfred A. Knopf, 2014), p.51.
116 Harris, *Brandywine*, p.27
117 NARA: M804, W9554, Peter McDonald pension.
118 Lyon Gardiner Tyler (ed.), *Encyclopedia of Virginia Biography* (New York: Lewis Historical Publishing, 1915), vol.2, p.172.

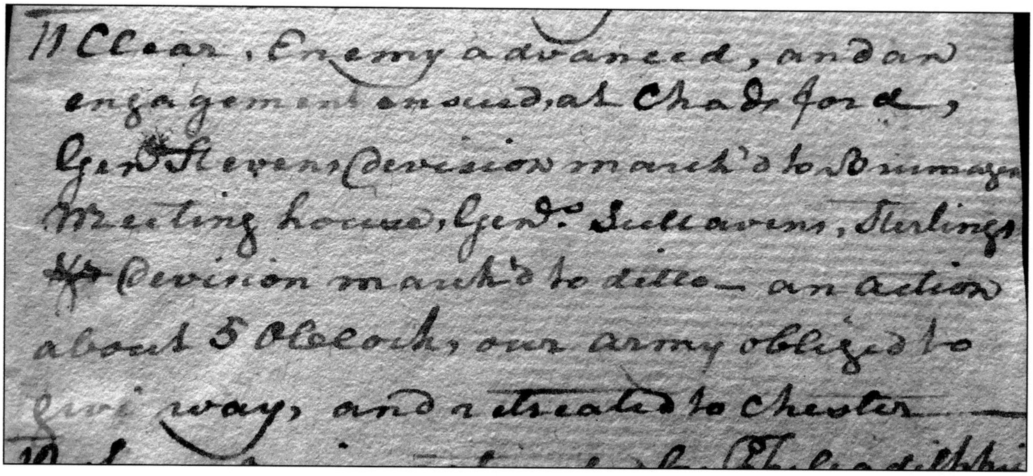

11 Clear, Enemy advanced, and an engagement ensued, at Chadsford, Genl Stevens Devision march'd to Birmingham Meeting house, Genls Sullivans, Sterlings Devision march'd to ditto — an action about 5 O'Clock, our army obliged to give way, and retreated to Chester

Jonathan Clark's diary entry for the day of Brandywine. (The Filson Historical Society, Louisville, KY)

the river, holding their weapons and cartridge boxes in the air. Most of the militia ran off, but Maxwell's men, whom the Hessians called 'nothing but sharpshooters', moved closer to the ferry and began picking off the vulnerable Redcoats and Hessians as they crossed. The Pennsylvania artillery moved forward and fired grapeshot. East of the ferry's causeway, Wayne's Pennsylvanians positioned themselves to make a stand using ditches and a few structures in the floodplain along Harvey Run.[119]

When the first Redcoats across captured the Pennsylvania cannons, Maxwell's skirmishers retreated to Wayne's improvised defences.[120] Here, John Chenoweth remembered 'a hot engagement' as they held off the Crown forces for as long as they could. The intensity of fire at Harvey Run matched the exchange at Birmingham Hill. Sergeant Parett boasted later that 'he used his gun with great effect and success.' William Moody, the Maryland veteran of the siege of Boston, was 'wounded in the left arm and on the head' just three months after taking a ball in the knee at Short Hills. David Williams of Captain Croghan's Company, now a veteran of 'fifteen battles and skirmishes', was 'shot through the leg and had part of his jaw and teeth carried away.'[121] Moses Crawford, who had been wounded in the arm at Cooch's Bridge, was shot again in the hand.[122] Parett, 'having shot away his entire stock of ammunition, which comprized 22 rifle balls … got another supply of ammunition whilst the battle lasted.'[123] A 5th Virginia soldier remembered that he and Crawford were talking 'just as the Retreat was ordered'; having held out for as long as they could, Wayne's and Maxwell's men withdrew.[124]

119 Harris, *Brandywine*, pp.257, 325–327, 338–339.
120 Harris, *Brandywine*, p.334.
121 NARA: J. Chenoweth pension, W. Moody pension, D. Williams pension.
122 NARA: M804, W910, Moses Crawford pension.
123 NARA: J. Parret pension.
124 Chase et al (eds), *Papers of Washington* (Revolution), vol.11, pp.200–201.

While Darke and about 50 8th Virginia men were falling back up Harvey Run, Colonel Bowman and the rest of the regiment were retreating up the eastern end of Sandy Hollow, where Stephen's and Stirling's Divisions formed up to make another stand. This started a fighting retreat that extended for about three miles and half a dozen fence lines.[125] One man said 'every inch of ground' was disputed.[126] The British advanced with their bayonets as the Americans fired 'from hill to hill and from wall to wall', through Sandy Hollow all the way to Dilworthtown.[127] The Americans' lack of practice and discipline was on display all day, but there was a small upside to their lack of training. A British soldier discerned that the rebels' 'chief qualification is agility in running from fence to fence and thence keeping up an irregular, but galling fire on troops who advance with the same pace as at their exercise.'[128]

As long shadows faded into dusk, Nathanael Greene's Division covered the retreat of the exhausted and jumbled army moving south on the Wilmington Road beyond Dilworthtown. Greene's, Muhlenberg's, and Weedon's Brigades had yet to engage in heavy action that day. Muhlenberg's role at this time is not well recorded, but Weedon's Brigade performed splendidly. The men who fought at Birmingham and Sandy Hollow met Wayne's and Maxwell's men about where the Wilmington and Chester Roads intersected and took the latter path east in the darkness.[129] Their tired enemy followed no farther.

125 Wilkin, *Some British Soldiers*, p.230.
126 Agnew, 'Sketch of Howell', p.224
127 Kipping and Smith (trans. and ed.), *Muenchhausen Diary*, p.31; Tustin (ed.), *Ewald Journal*, pp.86.
128 Wilkin, *Some British Soldiers*, p.245.
129 Anon. (ed.), 'Diary of Joseph Clark', p.99; Harris, *Brandywine*, pp.351–365.

11

Smoke

After Brandywine, Jonathan Grant and Thomas Owens followed behind the retreating army with Maxwell's corps, rounding up stragglers.[1] The army spent the next several days resting and repositioning itself to blunt the British Army's next advance toward Philadelphia. They crossed the Schuylkill River on the city's pontoon bridge, marched upstream and camped again at the river's falls near Germantown. Lieutenant Curry and his recruits for Higgins' Company finally joined the regiment.[2] After a respite, the army marched upstream to the fords where the British were expected to cross and waded through the river back into Chester County.

Chester County was crossed diagonally by a wide geological feature known as the Great Valley. Its southeastern rim, the 'South Valley Hills', met the Schuylkill opposite Matson's Ford (Conshohocken). Its northwestern rim, the 'North Valley Hills', met the river at Fatland Ford, close to the soon-to-be-important Valley Forge. Swede's Ford Road ran up the centre of the valley to a river crossing of the same name. It was a branch of the Conestoga Road, which crossed the valley from the west and then paralleled the southeastern rim for a few miles on its way to Philadelphia. The army camped along the road, with its vanguard in the valley near the White Horse Tavern and its rear at the Warren Tavern, about where the road descended into the basin. This put the Americans directly across the Redcoats' path.[3]

The Battle of the Clouds, 16 September 1777

Thomas Owens was the last of Grant's original messmates recorded in Sergeant McCarty's 1776 notebook.[4] They had enlisted on the same day.[5] Of the other four men who shared their kettle, two were dead, one was given an early discharge after the winter campaign, and the fourth, never on the rolls, was probably a camp follower.[6] Owens reenlisted in March for another three years, but Grant had decided to finish out his two years and go home.[7] Now,

1 Chase et al (eds), *Papers of Washington* (Revolution), vol.11, pp.204–205.
2 NARA: R. Chambers pension.
3 LOC: Geography and Maps Divisions, G3791.S3 1777.P7, 'Progress of the army from their landing till taking possession of Philadelphia.'
4 WHS: Draper Mss, N, vol.2, p.4.
5 NARA: M246, f.211, p.3.
6 WHS: Draper Mss, N, vol.2, p.4; NARA: M246, f.211, pp.2–5.
7 NARA: M246, f.211, pp.3.

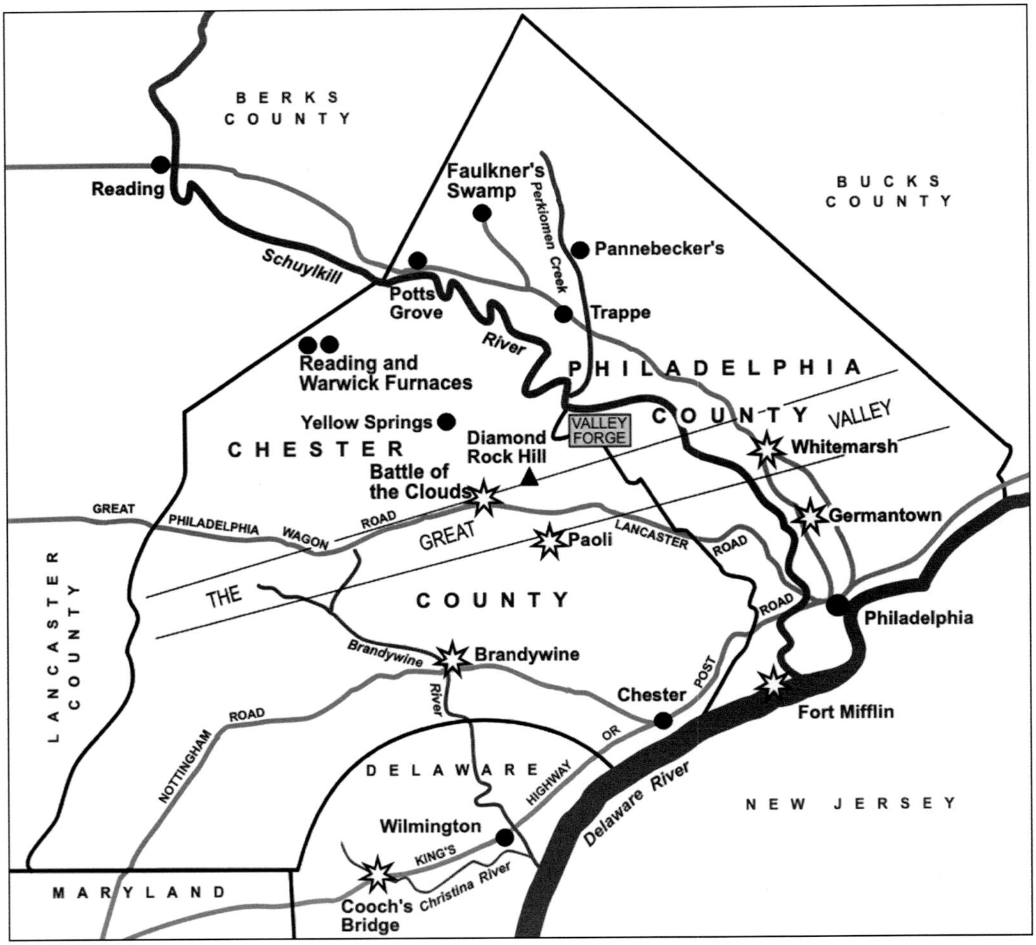

Chester and Philadelphia Counties.

on the morning of 16 September, the two frontiersmen were advanced toward the British with Captain Darke and William Maxwell near the Boot Tavern on what is now Phoenixville Pike. They were supported by Dunlap's Partisans, a militia unit of picked riflemen.[8] Far off to their left, Wayne's Division was similarly advanced from the other end of the American line, southeast of the White Horse Tavern, and also supported by militia. This was the second time Maxwell and Wayne were paired together for a dangerous duty. About noon, the rest of the army went down into the valley and up the northwest rim to take a more defensible position.[9] The Anglo-German army approached from the south in two columns.

8 NARA: A. Cummings pension.
9 Gary Ecelbarger, *George Washington's Momentous Year: Twelve Months that Transformed the Revolution* (Yardley: Westholme, 2024-), vol.1, pp.114–119; Gary Ecelbarger, 'Clement Biddle Partially Clears the "Battle of the Clouds"', *JAR*, 11 March 2021, <allthingsliberty.com/2021/03/clement-biddle-partially-clears-the-battle-of-the-clouds>, accessed 1 Sept. 2024.

It began to rain. Maxwell and Wayne both sent their militia farther forward to 'bring on' the attack.[10] Wayne's militia fired and quickly retreated. Dunlap's Partisans did the same.[11] This brought Darke's detached men into the action as the rain fell harder. A witness (confusing Maxwell's men for Morgan's) wrote, 'Morgan's rifelmen ware in a wood... The rifelmen begun the action with their advance guard' facing off against advancing Hessians.[12]

Grant, Owens, and the other marksmen maintained a retreating fire as the rain turned into an impressive downpour. Gunpowder turned to 'mush' on both sides.[13] 'All this time...' wrote the witness, the 'riflemen ware on the wings, next to the enemy, against the Hissions'. They had a brief advantage, 'as they could use their rifels, having bearskins over their locks.' On the north side of the valley, Scott's Brigade had been ordered to support Maxwell and Wayne, but the weather made that impractical. Scott turned Bowman's men around before the order was given, sparking another spat with Adam Stephen.[14] The American army retreated north to Yellow Springs in the middle of a powerful deluge, struggling to make the gruelling overnight slog over muddy fields and dangerously flooded creeks.[15] As they marched away, Bowman's men could hear sporadic gunfire well enough to distinguish the 'cracks' of the American long rifles from the muted reports of the shorter, larger-bore jäger rifles.[16] When their firearms became useless, the jäger shouldered them and charged at Maxwell's men with their swords.[17] Thomas Owens was killed as the skirmish petered out in a slippery, downhill retreat.[18] The 'Battle of the Clouds' was quickly over, but Maxwell's men were ordered to remain in the Great Valley to protect the removal of the baggage wagons and supplies stored at Valley Forge.[19]

Captain Knox at Freeman's Farm, 19 September 1777

The 8th Virginia marksmen attached to Daniel Morgan arrived in Albany, New York, on 31 August. They were put in Brigadier General Enoch Poor's Brigade and Major General Benedict Arnold's Division.[20] It took time to get Morgan's 400 men organised. Some in Captain Knox's Company, including an 8th Virginia man, remembered ardent Culpeper County patriot

10 NARA: M804, S30629, James Patten pension (Pa. militia).

11 NARA: J. Patten pension; Michael C. Harris, *Germantown: A Military History of the Battle for Philadelphia, October 4, 1777* (El Dorado Hills, Ca.: Savas Beatie, 2020), pp.52–53.

12 John C. Dann (ed.), *The Nagle Journal: A Diary of the Life of Jacob Nagle, Sailor, From the Year 1775 to 1841* (New York: Weidenfeld & Nicolson, 1988), p.10.

13 Harris, *Germantown*, p.55.

14 Octavius Pickering and Charles W. Upham, *Life of Timothy Pickering* (Boston: Little, Brown, and Company, 1867–1873), vol.1, pp.159–160; Chase et al (eds), *Papers of Washington* (Revolution), vol.11, pp.468–470.

15 Pickering and Upham, *Life of Pickering*, vol.1, pp.159–160; Chase et al (eds), *Papers of Washington* (Revolution), vol.11, pp.253.

16 Dann (ed.), *Nagle*, p.10.

17 Harris, *Germantown*, p.55.

18 NARA: M246, f.211, p.15.

19 Chase et al (eds), *Papers of Washington* (Revolution), vol.11, p.258.

20 Eric Schnitzer and Don Troiani, *Don Troiani's Campaign to Saratoga – 1777* (Guilford, Ct.: Stackpole Books, 2019), p.149; Zambone, *Daniel Morgan*, p.134.

Gabriel Long as their first captain. Soldiers admired Morgan as a gifted leader, and veterans were later quick to say that they knew him. Henry Wysor bragged, 'Morgan had been a neighbour and acquaintance of mine.' Solomon Hendricks boasted that he was 'selected by Col. Morgan (to whom he was personally known) as one of his rifle corps.'[21]

The Continental Army in the north was struggling. Burgoyne had recaptured Fort Ticonderoga on the night of 5 July. Congress, perhaps unfairly, relieved Major General Philip Schuyler of command and replaced him with Berkeley County's Horatio Gates. Morgan's arrival in Cambridge in 1775 had resulted in fights, but this time, he was welcomed in the north. Three hundred of 'the most able, active, and spirited' musketeers from the New England regiments were attached to Morgan as light infantry under Major Henry Dearborn, a veteran of Bunker Hill and Arnold's march to Quebec. Some Stockbridge Mohicans were also assigned to Morgan to serve as rangers and scouts.[22]

Thinking of the Patriots' success at Bunker Hill, Gates found an excellent high-ground position 25 miles up the Hudson from Albany at Bemis Heights. It gave the Continentals an unobstructed view looking north over forests and farmstead clearings and allowed an approaching army very little room to manoeuvre on either side. The right side was close to the Hudson River, and a swamp protected the left. The Americans fortified the heights and blocked the main road along the river by felling trees and dismantling bridges at the tributary creeks.[23]

Morgan bunked with Arnold in a farmhouse near the forwardmost point of the American entrenchments. Captain Knox led his men to a barn directly facing the Crown forces' likely approach.[24] As the line units worked on fortifications, Morgan's men scouted and patrolled the mostly wooded plain to the north.[25]

Burgoyne's army advanced in three columns on the 19th. His Germans made a show of approaching on the river road while other troops sought to get around the Americans to the west. Morgan, meanwhile, took his men out to 'observe their Direction, and harass their advance.' When they made contact on the cleared acres of John Freeman's farm, Morgan's Provisional Rifle Corps advanced in a crescent formation with the colonel signalling with a turkey call from the centre. Though the American rifles quickly bested the British muskets, Morgan's most advanced men pursued their retreating enemy too aggressively. Captain Van Swearingen (a Berkeley County native now detached from the 8th Pennsylvania) and several riflemen surrendered in a circle of bayonets, and the other riflemen were forced to scatter.[26] Dearborn's musketeers were not close enough to cover them.

After a pause and some confusion, Knox and his men heard Morgan summoning them back with his turkey call. The regiments of Enoch Poor's Brigade also arrived, forming a strong line that pushed Dearborn's men farther from the riflemen.[27] The sharpshooters,

21 NARA: H. Wysor pension, S. Hendricks pension.
22 Schnitzer and Troiani, *Campaign to Saratoga*, pp.149–151.
23 Henry P. Johnston (ed.) *The Correspondence and Public Papers of John Jay* (New York: G.P. Putnam's Sons, 1890–1893), vol.1, pp.165–167.
24 Zambone, *Daniel Morgan*, p.135.
25 Zambone, *Daniel Morgan*, p.135; Schnitzer and Troiani, *Campaign to Saratoga*, p.163.
26 Wilkinson, *Memoirs*, vol.1, p.237; Joseph Lee Boyle (ed.), 'Notes and Documents: From Saratoga to Valley Forge: The Diary of Lt. Samuel Armstrong', *PMHB*, 121:3 (1997), p.245.
27 Zambone, *Daniel Morgan*, p.137.

ready to reengage, took a position on the American right behind a deep ravine. They cut abatis with their tomahawks and positioned them along the edge of the valley in front of them. The battle began in earnest and lasted for hours, but King George's troops were unable to gain an advantage. Several of the riflemen sniped from the trees, focusing for maximum effect on officers and artillerymen. The British 62nd Regiment, directly opposite Morgan's men at the ravine, lost half its strength.[28]

Gates refused to send more men from the heights, and the arrival of Hessian reinforcements forced Arnold's division to retreat late in the day. Yet, the Americans fought well and did significant harm to Burgoyne's army before they withdrew. This outcome was due in great part to the performance of Morgan, Knox, and their riflemen. Arnold, who was later reviled, showed good instincts and a willingness to trust his subordinate officers in the field.

Maxwell's Light Infantry During the Paoli Massacre

One of Knox's riflemen was almost 300 miles away from his captain on the day of the Battle of Freeman's Farm.[29] Sixteen-year-old Abraham Hornback was in Pennsylvania, driving a team of horses hitched to a wagon that belonged to Captain Westfall.[30] He was in the vicinity of Milltown (Downingtown) in the Great Valley, on his way back from Virginia. What his errand was and why it required a wagon is not recorded. Perhaps he was retrieving some comrades who had been unfit to march in the spring.[31] His passengers, if he had them, were near their destination. Hornback, on the other hand, had to return the wagon to Abel Westfall and then find his way to Captain Knox in upstate New York.

Hornback came upon a large column of Maryland militiamen under the command of Brigadier General William Smallwood. They were on their way to reinforce Wayne and Maxwell farther up the valley. Wayne had sent a messenger to Smallwood telling him to hurry, and one thing that would help with that was another wagon.[32] Hornback's 'Waggon and Team,' the teenage rifleman reported, were 'Impressed from him Between the Town of Lancaster and the City of Philadelphia by the Maryland Militia Commanded [by] General Smallwood.' Smallwood should have given him a receipt, but there was no time for that.[33]

Meanwhile, Captain Darke and his detachment were on the north ridge of the valley with Maxwell. There were three prominent heights there between the army's last position and the river: Diamond Rock Hill, Mount Misery, and Mount Joy. Diamond Rock Hill was closest to the site of the Battle of the Clouds and was probably Maxwell's position. He has been criticised by some historians for not helping remove the stores at Valley Forge, but he was never tasked with doing that. In fact, the commander-in-chief initially ordered him to stay put. 'I would have you remain where you are,' Washington told him, 'untill that part of the Baggage & stores at the Valley can be got away, which I wish to be effected as expeditiously as possible,

28 Zambone, *Daniel Morgan*, pp.138–140; Schnitzer and Troiani, *Campaign to Saratoga*, p.179.
29 NARA: M246 f.26, pp.83.
30 NARA: M247 i.42, p.195.
31 NARA: M881, r.1045, Abraham Hornback.
32 Harris, *Brandywine*, pp.82–83.
33 NARA: M247 i.42, p.195.

& then Join us at Warwick by the shortest Route.' Further clarity is found in Washington's reference to 'General Maxwell's Quarters' as the place 'where the army last drew up' on the northwest rim of the valley.[34] Washington did direct Maxwell to impress horses if needed to get the baggage out of the valley, but the removal of both baggage and stores was the responsibility of the Quartermaster's Department. Realtime correspondence between Washington and the Quartermaster's Department leaves no doubt about this.[35] Maxwell's Light Infantry guarded against an approach by the British from the south side of the valley.

Then, from his new headquarters at Reading Furnace in the northwest corner of Chester County, Washington directed Wayne and Maxwell to harass the British rear while the waters of the Schuylkill subsided. 'Cutting the Enemys Baggage would be a great matter,' he told them, 'but take care of Ambuscades.' Though they were told to coordinate,[36] Wayne prioritised the first half of the order and Maxwell evidently focused on the second. Wayne moved to the South Valley Hills, near Paoli, and Maxwell stayed in the North Valley Hills. If Howe's army crossed at Swede's Ford, they would be positioned on both his flanks. Maxwell, however, also had his orders to guard Valley Forge. His movements are not recorded, but paralleling the British advance along the ridge toward Mount Misery would have taken him farther from Wayne. Maxwell was also in a better position than Wayne to know that Washington took the rest of the army back to the north side of the Schuylkill at Parker's Ford on the 19th.[37] Some correspondence from these days was intercepted, which may explain why Wayne was not aware.[38] He wrote the commander-in-chief the same day, 'I expect Genl. Maxwell on their left flank every Moment and as I lay on their Right, we only want you in their Rear – to Complete Mr Hows business.'[39] Washington was not coming, and if Wayne tried to coordinate with Maxwell, there is no other record of it. Carrying any message across the Great Valley at this point in time was a high-risk venture. Wayne's division was hit the next night with an attack so bloody and lopsided it is remembered as the 'Paoli Massacre.' Abraham Hornback's wagon was not enough to get Smallwood's men to Wayne in time. The 2,100 inexperienced Marylanders approached as the massacre was underway, and half of them fled.[40]

One of Dunlap's Partisans reported that 'the corpse to which' he belonged crossed the river on the same night as the Paoli Massacre.[41] Henry Muhlenberg reported in his diary two days later that 'a corps of American light infantrymen, a *scouting party*, was chased across the Schulkiel toward us by the British.' Maxwell was at Trappe when this entry was written, and his men are the likely subject of the report.[42] If both accounts are correct, Maxwell sent his militia across the river two days before he retreated himself. In that scenario, Captain Darke and his band of 8th Virginia riflemen were among the last Continentals to come across.[43]

34 Chase et al (eds), *Papers of Washington* (Revolution), vol.121, pp.251–252, 258; Ecelbarger, 'Clement Biddle.'
35 Chase et al (eds), *Papers of Washington* (Revolution), vol.11, pp.244–246, 259, 265.
36 Chase et al (eds), *Papers of Washington* (Revolution), vol.11, pp.265–266.
37 Ecelbarger, *Washington's Momentous Year*, vol.1, pp.124–126.
38 John F. Reed, *Campaign to Valley Forge, July 1, 1777-December 19, 1777* (Philadelphia: University of Pennsylvania Press, 1965), pp.159, 167; Harris, *Germantown*, p.78.
39 Chase et al (eds), *Papers of Washington* (Revolution), vol.11, pp.273–274.
40 Harris, *Germantown*, pp.102–103.
41 NARA: J. Patten pension.
42 Tappert and Doberstein (trans), *Journals of H.M. Muhlenberg*, vol.3, p.79; Harris, *Germantown*, pp.102–103.
43 It has been previously assumed that Maxwell crossed the river before Paoli.

Faulkner Swamp and Perkiomen Creek

On a clear 22 September, Captain Clark's diary tells us the 8th Virginia 'march'd about Six miles to the Swamp and encamped.'[44] Falckner Schwamm (Falckner Meadows) was the site of New Hanover Church,[45] the oldest German Lutheran congregation in Pennsylvania.[46] English speakers called the place Faulkner Swamp, though there was no actual swamp. Peter Muhlenberg and Chaplain Christian Streit knew the community well. The general's father had preached there regularly since 1743.[47] When the present stone church was dedicated in 1768, a not-yet-ordained Streit delivered an English-language address during the ceremonies.[48]

An estate known as Pottsgrove sat four miles to the south, where Pottstown is now. It was the home of the late John Potts, the iron baron who owned the furnace at Warwick and forges at Coventry, Mount Joy ('the valley forge'), and elsewhere. Potts' children now ran the business, and his widow lived in the house.[49] Washington's letters from the next few days were dated 'Camp near Pots Grove.'

Twenty miles downriver, Howe's army crossed the Schuylkill virtually unopposed on 23 September. Washington made a conscious choice not to resist it.[50] Protecting Philadelphia was no longer realistic; Congress left the city and reconvened 100 miles west at York. The best the army could do for the city now was to reinforce the forts guarding the Delaware River and prevent the British from receiving supplies. Samuel Smith, a lieutenant colonel from the Maryland Line, was sent off with a detachment of 200 men for this purpose.[51] At least a dozen of these men were from the 8th Virginia Regiment, apparently led by Sergeant John Roberts of Captain Darke's Company.

Darke himself was halfway between Washington and Howe near Brigadier General Muhlenberg's hometown, Trappe. Maxwell's Light Infantry camped there on the west side of Perkiomen Creek.[52] Captain Clark's Company was also sent forward to set up a picket at the house of George Hepler, a member of Henry Muhlenberg's congregation.[53] Anthony

44 FHS: Clark Diary, 22 Sept. 1777.

45 Henry S. Dotterer, 'Folk-Names of Places in the Perkiomen Valley,' *The Perkiomen Region, Past and Present*, 1:1 (1894), pp.5–6; Robert Wood, 'Early Church Schools,' *The Goschenhoppen Historians*, <goschenhoppen.org/early-church-schools>, accessed 28 Nov. 2023.

46 John Jacob Kline, *The Lutheran Church in New Hanover, Pa.* (New Hanover, Pa: New Hanover Lutheran Church, 1910), pp.8, 21.

47 Tappert and Doberstein (trans), *Journals of H.M. Muhlenberg*, vol.1, pp.20, 66–67, 84, 97 and passim.

48 Tappert and Doberstein (trans), *Journals of H.M. Muhlenberg*, vol.2, pp.364–365; Kline, *New Hanover* Church, pp.28–31.

49 Daniel A. Graham, 'The Family of John Potts (1709/10–1768), Ironmaster, and Ruth Savage (1715/16–1786) of Pottstown, Pennsylvania Through the Fourth Generation: A Genealogical Sketch,' <montgomerycountypa.gov/DocumentCenter/View/20669/Dan-Graham-Research>, accessed 27 Nov. 2023.

50 Gary Ecelbarger, 'The Feint That Never Happened: Unheralded Turning Point of the Philadelphia Campaign,' *JAR*, 19 Nov. 2020, <allthingsliberty.com/2020/11/the-feint-that-never-happened-unheralded-turning-point-of-the-philadelphia-campaign>, accessed 27 Nov. 2023.

51 Harris, *Germantown*, pp.102–103, 146.

52 Chase et al (eds), *Papers of Washington* (Revolution), vol.11, p.316.

53 FHS: Clark Diary, 24–26 Sept. 1777; Anon (ed.), 'Mennonite Historians of Eastern Pennsylvania Cemetery Database Report,' <mhep.org/files/PDF/CemeteryDatabase/surname-H-report.pdf>, accessed 28 Nov. 2023.

Chaplain Christian Streit gave an English-language address at the dedication of New Hanover Lutheran Church's new stone building in 1768. A 1972 mural by George F.H. Walters depicts the new church, the old log building and a procession of clergy led by Rev. Henry Muhlenberg. The Ministerium of Pennsylvania was the only Lutheran 'synod' in North America at the time and invitations may have been sent to congregations as far away as New York and the Carolinas. (Courtesy of New Hanover Lutheran)

Wayne reappeared after his shellacking at Paoli and resumed his coordination with Maxwell. Washington was suspicious when he learned the British had still not entered Philadelphia and sent Count Casimir Pulaski's cavalry forward as well.[54] The growing collection of Continentals at Perkiomen Creek warranted a major general's presence, so Lord Stirling came forward to command.[55] On the 25th, Washington asked the putative earl to consult the other forward generals 'and determine whether it will be best for you to March back the Picquets, & for Maxwells Corps to join their respective Brigades immediately, or wait till to morrow.'[56] They waited another day.[57]

This was indeed the end of the road for Maxwell's Light Infantry, and Darke's 45 or 50 8th Virginia men returned to their captains. Although two veterans remembered it operating past the first of October,[58] the decision to disband the light infantry was probably made on the 24th. Maxwell pulled the cork too often and could not escape unflattering comparisons to Daniel Morgan. 'Maxwells Corps 'Twas expected would do great things,' complained William Heth, who served under both men, 'we had opportunities – and any body but an old-woman, would have availd themselves of them – He is to be sure – a Damnd bitch of a General.'[59] A fairer assessment is that Maxwell's corps performed well most of the time despite a lack of cohesion and other challenges. Nevertheless, Washington wrote to Horatio Gates on 24 September asking him to send Daniel Morgan back.[60]

54 Tappert and Doberstein (trans), *Journals of H.M. Muhlenberg*, vol.3, p.80.
55 Tappert and Doberstein (trans), *Journals of H.M. Muhlenberg*, vol.3, p.80; Chase et al (eds), *Papers of Washington* (Revolution), vol.11, p.316.
56 Chase et al (eds), *Papers of Washington* (Revolution), vol.11, p.321–323.
57 FHS: Clark Diary, 26 Sept. 1777.
58 NARA: M804, S5582, Robert Humphrey pension (Pa. State Rgt); J. Nicholson pension.
59 Flickinger (ed.), 'Diary of Heth,' p.33.
60 Chase et al (eds), *Papers of Washington* (Revolution), vol.11, pp.310–311.

Pannebecker's Mill

Peter Muhlenberg and Christian Streit were not the only 8th Virginia men with ties to upper Philadelphia County (now Montgomery County). Decades earlier, in 1728, settlers from the area sent a petition to the governor of the Quaker colony begging for protection from Indian attacks. One of the signers was Colonel Bowman's grandfather, Jost Hite.[61] Now, on 26 September, the army moved a few miles east and camped on the 500-acre property of Samuel Pannebecker. This was Hite's old home. He purchased the land in 1718 when Colonel Bowman's mother was 11 years old and built a stone home and a wooden grist mill there.[62] Hite took his family to Virginia 14 years later, leading the way for thousands more. Bowman had almost certainly never been to the place before, and may never have learned of his connection to it.

Colonel Bowman's grandfather built the original section of this house near modern Schwenksville, Pa. The original house was 30 feet square, consisting of the three right bays of the main section. The additions, dormers, porch, and six-over-one windows were added by Pennsylvania Gov. Samuel Pennypacker in 1901. (Carl Klase, Courtesy of Pennypacker Mills, County of Montgomery, Schwenksville, Pa.)

61 Pennypacker Mills Collection: Cat. No. P81.179, John Roberts et al, petition to Gov. Patrick Gordon, 10 May 1728; Samuel W. Pennypacker, 'Bebber's Township and the Dutch Patroons of Pennsylvania', *PMHB*, 31:1 (1907), pp.11–14.

62 Nancy K. Gaugler and Ralph Conner, 'Jost Hite: From the Neckar to the Shenandoah', *Pennsylvania Folklife*, 37:1 (1987), pp.15–32; Stephen L. Kehs and Madeline L. Cohen, 'The Pennypacker Mansion,' Montgomery Co., Pa., National Register of Historic Places nomination, 1976, NPS ref. no. 76001657.

After Captain Clark's Company joined the encampment at Mr. Pannebecker's they spent three days collecting new tents and visiting farms across the Schuylkill in Pikeland and Charlestown townships, probably purchasing or impressing supplies.[63] Meanwhile, as Major Helphenstine lay dying in Winchester, the disruptive, year-long fight over his job finally came to an end. Washington accepted the board of officers' recommendation and Darke was given a major's commission, predated by almost nine months. Campbell, too, was properly promoted to major and transferred to the 13th Virginia.[64] This put him over Captain Beall's 8th Virginia veterans and back under Brigadier General Peter Muhlenberg's command.

The Route from Chads' Ford to Supplee's Chapel
11 Sept: Retreat from Brandywine to Chester
12 Sept: Falls of the Schuylkill River
14 Sept: Across Schuylkill into Chester Co.
15 Sept: White Horse Tavern
16 Sept: Battle of Clouds to Yellow Springs
17 Sept: Across French Creek to Vincent Twp
18 Sept: Warwick Furnace
19 Sept: East Bank of Perkiomen Creek
20 Sept: Pawling's Ford
21 Sept: West of Trappe
22–25 Sept: Faulkner Swamp
26–28 Sept: Pannebecker's Mill
29 Sept: Arrive Supplee's Chapel[65]
(Approximately 140 miles)

Other promotions opened the way for George Slaughter to become major of Colonel Woods' 12th Virginia, which shared a brigade and much of its recruiting geography with the 8th. The date of his commission was 4 October, and pay records indicate he was with his new regiment during the events of that day. John Graves took command of Slaughter's old company for the winter. He was overdue for a promotion and received a captain's commission backdated to 4 January.[66]

The Battle of Germantown, 4 October 1777

After the British entered Philadelphia, the Continentals moved a few miles closer and the generals met to decide on their next move.[67] Howe had divided his force, leaving somewhat fewer than 9,000 men outside the city at Germantown. Including militia, Washington now

63 FHS: Clark Diary, 26–30 Sept. 1777; Futhey and Cope, *Chester County*, pp.170–201.
64 Chase et al (eds), *Papers of Washington* (Revolution), vol.11, p.343.
65 FHS: Clark Diary; Boyle (ed.) 'McMichael Journal, Sept.-Dec. 1777.' Supplee's Chapel is now Bethel Hill United Methodist Church.
66 NARA: M246, f.215, pp.2; f.208, pp.2, 57, f.298, pp.9, 35.
67 Chase et al (eds), *Papers of Washington* (Revolution), vol.11, pp.346–347.

had about 16,000 soldiers.[68] It was a clear opportunity. No details were shared with the enlisted men, but on 3 October their weapons were inspected, they were told to cook available rations, and each musketeer was given 40 paper cartridges. 'We naturally concluded,' one soldier remembered, 'there was something serious in the wind.'[69]

The sun set at 5:42 p.m. and twilight succumbed to darkness 20 minutes later. With Higgins' tiny company present (and Knox's and John Stephenson's companies dissolved), all the 8th Virginia's companies prepared to take the field together for the first time. Major Darke sat astride a horse, ready to charge about relaying orders to the company commanders. David Williams, the soldier who lost part of his face at Brandywine, was told to stay behind and guard the regiment's wagons.[70] Brigadier General Scott's nervous brigade major, William Johnson, approached Sergeant Parett of Captain Clark's Company to extract a promise that he would 'bear him from the field of Battle and take care of him, if he should be wounded, and not let him fall into the hands of the enemy.'[71]

Colonel Bowman was on leave for unrecorded reasons, leaving Lieutenant Colonel Markham to make his debut in command of the regiment. Markham's Piedmont origins, recent arrival, and apparent lack of combat experience would all work against him. He was without question less familiar than Bowman with the character and capabilities of the men he was responsible for. The recent churn among company commanders did not help. Darke's Company was now led by Lieutenant Israel. John Graves commanded Major Slaughter's old company. Campbell's Company was led again by Mathias Hite (who was still a lieutenant and not happy about it).[72] Above Markham, Scott and Stephen still led the brigade and the division. William Woodford, however, had been wounded at Brandywine, so Scott's sister brigade in the division was led by Colonel McClanahan of the 7th Virginia.

The plan required four columns to leave at different times and arrive at specific places in an operation that had to be synchronised but was impossible to coordinate in real-time. Every possible effort was made to ensure success. The generals kept the plan secret, enforced strict silence on the march, and built extra time into the schedule for rest and contingencies. Smallwood's column of Maryland and New Jersey militia was the first to march. Tasked with getting around the British right flank, his men had the farthest to go. Greene's column followed on the same road about 30 minutes later. Stephen's Division brought up the rear of Greene's column, following Alexander MacDougall's recently arrived Connecticuters and Greene's own division under the temporary command of Peter Muhlenberg.[73] While Colonel Russell led Muhlenberg's brigade, command of the 13th Virginia fell to its new major, Dick Campbell.[74]

---

68 Ecelbarger, *Washington's Momentous Year*, vol.1, pp.146, 148, 152–153.

69 Joseph Plumb Martin, *A Narrative of Some of the Adventures, Dangers and Sufferings of a Revolutionary Soldier* (1830, reprinted Eastern Acorn Press, 1991), p.72.

70 NARA: D. Williams pension; M804, S40735, Christopher Young pension.

71 NARA: J. Parret pension; Chase et al (eds), *Papers of Washington* (Revolution), vol.9, p.408; David A. Clary and Joseph W.A. Whitehorne, *The Inspectors General of the United States Army, 1777–1903* (Washington: U.S. Army, 1987), pp.36, 39, 43.

72 NARA: M246, f.208, pp.4–5, 14, 57, f.212, p.30.

73 Chase et al (eds), *Papers of Washington* (Revolution), vol.9, pp.361–362; Harris, *Germantown*, pp.253–258.

74 Lt. Col. John Gibson was at Fort Pitt. (Gary S. Williams, *'No Man Knows This Country Better': The Frontier Life of John Gibson* (Akron: University of Akron Press, 2022), p.51.

Germantown was everything its name suggested. The Pennsylvania Dutch called it Deitscheschteddel. The borough was founded in 1683 on land purchased by mostly German-speaking immigrants from William Penn and had for decades been the wellspring of both 'plain' (Mennonite) and 'fancy' (Lutheran and Reformed) Pennsylvania Dutch culture and settlement. Germantown and Woodstock were two ends of one long cultural chain.

The 8th Virginia Regiment, Captain Clark noted, 'march'd from dark all night toward the enemy.' They shuffled silently along the dirt roads under a moon two days past new. The nighttime approach may have seemed almost routine to Captain Croghan's veterans, who had marched in the dark to Mamaroneck, Trenton, and Princeton.[75] The British pickets' most recent locations were known from reconnaissance, but that sort of information grew stale quickly.[76] The generals planned to pause at 2:00 a.m. and let the men rest for an hour. At 3:00 a.m., the pickets were to capture the outmost enemy pickets without discharging firearms. Then, after resting again if there was time, they were to form into a line of battle and attack the British camp at five o'clock, 30 minutes before dawn and almost 12 hours after setting out.[77] A number of men steeled themselves with rum or whiskey along the way.[78] Perhaps a mile ahead of Markham's regiment, one of Smallwood's men stopped to relieve himself in the woods. When he was done, he rushed to catch up with his company in the dark but took a wrong turn onto Lime Kiln Road. The lost soldier, whose name was Fynn, came upon a British sentry and was taken prisoner.[79]

James Curry, meanwhile, marched through the night, stalked by death as usual. He had watched his siblings' lifeless bodies fall into the sea in 1762 and still struggled with his 1774 wound from Point Pleasant, which left him unable to raise a glass of water with his right hand.[80] The 25-year-old lieutenant had recruited the bulk of Captain Higgins' woefully understrength company, and guided them now into their first battle.[81] 'About dusk the whole force was in motion,' Curry later told his son, but the men were moving slowly.[82] Like a traffic jam, any obstacle met by the front of the column forced those behind to stop as well, and it took time to get everyone going again. Another officer described a sequence of 'short marches and frequent halts.'[83]

'Unavoidable delays,' Curry remembered, 'occasioned by the ammunition wagons and artillery, together with the fatigues of a night march, so far overcame the watchfulness of the troops that many of the files were actually dozing, and would have halted and slept upon their feet, had it not been for the impulse given them by other files immediately succeeding them.' Wet roads also slowed them down. 'Still farther inconvenience was experienced

75 NARA: J. Grant pension.
76 Harris, *Germantown*, pp.249, 297.
77 Henry Steele Commager and Richard B. Morris (eds), *The Spirit of Seventy-Six: The Story of the American Revolution as Told by its Participants* (1958; reprinted Edison, N.J.: Castle Books, 2002), p.629.
78 NARA: M804, S2035, James Wheeler pension (5th Conn.); Chase et al (eds), *Papers of Washington* (Revolution), vol.11, pp.604–606; Harris, *Germantown*, pp.364–365.
79 McGuire, *Philadelphia Campaign*, vol.2, pp.61–64.
80 Durant, *Union County*, p.295.
81 NARA: M246, f.208, pp.60–61.
82 Durant, *Union County*, p.296.
83 Commager and Morris (eds), *Spirit of Seventy-Six*, p.629.

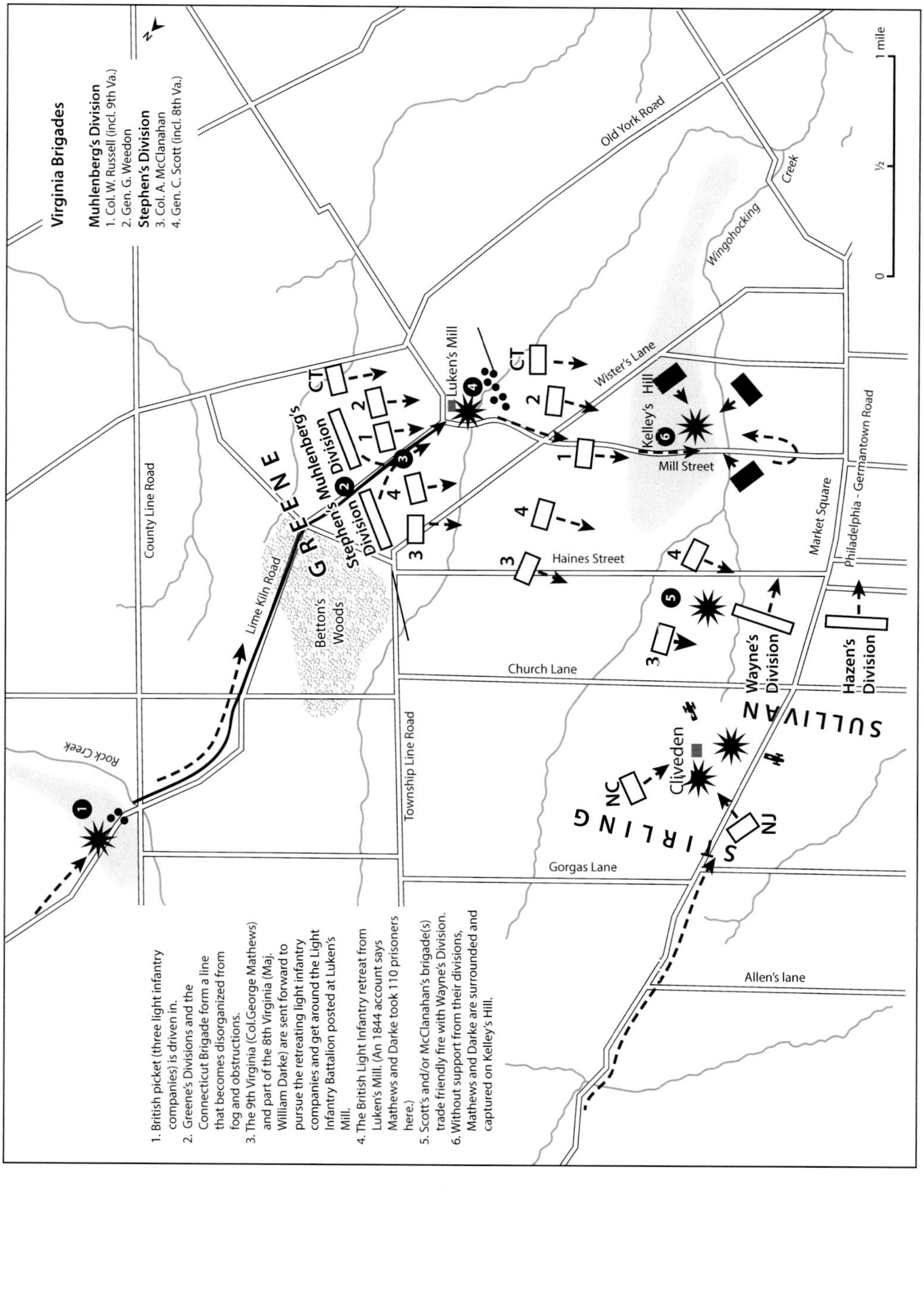

The Battle of Germantown, 4 October 1777.

on account of the road being in many places obstructed by shallow pools of water. The advancing platoons filed off to right and left for the purpose of passing with dry feet, a movement which could not be accomplished without considerable delay.' In Curry's telling, Washington personally exhorted the officers to stop the men from bypassing the puddles. 'Gentlemen, Officers,' Washington said, 'I call upon you to exert yourselves. If you keep filing around every mud-puddle in this manner, when shall we reach the enemy?' After this corrective order, Curry said, 'There was no more going around the puddles, obstacles were unheeded, and there seemed to be no feeling but to reach the British quarters in the quickest time possible.'[84]

Markham's tired infantry regiment turned onto Lime Kiln Road as the first colours of daylight showed in the east.[85] Except for Mr Fynn, Smallwood's Maryland and New Jersey militia were somewhere to the left. Sullivan's column of mostly Maryland and Pennsylvania Continentals was two miles to the right.[86] On the far right, a column of Pennsylvania militia advanced beside the Schuylkill River. Greene's command had one very specific task: driving the British against the river, where they could either swim or surrender. Sullivan explained: 'The Reason of our Sending So many Troops to attack their right was because it was supposed That if This wing of the Enemy could be forced their army must have been pushed into the Sculkill or have been compelled to Surrender. Therefore Two Thirds of the Army at Least were Detached to oppose the Enemys Right.'[87]

Greene's column encountered a British picket, three companies of the 1st Light Infantry Battalion, farther out than expected. Approaching now from above Germantown, Curry said they 'came upon the picket guard of the enemy at Chestnut Hill, which retreated precipitately, after discharging a field piece to give the alarm to the main body.'[88] The actual geography suggests a location on the high ground north of Rock Creek (southwest of the Curtis Arboretum). Markham and his men were still more than two miles from Luken's Mill, where they had expected first contact, and almost four road miles from the centre of Germantown.[89] They had failed to keep the picket from firing their muskets. Even worse, a signal cannon had been fired. Thanks to Mr Fynn's bladder, their approach had been expected. As gunfire from Sullivan's column became audible from the southwest, Scott's brigade major reminded Sergeant Parett not to leave him wounded on the field.[90]

Greene decided it was time to form his column into a line of battle, and Stephen marched his division forward from the rear. This brought the 8th Virginia next to Colonel George Mathews' 9th Virginia.[91] Stephen, always prone to impulsive commands, ordered Mathews to chase the withdrawing Redcoats. He may have been drunk, but he denied it.[92] Muhlenberg,

84 Durant, *Union County*, p.296. Washington did not advance with Greene's column, so it appears something was lost or added in the retelling of this story.
85 Muhlenberg, *General Muhlenberg*, p.108.
86 Harris, *Germantown*, p.256.
87 Otis G. Hammond (ed.), *Letters and Papers of Major-General John Sullivan* (Concord: New Hampshire Historical Society, 1930), vol.1, p.543.
88 Durant, *Union County*, p.296.
89 Harris, *Germantown*, p.297.
90 NARA: J. Parret pension.
91 Muhlenberg, *General Muhlenberg*, p.108; Harris, *Germantown*, p.300.
92 Showman et al (eds), *Papers of Greene*, vol.2, pp.188–189.

on the other hand, was commanding a division for the first time and carefully stuck to his knitting. The Berkeley general then decided that the 9th was insufficient for the task, turned to John Markham, and directed the 8th Virginia to follow.[93]

Markham baulked at the order. After the battle he was charged with 'Delay when ordered to support the advanced guard.' Major Darke, who was never afraid of a fight, stepped up to support Mathews and advanced with a substantial part of the regiment.[94] They disappeared into a dense fog the morning sun had begun to lift from the ground. Peter McDonald of Captain Westfall's Company recalled that 'Markam was our Colonel but he gave up the command to Major Darke ... who advanced and brought on the attack.'[95] Stephen did not criticise Markham in his written report. 'I detachd Col. Mathews,' he wrote, 'who was nearest to me & advancing wt. Spirit; to Support him I orderd Major Dark with part of the Eight Regiment.'[96] Stephen's desire to quickly capture the picket at Luken's Mill was perfectly proper and according to plan.

Markham's conduct aside, however, there was a serious problem: the 9th Virginia belonged to Muhlenberg's Division, not Stephen's.[97] Command and control are essential on any battlefield. Yet here, Markham was refusing to follow orders while Stephen was interfering with a separate chain of command. Captains and corporals would have been justified in asking just who was in charge, and indeed, they may have begun to wonder.

Greene's five brigades followed Darke and Mathews into what Henry Gaddis of Captain Croghan's Company called 'a severe battle.'[98] 'After a short but rapid pursuit,' Lieutenant Curry remembered:

> ... we found ourselves suddenly confronted by the British lines at Germantown ... in a few moments the random firing, which had been previously kept up, was succeeded by an almost unremitted crash of small arms and artillery, along the whole extent of the contending armies. The morning was darkened by a heavy fog, which blended with the smoke of the firing, had became so thick that we were unable to distinguish the British uniform at twenty paces, and were only assured of their locality by the streams of fire emitted from their pieces, which were leveled toward us. The enemy very soon gave way, and were unable to make a decided stand...[99]

So far, so good. Sullivan's Division, however, was firing and advancing on an axis at a near right angle with Greene's approach, and neither column could see the other. Muhlenberg's great-nephew and first biographer said that because Greene's column 'arrived about half an hour after Sullivan's, Wayne's division was directly in front of the position properly occupied by Stephen.'[100] The extent of Greene's late arrival is debated, and reports vary from 15

93 Chase et al (eds), *Papers of Washington* (Revolution), vol.11, pp.375–380, 468–470, vol.12, pp.1–2; NARA: P. McDonald pension; Durant, *Union County*, p.296.

94 Chase et al (eds), *Papers of Washington* (Revolution), vol.11, pp.468–470, vol.12, pp.1–2.

95 NARA: P. McDonald pension.

96 Chase et al (eds), *Papers of Washington* (Revolution), vol.11, pp.468–470.

97 Harris, *Germantown*, p.301.

98 NARA: H. Gaddis pension.

99 Durant, *Union County*, p.296.

100 Muhlenberg, *General Muhlenberg*, p.108.

to 45 minutes.[101] Shorter estimates may discount the distance Greene's wing had to cover following its first engagement at Rock Creek. Either way, a delay of some length, a variety of obstacles, and low visibility were at this moment creating a fatal misalignment of forces.

Fences, hedges, walls, and fields thick with grain threw Greene's division out of formation. The order to advance in a line was remembered as 'impracticable' by a frustrated officer in the 3rd Virginia. Disordered, distracted, and blind, the brigades drifted away from each other as they pressed forward.[102] Still, they pushed back the British 4th Regiment and lost no momentum when the 49th Regiment came up to assist. Stephen, whose account was written defensively, reported this initial success.

> I sent Mr Black who acted as Aid de Camp, to order up a Body of troops unemployd on my Right; to Attack the Reinforcement ... Upon Seeing them Advance, the troop formerly engagd, pushd the Enemy so Closely, that I calld to them 'give them the Bayonet['] – Upon hearing this, The Enemy Officers on horse back rode to their Rear out of Sight; Many of their Men running After them; whilst a party Run towards Our troop crying Quarters.[103]

The success was fleeting. Curry remembered, 'Our troops being imperfectly disciplined and flushed with success, were unfortunately in disorder at this critical juncture.'[104] By his own account, Stephen was again giving orders to officers not under his command.[105] He should have been focused on ensuring McClanahan's brigade aligned properly with Wayne's. Instead, as the British retreated, Stephen's two separated brigades came blindly upon Wayne's left flank, Scott in front of them and McClanahan behind. Unable to see far through the fog and smoke, one or both of Stephen's brigades exchanged fire with the Pennsylvanians, and the entire operation began to unravel.[106]

On Sullivan's approach, British soldiers took cover in several stone buildings, the most notable of which was Cliveden, the country home of jurist Benjamin Chew. Determined that leaving 100-odd soldiers barricaded inside the house would be 'unmilitary,' Brigadier General Henry Knox convinced Washington to attack it in force.[107] It was a bad mistake. The house proved impenetrable, even to field artillery. The futile effort halted Washington's reserve, which should have continued forward. The sound of the cannons also lured McClanahan's brigade away from Scott's and convinced Wayne's division the British were in their rear.[108]

---

101 Harris, *Germantown*, p.298; Theodore Thayer, *Nathanael Greene: Strategist of the American Revolution* (New York: Twayne Publishers, 1960), p.202.

102 Harris, *Germantown*, p.311.

103 Chase et al (eds), *Papers of Washington* (Revolution), vol.11, pp.468–470.

104 Durant, *Union County*, p.296; Harris, *Germantown*, p.310.

105 Harris, *Germantown*, p.310.

106 Chase et al (eds), *Papers of Washington* (Revolution), vol.11, pp.468–470; Anon. (ed.), 'Diary of Joseph Clark', p.101; Harris, *Brandywine*, pp.311–312, 334, 340, 352–353.

107 Chase et al (eds), *Papers of Washington* (Revolution), vol.11, pp.468–470; Harris, *Germantown*, pp.328–329.

108 Harris, *Germantown*, pp.343–344.

As Sullivan's line stepped backward and McClanachan's fractured, Scott's Brigade and Muhlenberg's division were left exposed. Greene attempted a short tactical retreat to organise his line, but he lost control as the tide of battle turned.[109] Joseph Parett heard Major Johnson calling him and saw that the officer had been shot. With a comrade, Parett 'carried him where he was safe from further injury.' They 'returned, and in the midst of the battle resumed their positions in the line,' but then Parett was 'disabled by a wound in the right leg, just above the ancle.'[110] Jonathan Grant was also wounded in the leg.[111] A soldier in Muhlenberg's division remembered that 'by this time we sustained a fire from front, left and part of the rear,' and Stephen told his colonel to 'evacuate the ground from the right of Sub-Divisions by files.'[112] Yet again, Stephen appears to have given orders to men not under his command. Lieutenant Curry said, 'after a hard struggle' they were 'forced literally to retreat from victory.'[113] With his wounded ankle, Sergeant Parett said 'it was with the greatest difficulty' that he 'secured himself during the retreat.'[114]

The 13th Virginia and its 8th Virginia veterans got caught up in the finger-pointing that followed. An officer in the Pennsylvania State Rifle Regiment asserted that 'the Pusillanimity of the 13th Virga. Regt. gave the Enemy an opportunity of comming round our left flank.'[115] The 13th was clearly in the thick of the fighting and the claims against Major Campbell's men were found to be without merit.[116] 'I got wounded in my leg in a very desperate manner,' John Vance of Robert Beall's Company recounted, 'and was also wounded through the cheek with a Bayonet.'[117] Campbell himself was wounded seriously enough to give up command for the rest of the day.[118]

The 14th and 12th Virginia regiments covered the retreat. 'Col. Lewis & Col. Wood kept the field with their Regiments untill they were Orderd to Retire,' Stephen reported. He also said, 'Col. Lewis, & Col. Russel of Genl Greens Division Col. Wood wt. his Regiment & Major Campbell of the Right of My Division behavd Gallantly during the Action.'[119] He had nothing to say about John Markham.

Major Darke's Advance with the 9th Virginia

Greene's column was pushing forward with little opposition when Colonel Mathews and Major Darke were sent ahead. An 1844 account says they took 110 prisoners at Luken's Mill and continued down Luken's Mill Road (Church Lane), across Wingohocking Creek, all the way to the town's central market square.[120] Another account says they captured some

109 Harris, *Germantown*, pp.360, 391.
110 NARA: J. Parret pension
111 NARA: J. Grant pension.
112 Boyle (ed.) 'McMichael Journal, Sept.-Dec., 1777,' 4 Oct. 1777.
113 Durant, *Union County*, p.296.
114 NARA: J. Parret pension.
115 Joseph Lee Boyle (ed.) 'The James McMichael Journal, September 12-, 1777-December 23, 1777,' *JAR*, <allthingsliberty.com/2018/03/the-james-mcmichael-journal-september-12–1777-december-23–1777/>, accessed 7 Oct. 2024, 4 Oct. 1777.
116 Chase et al (eds), *Papers of Washington* (Revolution), vol.12, pp.1–2.
117 NARA: J. Vance pension.
118 NARA: M804, S40516, David Steele pension (13th Va.).
119 Chase et al (eds), *Papers of Washington* (Revolution), vol.12, pp.1–2.
120 John F. Watson, *Annals of Philadelphia and Pennsylvania in Olden Time* (Philadelphia: Penington & Hunt, 1844), vol.2, p.37.

A photograph of Luken's Mill. The structure, later known as Robert's Mill, was built in 1683 and demolished in 1873. (Library Company of Philadelphia)

British cannons.[121] They expected Stephen's and Muhlenberg's divisions to quickly follow and learned too late that things were falling apart. Peter McDonald told his family, 'Darke led his command too far in pursuit of the enemy and they found that they were cut off from the main Army and had to surrender as prisoners of war.'[122] A 9th Virginia man recalled 'not knowing that our army had falen Back. Our Rege't. was there cut up and the survivers worn out with fateag was made Prisoners.'[123] An 1822 biography of Nathanael Greene asserted that Mathews 'made so many prisoners as to encumber his retreat' and was consequently surrounded.[124] Philadelphia lore recorded 60 years later tells us, 'These Virginians had just before captured a party of British in the fog, and set up a great hurrah, which brought a greater force upon them, and caused their own capture.'[125]

Contemporary accounts focus on the 9th Virginia because of Mathews' seniority and the 8th Virginia's fractional participation.[126] John Eager Howard of Maryland remembered that that it involved 'a part of Muhlenberg and Scott's Brigades, from the left wing, particularly the ninth Virginia Regiment, commanded by Col. Matthews.'[127] None of Jonathan Clark's or David Stephenson's men were taken, which may mean those captains chose to stay with

121 John Eager Howard, 'Col. John Eager Howard's Account of the Battle of Germantown', *Maryland Historical Magazine*, 4 (1909), p.319.
122 NARA: P. McDonald pension.
123 NARA: M804, W6427, Samuel Waples pension (9th Va.). Edited for clarity.
124 William Johnson, *Sketches of the Life and Correspondence of Nathanael Greene* (Charleston: A.E. Miller, 1822), vol.1, p.87.
125 Townsend Ward, 'The Germantown Road and Its Associations', *PMHB* 6:3 (1882), p.277.
126 Harris, *Germantown*, pp.362–364.
127 Howard, 'Account of Germantown', p.319.

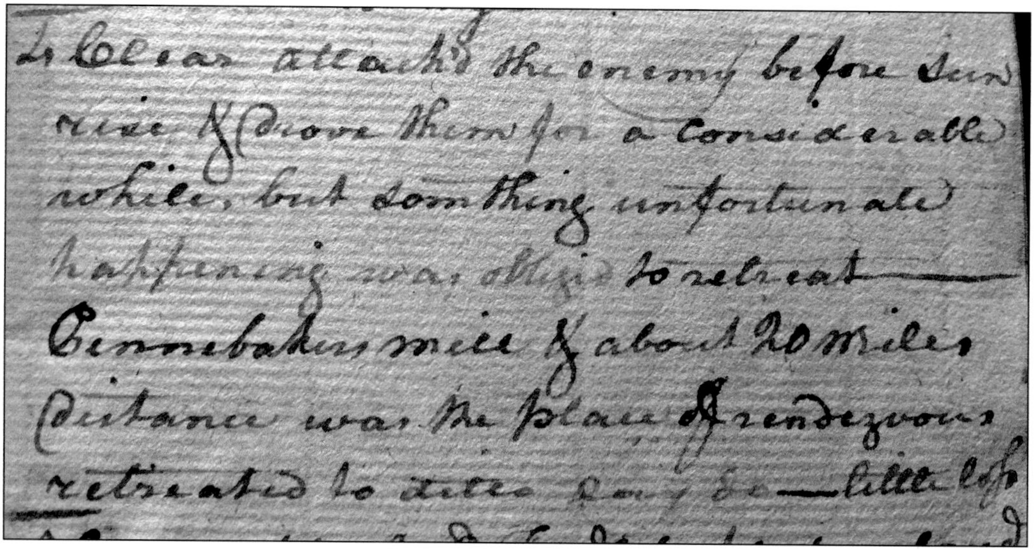
attack'd the enemy before Sun
rise & drove them for a considerable
while, but somthing unfortunate
happening was obliged to retreat —
Pennebakers mill & about 20 miles
distance was the place of rendezvous

Jonathan Clark's diary entry for the Battle of Germantown. (The Filson Historical Society, Louisville, KY)

Markham. On the other hand, Hampshire County blacksmith John Chenoweth appears to have been entirely unaware that Markham refused to advance. 'I ware taken prisoner,' he wrote, 'in the battle with the rest of our rigment & the 9 rigment along with ous.' The trapped men went down fighting in what Chenoweth called 'a seane of carnage.'[128] Even Mathews received several bayonet wounds.[129] According to a British account, 'those that Escap'd the Bayonet run into the Camp … threw down their Arms & beg'd for Mercy.'[130] The surrender, if the 1844 source is correct, occurred on Kelley's Hill, meaning the Virginians made it about a third of the way back to the mill before laying down their arms.[131]

British Major General James Grant claimed many of the captured Americans were drunk. 'They got Rum three times,' he said, 'Before they set out – halfway – and at Chesnut Hill, when they drew near if I may judge from the situation I found a Colonel & two Majors in, they were certainly all drunk.'[132] Grant can only have been referring to Major Darke and the two surviving field officers of the 9th Virginia: Colonel Mathews and Major Levin Joynes. (Lieutenant Colonel John Sayres of the 9th was killed.)[133] While there is no reason to doubt that rum or whiskey was dispensed on the march, Grant probably confused extreme exhaustion for inebriation. Several men fainted from fatigue that day and even Peter Muhlenberg reportedly fell asleep in his saddle.[134]

128 NARA: J. Chenoweth pension, S. Waples pension.
129 Howard, 'Account of Germantown,' p.319; NARA: S. Waples pension.
130 Harris, *Germantown*, p.364.
131 Watson, *Annals of Philadelphia*, vol.2, p.37.
132 Harris, *Germantown*, pp.364–365.
133 Sanchez-Saavedra, *Virginia Military Organisations*, pp.58–59.
134 Anon., 'Contemporary Account of the Battle of Germantown,' *PMHB*, 11:3 (1887), p.331; Muhlenberg, *General Muhlenberg*, pp.113–114.

Chenoweth recalled that after he was detained, his captors 'ware still taking small partties of our popple.' He also said, 'we ware taken when veary thin cloathd and without blankets.'[135] That did not bode well for captives in the hands of unkind jailors going into winter.

Elsewhere, Markham's men retreated in reasonably good order. 'We were pursued by the enemy a distance of two or three miles,' said Lieutenant Curry, 'until we attained a favorable position on some rising ground, from whence we were enabled to check their progress by a few discharges of artillery.'[136] This effort to cover the retreat at Whitemarsh Church was not as well-executed as Curry remembered. Charles Scott approached Adam Stephen, the senior commander on site, urging him to organise the men and artillery to hold back their pursuers. 'But,' concluded a court martial, 'the General went off under pretence to reconoitre. Ordering off the Artillery at the same Time and left his Division behind; for want of this necessary Disposition tis supposed many Stragglers fell into the Enemys hands.'[137] Anthony Wayne covered the retreat with a single cannon.[138]

Those who made it out marched past their starting point all the way back to Perkiomen Creek, where they could make a stand if they had to. This means some of the men had marched 40 miles in less than 24 hours without any sleep.[139] One soldier described the two days as so gruelling 'it was almost an unspeakable fatigue.'[140]

Though the numbers are tiny compared to what malaria had already done, Germantown was the 8th Virginia's largest battlefield casualty event of the war. Two of Captain Croghan's men were killed. Thirty-nine men were captured, most or all of them with Major Darke. Several more were reported wounded, newly 'sick, absent', discharged early, or missing. The regiment's wounded men were cared for as all wounded soldiers were before the age of modern medicine. A militiaman recalled entering 'an apartment called the hospital … and there beheld a most horrid sight. The floor was covered with human blood; amputated arms and legs lay in different places in appalling array, the mournful memorials of an unfortunate and fatal battle, which indeed it truly was.'[141]

Captain Knox at Bemis Heights, 7 October 1777

Two days after Germantown, Captain Knox took his unit scouting near the enemy lines north of Saratoga with Daniel Morgan and Henry Dearborn's combined force of 800 men.[142] The attack they expected after their success at Freeman's Farm had not materialised. Instead, the British dug in and waited for support from New York City. But time was working against them. More than 100 Oneida warriors and thousands of militiamen reinforced Gates' rebel army. The Oneida were assigned to Morgan's command.[143] Benjamin Lincoln arrived with

135 NARA: J. Chenoweth pension.
136 Durant, *Union County*, p.296.
137 Showman et al (eds), *Papers of General Greene*, vol.2, pp.188–189.
138 Harris, *Germantown*, p.384.
139 Harris, *Germantown*, pp.386–388.
140 Boyle (ed.) 'McMichael Journal, Sept.-Dec. 1777,' 4 Oct. 1777.
141 Dann (ed.), *Revolution Remembered*, p.151.
142 Anon. (ed.), *Journals of Henry Dearborn, 1776–1783* (Cambridge: John Wilson and Son, 1887), p.8.
143 Boyle (ed.), 'Samuel Armstrong Diary,' p.246.

Germantown Casualties

Field Officer: Captured: Maj. William Darke								
Clark's Company	**Westfall's Company**	**Stephenson's Company**	**Berry's Company**	**Croghan's Company**	**Graves' Company†**	**Higgins' Company**	**Hite's Company‡**	**Israel's Company§**
Wounded: William Means.	Captured: Fifer Michael Howell, John Anderson, Burket Borer, James Brandy, John Chenoweth, James Hornbeck, Peter McDonald, Daniel Parks. Wounded: Richard Cain William Henesey, James Hornback.	Wounded: 2nd Lt. Benjamin Kinley. Missing: Charles Sanders.	Wounded: Drummer Benjamin Carter.* Missing: Edward Golleyhor.	Killed: Richard Evans, Henry Saltsman. Captured: Ens. Jonathan Smith, Harmon Commins, Benjamin Cowen, Jesse Davis, John McDonald, Jr., Christian Stydner. Wounded: Josiah Arnold, Jonathan Grant, John McCollaster, Paul McGowan, Missing: George Watts.	Captured: 2nd Lt. Reuben Field, Ens. Philip Huffman, Drummer Meshack Pearson, William Fincham, Thomas Freeman, Isaac Hiers,* Jeremiah Johns, William Kennedy, William Payne, James Rains, Elzaphan Rucker, Thomas West. Wounded: William Robert, Richard Roberts,* Bryant Sloan,* John Sloan, William Smith.*	Captured: Capt. Robert Higgins, 2nd Lt. John Clark, Zachariah DeLong, Daniel McNaughton, John Roberts, Henry Ruyle, Michael Sword, Benjamin Weeser.	Captured: Solomon Smallin, Peter Smith. Wounded: Nicholas Foster, Barton Whitehorn, Missing: Jessy Allison, Henry Minor.*	Captured: 2nd Lt. Christopher Moyer, Nathan Willett.

*Newly hospitalized, 'sick absent,' or discharged without explanation. †Previously George Slaughter's Company. ‡Previously Richard Campbell's Company. §Previously William Darke's Company.

even more men after the Battle of Bennington. Burgoyne's numbers, meanwhile, were dwindling. One day, American patrols took 18 prisoners. On another, 10 deserters came in. On the third day of October, 40 prisoners were taken.[144] Most or perhaps all this skirmishing involved Morgan's Rifles and Dearborn's Light Infantry, which developed into an effective combined-arms force.

Another foray on 7 October netted seven more British prisoners, but rain and darkness colluded to get the skirmishers lost in the woods. Rather than wander, they bivouacked in a heavy downpour with no tents or shelter. Silence was enforced the whole night as they were 'just by the enemy.'[145] In the morning, the tired warriors made their way to camp and got some food in their bellies. They needed rest, too, but that had to wait. The British were finally coming.[146]

Captain Knox and his lieutenants James Craig and William Lewis Lovely had led their men into many fights before, but this day they performed their most valuable service of the war. Morgan and Dearborn's performance was nearly perfect. Mutual support allowed the riflemen to take full advantage of their weapons' range and accuracy under the protection of Dearborn's muskets and bayonets. They enfiladed the advancing enemy's right (western) flank and poured out a deadly fire. '[T]he Rifle men & Light Infantry fell on upon the Enimys Right flank & Partly in their rear,' wrote Dearborn, 'which soon Obliged them to Quit their heavy Artillery & a Considerable Number of waggons with Amonition & other stores.' Then, 'finding us in their Rear, their main Body Gave way, Leaving several other Pieces of Cannon.'[147]

The opposition that day was a reconnaissance in force, amounting to about a third of Burgoyne's army. On the American side, Morgan's 800 men were just one end of a long American line. Nevertheless, their performance was crucial to a major American victory. Two days later it was 'found the Enimy had Evaquated the whole of their Lines & had Left about 500 sick & wounded on the ground & a Considerable Quantity of Provision.' Knox's men helped take possession of the British entrenchments and skirmished with Burgoyne's weak army as it retreated north toward the village of Saratoga.[148] Finally, on 13 October, Burgoyne asked for terms and on 17 October he surrendered. Sergeant Wysor proudly remembered that he was 'at the taking of Burgoyne.'[149] Major Dearborn called it 'the greatest Conquest Ever known.'[150] 'Burgoyne' joined the vocabulary of the Continental Army as a verb. Saratoga was a major turning point, but Independence had still not been won. The Burgoyning of Lieutenant General Charles, Earl Cornwallis was still four years away.

---

144 Anon. (ed.), *Dearborn Journals*, pp.7–8; Boyle (ed.), 'Samuel Armstrong Diary', pp.246–247.
145 Anon. (ed.), *Dearborn Journals*, p.8; Schnitzer and Troiani, *Campaign to Saratoga*, p.230.
146 Anon. (ed.), *Dearborn Journals*, p.8.
147 Anon. (ed.), *Dearborn Journals*, p.8; Boyle (ed.), 'Samuel Armstrong Diary,' p.248; Schnitzer and Troiani, *Campaign to Saratoga*, pp.225–244.
148 Anon. (ed.), *Dearborn Journals*, p.8–9.
149 NARA: H. Wysor pension.
150 Anon. (ed.), *Dearborn Journals*, p.10.

12

The Reckoning

Harmon Commins, one of Captain Croghan's men, recalled that he was 'taken prisoner sent to Philadelphia and confined in jail on scanty allowance.'[1] After Germantown, officers and enlisted men alike were thrown into the 'new gaol' on Walnut Street, directly behind the State House and conveniently across the street from the potter's field that is now Washington Square. The officers' gorgets were wrenched from their necks by guards who promised to replace them with nooses. It was an empty threat. After three days, the officers and the wounded were taken to the State House.[2]

The semiliterate John Chenoweth was more explicit than Commins in describing his confinement, calling it 'the dredfullest suffering that ever mortaly did to live.' For a 'good lenth of time', he wrote, they buried seven or eight of their comrades a day. It would have been even worse, he said, 'had it not ben for the pople cald quakers.'[3] The Philadelphia Society for Assisting Distressed Prisoners had been established one year earlier. Its members went door to door with a wheelbarrow collecting donations of food. The British shut the ministry down, but not before it provided Chenoweth and his comrades with a few desperately needed meals.[4]

The cold and hungry prisoners were told they could enlist in the Queen's Rangers, and a few took the offer seriously.[5] '[S]ome of my mess concluded we had better doo it than to dey in that misrabel state of starvation,' Chenoweth remembered. 'I remonstrated to the caus we ware on & that we had taken the oath of Ealeganas [allegiance] to the united States.' If the Revolution succeeded, he warned the other prisoners, they would be hanged as traitors. 'I din sooner prefeir death bitter as it might be than agre to their proposials.' He lamented that 'a number of ous did agree to that misarable death & numbers died I belive in that resolution.'[6]

1 NARA: H. Commins pension.
2 WHS: Draper Mss., L, vol.1, p.39; S. Waples pension; Frazer (ed.), *Frazer Memoir*, p.164; Robert Morton, 'Diary of Robert Morton', *PMHB*, 1:1 (1877), p.16.
3 NARA: J. Chenoweth pension.
4 Negley K. Teeters, *They Were in Prison: A History of the Pennsylvania Prison Society, 1787–1937* (Philadelphia: John C. Winston Co., 1937), pp.14–15.
5 John Graves Simcoe, *Simcoe's Military Journal: A History of the Operations of a Partisan Corps Called The Queen's Rangers* (New York: Bartlett & Welford, 1844), p.19.
6 NARA: J. Chenoweth pension.

American soldiers captured at Germantown were taken to the Walnut Street Jail in Philadelphia, where poor treatment led to malnutrition, illness, and some deaths. William Russell Birch, 1804. (Library Company of Philadelphia)

Finger-Pointing and Consequences

While Horatio Gates was congratulating himself in upstate New York, Washington's chastened army huddled at Pannebecker's for a few days, resting, healing, burying the dead, and collecting stragglers. Four men from Stephenson's, Croghan's, and Lieutenant Hite's companies were still missing when the September muster was taken in mid-October.[7]

The army moved from Pannebecker's to Towamencin Township on 8 October, to Worcester Township on the 16th, and then to Whitpain Township on the 21st.[8] Once rested, the soldiers busily sewed moccasins to replace worn-out shoes and prepared thousands of paper cartridges for their next engagement. When slightly premature news of Burgoyne's

7 NARA: M246, f.211, p.15; f.214, p.13; f.218, p.11.

8 William S. Baker, *Itinerary of General Washington from June 15, 1775 to December 23, 1783* (Philadelphia: J.B. Lippincott, 1892), pp.95–103.

formal surrender arrived, Washington ordered a *feu de joie*. The British could hear it in Philadelphia, and they knew what it meant.[9]

Amid the celebration, there was a stark realisation that changes had to be made. The generals in upper Philadelphia County understood that the triumph at Saratoga made their own failures more glaring. The obnoxious Mathias Hite was the first to feel the sting. A 'General Court martial' was announced on 7 October 'for the trial of divers officers, accused of cowardice.'[10] Hite resigned the same day.[11] Immediately after his resignation, General Washington announced what the lieutenant from Dunmore County already knew: 'Promotions, in consequence of the late deaths and resignations, will now take place as a reward to the merit of deserving officers … Officers who are under the imputation of *cowardice*, or whose characters in other respects are impeachable, are to be noted; as the General is determined to discriminate between the good & bad.'[12] Hite's departure so soon after Campbell's promotion left more than 50 men in the care of two junior officers: 2nd Lieutenant John Steed and Ensign Robert Breckenridge.[13] Steed and Breckenridge were capable men who received prompt promotions and served to war's end.[14] The new policy worked.

False accusations aside, the courts martial did determine that alcohol played a role in the failure at Germantown. Cowardice, too. Two Connecticut lieutenants were found guilty of being so drunk they could not perform their duties on the battlefield. Captain Goodrich Crump of the 1st Virginia was found guilty of cowardice 'and sentenced to be cashiered – and his name – place of abode, and his punishment, published in the News-papers … After which, it shall be deemed scandalous, for any officer to associate with him.' Among those vindicated was the 13th Virginia's Lieutenant Simon Morgan, one of Captain Robert Beall's 8th Virginia veterans. Though accused of cowardice, he was 'Acquitted with honor by the unanimous opinion of the court.' Two other officers from the 13th were similarly acquitted,[15] which must have been a great relief to Major Campbell.

The reckoning worked its way through the officer corps. Courts of inquiry were formed to investigate generals Sullivan, Wayne, and Maxwell for their performances at Staten Island, Paoli, and at the head of the light infantry. Maxwell was accused of having once been 'disguised with liquor in such a manner, as to disqualify him in some measure, but not fully, from doing his duty.' All three of the generals were acquitted.[16] Soon, Lieutenant Colonel Markham and Major General Stephen would take their turns under the microscope.

---

9 Chase et al (eds), *Papers of Washington* (Revolution), vol.11, pp.428–429, 523–524, 535, 541–542; Anon. (ed.), 'Diary of Joseph Clark,' p.101.
10 Chase et al (eds), *Papers of Washington* (Revolution), vol.11, pp.415–416.
11 NARA: M246, f.208, p.57.
12 Chase et al (eds), *Papers of Washington* (Revolution), vol.11, pp.471–473.
13 NARA: M246, f.214, p.13.
14 NARA: M246, f.208, p.57.
15 Chase et al (eds), *Papers of Washington* (Revolution), vol.11, pp.553–555, 604–606, vol.12, pp.1–2.
16 Chase et al (eds), *Papers of Washington* (Revolution), vol.11, pp.480–482, 512–514, 592–593, vol.12, pp.1–2, 74–76, 113.

The Siege of Fort Mifflin

It took Major John Green several months to recover after he was shot at Mamaroneck, but he received a promotion and appeared at Fort Mifflin with reinforcements on 18 October 1777. The small garrison was glad to see him, perhaps especially the 8th Virginia's Ezekiel Abel, George Ashby, and Thomas Griffith, who had served under him in the north. They were near the end of their first month performing the difficult job of keeping British ships from supplying occupied Philadelphia. Lieutenant Colonel Smith, the Maryland officer who led the Continentals there in September, was less enthusiastic about Green's arrival. Though they held the same rank, Green was senior to him.[17]

8th Virginia Men Detached to Fort Mifflin
Sergeant John Roberts (Israel's Company)
Ezekiel Abel (Croghan's Company)
George Ashby (Campbell's Company)
Robert Chambers (Higgins' Company)
John Dowland (Israel's Company)
Philip Faint (Westfall's Company)
George Faint (Westfall's Company)
Thomas Griffith (Croghan's Company)
George McVey (D. Stephenson's Company)
Zachariah Pigman (Westfall's Company)
Matthew Plumley (Hite's Company)
John Simpson (Berry's Company)
Bryant Sloan (Slaughter's Company)[18]

Command disputes were just one of the issues hampering the fort's operations. When Smith's 200 men arrived on Mud Island late in September, they found a weak garrison of Pennsylvania militia that had little training and no idea how to operate the post's artillery. Coordination with Pennsylvania Navy river patrols was difficult. The fort itself was a mess: it had been partially constructed before the war, abandoned, and then hurriedly finished. Dykes held back the tide to keep the aptly named island dry.[19] The fort was highly vulnerable and the mission extremely dangerous.

The prisoners starving in the Walnut Street Jail had a particular understanding of the fort's importance. 'I beleive they wold not hav [been] qit so inhuman if they cold have got there shiping up,' John Chenoweth wrote of his captors, 'let ous wake night or day the cannon ware playing at this little mud island fort.' The river blockade and land-based disruption of Crown forces foraging left the British and their horses increasingly hungry. His captors, Chenoweth believed, 'ware much stinted themselves or at least the gard told ous soo.'[20]

17 McGuire, *Philadelphia Campaign*, vol.2, p.186.
18 NARA: Revolutionary War Rolls. Zachariah Pigman uncertain and assessed from records.
19 McGuire, *Philadelphia Campaign*, vol.2, pp.182–184.
20 NARA: J. Chenoweth pension; Morton, 'Morton Diary', p.19.

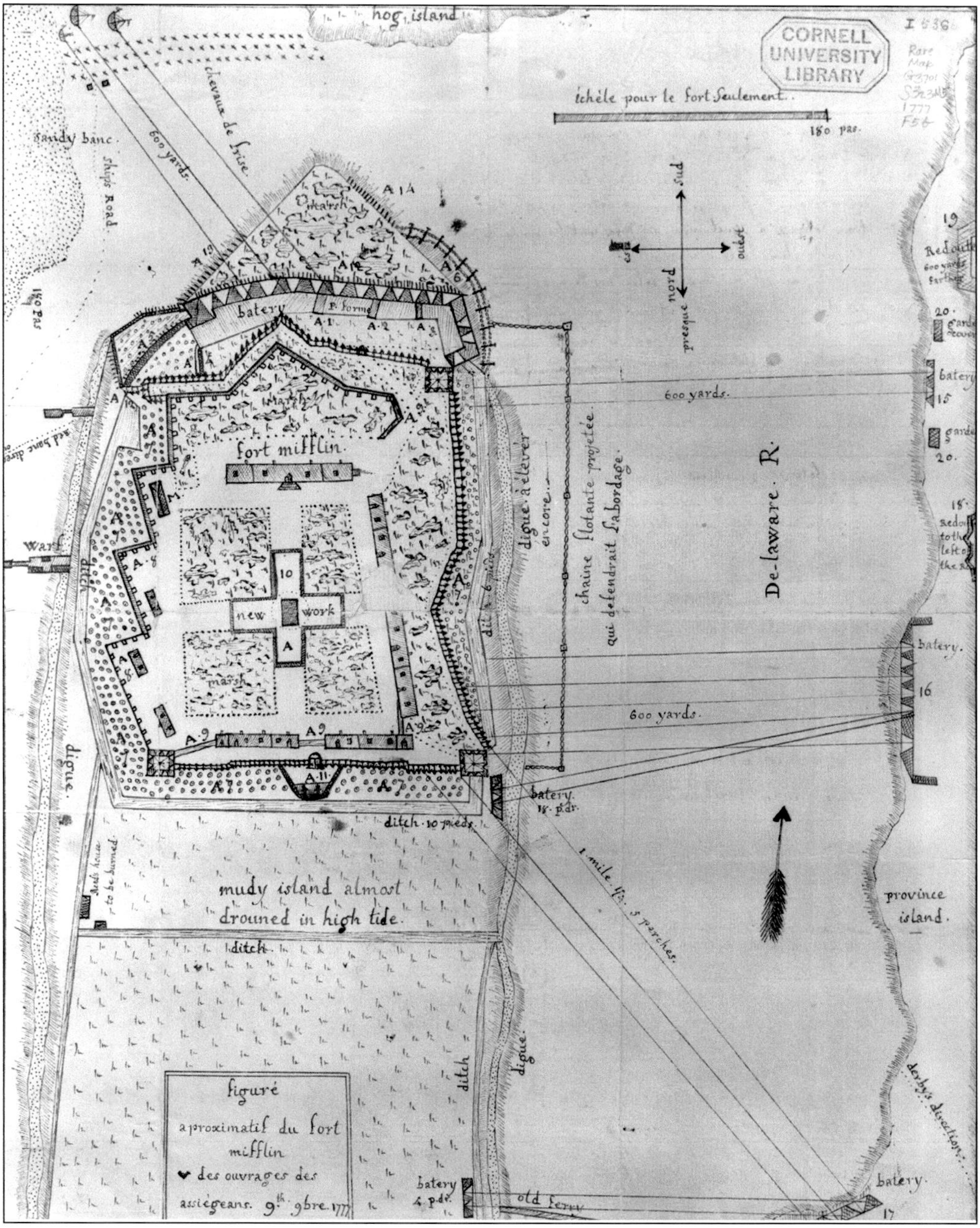

French engineer Francois de Fleury drew this map of Fort Mifflin while on the island and under fire. (Division of Rare and Manuscript Collections, Cornell University Library)

An assault led by Hessian *Oberst* Carl von Donop against Fort Mercer failed in dramatic fashion on 22 October. This was Fort Mifflin's sister fort on the New Jersey side of the river. Three warships, including the 64-gun HMS *Augusta*, approached Mud Island to provide suppressing fire for a 200-man grenadier assault. The cannonade was intense. The Pennsylvania Navy responded by launching fire rafts at the vessels while the fort's garrison hurled hot shot at them. The *Augusta* caught fire and burned for three hours. When the flames reached its magazine, a gigantic explosion killed 60 crewmen.[21] Windows shattered in Philadelphia.[22] Houses shook 35 miles away.[23] The sound was compared to an earthquake 60 miles away in Lancaster.[24]

The victory at Fort Mercer and the explosion of the *Augusta* only bought the Americans some time. The British took several days to place guns on nearby Carpenter's Island and proceeded to pound Fort Mifflin for days. Naval artillery then joined in, and no part of the fort was safe. Colonel Smith was wounded and evacuated. HMS *Vigilant* came right up to the island on 15 November and began firing from just 20 yards away. Men who remained standing were 'cut up like cornstalks.' Men who tried to crouch were 'split like fish to be broiled.' The entire garrison evacuated that night, leaving a 13-stripe flag defiantly flying.[25]

One of the wounded men from Mud Island was George Ashby. His Shenandoah Valley roots ran deep: his grandfather gave his name to the gap in the Blue Ridge where Captain Berry's Company first collected in 1776. His father carried a chain in George Washington's first surveying expedition in 1748.[26] When Ashby got back to camp, Charles Scott took one look at his leg and furloughed him for the remainder of his enlistment.[27]

Truth and Consequences

The courts martial continued in Whitpain Township. John Markham was charged with 'Having left the regiment in time of action', doing it again during the retreat, and 'Delay when ordered to support the advanced guard.' He was found guilty 'by the unanimous opinion of the court … and sentenced to be cashiered.' General Washington approved the sentence.[28] Markham returned to Virginia but moved away from his home in Chesterfield County. He used a substantial inheritance to start a new life 150 miles to the west in Pittsylvania County.[29]

21 Morton, 'Morton Diary', p.23; McGuire, *Philadelphia Campaign*, vol.2, p.172–173
22 McGuire, *Philadelphia Campaign*, vol.2, p.173; Edwin Martin Stone (ed.), *The Invasion of Canada in 1775: Including the Journal of Captain Simeon Thayer* (Providence: Knowles, Anthony & Co., 1867), pp.76–77.
23 Tappert and Doberstein (trans), *Journals of H.M. Muhlenberg*, vol.3, p.91.
24 E.W. Spangler, (ed.), 'Memoir of Major John Clark, of York County, Pennsylvania', *PMHB*, 20:1 (1896), pp.77–86, 83–84.
25 Martin, *Narrative of Adventures*, pp.92–94.
26 J.M. Toner (ed.), *Journal of My Journey Over the Mountains; by George Washington, While Surveying for Lord Thomas Fairfax, Baron of Cameron, in the Northern Neck of Virginia, Beyond the Blue Ridge, in 1747–1748* (Albany: Joel Munsell's Sons, 1892), pp.28, 39, 55; Jackson (ed.), *Diaries of Washington*, vol.1, pp.1–5.
27 LVA: Revolutionary War Bounty Land Claims, George Ashby.
28 Chase et al (eds), *Papers of Washington* (Revolution), vol.12, pp.1–2.
29 Garrett, 'John Markham', pp.2–6.

Many first-hand accounts of Germantown describe the defeat as inexplicable. 'What happened?' was the question on every soldier's tongue. Captain Clark wrote that after driving the British forces for a considerable time, 'something unfortunate happening was obliged to retreat.'[30] Colonel Walter Stewart of the 13th Pennsylvania wrote, '[E]verything appeared in our favour when the Unfortunate retreat took place, which cannot be accounted for.'[31] Adam Stephen said they 'fled from victory.'[32]

Many things went wrong: the British had pickets farther out than expected, visibility was limited by fog and smoke, the army was exhausted, the reserve was tied up by the unwise siege of Cliveden, Greene's column arrived late and formed into a line too early, MacDougall's brigade never found its place in the line, there was an incident of friendly fire, and some men were drunk. None of these factors, however, prevented the Continental divisions from pushing deep into Germantown until, as if controlled by an unseen hand, they suddenly began to withdraw. He insisted he did everything he could to prevent it, but Adam Stephen was the only general known to have actually ordered men to retreat. In his 12 October letter, Stewart reported, '...it is left on Genl. Stevens who certainly gave the order to the left wing, he is suspended and to day a Court of Enquiry sits of which Lord Sterling is President.'[33]

A statement by the Marquis de Lafayette, who did not participate in the battle, may be the key to understanding Stephen's behaviour. Lafayette recorded that Greene's column was 'retarded by an absurd precedence dispute between divisions.'[34] Stephen did not merely have a bad day at Germantown. Drunk or not, he repeatedly interfered with Muhlenberg's command, neglected his own command, failed to properly support Mathews and Darke, and undermined efforts to cover the retreat at Whitemarsh Church.

The former Berkeley County Sheriff had done much in his career to make people dislike him. He had a long history of being petulant, impulsive, combative, dishonest, and self-aggrandising. His protracted fight with Jacob Hite cannot have been forgotten by the many Hite friends and family members in his own division. In his personal life, he preferred a disgraceful relationship with his brother's housekeeper to a marriage.[35] He argued with his brigadiers, particularly Charles Scott. He jeopardised the attack on Trenton. Washington rebuked him in May for exaggerating enemy casualty counts and had to tell him repeatedly to stand down from ill-conceived schemes in New Jersey.[36] After Germantown, Scott reported Stephen's failures directly to Washington. In a defensive letter that probably backfired, Stephen retorted, 'I am Compelld to inform your Excellency, that General Scot has been an incumbrance to Me for Some time.' He described long-running acrimony dating at least to Brandywine. 'I had great inclination to let all these things pass,' Stephen wrote, 'hoping that the least Reflexion would have brought him to Alter his Conduct; but besides Aspersing me to your Excellency; he goes through the Division alienating the Affection of

30 FHS: Clark Diary, 4 Oct. 1777.
31 Anon. (ed.), 'Unpublished Papers Relating to the Battle of Germantown', *PMHB*, 1:4 (1877), p.400.
32 Chase and Lengel (eds), *Papers of Washington* (Revolution), vol.11, pp.468–470.
33 Anon. (ed.), 'Unpublished Papers Relating to Germantown', p.400.
34 Idzerda (ed.), *Lafayette Papers*, vol.1, p.97.
35 Ward, *Stephen*, pp.5, 66, 97, 219; Ward, *Scott*, pp.43–44.
36 Chase et al (eds), *Papers of Washington* (Revolution), vol.9, pp.406, 458–459, 481–482, 523.

the Officers; & breeding bad blood.'[37] Washington knew both generals well enough to make his own assessment.

On 26 October, a court of inquiry met to investigate three charges: 'Unofficerlike behavior on the march from the Clove,' unofficerlike behavior at the battles of Brandywine and Germantown, and 'Drunkenness, or drinking so much, as to act frequently in a manner, unworthy the character of an officer.'[38] Stephen was not specifically charged with being drunk at Germantown. A court martial convened to try him and, after an extended and frequently interrupted trial, announced on 20 November:

> The Court having considered the charges against Major General Stephen, are of opinion, that he is guilty of unofficerlike behaviour, in the retreat from Germantown, owing to inattention, or want of judgement; and that he has been frequently intoxicated since in the service, to the prejudice of good order and military discipline ... Therefore sentence him to be dismissed the service – The Court find him not guilty of any other crimes he was charged with, and therefore acquit him, as to all others, except the two before mentioned.[39]

It had been a long time coming. When Washington was appointed commander in chief in 1775, Stephen whispered to Benjamin Rush, 'He is a *weak man*. I know him well. I served with him during the last French war.'[40] Now he wrote to the new President of Congress, South Carolina's Henry Laurens, pleading, 'It has been my misfortune to become the Object of hatred of a Person of high Rank, for no other reason that I know, but for delivering my Sentiments on the Measures persu'd this Campaign, with that Candour and Boldness which becomes an old officer of Experience, who had the Interest of America at heart.' Whatever sympathy the general's appeal stimulated in Laurens' mind was surely dispelled by Stephen's acerbic charge 'that instead

The Adam Stephen Monument is collocated with his grave in Martinsburg, West Virginia. (Author's photo)

37 Chase and Lengel (eds), *Papers of Washington* (Revolution), vol.11, pp.468–470.
38 Chase and Lengel (eds), *Papers of Washington* (Revolution), vol.11, pp.604–606.
39 Chase et al (eds), *Papers of Washington* (Revolution), vol.12, pp.327–328.
40 L.H. Butterfield (ed.), *Letters of Benjamin Rush* (Princeton: Princeton University Press, 1951), vol.2, p.1120.

of a Court Martial it was a Court of Inquisition, unparalleled in any Army to the Westward of Asia.'[41] Laurens knew this was not true.[42] Even Benjamin Rush, who had once listened to Stephen, now believed he was 'a sordid, boasting cowardly sot.'[43] Stephen was finished.

Knox's Missing Money

James Knox left Saratoga with Morgan's Provisional Rifle Corps the day after Burgoyne surrendered.[44] After a long march, the riflemen arrived at Whitemarsh in mid-November to a well-deserved heroes' welcome.[45] For Captain Knox, however, the joy was short-lived.

The long hunter's assignment to Morgan's Rifles had forced him to quicky wrap up his business in July. The most important matter before him at that time was paying the soldiers of his defunct company of Fincastle men. At Middle Brook 'he received of the Continent a considerable Sum of Money for the purpose of paying the Wages and arrears of pay due to the Officers and Soldiers that were under his Command in Carolina.'[46] Paying these men was not a simple matter. In addition to Knox, 1st Lieutenant James Craig, and 2nd Lieutenant William Lewis Lovely, there were exactly seven men left in the company, three of whom were at remote hospitals. The rest had died, deserted, been too sick to hobble home from the south, or transferred into the South Carolina Line. The 8th Virginia's paymaster, Hezekiah Stoakes, was in camp but evidently relied on Knox to make the payments.[47] Knox paid the men he could find, left the balance of the money with Captain Berry, and left with Colonel Morgan for New York. Now that he was back, he and Berry went to the latter captain's company wagon and discovered that, though the box was still there and locked, its hinges were broken, and most of the money was gone.[48] The rifle captain was on the hook for every penny.

Needing help, Knox went to the most senior officer he knew: Brigadier General Peter Muhlenberg. The general advised him to draft a petition to George Washington and offered to deliver it himself. 'Capt. Knox humbly begs leave to submit his Case to your Excellency,' said the formal third-person plea. The money in question, counted in the odd denominations of Continental bills, was 'Nineteen Thirty Dollar Bills, Eighteen Two Dollar Bills, & four Three Dollar Bills amounting to six hundred & Eighteen Dollars.'[49] '[S]ome of the People are now come and claim their wages, he thinks it hard to pay so large a Sum out of his own pocket. he therefore prays your Excellency will be pleased to order an Examination into this Affair, and afford him such Relief as the Nature of the Case will admit of.'[50]

41 NARA: M247, r.179, p.235, Adam Stephen to Henry Laurens, 6 Dec. 1777.
42 Ward, *Stephen*, pp.197–199.
43 S. Weir Mitchell (ed.), 'Historical Notes of Dr. Benjamin Rush, 1777', *PMHB* 27:2 (1903), p.147.
44 Zambone, *Daniel Morgan*, p.152; John F. Luzader, *Saratoga: A Military History of the Decisive Campaign of the American Revolution* (New York: Savas Beatie, 2008), p.338.
45 Idzerda (ed.), *Lafayette Papers*, vol.1, p.159.
46 Chase et al (eds), *Papers of Washington* (Revolution), vol.12, pp.318–319.
47 NARA: M246, f.208, pp.6, 8, 10.
48 NARA: M247, i.41, pp.75–76, Depositions of Thomas Berry and John Kay, 31 March 1778.
49 NARA: M247, i.41, pp.72–74, 'Petition of Capt. Knox.'
50 Chase et al (eds), *Papers of Washington* (Revolution), vol.12, pp.318–319.

Three days later, one of Washington's aides de camp sent a note back to Muhlenberg with instructions for Captain Knox. 'He will prepare the fullest proof of the circumstances related, & present them to Congress as his Excellency has not power to determine in a matter of this nature.' Paymaster General William Palfrey was preparing to visit Congress and offered to take the petition with him.[51] Everything was lined up for an effective presentation, but Knox was now gone. He marched to New Jersey with Morgan's Rifles the day after he wrote his petition and two days before Muhlenberg received Washington's reply.[52] Palfrey was long gone by the time Knox returned, and the Fincastle captain's two best witnesses, Captain Berry and Lieutenant John Kay, were back in Virginia on winter furloughs.[53]

When they returned in the spring, Berry and Kay signed depositions that were submitted to Congress with Knox's original petition. The documents were read in Congress on 18 April 1778 and referred to the Board of Treasury.[54] In August (almost a year after the incident), the sceptical board reported that 'nothing is offered to prove that the petitioner was authorised to receive money' in the first place. Distributing wages was the paymaster's job. Moreover, 'supposing him justifiable in this, no evidence is adduced to shew that it was not through his neglect that the money which he drew for the officers and men of his company, remained in his hands when ordered to join Colonel Morgan's corps.' There were probably good answers on these points, but the board had further objections.

> That in the petition, it is set forth, that only six hundred and eighteen dollars belonging to the said officers and soldiers, were delivered to Captain Berry at the time of his receiving the order to join Colonel Morgan; whereas, by the deposition of Captain Berry, it appears that fifteen hundred and twelve dollars had been delivered to him by the petitioner, of which 618 dollars had been lost; that the evidence of John Key, relative to the breaking open the chest, appears unfavourable to the petitioner.

The depositions aligned with Knox's petition on the sequence of events and the theft of $618, but other details did not match. Knox said he had put the money in Berry's chest and Berry said Knox put the money in his own chest and left it with the key. Knox said he left Berry with $618, while Berry said Knox left $1,512 dollars of which $618 was stolen. Lieutenant Key, similarly, said he 'was present when the said Capt. Knox examined a bundle of money that was in his chest and declared he had been robbed.'[55] Why, one must wonder, would a thief not take *all* of the money? In Lieutenant Kay's account, the officers 'found that the hinges of his chest had been drawn' and there was 'an ax laying by the wagon.' It seems the Board of Treasury thought this story was a little too perfect. Congress decided to grant Captain Knox 'leave to withdraw his petition.'[56]

51 NARA: M247, i.41, p.71, William Kidder Meade to Peter Muhlenberg, 22 Nov. 1777.
52 Chase et al (eds), *Papers of Washington* (Revolution), vol.12, pp.349–350.
53 NARA: M246, f.209, pp.19, 22.
54 Ford (ed.), *Journals of Congress*, vol.10, p.366.
55 NARA: M247, i.41, pp.75–76, Depositions of Thomas Berry and John Kay, 31 March 1778.
56 Ford (ed.), *Journals of Congress*, vol.11, pp.842–843.

Whitemarsh

When Knox went to New Jersey with Morgan, it was to help isolate the British in Philadelphia. Fort Mercer was still in American hands, and more troops were on the way from the north following Burgoyne's surrender. When Nathanael Greene was sent to coordinate,[57] Lafayette volunteered to go with him. The ardent Frenchman's wound from Brandywine was not fully healed, so he rode without a boot on his left foot. Their efforts across the Delaware were short-lived; they withdrew when a large British force crossed the river. But Lafayette did get a chance to prove his courage again in a small engagement near Gloucester.[58]

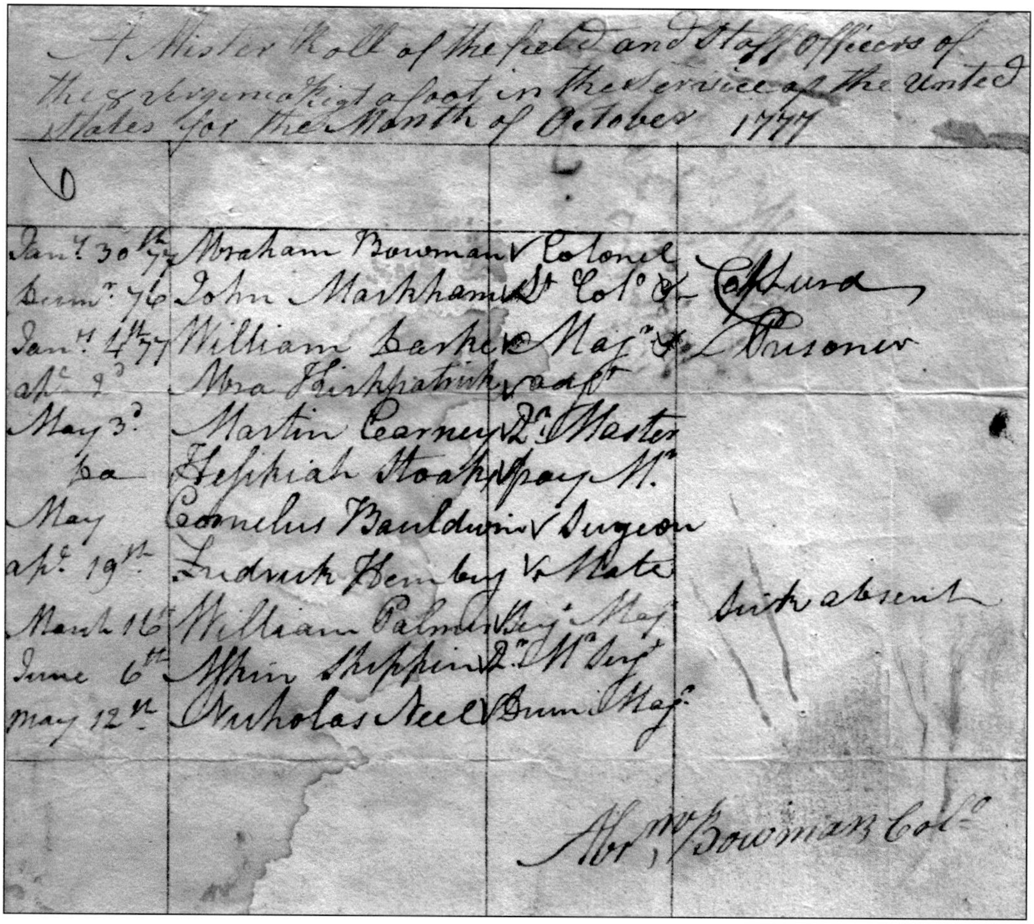
A Muster Roll of the field and Staff Officers of the 8th Virginia Regiment afoot in the Service of the United States for the Month of October 1777

Abraham Bowman Colonel
John Markham Lt Col.
William Darke Majr
Abra Kirkpatrick Adjt
Martin Carney Qr Master
Hezekiah Hoak Pay Mr
Cornelius Bauldwin Surgeon
Ludwick Hemby Mate
William Palmer Serjt Maj
Aphin Shippin Qr Mr Serjt
Nicholas Neel Drum Major

Captured Prisoner

Sick absent

Abram Bowman Col.

A roll of field, staff, and warrant officers recorded after the Battle of Germantown. (National Archives)

57 Chase et al (eds), *Papers of Washington* (Revolution), vol.12, pp.349–350.
58 Idzerda (ed.), *Lafayette Papers*, vol.1, pp.100, 158–161.

Washington, meanwhile, moved the army forward from Pannebecker's to Whitemarsh to keep a closer eye on the city. On 4 December, Howe came out of the Philadelphia with 15,000 men and camped on the north end of Chestnut Hill. American alarm guns fired between three and four o'clock the next morning,[59] but the Whig army was safe in a strong position on high ground. If the British wanted a battle, they would have to draw the Patriots out.

At Whitemarsh, the 8th Virginia was just a skeleton of a regiment and had no field officers. Colonel Bowman was at home in Strasburg, Markham had been cashiered, and Major Darke was a prisoner. Captain Westfall resigned in November, bringing the number of companies commanded by lieutenants to four. Jonathan Clark was now the senior captain and in command of the regiment in Bowman's absence. Casualties, illness, desertion, furloughs, and detached duty whittled every company down to a fraction of its original size. Lieutenant Richard Eastin of Captain Berry's Company led the largest company with a second lieutenant and 26 enlisted men in camp. Lieutenant Isaac Israel's Company (originally Darke's) was down to just two corporals. Early in December, finding no one more senior in camp, William Croghan signed an officers' muster as 'captain commandant.'[60] He had once been the most junior of 10 captains.

The 8th Virginia Regiment, November 1777[61]

Field Officers: Col. Abraham Bowman* Maj. William Darke†		**Staff Officers:** Adj. Abraham Kirkpatrick* Surg. Cornelius Baldwin Surg. Mate Frederick Heimberger* Paymstr. Hezekiah Stoakes* Qtr. Master Martin Carney*		**Warrant Officers:** Qtr. Mst. Sgt. Ashkenaz Shappee* Sgt. Maj. William Palmer* Drum Maj. Nicholas Neal*	
Company	**Captain**	**1st Lieutenant**	**2nd Lieutenant**	**Ensign**	**Enlisted Men**
Clark's	Jonathan Clark	Leonard Cooper		Philip Eastin	24/36 present
Stephenson's	David Stephenson		Benjamin Kinley	James Hooke	14/33 present
Berry's	Thomas Berry*	Richard Eastin	Francis Baldwin	John Kay*	26/40 present
Croghan's	William Croghan	Abraham Kirkpatrick‡*	James Higgins		24/42 present
Higgins'	Robert Higgins†	James Curry	John Clark†	Peter Higgins	6/12 present
Israel's		Isaac Israel*		Thomas Miller*	2/26 present
Steed's		John Steed		Robert Breckenridge	24/47 present
Berwick's			James Berwick	Cornelius Westfall*	8/26 present
Graves'			John Graves*		14/34 present
142/296 enlisted men present. 154 Absent. Lt. Israel's Co. previously Darke's. Lt. Steed's Co. previously Campbell's. Lt. Berwick's Co. previously Westfall's. Lt. Graves' Co. previously Slaughter's. Company musters recorded on various dates in December. *Absent. †Prisoner. ‡Adjutant.					

59 Anon. (ed.), 'Diary of Joseph Clark,' p.102; Kipping and Smith (trans. and ed.), *Muenchhausen Diary*, p.45; Ecelbarger, *Washington's Momentous Year*, vol.1, p.214.

60 NARA: M246, f.208, pp.12, 14, f.209, p.22.

61 NARA: M246, f.208, p.14; f.209, pp.22–23; f.210, pp.16–17; f.211, pp.20–21; f.212, pp.13–14; f.213, pp.10–11; f.214, pp.18–19; f.217, pp.22-23; f.218, p.17; f.219, pp.21–22

Clark was only gone briefly, carrying messages under a flag of truce to the Rising Sun Tavern in Germantown. He was back in command when the British approached from Chestnut Hill on 5 December.[62] The regiment and most of the army remained up on the ridge while Morgan's Rifles protected the left and the 2nd Connecticut Regiment, acting as light infantry, protected the right. Each flank also had some militia and light dragoons for support.[63] As he had in the Watchung Mountains, Washington refused to be drawn into a full battle, so the armies did little more than sit and watch each other. The British withdrew into Germantown and came out again onto Edge Hill on the 7th, facing the left side of the American line. Washington sent out his skirmishers. Knox's men followed Morgan out on the left, accompanied by Colonel Mordecai Gist's Maryland militia. The 2nd Connecticut did the same on the right, supported by Pennsylvania militia. The latter force engaged but quickly retreated. Morgan and Gist advanced into the dense woods of Edge Hill and got into a serious fight. They were attacked from two directions and forced to retreat. One participant recalled, 'Morgan with 500 riflemen ... attacked them and greatly annoyed them driving them frequently from their Cannon, but they opportunely received a reinforcement and we were compiled [compelled] to give back.'[64] Major Joseph Morris, Morgan's third in command, took a musket ball through his mouth that ripped out his teeth and lodged in the back of his neck. He lived long enough to die at home in New Jersey.[65]

The Route from Germantown to Valley Forge

4 Oct: Retreat from Germantown
5 Oct: West bank of Perkiomen
8 Oct: Towamencin Twp
16 Oct: Supplee's Chapel
21 Oct: Whitpain Twp
2 Nov: Whitemarsh Twp
11 Dec: Swede's Ford
13 Dec: Gulf Mill
19 Dec: Valley Forge[66]
(Approximately 70 miles)

Up on the ridge, Captain Clark and the 8th Virginia Regiment saw no action. The regiment was in the encampment's second line, and the fighting was limited enough that they were only vaguely aware of the 'Battle of Whitemarsh'. Clark recorded 'an alarm' on 5 December, with a note that the 'enemy moved to Chestnut Hill.' He recorded 'some schirmish'g', on the 7th and, after another two days, noted that the 'enemy ret'd to Philadelphia.'[67] But they spent these days freezing on the windswept high ground. The tents and baggage had been sent off

62 FHS: Clark Diary, 2–3 Dec. 1777; NARA: M246, f.208, p.12,

63 Chase et al (eds), *Papers of Washington* (Revolution), vol.12, pp.534–535, vol.14, pp.147–150.

64 NARA: M804, S30392, Charles Eads pension (5th Va.).

65 NARA: M804, S42233, John Ryan pension (1st Pa.); Samuel Hays, 'A Sketch of Major Joseph Morris,' *The Record*, First Presbyterian Church of Morristown, N.J., 5:34–35 (1885), pp.182–184, 186–188, 187.

66 FHS: Clark Diary; Boyle (ed.) 'McMichael Journal, Sept.-Dec. 1777;' Baker, *Itinerary of Washington*, pp.95–110.

67 FHS: Clark Diary, 5–9 Dec. 1777; Morton, 'Morton Diary', p.34.

when the alarm guns fired.[68] From the perspective of Knox, Craig, and Lovely, however, the fighting had been plenty intense. General Washington held up the riflemen as exemplary soldiers in his general orders: 'The Commander in Chief returns his warmest thanks to Col. Morgan, and the officers and men of his intrepid corps, for their gallant behaviour in the several skirmishes with the enemy yesterday.'[69] The King's German auxiliaries, meanwhile, vented their frustration by committing 'great outrages on the inhabitants' on their way back to Philadelphia. They set fire to the Rising Sun Tavern.[70]

Lafayette in Command

The Marquis de Lafayette was a major general without a command, and he was eager to change that. He was young, but his title, his wealth, his connections, and the hoped-for French alliance all weighed in his favour. He pursued his goal with charm and a confirmed willingness to stand in harm's way. 'The Marquis,' Nathanael Greene commented, 'is determined to be in the way of danger.'[71] After leading the attack in New Jersey, Lafayette told Henry Laurens it was 'very trifling' and gave all credit to Morgan's men and the New Jersey militia. He said, 'no kind of merit at all can be on the account of the general officer who was by chance with them, however I have had the greatest pleasure to see by my own eyes with what bravery and alacrity a little reconnoitring party … has repulsed very far with a great loss a body of 350 hessians with field pieces'.[72]

General Washington liked Lafayette and told President Laurens, 'He is extremely solicitous of having a Command equal to his Rank.' Washington advised that from 'the attachment which he has manifested to our cause, and the consequences, which his return in disgust might produce, that it will be adviseable to gratify him in his wishes.' Adam Stephen's disgrace opened a spot the marquis thought 'would be the most agreeable.'[73] On 1 December, Congress gave him his wish.[74]

Lafayette inaugurated his command with a flattering letter to a man he had never met, Governor Patrick Henry, 'I am highly sensible of all the advantages I obtained in being entrusted with the command of a virginian division,' he professed, 'and I dare entertain the idea that such a favor will intitle me to some connexions with that state. I hope that Virginia will be satisfied with the conduct of those of her brave sons I'l have the honor to fight with.'[75]

The 8th Virginia's new divisional commander performed well. The regiment's 1776 recruits spent most of their two years under Major Generals Lee and Stephen, but the 1777 men associated their service with the French commander. Lieutenant Curry, for instance, recalled

68 Anon. (ed.), 'Diary of Joseph Clark', p.103.
69 Chase et al (eds), *Papers of Washington* (Revolution), vol.12, pp.571–573.
70 Morton, 'Morton Diary', pp.34–35.
71 Chase et al (eds), *Papers of Washington* (Revolution), vol.12, pp.408–411.
72 Idzerda (ed.), *Lafayette Papers*, vol.1, pp.158–161.
73 Chase et al (eds), *Papers of Washington* (Revolution), vol.11, pp.505–508, vol.12, pp.78–85.
74 Ford (ed.), *Journals of Congress*, vol.9, pp.982–983.
75 Idzerda (ed.), *Lafayette Papers*, vol.1, p.211.

A ca. 1786 bust of the Marquis de Lafayette, attributed to Jean Antoine Houdon. (Diplomatic Reception Rooms, U.S. Department of State)

that 'the principal part of my time ... General Lafayette commanded our Division of Virginia troops.'[76]

Valley Forge

Henry Redman and his three boys received passes to go home. A fourth son recalled, 'in the winter they all came hom on furloaug.'[77] They were less than a year into their three-year 1777 enlistments and were expected back in the spring. Virginia's two-year 1776 enlistments may have saved the Revolution the previous winter, but now most of them were close to expiring. These were some of the army's very best soldiers, and their colonels proposed a plan to keep them in service. Washington explained to Governor Henry:

> The time, for which the original Men of the Nine old Virginia Regiments were raised, will expire in February and from that to April; and it is much to be doubted, whether they will reinlist upon the common Bounty if at all. They will be a loss to the Service as they are seasoned Soldiers and well acquainted with their duty. The Officers commanding the Regiments proposed as an inducement to the men to reinlist to permit them to go home about xmass and remain there till March.[78]

What this meant in practice was that everyone could go home except for short-timers who declined to reenlist. Most of the officers also went home, which annoyed the commander-in-chief. When new, the 8th Virginia had about 700 enlisted men on the rolls. When they arrived at the Valley Forge encampment, there were just 79 present at or near camp. Cornelius Baldwin and Sergeant Major William Palmer were the only members of the regimental staff

76 LVA: J. Curry petition.
77 NARA: H. Redman pension.
78 Chase et al (eds), *Papers of Washington* (Revolution), vol.12, pp.240–242.

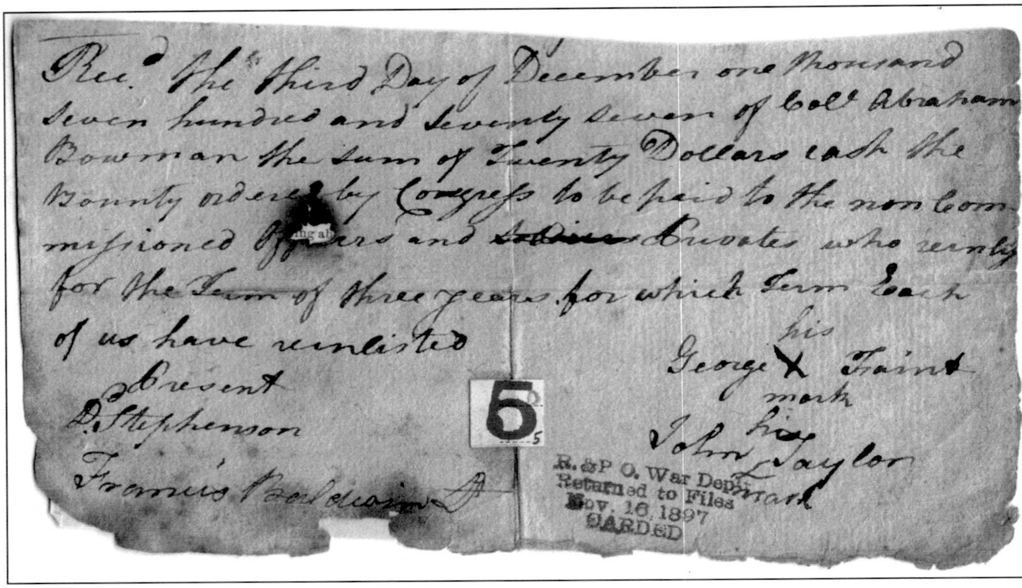

George Faint and John Taylor received $20 each for reenlisting on 3 December 1777. (National Archives)

there. Captain Croghan was once again the senior commissioned officer. James Higgins, his longtime lieutenant and George Rogers Clark's early exploration partner, stayed with him. Lieutenant James Curry and Ensign Peter Higgins from Robert Higgins' barely extant company were there as well. Every other officer was gone.[79]

Corporal Henry Gaddis remembered, 'we marched to Valley Forge whare we built houses and camp'd thare for the winter.'[80] The site of the encampment was far enough from Philadelphia to be safe from surprises but close enough to disrupt British foraging.[81] Valley Creek ran northeast through the Great Valley but turned sharply north through the hills before pouring into the Schuylkill. Mount Joy and Mount Misery rose on either side of the creek. East of Mount Joy, two ridges ran not quite parallel to each other to the river, bracketing a plain in between. Most of the brigades built their huts on the Z-shaped south ridge, which took the name 'Front Line Hill.'[82] Scott's Brigade built 109 huts on the west end of this ridge looking west toward Mount Joy.[83]

Hut building was the top priority, but there were other urgent needs. Shoes and clothing were desperately wanted as the weather grew colder. The commissaries were almost empty, with no means to restock. Nearly all the army's wagons were broken or missing, and the draft horses were worn out, crippled, or dead. Distrustful Pennsylvania farmers refused to provide the army with food, animals, or wagons. When his soldiers began to starve and

79 NARA: M246, f.208, pp.37–38. James Higgins was not related to Robert and Peter.
80 NARA: H. Gaddis pension.
81 Anon. (ed.), 'Diary of Joseph Clark', p.104.
82 Thomas Blake, 'Lieutenant Thomas Blake's Journal', in Frederick Kidder, *History of the First New Hampshire Regiment in the War of the Revolution* (Albany: Joel Munsell, 1868), p.40; Henry Woodman, *The History of Valley Forge* (Oaks, Pa.: John U. Francis, Sr., 1922), pp.53–54.
83 Calculation by Gary Ecelbarger.

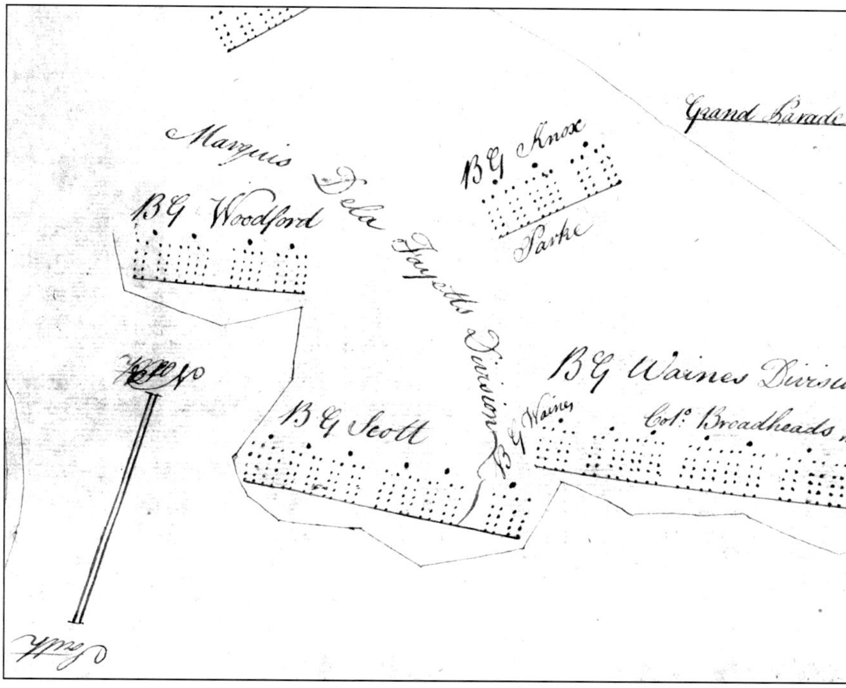

Detail of a map drawn early in the Valley Forge encampment showing the position of Lafayette's Division. (MS.2011.1.1, Collection of the Newport Historical Society)

steal, Washington authorised impressment, but farmers responded by hiding things in the woods.[84] A distressed Pennsylvania officer said there was 'not a blanket to Seven men'.[85] Lafayette saw men in his division sleeping in shifts for the same reason.[86] He remembered, 'The unfortunate American soldiers lacked everything – coats, hats, shirts, and shoes. Their feet and legs turned black with frostbite, and often had to be amputated.'[87] He and Washington individually urged Patrick Henry to send clothing for the Virginia Line, and the willing governor got to work immediately.[88] When logistical problems delayed a shipment at York, still the seat of Congress, Lafayette pressed Henry Laurens to speed it along.[89] Blankets, stockings, and shoes for the Virginians finally arrived about 10 January, followed by 'a great quantity of clothing' two months later.[90]

The camp huts were a simplified version of the log houses many 8th Virginia men grew up in. They had no foundations, the logs were not squared, and turf or thatch covered the roofs. Fireplaces made the cabins warm, but in-ground floors and sod roofs made them damp. Twelve men lived in each 14-foot by 16-foot cabin, making the shelters incubators for lice and disease. Officers had better accommodation, but even Charles Scott had a log hut built

84 John W. Jackson, *Valley Forge: Pinnacle of Courage* (Gettysburg: Thomas Publications, 1992), pp.63, 80–86.
85 Hazard et al (eds), *Pennsylvania Archives*, ser.1, vol.6, pp.252–253.
86 Jackson, *Valley Forge*, p.157.
87 Idzerda (ed.), *Lafayette Papers*, vol.1, p.170.
88 Chase et al (eds), *Papers of Washington* (Revolution), vol.13, pp.17–18; Idzerda (ed.), *Lafayette Papers*, vol.1, p.211.
89 Idzerda (ed.), *Lafayette Papers*, vol.1, pp.209–210.
90 Anon. (ed.), 'Diary of Joseph Clark', p.103, 105.

for him by the men of the 12th Virginia.[91] Some men were detailed to build a bridge across the Schuylkill to facilitate foraging and skirmishing. Each brigade on Front Line Hill was tasked with building an outer breastwork parallel to their line of huts.[92]

Viruses and vermin were not the only health issues. Some men arrived with wounds, including two of Captain Croghan's men who were hurt at Brandywine. Alexander Moore was allowed to go home 'in consequence of a wound received at the Battle of Brandywine which prevented his performing the duties of a soldier.'[93] David Williams, who had lost part of his jaw, was required to stay. He 'laid all winter at the Valley Forge' waiting for his enlistment to end.[94]

It took three months to resolve the supply issues, and life remained hard that whole time. Broken equipment, half-frozen horse carcasses, and waste (human and otherwise) collected around the huts. Gambling and black-market commerce became popular in the camp while 'tippling houses' and prostitutes began operating outside its perimeter.[95] On 28 January, a court-martial sentence was announced for 8th Virginia fifer Stephen Rice, who was an April 1777 recruit of George Slaughter's. His company was now commanded by Lieutenant John Graves, but Sergeant Robert Spilman was the senior man in camp.[96] After three months of confinement, he was found guilty of 'plundering the inhabitants of the Country.'[97] He was punished with 'one hundred lashes on his naked back well laid on.'[98]

Rice's former captain, meanwhile, found himself wanting a furlough just when General Washington decided to crack down on them.[99] Major Slaughter received news from Culpeper that his house had burned and his uninoculated family had no place to hide from a smallpox outbreak. He asked for a furlough, which was peremptorily denied. Angry and eager to get home, Slaughter resigned from the 12th Virginia and left. A month later, he wrote a contrite letter to Washington asking to come back.

> The abrupt manner in which you was pleased to refuse me leave of absence: the difficulties and hardships that an American Officer inevitably labours under; the ridicule, that I shall probably incur from the unthinking, for my apparent mutability of temper, would I Apprehend, deter the generality of mankind from an Application Similar to this: but the attachment I have to your Excellency, for the faithfull discharge of the important trust you hold, & the Ardent desire that posseses me of Supporting the Just claims of my Country, Urges me on with an irresistible impulse to ask for the post, that I resigned, perhaps rather rashly – I hope however, your Excellency will not think so, when I inform you that

91 Chase et al (eds), *Papers of Washington* (Revolution), vol.12, pp.626–628; Jackson, *Valley Forge*, pp.42–55.
92 Blake, 'Journal', p.40.
93 NARA: M246, f.211, p.23; NARA: M804, S41893, Alexander Moore pension.
94 NARA: D. Williams pension.
95 Jackson, *Valley Forge*, pp.65, 81, 103–104, 127, 169.
96 NARA: M246, f.208, p.34.
97 NARA: M246, f.217, pp.17, 20, 23; Chase et al (eds), *Papers of Washington* (Revolution), vol.13, pp.369–370.
98 Chase et al (eds), *Papers of Washington* (Revolution), vol.13, pp.369–370.
99 Chase et al (eds), *Papers of Washington* (Revolution), vol.12, pp.662–665.

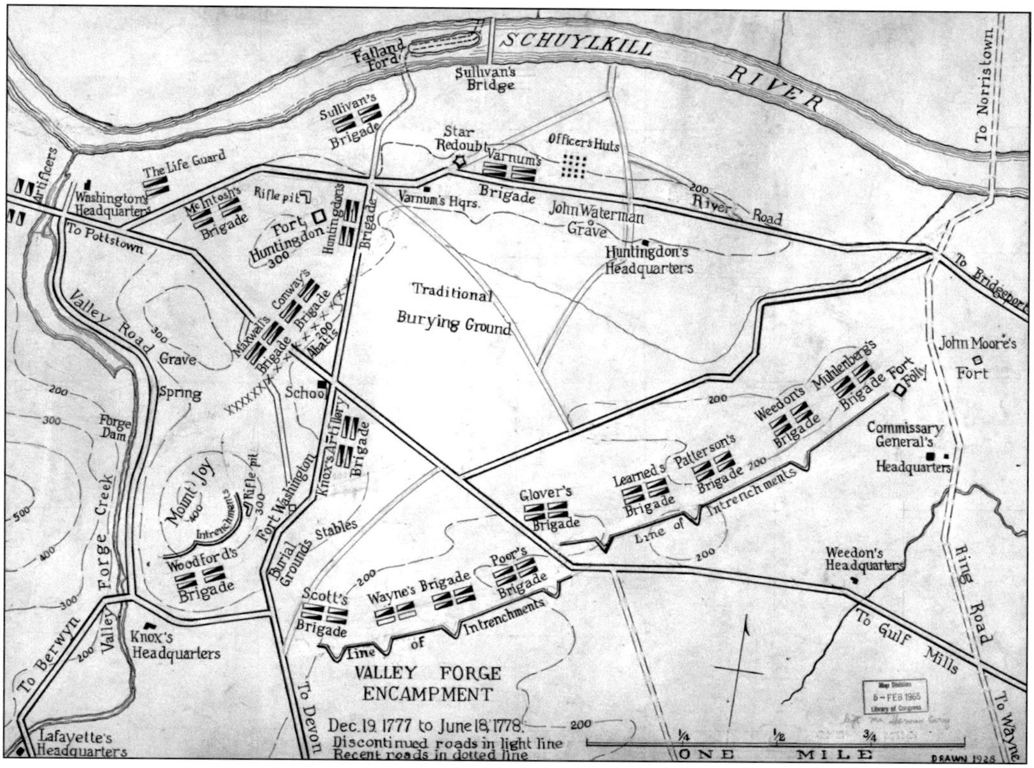

A 1928 map of the Valley Forge encampment. (Library of Congress)

> domestick calamities was the only cause; The misfortune of haveing my house burnt, & my family daily threatened with the small pox, which had got it before I reached Virginia – made my presence at home absolutely necessary. I should have mentioned The above particulars to your Excellency, had not the hasty manner in which you was pleased to answer me rendered it impracticable … if my reenstation can take place with propriety, it will afford me great satisfaction; if not, I hope I can Acquiesce without murmuring, and serve my country to the utmost of my power in a civil Capacity.[100]

Washington refused the request.

Lafayette and the Conway Cabal

Soon after Lafayette took command of the division, he was pulled away by Congress's Board of War to launch an attack on Canada. The order was part of an effort by the 'Conway

100 Chase et al (eds), *Papers of Washington* (Revolution), vol.13, pp.438–439.

Cabal' to separate Washington from his strongest allies as they worked to replace him with Horatio Gates. One ill-advised invasion of Canada had already failed, but the notion that Lafayette could more effectively appeal to the people of the former French colony had gotten traction. When he learned that Washington had not been consulted on the plan, Lafayette travelled directly to York, asked for explicit orders, and insisted that his command not be independent of Washington (as Gates' had been at Saratoga). He intentionally embarrassed Washington's critics by offering a toast to the commander-in-chief over dinner, obliging them to raise their glasses.[101]

When Lafayette arrived in Albany, he conferred with the officers there and wrote an uncharacteristically furious letter to Henry Laurens to 'let him know which hell of blunders, madness, and deception I am involved in.' He understood what Gates' supporters had done. 'You know,' he wrote, 'that the whole expedition has been put on foot in order to satisfy one single Man's ambition.'[102] He returned to Pennsylvania and resumed command of his division.[103]

The Departure of the Two-Year Men

Circumstances began to improve at Valley Forge in the second and third months of 1778. Food and clothing arrived, and the weather grew warmer. Shad spawned in the Schuylkill, briefly offering all the fish a soldier could catch. There were Sunday services in each brigade, and plays were performed for the officers. Soldiers played rounders and wicket (games related to baseball and cricket).[104] In March, Major General Friedrich Wilhelm, Baron de Steuben began to teach a uniform drill to make the army more effective on the battlefield.

Several men who were previously listed as sick and absent appeared in camp on 16 February to receive the extra month's pay Congress approved 'as a reward for the virtuous patience and Zeal of the troops under the Inconvenience of their present situation.'[105] This briefly brought the number of 8th Virginia men in camp to over 100, but the count dropped quickly from there. Departures began in January when the enlistments of the two-year men began to expire. Late in February, however, Sergeant John McDonald of Captain Croghan's Company unexpectedly showed up in camp. He had been captured at Germantown but escaped from the Philadelphia jail on St Valentine's Day. He made his way to Valley Forge, picked up his discharge, and went home.[106] Musters were not taken again until April, but more than half of the two-year men were gone by the end of February, and all were free to go by 10 April. Charles Scott signed their discharges.[107]

101 Idzerda (ed.), *Lafayette Papers*, vol.1, p.245.

102 Idzerda (ed.), *Lafayette Papers*, vol.1, pp.246–279, 297–300.

103 Chase et al (eds), *Papers of Washington* (Revolution), vol.14, pp.459–464.

104 Jackson, *Valley Forge*, pp.101–102, 167, 177–179.

105 NARA: M246, f.208, p.40; Chase et al (eds), *Papers of Washington* (Revolution), vol.13, pp.542–544.

106 NARA: M246, f.208, p.37, f.211, pp.45.

107 NARA: S37725, Philip Barr pension, S30994, William Dodson pension, S38269, James Oliver pension, W310, James Range pension, S38132, George Seifret pension, A. Bible pension, A. Cabbage pension, J. Campbell pension, William Combs pension, William Dodson pension, J. Engle pension, J. Fetzer

The departing veterans had enlisted for two years when every other state required men to serve just one. They had collectively experienced almost the entirety of Virginia's part in the war. Jonathan Grant stood just a few yards from Washington at Trenton and no farther from Hugh Mercer at Princeton. His comrade David Williams remembered those hard days as just two of 15 battles and skirmishes he fought in.[108]

A few men agreed to remain beyond their terms. Grant remembered that he 'afterwards at the request of General Washington served three months as Volunteer.'[109] As he watched his comrades leave, the events of two difficult years were surely on his mind. On 10 April he must have felt like the last man standing. If so, it was a false sensation. Forty-three of the 1776 men had reenlisted and would soon be back with the three-year men and new recruits.

Malnourished Prisoners

Life for the prisoners in Philadelphia remained hard, especially for the enlisted men. John Chenoweth's brief account of 'the dredfullest suffering' is a rare voice from what is otherwise a black void from which many did not return. Treatment was unequal, to be sure. Officers were separated from the enlisted men, permitted to correspond with their friends, and granted limited paroles to recover from illnesses. Lieutenant John Clark corresponded with his brother, filling every letter with requests for money and clothing. From the State House in December, he asked Jonathan to 'get me some cloth for a Regimental Coat such as our Regt. wears, if not to be got scarlet or light blue and have it made by your own measure for if I stay here this winter as there is no likelihood of any thing else shall be very bad for one.' He asked his brother to send him money by collecting his pay and settling accounts with soldiers who were indebted to him. 'You say you have old Virga. Money at home that will be of service to me,' he responded in the same letter, 'but not so good as silver or gold.' In a city under British occupation, Virginia currency was less negotiable than precious metal specie.[110] Jonathan, certainly through sacrifice and effort, sent his brother a gold piece worth 45 shillings. Others helped, too. 'Maj. Slaughter,' Clark wrote, 'has been very kind in letting me have the money mentioned. Shall not forget him.'[111]

'I Received your letter yesterday,' Major Darke wrote to Captain Clark, 'in which you desired me to give you an account of the state of the Eighth Regiment that are prisoners heare.' He was unable to say much. 'I came out of gaol about the 15th of Jany and have bean sick almost ever sinc[e,] Most of the time scarce able to get out of My bed & when I was [, I was] not alowed to go to them.' He did offer an update on the officers. 'I beleve the officers are all well Except your brother Who is unwell with a swelling and soreness on one of his legs but he has been out of gaol some time and like to get well soon.'[112]

pension, J. Grant pension, M. Hennen pension, J. Johnston pension, G. Spickard pension, W. Taylor pension.

108 NARA: D. Williams pension.

109 NARA: J. Grant pension. See also S16984, Alexander Monroe pension (Grayson's Additional).

110 Morton, 'Morton Diary', p.8, 32–33.

111 WHS: Draper Mss, L, vol.1, p.39.

112 WHS: Draper Mss, L, vol.1, p.44.

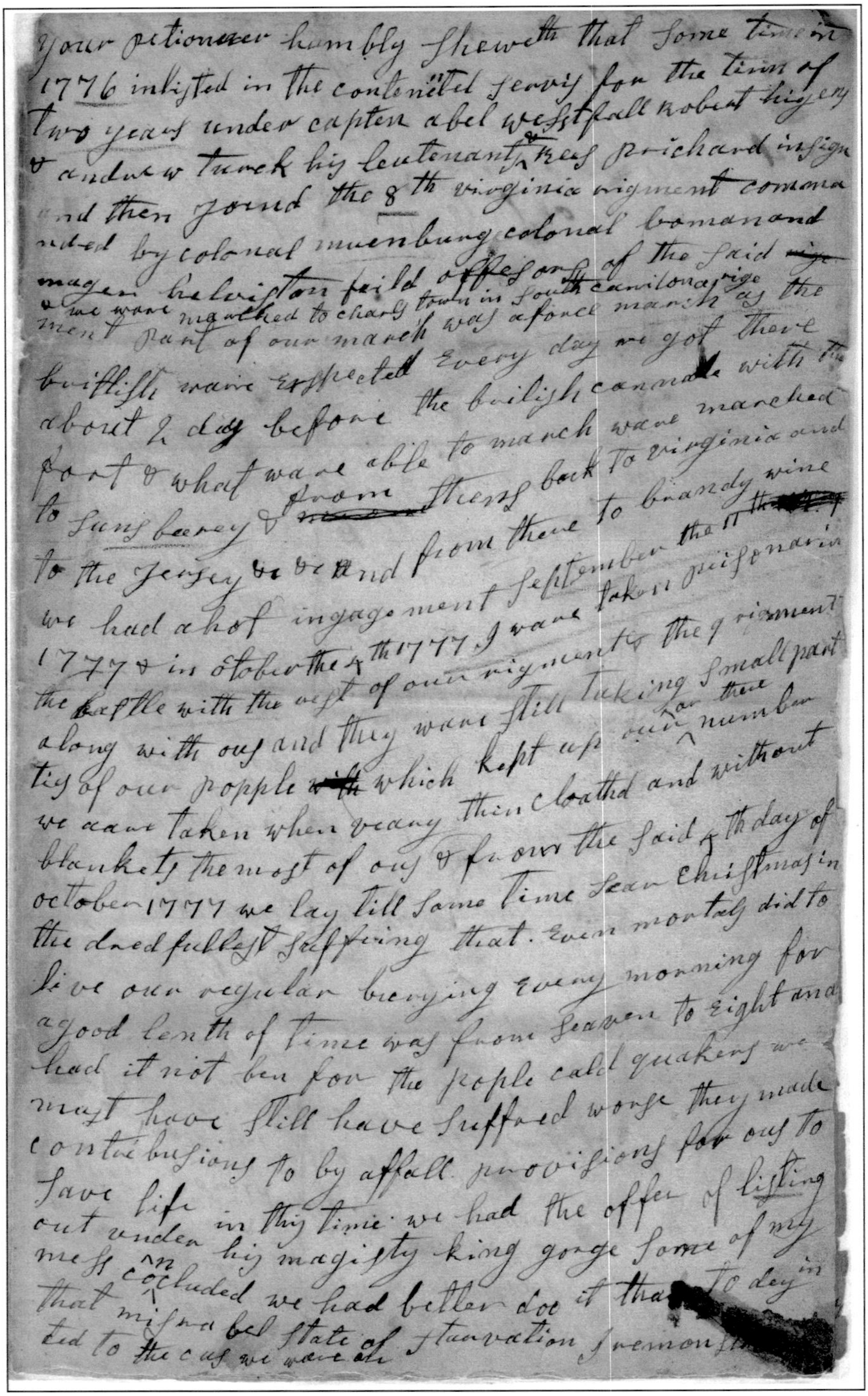

your petioneer humbly Shewetth that Some time in
1776 inlisted in the contenittel seavis for the term of
two years under capten abel westfall robert higery
& andrew turck his leutenants & rees prichard insign
and then joind the 8th virginia rigment comma
nded by colonal muenburg colonal bomanand
mager helviston field offesars of the said rig
ment & we ware marched to charls town in South carilona rige as the
part of our march was a force march as there
brittish ware expected every day we got there
about 2 day before the brittish came with the
foot & what ware able to march ware marched
to Sansbeary & from thens back to virginia and
to the jersey &c &c and from there to brandy wine
we had a hot ingagement September the 11th
1777 & in otober the 4th 1777 I ware taken prisonar in
the battle with the rest of our rigment to the 9 rigment
along with ous and they ware still taking small part
ties of our popple which kept up our number or there
we ware taken when veary thin cloathd and without
blankets the most of ous & from the said 4th day of
october 1777 we lay till Some time sear chistmas in
the dreadfullest suffering that even mortals did to
live our regular berying every morning for
a good lenth of time was from seaven to eight and
had it not ben for the people cald quakers we
must have still have suffered worse they made
contributions to by afall provisions for ous to
save life in this time we had the offer of listing
out under his magisty king gorge some of my
mess concluded we had better doe it than to dey in
that misarabel state of starvation I remonst
tid to the ous we ware

The first page of John Chenoweth's petition to Congress details his capture at the Battle of Germantown and suffering in the Walnut Street Jail. (National Archives)

The younger Clark brother had scurvy, which was a consequence of malnutrition and thus evidence that even officers were denied fresh food. 'I have for the Present my Parole to a limited house only,' Clark wrote from the home of 'Mr. Scot.' He explained further, 'The reason of my Parole was owing to my health. I have a scurvatick umor that has fell into my legs which has disabled me from walking. I am in know danger. I am in hopes as soon as I can recover so as to be able to walk about I shall be allowed more indulgences.' Though he relied on humoral theory (the 'four temperaments') to explain his illness, the cure for scurvy was better food, which his host seems to have provided. In the same letter, John shared more bad news with his brother: 'the Piese of Gold of 45/ that you sent to me ... was Counterfit.' The balance of the letter was filled with the schemes of a prisoner trying to lessen his own suffering.'[113] Most of Major Darke's letter was similar.

The First Drafted Soldiers

Back in Virginia, officers spent the winter doing the now-impossible job of recruiting. The romance of war was gone, and the Old Dominion's eager and willing men were already in service. Enlistment terms had been stretched from one year to two, and from two to three. Virginia had already resorted to a draft to help the 10th through 15th regiments fill their ranks. In October of 1777, the General Assembly extended the draft to cover recruiting for all its regiments and added an extra bounty for volunteers.[114] The legislature backtracked and allowed men, for a reduced bounty, to join for one year.[115]

County militia organizations administered the draft, and in 1778 there were some new counties. One was carved out of Augusta and named for Charles Watson-Wentworth, 2nd Marquess of Rockingham, the prime minister who oversaw the repeal of the Stamp Act and continued to advocate for American rights. Rockbridge County was carved out of Augusta and Botetourt at the same time.[116] Dunmore County finally shed its hated name to become Shenandoah County.[117]

Sixteen-year-old William Pollard of Winchester agreed to serve in Captain Berry's Company for a year. 'Richard & Philip Easton was the Lieutenant & Ensign,' he remembered about his enlistment, noting that they 'were brothers from my neighborhood.'[118] Shenandoah County resident Elias Turner signed on for a year 'in the company commanded by Captain John Steed.'[119] Steed was promoted in Richard Campbell's old company on March 30th.[120]

Counties that fell short of volunteers proceeded to conduct a draft. Peter Van Pelt, James Blaine, and Jacob Crow were among those drafted in Augusta County. 'Peter Van Pelt and myself were drafted at the same time and place,' remembered Blaine, '& received $15 each

113 WHS: Draper Mss., L, vol.1, p.43.
114 Hening (ed.), *Statutes*, vol.9, pp.337–349.
115 Hening (ed.), *Statutes*, vol.9, pp.275–280, 337–349.
116 Hening (ed.), *Statutes*, vol.9, pp.420–424.
117 Hening (ed.), *Statutes*, vol.9, pp.424.
118 NARA: M804, S17638, William Pollard pension.
119 NARA: M804, R10758, Elias Turner pension.
120 NARA: M881, r.938, John Steed.

bounty.' The draft term was for one year, and only single men were eligible. Van Pelt, however, quickly married his fiancée before leaving for Valley Forge.[121] Ten days after the wedding, General Washington sent a letter to Abraham Bowman calling him back to camp.[122] The colonel was already collecting his men when he received the order.

Some men hired substitutes. William Phillips of Captain Berry's Company was employed over the winter by Quaker silversmith William Richardson, who had a shop south of Winchester.[123] When furloughs ended, 'he was prevailed upon by Mr. Richardson to procure a substitute, which he did, and paid him seventy-five pounds Virginia currency in money and a pair of silver shoe buckles.'[124] A few who took the reenlistment bounty never appeared. William Morrow from Captain Berry's Company was recorded as a deserter. So was Edward Stapleton, formerly of Captain Knox's Company. Stapleton had deserted before. In Pittsburgh, Captain Croghan's men had their own rendezvous where William Brown failed to appear. In his case, however, he had been listed as 'sick, absent' since Germantown.[125]

The men who did show up were a mix of the reluctant and the ready, the amateur and the able. 'I engaged to serve twelve months,' wrote William Pollard, 'but there was some that enlisted for a longer time, Also there was a draft for twelve months.' On 1 April, this motley assortment of hardened veterans and scared youths 'all marched from Winchester together & joined the Army at Valley Forge.'[126]

Captain Clark arrived at Valley Forge from Caroline three days after the last of the unrenewed 1776 enlistments expired.[127] Jonathan Grant was still in camp, but the cabins built by Scott's Brigade in December were mostly vacant and waiting for new occupants. Messes were organised, and the men picked bunks in the damp huts. James Blaine and Peter Van Pelt shared a mess. The teenage William Pollard was assigned to a mess with Dan Anderson, the veteran sergeant of Daniel Morgan's 1775 rifle company. Also living in their cabin were Jonathan Sandusky, who had enlisted in 1777, and Bean Smallwood and Solomon Redman, who had reenlisted.[128]

The arrival of fabric for the Virginia Line allowed 8th Virginia men to receive new clothing. 'Shirtmen' no longer, they wore the now-familiar blue coats that became the official uniform in 1779.[129] The new arrivals began learning Steuben's drill and participated in several events and observances. Fast Day, a spring counterpart to Thanksgiving most

121 NARA: M804, W18198, Peter Van Pelt pension.

122 Chase et al (eds), *Papers of Washington* (Revolution), vol.14, p.323.

123 George Barton Cutten, *The Silversmiths of Virginia, Together with Watchmakers and Jewelers, from 1694 to 1850* (Dietz Press, 1952), pp.216; Edward C. Chandlee, *Six Quaker Clockmakers* (Philadelphia: Historical Society of Pennsylvania, 1943), p.105.

124 NARA: W. Phillips pension.

125 NARA: M246, f.209, p.25, f.211, p.26.

126 FHS: Clark Diary, 1 April 1778; NARA: W. Pollard pension.

127 FHS: Clark Diary, 13 April 1778.

128 NARA: W. Pollard pension.

129 Chase et al (eds), *Papers of Washington* (Revolution), vol.12, pp.240–242, 352–353, 564–566, vol.14, pp.422–423, vol.22, pp.581–582; Mary R.M. Godwin, *Clothing and Accoutrements of the Officers and Soldiers of the Virginia Forces: 1775–1778*, Colonial Williamsburg Foundation Library Research Report Series RR0049, Colonial Williamsburg Foundation, June 1962, pp.139–140. Thanks to David Ervin.

popular in New England, was held on 22 April.[130] The first day of May was King Tammany's Day, which honoured the 'affable' Delaware chief who helped William Penn establish his 'peaceable kingdom.'[131] The army celebrated news of the French alliance with another *feu de joie* on 6 May.[132] Lafayette represented his country at this celebration by wearing a white sash.[133] On 12 May, Lafayette administered a new oath of allegiance to the men of the division.[134] Then, as the weather got warmer, the soldiers started knocking the clay out from between the logs of their huts to let in the fresh spring air.[135] They moved into tents on 8 June, ready for the regiment's third season of war.[136]

---

130 FHS: Clark Diary, 22 April 1778; Anon., *Religion and the Founding of the American Republican* (exhibition), Library of Congress, <loc.gov/exhibits/religion/rel04.html>, accessed 13 Feb. 2024; Donna Gilbreth, 'Fast Day,' *New Hampshire Almanac*, <nh.gov/almanac/fast-day.htm>, accessed 13 Feb. 2024.

131 Thomas Ewing (ed.), *George Ewing, Gentleman: a Soldier of Valley Forge* (Yonkers, N.Y.: T. Ewing, 1928), p.44; Martin W. Walsh, 'May Games and Noble Savages: The Native American in Early Celebrations of the Tammany Society,' *Folklore*, 108 (1997), pp.83–91.

132 FHS: Clark Diary, 6 May 1778.

133 Idzerda (ed.), *Lafayette Papers*, vol.2, p.7.

134 NARA: J. Curry pension; Jackson, *Valley Forge*, p.193.

135 Jackson, *Valley Forge*, p.213.

136 FHS: Clark Diary, 8–10 June 1778.

13

Monmouth

The regiment's 'Old Friend' Charles Lee was paroled by his captors in April and exchanged in May. He rejoined the army and took command of Nathanael Greene's division when the Rhode Islander became quartermaster general. The Continental Army had changed considerably during Lee's absence, but he had not changed one bit. He conceded that he 'hardly knew a single man or officer' under his command.[1] Because his own strong opinions left him inept at picking up on social and political cues, he underestimated Washington's heightened standing and the political imperative of a successful offensive.[2] It cost him dearly.

Prisoners in Philadelphia continued to suffer and die. Zachariah Pigman, one of Captain Westfall's recruits, and Zachariah DeLong of Captain Higgins' Company both died in February.[3] When Lieutenant Clark recovered from scurvy, he was sent back to the Walnut Street Jail.[4] An episode from Major Darke's captivity was recorded, with some apparent embellishment, in 1913. Elements of the story, learned from a descendant, place it in June of 1778. News of the French alliance forced Britain to consolidate its forces in New York and the Caribbean. Darke's wife, Sarah, came to visit him in Philadelphia just as prisoners were being put on ships for transport. Darke was 'confined in a man-of-war outside Philadelphia,' preparing to sail north. He said, according to the narrative, 'the English soldiers would shove him a bowl of soup and say, "There, drink, you rebel dog."'

> Mrs. William Dark dressed herself as a cabin boy, tied her hair in a queue and got on board the ship to see her husband. According to a portrait she was a slender, black-eyed, rosy cheeked, daring young Virginia lady. The commander of the English man-of-war had a keen eye for beauty and he discovered her sex almost immediately, but was so filled with admiration of her courage and daring, that when she left the ship he gave her a chest filled with fine linen and lace. A remnant of the latter is still preserved as a family heirloom.[5]

1 Anon. (ed.), *Proceedings of a General Court-Martial, Held at Brunswick, in the State of New Jersey, By Order of His Excellency Gen. Washington, Commander-in-Chief of the Army of the United States of America, for the Trial of Major-General Lee, July 4th, 1778* (New York: J.M. Bradstreet & Son, 1864), p.137.

2 Papas, *Renegade Revolutionary*, p.46.

3 LVA: Revolutionary War Bounty Land Claims, Zachariah Pigman and Zachariah DeLong.

4 WHS: Draper Mss., L, vol.1, p.42.

5 Elizabeth Paschal O'Connor (Mrs. T.P. O'Connor), *My Beloved South* (New York: G. P. Putnam's Sons, 1913), pp.100–101.

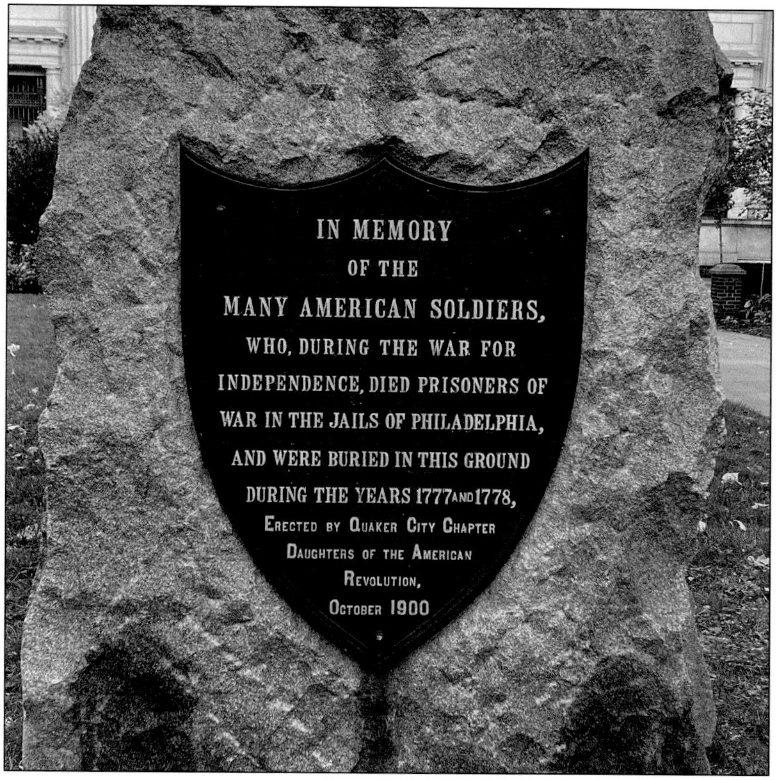

Between 2,000 and 3,000 Revolutionary War soldiers are buried in Philadelphia's Washington Square. (Author's photo)

The British withdrawal to New York created opportunities for some prisoners to escape. Lieutenant Christopher Moyer and Ensign Philip Huffman got away on 1 June and appeared at Valley Forge in time to be counted six days later. They were put in George Slaughter's old company, commanded by Isaac Israel, who was now a captain.[6] Drummer Meshack Pearson, the triplet from Culpeper, escaped and 'continued in the Army, as a Waggoner, until after the capture of Cornwallis.'[7] Captain Kirkpatrick, meanwhile, took command of Darke's and Westfall's remnants, now combined into one company. Lieutenant James Berwick remained from Westfall's Company, and Thomas ('Tommy') Miller came from Darke's Company as ensign.[8] With Knox's Company long gone, this brought the regiment down to eight companies, a Continental Army standard Virginia had not previously complied with.[9]

The British completed their evacuation of Philadelphia on 18 June. Prisoners and Loyalists were taken to New York by ship. There, Darke and other officers were held at various places around New Utrecht on Long Island with limited paroles. John Clark was housed at the home of prosperous but elderly Colonel Nicholas Stillwell near the village of Gravesend. 'I am in a very agreeable family and Neighborhood,' he wrote. 'Likewise am in hopes to

6 NARA: M246, f.217, p.28.
7 NARA: M804, f.208, p.43; M. Pearson pension.
8 NARA: M246, f.215, pp.2, 5, 8.
9 Ford (ed.), *Journals of Congress*, vol.3, p.322; Wright, *Continental Army*, pp.46, 70, 108, 142.

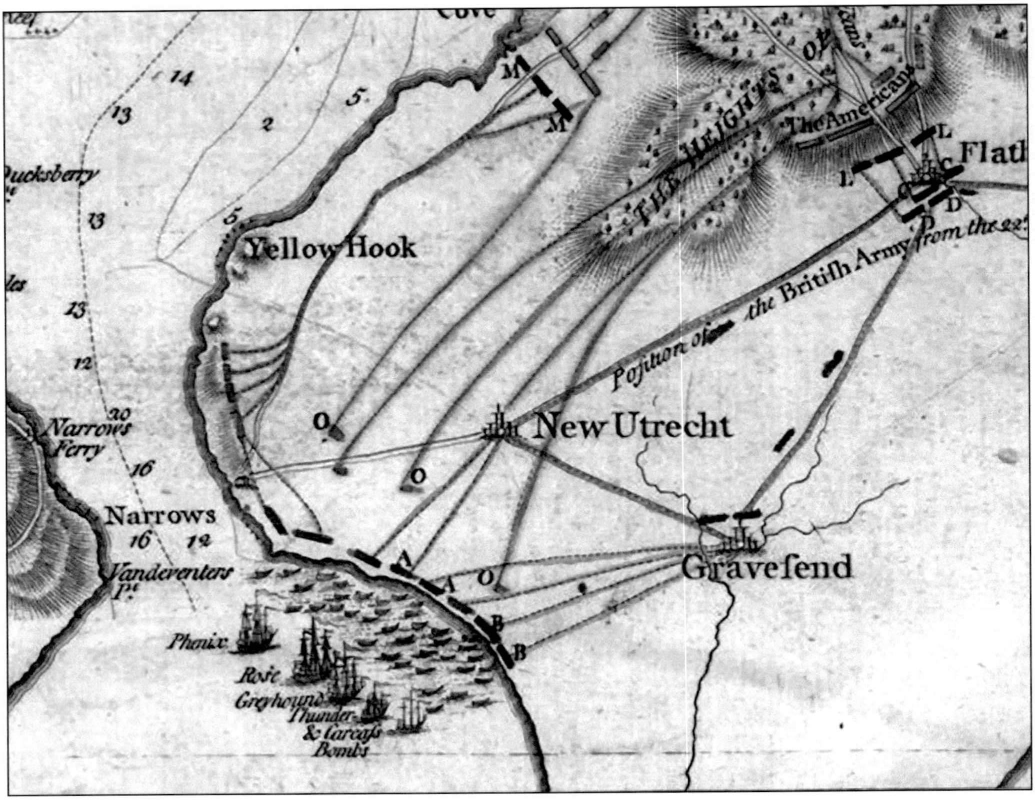

A British map of the Battle of Long Island shows the locations of Gravesend and New Utrecht south of Brooklyn near the western tip of the island. (Library of Congress)

enjoy myself very happily among them, my health is considerably recovered.' Predictably, he asked again for money. 'Hard money is an article I shall be in great want of here on account of paying my Board. I am in hopes if there [is] any to be got you will supply me by the first opportunity, as for cloaths I have a sufficiency at present.'[10]

For the enlisted prisoners, conditions only got worse. In Lafayette's account, 'The prisoners were crowded together in a ship at New York, where they had to breathe foul air and suffered everything that the grossest insolence could add to starvation, filth, disease, and complete neglect … As each victim succumbed to such treatment, the other Americans were told, "Good, there is one less rebel."' When a prisoner swap was negotiated in August, it was learned that 'Five hundred Americans, half dead, had been brought ashore. Most of them died there, and General Washington quite naturally refused to count them in the exchange.'[11] How many 8th Virginia men died this way cannot be discerned, but John Chenoweth was among the survivors. He said he returned home with 'my health so much

10 WHS: Draper Mss., L, vol.1, p.46.
11 Idzerda (ed.), *Lafayette Papers*, vol.2, p.9.

impard that there ware no hissetation in quiting me from mustering & all millyteary service till a little time before cornwallace was taken.'[12]

Except for Loyalists, who were regarded as traitors, prisoners in American hands were generally treated better. There were no prison ships, and many German Auxiliaries opted to remain in America after the war.

The 4th-8th-12th Virginia Regiment

At Valley Forge, a 31 May head count recorded that the 8th Virginia had just 98 out of its 188 men present and fit for duty. More than half of those present were officers, sergeants, musicians, and staff. The 45 private soldiers present were too few to fill out even one company. Another 52 were 'on command' performing separate services, but their return would not have gotten Colonel Bowman to two full companies. The 'poor old 8th reduced Reg't,' as it was called in a letter, had too many officers and too few enlisted men.[13]

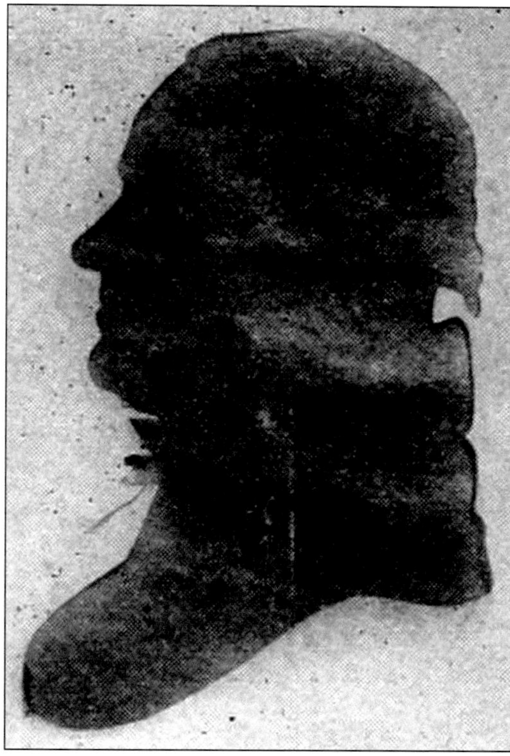

Silhouette of Lieutenant Colonel John Neville, from *Memoirs of Allegheny County Pennsylvania* (Madison: Northwest Historical Association, 1904)

The other regiments in Scott's Brigade were also understrength. The 4th Virginia's colonel had resigned, its lieutenant colonel had died, and it could only field 72 of its 181 men, officers included. The newer 12th Virginia was in somewhat better shape. Major Slaughter had resigned in December, but Colonel James Wood and Lieutenant Colonel John Neville were both present and leading 275 men out of a paper strength of 442. Colonel William Grayson was the lone field officer in his 'Additional' Continental regiment, mustering 106 of 202 men. Lieutenant Colonel John Parke of Patton's Additional Continental Regiment had 83 of 143 of his men in camp.[14]

12 NARA: J. Chenoweth pension.

13 George H. Farrier (ed.), *Memorial of the Centennial Celebration of the Battle of Paulus Hook* (Jersey City: M. Mullone, 1879), p.86; Lesser (ed.), *Sinews*, p.68.

14 NARA: M246, f.106, pp.12–19, f.119, p.18, f.145, p.21, f.298, p.27; Lesser (ed.), *Sinews*, p.68.

The 4th-8th-12th Virginia Regiment, June 1778[15]

Field Officers: Col. James Wood Lt. Col. John Neville *Maj. Jonathan Clark*		**Staff Officers:** Adj. William Kelly* Adj. Henry Bowyer Surg. William McMachen *Surg. Cornelius Baldwin* Surg. Stephen Ranny* Surg. Mate Charles Grier Surg. Mate Hugh Martin Paymstr. Benjamin Lawson *Paymstr. Hezekiah Stoakes* Paymstr. William Baylis Qtr. Master Nathaniel Lucas* *Qtr. Master Martin Carney* Qtr. Master Achilles Foster		**Warrant Officers:** Qtr. Mst. Sgt. John Watkins Qtr. Mst. Sgt. Sgt. Thomas Sewell Sgt. Major Richard Morgan *Sgt. Major John Harding** Sgt. Major Vincent Tapp* Drum Maj. Alexander Wilson *Drum Maj. Nicholas Neal* Drum Maj. William Coventry *Fife Maj. William Lipscomb* Drill Sgt. Thomas Creed	
Company	**Captain**	**1st Lieutenant**	**2nd Lieutenant**	**Ensign**	**Enlisted Men**
Colonel's		Robert Gamble†*	*Philip Eastin*		45/80 present
Lt. Colonel's		William Rogers	James Holloway		49/79 present
Major's		Presley Neville‡	William Porter		44/78 present
Croghan's	*William Croghan*	*James Higgins*		*Peter Higgins*	36/81 present
Waggener's	Andrew Waggener	Abraham Hite	Albert Russell		28/77 present
Walls'	George Walls	Nathaniel Lucas§	William O'Callis		31/81 present
Bowyer's	Michael Bowyer	Joseph Swearingen*	John McDowell		51/80 present
Kirkpatrick's	*Abraham Kirkpatrick*	*James Curry*	*Robert Breckenridge*		37/77 present
Stith's	John Stith	William Boyce	James Morton		28/77 present

8th Virginia officers in italics. Rogers, Walls, and Stith from 4th Va. Wood, John Neville and Presley Neville, Gamble, Bowyer, and Waggener from 12th Va. 349/710 enlisted men present. 361 absent. *Sick, absent or transferred during period. †Captain-lieutenant. ‡Aide de camp to Lafayette. §Quartermaster.

A formal consolidation was deferred, but the 4th, 8th, and 12th Virginia regiments were united into one unit under Colonel Wood. Jonathan Clark was elevated to major and third in command after Lieutenant Colonel Neville. The 8th Virginia's private soldiers were put into two companies commanded by William Croghan and Abraham Kirkpatrick. David Stephenson was promoted to major and moved to the 5th Virginia.[16] Otherwise, the consolidation left several 8th Virginia officers 'supernumerary,' including Colonel Bowman.[17] Unlike most of the extra officers, however, Bowman was senior to many others of his rank. He was, however, junior to Colonel Wood. He remained in service for the time being, but

15 NARA: M246, f.122, pp.2, 5, 8, 11; f. 123, p.2; f.124, pp.2–3; f.125, p.3; f.126, p.3; f.127, p.3; f.128, p.3; f.129, pp.2–3; f.130, pp.2–3; f.131, pp.2–3)

16 Sanchez-Saavedra, *Virginia Military Organisations*, p.45.

17 NARA: M246, f.364, p.6.

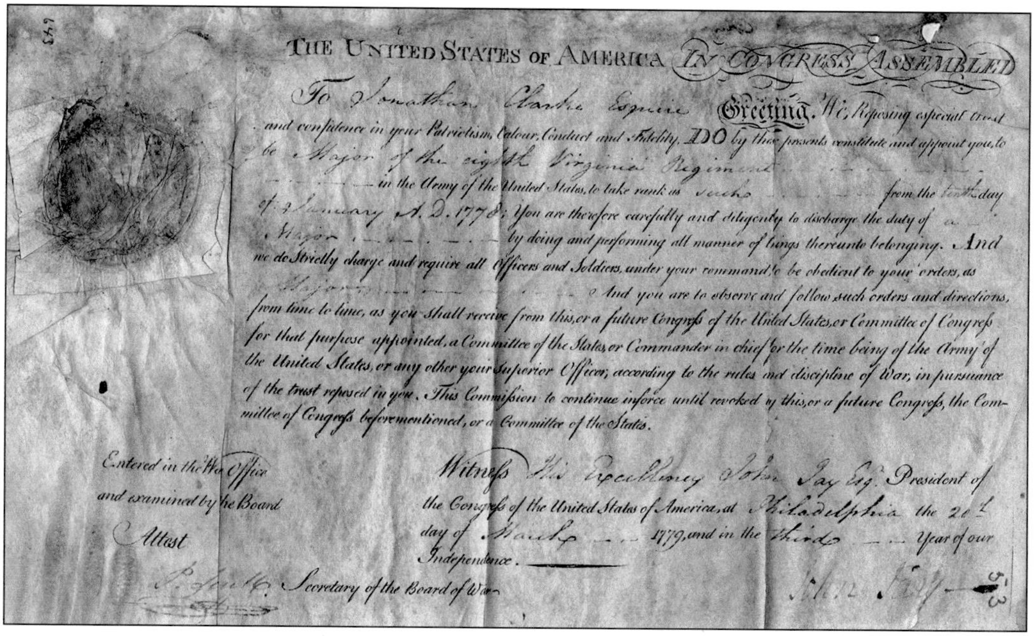

The United States of America In Congress Assembled

To Jonathan Clarke Esquire Greeting. We, reposing especial trust and confidence in your Patriotism, Valour, Conduct and Fidelity, DO by these presents constitute and appoint you, to be Major of the eighth Virginia Regiment in the Army of the United States, to take rank as such from the tenth day of January A.D. 1778. You are therefore carefully and diligently to discharge the duty of a Major by doing and performing all manner of things thereunto belonging. And we do strictly charge and require all Officers and Soldiers, under your command, to be obedient to your orders, as Major. And you are to observe and follow such orders and directions, from time to time, as you shall receive from this, or a future Congress of the United States, or Committee of Congress for that purpose appointed, a Committee of the States, or Commander in chief for the time being of the Army of the United States, or any other your superior Officer, according to the rules and discipline of War, in pursuance of the trust reposed in you. This Commission to continue in force until revoked by this, or a future Congress, the Committee of Congress beforementioned, or a Committee of the States.

Entered in the War Office and examined by the Board

Attest

[illegible] Secretary of the Board of War

Witness His Excellency John Jay Esq. President of the Congress of the United States of America, at Philadelphia the 20th day of March 1779, and in the third Year of our Independence.

John Jay

President of Congress John Jay signed this commission on 20 March 1779, more than a year after Jonathan Clark's promotion to major and even longer after its retroactive effective date. (Draper Manuscripts Collection, Wisconsin Historical Society)

without a command. Duplicate staff and warrant officers were carried on the rolls for the time being, but most supernumerary commissioned officers went home.

Three of Washington's five divisions were now under the command of men with European titles: William Alexander, Earl of Stirling;[18] Gilbert du Motier, Marquis de La Fayette; and Johann von Robais, Baron de Kalb, who was sick and absent. Though the son of a soldier, Charles Lee had rubbed elbows with monarchs. Anthony Wayne had no such status and was the only brigadier general of the five. He was technically filling in for Major General Benjamin Lincoln. The North Carolina brigade was added to Lafayette's Division. Its previous commander, Brigadier General Lachlan McIntosh, was familiar to the 8th Virginia's veterans of Sunbury. In May, however, he was given command of the Western Department and left for Pittsburgh, taking Major Richard Campbell and the homesick men of the 8th Pennsylvania and the 13th Virginia regiments with him.[19] On 6 June 1778 Lafayette's Division consisted of:

Woodford's Brigade

3rd-7th Virginia Regiment, Lieutenant Colonel Holt Richardson
11th-15th Virginia Regiment, Lieutenant Colonel John Cropper
(50 officers, 17 staff, 838 enlisted present)

18 Alexander's claim this previously lapsed title was recognized in Edinburgh but not in London (Nelson, *Lord Stirling*, p.36–40).

19 Chase et al (eds), Papers of Washington (Revolution), vol.15, pp.108–110, 204–205, 372–373, 424–427.

Scott's Brigade
4th-8th-12th Virginia Regiment, Colonel James Wood
Grayson's Additional Regiment, Colonel William Grayson
Patton's Additional Regiment, Lieutenant Colonel John Parke
(60 officers, 16 staff, 982 enlisted present)

North Carolina Brigade
1st North Carolina Regiment, Colonel Thomas Clark
2nd North Carolina Regiment, Colonel John Patten
(78 officers, 19 staff, 1,078 enlisted present)[20]

Chasing the British Army

The Continentals were quick to march in June when confirmation came that the British had left Philadelphia.[21] Augusta County draftee James Blaine was now in Captain Croghan's consolidated company. He remembered that 'from Valley Forge we marched with the Army in pursuit of the British, through New Jersey.'[22] Major Clark recalled that they crossed the Schuylkill on the 19th and the Delaware on the 21st. They crossed at Coryell's Ferry,[23] about 50 river miles above where the Crown forces had crossed from Philadelphia four days earlier.

Colonel Bowman 'started on' with the army into New Jersey but 'was taken with the fever & ague & was detained in Trenton New Jersey several weeks.'[24] 'Indisposition' was a common excuse in those days, but this third-party account sounds like an episode of resurgent malaria. This could explain Bowman's absence from the Battle of Germantown as well. Colonel Wood, ironically, had reported being in an 'Extreme ill state of Health' three months earlier.[25] He, too, was evidently absent, leaving Lieutenant Colonel Neville in charge of the 4th-8th-12th Regiment.[26] Shenandoah County draftee Henry Aleshite remembered that the regiments were 'put together and then commanded by Col. John Nevill, in Gen Scott's Brigade Va. Line. From Valley Forge we marched in pursuit of the British into the Jerseys.'[27]

The American generals debated the wisdom of an attack, but Washington was intent on precipitating an engagement. General Henry Clinton, who had taken over from William Howe on the British side, was travelling northeasterly across New Jersey on the King's Highway.[28] The Continentals were above him longitudinally but on an intersecting route.

20 The North Carolina Brigade Commanded by Colonel Thomas Clark. NARA: M246, f.14, pp.59–60.
21 FHS: Clark Diary, 8–18 June 1778.
22 NARA: P. Van Pelt pension.
23 FHS: Clark Diary, 19–21 June 1778.
24 NARA: W. Pollard pension.
25 Chase et al (eds), *Papers of Washington* (Revolution), vol.15, pp.182–183.
26 NARA: M246, f.131, p.2; f.298, pp.15.
27 NARA: M804, S29579, Henry Aleshite pension.
28 Locally known by various names at the time, since 1798 as Monmouth Road, and now also as a section of County Route 537. Anon., 'History of the Burlington Path,' <twp.freehold.nj.us/398/History-of-the-Burlington-Path>, accessed 18 Feb. 2024.

William Maxwell's New Jersey brigade had been sent ahead in May to harass and slow the British, and additional forces were now sent forward to support him.

Orders of battle become complicated in the second half of the Revolution for two reasons. First, because Congress declined to appoint lieutenant generals, Washington routinely assigned three major generals to command a left wing, a right wing, and a reserve or 'second line' on the battlefield. The down-command effects of this were evident at Germantown: Greene was elevated to command the Continentals' left wing, Muhlenberg was pulled from his brigade to command Greene's Division, Colonel Russell was taken from his regiment to command Muhlenberg's Brigade, and Major Campbell commanded the 13th Virginia in Russell's stead. The second source of confusion is the expanded practice of detaching picked men for specific operations. Troop detachments were nothing new: 8th Virginia men had previously been sent off for weeks or months under Croghan, Morgan, Maxwell, and others. In the main battle of 1778, however, large numbers of men were pulled from their companies to serve for just a few days in ad hoc detachments.

Morgan's Rifles were sent to support Maxwell. Captain Knox still commanded his rifle company with lieutenants Craig and Lovely, but only two other 8th Virginia veterans remained: William Courtney and Osborne Flynn.[29] Washington more than offset such attrition by ordering each of the army's brigades 'to furnish an active, spirited Officer and twenty five of it's best marksmen' to bolster Morgan's corps.[30] Who was chosen from the 4th-8th-12th is not known, but the 8th and the 12th were good sources for sharpshooters. Washington also lent Morgan most of his Life Guard, possibly including Michael Tullis and Robert Wadsworth, formerly of Darke's and Westfall's companies.[31] Thus bolstered, the Provisional Rifle Corps headed south to coordinate with Maxwell. Morgan operated on the far side of the British columns, making communication difficult.[32]

The American generals continued to disagree about the wisdom of an offensive move. Lee believed it would be 'to the last degree criminal' to attack a better-trained force when the new French alliance had already forced Clinton to scale back British operations.[33] Washington, thinking of Congress's expectations, public opinion, and the morale of his men, was determined to attack. He did not, however, intend to risk a catastrophic loss. He planned to hold back most of the army unless there was a meaningful opportunity for a victory. To that end, Charles Scott was pulled from command of his brigade and sent off with another detachment of 1,500 'picked men.'[34] Captain Croghan went with him.[35] So did Sergeant Anjer Price, who had reenlisted after two years in Richard Campbell's Company.[36] Draftee William George was taken from Captain Kirkpatrick's Company. He recalled that

29 NARA: M246, f.26, pp.91, 93, 101, 103.

30 Chase et al (eds), *Papers of Washington* (Revolution), vol.15, pp.492–495.

31 NARA: M. Tullis pension; R. Wadsworth pension.

32 Chase et al (eds), *Papers of Washington* (Revolution), vol.15, pp.518, 522–523.

33 Chase et al (eds), *Papers of Washington* (Revolution), vol.15, pp.457–458; Anon. (ed.), *Court Martial of Charles Lee*, p.95; Mark Edward Lender and Garry Wheeler Stone, *Fatal Sunday: George Washington, the Monmouth Campaign, and the Politics of Battle* (Norman: University of Oklahoma Press, 2016), pp.173.

34 Lender and Stone, *Fatal Sunday*, p.452.

35 Anon. (ed.), *Court Martial of Charles Lee*, pp.38–39.

36 NARA: Anjer Price pension.

Colonel William Grayson. (Library of Congress)

a certain number were 'taken from each company of our regiment' and 'placed under the command of Gen'l. Scott, as light infantry, for the purpose of pursuing the British, who were then marching toward Sandy Hook.'[37] William Grayson, the senior colonel present, took temporary command of Scott's Brigade. He was mostly left with the greenest and least capable men, but retained a few veterans like Bean Smallwood.

When Washington decided to send off yet another detachment of 1,000 men under Anthony Wayne, a major general was needed to coordinate forward operations. Lee passed on the command, assessing that the scale of the harassing manoeuvres was not large enough to require the army's second-most-senior officer. Lafayette, however, was quick to accept and 'in raptures' over the opportunity.[38] Overeager, the 20-year-old Frenchman pushed the advanced forces unreasonably hard under a hot sun for two days and took them too far from support. Washington pulled him back and ordered him to rendezvous at Englishtown with Lee, who brought two more brigades and took command.

Washington rode forward to Englishtown to meet with Lee. Maxwell, Scott, and Wayne attended as well and understood that Washington wanted Lee to attack. How much discretion Lee was left with later became a point of contention.[39] Lee voiced no objection to the plan during the council.[40] Still, he worried about command and control, noting later that the regiments had 'no uniforms or distinguishing colors [flags]' and conceded that he was 'unhappily almost an utter stranger to the names and faces of the commanding officers of the respective corps.'[41] He knew almost nothing of the terrain ahead and had nothing close to real-time intelligence on the British army's movements. An attempt to get information from locals was fruitless. 'The people here are inconceivably stupid,' Lee complained in an update to Washington. 'I have sent two lively young footmen (for they have no horses) to reconnoitre.'[42]

37 NARA: M804, S3390, William George pension. (Pension shows signs of memory loss.)
38 Chase et al (eds), *Papers of Washington* (Revolution), vol.15, p.536.
39 Anon. (ed.), *Court Martial of Charles Lee*, pp.7, 14.
40 Bunbury (ed.), *Lee Papers*, vol.2, p.430.
41 Anon. (ed.), *Court Martial of Charles Lee*, p.213.
42 Bunbury (ed.), *Lee Papers*, vol.2, p.426.

The Battle of Monmouth, 28 June 1778

Colonel Grayson led Scott's Brigade with the main body of the American army east on Cranbury Road. They funnelled across the bridge over the Manalapan River to Englishtown. From there, the road continued past Tennent's Presbyterian meeting house to the Monmouth County courthouse in Freehold Township.[43] The village was surrounded by farms, which enjoyed a belt of fertile soil that ran along the north edge of New Jersey's pine barrens.[44] Fields of golden, five-foot-tall stalks with heavy, drooping heads announced that the rye was ripe for harvest[45] The land east of Freehold was drained by a trio of creeks known then as Spotswood North Brook, Spotswood Middle Brook, and Spotswood South Brook. Each had associated tributaries, wetlands, and ravines.[46] Most of the area's land was cleared for farming, but woodlots and forest patches still covered substantial ground. It was at Freehold that the British route north on the King's Highway intersected with the American path east on the Cranbury Road. As William Pollard recalled, 'our Army & the enemy met at Monmouth Court house in New Jersey & had a sever battle.'[47]

The Route from Valley Forge to Monmouth

19 June: Depart Valley Forge
21 June: Coryell's Ferry
22 June: Across Delaware River
23 June: Hopewell, N.J.
25 June: Near Kingston, N.J.
26 June: Through Cranbury, N.J.
27 June: Englishtown, N.J.
28 June: Battle of Monmouth[48]
(Approximately 87 miles)

At 3:00 a.m. on 28 June, Grayson was roused to read new orders.[49] The commander in chief was worried that the King's army might march off before he could hit them. Lee ordered Grayson to get the brigade ready immediately. With the support of Brigadier General James Mitchell Varnum's New England brigade (under the command of Colonel John Durkee), Grayson was going to go and get the enemy's attention. The same orders went to Daniel Morgan, but the 1:00 a.m. letter's carelessly incorrect reference to 'tomorrow' caused Knox, Craig, and Lovely to miss the day's events entirely.[50]

The sun came up while Croghan's and Kirkpatrick's consolidated companies trotted into Englishtown. Grayson reported to Lee and was handed Washington's attack orders by

43 Lender and Stone, *Fatal Sunday*, p.201.
44 Anon. (ed.), *Court Martial of Charles Lee*, p.185; Lender and Stone, *Fatal Sunday*, p.204.
45 NARA: M804, S7687, William Taylor pension (7th Md.).
46 Now McGelliard's Brook, Weamaconk Creek, and Wemrock Brook. Spotswood is a small village downstream and to the northwest.
47 NARA: W. Pollard pension
48 FHS: Clark Diary; Baker, *Itinerary of Washington*, pp.132–135.
49 Anon. (ed.), *Court Martial of Charles Lee*, pp.40, 185; Lender and Stone, *Fatal Sunday*, p.194.
50 Anon. (ed.), *Court Martial of Charles Lee*, p.138.

one of Lee's aides. The local guides Grayson needed had disappeared, so Lee sent his aide de camp, Captain Evan Edwards, to go bang on doors and find new ones. The delay was finally resolved when a militia general offered to provide men for the job.[51] It was 6:00 a.m. when Grayson's brigade marched toward the British position at the courthouse. The sun rose higher, and the remaining men of the 8th Virginia could tell that it was going to be another very warm day. They left their packs, blankets, and uniform coats behind.[52] They were joined by gunners with four cannons, and a few light horsemen led the way.[53]

Lee's intentions may have changed over the course of the morning, but Grayson's ultimate orders were to find and 'lie very near the enemy as a party of observation, in case of their moving off to give the earliest intelligence of it, and to skirmish with them so as to produce some delay, and give time for the rest of the troops to come up.'[54] This was a dangerous assignment, made more so by the fact that Morgan's Rifles would not be helping. While Lee was following with the rest of the 'advanced guard' (Maxwell and the picked detachments under Scott and Wayne), Washington and the bulk of the American forces were still all the way back at Manalapan Bridge.[55]

Who commanded the 4th-8th-12th Regiment at Monmouth is not clear, but the evidence that exists suggests it was Jonathan Clark. Colonel Wood is unmentioned in the records. Veterans consistently mention Lieutenant Colonel Neville as leading during this period but apparently never in specific reference to Monmouth. Major Clark was there, among the forward troops, and probably in command.[56] Captain Croghan was next in seniority, but he was leading men in Scott's detachment.[57]

Grayson's 'party of observation' moved forward as the sun climbed high into the sky. One Virginian remembered it as 'the hottest day he has ever been in.'[58] When they approached Spotswood Middle Brook, several groups of New Jersey militia rushed past them, going the other way. The retreating men were convinced that 'the main body of the enemy' was coming after them. One of Lee's aides de camp told Grayson to halt despite his orders. The sound of musket fire confirmed that some British soldiers were close.[59] Brigadier General Philemon Dickinson of the militia insisted that if they crossed the causeway and bridge over the 'West Morass' (Spotswood Middle Brook), the British would come down a parallel road and flank them. Still, he asked Major Clark and the 4th-8th-12th to run across the bridge and cover the militia retreat, which they did.[60]

Lee was sceptical when he received Dickinson's report but nevertheless halted the line, sent Wayne to take command at the head of the column, and rode forward to look for

51 Anon. (ed.), *Court Martial of Charles Lee*, pp.40, 118, 185.
52 Anon. (ed.), *Court Martial of Charles Lee*, p.10; Lender and Stone, *Fatal Sunday*, p.198.
53 Anon. (ed.), *Court Martial of Charles Lee*, p.150, 164.
54 Anon. (ed.), *Court Martial of Charles Lee*, p.12. Grayson was given various orders to start, stop, and proceed carefully, but this order describes his mission.
55 Anon. (ed.), *Court Martial of Charles Lee*, p.186; Lender and Stone, *Fatal Sunday*, pp.233–234.
56 FHS: Clark Diary, 28 June 1778.
57 Anon. (ed.), *Court Martial of Charles Lee*, pp.38–39.
58 NARA: M804, S1651, John Chambers pension (14th Va.).
59 Anon. (ed.), *Court Martial of Charles Lee*, p.41, 186.
60 Anon. (ed.), *Court Martial of Charles Lee*, pp. 22, 41, 151, 161, 186; Lender and Stone, *Fatal Sunday*, pp.241–249.

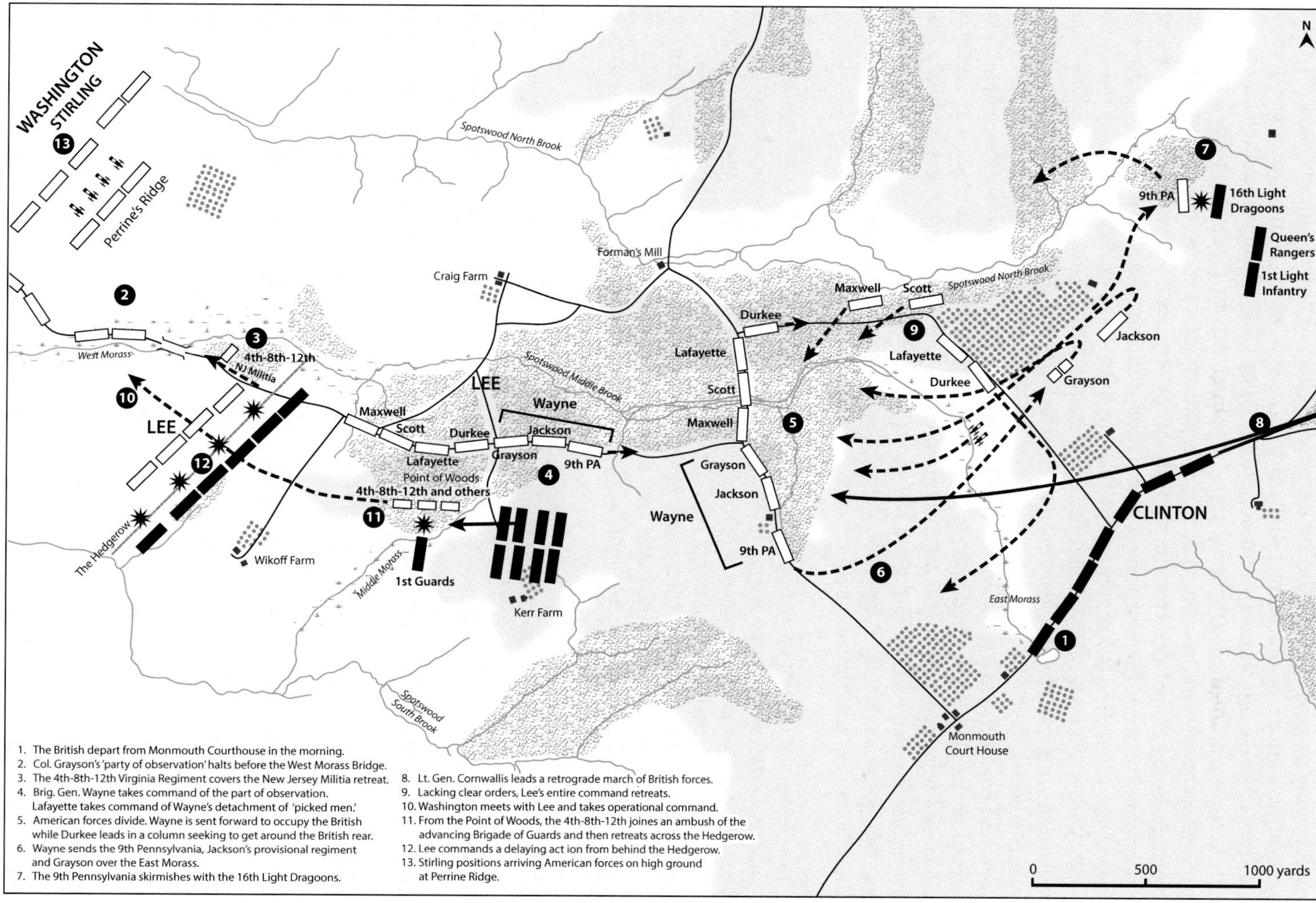

The Battle of Monmouth, 28 June 1778.

himself. Seeing no evidence that the British were coming, he ordered the entire 4,500-man advanced guard to proceed. Colonel Richard Butler's 9th Pennsylvania Regiment (pulled from Scott's picked detachment) went first, followed by Colonel Henry Jackson's consolidated 'detachment' of three understrength New England regiments, Grayson's (Scott's) brigade, Durkee's (Varnum's) brigade, Wayne's picked detachment (now commanded by Lafayette), Scott's picked detachment, and Maxwell's Brigade.[61] They marched to a point about half a mile from the courthouse and halted. Reconnaissance spotted the Queen's Rangers, but when the artillery started detaching guns from limbers, Lee ordered them to wait. Rather than show too much force, he directed Wayne to take his skirmishers forward and simply keep the enemy occupied while Durkee led an effort to get around the Loyalists' left.[62]

Scott and Maxwell were positioned to support an encirclement, but neither general was informed of the plan.[63] They had been told to keep to the trees and out of sight as much as possible and were consequently hard to find when they were needed. Fighting broke out between Butler's men and the 16th Light Dragoons past the 'East Morass' north of the courthouse. The gentle nudge Lee hoped would keep the British forces in place was impossible to calibrate. Grayson reported soon after:

> I then saw the enemy drawn up in order of battle, in much greater numbers than before, and they cannonaded us from two or three pieces of cannon. I hallooed to Colonel Jackson to come and form upon the top of the hill upon my left, who asked me if I had any artillery, I told him I had not … I saw Colonel Jackson's regiment retreating, and [Lee's aide] Major Mercer told me to go off in the rear of Colonel Jackson's regiment the way I had come. We retreated or went back, recrossed the morass, where General Scott's detachment was halted in a wood, where we halted also.[64]

Grayson ducked back out of the woods to observe and saw the Crown forces approaching 'in force.' While Grayson was watching, a New Hampshire colonel in Scott's detachment sent 'Captain Croghan and … [Adjutant William] Kelly in pursuit of General Scott, to inform him that the enemy were coming down in two columns.' Scott promptly 'sent back Kelly and Croghan to order' the Yankee colonel 'to retreat by the left of battalions in columns.' When Grayson returned to the woods he found 'the whole of the troops that had retreated with me had marched.'[65] Things were beginning to fall apart.

Lee moved Lafayette's detachment to protect his right. This, combined with Jackson's tactical retreat, looked to the other detachments like an ordered withdrawal. Major Mercer and Colonel Grayson had opposite understandings of where the 4th-8th-12th was

61 Anon. (ed.), *Court Martial of Charles Lee*, p.121.

62 Anon. (ed.), *Court Martial of Charles Lee*, pp.17, 22–23; Lender and Stone, *Fatal Sunday*, pp.254–256, 446.

63 Lender and Stone, *Fatal Sunday*, p.256.

64 Anon. (ed.), *Court Martial of Charles Lee*, p.44.

65 Anon. (ed.), *Court Martial of Charles Lee*, pp.38–39, 44.

supposed to be.[66] Scott and Maxwell did not know what they were supposed to do, and Lee did not even know where they were.[67] Consequently, the two generals had to decide what to do solely on the basis of what they could see.[68] Within minutes, Lee's entire 4,500-man advanced guard was retreating, and the general was looking for somewhere in the rear to make a stand.[69]

Lee failed to maintain command and control and then failed to advise Washington of the withdrawal. When the commander-in-chief arrived on the field, he was 'exceedingly alarmed, finding the advance corps falling back upon the main body, without the least notice given to him.' Among the first men Washington encountered were Patton's and Grayson's 'additional' regiments, under the command of Lieutenant Colonel Parke. The commander in chief ordered the thoroughly exhausted and dangerously dehydrated men into the shade.[70] Clark's 4th-8th-12th men followed closely behind and then Major General Lee rode up to speak to Washington.

There are several accounts of what was said, but Lieutenant Curry, who was now in Kirkpatrick's Company, said he heard the exchange himself. He related many times at his postwar Ohio home that Washington demanded an explanation for the retreat. 'Sir,' he asked, 'what means this disorderly retreat?'

Lee responded by insulting the Continental Army. 'Sir, your raw militia cannot cope with the British regulars.'

'You have not tried them,' Washington replied as he turned his horse around. 'Will you command?'

'Yes,' Lee replied, clinging to his honour, 'and I will not be the first to leave the field.'[71] Satisfied for the moment, Washington rode off to restore order.

To his credit, Lee had already identified the stronger ground that Washington used to make a stand. But the Americans had to buy time.[72] Washington directed Clark's 4th-8th-12th and two other battalions into a 'point of woods' on the north side of the battlefield, roughly midway between the east and west morasses. Wayne was sent to command.[73] Between the point of woods and the West Morass, Durkee and others were positioned behind an overgrown fence that was called 'the hedgerow.'[74]

Behind the West Morass, Lord Stirling organised the bulk of the army on high ground known as Perrine Ridge. Nathanael Greene, meanwhile, was leading Continental artillery on a long loop to high ground on the south side of the battlefield.[75] If the soldiers in the woods could hold their ground long enough and if the men at the hedgerow did the same, the Continental Army would be well-positioned to stand their ground against the Crown's forces and perhaps even prevail.

---

66 Anon. (ed.), *Court Martial of Charles Lee*, p.43
67 Anon. (ed.), *Court Martial of Charles Lee*, p.141; Lender and Stone, *Fatal Sunday*, pp.256, 263, 265, 269
68 Lender and Stone, *Fatal Sunday*, p.266.
69 Anon. (ed.), *Court Martial of Charles Lee*, pp.189–190.
70 Anon. (ed.), *Court Martial of Charles Lee*, pp.71, 73, 74, 83–84, 92.
71 Durant, *Union County*, p.297.
72 Lender and Stone, *Fatal Sunday*, p.291.
73 Anon. (ed.), *Court Martial of Charles Lee*, pp.86–87; Lender and Stone, *Fatal Sunday*, pp.292, 448.
74 Lender and Stone, *Fatal Sunday*, pp.206–208; Anon. (ed.), *Court Martial of Charles Lee*, pp.68, 129.
75 Lender and Stone, *Fatal Sunday*, pp.297, 333.

The Point of Woods

With 'Mad Anthony' Wayne in command, the last men of the 8th Virginia hurriedly formed in the woods while cannons roared and small arms popped. They positioned themselves as Curry and others had done at Point Pleasant in 1774, standing behind trees and crouching behind bushes.[76] Within minutes, the elite British Guards came across the field in a line with their right flank facing the woods. Black powder smoke obscured the field but cleared at the right moment. The Patriot skirmishers hurled a cloud of lead balls at the marching men.[77] It was a nearly perfect enfilade, and dozens of Redcoats fell to the ground. Enraged, the rest of the Guards turned and charged. A desperate melee ensued.[78] British cavalry rode in, adding the slashing of sabres to the thrusting of bayonets. Overwhelmed, Wayne's attackers fled through a hay field toward the hedgerow.[79]

Virginia accounts of this fight are virtually non-existent. Bean Smallwood was wounded twice, most seriously in his left thigh. A 12th Virginia man called it 'a sore engagement.'[80] Another participant described a terrifying chase in which anyone too brave or too slow was cut down. 'Damn the rebel!' British soldiers called to each other. 'Why don't you kill

Anthony Wayne, ca. 1782. (Library of Congress)

The site of the melee in the point of woods. The tree line has been straightened and the 'point' removed. (Photo: William R. Griffith IV)

76 Lender and Stone, *Fatal Sunday*, p.300; Williams, *Dunmore's War*, pp.284–290.

77 Emory Washburn, *Historical Sketches of the Town of Leicester, Massachusetts, During the First Century from its Settlement* (Boston: John Wilson and Son, 1860), p.260; Lender and Stone, *Fatal Sunday*, p.292.

78 Anon. (ed.), *Court Martial of Charles Lee*, p.130.

79 Washburn, *Historical Sketches*, pp.260–261.

80 NARA: M804, R8738, Bean Smallwood pension, R2869, Andrew Demoss pension (12th Va.).

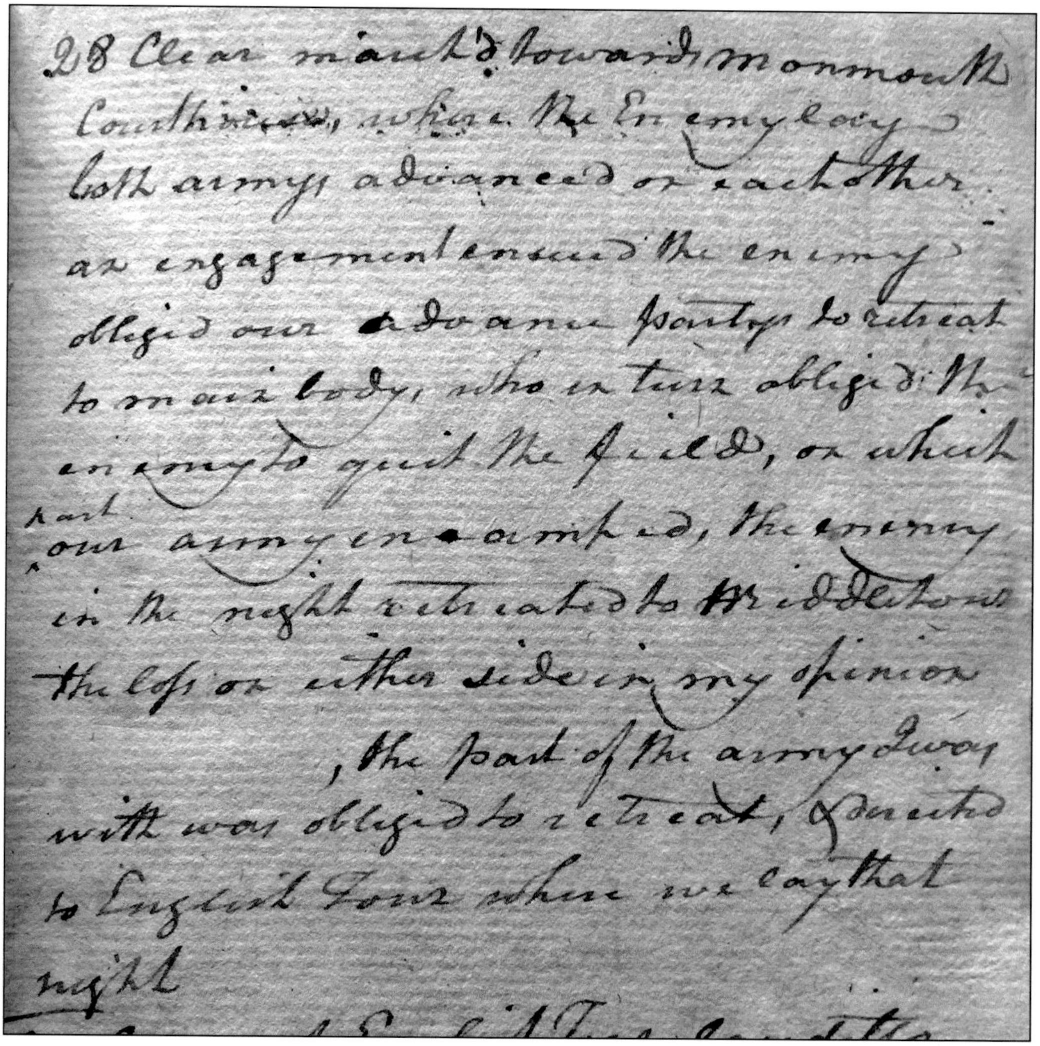
28 Clear march'd towards Monmouth Courthouse, where the Enemy lay both armys advanced on each other an engagement ensued the enemy obliged our advance partys to retreat to main body, who in turn obliged the enemy to quit the field, on which part our army encamped, the enemy in the night retreated to Middletown the loss on either side in my opinion

, the part of the army I was with was obliged to retreat, & directed to English Town where we lay that night

Major Clark's brief diary account of the Battle of Monmouth. (The Filson Historical Society, Louisville, KY)

him?'[81] When Clark's men got over the hedgerow to Perrine Ridge, a sharp contest developed across the overgrown fence. It took a while for the British to break through, and when they did, Stirling was ready. His men on the ridge hammered the advancing forces with cannon fire. The British pulled back and responded with their own guns, beginning an artillery duel that lasted for two hours.[82] Then, finally in position, Nathanael Greene's cannons opened an enfilading fire from Comb's Hill, forcing Henry Clinton's army to retreat. American skirmishers pursued them, but the sun set, and combat ceased.

81 Washburn, *Historical Sketches*, p.261.
82 Lender and Stone, *Fatal Sunday*, pp.315, 318–320.

Major Clark's account of the battle was characteristically brief: 'both armys advanc'd on each other, an engagement ensued, the enemy obliged our advance partys to retreat to main body, who in turn obliged the enemy to quit the field.' Like most American accounts, however, he noted that many of the Americans slept on the battlefield that night.[83] William George, one of Scott's picked men from Kirkpatrick's Company, dispassionately recalled:

> We were ordered by Gen'l. Lee to retreat, at the commencement of the battle in order [to] gain more advantageous ground. We retreated (I think about half a mile) then halted and fought for some time – at length both sides withdrew. We lay on our arms all night, expecting to have another battle on the next morning, but when morning came the British were all gone.[84]

Clinton never intended to remain at Monmouth, but holding the field was a recognized definition of victory, and the Continentals were ecstatic. Another of Scott's soldiers from that day boasted 'that he well remembers they gained the victory, and kept the ground, and that night they lay on the field of battle.'[85] Not everyone slept there. Major Clark's worn-out men saw no more fighting after the point of woods and were 'directed to English Town where we lay that night.'[86]

In 1837, Agnes Van Pelt remembered that her husband 'was not immediately engaged in the battle himself, he having been appointed one of the guard for the baggage wagons on that day.' Though miles in the rear, Peter 'was within hearing of the whole engagement.' Another draftee, William Clark, was among the sick 70 miles away at Valley Forge. He could hear the battle too.[87]

There was a brief pursuit in the morning. 'We followed them part of the way to Sandy hook,' said one of Kirkpatrick's men, 'but finding that we could not overtake them returned to Monmouth, buried our dead and remained there several days.'[88] The short-term detachments were dissolved and their men returned to their companies. There was work to do. The aftermath of the battle was made especially horrid by the summer heat. Black and bloated bodies littered the area. 'The stench from the woods was intolerable,' said one officer, 'they being filled with dead men and horses.'[89]

The Route from Monmouth to White Plains

1 July: Depart Monmouth to Spottswood, N.J.
2–6 July: Brunswick, N.J.
6 July: Quibbletown, N.J.
7 July: Springfield, N.J.
9 July: Acquackanonk Twp, N.J.

83 FHS: Clark Diary, 28 June 1778. Edited for clarity.
84 NARA: W. George pension.
85 NARA: A. Demoss pension.
86 FHS: Clark Diary, 28 June 1778.
87 NARA: P. Van Pelt pension, W. Clark pension.
88 NARA: W. George pension.
89 Anon (ed.), 'The Papers of General Samuel Smith,' *The Historical Magazine*, 7:2 (1870), pp.81–92, 92.

11 July: Paramus, N.J.
14 July: Kakeate, N.Y.
15 July: King's Ferry, N.Y.
17 July: Across Hudson River to Peekskill, N.Y.
18 July: Croton River
20 July: North Castle, N.Y.
24 July: White Plains, N.Y.[90]
(Approximately 137 miles)

A pencil caricature of Charles Lee titled 'Suspended General' drawn by Colonel Tadeusz Kościuszko after the general's conviction. Several sources confirm that Lee had a large nose. ('Caricature of General Lee,' Thaddeus Kosciuszko, Richard Peters Papers, #0498, Historical Society of Pennsylvania)

On 1 July, Clark and his men left Englishtown, marched 10 miles, and camped at the village of Spotswood.[91] Officers were selected there to form a court to try Major General Lee for failure to attack as directed, misbehaviour on the battlefield, and disrespecting the commander-in-chief. The court met off and on for weeks. Lee's culpability on the first two points is still debated, but his words after the battle left him unquestionably guilty of the third, and he was convicted of all three. He was suspended for a year and never returned to service.[92]

From Spotswood, James Blaine remembered they continued 'to Brunswick under the same Officers and from thence to Kings Ferry, and then to White Plains in York State, where we were stationed about two months.'[93] At White Plains in September, Virginia's senior officers congregated in William Woodford's quarters and worked out a plan to reduce the Commonwealth's 15 regiments to 11.[94] After two and a half years of tough service, the old 8th Virginia was folded into the 4th Virginia and the larger 12th Virginia was given its number. Several officers were let go. Supernumerary status was determined by seniority within a rank, so just-promoted officers like Major James Knox, Captains James Craig and James Higgins, and 1st Lieutenant Benjamin Kinley were all dismissed.[95]

90 FHS: Clark Diary; Baker, *Itinerary of Washington*, pp.135-139.
91 FHS: Clark Diary, 1 July 1778.
92 Anon. (ed.), *Court Martial of Charles Lee*, pp.113–116.
93 NARA: P. Van Pelt pension.
94 FHS: Clark Diary, 11 Sept. 1778.
95 LVA: Revolutionary War Bounty Land Claims, Austin Sandridge (2nd Va.); NARA: M246, f.364, pp.6, 79–93; Gwathmey, *Register*, p.448.

John Neville was promoted and took command of the 4th Virginia with William Croghan as his major. Major Clark went to the new 8th Virginia under Colonel Wood. With a nod to economy, each field officer now commanded a company, reducing the number of captains. The senior lieutenant of the colonel's company was known as a 'captain-lieutenant' and performed the duties of a captain. Other company officers took on staff roles. Captain Kirkpatrick, for instance, doubled as the Charles Scott's brigade major,[96] a job some 8th Virginia men remembered incorrectly as a rank promotion. Draftee William Clark later tried to explain, 'Captain KeelPatrick, KilPatrick, KirkPatrick or whatever his name was, was promoted to the office of Major but cannot recollect who was made Captain in his place.'[97] Five of the 4th Virginia's seven populated companies had veterans of the old 8th Virginia as officers: Captains Abraham Kirkpatrick and John Steed, Captain-Lieutenant Leonard Cooper, and Lieutenants James Curry and Christopher Moyer. Most, but not all, of the 8th Virginia's rank and file were put under Kirkpatrick and Steed. Captain Israel also belonged to the combined regiment, but he was absent with no actual command.[98]

The 4th Virginia Regiment, December 1778[99]

<table>
<tr><td colspan="2">Field Officers:
Col. John Neville
Lt. Col. Robert Ballard*
Maj. William Croghan</td><td colspan="2">Staff Officers:
Adj. William Kelly
Surg. William McMachen*
Surg. Mate Charles Greer
Paymstr. Benjamin Lawson
Qtr. Master Martin Carney*</td><td>Warrant Officers:
Qtr. Mst. Sgt. John Watkins
Sgt. Maj. John Harding
Sgt. Maj. Richard Morgan*
Drum Maj. Nicholas Neal*
Drum Maj. Alexander Wilson*
Fife Maj. William Lipscomb*
Fife Maj. Conrad Pannebaker</td></tr>
<tr><td>Company</td><td>Captain</td><td>1st Lieutenant</td><td>2nd Lieutenant</td><td>Enlisted men</td></tr>
<tr><td>Colonel's</td><td></td><td>Leonard Cooper†</td><td>William Kelly‡</td><td>22/44 present</td></tr>
<tr><td>Lt. Colonel's</td><td></td><td>James Curry</td><td>Philip Huffman*</td><td>27/49 present</td></tr>
<tr><td>Major's</td><td></td><td>Christopher Moyer</td><td>Peter Higgins*</td><td>16/40 present</td></tr>
<tr><td>Walls'</td><td>George Walls*</td><td>John Wilson</td><td>Martin Carney§*</td><td>18/42 present</td></tr>
<tr><td>Stith's</td><td>John Stith</td><td>James Morton</td><td>Benjamin Lawson||</td><td>18/45 present</td></tr>
<tr><td>Kirkpatrick's</td><td>Abraham Kirkpatrick¶</td><td>Robert Breckenridge</td><td>Thomas Miller</td><td>16/41 present</td></tr>
<tr><td>Steed's</td><td>John Steed</td><td>William Lews Lovely**</td><td>Philip Eastin*</td><td>24/44 present</td></tr>
</table>

Old 8th Virginia officers in italics. 141/305 enlisted men present (including NCOs). *Absent. †Captain-lieutenant. ‡Adjutant. §Quartermaster. ||Paymaster. ¶Brigade major. **Commissary. Lt. Colonel's Co. data from November.

Colonel Bowman's situation was more complicated. He had already lost his command to James Wood at Valley Forge when the old 8th was provisionally combined with the 4th and the 12th. It did not matter that Wood was himself absent when they marched to Monmouth.

96 Chase et al (eds), *Papers of Washington* (Revolution), vol. 18, pp.519-520.
97 NARA: W. Clark pension.
98 NARA: M246 f.364 pp.212–219.
99 NARA: M246, f.118, p.11, 51; f.119, pp.12, 49; f.120, p.12; f.121, pp.8, 44

Sick, angry, or simply having nothing to do, Bowman went to Trenton.[100] On the day the army camped at Spotswood, Charles Scott ordered him in writing 'to return to Virginia and call upon the Governor of Virginia for money to recruit the regiment.'[101] According to Peter Muhlenberg, Bowman had 'orders to hold himself in readiness to Join the Army whenever call'd upon.'[102] It is unclear whether Bowman went to see Scott at Spotswood or if the order was sent to Trenton.

Colonel Bowman dutifully travelled to Williamsburg to see Patrick Henry, but Virginia did not need him. '[I] met with no success in the recruiting business,' he wrote to Major Clark late in October with what might have been an affected cheerfulness, 'the governor told me that he had appointed officers for that purpose, so that I have nothing to do but spank the girls and drink groog.' On the subject of alcohol, he merrily added, 'I wish you had some of my old Wiskey. I think it would make you quite well.'[103] Bowman asserted later that he 'remained an officer during the War without being again called into service.'[104]

The consolidation of the Virginia Line from 15 to 11 regiments occurred shortly after Bowman's return to Virginia. Though he was among the more senior colonels, he was left out of the new arrangement. His name appears on a list of 'Field Officers Omitted' with the note: 'Supposed will resign.'[105] What happened to him is plain to see: there were not enough colonelcies to go around, and Bowman was 300 miles away. It is revealing that nobody bothered to tell him. The injustice of it was noticed at the highest level and Peter Muhlenberg was finally assigned the job of telling him. 'He was derang'd at White Plains,' wrote the general, 'but was not informed of it until some time in 1779 when I was directed by the Commander in Chief to inform [him.]'[106]

100 NARA: W. Pollard pension.
101 NARA: M804, W396, Abraham Bowman pension. The date of the order was noted by General Muhlenberg in 1784.
102 LVA: Revolutionary War Bounty Land Claims, Abraham Bowman.
103 Draper Mss, L, vol.1, p.50. Edited for clarity.
104 NARA: A. Bowman pension.
105 NARA: M246, f.364, p.6.
106 LVA: A. Bowman bounty claim.

14

Veterans

Colonel Bowman and many 8th Virginia veterans turned their attention to the West when their service ended. This included early deserters like Martin Maney and Greenberry Choat, who joined William Christian's expedition against the Cherokee in 1776.[1] Most of the Cherokee sued for peace after that, but a radicalised faction under Dragging Canoe split away to become the Chickamauga. Maney, Choat, and Major George Slaughter participated in an expedition against the Chickamauga under Colonel Evan Shelby in 1779.[2] The inhumanity of these conflicts was unambiguous. A friend recalled that Maney once discovered an Indian who had 'secreted himself in the fork of a tree.' Maney shot him, removed his head, and brought it back to camp as a trophy.[3]

Some turned their attention to the West while still in service. When Washington sent the 8th Pennsylvania and 13th Virginia back to the forks of the Ohio, Richard Campbell was elevated to lieutenant colonel.[4] In a fatiguing three months on horseback, he travelled from Valley Forge to York, back to Valley Forge, back to York, to Williamsburg, and then to Fort Pitt on various errands.[5] The two regiments were certain to squabble over the Virginia-Pennsylvania boundary question, but Brigadier General Lachlan McIntosh, the new commander of the Western Department, was from Georgia and could be counted on to be neutral.[6]

McIntosh's top military concern in 1778 was the British garrison at Detroit. From there, Lieutenant Governor Henry Hamilton armed Native proxies and directed them to attack as far south as Kentucky. Convinced that Hamilton paid the Indians for scalps, the Americans called him the 'hair buyer general.'[7] Fort Pitt was also the venue for planned treaty

1 NARA: M246, f.216, p.8; G. Choat pension.

2 Anon. (ed.), *Journal of the House of Delegates*, 1784 (Richmond: Commonwealth of Virginia, 1828), pp.13–14; NARA: A. Cabbage pension. English, *Life of General Clark*, vol.2, pp.692–693; Thwaites and Kellogg, *Dunmore's War*, p.197.

3 NARA: M. Maney pension.

4 Chase et al (eds), *Papers of Washington* (Revolution), vol.13, pp.656–657, 686–688; Williams, *Life of John Gibson*, p.51.

5 Chase et al (eds), *Papers of Washington* (Revolution), vol.15, pp.208, 316–318, 345; H.R. McIlwaine (ed.), *Official Letters of the Governors of the State of Virginia* (Richmond: Virginia State Library, 1926), vol.1, pp.296–298; Kellog (ed.), *Frontier Advance*, pp.57–60, 78–79.

6 Chase et al (eds), *Papers of Washington* (Revolution), vol.15, pp.108–110.

7 James (ed.), *Clark Papers*, pp.97, 159.

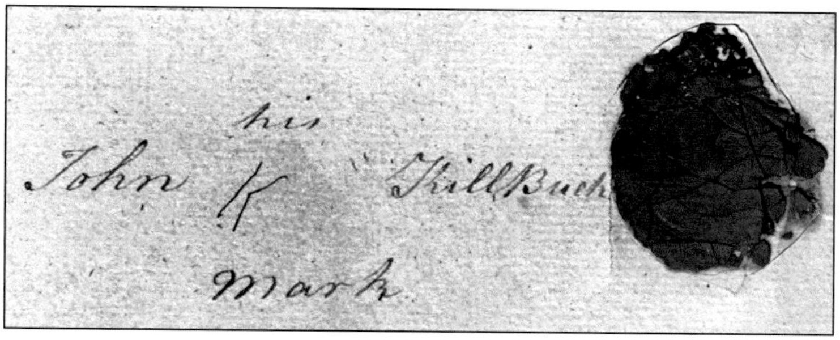

Gelelemend (John Killbuck, Jr.) signed the Treaty of Fort Pitt with a 'K.' (National Archives)

negotiations with the Delaware Tribe. Andrew Lewis and his brother Thomas negotiated with three 'deputies and chief men': White Eyes (Koquethagechton), Captain Pipe (Hopocan or Konieschquanoheel), and John Killbuck, Jr. (Gelelemend). War parties under Gelemend's father had chased Robert Higgins at Fort Pleasant and killed Ned McCarty's father at New Creek during the French and Indian War. For both sides, the negotiations required wisdom, foresight, and forgiveness. The resulting pact guaranteed McIntosh passage through their territory and obliged him to contribute to tribal defence by building and garrisoning a fort at their main village of Coshocton. John Stephenson, now a Yohogania County justice and colonel of the 1st Battalion of Yohogania Militia,[8] signed the treaty as a witness.[9]

The Continental regiments at Fort Pitt were supported by Virginia militia from Ohio, Monongalia, Yohogania, Hampshire, Berkeley, and Shenandoah counties. A July muster shows 402 militiamen plus officers.[10] Extreme measures were taken to preserve this force. A Hampshire man remembered McIntosh 'threatened them with attack by the regulars, if they should attempt to leave him' when their terms ended.[11] Leveraging the border dispute, John Stephenson strongarmed men registered with the Pennsylvania militia into Virginia service. Pennsylvanians were abducted by a roaming band of Virginians, brought to Stephenson's home on Jacobs Creek, bound, and locked in his smokehouse. They were tried before a sham court martial for mutiny, desertion, and disobeying orders, sentenced to serve an immediate tour of duty, and fined two months' pay. They were then taken 30 miles to Fort McIntosh and put into service. Governor Henry, who was almost 400 miles away in Williamsburg, was not pleased when he learned about the practice.[12]

McIntosh built a fort named after himself at the mouth of the Beaver River. Constructed on the 'Indian' side of the Ohio's counterclockwise loop, it communicated offensive intent. By October, however, the general from Georgia knew it was too late in the year to start an expedition against Detroit. He was, however, determined to build the fort at Coshocton.[13] Doing so would meet the United States' treaty obligation and set the stage for an expedition against Detroit in 1779.

8 Crumrine (ed.), *Yohogania Minute Book*, pp.211, 216, 348, 397.
9 NARA: Record Group 11, 'Ratified Indian Treaty 8: Delaware – Fort Pitt, September 17, 778.'
10 NARA: M246, f364, p34.
11 NARA: M804, R2590, John Cuppy pension (Hampshire militia).
12 LVA: State Government Records Collection, Accession 36912, Patrick Henry letter and depositions, 27 Nov. 1778.
13 Eric Sterner, 'The Siege of Fort Laurens, 1778–1779', *JAR*, 17 Dec. 2019.

Four 8th Virginia veterans commanded at Fort McIntosh: Richard Campbell, Robert Beall, Simon Morgan, and Benjamin Biggs. (Photo: Bruce Bell)

McIntosh marched into the trans-Ohio country from his namesake fort on 4 November 1778.[14] Colonel Stephenson was instructed to organise his best riflemen into light infantry companies to walk as flankers for the westbound column. The procession included a number of 8th Virginia veterans, including Stephenson's former soldiers now in Captain Beall's Company and an unknown number of men who, like Stephenson himself, were now in the militia. James Berwick joined as a volunteer.[15] The former clerk of the West Augusta Committee had risen from ensign under Captain Croghan to 1st lieutenant of Captain Westfall's company before becoming supernumerary when the 4th-8th-12th Regiment was formed. Richard Campbell was left in command at Fort McIntosh with instructions to finish its construction, collect supplies, and maintain order.[16]

14 Edward G. Williams (ed.), 'A Revolutionary Journal and Orderly Book of General Lachlan McIntosh's Expedition, 1778', *Western Pennsylvania Historical Magazine*, 43:1 (1960), p.11, 43:3 (1960), p.269.

15 Williams (ed.), 'Journal of McIntosh Expedition', pp.167, 169, 175, n.14, 269.

16 Kellogg (ed.), *Frontier Advance*, pp.164–165; Williams (ed.), 'Journal of McIntosh Expedition', pp.268.

The journey from Fort McIntosh was frightening. Two men who strayed ahead of the column were found scalped and dead on the path.[17] Heavy snow, restless militia, and dwindling supplies ground the expedition to a halt well short of Coshocton. In lieu of the fort promised to the Delaware, a stockade was built on the Tuscarawas River and named for Henry Laurens. Its garrison was reduced to eating leather before the winter ended.[18]

Stony Point and Paulus Hook

Back east, Charles Scott led his men from White Plains to the Hudson Highlands. His reorganised brigade consisted of Virginia's 4th Regiment (formerly the 4th and 8th), 6th Regiment (formerly the 10th), and 8th Regiment (formerly the 12th), along with the Delaware Regiment.[19] One of Kirkpatrick's men remembered they 'marched to Robinson's farm on North river [the Hudson] Where he lay until late in the fall.'[20] The camp was on the east side of the Hudson near modern Garrison, New York, opposite and a little below West Point.[21] Major General Israel Putnam commanded Scott's and Muhlenberg's Brigades until November, when the Fighting Parson took over.[22]

Scott had been advocating for a 1,000-man, half-musket, half-rifle light infantry corps, and he got his way that fall.[23] He was a busy man, with duties including reconnaissance above New York City, coordinating with the army's spy network inside the city, and command of his own brigade. He wore himself out and went home sick to Virginia, leaving his brigade to Colonel Russell.[24] When cold weather came, Scott's light infantrymen rejoined their regiments and returned to Middle Brook for the winter.[25] As had been done at Valley Forge, men with expiring enlistments (draftees and other one-year men this time) were given winter furloughs if they signed up for another term.[26] Colonel Neville was surprised at how many were willing to do so.[27]

17 Williams (ed.), 'Journal of McIntosh Expedition,' pp.12, 14, 271; NARA: M804, S2051, Ephraim Bates pension (Monongalia Militia).
18 Kellogg (ed.), *Frontier Advance*, pp.24, 172–175, 183–184, 257.
19 Chase et al (eds), *Papers of Washington* (Revolution), vol.16, pp.121–123, vol.17, pp.78–80; Lesser (ed.), *Sinews*, pp.84–88.
20 NARA: M804, S16303, John Wyatt pension.
21 FHS: Clark Diary, 20 Sept. 1778; S.E. Tillman, 'A Review of West Point's History', *Quarterly Journal of the New York State Historical Association*, 2:3 (1921), pp.151; Anon. (ed.), 'Diary of Joseph Clark', pp.108, 109.
22 FHS: Clark Diary, 22 Sept. 1778; Chase et al (eds), *Washington Papers* (Revolution), vol.17, pp.78–80; Muhlenberg, *General Muhlenberg*, pp.160, 167–168.
23 Chase et al (eds), *Papers of Washington* (Revolution), vol.13, pp.240–241, vol.16, pp.266–268; Anon. (ed.), 'Diary of Joseph Clark', p.109.
24 Chase et al (eds), *Papers of Washington* (Revolution), vol.18, pp.166–167, 195–196, 477; Ward, *Scott*, pp.52–57; David C. Bonk, *'Men Who Are Determined to be Free:' The Assault on Stony Point, 15 July 1779* (Warwick: Helion & Company, 2018), pp.62–63.
25 FHS: Clark Diary, 28 Nov.-9 Dec. 1778; Anon. (ed.), 'Diary of Joseph Clark', p.109; Bonk, *Stony Point*, p.63.
26 Chase et al (eds), *Papers of Washington* (Revolution), vol.17, pp.394–395, 417–418, 425–426, vol.18, p.480.
27 Chase et al (eds), *Papers of Washington* (Revolution), vol.18, p.477.

Major Croghan enjoyed his time at Middle Brook over the winter of 1778–1779. 'We Spend our time very Sociable here, Are never disturbed by the Enemy, have Plenty of Provisions, & no want of Whiskey Grog ... We have a Variety of Amusements. Last Evening the Tragedy of Cato was performed at Brunswick, by the officers of the Army. Will the Congress be Displeased.'[28] The spring of 1779 was equally uneventful. Scott remained in Virginia to oversee recruiting, and his brigade in New Jersey was dissolved. Once again, the Virginia Line had too many officers for too few soldiers. The 3rd and 4th regiments were provisionally merged and as the '3rd and 4th Virginia Regiment' under Colonel Neville and reassigned to General Woodford.[29] Under this arrangement, Leonard Cooper retained the rank of captain-lieutenant, each of the other companies was led by a captain, and the field officers were not assigned company commands.

The 3rd & 4th Virginia Regiment, June 1779[30]

Field Officers:	**Staff Officers:**	**Warrant Officers:**
Col. John Neville Lt. Col. Thomas Gaskins *Maj. William Croghan*	Adj. John Hawkins Adj. William Kelly Surg. William McMachen Surg. Mate Charles Greer Paymstr. William Bentley Paymstr. Benjamin Lawson Qtr. Master Arthur Lind Qtr. Master James Morton	Sgt. Maj. Anderson Freeman *Sgt. Maj. John Harding* Qtr. Mstr. Sgt. Robert Chapple Qtr. Mstr. Sgt. John Watters Drum Maj. Henry Anderson *Drum Maj. Nicholas Neal** Fife Maj. Richard Thompson Fife Maj. Conrad Pannebaker

Company	Captain	1st Lieutenant	2nd Lieutenant	Enlisted Men
Stith's	John Stith	James Morton†	Benjamin Lawson‡	32/47 present
Kirkpatrick's	*Abraham Kirkpatrick**	*James Curry*	*Robert Breckenridge*	34/50 present
Anderson's	John Anderson*	John Fitzgerald	Nathaniel Anderson*	43/59 present
Blackwell's	John Blackwell	Leroy Edwards	John Raney	25/43 present
Peyton's	Valentine Peyton	Arthur Lind†*	Lipscomb Norvel	29/46 present
Steed's Company:	*John Steed**	*William Lewis Lovely**	John Wilson *Philip Eastin*	33/44 present
Bentley's	William Bentley‡*	John Hawkins§	William Stephen	27/53 present
Cooper's	*Leonard Cooper*‖	*Philip Huffman*	William D. Kelly§	31/54 present

Old 8th Virginia officers in italics. 254/396 enlisted men present (including NCOs). *Absent. †Quartermaster. ‡Paymaster. §Adjutant. ‖Captain-lieutenant.

In June, Washington responded to British forays out of New York by repositioning the army into the Clove near the Hudson Highlands.[31] Like Morgan, Maxwell, and Scott before

28 William Croghan to Bernard Gratz, 1 March 1779, quoted in Samuel W. Thomas, 'William Croghan, Sr. [1752–1822]: A Pioneer Kentucky Gentleman', *Filson Club Quarterly*, 43:2 (1969), p.38

29 NARA: M246, f.97, pp.2–50; Chase et al (eds), *Papers of Washington* (Revolution), vol.20, pp. 444–445, vol.21, pp.138–141.

30 NARA: M246, f.97, p.2; f.98, p.6; f.99, p.5; f.100, p.6, 40; f.102, p.5; f.103, p.6; f.104, p.6; f.105, p.6.

31 Chase et al (eds), *Papers of Washington* (Revolution), vol.21, pp.24–25, 85–86.

him, Anthony Wayne took command of a corps of detached light infantry.[32] The King's army took Stony Point and Verplank's Point, which were important positions that faced each other across the Hudson. That and a British incursion into Connecticut compelled the long-idle Americans to respond.

Courageously obtained intelligence paved the way for an attack on Stony Point during the dark early hours of 15 July 1779.[33] Most of the light infantry, Virginians and others commanded by Colonel Christian Febiger, waded silently through two feet of water along the shore below the fort.[34] Among them was William Lewis Lovely,[35] who was now Captain Steed's senior lieutenant.[36] So too were Moses Crawford and John Redman who were now in Captain-Lieutenant Leonard Cooper's company.[37] There is evidence that Major Clark participated.[38] Robert Chambers, also in Cooper's company but not in the light infantry, recalled that he was positioned with Peter Muhlenberg to support Wayne if the operation failed.[39]

Pennsylvania's Richard Butler simultaneously led most of the other light infantry from the north, while a small group feigned a frontal attack.[40] Silence, speed, and early morning darkness were the keys to success. Roads were blocked, secrecy was maintained until the last minute, and a man was killed by an officer for trying to fire his weapon prematurely. Febiger's van splashed around the first ring of abatis and rapidly climbed the fascine walls into the fort.[41] A soldier in the 'new' 8th Virginia said that 'he escaped receiving any wounds although his hat & cloaths were literally riddled.'[42] On the north side, Butler's men successfully chopped their way through the sharpened sticks.[43] Once the light infantry got inside the fort, it was quickly theirs.

Stony Point's capture was an unmitigated success. So much so, that another attack was organised in August against the British position at Paulus Hook in New Jersey. Sixty-five unidentified men from the 4th Virginia participated.[44] The raid, conceived by Major Henry Lee was flawed in every phase but still resulted in nearly 160 prisoners.[45] Lee reported that Jonathan Clark's column, on the right, 'broke through all opposition, and found an entrance to the main work. So rapid was the movement of the troops, that we gained the fort before the discharge of a single piece of artillery.' The 23-year-old Lee was showered with praise and awarded a gold medal by Congress.

---

32 Chase et al (eds), *Papers of Washington* (Revolution), vol.19, p.220, vol.21, pp.212–213.
33 Bonk, *Stony Point*, p.83.
34 Bonk, *Stony Point*, pp.94, 122.
35 Robert A. Rutland et al (eds), *The Papers of James Madison: Presidential Series* (Charlottesville: University Press of Virginia, 1984–2020), vol.9, pp.570–573.
36 NARA: M246, f.104, pp.2–20.
37 NARA: M246, f.100, p.42; NARA: M804, S43913, John Redman pension; W910, Moses Crawford pension.
38 NARA: M804, S38443, William Tiller pension (12th Va.); FHS: Clark Diary, 15 July 1779.
39 R. Chambers pension; Muhlenberg, *General Muhlenberg*, pp.173–174.
40 Maria Hull Campbell, *Revolutionary Services and Civil Life of General William Hull* (New York: D. Appleton & Co., 1848), p.164.
41 NARA: W. Tiller pension
42 NARA: I. Jackson pension.
43 Bonk, *Stony Point*, pp.87–102
44 Farrier (ed.), *Paulus Hook*, p.63.
45 Draper Mss, L, vol.1, p.60; Farrier (ed.), *Paulus Hook*, pp.41–53.

The British post at Paulus Hook. Edward Lamson Henry (1841–1919). Watercolour and gouache. (New Hampshire Antique Co-op)

Major Clark, however, was the senior officer in the engagement and many in the Virginia Line were furious at Lee.[46] William Croghan, Clark's comrade, friend, and future brother-in-law, was angriest of all. He fumed, 'The Magazine was not blown up, the Barricks not sett on fire, the cannon not spiked, no article of Stores … was the least damaged; in fact, nothing further was done than rushing into the Garrison in confusion and driving out the prisoners, mostly without their clothes.' Croghan and others asserted that Lee gained the command by lying to Clark about the date of his commission. Croghan wrote in a letter:

> Several officers have been much injured in the Virginia line, on account of giving Major Lee the command of 300 of our men to reduce Powel's Hook, and unjust methods taken by him to have the command, by telling one of our Majors, who marched with the 300 men, that his commission was older than it really is – otherwise he would not have had the command over him. I believe Major Lee will be arrested.[47]

Clark corrected his own diary on the point of seniority, recording that he was 'detach'd ~~under~~ *with* Majr Lee & surprizzed ye fort at Powles Hook & took 157 Prisoners.'[48] Lee was wisely careful to praise Clark's conduct in the operation. 'At every point of the enterprise,' he professed, 'I stood highly indebted to Major Clarke for his zeal, activity, and example.'[49] The two majors met privately, and Lee apologised to Clark in writing.[50] So did Lord Stirling, who was culpable for letting the dispute arise.[51]

46 Farrier (ed.), *Paulus Hook*, pp.65, 77, 82.
47 Farrier (ed.), *Paulus Hook*, p.73.
48 FHS: Clark Diary, 18 Aug. 1779. Emphasis added.
49 Farrier (ed.), *Paulus Hook*, p.67.
50 FHS: Clark Diary, 21 Aug. 1779; Draper Mss, L, vol.1, p.62; Farrier (ed.), *Paulus Hook*, p.87.
51 Draper Mss, L, vol.1, p.61.

As Croghan wanted and predicted, Major Lee was arrested and tried. 'Major Clarke,' wrote a Massachusetts officer, 'who is exceedingly the gentleman, advised and endeavored to dissuade those officers from the prosecution, but in vain. On the trial, he supported this character; though the only person who could reasonably be thought to be injured by Major Lee's having the command, his whole evidence ... might be considered as an encomium on his conduct.'[52]

The court ruled: 'Major Lee did thro' inattention give Major Clark a wrong date of his Commission, but by no means intended to impose on Major Clark by assuming Command of him, having express Orders from his Excellency the Commander in Chief for that special Command.' The attack had been Lee's idea, but he still knew he was in Clark's debt. 'I am under great obligations to you,' he told him, 'for the temper and coolness with which you conduct yourself.'[53]

What was really at issue, of course, was credit and glory, and Lee received more of both than he deserved. Even from afar, Daniel Morgan figured out what happened and wrote Clark to say so. 'I now congratulate you on your success at Powlus Hook; but I assure you till lately, and within these few days, I did not know you ware in the Scuffle; but since I have found out, I endeavored to make it as public as possible, as it was alwais my wish, that Every Man's Merits should be made publick.'[54]

Charles Scott's Recruit Detachment Battalions

In the spring of 1779, John Wyatt and other reenlisted veterans congregated at Petersburg, a hub of Virginia's tobacco trade at the falls of the Appomattox River. Wyatt was a 1778 one-year man who began his service in the 8th Virginia. He fought at Monmouth, camped at White Plains and Robinson's Farm, and reenlisted at Middle Brook, which earned him a winter furlough at home in Botetourt County.[55] Other 8th Virginia veterans were entering their fourth years of service. William Kennedy, for example, was one of George Slaughter's original men from Culpeper. He was captured at Germantown, escaped, returned to service, and reenlisted. William Scott was a former James Knox recruit beginning his third enlistment. As always, there were a few men who cheated the system. William George of Captain Steed's Company took the furlough and never showed up again. He successfully applied for a pension in 1832, admitting only that he 'never received a written discharge.'[56]

The British had taken Savannah, and all eyes were now on the south. Charles Scott, who was still in Virginia, was directed to organise recruits into three battalions and send them south under recalled supernumerary officers.[57] Veterans were initially kept separate but

52 Josiah Quincy (ed.), *The Journals of Major Samuel Shaw, the First American Consul at Canton* (Boston: Wm. Crosby and H.P. Nichols, 1847), p.68.
53 Farrier (ed.), *Paulus Hook*, pp.82, 87.
54 Draper Mss, L, vol.1, p.67.
55 NARA: J. Wyatt pension.
56 NARA: M246, f.102, p.20, f.104, p.20, f.208, p.43; W. George pension.
57 Chase et al (eds), *Papers of Washington* (Revolution), vol.20, pp.342–343.

were eventually thrown in with the recruits.[58] The soldiers were rightly afraid of going to the coastal south in the summertime. One officer fretted, 'there is ten to one against my returning, as the Country is so sickly.'[59] Supply shortages and a British raid in the Chesapeake delayed their departure, but the first of the three battalions left for the south in June.[60]

The terms used to describe elements of the Virginia Line from this point in the war forward were inconsistent. They referred to the circumstances of their creation and to ad hoc commands rather than to actual standing regiments. An official organisation was preserved on paper, but it served little purpose beyond tracking officers' relative seniority and confusing future generations of historians and genealogists. Despite the inclusion of veterans, the units organised by Charles Scott at Petersburg are usually referred to as 'recruit detachment battalions' or simply as the 1st through 3rd 'Virginia Detachments' of Scott's new brigade.[61] No effort was made to keep 8th Virginia veterans together. Moses Crawford, one of William Croghan's early recruits entering his fourth year of service, left Petersburg with the 1st Virginia Detachment in June under Colonel Richard Parker.[62] Wyatt left with the 2nd Detachment in October under Colonel William Heth. Richard Bennett, previously of George Slaughter's Company, was assigned to Colonel Abraham Buford's 3rd Detachment, as was Adam Dietz, the now 10- or 11-year-old child volunteer who had followed Captain Kirkpatrick. Buford's detachment could not leave Petersburg for lack of clothing and supplies.[63]

Charles Scott's Brigade of 1780.[64]

1st Detachment	2nd Detachment	3rd Detachment
Field Officers: Col. Richard Parker* Lt. Col. Samuel Hopkins Maj. Richard Clough Anderson Also: *Moses Crawford*	**Field Officers:** Col. William Heth Lt. Col. Gustavus Wallace Maj. James Lucas† Maj. William Lewis Also: *John Wyatt.*	**Field Officers:** Col. Abraham Buford Lt. Col. Robert Ballard† Maj. Thomas Ridley Also: *Richard Bennett, Adam Dietz*

8th Virginia veterans in italics. *KIA at Charles Town. †Resigned.

58 Chase et al (eds), *Papers of Washington* (Revolution), vol.20, pp.342–343; NARA: J. Wyatt pension.
59 Palmer et al (eds), *Calendar*, vol.1, p.319.
60 Ward, *Scott*, pp.68–72.
61 Jim Gallagher, 'Virginia Continental Line Reorganisation of 1778 and 1779', *7th Virginia Regiment of the Continental Line*, <7vr.org/single-post/2018/01/07/virginia-continental-line-reorganisation-of-1778-and-1779>, accessed 5 May 2024.
62 NARA: M. Crawford pension.
63 NARA: M804, S36412, Richard Bennett pension.
64 NYPL: MssCol 927, 'A General List of the Continental officers included in the Capitulation of Charles Town May 12th 1780' and 'A List of Officers Late at Haddrel's Point, 4th August 1781'; Sanchez-Saavedra, *Virginia Military Organisations*, p.179; John U. Rees, *Examples of the Complexity of Continental Army Unit Lineage* (The Virginia, Pennsylvania and Massachusetts Continental Lines), <scribd.com/doc/307784931/Examples-of-the-Complexity-of-Continental-Army-Unit-Lineage-The-Virginia-Pennsylvania-and-Massachusetts-Continental-Lines>, accessed 30 April 2024.

The Kirkpatrick-Cooper Duel

To the north, on 23 September 1779, senior officers of the Virginia Line congregated at William Woodford's quarters at Camp Ramapo to sort out rank and promotion issues yet again. Most of the officers present had commanded the 8th Virginia's men in one capacity or another: Brigadier General Peter Muhlenberg, Colonels James Wood and John Neville, and Majors Jonathan Clark, David Stephenson, and William Croghan. A key question before them was how to determine the relative ranks of officers such as William Darke, Robert Higgins, and John Clark, who were prisoners of war without actual commands. Though a captive, Darke was promoted to lieutenant colonel.[65] The officers noted that Captain Israel had not been seen for 16 months. He had been 'repeatedly called upon to join his Regiment without effect.' He had previously offered to resign, and there was 'reason to believe that he did not consider himself in the line.' Among the 3rd-4th Virginia officers present, Leonard Cooper and James Curry were due promotions to captain, which positioned William Lewis Lovely to succeed Cooper as captain-lieutenant. Philip Eastin, Philip Huffman, Peter Higgins, and Tommy Miller were technically still ensigns and owed commissions as lieutenants. Eastin had been waiting more than a year. In Colonel Woods' 'new' 8th Virginia, Jonathan Clark was due a lieutenant colonel's commission.[66] Washington accepted all these recommendations and asked Congress for the papers.[67]

Several days after the senior officers met, Abraham Kirkpatrick attacked Leonard Cooper in camp.[68] There was no contest between them in seniority, but Cooper's promotion may have lit another fuse. Colonel Wood recorded that 'a Dispute arose in the Parade, while the army lay at Pompton Plains in the State of New Jersey, between Captain Abraham Kirkpatrick, and Captain Leonard Cooper, after much abuse and ill Language on the part of Kirkpatrick, he proceeded to strike the said Captain Cooper several strokes with a cane.'

Whatever the issue, Cooper's first inclination was to let the matter go. That, however, was not going to fly. According to Colonel Wood, 'Captain Cooper not shewing a disposition to demand satisfaction, was informed by many officers of his own Corps, that unless he did, he must leave the Regiment, as they were Determined he should not rank as an Officer.' Under this duress, Cooper 'gave the said Kirkpatrick a Challenge, which was Accepted, and a Duel fought with Pistols.'[69]

The purpose of duelling was never revenge but rather the restoration of honour. Kirkpatrick clearly knew what he was doing when he escalated the quarrel. Caning a fellow officer was the ultimate insult. A history of southern duelling explains, 'A gentleman fought another gentleman with a pistol on the field of honor, according to the rules. A gentleman horse-whipped or caned a person of the lower estates.' Enslaved people were abused this way.[70]

65 NARA: M881, r.1042, pp.120, 125–126, 129, 133.

66 NARA: M246 f.364 pp.212–219.

67 Chase et al (eds), *Papers of Washington* (Revolution), vol.22, pp.543–544.

68 FHS: Clark Diary, 10 Oct. 1779.

69 LVA: Revolutionary War Pension Applications, pen. 92, Leonard Cooper.

70 Jack K. Williams, *Dueling in the Old South: Vignettes of Social History* (College Station: Texas A&M University Press, 1980), p.26.

Failure to demand satisfaction would, under the code of honour, have exposed Cooper as a coward unworthy of his commission.[71]

Kirkpatrick arrived for the contest with Captain James Curry as his second.[72] Kirkpatrick feared no one, seemingly to the point of being a bully.[73] As for Curry, his wound from Point Pleasant still left him with only partial use of his right arm.[74] We do not know who Cooper's second was. The seconds' first duty, in most cases, was to pursue reconciliation. In this case, however, where the insult was both public and violent, there was no point in that. Pistols were the only means of resolution.[75]

The entire event was governed by the seconds. They spoke for the contestants, measured the distance, loaded the weapons, and enforced the rules. If either duellist fired prematurely, the other's second was at liberty to shoot him. If the premature fire hit the other contestant, the second was required to shoot the offender. If either party tried to back out, it was his second's duty to declare him a coward and post a public notice to that effect. A surgeon, perhaps the 3rd-4th Virginia's William McMachen, was on hand with however many witnesses the seconds had agreed to.[76]

When all was set, Kirkpatrick and Cooper faced each other 10 or 20 paces apart with their loaded pistols held down at their sides. When the word was given, they fired. Cooper may have been the better man, but Kirkpatrick was the better shot. The junior captain was seriously wounded high in his right leg. If they adhered to protocol, Cooper's second then asked Curry for permission to leave the ground. The duel was over, and Cooper's honour was restored.[77]

Bowman's Station

At his home near Strasburg, Colonel Bowman missed his friends in the army. He sent a letter to Major Clark mirthfully scolding him for not writing. He was, he said, willing to overlook past sins, but if Clark did not mend his ways, he would put him 'under arrest & have you tried by a Court martial of young ladies.' Feigning his former authority, he 'granted' his friend a furlough to come visit him in Shenandoah County. 'There is a great to do here about some songs that is lost and is requested you would rite them over & bring them up yourself.'[78]

Bowman learned he was supernumerary about the time he turned 30. Disappointed, perhaps, but nevertheless free of military obligations, he packed up and moved to Kentucky.[79]

---

71 John Lyde Wilson, *The Code of Honor or Rules for the Government of Principals and Seconds in Duelling* (Charleston: James Phinney, 1858), pp.4–8, 11, 38.

72 Durant, *Union County*, p.297.

73 Bigham, *Kirkpatrick*, p.10.

74 Durant, *Union County*, p.295.

75 Wilson, *Code of Honor*, pp.11–20, 32.

76 Wilson, *Code of Honor*, pp.24, 27, 29.

77 LVA: Revolutionary War Pension Applications, pen. 92, Leonard Cooper; Wilson, *Code of Honor*, pp.27–28.

78 Draper Mss, L, vol.1, p.56.

79 Draper Mss, L, vol.1, p.63.

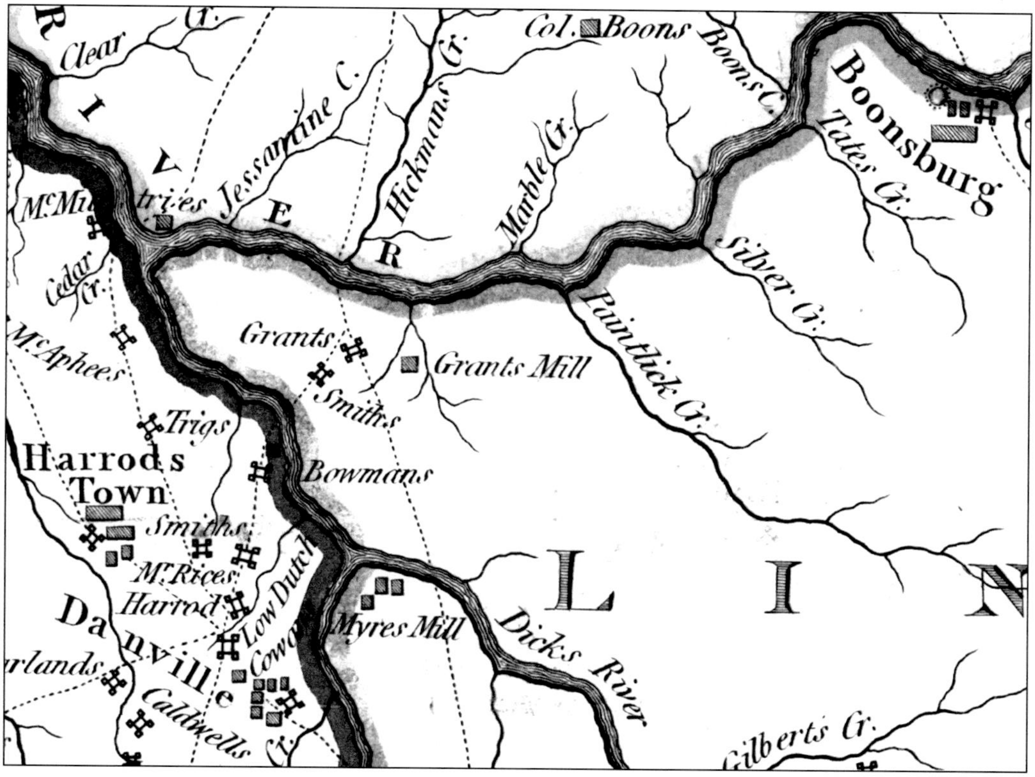

Detail of a 1784 map by John Filson shows Bowman's Station below the Dix River's junction with the Kentucky River. (Library of Congress)

Still single himself, he led 22 families down the Wagon Road in September to Big Lick (Roanoke) and turned onto the still-rough Wilderness Road to the West.[80] They abandoned their wagons at the Cumberland Gap and continued on as a packhorse train, riding or walking beside their horses and oxen.[81] Bowman brought the settlers to a spring seven miles east of Harrodsburg and established Bowman's Station. The water running from the ground formed Spring Branch, which flowed north through sugar maples to Cane Run and on to the Dix River. The settlement was on land owned by John Bowman, but adjacent plots were owned jointly or individually by Abraham, John, and Joseph.[82] The Dix, which looped about on the east side of the settlement, had been named by James Knox for a friendly Cherokee he called 'Captain Dick' a few years before the Revolution.[83]

80 Beckner (ed.), 'Interview with Elijah Foley', p.255; Draper Mss. 1, vol.1, p.65.

81 Elijah Foley, undated letter in private collection, in Nancy Foley Johnson, 'The History of Elijah Foley and His Family, After Whom "Foley's Landing" Subdivision is Named', <sites.rootsweb.com/~kyfayett/nfj/elijah_foley.htm>, accessed 2 April 2024.

82 Hammon and Taylor, *Western War*, pp.103.

83 WHS: Draper Manuscripts, C, vol.5, p.43.

Bowman's caravan had been planned for years, and he knew his destination.[84] He had explored Kentucky at least once before the war. In early 1776, he established 'Hite, Bowman & Co.' with a cousin and his brothers to invest in Kentucky land.[85] In 1778 'Colonel Bowman' planted corn on property near Harrodsburg for the use of the settlement and left 'a negro man to tend it.'[86] John held the rank of colonel in the Kentucky County militia, but Abraham could just as well have visited the site during the year that had passed since his meeting with Governor Henry.

Kentucky was still subject to Indian attacks from north and south, but Virginia triggered a land rush by making parcels available at low cost. The Commonwealth made land accessible to 'bona fide' early settlers who had occupied and improved land (or paid others to do so) before 24 June 1776, often at little or no cost beyond minor fees. For those who came later, land was sold through the Virginia Land Office or granted as bounties to Revolutionary War veterans.[87] Moving to Kentucky was worth the risk in an era when land was the only secure form of wealth. In 1780, Kentucky County was split into Fayette, Jefferson, and Lincoln counties.

The winter of 1779–1780 remains the harshest ever in recorded in North America.[88] Every coastal river north of the Carolinas froze solid. People walked across Chesapeake Bay and New York Harbor.[89] In Kentucky, settlers starved, and wild animals froze to death. The Kentucky River froze to a depth of two feet and a traveller described the nights as 'violently cold.'[90] Bowman's pioneers reached their destination in mid-December and endured the season in makeshift shelters. 'There was nothing but a camp there, till some time in March' remembered one settler, 'because it was too cold to work.' One man died, unable to subsist on emaciated wild game.[91]

When spring came, they tapped the maple trees and boiled the sap down into sugar, which they used to make beer, vinegar, and spirits. In frontier parlance, a 'station' was a place of safety, but usually something less than a fort. The settlers at Bowman's Station got to work building lines of log houses in what was described as a 'half H' formation, facing each other across the stream. Livestock were corralled in the 150-yard-wide valley in between.[92] There was no stockade.

When he first arrived at Spring Branch, Colonel Bowman learned that his brother Joseph had died after playing an important part in George Rogers Clark's daring capture of Vincennes.[93] Joseph was terribly burned in a gunpowder explosion and died in August 1779.[94] News also arrived that the oldest Bowman brother, Jacob, a Loyalist, was killed in

84 Wayland, *Bowmans*, pp.63–64; NARA: A. Cabbage pension. English, *Life of General Clark*, vol.2, p.979.

85 Wayland, *Bowmans*, pp.44–45, 64.

86 Beckner (ed.), 'Interview with Elijah Foley', p.259; Collins, *Sketches of Kentucky*, vol.1, p.513.

87 Hening (ed.), *Statutes*, vol.9, pp.355–356, vol.10, pp.50–65.

88 David M. Ludlum, *Early American Winters: 1604–1820* (Boston: American Meteorological Society, 1966), p.117.

89 Thomas Jefferson, *Notes on the State of Virginia* (Boston: Lilly and Wait, 1832), p.83; Ludlum, *Early American Winters*, p.115.

90 Fleming, 'Travels in Kentucky', pp.628, 630.

91 Beckner (ed.), 'Interview with Elijah Foley', pp.255, 257.

92 Fleming, 'Travels in Kentucky', pp.231–232, 255.

93 NARA: A. Cabbage pension. English, *Life of General Clark*, vol.1, pp.557–578.

94 NARA: A. Cabbage pension. English, *Life of General Clark*, vol.1, pp.374, 575.

A plaque on the Bowman Memorial Gate in Harrodsburg, Ky. memorializes the achievements of the four best-known Bowman brothers. (Author's photo)

the Carolinas, possibly at the Battle of Ramsour's Mill.[95] When Abraham heard the news he stoically said it was 'It was no matter at all; no matter.'[96]

485 Miles in the Cold

About the time Bowman's pioneers burrowed into their brush huts to stay warm, the Virginia Continentals moved out of their cabins at Morristown. Word came just as they were finishing their construction. 'In a few days after we got there,' remembered a soldier, 'orders came for us to march to the South.'[97] An attempt to expel the British from Savannah had failed, and all eyes were turning to Charles Town. A few days after their soldiers marched from camp, Major Croghan and Brigadier General Woodford stood frustrated on the bank of the partially frozen Delaware, watching pedestrians carefully exit a boat at

95 Wayland, *Bowmans*, pp.116–117.
96 Beckner (ed.), 'Interview with Elijah Foley', p.257; Wayland, *Bowmans*, p.8.
97 NARA: W. Tiller pension.

Howell's Ferry. The boat stopped at the edge of the ice lining the shore and its passengers nervously walked the rest of the way on a plank. The officers knew this was not going to work for horses, wagons, artillery, and a brigade of men. After inspecting four different crossings, the officers decided to hold the troops in New Jersey until the river froze solid and they could cross on foot. Woodford and Croghan, meanwhile, took a boat across at Cooper's Ferry (Camden) directly to Philadelphia. Croghan rode on to Lancaster to visit his aging uncle while Woodford met with political leaders in William Penn's city.[98]

Woodford explained to the Board of War 'how Much More Convenient it would be for the Virginia Troops to be Divided in 3 or 4 Divisions.' The Board agreed to further consolidation of command, and the officers Croghan called 'Overplus' were allowed to leave until called upon.[99] Captain Steed and Lieutenants Lovely, Eastin, and Huffman were all sent home. Abraham Kirkpatrick had been on leave since his duel with Captain Cooper.[100] The remaining officers in Woodford's Brigade were organised under Colonels Russell, Neville, and Nathaniel Gist. These 'divisions' were referred to in various ways but are called 'battalions' here for clarity. Croghan had been Woodford's brigade major since May. He kept that position while also serving as major of William Russell's 1st Virginia Battalion.[101] John Neville commanded the 2nd Virginia Battalion along with Lieutenant Colonel Nicholas Cabell of Amherst County and 8th Virginia veteran Major David Stephenson. Jonathan Clark was lieutenant colonel of the 3rd Virginia Battalion under Colonel Gist.

William Woodford's Brigade of 1780.[102]

1st Battalion	2nd Battalion	3rd Battalion
Field Officers: Col. William Russell Lt. Col. Burgess Ball *Maj. William Croghan**	**Field Officers:** Col. John Neville Lt. Col. Nicholas Cabell *Maj. David Stephenson* Also: *Capt. James Curry, Lt. Robert Breckenridge, Robert Chambers, Michael Sword*	**Field Officers:** Col. Nathaniel Gist *Lt. Col. Jonathan Clark* Maj. Andrew Waggener Also: *Surg. Cornelius Baldwin,* Ens. Edmund Clark

8th Virginia veterans in italics. *Brigade major.

98 Randy F. McNew Crouse (ed.), *The Revolutionary War Diary of Major William Croghan of the Virginia Continental Line, 1779–1780*, 3rd ed. (Huntsville, Ala.: R.F.M. Crouse, 2013), pp.9–16.

99 McNew (ed.), *Croghan Diary*, pp.9–16.

100 NARA: M246, f.102, pp.17–20.

101 NYPL: MssCol 927, 'A General List of the Continental officers included in the Capitulation of Charles Town May 12th 1780' and 'A List of Officers Late at Haddrel's Point, 4th August 1781'; Sanchez-Saavedra, *Virginia Military Organisations*, p.179; John U. Rees, *Examples of the Complexity of Continental Army Unit Lineage* (The Virginia, Pennsylvania and Massachusetts Continental Lines), <scribd.com/doc/307784931/Examples-of-the-Complexity-of-Continental-Army-Unit-Lineage-The-Virginia-Pennsylvania-and-Massachusetts-Continental-Lines>, accessed 30 April 2024.

102 NYPL: MssCol 927, 'A General List of the Continental officers included in the Capitulation of Charles Town May 12th 1780' and 'A List of Officers Late at Haddrel's Point, 4th August 1781'; Sanchez-Saavedra, *Virginia Military Organisations*, p.179; John U. Rees, *Examples of the Complexity of Continental Army Unit Lineage* (The Virginia, Pennsylvania and Massachusetts Continental Lines), <scribd.com/doc/307784931/Examples-of-the-Complexity-of-Continental-Army-Unit-Lineage-The-Virginia-Pennsylvania-and-Massachusetts-Continental-Lines>, accessed 30 April 2024.

The freezing of the upper Chesapeake dashed any hope of travelling by water, so the battalions marched separately into mercilessly cold weather during the second week of January, two or three days apart.[103] Colonel Neville allowed his men to march 'in companies' so they could stay in motion and huddle together. The consequences of the march came quickly. 'Several have their Hands, Feet & Other parts of their Bodys Frozen,' noted Croghan in his diary, describing frostbite. According to Captain Curry:

> The snow was the deepest that had ever been known, and was badly drifted. It was crusted over, however, as to uphold horses and wagons, and was so deep that artillery even could be hauled over the tops of the fences. But in low places and along the streams wagons and artillery were constantly breaking through, entailing the hardest work to get them again onto solid snow.[104]

Croghan said the ocean of white made it hard to follow the thoroughfare, despite it being 'as public a Road as any on the Contanent.' They were able to advance, 'but with Inexpressable Difficulty.'[105] The cold continued and seemed to deepen still further when they crossed on the ice of the Susquehanna River. The bodies of horses and men became 'Extremely White with Frost' facing away from the sun.

They trudged along on the Great Wagon Road to Frederick, Maryland, where excited locals begged Colonel Neville to fire his cannons. He agreed, but the concussive blasts shattered several of the town's windows. Across the Potomac in Virginia, the shivering soldiers continued south along the Carolina Road on the east side of the Blue Ridge. After they traversed the frozen Rappahannock River, Croghan recorded seeing 'the Ground bare of Snow for the first time Since our March from the Jerseys.'[106] At Fredericksburg, they joined an extravagant celebration of Washington's 48th birthday. They celebrated it again at Richmond 11 days later, this time following the old Julian calendar. Finally, on the second day of March 1780, Colonel Neville's battalion arrived at Petersburg.[107] After a march of 485 miles, winter was over.

The Siege of Charles Town, 31 March–12 May 1780

Major General Scott and Colonel Buford were still in Petersburg when Woodford's frostbitten brigade arrived. Major Croghan was happy to see Scott and transferred into his brigade. He performed double duty as brigade major and major of Buford's 3rd Virginia Detachment. After a week of warmth and rest, Woodford's Brigade marched for Charles Town, which was now under immediate threat. Scott, Croghan, and 'Captain Minzies' (likely Callohill or Holman Minnis) rode south on their own three days later. They left

103 McNew (ed.), *Croghan Diary*, p.14; FHS: Clark Diary, 13 Jan. 1780.
104 Durant, *Union County*, p.297.
105 McNew (ed.), *Croghan Diary*, pp.12–14.
106 McNew (ed.), *Croghan Diary*, pp.19–21.
107 McNew (ed.), *Croghan Diary*, pp.21–25.

Buford and his unequipped men behind, but the 1st and 2nd Detachments were in Georgia. With no foot soldiers to slow them down, Croghan and Scott made good time.[108]

Jonathan Clark, David Stephenson, and the other 8th Virginia veterans in Woodford's Brigade travelled through Halifax, Cross Creek, and Camden on roads that were familiar from the spring of 1776.[109] Croghan and Scott took a wider western route through Hillsborough, Cheraw, and Georgetown but arrived in Charles Town a week before Woodford on 30 March.[110] Scott called it 'the most disagreeable journey ... that I ever experienced.'[111] Parker's and Heth's detachments met them there, and Scott took command as their brigadier. Morale was good for a short time but soon declined. 'We arrived the evening before the siege commenced,' Scott wrote to a friend, 'during which, – not having the most distant hope of success, – you may easily figure to yourself my feelings.'[112]

The city sat at the south tip of a peninsula formed by the junction of the Ashley and Cooper rivers. The large French and Indian War-era fortress known as the Horn Work sat nearly a half mile north of town, bracketed by tidal creeks jutting in from the rivers. Longer-serving 8th Virginia veterans remembered seeing a man hanged there in the summer of 1776.[113] North of it, a zig-zag line of defensive works had been erected between the creeks.[114] When Croghan wrote that they arrived 'the evening before the siege commenced', he meant the British began moving dirt the next day.[115] Siege operations usually followed a defined choreography. An initial line of trenches was dug just within artillery range, in this case at 'Ten or Twelve hundred yards.' A connecting trench was then excavated toward the town, from which a second siege line was dug. Guns were moved forward to a more effective range in the new trench, and the process was repeated. Defenders did their best to disrupt the operation with their own artillery and by sending out sorties. Nearly two weeks of spade-work had to be done before the British siege guns could open fire, but the American guns started hurling iron immediately.[116]

When Woodford's Brigade approached Charles Town, his soldiers were put into small boats and crossed the Cooper River at night. Captain Curry's boat lost sight of Charles Town's lights and got lost in the harbour. He and his men were rescued by a French vessel, the captain of which did his best to encourage them by insisting, 'The English can *no possible* take Charleston.'[117] However, when the Virginians got to the city in the morning, frightened civilians used their empty boats to flee.[118]

---

108 McNew (ed.), *Croghan Diary*, pp.21–26; Ward, *Scott*, p.74.
109 FHS: Clark Diary, 8 March–6 April 1780.
110 McNew (ed.), *Croghan Diary*, pp.26–32; Boston Public Library (BPL): American Revolutionary War Manuscripts Collection, MS G.380.38, 'Letter book of General Lincoln containing copies of 339 letters written at the time of the siege of Charleston', vol.2, p.36.
111 William Vincent Byars (ed.), *B. and M. Gratz: Merchants in Philadelphia, 1754–1798* (Jefferson City: Hugh Stephens Printing, 1916), p.203.
112 Byars (ed.), *Gratz Papers*, pp.203–204.
113 Elliott, 'Diary', pp.231, 234.
114 Borick, *Gallant Defense*, pp.115–116.
115 BPL: Lincoln Letter Book, vol.2, p.36.
116 McNew (ed.), *Croghan Diary*, pp.38–39.
117 Durant, *Union County*, p.297.
118 Carl P. Borick, *A Gallant Defense: The Siege of Charleston, 1780* (Columbia: University of South Carolina Press, 2012), p.130.

A British map of the 'Investiture of Charleston', 1780. (Library of Congress)

The officer in charge at Charles Town, Major General Benjamin Lincoln, was a long way from his Massachusetts home. When Woodford's 'Hardy Veterans' (as they were called) marched into town, church bells rang and a *feu de joie* was organised.[119] Lincoln knew, however, that the situation was not promising. He assembled the generals on 13 April and asked them to start thinking about an evacuation. The British siege guns opened fire just as the meeting adjourned.[120] Croghan said cannonballs 'flew through the streets' as people ran for their cellars.[121] Mortars fired incendiary bombs called 'carcasses' that set houses ablaze.[122] One of Colonel Neville's men wrote:

> the brittish open there batrys upon us about eight or nin aclock in the morning, with there cannon, ther bem shels, ther cerkises, the Smawl arms, and everything that theay couald destroy us with, and it continued night and day. We never had the chance to pul of[f] our clo[thes] but fore tims. For foore weakes we had to fight nit and day.[123]

The 'Smawl arms' fire came from the rifles of the Jägerkorps. The Patriots countered by throwing up a breastwork for American riflemen just outside the main defences on the Cooper River side. Augusta County's Major David Stephenson commanded these marksmen, and they performed well.[124] One of his men caught an enemy soldier peeking out of his trench and shot him in the eye. With artillery support, they forced the British to abandon their first connecting line and start a better one on the Ashley side.[125]

The siege lines advanced, and the Royal Navy pushed past Sullivans' Island into the harbour. The British already controlled the Ashley side of the city and sent troops across the Cooper and a tributary, the Wando River, to begin the encirclement of the town. Sleep, silence, and food all became scarce. Clark wrote 'firing continued' in his diary day after day.[126] Soldiers were issued the same rations for every meal: rice, increasingly bad meat, some coffee, and sugar.[127] Captain Curry, whose right arm was already impaired, was 'severely wounded in the hand by the bursting of a shell.'[128] Governor John Rutledge left the city to ensure continuity of government.[129] About midnight on the 17th, a bomb tore through Major Croghan's tent, smashed through his table, and burrowed more than a foot into the ground. Seeing that its fuse had gone out, he pulled out the unexploded shell and gave it to an artillery officer, who fired it back at the British lines.[130]

American efforts to keep the city open now focused on a redoubt at Lempriere's Point, where Hobcaw Creek poured into the Wando.[131] Brigadier General Scott led 300 men up

119 Hamer et al (eds), *Papers of Laurens*, vol.15, p.273; McNew (ed.), *Croghan Diary*, p.42.
120 Borick, *Gallant Defense*, pp.138–139.
121 McNew (ed.), *Croghan Diary*, p.47.
122 FHS: Clark Diary, 13 April 1780.
123 NARA: W. Tiller pension. Edited for clarity.
124 NARA: H. Aldred pension.
125 Borick, *Gallant Defense*, pp.164–165.
126 FHS: Clark Diary, 14 April–7 May 1780.
127 McNew (ed.), *Croghan Diary*, p.67.
128 Durant, *Union County*, pp.295, 297.
129 Borick, *Gallant Defense*, p.141
130 McNew (ed.), *Croghan Diary*, p.50.
131 BPL: Lincoln Letter Book, vol.2, p.33.

the Cooper during the night of 18 and 19 April to defend the strategic location, but did not stay. He returned to Charles Town for a meeting at which Lieutenant Governor Christopher Gadsden and members of the Privy Council 'very Rudely' chided the Continental officers for contemplating an evacuation. Outrageously, Thomas Ferguson vowed that if they attempted to leave 'he would be among the first who would open the Gates for the Enemy and assist them in attacking us before we got aboard.'[132] Major Croghan explained to his diary that 'Lieut Governor Gadsden, Mr. Ferguson, and Colonel Pinkney have very Extensive fortunes in the Garrison & State of South Carolina.'[133]

It was too late to get out anyway. On the 21st, Lieutenant Colonel Clark recorded that Lincoln sent 'a flag to the enemy offering [terms] which was refused, and a very heavy cannonade ensued which cont[inue]d ye greatest part of the night.' At Lempriere's Point, Croghan had 'an exceeding good view of the Firings on Both Sides, which far Exceeded my Ideas.' Mesmerized, he stood and watched for two hours as 'the American and British lines Seem'd in a Constant Blaze, which with the throwing and Bursting of Shells, the unremitting roar of heavy Cannon &c – Made an awful yet pleasing appearance.' Lincoln ordered Croghan back to Charles Town in the morning. 'I was Sorry to receive Such orders,' he wrote, 'being in great doubt of my ever having it in my power, if I once return'd to Town if I could again leave it Except as a prisoner.'[134]

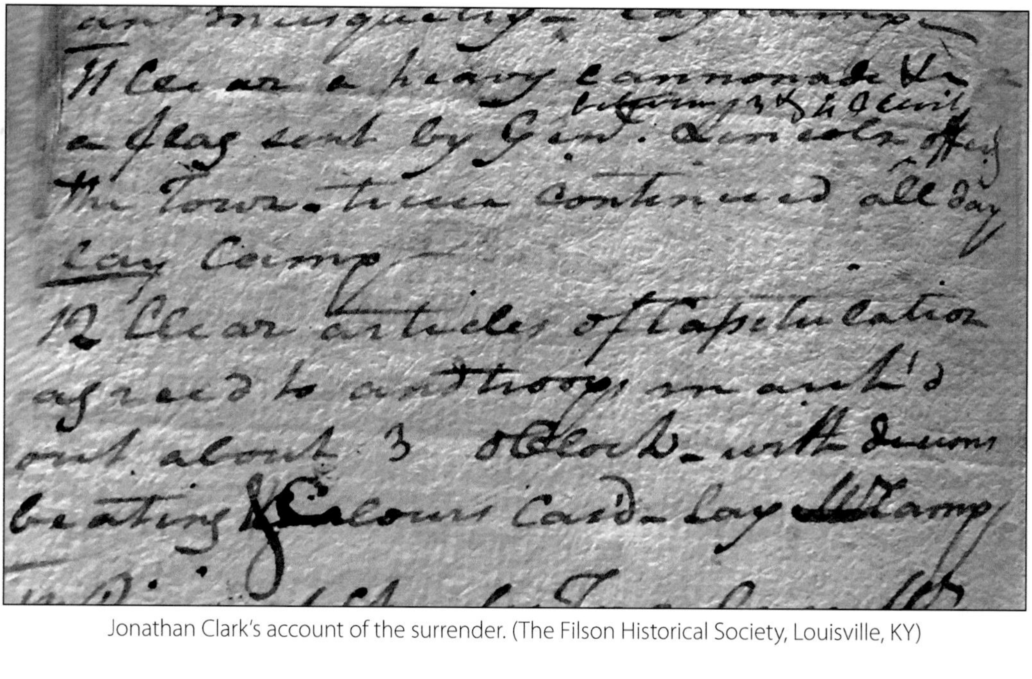

Jonathan Clark's account of the surrender. (The Filson Historical Society, Louisville, KY)

132 Lilla Mills Hawes (ed.), *Lachlan McIntosh Papers in the University of Georgia Libraries* (Athens: University of Georgia Press, 1968), pp.103–104; McNew (ed.), *Croghan Diary*, p.55.
133 McNew (ed.), *Croghan Diary*, p.56.
134 McNew (ed.), *Croghan Diary*, pp.58–59.

Indeed, a week later, the major looked back to see the British flag flying above Lempriere's Point. He wrote '…alas we are now Entirely Surrounded.'[135] Lincoln surrendered the city on 12 May. Clark said the 'articles of Capitulation' were agreed to and the 'troops march'd out about 3 o'clock with drums beating & Colours cas'd.'[136]

Knox and Slaughter in the West

Virginia's western charter lands had developed into an active war zone on both sides of the Ohio. Aside from a few unsuccessful Continental forays out of Fort Pitt, Virginia fought in the West alone. Most Cherokee and Shawnee leaders had recognised the Big Knife's possession of Kentucky, but Lieutenant Governor Hamilton actively directed Indian proxies to attack south of the Ohio, and Virginians crossed to the north to respond. Patrick Henry approved a secret plan to counter with an attack on former French settlements near the Mississippi River. The campaign, led by George Rogers Clark and Joseph Bowman (two brothers of 8th Virginia officers), exceeded all expectations. Hamilton himself was taken prisoner on 25 February 1779, and Virginia incorporated the north side of the river as Illinois County.[137] Clark's volunteers were augmented and organised on state establishment as the Illinois Regiment and set about securing the northwestern territory. The Virginians garrisoned the francophone villages at Kaskaskia, Cahokia, and Vincennes and built Fort Jefferson near the Iron Banks of the Mississippi, just below the mouth of the Ohio.[138]

George Slaughter was barred from Continental service but determined to remain engaged, and that meant he needed a state commission. The Old Dominion was looking for good officers to command four new battalions of six-month state volunteers. His long experience in Pontiac's War, Dunmore's War, and the first years of the Revolution stood out and the governor appointed him commanding lieutenant colonel of the 2nd Virginia Volunteer Battalion. His orders were to supervise the recruiting of 500 men in 10 companies and reinforce Washington in New Jersey.[139] On the advice of Congress, however, the plan was abandoned, and Slaughter was once again out of a job.[140] He returned to the West, participated in Evan Shelby's campaign against the Chickamauga, and he spent the summer of 1779 in Kentucky.[141]

British attacks in the Chesapeake convinced Virginia to try again to step up its defences. The legislature passed an act in June authorizing four new battalions, 'two for the defence of the western frontiers and two for the defence of the eastern limits of this state.'[142] Joseph

135 McNew (ed.), *Croghan Diary*, p.64.
136 FHS: Clark Diary, 12 May 1780.
137 Draper Mss, L, vol.1, pp.54–55; Eric Sterner, *Till the Extinction of This Rebellion: George Rogers Clark, Frontier Warfare, and the Illinois Campaign of 1778–1779* (Yardley: Westholme, 2024).
138 NARA: A. Cabbage pension. English, *Life of General Clark*, vol.2, p.673.
139 McIlwaine et al (eds), *Council of the State of Virginia*, vol.2, pp.153–154; Hening *Statutes*, vol.9, pp.445–449.
140 McIlwaine et al (eds), *Council of the State of Virginia*, vol.2, pp.174–175.
141 Louise Phelps Kellogg (ed.), *Frontier Retreat on the Upper Ohio, 1779–1781* (Madison: Wisconsin Historical Society, 1917), pp.179–180, n.2.
142 Hening (ed.), *Statutes*, vol.10, pp.32–34.

Crockett and James Knox were picked to lead the western battalions as lieutenant colonels.[143] A frequent pair, Knox and Crockett had served in William Russell's 1775 independent provincial frontier company and were dropped as supernumerary majors at the same time.[144] George Walls, the Berkeley captain whose quest for vengeance imperilled the attack on Trenton, resigned from the 2nd Virginia Battalion to be Knox's major.[145] Knox and his men were at Lynch's Ferry (Lynchburg) in December,[146] but spent the rest of the bitter winter camped farther west in Powell's Valley between the Cumberland and Clinch ridges. There, perhaps from the half-acre stockade called Rye Cove Fort,[147] they coordinated with locals to guard against Native incursions through the Cumberland and Moccasin gaps.[148]

By spring it was obvious that the complex statewide recruiting system for the four state battalions had failed. Virginia abandoned the eastern units and merged the western battalions under Crockett, who was senior. Knox was supernumerary once again and his military career thus came to an end.[149] He turned his attention to the settlement of Kentucky, leading packhorse trains of settlers through the Cumberland Gap and,[150] beginning in 1795 (again with Crockett), managing the task of widening the trace so wagons could make it through on what came to be known as the 'Wilderness Road.'[151] Four years later, the land on the Kentucky side of the gap was organised as Knox County. Knox County and Knoxville, Tennessee are usually said to be named after artillerist Henry Knox, but some old accounts say the two places were named in honour of the long hunter, warrior, and road builder.[152] The Knoxville theory is easily discounted. The Knox County claim, however, has real weight, supported by the specific geography, the Antifederalist views popular in Kentucky at the time it was formed, and the names given to other counties in the same period.

Lowering its expectations, Virginia moved yet again to raise men for frontier defence. George Slaughter was tasked in November 1779 with recruiting 100 men and leading them west.[153] The Culpeper veteran relied on his reputation, his family, and his friends to collect the new force. His nephew James Slaughter remembered being 'appointed a Lieutenant in

143 Boyd et al (eds), *Papers of Jefferson*, vol.3, pp.50–52.
144 LVA: A. Sandridge bounty claim.
145 LVA: Legislative Petitions, Accession 36121, Robert Powell (Crockett's Western Battalion).
146 Boyd et al (eds), *Papers of Jefferson*, vol.3, pp.252–253.
147 Redd, 'Reminiscences', 7:1 (1899), p.3.
148 Boyd et al (eds), *Papers of Jefferson*, vol.3, pp.160–161.
149 Hening (ed.), *Statutes*, vol.10, pp.215–216; Boyd et al (eds), *Papers of Jefferson*, vol.3, pp.540–541; LVA: R. Powell legislative petition.
150 Redd, 'Reminiscences', 7:3 (1900), p.245; Chester Raymond Young (ed.), *Westward into Kentucky: The Narrative of Daniel Trabue* (Lexington: University Press of Kentucky, 1981), pp.81–82; D.W. Clark, *Memoir of Mrs. Jane Trimble: A Tribute of Affection from Her Grandson* (Cincinnati: Methodist Book Concern, 1861), pp.40–61; Waddell (ed.), *Annals of Augusta*, pp.451–453.
151 Jouett Taylor Cannon (ed.), 'State Archives – General Expenditures 1792–1798', *Register of Kentucky State Historical Society*, 32:99 (1934), p.128; Neal Owen Hammon, 'Early Roads into Kentucky', *Register of the Kentucky Historical Society*, 68:2 (1970), pp.91–131, p.94.
152 Draper Mss, C, vol.5, p.50; Oren F. Morton, *Annals of Bath County, Virginia* (Staunton: McClure Co., 1917), pp.195–196.
153 Anon. (ed.), *Journal of Delegates*, 1779, p.40.

James Knox and Joseph Crockett oversaw improvement of the Wilderness Road into a thoroughfare passable by wagons. (Photo: Duane Hall, HMdb.org)

Captain Benjamin Roberts' Company of Major George Slaughter's Corps' and marching 'with said Company from Culpeper County to the falls of Ohio.'[154]

Major Slaughter's 100 men were 'attached to, and considered as part of' Lieutenant Colonel Crockett's consolidated battalion,[155] but started off for Kentucky while Crockett was detained in the east.[156] They took Braddock's Road toward Fort Pitt but got stuck in the Allegheny Mountains when the historically hard winter came.[157] They toughed out the hostile weather much as Abraham Bowman's settlers did and finally reached Fort Pitt in April or May of 1780. Former 8th Virginia captains John Stephenson and Richard Campbell were both there at the time, allowing for a small reunion about the time when Jonathan Clark, David Stephenson, and William Croghan were giving up the fight at Charles Town.[158] Slaughter's 100 soldiers left for the falls of the Ohio in canoes on 20 May and gained another 50 men recruited by John Bowman when they got there.[159]

154 NARA: M804, S31370, James Slaughter pension (Crockett's Western Battalion).
155 Hening (ed.), *Statutes*, vol.10, p.215.
156 NARA: A. Cabbage pension. English, *Life of General Clark*, vol.1, pp.258–259.
157 NARA: M804, S6584, James Ballard pension (Crockett's Western Battalion); Kellogg (ed.), *Frontier Retreat*, pp.179–180, n.2.
158 Chase et al (eds), *Papers of Washington*, vol.25, pp.62–63.
159 Hazard et al (eds), *Pennsylvania Archives*, ser.1, vol.12, pp.232, 238–239; Boyd et al (eds), *Papers of Jefferson*, vol.3, pp.160–161.

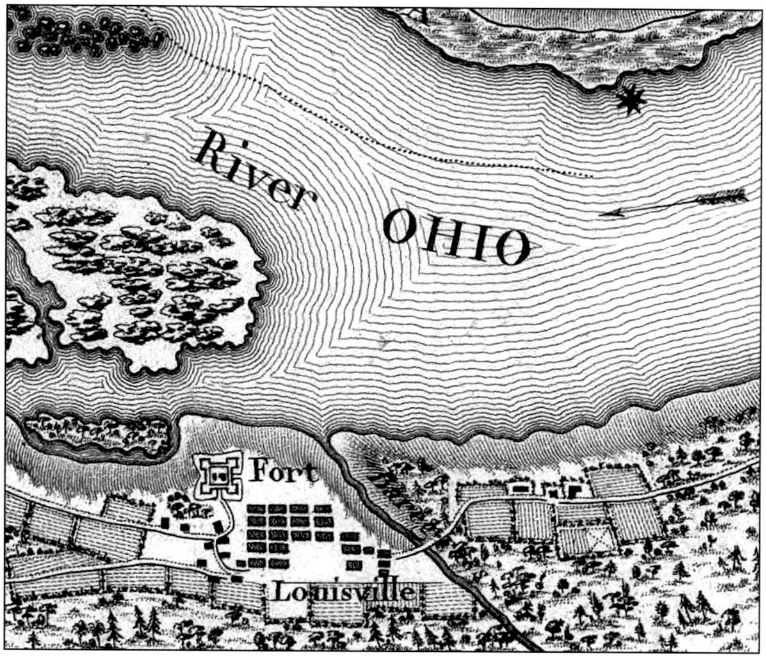

A detail from 1796 map of shows the arrangement of Louisville and Fort Nelson at the falls of the Ohio River. George Henri Victor Collot. (David Rumsey Map Collection, David Rumsey Map Center, Stanford Libraries)

In the summer, Slaughter played a central role in organising Colonel George Rogers Clark's expedition into Ohio that culminated in the Battle of Piqua on 8 August.[160] The tough winter and the summer's perilous service took a heavy toll that left them ill-prepared for the winter that followed. One Kentuckian reported on 25 August, 'we have very small expectations from Colo Slaughter's Regiment as it does not exceed forty effective men, who must suffer this winter for clothing.'[161] The condition of the men, dwindling supplies, and the diversion of Crockett away from the west imperilled Virginia's western gains.[162] George Rogers Clark returned to Virginia at the end of 1780 to seek support in person, leaving Major Slaughter in command at the settlement now incorporated as Louisville.[163] Slaughter was one of the town's original trustees and oversaw the construction of Fort Nelson to replace an existing stockade.[164]

Slaughter reported on his supply problems to Governor Thomas Jefferson in December. 'My Men,' he wrote, 'have never drawn any thing from the State but Cloth and thirty Blankets at Williamsburg ... They now [have] no Shirts, Hats, Blankets or Breeches, not having drawn Cloth for that purpose, Shoes, Stockings [or] Mocasons, so that they are totally unfit for duty.' They suffered this way through the whole winter of 1780–1781 and were no better off in the spring when Slaughter reported, 'We are here without money, Clothing, or any thing else scarsely to subsist on.' The surrounding security situation was equally poor. 'The

160 Kellogg (ed.), *Frontier Retreat*, p.186.
161 Kellogg (ed.), *Frontier Retreat*, p.266.
162 NARA: M804, R17484, William Roberts (Crockett's Western Battalion).
163 NARA: A. Cabbage pension. English, *Life of General Clark*, vol.2, pp.688, 702.
164 Hening (ed.), *Statutes*, vol.10, pp.293–295; Kellogg (ed.), *Frontier Retreat*, pp.179–180, n.2.

An illustration of Fort Jefferson by Rick Mjos based on research by Ken Carstens. (Courtesy of Ken Carstens)

Savages have been very troublesome this Spring,' he complained, 'almost every other day we have accounts of some one being either kill'd or Captured; upwards of 40 Men, Women and Children have fallen a prey to them within the County of Jefferson in the course of 2 Months past and we have not had the satisfaction of getting but one of there Scalps.'[165]

One of Slaughter's men was William Smith, a Culpeper veteran of his 8th Virginia company.[166] At some point that winter, Smith 'was sent by Major George Slaughter as an express to the Iron Banks, which duty he performed with success.'[167] Smith's mission was no walk in a park. There and back, it was a 500-mile journey through hostile wilderness. However, he found at least one familiar face when he arrived at Fort Jefferson in the person of Martin Carney. Carney had been quartermaster of the 8th Virginia (and the 4th), but Charles Scott called him 'a Rascul who Ought not to Have Born the rank of a Corporal.' Unable to 'Support a Charge Suffecent to Brake him,' Scott accepted Carney's resignation at Petersburg, viewing it as 'a favourable oppertunity to get Him aut of the Service.'[168] Now Carney was quartermaster at Fort Jefferson and quite miserable about it. He wrote to George Rogers Clark in April to complain about the 'Disagreeableness of so long and Close a confinement as I have laboured under Since my Arrival at this place.'[169] Carney had survived a siege by Choctaw and Cherokee warriors and the reduction of the garrison to 'a very small number...occasioned by famine, desertion, and numbers daily dying.'[170] After a year of sometimes terrifying isolation 800 miles from Williamsburg, he begged to be relieved.

165 Boyd et al (eds), *Papers of Jefferson*, vol.4, p.188, vol.5, pp.493–494. Kentucky County was split into Jefferson, Lincoln, and Fayette counties in 1780.

166 NARA: M804, S7548, William Smith pension.

167 NARA: W. Smith pension.

168 Chase et al (eds), *Papers of Washington*, vol.21, pp.588–590.

169 Missouri Historical Society Archives (MHSA): Clark Family Collection, 1766–1991, Martin Carney to George Rogers Clark, 22 April 1781.

170 NARA: A. Cabbage pension. English, *Life of General Clark*, vol.2, pp.673–675, 688–689; Hammon and Taylor, *Western War*, pp.132–133.

Defeats at the Waxhaws and Camden

After waiting months for clothing and equipment, Colonel Abraham Buford's 3rd Virginia Detachment finally marched from Petersburg. Among Buford's men racing to aid the defence of Charles Town were Richard Bennett and the boy Adam Dietz. They were within 50 miles of the city when news came that Benjamin Lincoln had surrendered. Lieutenant Colonel Banastre Tarleton's British Legion chased the Virginians to the Waxhaws, just short of the North Carolina line. When Buford refused to surrender on 29 May 1780, many of his men were cut down and Dietz and Bennett were both taken prisoner.[171]

Following Lincoln's surrender and Buford's defeat, Congress appointed Berkeley's Major General Horatio Gates commander of a new southern army. It was composed mostly of Maryland and Delaware Continentals supported by regional militia. Gates, too, was soundly defeated at Camden, South Carolina, on 16 August 1780. James Young, an 8th Virginia veteran who was probably in militia service, said, 'at the defeat of General Gates,' he 'became separated from the American army, was taken prisoner by the tories, and in consequence of the retreat of the army towards the north, was unable again to join it.'[172] Thus, by the fall of 1780, the Virginia Line had surrendered at Charles Town and seen its remnants thrashed at the Waxhaws and Camden. Georgia and South Carolina seemed firmly in British hands, and Virginia had no army left with which to defend itself.

Prisoners in Charles Town

Adam Dietz, Richard Bennett, and James Young were marched to the coast and thrown in with the Continentals taken in the surrender of Charles Town. The officers were held at a brick barracks about a mile inland from Haddrell's Point on limited paroles.[173] The enlisted men were kept at a barracks in town while Loyalists, pretended and real, streamed into town to accept the King's 'protection.' Bennett, who had begun his service in George Slaughter's Company, recalled that 'a few months after I was made a prisoner I ran away from the British & came on to Fredericksburgh in Virginia' and reported for duty.[174] John Wyatt, the Jonathan Clark recruit now in the 2nd Virginia Detachment, remained at the barracks for about six months. He then traded a quart of rum for a pass belonging to 'one Joseph Seal who had been made a prisoner at Waxhaw & had taken protection under the British, and enlisted with them.' Using the pass, he 'effected his passage through the British lines made his escape and returned home to Botetourt.'[175]

So many men snuck out of Charles Town that the British clamped down hard. Robert Chambers, formerly of Captain Higgins' Company, remembered that under the terms of capitulation, they 'were to receive rations as a British Soldier ... we were to have the Barracks for our resident and the liberty of the town but instead of complying with these articles

171 NARA: A. Deets pension; R. Bennett pension.
172 NARA: M804, R11976, James Young pension.
173 Anon., 'Revolutionary War in Mount Pleasant.'
174 NARA: R. Bennett pension.
175 NARA: J. Wyatt pension.

they confin'd us on board prison ships where our distressed situation was too great to be express'd.'[176]

As they had in Philadelphia, the British leveraged the frightful conditions to induce men to enlist in their army. Captain Curry remembered Lord Charles Montagu, three-time colonial governor of South Carolina, 'Attempting to enlist a Corps from the prisoners.' Most refused to sign on, but after many months of confinement and abuse, a number of men lost the will to resist. Beatings and threats of impressment into the Royal Navy eventually prompted 500 men to enlist,[177] including Osborn Flynn (originally of Westfall's Company), John Roberts (of Darke's), and John Harden, William McCoy, and James Patterson (all of David Stephenson's Company).[178] Montagu 'succeeded in getting a number who expected to be taken into the Country and then make their escape,' Curry recalled, 'but they were immediately put in [ships] and sent to the West Indies.'[179]

There was not enough room in the barracks at Haddrell's Point for all the officers. The most senior found rooms in local homes, while ensigns built huts in the woods. Benjamin Lincoln was allowed to go home on parole and an ailing William Woodford was taken to New York, where he died. This left Charles Scott as the senior Virginian and he did everything he could to care for his men. Food was scarce, in part because it was retrieved using a boat so leaky anyone using it had to have one hand 'almost constantly employed' to bail water. To make up the difference, they caught crabs and fish.[180] Medicine, too, was hard to come by as they entered the season for mosquito-borne diseases. Scott wrote to friends in the north, tried to sell his personal possessions, including people, and used his personal credit to raise hard money.[181] Many officers accrued smaller debts, while Major Stephenson and others were able to avoid borrowing.[182] Tobacco and flour was shipped to them from Virginia, which they sold in Charles Town to get other food and supplies.[183]

Since officers were allowed to retain their waiters, there were several enlisted men at Haddrell's Point. Andrew Wolfe, a 1778 Clark enlistee, had been serving as Adjutant William Kelly's waiter since the provisional consolidation at Valley Forge. Captain Curry affectionately called him 'a poor uncultivated dutch boy.'[184] Still a lieutenant, Kelly worked as adjutant and aide to Charles Scott, handling his paperwork and correspondence. He was also the only Virginia officer to defect to the British from Haddrell's Point. Kelly tried to get Andrew Wolfe to go with him, but the 'uncultivated dutch boy' refused.[185] The disloyal

176 NARA: R. Chambers pension.

177 NARA: M247, item 156, p.42.

178 C. Leon Harris (ed.), 'Prisoners of War from the Siege of Charleston and the Battle of Camden Who Joined the British in the Duke of Cumberland's Regiment', *Southern Campaigns American Revolution Pension Statements and Rosters*, <revwarapps.org/b406.pdf>, accessed 16 May 2024.

179 NARA: M804, S46413, Andrew Wolfe pension; Lewis Namier, 'Lord Charles Greville Montagu (1741–84)', in Lewis Namier and John Brooke, *The History of Parliament: The House of Commons, 1754–1790* (London: Secker & Warburg, 1964), vol.3, p.153.

180 Moultrie, *Memoirs*, vol.2, pp.112–118.

181 Byars (ed.), *Gratz Papers*, p.204; Ward, *Scott*, pp.78–80.

182 Palmer et al (eds), *Calendar*, vol.2, p.373.

183 Draper Mss, L, vol.2, pp.9–11; Idzerda (ed.), *Lafayette Papers*, vol.4, pp.218–219.

184 NARA: A. Wolfe pension.

185 NARA: A. Wolfe pension.

adjutant took all of Scott's papers with him, leaving the financially strapped general unable to get reimbursed for much of what he provided for the men.[186]

Lieutenant Colonel Clark's diary from Haddrell's Point contains little more than repetitive weather reports, exhibiting a dreary time in captivity.[187] Captain Curry, on the other hand, appears never to have been bored. He served as a second in another duel, this time for Colonel Gist, who faced off against South Carolina Captain Wade Hampton. Neither man was injured.[188] On another day, while walking near the city with his captors, Curry saw a rabbit. 'Drawing his sword he made a plunge, and splitting the unfortunate animal, turned, and with a polite bow, extended it to the principal officer of the party.'[189] Or so he claimed.

On 4 July 1780, Clark noted 'a meeting of the officers to celebrate the anniversary of Independence.' Though it rained in the evening, the barracks was illuminated with a lamp or candle in every window.[190]

Virginia's War in the West

As much as anything, it was vast expanses that made America the land of opportunity. Undeveloped terrain was considered 'waste' under English and American law, though it was still off limits unless acquired from Natives by purchase and treaty.[191] The United States earned a reputation for breaking its Indian treaties, but the decentralised nature of the Indians' own politics led to noncompliance on that side as well. Private deals 'by persons pretending to derive titles from Indian deeds and purchasers' were another problem. In 1776, the Virginia Convention barred private purchases of Indian land while also declaring 'all persons who are now actually settled on any unallocated or unappropriated lands in Virginia … shall have the pre-emption, or preference, in the grants of such lands.'[192] In 1777, the size of pre-emption grants was limited to 400 acres, but actual settlers were allowed to purchase another 1,000 acres, and a land office was set up at St Asaph (Logan's Station), Kentucky to do the paperwork. The Commonwealth also began promising grants of bounty land as an enlistment incentive.[193]

The Bowman family was at the vanguard of the resulting land rush and consequently embroiled in the ongoing western conflict. After Indians laid siege to Boonesborough in 1778, John Bowman crossed the Ohio with Kentucky militia to attack the Shawnee village of Chillicothe in 1779. British Captain Henry Bird came south from Detroit in 1780 with an army of Canadian rangers, Native warriors, and artillery. Abraham Bowman's sister,

186 Ward, *Scott*, p.80.
187 FHS: Clark Diary, 20 May–31 Dec. 1780.
188 Durant (ed.), *Union County*, p.297; Ronald E. Bridwell, 'Wade Hampton I,' South Carolina Encyclopedia, <scencyclopedia.org/sce/entries/hampton-wade-i/>, accessed 18 May 2024.
189 Durant (ed.), *Union County*, p.297.
190 FHS: Clark Diary, 4 July 1780.
191 Williams, *Dunmore's War*, pp.12–15.
192 Anon (ed.), *Proceedings of the 5th Convention*, p.63.
193 Hening (ed.), *Statutes*, vol.9, pp.179, 213–214, 355–356, vol.10, pp.26–27, 35–65; Hammon and Taylor, *Western War*, pp.104, 109.

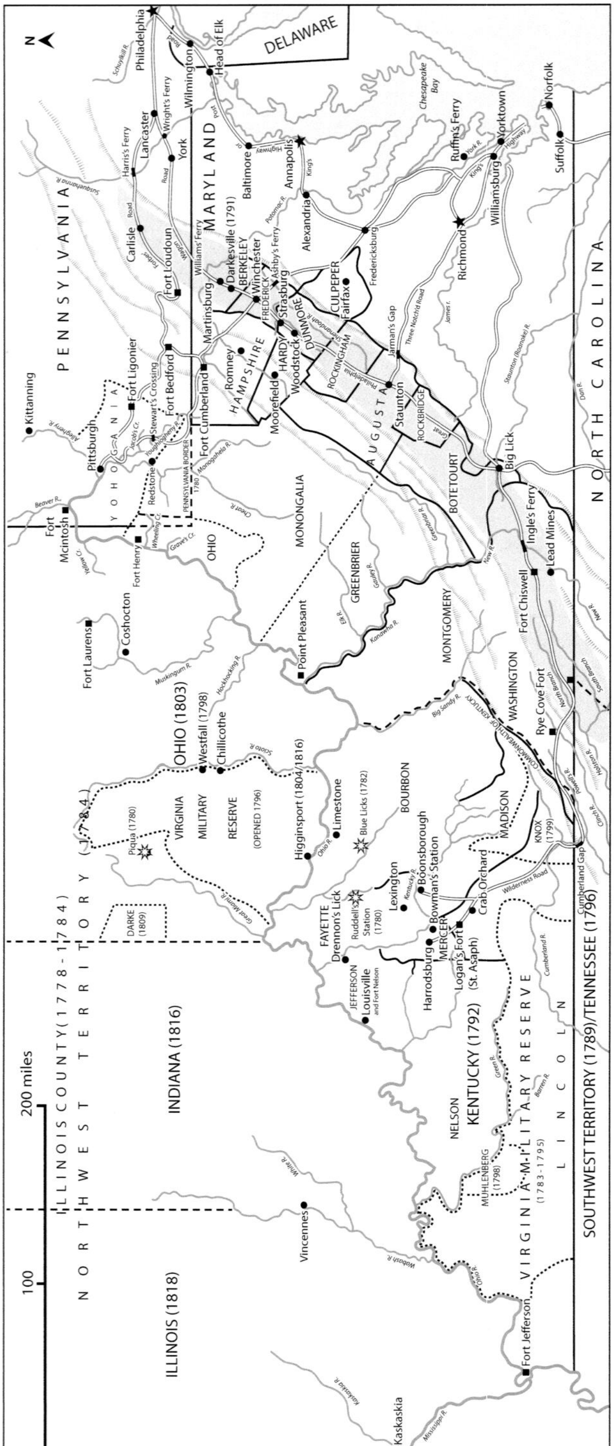

The Later Virginia Frontier.

Elizabeth Ruddell, was taken captive with her husband and five children.[194] They trudged all the way to Detroit, where their youngest child was burned to death.[195] The Shawnee adopted eight-year-old Stephen and four-year-old Abraham and sent the rest of the family to Montreal. George Slaughter, meanwhile, helped George Rogers Clark organise a retaliatory expedition against the Shawnee settlement at Piqua (Peckuwe).[196]

George Rogers Clark, now a Virginia state general, passed through Pittsburgh on his way back to the frontier in the spring of 1781. He carried blank commissions signed by Governor Jefferson for a new troop of cavalry for western service. He and Captain Benjamin Field (brother of the 8th Virginia's Reuben Field) got to work recruiting. Eighth Virginia veteran Thomas Ravenscraft accepted a lieutenancy. Samuel Murphy, another veteran of John Stephenson's Company, enlisted.[197]

Clark and his recruits floated down the Ohio to the falls and linked up with the Illinois Regiment and Crockett's Western Battalion. Captain John Chapman, once one of Thomas Berry's sergeants, was among the men who greeted them. So was George Slaughter, who had struggled through the winter at Fort Nelson. The reunion coincided with a worsening security situation. Chapman and another captain were killed when Mohawk chief and commissioned British officer Joseph Brant invaded Kentucky with an Anglo-Native force.[198] A third officer remembered, 'three of us, Capt. Chapman, Capt. Tipton and I, on a ride to Col Floyds station about six miles from the falls, were fired on by a party of Indians and Capt Chapman and Tipton, the one before and the other behind me, were shot down.'[199]

Eleven days later, Lieutenant Ravenscraft was tasked with evacuating settlers from Squire Boone's Station (Painted Stone Station), which sat exposed on the Kentucky River.[200] Ravenscraft was the ranking officer while Captain Field was away. The mission involved escorting a caravan of mostly women and children 21 miles west on Boone's Wagon Road to greater safety at Linn's Station on Beargrass Creek. A militiaman recalled that Ravenscraft's procession was 'attacked by a large body of Indians, and men women & children were slain by the savages, and nearly every man of the Troop of Captain Field was killed and taken prisoners.'[201] Ravenscraft was unhurt but Samuel Murphy was wounded in the left hip.[202] 'Boone's Defeat' or the 'Long Run Massacre' was perpetrated by 50 Miami warriors who had split off from Brant's invaders.[203]

194 Otto A. Rothert (ed.), 'John D. Shane's Interview, in 1841, with Mrs. Wilson of Woodford County', *Filson Club History Quarterly*, 16:4 (1942), p.228.

195 *Virginia Gazette* (Hayes), 31 May 1783; Rothert (ed.), 'Mrs. Wilson', p.231.

196 John F. Winkler, *Peckuwe, 1780: The Revolutionary War on the Ohio River Frontier* (Oxford: Osprey Publishing, 2018), pp.50–81.

197 NARA: T. Ravensraft pension, S. Murphy pension.

198 NARA: M804, R18512, Abraham Tipton pension.

199 NARA: M804, S16948, Hugh McGavock pension (Crockett's Western Battalion). Edited for clarity.

200 WHS: Draper Mss, CC, vol.13, pp.226, 228.

201 LVA: Federal Government Records Collection, Virginia Half Pay and Other Related Revolutionary War Pension Application Files, Benjamin Field.

202 NARA: S. Murphy pension.

203 Vince Akers, 'A Detailed History of Painted Stone Station', *Painted Stone Settlers*, <paintedstonesettlers.org/detailedhistory.html>, accessed 23 Nov. 2024.

John Floyd, who had explored Kentucky with James Knox before the war now held the job of Jefferson County lieutenant. He organised an immediate counteroffensive, but because the Indians had killed or stolen many horses, just 27 men rode out with him. A mixed group of Floyd's militia and Ravenscraft's surviving state regulars rode in three nine-man columns led by Ravenscraft, Floyd, and Peter A'Sturgis. Brant's full 200-man Miami and Huron force attacked them on the road.[204] Ravenscraft survived this uneven fight known as 'Floyd's Defeat,' but he had a rough start to his captivity. 'They made him run the gauntlet,' remembered another captive, 'and nearly killed him.'[205] He 'was tomahawked by the Indians on the head' and never fully recovered.[206] Murphy and Ravenscraft, after a long trek, joined Abraham Bowman's sister as captives in the north. Murphy explained that 'he was taken prisoner by the Indians ... and taken to Detroyet – and some time in November of the same year he was sold to the British and was taken to a place cald prisoners Island,' which was probably near Montreal.[207]

Woodlands Indian tribes sometimes made captives 'run the gauntlet.' (Edward Eggleston and Lillie Eggleston Seelye, *Tecumseh and the Shawnee Prophet* (New York: Dodd, Mead & Company, 1878))

Though the fighting was fierce, and the frontier was vast, there were signs to remind the combatants of how close-knit the sparsely populated West had once been. John Stephenson's former lieutenant, Simon Girty, played a key role in Bird's 1780 attacks. Joseph Brant was Major William Croghan's cousin by marriage: his wife was the daughter of George Croghan and a Mohawk woman.[208]

Bowman's Station was never attacked, but its men responded to several regional emergencies. One of them died fighting alongside George Slaughter at Piqua in 1780. Abraham Bowman married that man's widow, Sarah (née Henry). Bowman himself survived a deadly

204 Akers, *Painted Stone Settlers.*
205 Rothert (ed.), 'Mrs. Wilson', p.231.
206 NARA: T. Ravenscaft pension; James (ed.), *George Rogers Clark Papers*, p.604.
207 NARA: S. Murphy pension.
208 Phillip W. Hoffman, *Simon Girty, Turncoat Hero: The Most Hated Man on the Early American Frontier* (Franklin, Tenn.: Flying Camp Press, 2009), pp.183–194; Isabel Thompson Kelsay, *Joseph Brant, 1743–1807: Man of Two Worlds* (Syracuse: Syracuse University Press, 1984), pp.276–277.

clash at Blue Licks in 1782, but five of his Bowman's Station comrades perished.[209] Blue Licks was the last significant battle of the Revolutionary War fought on American soil.

Ravenscraft and Murphy both tried to escape from 'Prisoners Island.' Ravenscraft ran away in June of 1782, but was captured at Saint-François-du-Lac. He was taken back to Montreal,[210] where Isaac Ruddell was suspected of having tipped off the British to his departure.[211] Murphy had more luck, remembering that 'on the 11th day of July 1782 he in company with Ezekial Louis made his escape and returned home having been absent about one year.'[212]

Ravenscraft was exchanged after the war and went on to lead troops in the War of 1812. 'Old as the Old Gentleman was,' a neighbour commented in 1825, 'he led a Company to the field in the last war; never was there a better soldier, or a man who possessed better feelings toward his Country, and his fellow man, than Capt. Ravenscraft.'[213]

The Ruddell boys, like many other child captives, completely embraced their lives as Indians. They were adopted by the family of Tecumseh, the famous Shawnee war chief. Among their Indian friends was a brother of William Ward, the original ensign of James Knox's Company. Stephen Ruddell later wrote out an account of his life as a Shawnee warrior, describing combat alongside Tecumseh opposite frontiersman Simon Kenton and against Anthony Wayne's army at Fallen Timbers in 1794. Ward's brother, who lived as an Indian from the age of three, died in combat. Colonel Bowman's nephews were turned over with many other captives after the Treaty of Greenville in 1795, having lived in Indian society for 15 years.[214] While searching for them, an officer found an Indian who could speak a little English and asked if he knew Stephen Ruddell. 'Me,' said the Indian, striking his hand on his chest, 'Me, Stephen Liddle.' Abraham Ruddell spoke no English at all.[215]

Release from Long Island

John Clark's life as a prisoner on Long Island was not very different from his brother's at Haddrell's Point. Boredom, meagre supplies, and a need for money plagued them both. The younger Clark, Robert Higgins, Reuben Field, and Jonathan Smith lived on farms around New Utrecht and Gravesend for more than two years. They had to pay for their room and board but had no way to get money other than begging in their letters home. Lieutenant Colonel Darke was allowed to go home for a while but returned when the British recalled paroled American officers in 1779.[216]

---

209 Beckner (ed.), 'Interview with Elijah Foley', pp.257–259.

210 Douglas Brymner (ed.), *Report on Canadian Archives, 1887* (Ottawa: MacLean, Roger & Co., 1888), p.307.

211 Rothert (ed.), 'Mrs. Wilson,' p.231.

212 NARA: S. Murphy pension.

213 NARA: T. Ravenscraft pension.

214 WHS: Draper Mss, YY, vol.2, pp.120–133, CC, vol.8, p.24.

215 Young (ed.), *The Narrative of Daniel Trabue*, p.139–140.

216 NARA: M246, f.4, p.12; Thomas M. Strong, *The History of the Town of Flatbush in King's County, Long Island* (New York: Thomas R. Mercein, 1842), pp.158–159; Draper Mss, L, vol.1, p.42; Chase et al (eds), *Papers of Washington* (Revolution), vol.19, pp.152–154, n.1., vol. 24, pp.68–70.

In 1780, Darke cosigned a 'memorial' to Governor Jefferson, begging for help. Following the style of a petition, the officers referred to themselves in the third person. 'A whole year has now elapsed,' they complained, 'since they have received the smallest supply, and the scanty pittance then handed them, was barely sufficient.' The only thing Virginia had to offer them was tobacco. The legislature offered to send a shipment of it to New York, hoping the officers could sell it or barter with it. Washington advised Jefferson that the British would not allow it and suggested the Commonwealth sell the tobacco itself and forward the proceeds.[217]

Late in 1780, Governor Jefferson agreed to trade Lieutenant Governor Henry Hamilton (the 'hair buyer') in a trade for the men on Long Island.[218] The Virginia officers were finally free and headed home. According to a tradition recorded in 1910 Darke was 'obliged to walk all the long weary way back to his home in Virginia. On the road he stopped at the cottage of a settler for food and rest. A bird was hanging in its cage near the door. Darke offered the owner one of his few "hard dollars," bought the bird, and immediately opened the cage door, and let it fly.'[219]

Jacob Rinker's Militia Company

Though Tommy Miller was one of the 8th Virginia veterans helping rebuild the Virginia Line, he was not really a Virginian. He was from Cecil County, Maryland, where his father was an elder of the important West Nottingham Presbyterian Church. His father was also 'a man of austere bearing' who 'kept his children at too great a distance.' Miller was just 16 years old when he received his ensign's commission 'through the intervention of some friend.' That friend may have been Abraham Kirkpatrick, who grew up in Cecil County and knew the Miller family.[220] Miller fought at Brandywine and was briefly missing after the chaotic retreat from Germantown.[221] He was promoted to lieutenant, fought at Monmouth, and was among the officers sent home when Woodford consolidated the Virginia Line into three battalions at Philadelphia. After the triple defeats of 1780, he was stationed at Chesterfield Court House as a recruiting officer, helping the Old Dominion rebuild its Continental forces. He was at that time 'an agreeable and handsome young man' and 'a gallant officer' who quickly caught the eye of Nancy Ball.[222] Nancy came from a good family and was related to George Washington, but not closely.

Muhlenberg, meanwhile, returned to Virginia in April to take charge of recruiting.[223] Not counting the commander-in-chief, he was the last Virginia general still free and in active Continental service. As Muhlenberg and Miller enrolled new soldiers at Chesterfield Court House, the tide started to turn in the south. A decentralised army of frontiersmen

217 Boyd (ed.), *Papers of Jefferson*, vol.3, pp.388–391, 458, 481; Chase et al (eds), *Papers of Washington* (Revolution), vol.28, pp.26–29.

218 Chase et al (eds), *Papers of Washington* (Revolution), vol.28, p.96; Boyd (ed.), *Papers of Jefferson*, vol.4, p.68.

219 Dandridge, *Historic Shepherdstown*, p.257.

220 Samuel H. Miller (ed.), *Life of Samuel Thomas Miller* (Lynchburg: J.P. Bell Company, 1911), pp.7, 9.

221 NARA: T. Miller pension; M246, f.212, p.11.

222 Miller (ed.), *Life of Miller*, p.12.

223 Muhlenberg, *General Muhlenberg*, pp.181–184.

described by their enemies as 'crackers', 'riff-raff', and 'little more than white Indians' bested a small force of Loyalists at Musgrove's Mill, South Carolina just two days after Gates' loss at Camden.[224] This presaged a much larger victory at King's Mountain a few weeks later. There, an army of 'overmountain men' and western militia defeated a large force of Loyalists and proved that the backcountry could be occupied but never subdued.

Daniel Morgan was promoted to brigadier general while this was happening and headed south to help. He was followed by Major General Nathanael Greene, who replaced Horatio Gates as commander of the Southern Department.[225] It was hoped that Greene had the strategic and logistical skills to succeed with few resources. Baron de Steuben came with him as far as Virginia, tasked with training an army from scratch.[226] Tommy Miller went south with Greene, but proposed to Nancy before he left.[227]

Back beyond the Blue Ridge, Abraham Burner was drafted into active militia service. The Shenandoah County veteran had served a partial term as a substitute in Richard Campbell's Company in 1777. Now his militia captain was Jacob Rinker, the Swiss surveyor who had been Jonathan Clark's original second-in-command. Rinker's brother George, the militia company lieutenant, remembered that a just-released 'Colonel Darke ... was the officer under whom they mustered.' Burner's admission that he was drafted illustrates how hard it was to get men to step forward, even after a pep-talk from William Darke. In neighbouring Frederick, a man found himself activated when 'some one slipped County money into my pocket and told me I was enlisted.'[228]

Rinker's militiamen congregated at Woodstock, marched south on the Wagon Road, crossed the Blue Ridge through Rockfish Gap, and made their way through North Carolina.[229] In South Carolina, Major General Greene made the bold decision to divide his force. The Southern Department commander sent Morgan west of the Catawba River with his best soldiers as a 'flying army' or ad hoc 'legion' while he settled into a 'camp of repose' with his newer troops at Cheraw.[230] Lieutenant Miller went with Morgan and the Shenandoah militia stayed behind.[231] They were compelled to stay long past their enlistments and then marched home with a herd of British prisoners after Morgan pulled off a stunning victory at Cowpens.[232]

224 John Buchanan, *the Battle of Musgrove's Mill: 1780* (Yardley: Westholme, 2022), p.11.

225 George Washington Greene, *The Life of Nathanael Greene* (New York: G.P. Putnam and Son and Hurd and Houghton, 1867–1871), vol.3, pp.54–65; Graham, *Morgan*, p.237

226 Paul Lockhart, *The Drillmaster of Valley Forge: The Baron de Steuben and the Making of the American Army* (New York: Harper Collins, 2008), pp.234–235.

227 Miller (ed.), *Life of Miller*, p.12.

228 NARA: M804, S19452, Henry Roarer pension (Va. Militia); W18515, Christian Miller pension (Va. Militia), W24693, Abraham Burner pension, S32485, George Rinker pension (Va. Militia); S40649, Thomas Waters pensions (Gaskins' Provisional Rgt), 10416½, Jacob Taylor pension (Va. Militia).

229 NARA: M804, S9142, John Camper pension (Va. Militia); S16486 George Miller pension (Va. Militia); C. Miller pension; H. Roarer pension; J. Miller pension.

230 Andrew Waters, *To the End of the World* (Yardley: Westholme, 2022), pp.62–71.

231 LOC: George Washington Papers, Ser.4, General Correspondence: Daniel Morgan to Nathanael Greene, January 19, 1781, with List of Commissioned Officers in January 17th Action; John Burk, Skelton Jones, and Louis Hue Girardin, 4 vols, *The History of Virginia* (Petersburg: Dickson & Pescud, 1804–1816), vol.4, p.477.

232 NARA: A. Burner pension, J. Camper pension; G. Rinker pension, H. Roarer pension C. Miller pension.

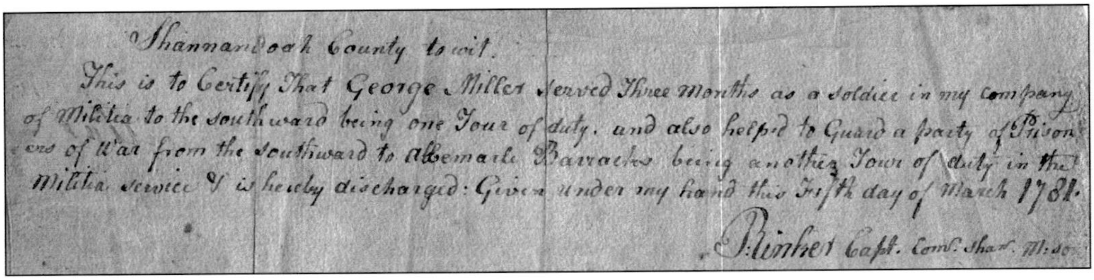

Shannandoah County to wit.
This is to Certify That George Miller Served Three months as a soldier in my company of Militia to the southward being one Tour of duty. and also helped to Guard a party of Prisoners of War from the southward to Albemarle Barracks being another Tour of duty in the militia service & is hereby discharged: Given under my hand this Fifth day of March 1781.
G. Rinker Capt. Comd. Shan. Milo

A militia discharge signed by George Rinker after the delivery of prisoners taken at Cowpens. (National Archives)

With Nathanael Greene in the South

Abraham Burner's former captain, Richard Campbell, was still out on the northwest frontier. Campbell's postings at Fort McIntosh and Fort Laurens were not as remote as Martin Carney's exile at Fort Jefferson, but they felt about the same.[233] In the spring of 1780, he wrote to his highest-ranking friend, Peter Muhlenberg, asking for help getting a transfer.[234] He also wrote directly to George Washington, using the improvised spelling common to western men.

> If your Excellency thinks Proper to Con[t]inue the Reigt in this Department, I will thank your Excellency for leave to Join Some Other Coare… When I Stept forth in the Armey it was my determination to Render my Cuntry Ever Service, In my Power & wish to be allways where i Could take an Active Part, & as there has Been Officers Ordered from Differant Reigts To Command Troops to the Southward I should be Glad to meet with the Same Indulgance if Your Excellency Thought Proper. I am Sensible your Excellency is not Unaquainted with my Charrictor While with the Meine Armey therefore I Will not Trouble you Any Further & hope to Receive Your Excellencyes Answer.[235]

Campbell may also have communicated his desire during a December visit to Richmond.[236] He got his wish. The 13th Virginia Regiment, now called the 9th, was reduced to two companies and 'surplus' officers were ordered to Chesterfield Court House.[237] Campbell was put in command of a provisional Continental regiment of mostly new draftees on 18-month enlistments and led them south to reinforce Greene. He secured an ensign's commission for his teenage son Archibald and brought him along.[238]

233 Gabriel Neville, 'Shenandoah Martyr: Richard Campbell at War', *JAR*, 3 Dec. 2019, <allthingsliberty.com/2019/12/shenandoah-martyr-richard-campbell-at-war>, accessed 27 May 2024.
234 LOC: George Washington Papers, Ser.3B, Continental and State Military Personnel, 1775 to 1783, George Washington to Peter Muhlenberg, October 17, 1780.
235 Chase et al (eds), *Papers of Washington* (Revolution), vol.25, pp.62–63.
236 Boyd (ed.), *Papers of Jefferson*, vol.4, pp.214, 239–240.
237 Kellogg (ed.), *Frontier Retreat*, pp.335–336.
238 NARA: M804, W22543, Oliver Wallace pension (Gaskins Provisional Rgt).

The Virginia brigade under Greene was commanded by Brigadier General Isaac Huger of South Carolina. Huger had, when a colonel in 1776, pulled several 8th Virginia men into his 5th South Carolina Regiment. One soldier named Collin Mitchum had enlisted in Richard Campbell's original company, transferred to Huger's regiment, and served in the South Carolina Line until 1780. Now, coincidentally, he was under the command of both men.[239] There were other familiar faces in the new Virginia brigade. Colonel John Green, the veteran of Mamaroneck and Fort Mifflin, commanded another provisional regiment.[240] Lieutenant Tommy Miller, fresh from the glory of Cowpens, was there.[241] Philip Huffman, another of the 10 ensigns of 1777, was a lieutenant.[242] Simon Morgan, John Stephenson's first ensign, was one of Campbell's captains.[243]

Greene's first southern engagement against the British occurred at Guilford Court House, North Carolina on 15 March 1781. Mitchum took a wound to his thigh and Captain Huffman was killed.[244] Lieutenant General Earl Cornwallis held the ground at the end of the day, but Greene's army made him pay dearly for the victory. The armies met again at Hobkirk's Hill, South Carolina late in April and Greene allowed his enemy another costly victory. Lieutenant Colonel Campbell was injured with a contusion to his thigh.[245] In June, the Americans laid siege to the British fortifications at Ninety-Six, South Carolina. They dug trenches in the classic fashion, but Campbell organised a direct assault when British reinforcements were reported on the way. Riflemen fired into the fort from a tower while others chopped through a row of abatis. Lieutenant Miller was 'severely wounded' when two groups of defenders raced around the fort from the rear on opposite sides and charged Campbell's men with bayonets.[246] Greene gave up and moved his army on while he still could.

About this time, Campbell's son got himself into a bind that was memorialized in 1828 as 'An instance of romantic gallantry.'

> His son, who bore a Subaltern's commission in his Regiment, had quarrelled with a brother officer, and some harsh expressions were eventually exchanged, when the dispute appeared to terminate. The indignant parent, insisting that a war of words was ill-suited to military characters, compelled him to call his adversary to the field, and accompanied him to it as his second.[247]

239 NARA: C. Mitchum pension; LVA: Auditor of Public Accounts (1776–1928), Collin Mitchum; C. Mitcham petition.

240 Showman et al (eds), *Papers of Greene*, vol.6, p.584.

241 NARA: T. Miller pension.

242 LVA: Revolutionary War Bounty Land Claims, Philip Huffman.

243 NARA: M804, S42730, William Freehold pension (Campbell's Provisional Rgt); S16420, Ambrose Hoffman pension (Campbell's Provisional Rgt).

244 LVA: C. Mitcham petition; Bobby Gilmer Moss, *Roster of South Carolina Patriots in the American Revolution* (Baltimore: Genealogical Publishing, 1983), vol.2, p.688; LVA: P. Huffman bounty claim.

245 Banastre Tarleton, *A History of the Campaigns of 1780 and 1781 in the Southern Provinces of North America* (London: T. Cadell, 1787), p.470; NARA: M804, W8681, Guilford Dudley pension (Halifax, N.C. Militia).

246 Showman et al (eds), *Papers of Greene*, vol.8, pp.408–409; NARA: T. Miller pension.

247 Alexander Garden, *Anecdotes of the American Revolution*, Second Series (Charleston: A.E. Miller, 1828), p.196.

Archibald survived the duel unscathed but saw his father die soon after at the Battle of Eutaw Springs on 8 September.[248] Collin Mitchum, who had recovered from his wound at Guilford, was 'Crippled in his right Shoulder.'[249] Tommy Miller was hurt again.[250] The long-serving Simon Morgan 'was severly wounded' and assisted off the ground by one of his men. Accounts of Richard Campbell's death vary in detail, but it is certain he took a ball to the chest and died within minutes.[251] Greene reported, 'Lt Colo Campbell fell as he was leading his Troops to the charge, and tho' he fell with distinguished marks of honor, yet his loss is much to be regretted. He was the great Soldier and the firm patriot.'[252] The enlisted men regretted Campbell's death as well. While he was alive, they affectionately called him 'Dick Campbell.'[253] Decades later, one old man who had served under him still called him 'the brave Col. Campbell,' even in a passing mention.[254]

Over the next decade, Campbells' friends from the old 8th Virginia looked out for Archibald. Muhlenberg went out of his way to help the young officer find opportunities for advancement.[255] A decade later, William Darke gave him a position in the army that Arthur St Clair took against the Indians in northwest Ohio. Darke was wounded there, and Archibald was killed.[256]

Tory Uprisings

When the Crown forces turned their attention to Virginia, the Old Dominion's government wisely moved from Williamsburg to the fall line at Richmond. Nevertheless, the hated traitor Benedict Arnold came up the north side of the James and attacked the new capital. The raiders looted and torched the town and destroyed the nearby Westham cannon foundry and arsenal. Then, Arnold's men crossed the James River to Chesterfield County to burn and loot some more.[257]

The incursion was intended to sever Nathaniel Greene's supply lines and set the stage for a reconquest of Virginia. It also emboldened the First Colony's quiescent Loyalists and dissidents. Disgruntled Germans in the remote hollows of Hampshire County had been resisting state authority for some time.[258] A man named John Claypool chose this time to

248 WHS: Draper Mss, DD, vol.1, p.223; LVA: Revolutionary War Bounty Land Claims, Richard Campbell and Archibald Campbell.

249 LVA: C. Mitcham petition.

250 NARA: T. Miller pension.

251 Lee, *Memoirs of the War*, vol.2, p. 473; NARA: M804, S3257, William Davis pension (Lee's Legion); David Ramsay, *The History of the American Revolution* (Philadelphia: R. Aitken & Son, 1789), vol.2, p.253; NARA: W. Freehold pension.

252 Showman et al (eds), *Papers of Greene*, vol.9, pp.328–333.

253 NARA: M804, W5933, Jeremiah Brann pension (Campbell's Provisional Rgt); G.H. Puntenney pension.

254 NARA: M804, W1912, Zackquil Morgan pension (Monongalia Militia).

255 Harlan Crow Library, Peter Muhlenberg to Anthony Walton White, 3 Jan. 1782.

256 LVA: Revolutionary War Bounty Land Claims, Richard Campbell; John F. Winkler, *Wabash 1791* (Oxford: Osprey Publishing, 2011), pp.75–76.

257 Mark Edward Lender and James Kirby Martin, 'A Traitor's Epiphany: Benedict Arnold in Virginia and His Quest for Reconciliation', *VMHB* 125:4, p.332

258 Wust, 'Disaffection in the Rear,' pp.66–73.

lead a significant uprising near Romney. Daniel Morgan, who had been resting his damaged spine at home in Winchester, raised a force to quash it. Jacob Rinker joined him with the Shenandoah Militia.[259] William Phillips, the silversmith, came with the Frederick Militia.[260] Claypool's Rebellion was largely a tax rebellion, and its leader was commendably contrite when it ended.[261]

In Virginia's southwest, a Tory uprising was foiled by a single 8th Virginia veteran. After trading a quart of rum for a pass out of Charles Town, John Wyatt returned home to Botetourt and was summoned by some of the regions' senior military leaders, Andrew Lewis, William Preston, William Christian, and Hugh Crockett. They 'prevailed upon him not to rejoin the Army as they would have him excused.' Instead, they wanted him to 'to act as a spy among the Tories on New River' using his Charles Town pass as a Loyalist credential. Crockett found an old captain's commission signed by Lord Dunmore and altered it to show the name on the pass. With these documents and some appropriately dated Charles Town newspapers, Wyatt made his way to the Tory settlements and introduced himself as a captain in British service. He was 'kindly received and entertained by them.' He stayed with them for a while and eventually learned 'it was their intention to attack, breakup and destroy Chizzel's lead mines on New River, and to attack the homes, destroy the property and take the lives of our leading men in that section of the country.' Posing as a Loyalist officer, 'he obtained from them a written list of their force, which amounted to a considerable number.' He also persuaded them to delay their attack, promising 'that in a short time there would be British troops in the neighborhood who would assist them in their enterprise.' He left them, then, to report to Patriot militia officers, 'who immediately raised the militia and took a large number of the Tories prisoners.'[262]

259 NARA: M804, R5828, George Keller pension (Shenandoah Militia); S4017, Jacob Surber pension (Shenandoah Militia); G. Rinker pension.

260 NARA: M804, W1471, William Phillips pension.

261 NYPL: MssCol 2091, 'John Claypool to General Morgan, 31 May 1781'; Palmer (ed.), *Calendar*, vol.2, pp.682–683.

262 NARA: J. Wyatt pension.

15

Yorktown

When Richard Campbell led his Continental recruits south from the Chesterfield Barracks in February, he left several old friends behind. Captains Abraham Kirkpatrick, William Lewis Lovely, and Reuben Field had once been junior officers under Croghan, Knox, and Slaughter. Field had come the farthest, having started out as an enlistee.[1] Now, they were preparing to form companies under Lieutenant Colonel Thomas Gaskins of Northumberland County.[2] Field was an exchanged prisoner taken at Germantown and may have joined somewhat later.

Captain Kirkpatrick billeted for a time in the home of Chesterfield County militia lieutenant colonel, Edward Friend. 'I got verry wet coming to this place,' he complained in January, 'have caught a Violent cold and am hardly able to write.'[3] But he had a roof over his head, which was a luxury the enlisted men did not have. One hardship he did share with the enlisted men was a desperate need for new footwear. He wrote a letter to Steuben's chief aide,[4] Colonel William Davies, asking him to tell the clothier to let him have a new pair.[5]

East of Chesterfield and south of the James River, Peter Muhlenberg commanded a militia army populated with many former Continentals. This brought him back to the area where he first took actual command of the 8th Virginia in 1776. Reprising his mission from that year, he camped at Suffolk to keep Benedict Arnold hemmed in at Portsmouth.[6] On 2 March, he pushed Arnold in by taking Great Bridge, another replay of the early war.[7] Both sides were then reinforced, but British help arrived first and Muhlenberg had to back away.

Lieutenant Colonel Darke was also in the field with the militia because he had no Continental command. A militia officer from Rockingham County recalled serving under him as early as November, just a month after his exchange. A Stafford County man also remembered serving under Darke that winter. Early in 1781, 'He made several excursions (under Colonel Dark) on James River, sometimes in pursuit, and at other times under retreat from the enemy.'[8]

1 VMHC: Marquis de Lafayette Papers, Mss2 L1314 b 6: 'Proceedings, August 9, 1781, Camp Bottom's Bridge, of the court-martial of James Grant for assaulting [Abraham] Kirkpatrick.'
2 LVA: Governor's Office, A. Kirkpatrick to W. Davies, 7 Jan. 1781, 15 Jan. 1781, 14 May 1781.
3 LVA: A. Kirkpatrick to W. Davies, 12 Jan. 1781.
4 Lockhart, *Drillmaster of Valley Forge*, pp.237–238.
5 LVA: A. Kirkpatrick to W. Davies, undated.
6 Boyd (ed.), *Papers of Jefferson*, vol.6, p.9.
7 LOC: Steuben Papers, r.4, p.211, Gaskins to Steuben 8 March 1781, p.261, 4 March 1781.
8 NARA: M804, R9780, Joseph Smith pension (Rockingham Militia), W1634, Aaron Munday pension (Stafford Militia).

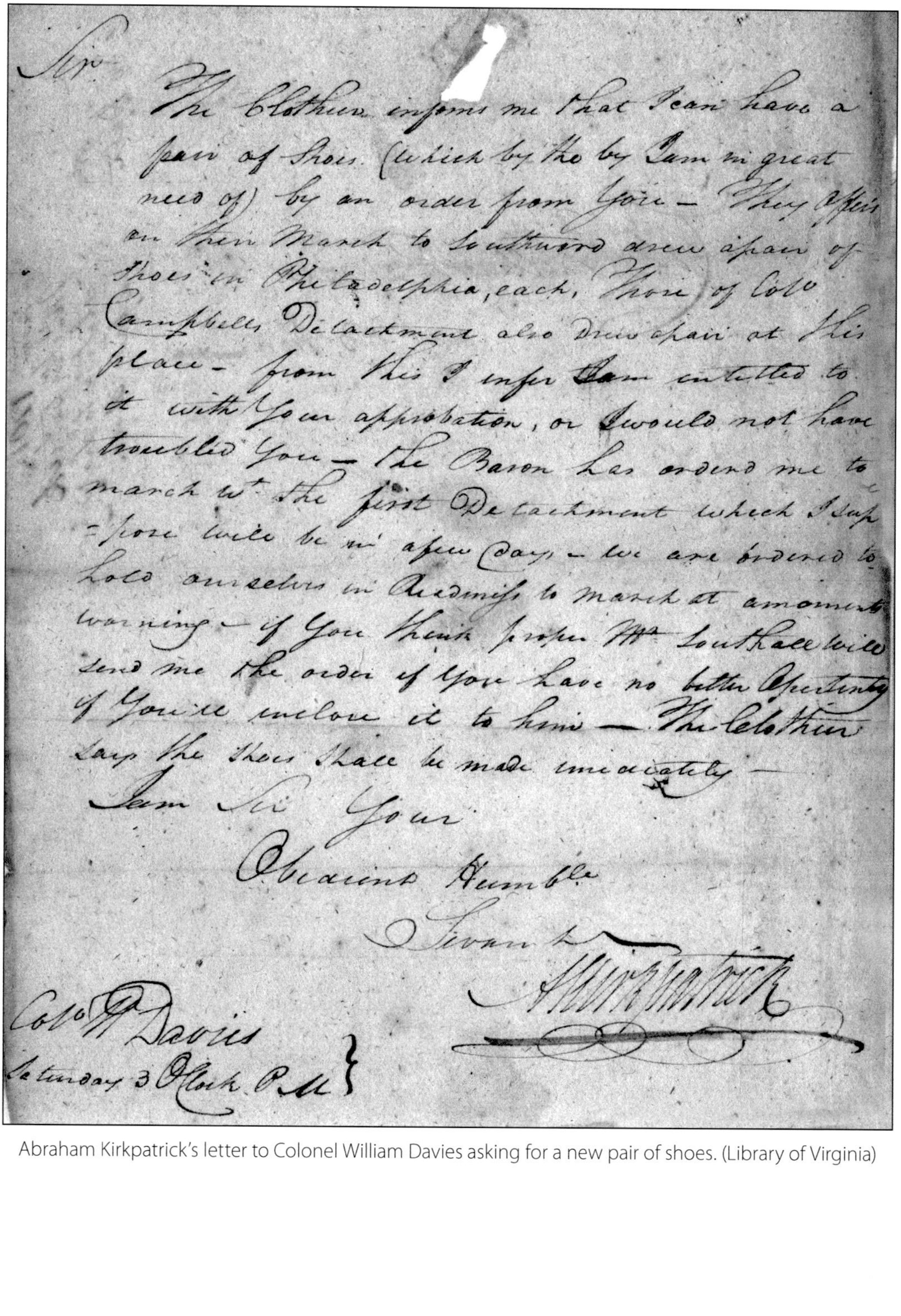

Sir

The Clothier informs me that I can have a pair of Shoes (which by the by I am in great need of) by an order from You — They Officers on their March to Southward drew a pair of Shoes in Philadelphia, each, Those of Colo Campbells Detachment also drew a pair at this place — from this I infer I am entitled to it with Your approbation, or I would not have troubled You — the Baron has ordered me to march wt the first Detachment which I suppose will be in a few Days — we are ordered to hold ourselves in Readiness to march at a moment's warning — If You think proper Mr Southall will send me the order if You have no better Opertunity If You'll inclose it to him — The Clothier says the shoes shall be made immediately —

I am Sir Your

Obedient Humble

Servant

A Kirkpatrick

Colo W Davies

Saturday 3 OClock P.M.

Abraham Kirkpatrick's letter to Colonel William Davies asking for a new pair of shoes. (Library of Virginia)

Point of Fork, where the Rivanna River flows into the James. The supply depot was some distance back from the actual point. (Author's photo)

In March, Arnold ceded command to Major General William Phillips, who moved inland again on the south side of the James toward Chesterfield. Muhlenberg's force made a courageous stand at Blandford (near Petersburg) before retreating. Henry Aleshite, formerly of Clark's and Steed's companies, noted the battle when he applied for a pension.[9] The Redcoats followed them north to Chesterfield and burned the training centre there. The Marquis de Lafayette, meanwhile, came south to Virginia with Continental reinforcements, and the King's men pulled back to Jamestown.

Muhlenberg and Lafayette kept close to the British, but the supply depot and training operation moved farther west with the state government for greater safety. The General Assembly went to Charlottesville and Governor Jefferson returned to his nearby home. Military stores were moved to Point of Fork where the Rivanna River emptied into the James.

The inland training operations remained under the command of Baron de Steuben, who had quickly developed a deep mutual enmity with Virginia's political leaders. The Prussian general grew eager to leave and join Greene in the Carolinas. To that end, he accelerated the training of Gaskins' recruits. There was little he could do, however, to get them properly equipped. Virginia's supply system was broken, and its treasury was empty. An officer protested in January that the recruits had 'not a remnant of cloathing larger than a good napkin to cover their nakedness.' Steuben complained, 'Colonel Gaskins' battalion is equipped with arms which have arrived from Philadelphia, but they have not had a single cartridge box ... Here is this poor battalion camped in the forest, which cannot be put in service or even drilled because they lack shoes and shirts.'[10]

When the stores were moved to Point of Fork, the rendezvous and training activities moved even farther up the James to Albemarle Old Court House (Scottsville).[11] A local boy

9 NARA: H. Aleshite pension.

10 Boyd (ed.), *Papers of Jefferson*, vol.4, pp.445–447, vol.6, pp.75–76.

11 Palmer et al (eds), *Calendar*, vol.2, pp.119–120.

walked by Kirkpatrick's tent one day, playing a fife. The captain and Lieutenant William Eskridge invited him in for a friendly chat and suggested he enlist as their company fifer. They told him they would give him 40 dollars, 'stating at the same time that they had no money then but would pay it afterwards.' The boy took the oath and remembered half a century later that he came to be 'well acquainted' with the two officers, 'in fact he almost lived with them all the time he was there.' Another recruit, a man from Hampshire, remembered that Kirkpatrick had an odd culinary fetish. 'He used … to send some of the Soldiers to hunt black snakes for him to eat, which he called bush Eals.'[12] Captain Lovely fell ill at this time and headed to the warm waters of Sweet Springs in Botetourt to recover. The resort was owned by William Lewis, a brother of Andrew Lewis. After Lovely passed through New London, an officer reported 'Capt. Lovely went through this Town to the Sweet Springs, he was very unwell at the time – I expect he is dead as I have heard nothing of him since he went away.'[13] But Lovely was back with Gaskins' Regiment by July.

Steuben arrived at Albemarle Old Court House on the 24th. He disliked the location and sent Kirkpatrick and another captain 'to reconnoitre a place eight miles up the river.'[14] The general was determined to head for North Carolina and decided he was tired of waiting. He sent Captain Kirkpatrick ahead with a letter to Governor Abner Nash, advising him that he was coming and asking him to provide Gaskins' men with shoes and clothing when they arrived.[15]

When he sent Kirkpatrick off, Steuben was unaware that Cornwallis had just brought his army north to Petersburg and taken command of British operations in Virginia. This brought the number of Redcoats in the Commonwealth far beyond what Arnold or Phillips had previously had. When news of Cornwallis's presence came, Steuben's men raced 30 miles back to Point of Fork to remove the stores there to a safer location.[16] As feared, Cornwallis turned his forces inland. The British Legion, under Banastre Tarleton, and the Queen's Rangers, under John Graves Simcoe, charged west on either side of the James. Tarleton hoped to capture Governor Jefferson and the legislature while Simcoe headed for the stores at Point of Fork.[17] Kirkpatrick's first serious fight as a Continental soldier had been against the Queen's Rangers at Mamaroneck. That attack succeeded in part because the Rangers were untrained and commanded by an aging drunk. The Queen's Rangers were a different organisation now, and Steuben had to choose between moving the stores and ensuring the survival of his command. He chose the latter, moving Gaskins' 645 men with 300 recently arrived militiamen south after a short skirmish.[18]

Steuben's southern march had been approved by Greene (who wanted support) and by Lafayette (who wanted Steuben out of Virginia). However, the approvals were given before Cornwallis moved north and now the move made no sense. Governor Nash, meanwhile,

12 NARA: M804, R6406, James Loden pension (Gaskins' Provisional Rgt), W4906, David Buffington pension (Gaskins' Provisional Rgt).
13 Palmer et al (eds), *Calendar*, vol.2, p.93.
14 Palmer et al (eds), *Calendar*, vol.2, pp.119–120.
15 Boyd (ed.), *Papers of Thomas Jefferson*, vol.6, pp.627–628.
16 LOC: Steuben Papers, r.5, p.108, Steuben to Lafayette, 28 May 1781.
17 John R. Maas, '"The Greatest Terror Imaginable:" Cornwallis Brings His Campaign to Goochland, June 1781', *Goochland County Historical Magazine*, 41 (2009), p.39.
18 LOC: Steuben Papers, r.5, p.301; NARA: O. Wallace pension.

was not where Kirkpatrick expected him to be, so the Cohee captain conferred instead with Brigadier General Jethro Sumner.[19] Kirkpatrick sent a report to Steuben that was blunter than might be expected from a captain to a major general.

> General Sumner shew'd me his last Orders from Genl Greene which directed him to march his new rais'd troops into Virga if Cornwallis should go into that State, which is the case. The Gentlemen here think it Verry extraordinary that Troops should march out of Virga. at a Time when almost all the enemys force is there and Genl Greenes forces more than adequate to their Task in South Carolina [and he] has more Troops than he can support and twill be only adding to the distress of both troops and inhabitants … I don't mean to Dictate, but only to draw a true picture of the distresses of this Country. Carolina would I believe rather send Men out than any should come into it.[20]

Steuben was just 35 miles from the North Carolina line when he decided to pause at Cole's Ferry to reconsider what he was doing.[21] The roll was called and revealed that 60 men had deserted.[22] Then Kirkpatrick's message arrived, and Steuben ordered Gaskins' men to turn around.[23] They marched northeast and joined Lafayette in Hanover County on 19 June.[24]

Freed from Charles Town

The officers at Haddrell's Point began angling to go home on parole as soon as they were taken captive, and Major Croghan found he had a potentially useful connection. George Croghan had, during Pontiac's War, permitted his daughter Susannah to marry Augustine Prévost, an officer in the 60th (Royal American) Regiment, the same organisation Peter Muhlenberg belonged to briefly in 1766.[25] Prévost's father was a major general in command of British forces in East and West Florida, but he was in declining health and relocated for a time to Charles Town. Major Croghan did his best to cultivate the tenuous relationship.

He wrote in June of 1780 that Prévost was being 'Exceedingly kind in Endeavoring to get me a Parole to go to the Northward & in every respect to Serve me.'[26] In fact, the Prévosts' efforts, if they really undertook any, may not have made much difference. It was not until 22 January 1781 that Jonathan Clark recorded that he had been 'at Charles Town on publick

19 William L. Saunders et al (eds), *The Colonial and State Records of North Carolina* (Goldsboro: Nash Brothers, 1886–1914), vol.22, p.535.
20 Boyd (ed.), *Papers of Thomas Jefferson*, vol.6, pp.627–628.
21 Idzerda (ed.), *Lafayette Papers*, vol.4, pp.182–183.
22 LOC: Steuben Papers, r.5, p.184, 'List of Deserters,' 12 June 1781.
23 LOC: Steuben Paperts, r.5, p.173; Lockhart, *Drillmaster of Valley Forge*, 265.
24 Richard K. MacMaster (ed.), 'News of the Yorktown Campaign: The Journal of Dr. Robert Honyman, April 17, 1781-November 25, 1781,' *VMHB* 79:4 (1971), p.405; Lockhart, *Drillmaster of Valley Forge*, p.265.
25 Alexander V. Campbell, *The Royal American Regiment: An Atlantic Microcosm, 1755–1772* (Norman: University of Oklahoma Press, 2010), p.207.
26 Potts, *Clark and Croghan*, p.85.

business' and 'obtained a parole.'[27] Croghan, Clark, and Clark's brother Edmund, a lieutenant in Colonel Gist's 3rd Virginia Battalion, sailed with others from Charles Town on 7 February and were dropped off at Edenton, North Carolina.[28] From there, with significant difficulty, they travelled to the Clark family home in Caroline.[29]

Brigadier General Scott was paroled about a month later and arrived home so 'feeble as to be unable to walk.'[30] Finally, a 'cartel' was agreed to on 3 May 1781, and enlisted prisoners and more officers were traded.[31] Major Stephenson and Captain Curry were dropped at Jamestown in July with nearly 900 men.[32] It took 'six ships and seven brigs to take us round to James town in virgina', said one enlisted man, 'and thear we was landed and exchanged man for man.' The enterprising John Kercheval, now about 18 years old, was there to help process them. After various adventures, he was now in the quartermaster department.[33]

As the senior officer on site, Stephenson spent days signing discharges and then marched the released men through Williamsburg to Richmond.[34] The soldiers were in terrible shape. Robert Chambers remembered:

> When we were discharg'd we were far from home. We were entirely destitute of money and almost every other necessary. We had suffered a long and severe captivity during which we had receiv'd neither clothing nor pay except two dollars from the commissary of the Southern Department. Never [a] poor man wanted a little money worse than we did. Our officers sympathized with us in our distress and would fain have relieved us but they were too much in our own situation to afford us any relief. The most of us thought of no alternative but begging our way home. One of the men said he thought it would be best to go to the Governor and make our case known to him perhaps he could and would relieve us. We mutually agreed to his proposal [and] we went to him. He was in his palace in Richmond and that worthy Gentleman compassionately and generously and immediately furnished us with money sufficient to bear our expenses home like gentlemen besides treating us with honourable and genteel respect. I wish I could remember his name but I have forgot it ... If he is alive he is worthy of peculiar Honour and if he is dead he is gone to heaven to receive an eternal reward. A friend in need is a friend indeed.[35]

The governor Chambers could not name was Thomas Nelson. David Stephenson learned what had occurred on the prison ships while he was signing discharges and angrily went

27 FHS: Clark Diary, 22 Jan. 1781; Draper Mss, L, vol.2, p.9.
28 McNew (ed.), *Croghan Diary*, p.71; FHS: Clark Diary, 15 Feb. 1781.
29 FHS: Clark Diary, 2 March 1781.
30 Ward, *Scott*, p.81.
31 LVA: J Curry petition.
32 NARA: M804, S6105, John Sizer pension (2nd Va. Detachment).
33 NARA: W. Tiller pension, J. Kercheval pension.
34 LVA: Revolutionary War Bounty Land Claims, David Brookes (3rd Va. Battalion), Drury Covey (3d Va. Battalion), John Winphrey (2nd Va. Detachment), William Green (1st Va. Battalion), Henry Rains (3rd Va. Battalion), Nathaniel Brooks (1st Va. Battalion), Jesse Rose (2nd Va. Battalion), David Berry (2nd Va. Battalion), William Griggory (2nd Va. Battalion).
35 NARA: R. Chambers pension. Edited for clarity.

to work collecting accounts into a memorial to the Marquis de Lafayette: 'We will not enumerate the many breaches of a sacred Capitulation. What we would principally beg leave to lay before you is, the conduct of the Enemy in confining our Soldiers on board Prison-Ships, and afterwards, compelling them into their Service'. The signers requested 'some speedy effectual mode of retaliation.'[36]

Michael Gold, one of Stephenson's own recruits from 1776, was among the soldiers forced into enemy service. '[U]pon the Exchange of prisoners in the Southern department,' Stephenson wrote, 'I was informed by Several of the other Soldiers that he was press'd from on board the Prison Ship in to the British Naval Service.' Stephenson wrote this in 1783 to help Gold get his bounty land despite his apparent treason. Stephenson assured the land commissioners that 'during his service in my Company he was A faithfull soldier to the utmost of his Ability.'[37] Gold got his land warrant.

Paroled but not exchanged, most of the released officers returned to their homes. Jonathan Clark spent the next six months with his parents in Caroline.[38] His friend William Croghan was a guest there for some of this time, so it was perhaps then that he got to know Jonathan's diminutive redheaded sister, Lucy, whom he would later marry.[39] Then Croghan rode home to Pittsburgh.[40]

A Militia Law with Teeth

Fleeing from Tarleton at Charlottesville helped the General Assembly become more clear-minded on Virginia's desperate situation. The Old Dominion had no money, few supplies, and only a small number of regular soldiers within her borders. Their efforts to recruit new men by the usual means simply were not working.[41] What did seem to work was the occasional practice of raising new units on the basis of one man's reputation. Virginia had turned to George Slaughter to raise men on his own after a similar failure in 1779. Thomas Jefferson had handed George Rogers Clark a stack of blank commissions when he left to go back to Kentucky. Clark was unable to raise the hoped-for number of men, but he and Slaughter both outperformed the usual process, perhaps especially as measured by the quality of the men they drew. Now the General Assembly asked Thomas Jefferson to 'call for the immediate assistance of Brigadier General Morgan to take the command of such Volunteers, Militia or others as he may be able speedily to embody.'[42] Morgan's reputation as a field commander had no equal, but he was home in Winchester suffering from back pain. 'I sincerely wish your health may be so far reestablished as to permit you to take the field,' Jefferson wrote, 'as no one would count more than myself on the effect of your interposition. I inclose you Commissions for the officers of three battalions.'[43]

36 NARA: M247, i.156, p.238.
37 LVA: Revolutionary War Bounty Land Claims, Michael Gold.
38 FHS: Clark Diary, 2 March–21 Sept. 1781.
39 FHS: Clark Diary, 28 March 1781; Thomas, 'William Croghan, Sr.,' p.43.
40 LVA: Governor's Office, W. Croghan to W. Davies, 18 Aug. 1781.
41 Boyd (ed.), *Papers of Jefferson*, vol.5, pp.33–37.
42 Anon. (ed.), *Journal of the House of Delegates*, 1781 (Richmond: Thomas W. White, 1828) pp.9–10, 14.
43 Boyd, *Papers of Jefferson*, vol.6, pp.70–72.

Morgan accepted the assignment despite his damaged spine. Yet, even the Hero of Cowpens struggled to compete with the wheat harvest for manpower.[44] Farmers watched their fields carefully. If they harvested too soon, the grain would not be hard enough for grinding. If they harvested too late, the dry kernels would fall from the stalks as they were cut.[45] Though the loss of one's crop could be devastating, there was more at issue than the harvest. Muhlenberg had seen the year before that voluntary recruiting simply did not work anymore.[46] Even the draft was ineffective, as the militia and Continental systems (administered by the same local authorities) tripped over each other and noncompliance penalties were rarely applied.[47] Even Morgan's reputation was not enough to overcome the headwinds. The general decided to 'call on the best aid I could possibly get,' and convened a meeting of the lower valley's 'Gentlemen who I esteem of most influence.' William Darke, Charles Mynn Thruston, Horatio Gates, the county lieutenants, and others met with Morgan on 15 June and sent recommendations to the General Assembly for a 'decisive measure for procuring the number' of needed recruits.[48] An act was quickly passed to make militia service truly compulsory. Any man who failed to appear for a two-month militia tour would now be arrested and put into Continental service for six months. Stepped-up penalties for desertion included the death penalty for anyone who left with a government-owned weapon. Local officials who failed to try and punish deserters would now be penalized themselves.[49]

The tough measures Morgan, Darke, and Thruston pushed for worked. At least 22 companies from multiple Shenandoah Valley and Piedmont counties cycled in and out of Darke's command in 1781 on two- and three-month tours. Jefferson, now at the end of his governorship, urged retired Continental officers to help. So did Morgan. A good example is Taverner Beale, who had been a member of the Dunmore Committee, the Dunmore Volunteers, and a lieutenant in Jonathan Clark's Company. He was now colonel, and probably county lieutenant, of the Shenandoah County militia. Morgan wrote him from Winchester urging him to help.

> I am directed by the Legislature of Virginia to raise a Brigade of Volunteers for the term of three months for the immediate defense of this state... Colo. Triplett I have appointed to raise a Brigade below the Ridge in Fauquier and Loudon, Colo. Darke in Berkeley and Hampshire, Colo. Smith in Frederick and Shendooe, will you undertake to raise what men you can in your County and join Colo. Smith. The matter is just this, if we do not make head and oppose the enemy they will destroy us.[50]

Ned McCarty took command of a company in Hampshire County. War had virtually defined McCarty's life since his father was burned at the stake, and he showed little fear of

44 Anon (ed.), *Field Crops: Usual Planting and Harvesting Dates*, Agricultural Handbook Number 628 (Washington: U.S. Department of Agriculture, 2010), p.48
45 Harold B. Gill, Jr., 'Wheat Culture in Colonial Virginia,' *Agricultural History*, 52:3 (1978), p.387.
46 Muhlenberg, *General Muhlenberg*, pp.187, 195–198.
47 Boyd (ed.), *Papers of Jefferson*, vol.5, pp.128, 366
48 Palmer et al (eds), *Calendar*, vol.2, pp.162–163.
49 Anon. (ed.), *Journal of Virginia Delegates*, 1781, pp.22, 26, 28, 29, 32; Hening (ed.), *Statutes*, vol.10, pp.416–421.
50 Anon (ed.), 'Letters of Daniel Morgan and Peter Muhlenberg,' *PMHB*, 21:4 (1897), p.488.

Ruffin's Ferry Tavern on the Pamunkey River, photographed by Frances Benjamin Johnston in 1935. The Virginia Department of Historic Resources estimates the house, later known as 'Waterville' and 'Windsor Shades,' was built between 1750 and 1775. Lafayette's Continentals and Darke's militia were encamped at the ferry before the Siege of York Town and the officers may have stayed at the tavern. (Library of Congress)

violence. He enlisted under Captain Westfall in 1776, served in Maxwell's Light Infantry, and organised a group of volunteers to go after Tories on the South Fork after his discharge at Valley Forge.[51] McCarty organised his company immediately after the new draft law was enacted in June. His men were armed with a mix of rifles and muskets. They marched from Romney through Winchester and Bowling Green to Ruffin's Ferry, where Darke's militia were camped.[52] A soldier said that when their short enlistments expired, McCarty 'solicited earnestly that we should not return home but stay and defend the Country from the enemy as that soldiers at this time were scar[c]e and the demand great.' McCarty's men valiantly agreed to stay for 'an indefinate period.'[53]

In August, Henry Wysor, a veteran of Berry's Company and Morgan's Rifles, joined Captain George Bell's company in Frederick and marched south to join Lieutenant Colonel

51 NARA: J. Cuppy pension.
52 NARA: M804, S7727, David Tichnal pension (Hampshire Militia); R10544, John Thompson pension (Hampshire Militia); S4407, George Horn pension (Hampshire Militia).
53 NARA: M804, S31528, Thomas Ashbrook pension (Hampshire Militia).

Darke's regiment. Anjer Price, who had served under Richard Campbell and Abraham Kirkpatrick, accepted a militia commission and marched some men south in September.[54] Silversmith William Phillips was drafted into active militia service.[55] Even John Chenoweth was drafted after his ordeal on a prison ship in New York Harbor. '[T]he captain cald on me,' he recalled, and 'asked me if I ware fit for duty. I told him I thought I was. I was inrold & drawed number 2 or 3.'[56] This was how the 'brigade' Jefferson asked Morgan to raise actually came together. It was not the hoped-for band of cheerful militia and plucky volunteers inspired by Morgan's charisma and heroism. Most were forced into service, but Ned McCarty's success in getting his men to stay proved the legislature right on one point: leadership mattered.[57]

Feet Half Worn Off

Captains Kirkpatrick, Lovely, and Field joined Lafayette about the same time a brigade of Pennsylvania Continentals arrived under Anthony Wayne. Including militia, Lafayette now had a respectable army of 5,000 men. Danish Colonel Christian Febiger, a veteran of Morgan's Rifles and the assault on Stony Point, pulled rank and took Lieutenant Colonel Gaskins' command. He was appalled at the regiment's condition. 'But Lord have mercy upon us,' he wrote, 'a modest army of Women on examining Any Thing lower than the navel, would instantly take to their Scrapers' if they saw it. The men were 'literally naked, shirts and Blanketts excepted.' There were no more than 20 pairs of good shoes in the entire regiment, and many of Gaskins' men were 'left about the Country, with their Feet half worn off.'[58]

Gaskins regained command when Febiger moved on to help wrestle with the supply crisis.[59] Lafayette pleaded for help in every direction. 'We are in the greatest want of Shoes,' he wrote to George Weedon in June, 'for Gods sake my dear friend, if it is possible try to collect a supply of them, and send them to me with the greatest dispatch.'[60] In July, when shoes intended for Gaskins' men arrived at Colonel Friend's in Chesterfield, they were intercepted by Anthony Wayne and given to his Pennsylvanians. The Virginians were furious.[61] Governor Nelson wrote to Lafayette and called it the kind of behaviour that 'is not to be tolerated.' Wayne blithely said Virginia could have them back, but he would then remove his men from service until they were supplied from Pennsylvania.[62]

54 NARA: M804, R481, John Feely pension (Frederick Militia), S18167, Sampson Price pension (Shenandoah Militia).
55 NARA: W. Phillips pension.
56 NARA: J. Chenoweth pension. Edited for clarity.
57 Dandridge, *Historic Shepherdstown*, p.260.
58 Palmer (ed.), *Calendar*, vol.2, pp.193–194.
59 HSP: Anthony Wayne Papers, Wayne to Thomas Nelson, 7 Sept 1781.
60 Idzerda (ed.), *Lafayette Papers*, vol.4, pp.13, 21, 23, 25, 41, 48, 50, 166, 189, 201.
61 Palmer (ed.), *Calendar*, vol.2, p.263; Idzerda (ed.), *Lafayette Papers*, vol.4, p.328.
62 Idzerda (ed.), *Lafayette Papers*, vol.4, pp.293, 307–309.

Old Jack

Captain Robert Higgins was finally released from New Utrecht in the spring of 1781. He resigned his commission and went home.[63] When he left southern Hampshire County years before, he entrusted operation of his farm to Old Jack, the Africa-born man he had purchased during a cattle drive. When he got home, Higgins discovered that he was deeply indebted to a man who had every reason to despise him. A local history refers to Higgins as a colonel, a postwar militia rank.

> …the Colonel returned home, and found that 'Old Jack' had made an excellent manager and overseer. The plantation and buildings were in good shape, the crops large and well housed, and the servants in good condition. Also, during his absence, the Colonel's wife had died, and 'Old Jack' was caring for the motherless children as only a beloved servant can.[64]

Jack's decency had prevailed over his lot in life.

Adultery and Attempted Murder

James Grant did not want to stand guard. He had more pressing and personal matters to attend to – matters involving his wife and Captain Kirkpatrick.[65] Grant was a recent recruit and one of the few in this period who volunteered for the duration of the war. He was a 23-year-old shoemaker from Loudoun County. He was born in County Kilkenny, but his Scottish name told a longer story.[66] He brought his wife with him when he enrolled at Powhatan Court House, but he now wanted her to go home.

The army had been marching almost constantly, but it had seen no combat since a battle at Green Spring early in July. A month had passed since then and all they had done was move west across the James and Appomattox rivers to Chesterfield and then turn back again toward the Tidewater. On 8 August, they passed through Richmond and camped on the Gill family's farm, a little east of Virginia's new capital.[67] The tents of Gaskins' Continentals went up in their usual arrangement, and the sun dipped to the horizon. Wayne's Pennsylvanians camped separately.[68] Lafayette was about 40 miles away on the Pamunkey River with Darke, the militia, and his light infantry.[69]

---

63 LVA: Revolutionary War Bounty Land Claims, Robert Higgins.

64 Anon. (ed.), *Brown County*, part 5, pp.21–22.

65 VMHC: 'Proceedings of Court Martial.'

66 LVA: State Government Records Collection, Accession 24296, 'Register & Description of Noncommissioned Officers & Privates at Chesterfield Court House, Powhatan Court House, Carter's Ferry, Albemarle Old Court House, Cumberland Old Court House, Winchester Barracks, Enlisted at different times from 1777 to 1783' [Chesterfield Size Roll], p.55.

67 American Revolution Institute of the Society of the Cincinnati (ARISC): L2007G37, 'Revolutionary war diary by an officer of the Third Pennsylvania Continental Line, May 26, 1781–July 4, 1782', 8 August 1781.

68 VMHC: 'Proceedings of Court Martial.'

69 Idzerda (ed.), *Lafayette Papers*, vol.4, pp.299–301, 302–311.

After the war, Robert Higgins built this house in Moorefield, near his childhood home in what is now Hardy County, W.Va. (Author's photo)

While the generals focused on new intelligence that Cornwallis had moved into York (it was seldom called 'Yorktown' then), Grant was focused on saving his marriage. His camp-follower wife and Captain Kirkpatrick had become suspiciously friendly, and it was driving him mad. He bristled and was slow to comply that evening when he was ordered to stand guard. He was certain that Kirkpatrick had depraved motives for giving him the order. When Kirkpatrick saw that Grant was not at his post, he directed Sergeant Joseph Lloyd to enforce the order. When Lloyd found him, Grant asked if he could pay someone else to stand guard for him. The 19-year-old sergeant said he did not know, so Grant went ahead and found someone.

Grant knew there was nothing he could do to Kirkpatrick and decided in this moment to send his wife home. 'I immediately went to Colo. Gaskins,' he said the next day, 'for a provision to carry her on her way home as I meant to send her from Camp.' Gaskins was amenable and said he would approve it.

Meanwhile, Grant's absence from the guard did not sit well with Kirkpatrick. He punitively ordered Sergeant Lloyd to put Grant *and* his hired substitute on guard. Grant helplessly went to his post and stood there stewing and worrying through his shift. It was about nine o'clock and already dark when he was relieved.[70] He returned to his tent and found – as he had suspected – that his wife was not there, despite the hour. A soldier in a neighbouring tent told him that she had gone to Kirkpatrick's waiter's tent to get some bread. Grant's worst fears seemed to be confirmed. He went there and looked around, even peering under the captain's canvas, but could not see his wife or the suspect officer.

He stepped out into the darkness and waited. Before long he could hear their voices, whispering. Creeping back, he saw them lying face-to-face on the captain's cot. His anger, already at a boiling point, overtook him. He took a musket from a nearby fence, loaded it, and fired into his captain's tent.

Robert Bradshaw, a young sergeant in Captain Lovely's Company, heard the shot and the pained cry of a wounded man. He rushed to the scene and saw Grant holding a cartouche. 'Who fired that shot?' he demanded to know. 'It was me,' the jealous husband confessed, unconcerned with the consequences. 'I shot the captain. I wish I had also shot my wife.'

Bradshaw told him that he was sure to hang for what he had done. 'I would as soon be so as not,' Grant replied despondently. 'The captain was in bed with my wife.'

Kirkpatrick stumbled out of his tent, bleeding from his head. The musket ball had ripped out his left eye and a piece of his skull. Bradshaw approached him with the would-be killer. Mincing no words, the shooter told Kirkpatrick what he had done and why. Kirkpatrick's odd reply is open to interpretation. He said, 'Your wife and I parted this morning.' Grant was then carried away and locked in the guardhouse. While there, he expressed some remorse for having so grievously wounded his captain. 'I'm sorry Captain Kirkpatrick is so bad,' he said. 'I should much rather have killed my wife.' Plainly, when it came to virtue, more was expected of women than of men.[71]

In the morning, the army marched 14 miles to Bottom's Bridge on the Chickahominy River.[72] A court martial convened there with Major William Alexander of Pennsylvania presiding. There were 12 other officers on the panel, including 8th Virginia veterans William Lewis Lovely and Reuben Field.[73] Grant was charged with 'exciting a Mutiny as far as in his power, by entering the Tent of Captn. Kirkpatrick of the same Line between the hours of 9 & 10 oClock...and wantonly Shooting the said Captn. Thro the Left Eye & Temple.' It was a serious charge. The default penalty, set in the Articles of War, was death. Grant's fate was very much in the hands of the court.[74]

He pled guilty to shooting Kirkpatrick but not guilty 'of the other Instances exhibited in the charge.' He denied any intent to incite a mutiny. Sergeant Bradshaw testified, as did an officer who interviewed Grant in confinement. Grant tried to expose the captain's motives by asking Sergeant Lloyd to tell the court about Kirkpatrick's orders 'relative to putting me on Guard.' Lloyd related what the orders had been but offered no opinion about why they were given.

70 Ten o'clock according to modern daylight savings time.
71 VMHC: 'Proceedings of Court Martial.'
72 ARISC: 'Third Pennsylvania Diary', 11–12 August 1781.
73 VMHC: 'Proceedings of Court Martial;' Trussell, Pennsylvania Line, p.56.
74 Ford (ed.), *Journals of Congress*, vol.5, pp.788–807, 789.

Grant was ordered to defend himself. He told his story to the court, making no attempt to deny what was plainly true. 'I went to my Guard and returned to Camp in the night,' he said, 'and on finding she was in Captn. Kirkpatrick's Tent I loaded a Gun and shot at Random into it.'

He was asked, 'Did you see your Wife in bed with Captain Kirkpatrick previous to your shooting him?'

'Yes,' he replied.

The court deliberated and announced their ruling. 'The Court are of opinion the prisoner is guilty of the charge exhibited against him, being a breach of the 3rd Article 2nd Section of the Articles of War and sentence him to suffer Death, more than two thirds of the Court agreeing thereto.'[75]

The court had ruled, but only the commanding officer, Anthony Wayne, could issue the order to carry out the sentence. There cannot really have been any doubt about what he would do. Three months earlier, his Pennsylvanians had demanded to be paid with something other than nearly worthless Continental paper dollars. Those who refused to stand down were tried, sentenced, and hanged by their whimpering messmates.[76] Wayne had just hanged another man for 'marauding.'[77] When he received the judgment, however, Mad Anthony was sensitive to the politics of a Pennsylvania general ordering the execution of a Virginia soldier. He had already upset the Virginians by taking their shoes. He passed the buck to Lafayette. 'Inclosed is the proceedings of a Genl. Court Martial,' he wrote. 'Was it held on a soldier belonging to the Pennsa. Line I should not have the least difficulty or a moments hesitation in Confirming it because if this Culprit should pass with Impunity – it may open a door to worse. But as it is a private of the Virginia Line I beg leave to commit it to your Decission.'[78] Lafayette signed the document and ordered Wayne to carry out the sentence.[79]

Four days after his crime, Grant was escorted to the gallows by James Slaton, a private from Captain Lovely's Company.[80] The Continentals lined up to watch Grant hang, an example meant to be seared into their minds. 'This day,' diarized a Pennsylvanian, 'a soldier of the Virginia Line was executed for attempting the life of one of his officers.'[81]

Kirkpatrick went on leave to recover from his injury. One of his men recalled a new officer taking over 'after Captain Kirkpatrick our first Captain got his eye shot out.'[82] Kirkpatrick spent at least part of the time at Hanover Court House and missed the Siege of Yorktown. Three months later he affirmed in a letter to Colonel Davies, 'I have purty well recovered my health.'[83] He returned to service, but for the rest of his life he wore his hat pulled down over

75 VMHC: 'Proceedings of Court Martial.' Edited for clarity.

76 Horatio Newton Moore, *Life and Services of Gen. Anthony Wayne* (Philadelphia: John B. Perry, 1845), pp.131–132.

77 Anon (ed.), *Journal of Lieut. William Feltman, of the First Pennsylvania Regiment, 1781–1782* (Philadelphia: Henry Carey Baird, 1853), p.8.

78 Anthony Wayne to Lafayette, 9 August, 1781 and 10 August, 1781, Idzerda (ed.), *Lafayette Papers*, pp.307–311; VMHC: 'Proceedings of Court Martial.'

79 VMHC: 'Proceedings of Court Martial.'

80 NARA: M804, W9655, James Slaton pension (Gaskins' Detachment).

81 ARISC: 'Third Pennsylvania Diary', 12 August 1781; Anon (ed.), *Journal of William Feltman*, p.9.

82 NARA: M804: W2608, Lewis Goodin pension (Gaskins' Detachment).

83 Palmer et al (eds), *Calendar*, vol.2, p.623.

the left side of his face. There is no evidence that Kirkpatrick had any continuing interest in Grant's wife, whose name is not even known. Five years later, he married Mary Ann Oldham, whose sister was the wife of Colonel John Neville.[84]

Closing in on Cornwallis

Tidewater Virginians called it 'York' or 'Yorktown,' but western men referred to Cornwallis's new position as 'Little York' to distinguish it from the one-time seat of Congress in Pennsylvania. Now all eyes turned to this community on the York River 15 miles from Williamsburg. Lieutenant Colonel Darke continued with Lafayette for some time at Ruffin's Ferry, working with militia companies as they came in. He coordinated with Brigadier General Edward Stevens, whose brigade his troops belonged to, and Brigadier General (and governor) Thomas Nelson, who had overall command of Virginia's militia.[85] When a French fleet appeared outside the capes of the Chesapeake, it was obvious that something major was afoot.[86] Louis XVI's warships fended off George III's fleet on 5 September, denying Cornwallis both supply and exit by sea. Lafayette crossed Ruffin's Ferry with his Continentals and marched them to Williamsburg. When Darke followed, his mostly inexperienced men grew frightened. British forces were still travelling freely through the area.[87] Darke's adjutant, George Bedinger, recalled:

> A short time before York Town was besieged and when our army lay at or near Williamsburg Colonel Darke marched a detachment of I think less than 1,000, mostly militia, who were then or afterwards called the 'Forlorn Hope,' as it was then generally thought that on our arrival in the suburbs of the town the Brittish *horse and foot*, would Immediately Sally out upon us and cut us off as we had no other troops in sight of the enemy. When we got in sight of the enemy and were expecting an immediate attack from the cavalry, I, acting then as Adjutant, as the men had marched in platoons and open columns, marched them up into close, solid columns, faced outwards, front rank kneeling, but arms firm, fixed bayonets, leaning out to an angle of near 45 degrees. This maneovre having been performed, briskly and promptly, it is believed that the enemy though[t] us well disciplined, if not regular troops, and that we were only an advanced party, and that the U.S. army was close at hand.

The Redcoats fired a few shots from a distance and moved on.[88] Darke's nervous militia made it to Williamsburg without further incident.

84 Bigham, *Kirkpatrick*, pp.7, 15.
85 NARA: M804, R1743, James Carter pension (Frederick Militia); W1237, George Corbin pension (Hampshire Militia); S19292, Martin Fainter pension (Shenandoah Militia); W3845, Benjamin Morgan pension (Berkeley Militia); W8732, Nicholas Smith pension (Frederick Militia); R10544, John Thompson pension (Hampshire Militia).
86 ARISC: 'Third Pennsylvania Diary', 1 Sept. 1781.
87 Anon (ed.), *Journal of William Feltman*, p.13.
88 Dandridge, *Historic Shepherdstown*, pp.260–261.

General George Washington arrived on 14 September ahead of the main American and French armies. Lafayette's troops were paraded and Washington rode along the line, reviewing them on horseback. The officers were assembled two days later to pay their respects to the commander in chief.[89] Washington stood in a doorway as the commissioned men filed in, each receiving a salute and a handshake. Those who had not met Washington before were introduced to him by generals Wayne and Edward Hand. It was probably on this occasion that Colonel Darke presumptuously 'made the first motion.' Without being summoned, he broke protocol by walking right up to the commander-in-chief to start a conversation. It was inappropriate, but Darke had known the great man since the 1750s and did not think he needed an introduction. 'I have never been able to account for such a motion,' Bedinger commented. 'I suppose it was the Colonel's usual *fire and rashness,* and, that Washington perhaps had a desire to know what the enemy would do on such an occasion. It was in my opinion an extraordinary and, I think unnecessary temerity.'[90]

When the rest of the Franco-American army arrived, Washington proceeded to lay siege to Little York. The topography that made the town defensible was also useful in its encirclement. The town faced the York River to the north. The ravine and marshy banks of York Town Creek curled around to the west and south. The town was also the home of Governor Nelson, and a man from the company Kirkpatrick led until he was shot 'went down with the Flag of truce into Little York to move … Nelson's Family out, before the siege began.'[91] Darke's militia helped begin the operation by clearing British outposts below the creek. '[W]e were marched to Pigeon Hill to drive the British back into York', one of his men remembered. 'The British spiked there cannon, and retreated into York, and we occupied the ground they had left.'[92]

The next three weeks were a chance to pay the British back for Charles Town. An outer line of trenches was dug. The French were positioned on the left, and the Americans were on the right. Captains Lovely and Field were in the centre of the American wing, reporting up through Colonel Gaskins, Brigadier General Wayne, and Major General Steuben to General Washington. On the right end of the line, Brigadier General Muhlenberg commanded the 1st Brigade of Lafayette's Light Division. Darke's militia stood behind them under Edward Stevens in the second line.[93] One of Darke's men said they 'went to entrenching all places that were exposed to the shot of the enemy. The British kept up a Cannonading on us and while we we[re] entrenching every now and then a man was killed. One man was killed a rod or two from me.'

89 Anon (ed.), *Journal of William Feltman*, p.14.

90 Anon. (ed.), *Military Journal of Major Ebenezer Denny* (Philadelphia: J.B. Lippincott & Co., 1859), pp.38–39; Dandridge, *Historic Shepherdstown*, p.261.

91 NARA: T. Waters pension.

92 NARA: M804, W2139, Thomas Lowry pension (Stafford Militia); S5531, William Hill pension (Caroline Militia); Jerome A. Greene, *The Allies at Yorktown: A Bicentennial History of the Siege of 1781* (Denver: National Park Service, 1976), pp.94–97.

93 Greene, *Allies at Yorktown*, pp.116–123.

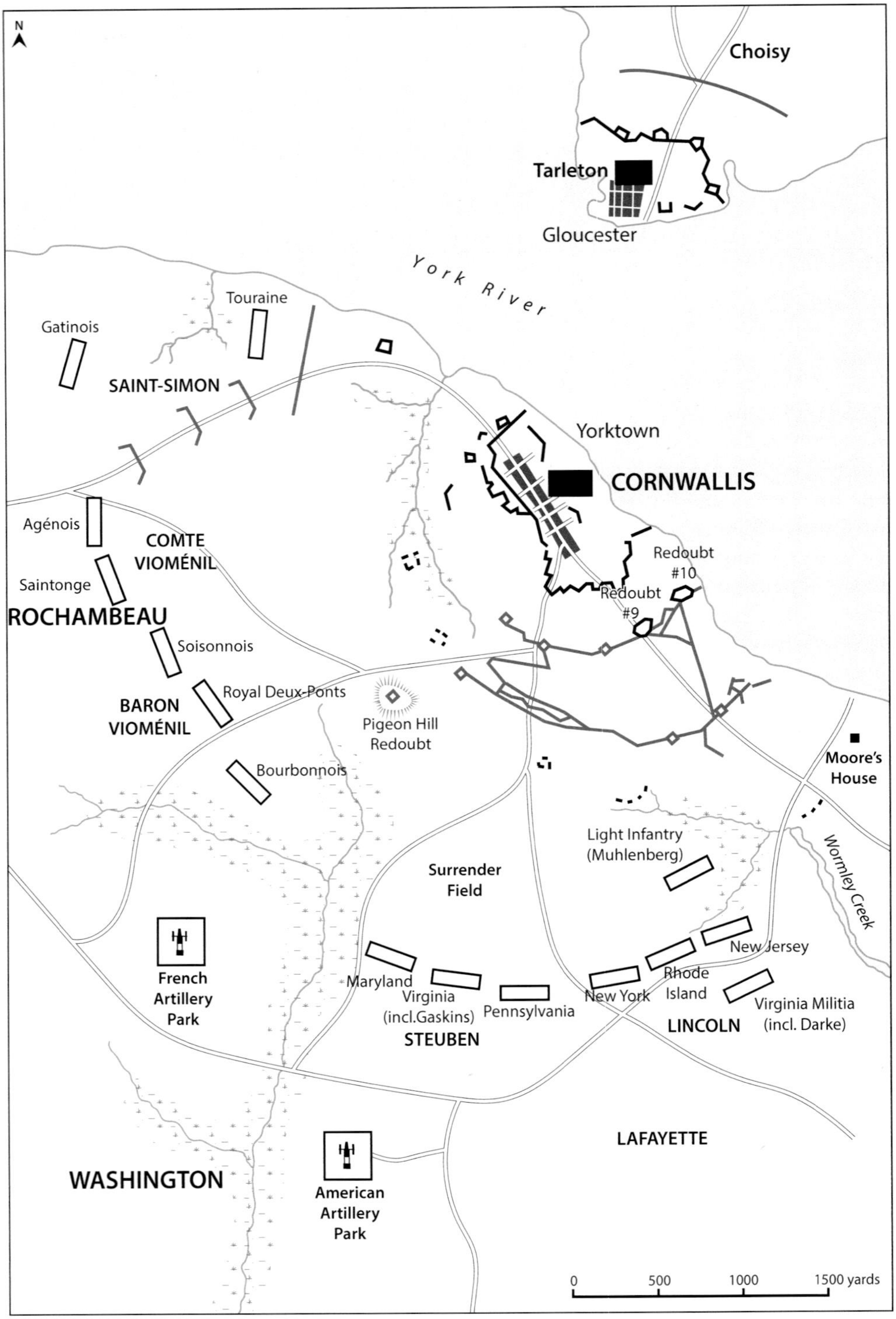

The Siege of Yorktown, September–October 1781.

8th Virginia Veterans at Yorktown[94]

Continental:	Militia:
Brig. Gen. Peter Muhlenberg	Col. Taverner Beale
Lt. Col. William Darke	Capt. Ned McCarty
Maj. William Croghan*	John Chenoweth
Capt. William Lewis Lovely	Henry Aleshite
Capt. Reuben Field	William Clark
Richard Bennett	William Phillips
John KerchKerheval†	John Simpson
Joseph Parett‡	George Spickard
	John Wyatt
	Henry Wysor

*Noncombatant on parole. †Quartermaster Dept. ‡Commissary Dept.

The Siege of 'Little York', 28 September–19 October 1781

Though Washington began his march to Little York in secret, word of it had spread quickly and many wanted to join. William Croghan was still on parole but decided to leave Pittsburgh anyway when he heard the news. On 'the first of October,' he wrote, 'flattering Myself I was Exchanged [I] settout to Join the Army at the Siege of York.'[95]

As the British had at Charles Town, the Americans advanced and dug a second line. To complete the second parallel, it was necessary to storm two British redoubts designated as numbers 9 and 10. John Kercheval was determined to participate. He 'applied to the officer appointed to command the Americans for permission to accompany them.'[96] The request was refused, perhaps by Peter Muhlenberg.[97]

Disappointed, he went to '*Major* Lamotte', a French officer he had met, who took him to the French commander. This time the answer was yes. Kercheval remembered that 'the parties marched in the night with silence moved each to the place of attack and almost at the same moment carried the places by storm.' This completed the second line, and it was now only a matter of time before the British surrendered. Kercheval remembered proudly, 'The French officer and Major Lamotte both gave a certificate highly complementary and recommended him in strong terms as worthy of a Commission in the regular service of the Virginia line.'[98] A few years later, Kercheval married Captain Thomas Berry's daughter, Jane.[99]

Major Croghan was less successful in his bid for glory. When he arrived, he learned that he was still on parole and could not participate. Nevertheless, he was there to see 'Cornwallis's

94 Incomplete list from pensions and other sources.
95 LVA: Governor's Office, W. Croghan to W. Davies, 18 Aug. 1781, W. Croghan to W. Davies, 30 Nov. 1781.
96 NARA: J. Kercheval pension.
97 Muhlenberg, *General Muhlenberg*, pp.270–276.
98 NARA: J. Kercheval pension.
99 Parry and Carr, 'Kercheval Family', pp.197–198.

Army lay down their Arms.'[100] William Clark, the 8th Virginia draftee who had trouble remembering Abraham Kirkpatrick's name, was posted as a sentinel at the river during the surrender ceremony and saw nothing. Afterward, however, he helped march British and German prisoners to Winchester.[101]

100 LVA: Governor's Office, W. Croghan to W. Davies, 30 Nov. 1781.
101 NARA: W. Clark pension.

16

Pioneers

The victory at Little York was not the end of the war. Eastern operations continued through most of 1782, the Treaty of Paris was not ratified by Congress until 14 January 1784, and the British did not evacuate their western forts until 1796. Several veterans of the 8th Virginia remained in service, including some of the original men. Cornwallis's defeat opened offensive opportunities in Georgia and South Carolina and a new battalion 'composed of different regiments of the Virginia Line' was thrown together under Lieutenant Colonel Thomas Posey. Abraham Kirkpatrick, back in action, commanded a company. Robert Breckenridge, once a sergeant in Knox's Fincastle company, doubled as a company lieutenant and as Posey's adjutant.[1]

Posey's enlisted men included Lewis Atkins, Michael Buckley, Thomas Elwell, George Lair, and Michael McKnight. These hardy warriors had been recruited by Captains Berry, Campbell, Clark, and Westfall in 1776. Of the roughly 700 men who enlisted into the 8th Virginia when it first formed, these five and one other are the only veterans identifiably still in service when the Continental Army disbanded.[2] The very last of the original enlisted men to be discharged was probably William Means, who had started in Clark's Company. He was guarding military stores at New London, Virginia when he was discharged by Abraham Kirkpatrick on 15 November 1783.[3]

Several officers continued to the end as well, but not always to the very end. Augusta County's Major David Stephenson quit on New Year's Day, 1783. By then, he was the senior major in the Virginia line. He explained himself in a letter to Washington:

> That when I entered the Service my fortune was very Small, And is now entirely expended, That extravagance has been no cause of my present Situation, nor is it from interested motives I would now wish to retire; but it is as really out of my power to equip myself decently as it is to purchase the Indies. Conscious that your Excellency will never wish to Continue an officer in Service whose appearance must be so inferior to his rank I rest Satisfied of your Approbation to retire.[4]

1 NARA: M246, f.338, pp.2, 16, 18, 64, 67.
2 NARA: M246, f.338, pp.2, 11, 13, 16, 18, 64, 67, f.209, p.2; f.210, p.2; f.338, pp.13, 29–30, 46, 67.
3 LVA: Revolutionary War Bounty Land Claims, William Means.
4 LOC: George Washington Papers, Ser.4, General Correspondence: David Stephenson to George Washington, 1 Jan. 1783.

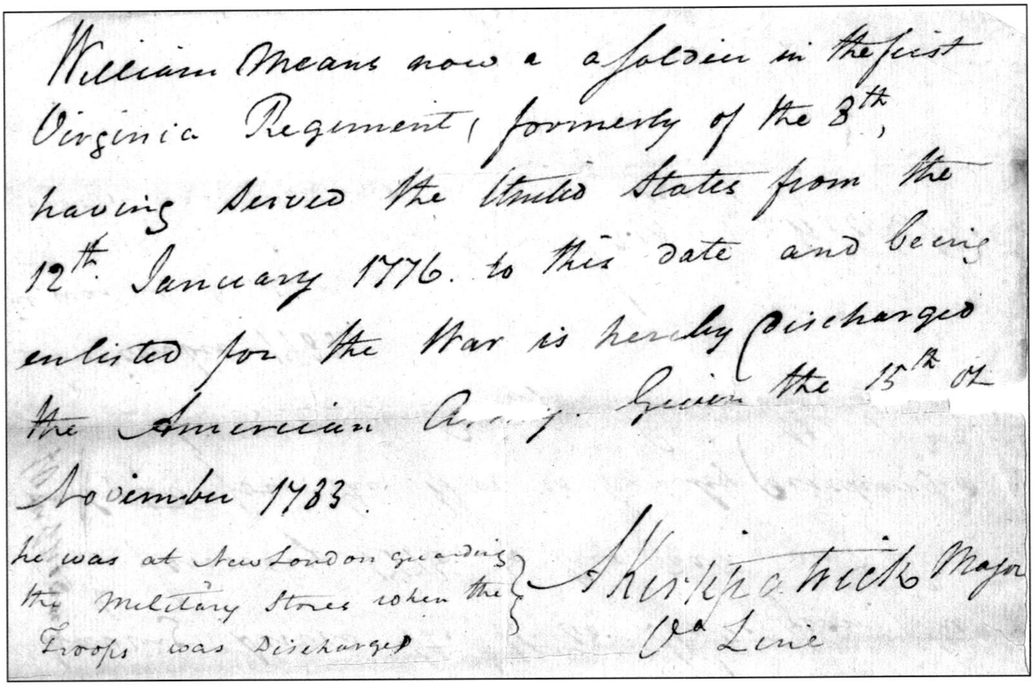

William Means now a a Soldier in the first Virginia Regement (formerly of the 8th, having Served the United States from the 12th January 1776. to this date and being enlisted for the War is hereby Discharged the American Army. Given the 15th of November 1783.

he was at New London guarding the Military Stores when the Troops was Discharged } A Kirkpatrick Major Va Line

William Means was the last of the 8th Virginia's original enlisted men to be dismissed. His discharge was signed by Brevet Major Abraham Kirkpatrick. (National Archives)

Major Croghan, now properly exchanged, was posted at Fort Pitt when operations ceased. Peter Muhlenberg wrote to him from Winchester on 13 July 1783, directing him 'to Discharge the Men belonging to the Virginia line.' He sent a stack of blank discharges and \$2,500 in 'Morris notes' for the men. Continental dollars were now worthless, but these circulating promissory notes were backed by the personal wealth of Philadelphia's Robert Morris.[5] Muhlenberg oversaw the discharges at Winchester himself. James Loden, the young fifer Kirkpatrick had promised 40 dollars to, was one of them. The general handed him his discharge and 'a little money of very inconsiderable sum saying it would befriend him on the road.' The officers, Loden recalled, had no money to pay the men what they were owed but made vague promises about contriving some way to get them back together when the funds were available. When Loden turned away unhappy, Muhlenberg called, 'stop fifer I give all my regulars a piece of land on Cumberland river.' Loden waited while the general 'wrote him a certificate' for land in Kentucky. He carried the document for years 'until he wore it out, pasted it together on another piece of paper and lost it.' Thus, aside from a little pocket money, he never realised anything of value for his service.[6]

5 HSP: Gratz Manuscript Collection, Peter Muhlenberg to William Croghan, 13 July 1783; Adam E. Zielinski, 'Robert Morris: The Financier of the Revolution', *American Battlefields Trust*, <battlefields.org/learn/articles/robert-morris-financier-american-revolution>, accessed 19 June 2024.

6 NARA: J. Loden pension.

Officers, too, were owed more than they ever received. Congress thanked them by giving 'all officers in the army, under the rank of major general, who hold the same rank now that they held in the year 1777, a brevet commission one grade higher than their present rank, having respect to their seniority.'[7] Peter Muhlenberg became a major general, John Neville became a brigadier general, and Abraham Kirkpatrick and William Lewis Lovely became majors. The promotions meant little, but they did entitle veterans to be addressed by the higher rank for the rest of their lives.[8]

The very last of the original 8th Virginia men to leave service was Captain Leonard Cooper. After his duel with Abraham Kirkpatrick, his leg was amputated and he enrolled in the Corps of Invalids, a unit of disabled men who served as guards and instructors. The Corps was led by Colonel Lewis Nicola, who became ignominious for urging General Washington to become king.[9] In 1781, Nicola described Cooper as 'in a most distressed situation, without a farthing of money or means of procuring any & reduced to one coat & that in rags, so much so that a few weeks will put it past hanging on.' Worse, Nicola reported, 'The captains wound is so high up his thigh that a very short stump remains & an attempt he made to use a wooden leg has renewed the wound made by the amputation.'[10] In 1782, Congress appropriated $16 to

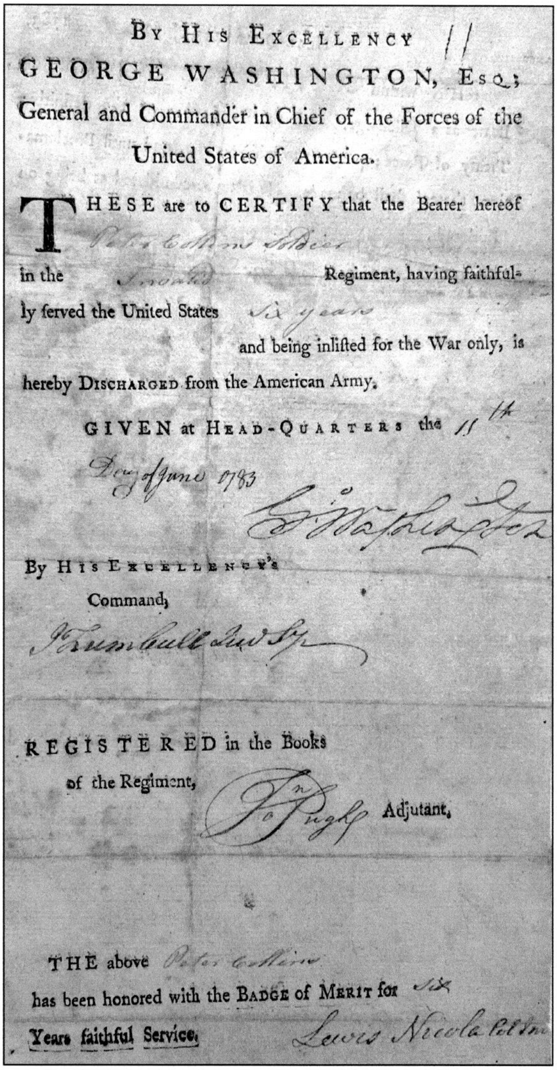
By His Excellency
GEORGE WASHINGTON, Esq;
General and Commander in Chief of the Forces of the United States of America.

THESE are to CERTIFY that the Bearer hereof Peter Collins soldier in the Invalid Regiment, having faithfully served the United States Six years and being inlisted for the War only, is hereby Discharged from the American Army.

GIVEN at Head-Quarters the 11th Day of June 1783

G Washington

By His Excellency's Command,
J Trumbull Jun Sec

REGISTERED in the Books of the Regiment,
Jno Pugh Adjutant,

THE above Peter Collins has been honored with the Badge of Merit for Six Years faithful Service,
Lewis Nicola Col Inv

Peter Collins spent the last years of the war with Captain Cooper in the Corps of Invalids. The veteran of Richard Campbell's Company was probably wounded at the Battle of Germantown. Collins' and Cooper's discharges were signed by George Washington and Lewis Nicola. (Library of Virginia)

7 Ford (ed.), *Journals of Congress*, vol.25, p.632.

8 William M. Welsh, 'Continental Army Brevets', *JAR*, 3 Nov. 2024, <allthingsliberty.com/2024/11/continental-army-brevets>, accessed 30 Jan. 2025.

9 John C. Fitzpatrick (ed.), *The Writings of George Washington* (Washington: Government Printing Office, 1931–1944), vol.24, pp.272–273, n.81.

10 Hutchinson et al (eds), *Papers of Madison*, vol.3, pp.165–166.

provide Cooper with a cork leg.[11] The Invalid Corps was disbanded in 1783 but Cooper and some others continued on in a Corps of Pensioners performing similar tasks well past the end of the war. He and the other pensioners were finally ordered discharged by Congress on 7 June 1785.[12] Of all the officers and enlistees who ever served in the 8th Virginia, Leonard Cooper, a one-legged soldier, was the last man standing.

Data Analysis

Outcomes for 1776 Enlistees[13]

Served Term	140
Reported Dead	101
Dropped from Rolls	101
Superannuated	95
Deserted	66
Reenlisted	43
Transferred	42
POW	21
KIA/MIA	13
Wounded	12
Promoted	5
Total men counted: 639	
Mortality range: 34.3% to 44.3%	
Casualties (no desertions): 53.6%	
Total attrition: 64.0%	

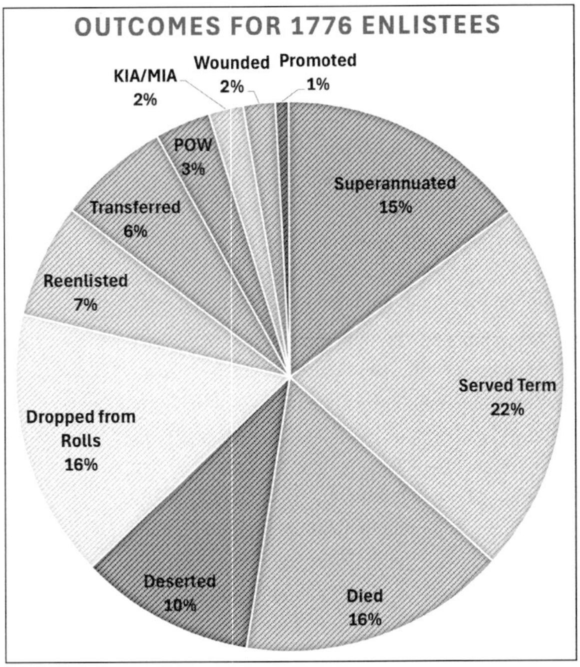

The data set for the table of outcomes includes the nine original companies recruited in early 1776. John Stephenson's 1775 company, for which no rolls survive, is not included. Knox's Company was 29 men short of its enlistment quota. Campbell's Company rolls are missing the names of 30 men dropped before April 1777. David Stephenson's Company rolls are missing the names of 51 men dropped before April 1777. At least 1,047 men served in the regiment at all ranks between December 1775 and September 1778. Officers continued to recruit on a continuous basis. Officers could resign at any time. The 639 men known to have enlisted in the nine counted original companies constitute the best data set for analysis, leaving 408 or more men excluded. Officers, staff, and warrant officers are not included. Enlisted men recruited after companies were certified by county committees are not included. 'Dropped from rolls' includes the 81 missing names from Campbell's and

11 Ford (ed.), *Journals of Congress*, vol.22, p.328.

12 LVA: Auditor of Public Accounts (1776–1928), Leonard Cooper; Hazard et al (eds), *Pennsylvania Archives*, ser.2, vol.11, p.275; NARA: M853, vol.134, p.240.

13 Muster and pay rolls at National Archives and August 1776 Croghan Detachment rosters in Draper Mss.

David Stephenson's companies and 16 others. 'Superannuated' includes 43 men discharged early, 35 left sick (not rejoined), one 'invalid,' and one man who hired a substitute. 'MIA' includes three battlefield MIAs and one man simply 'missing.' 'Promoted' men include three commissioned officers and one cadet. Only 36 percent of enlistees remained in service in the 8th Virginia when their two-year terms ended during the Valley Forge encampment. Seven percent reenlisted. Soldiers had only a one to two percent chance of being killed in battle (MIA and KIA at one percent each), but they nevertheless had a significant risk of dying in service. If half of 'dropped' and 'superannuated' men died along with a third of prisoners, then 34.3 percent of soldiers died from service-connected causes. There is no evidence of 'dropped' men surviving, so mortality among that group may be much higher. If 90 percent of 'dropped,' 75 percent of 'superannuated,' and 33 percent of POWs died, then 44.3 percent of soldiers died from service-connected causes. Some wounded and deserted soldiers may also have died of service-connected causes. A significant majority of mortally and seriously ill men contracted malaria in South Carolina and Georgia. Given the low number of battlefield casualties, an estimate of 80 percent of deaths from malaria, 10 percent from other disease, three percent from battle wounds and imprisonment, two percent from smallpox inoculation, and five percent from other causes seems reasonable. This no more than an educated guess. Many who remained in service after 1776 also suffered from disease. Most transfers were to the South Carolina Line and the Virginia Navy's row galley service. Most KIA, MIA, captured, and wounded were from the Battle of Germantown. Many men who served their terms without reenlisting and some men who deserted returned to service, often in activated militia duty. Among the five enlisted men who received commissions were Robert Breckenridge and Benjamin Biggs. Breckenridge became the first Speaker of the Kentucky legislature and a militia general. Benjamin Biggs became a general in postwar Virginia militia service and noted frontiersman.

The Bounty Land Lottery

John Clark was a little over 26 years old when he took his last breath. He died from tuberculosis contracted during his five long years of captivity. He was buried in Caroline County on 2 November 1783 with his parents and all nine sorrowful siblings looking on.[14] He had two older brothers, three younger brothers, and four sisters. His role model in life was his oldest brother, Jonathan. When Jonathan received a captain's commission, John replaced him as deputy clerk of Dunmore. A year later, he followed Jonathan into the 8th Virginia as a lieutenant in Captain Higgins' Company. George Rogers Clark, the second oldest, became a celebrated general in state service with another brother, Richard, by his side. The next brother was Edmund, who was captured with Jonathan at Charles Town. Sisters, Ann, Lucy, Elizabeth, and Frances remained at home during the war. Thirteen-year-old William, the youngest, would become the most famous of them all.[15]

14 FHS: Clark Diary, 29 Oct. 1783; Potts, *Clark and Croghan,* pp.121–122, 274–275.

15 English, *Conquest of the North-West,* vol.2, pp.991–1019.

Jonathan set off for Kentucky the day after the funeral, traveling with George, Richard, and possibly Edmund.[16] A large part of the territory west of Kentucky's Cumberland River was set aside for Virginia's war veterans, and those who attended an initial land lottery got the first pick of surveys.[17] Land could be claimed in Ohio as well, but it was not yet open for settlement. George was a commissioner and the principal surveyor in charge of the process for the Virginia State Line, with William Croghan acting as his chief deputy. Jonathan was a commissioner for the Virginia Continental Line. They rode to the Cumberland Gap and followed the Wilderness Road towards Louisville. Peter Muhlenberg, despite having moved back to Pennsylvania, oversaw the lottery.[18] He travelled to Pittsburgh, where he and Croghan took a flatboat down the Ohio to Louisville.

One of the first things Muhlenberg did when they arrived was visit the grave of John Chapman, who had been killed in 1781 by Joseph Brant's attackers.[19] Then Muhlenberg turned his attention to the lottery, which went smoothly. George Slaughter, James Knox, and Bob Breckenridge were there.[20] Many of the attendees had pockets full of land warrants belonging to friends, family, and neighbours. The actual surveys, which were supposed to be conducted immediately, were abandoned for the time being because of the challenges posed by squatters, the season, and the still-militant Chickamauga.

His work done, Muhlenberg set off for home, accompanied for several miles by George Slaughter. They stopped at Bowman's Station to visit Muhlenberg's one-time second-in-command, Abraham Bowman. For old times' sake, the malaria in Muhlenberg's liver chose this moment to work its evil. 'Immediately after my arrival I was taken with the fever and ague,' he wrote. He took some cinchona bark to treat his chronic condition and felt better after four days. When it was time to leave, Bowman gave him 'two bacon hams, and some dried buffalo-tongues for the journey.' Muhlenberg said goodbye and set off to English's Station, near Crab Orchard, to begin the dangerous journey home. George Slaughter escorted him there and then rode back to his home. The Fighting Parson left English's Station in the company of 45 strangers who, following common practice, travelled together for safety. They took Skaggs Trace to the Wilderness Road and the Cumberland Gap, encountering several dead bodies on the way. Muhlenberg emerged at Anderson's Block House on 31 May exhausted, filthy, and covered with ticks.[21]

William Croghan performed his duties as George Clark's deputy land commissioner capably and took over when the general turned his attention back to military matters. He married Lucy Clark, made a fortune in land speculation, acquired several slaves, and built an impressive home known as Locust Grove near Louisville. Lucy's sister Elizabeth married Lieutenant Colonel Richard Clough Anderson, George's counterpart for Virginia Continental Line surveys.[22] The entire Clark family, parents included, eventually relocated to Kentucky, but Jonathan was the last to move.[23]

16 FHS: Clark Diary, 3 Nov. 1783.

17 Hening (ed.), *Statutes*, vol.10, pp.23–27, 50–65, 159–162; vol 11, pp.309–313; Muhlenberg, *General Muhlenberg*, pp.294–295, 437–439.

18 Palmer, et al (eds), *Calendar*, vol.3, p.550; Muhlenberg, *General Muhlenberg*, pp.294–295; Potts, *Clark & Croghan*, pp.124–125.

19 Muhlenberg, *General Muhlenberg*, pp.425–439.

20 FHS: Clark Diary, 1 March 1784.

21 Muhlenberg, *General Muhlenberg*, pp.429, 439–440, 449–551.

22 Potts, *Clark and Croghan*, pp.124–125, 173–179.

23 FHS: Clark Diary, 29 Oct 1784, 2 Sept.-8 Oct. 1796; Ludie J. Kinkead, (ed.) 'How the Parents of George Rogers Clark Came to Kentucky in 1784–1785', *Filson Club History Quarterly* 3:1 (1928), pp.1–4.

A frontier home with a large community block house in the distance. A block house of this type was managed by John Anderson on the east side of the Cumberland Gap from 1775 until his death in 1817 (it burned down in 1876). (John F. Watson, *Annals of Philadelphia and Pennsylvania in Olden Time* (Philadelphia: Penington & Hunt, 1844))

William and Lucy (Clark) Croghan in their later years. Portraits by John Wesley Jarvis, 1820. (Courtesy of Historic Locust Grove)

Not everyone who moved to Kentucky prospered. Joseph Carman and his family were among the thousands of pioneers who floated down the Ohio River in the 1780s. He was a Croghan enlistee who served his two-year term and returned home from Valley Forge in 1778.[24] By 1787 he lived with his family at Well's Station, near the future site of Shelbyville. One day that fall, he and two companions set out to go buffalo hunting. They rode a few miles north toward Drennon's Lick (Drennon Springs), where salty water attracted large

24 WHS: Draper Mss, N, vol.2, p.16; NARA: M881, r.1040, Joseph Carman.

Locust Grove was the home of William and Lucy Croghan and the last home of George Rogers Clark. (Author's photo)

game. The hunters were ambushed there by a party of Indians who captured Carman while his companions ran for help. A rescue party followed a trail of blood for 200 yards to the Indians' campsite. There they found Carman's body 'dismembered and hung about on saplings.' His neighbours grimly 'gathered it up and took it back to Well's Station, for burial.' Carman left behind a wife and six children.[25]

In time, the sheer numbers of immigrants helped make Kentucky safer for those who came. It became the 15th state of the union when Virginia granted it independence in 1792. Robert Breckenridge helped draft the state's constitution and was the first Speaker of the Kentucky House of Delegates.[26] James Knox was a state senator.[27] Charles Scott was the new commonwealth's fourth governor.

The Constitution and the Whiskey Rebellion

Five years before Robert Breckenridge helped craft Kentucky's constitution, he helped ratify the Constitution of the United States. Two men from each Virginia county convened

25 WHS: Draper Mss., C, vol.19, pp.52–53.

26 Collins, Lewis and Richard H. Collins., *Historical Sketches of Kentucky* (Covington, Ky: Collins & Co., 1882), vol.1, p.275.

27 Cannon (ed.), 'General Expenditures 1792–1798', p.137.

Flatboats provided one-way travel for settlers who repurposed the lumber after reaching their destinations. Engraving by Alfred Rudolph Waud. (Historic New Orleans Collection, 1977.137.18.685)

at Richmond in 1788 to debate adoption of the new charter. Most of the Old Dominion's leading men were there: Patrick Henry, James Madison, John Marshall, George Mason, and others. So, too, were Breckenridge, William Darke, and Jacob Rinker.[28] A close contest between the Federalists and the Antifederalists was expected.

Two men dominated the debate. Patrick Henry, perhaps the greatest orator of his age, was strongly opposed concentrated federal power. His principal opponent was James Madison. Short and soft-spoken, Madison was the man most responsible for the document under consideration. The three 8th Virginia veterans mostly sat and watched Henry's eloquence wrestle with Madison's intellect. Even the opinionated Adam Stephen, Darke's partner from Berkeley, spoke just once or twice.[29] In the end, by leveraging a commitment to append a bill of rights to it, the convention voted to ratify the Constitution in a vote of 89 to 79.[30] Breckenridge, Rinker, Darke, and Stephen voted with the majority.

28 Leonard (ed.), *Assembly*, pp.172–174.

29 Rutland (ed.), *Papers of Mason*, vol.1, p.190; Boyd (ed.), *Papers of Jefferson*, vol.6, pp.204–205, College of William & Mary (CWM): John Marshall Papers, Mss. 39.1 M34, 'John Marshall to James Monroe, December 12, 1783'; William C. Rives, *History of the Life and Times of James Madison* (Boston: Little, Brown & Co., 1859–1866), vol.2, p.612.

30 David Robertson, *Debates and Other Proceedings of the Convention of Virginia, Convened at Richmond, on Monday the Second Day of June, 1788*, second edition (Richmond: Ritchie & Worsley and Augustine Davis, 1805), pp.466–469.

Ten months later, George Washington took the presidential oath of office in New York. He was dressed in civilian clothes but wore a sword that was given to him by William Darke. The blade is now in the collection of Morristown National Historical Park.[31] Among those at the inauguration was Peter Muhlenberg, a Pennsylvania member of the House of Representatives. His brother, Frederick, was the first Speaker. James Madison too was a member of the House. William Grayson, who had commanded the remains of Muhlenberg's regiment at Monmouth, was one of Virginia's first senators. The 1st Congress did important work: It approved the Bill of Rights and created the Departments of State, War, and Treasury. It established the District of Columbia and enacted groundbreaking laws governing patents and copyrights.

Muhlenberg and Representative George Mathews of Georgia (once colonel of the 9th Virginia) were among the members of Congress who opposed a tax on domestic distilled spirits.[32] The controversial excise, pushed through Congress by Alexander Hamilton, seemed calculated to injure western farmers. Spain had closed the port of New Orleans to American traffic, and the only practical method of shipping grain east from the Western Waters was by processing it into lower-volume, higher-value, shelf-stable whiskey. The tax on Western commerce was intended in part to force independent-minded Westerners to submit to federal authority. It was regressive and certain in time to concentrate production into the hands of a wealthy few.[33] Resentment was strongest along the forks of the Ohio, which Virginia had by then ceded to Pennsylvania. The protests looked much like the early days of the Revolution and began to turn violent.

The tax was just one of several controversies that arose during Washington's presidency. Another was caused by the catastrophic defeat of American forces by the Northwestern Indian Confederacy on the Wabash River in November of 1791. Archibald Campbell was killed there.[34] William Darke was the only officer to escape from the disaster with an improved reputation, and Virginia promptly named a town after him.[35] Still, he too was shot in the battle and helplessly watched his son die slowly from a head wound.

The defeat was the subject of the very first congressional oversight investigation and resulted in a pair of federal militia laws. The President was authorised to activate the states' militia to counter invasions, Indian attacks, and organised resistance to federal law. Under the new system, four major generals were responsible for broad Virginia geographies. Jonathan Clark, still resident in Virginia, was one. His counterpart responsible for the northwest was Daniel Morgan.[36] Two of the brigadier generals responsible for subsets of Morgan's command were Benjamin Biggs and William Darke, commanding the 10th

31 Erik Goldstein, Stuart C. Mowbray, and Brian Hendelson, *The Swords of George Washington* (Woonsocket: Mowbray Publishing, 2016), pp.63–67.

32 Anon (ed.), *Journal of the House of Representatives of the United States*, 1st Congress (Washington: Gales & Seaton, 1826), pp.356, 361, 363, 365.

33 Brady Cryzter, *The Whiskey Rebellion: A Distilled History of An American Crisis* (Yardley: Westholme, 2023), pp.xxv–xxviii.

34 LVA: R. Campbell bounty claim.

35 Hening (ed.), *Statutes*, vol.13, p.297.

36 LVA: State Government Records Collection, Accession 36902, 'Militia Establishment and Register of Militia Commissions of the Virginia Militia, 1792–1796', p.69.

Virginia named a town to honour Lieutenant Colonel William Darke in what is now Jefferson County, W.Va. (Author's photo)

and 16th brigades.[37] Biggs had risen far since his 1775 enlistment into John Stephenson's Company. He still lived in Ohio County, which had been trimmed by the border agreement with Pennsylvania. His brother Zachariah received what should have been a plum job as the local revenue officer under the whiskey law. Instead, he was subjected to intimidation and harassment by angry mobs.[38] The revenue inspector across the line in Pennsylvania had it even worse. John Neville, who had been brevetted a general at the end of the Revolution, found himself under siege in his own home. Bower Hill sat on the banks of Chartiers Creek, which flowed from the south into the Ohio River a few miles downstream from Pittsburgh. Neville was wealthy. Among his possessions were human chattels and a 500-gallon whiskey still. One day in July, he was awakened by dozens of armed protestors jeering and yelling in front of his house. He took a shot at them from a window, initiating a short firefight. His wife, his granddaughter, and a visiting girl loaded weapons for him in rotation. He shot four men, killing one of them.

The mob moved on, but Neville knew they would be back. He sent messages to friends and to the federal garrison in Pittsburgh asking for help. A small number of soldiers arrived with his wife's one-eyed brother-in-law, Major Abraham Kirkpatrick. Then, presumably to avoid capture, Neville bolted out of the house when the sound of drums signalled the

37 LVA: 'Militia Establishment and Register', pp.3–4, 70.

38 Kevin T. Barksdale, 'Our Rebellious Neighbors: Virginia's Border Counties During Pennsylvania's Whiskey Rebellion', *VMHB*, 111:1 (2003), pp.12–17.

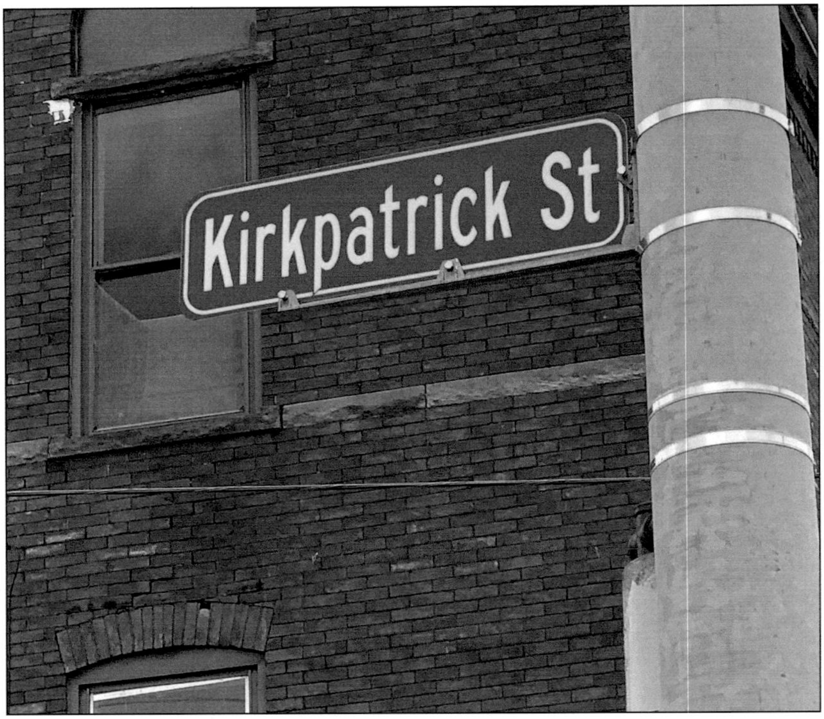

Kirkpatrick Street in Pittsburgh is named after Major Abraham Kirkpatrick. (Author's photo)

approach of a small army of whiskey rebels. An angry 600-person mob came brandishing rifles, pitchforks, axes, and swords. The tax protesters surrounded the house while one of them came forward with a flag of truce to demand that Neville come out and resign his office. Kirkpatrick coolly informed him that the general was not at home. The rebels wanted to search the house. There are conflicting reports of how the 8th Virginia veteran replied, but it was agreed that Neville's wife, granddaughter, and her visiting friend could leave. Another flag came with a demand that the soldiers in the house lay down their arms and surrender. Kirkpatrick refused and a battle began. Neville's outbuildings were burned, and then Bower Hill itself was torched, forcing Kirkpatrick and the federal troops to come out. Kirkpatrick attempted to get away, but the rebels captured him, intending to hold him hostage. Hours later, he was clandestinely released by a rebel leader.[39] By refusing to yield at Bower Hill, Kirkpatrick made himself the primary subject of the rebels' ire. His farm atop Coal Hill (Mount Washington) was burned to the ground.[40] When a mob prepared to burn his townhouse in Pittsburgh, a frantic effort was made to protect it. The brother of a man Kirkpatrick had killed at Bower Hill was brought forward to urge the arsonists to stand down. The man added, however, 'that if ever Kirkpatrick and he should meet, one of them should die.'[41]

39 Crytzer, *Whiskey Rebellion*, pp.78–82.

40 Hugh Henry Brackenridge, *Incidents of the Insurrection in the Western Parts of Pennsylvania in the 1794* (Philadelphia: John McCulloch, 1795), pp.67, 91.

41 Brackenridge, *Insurrection*, pp.16–17, 46, 53, 68, 82, 83, 88, 102, 111, 135, 152.

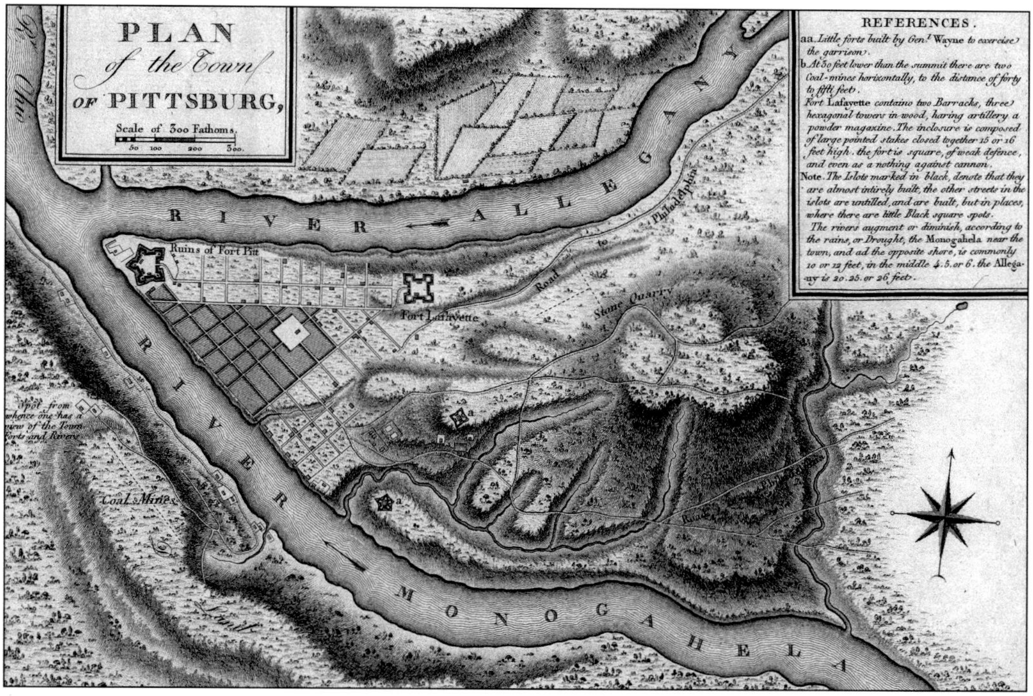

Pittsburgh in 1796. Abraham Kirkpatrick's town home faced the Monongahela in the settled (shaded) part of town. His farm that was burned by the whiskey rebels was across the river on the hill marked 'Coal Mines.' Fort Pitt, shown at the junction of the rivers, abandoned by this time; the troops that supported Neville came from Fort Fayette (Fort Lafayette), visible upstream on the Allegheney River. Map by George Henri Victor Collot. (David Rumsey Map Collection, David Rumsey Map Center, Stanford Libraries)

The whiskey tax was unfair, and Muhlenberg and Mathews both voted against it for that reason. Alexander White, who represented Morgan, Darke, and Biggs in Congress, voted for it but received just 17.6 percent of the vote in the next election.[42] It was White who read the mock proclamation at the Winchester burning of Thomas Gage in effigy in 1774.[43] However, the tax was no longer really the issue. Few of the men who shot at Kirkpatrick even owned a still. In September of 1794, Washington invoked the militia law to quell the rebellion, raising 13,000 men from Maryland, New Jersey, Pennsylvania, and Virginia. Darke's brigade marched west to Moorefield and then north to Cumberland, Maryland, joining with generals Morgan and Biggs along the way. Light Horse Harry stepped away from his duties as governor of Virginia to take overall command of the Virginians. Washington himself rode west to review the troops at Cumberland.[44] This was the last time Darke and Washington saw each other. Though by no means equals, Darke had known the President

42 Anon (ed.), *Journal of the House*, 1st Congress, pp.356, 361, 363, 365; Anon. (ed.), '3rd Congress: Virginia 1793', *Mapping Early America Elections*, <earlyamericanelections.org/maps/meae.congressional.congress03.va.county.html>, accessed 23 June 2024.

43 *Virginia Gazette* (Rind), 4 Aug. 1774; Maxwell and Swisher, *Hampshire*, p.740.

44 Barksdale, 'Rebellious Neighbors', p.25.

for 40 years, supporting him in war, business, and politics.[45] Washington returned to Philadelphia, and the militia army proceeded to Pittsburgh. The rebels fled.

A bottle of wine, perhaps one of several, sent to Abraham Kirkpatrick by President Washington for his courage during the Whiskey Rebellion. Kirkpatrick's descendants preserved the bottle and its now-evaporated contents. The gift is not otherwise documented, but a label put on the bottle when the cork was replaced in 1840 says, 'Washington Wine Imported in 1792 Rebottled [recorked] in 1840.' (Image Courtesy of Bonhams Skinner)

The Lives of Veterans

After the Revolutionary War, the 8th Virginia's original captains sought their fortunes in different ways and at various places. William Darke, David Stephenson, and Thomas Berry returned to their Shenandoah Valley homes. Darke went back to fighting Indians, but Stephenson and Berry grew old in quiet respectability. John Stephenson, George Slaughter, Jonathan Clark, William Croghan, and James Knox all moved to Kentucky. Croghan became wealthy. Slaughter signed the important but controversial Treaty of Fort McIntosh as a witness in 1785,[46] but then died penniless after serving a sentence in a debtor's prison.[47] His last preserved letters show him trying to trade worthless land in Ohio County for some kettles to boil salt in.[48] Abel Westfall and Robert Higgins moved to Ohio, where Higginsport and Westfall were named for them.[49] Westfall is now a ghost town, but a school district still carries the name. Richard Campbell lies somewhere in the ground at Eutaw Springs, South Carolina.

The regiment's veterans settled as far south as Alabama, as far north as New York, and in every state in between. John Redman, a drummer in Captain Campbell's Company and a veteran of the

45 Gabriel Neville, 'A Forty Year Bond: William Darke and George Washington in Politics, Business, and War', *Magazine of the Jefferson County Historical Society*, 84 (2018), pp.23–38.

46 NARA: M668, Ratified Indian Treaties, 1722-1869, 'Ratified Indian Treaty 10: Wyandot, Delaware, Chippewa and Ottawa – Fort McIntosh, January 21, 1785.'

47 *Field v. Slaughter and Others*, 22 Oct. 1808, Court of Appeals of Kentucky.

48 CWM: Archibald Woods Papers, Mss. 65 W87, 'George Slaughter, Kentucky, by Rob[er]t Woods, attorney, assignment of land to Archibald Woods', 10 Nov. 1795, 'George Slaughter, Louisville, to Archibald Woods, Wheeling, Va.,' 5 Aug. 1796, 'George Slaughter, Bourbon County, Ky, to Archibald Woods, Ohio County', 17 Nov. 1802, 'Geo. Slaughter, Kentucky Bourbon, to Archibald Woods, Ohio County', 2 Dec. 1803.

49 Anon. (ed.), *History of Franklin and Pickaway Counties, Ohio* (Place unknown: Williams Bros., 1880), p.322.

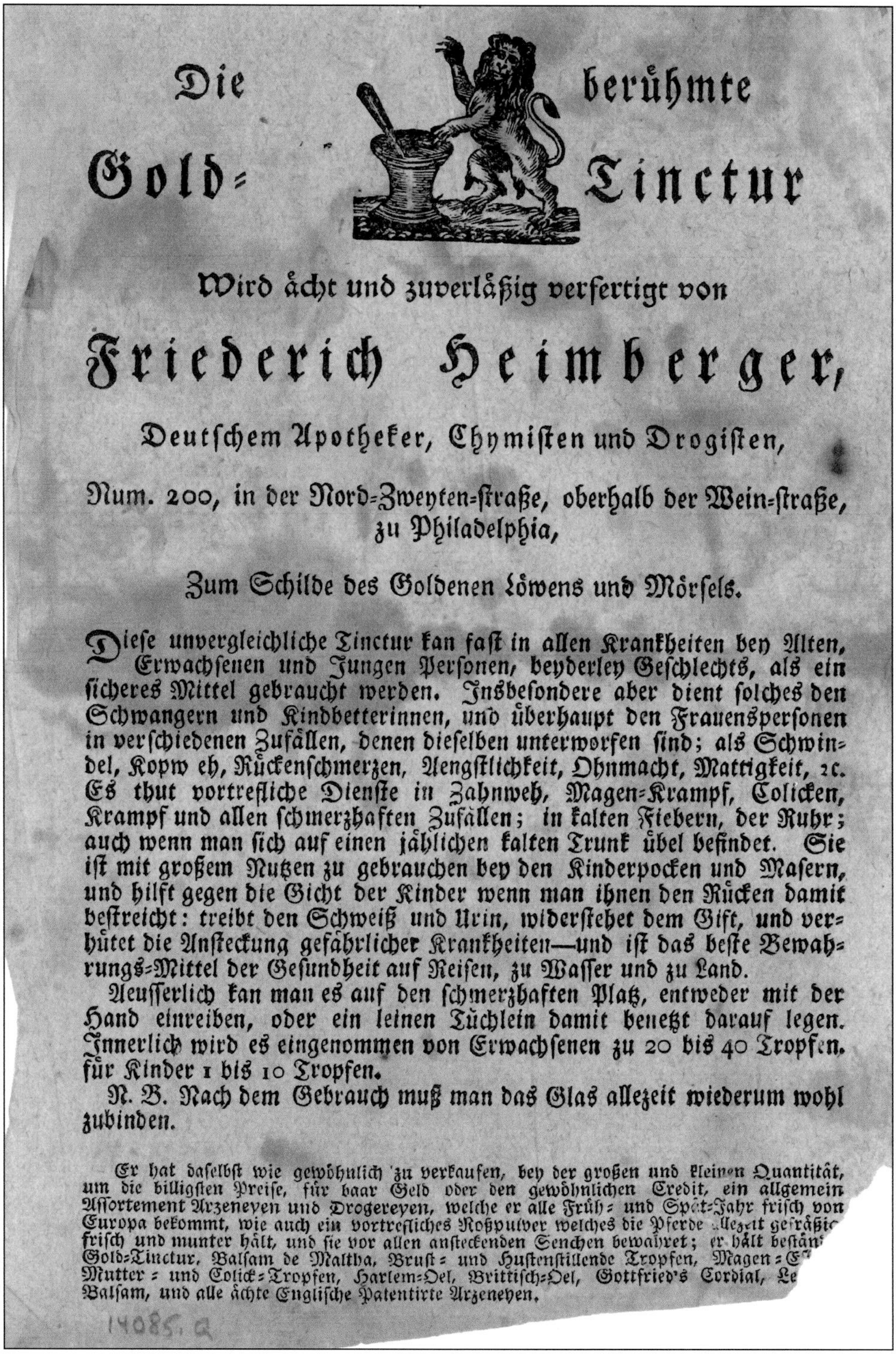

Die berühmte Gold= Tinctur

Wird ächt und zuverläßig verfertigt von

Friederich Heimberger,

Deutschem Apotheker, Chymisten und Drogisten,

Num. 200, in der Nord=Zweyten=straße, oberhalb der Wein=straße, zu Philadelphia,

Zum Schilde des Goldenen Löwens und Mörsels.

Diese unvergleichliche Tinctur kan fast in allen Krankheiten bey Alten, Erwachsenen und Jungen Personen, beyderley Geschlechts, als ein sicheres Mittel gebraucht werden. Insbesondere aber dient solches den Schwangern und Kindbetterinnen, und überhaupt den Frauenspersonen in verschiedenen Zufällen, denen dieselben unterworfen sind; als Schwindel, Kopweh, Rückenschmerzen, Aengstlichkeit, Ohnmacht, Mattigkeit, zc. Es thut vortrefliche Dienste in Zahnweh, Magen=Krampf, Colicken, Krampf und allen schmerzhaften Zufällen; in kalten Fiebern, der Ruhr; auch wenn man sich auf einen jählichen kalten Trunk übel befindet. Sie ist mit großem Nutzen zu gebrauchen bey den Kinderpocken und Masern, und hilft gegen die Gicht der Kinder wenn man ihnen den Rücken damit bestreicht: treibt den Schweiß und Urin, widerstehet dem Gift, und verhütet die Ansteckung gefährlicher Krankheiten—und ist das beste Bewahrungs=Mittel der Gesundheit auf Reisen, zu Wasser und zu Land.

Aeusserlich kan man es auf den schmerzhaften Platz, entweder mit der Hand einreiben, oder ein leinen Tüchlein damit benetzt darauf legen. Innerlich wird es eingenommen von Erwachsenen zu 20 bis 40 Tropfen. für Kinder 1 bis 10 Tropfen.

N. B. Nach dem Gebrauch muß man das Glas allezeit wiederum wohl zubinden.

Er hat daselbst wie gewöhnlich zu verkaufen, bey der großen und kleinen Quantität, um die billigsten Preise, für baar Geld oder den gewöhnlichen Credit, ein allgemein Assortement Arzeneyen und Drogereyen, welche er alle Früh= und Spät=Jahr frisch von Europa bekommt, wie auch ein vortrefliches Roßpulver welches die Pferde allezeit gefräßi[illegible] frisch und munter hält, und sie vor allen ansteckenden Senchen bewahret; er hält bestän[illegible] Gold=Tinctur, Balsam de Maltha, Brust= und Hustenstillende Tropfen, Magen=E[illegible] Mutter= und Colick=Tropfen, Harlem=Oel, Brittisch=Oel, Gottfried's Cordial, Le[illegible] Balsam, und alle ächte Englische Patentirte Arzeneyen.

14085. Q

A handbill advertising Frederick Heimberger's 'Famous Gold Tincture.' (Library Company of Philadelphia)

The postwar home of 8th Virginia Surgeon Cornelius Baldwin. He was from New Jersey but settled in Winchester after his release. (Author's photo)

attack on Stony Point, moved to New York City and became a tailor.[50] Surgeon's Mate Frederick Heimberger opened an apothecary shop in Philadelphia.[51] He catered to a German clientele, advertising his 'famous gold tincture' as a cure for just about any illness.[52] Jacob Sivley of Captain Clark's Company moved to Huntsville, Alabama, where his home became the subject of a buried-treasure legend.[53] Chaplain Christian Streit and Surgeon Cornelius Baldwin both decided they liked the Shenandoah Valley and settled in Winchester. Streit preached for the rest of his life in the church Peter Helphenstine helped build in 1764. The church burned down in 1854, but its ruins still preside over the graves of Helphenstine, Streit, Baldwin, and Daniel Morgan.

Some veterans became notable in other ways. Peter Muhlenberg was vice president of Pennsylvania's Supreme Executive Council (akin to lieutenant governor), a three-time member of the U.S. House of Representatives, and briefly a U.S. Senator before he accepted a lucrative patronage job as Collector of the Port of Philadelphia from President Jefferson.[54] William Darke played an important role in opposing to the Sedition Act during the presidency of John Adams.[55] John Chenoweth, the Welsh blacksmith from Hampshire County, became locally important in Randolph County (now West Virginia), serving at different times as

50 NARA: J. Redman pension.

51 LVA: Revolutionary War Rejected Claims, Frederick Heimberger.

52 Library Company of Philadelphia (LCP): Am 1800 Beruhm 14085.Q, 'Berühmte Gold Tinctur', ca. 1800.

53 Virgil Carrington Jones, 'The Sivley Treasure Recovered', in *True Tales of Old Madison County* (Huntsville: Historic Huntsville Foundation, 1992), pp.52–58.

54 Muhlenberg, *General Muhlenberg*, p.330.

55 *Aurora General Advertiser*, 19 Feb. 1799; *Gazette of the United States and Philadelphia Daily Advertiser*, 27 Feb. 1799; Boyd (ed.), Papers of Jefferson, vol.31, pp.491–494; Manning J. Dauer, *The Adams Federalists* (Baltimore: Johns Hopkins University Press, 1953), pp.216–217.

A postwar portrait of Cornelius Baldwin. Baldwin was taken captive with the Virginia Line at Charles Town in 1780. (Photo: Ben Ritter, Courtesy of Stewart Bell Jr. Archives)

Mary Baldwin (née Briscoe), wife of Cornelius Baldwin. Miniature. A matching portrait of Dr Baldwin has not been identified but is likely to exist. Watercolour on ivory, by Philippe Abraham Peticolas, 1797. (Smithsonian American Art Museum)

militia captain, state delegate, justice of the peace, coroner, constable, and sheriff.[56] Benjamin Biggs and Thomas Ravenscraft led troops in the War of 1812.[57] Some veterans' careers were memorialized in placenames: in addition to Darkesville, Westfall, and Higginsport, the counties of Muhlenberg, Knox, and Darke were created in Kentucky and Ohio.

Though never more than a lieutenant colonel in state or Continental service, Westerners addressed James Knox as 'general.'[58] In 1784, he led a giant caravan of settlers through the Cumberland Gap to Kentucky's bluegrass country. What began as eight or 10 families in Staunton grew along the way to a small army of 500 people, three-quarters of whom were children. At Bean's Station, a traveller remembered, 'they gave Gen. Knox, a Revolutionary officer, the entire command of their movements, and commenced their wilderness journey of two hundred and fifty miles.' As with Muhlenberg's return from the land lottery earlier

56 A.S. Bosworth, A History of Randolph County West Virginia (Elkins: publisher unknown, 1916), pp.67, 70, 73–74, 77, 235; Leonard (ed.), *Assembly*, p.205.

57 CWM: Archibald Woods Papers, Mss. 65 W87, 'Gen. Benj[ami]n Biggs to Archibald Woods', 11 Aug. 1813, 'Benjamin Biggs, West Liberty, to Col. Archibald Woods', 14 March 1814; NARA: T. Ravenscraft pension.

58 LVA: S. Bassett French Biographical Sketches, 'James Knox'; Clark, *Memoir of Jane Trimble*, pp.43–61.

the same year, 'It was thought necessary to march in military order.' Knox saw them through rushing river currents and attempted Indian attacks all the way to Crab Orchard before saying goodbye. 'Gen. Knox,' said a spokesman for the settlers

> I am authorized by this group of pioneers to tender you their acknowledgements for the kindness and care you have exercised toward them during the tedious and toilsome journey, and for the consummate skill displayed in their safely reaching their destination. They feel that it will be a pleasing duty to remember, while memory lasts, the services you have rendered them, and the strong and lasting obligation they are under to respect and love you.[59]

Most westward-bound veterans settled in Kentucky, but some chose Ohio when the Virginia bounty land reserve opened there in the 1790s. Others continued farther west. Sergeant James Lamb of David Stephenson's Company moved to Bourbon County, Kentucky, married a cousin of Daniel Boone, and then crossed the Ohio to Indiana. An abolitionist, he 'left Kentucky about 1818 on account of the evil influences of slavery.'[60] Others freed their slaves, but in different ways and perhaps for different reasons. In Kentucky, John Stephenson willed his property to his wife with the stipulation that when she died, their slaves were to be freed.[61] Back in the Shenandoah Valley, David Stephenson's widow provided in her will that their slaves were 'to be liberated and transported to some free State.'[62] In 1830, Michael Dean, a 92-year-old veteran of Thomas Berry's Company, went to the Bracken County, Kentucky courthouse to emancipate three people: a 30-year-old 'black' woman named Jenny and her two 'yellowish' children. He also left his home and 50 acres to Jenny in his will. Jenny had taken care of Dean and his wife when their own children abandoned them. One of those callous children was probably the father of Jenny's children.[63]

Philip Fine travelled all the way to Upper Louisiana, settling at St Louis by 1781. The French trading post founded there in 1764 had evolved into a small town under Spanish rule. Fine has long been recognised as the first 'American' resident of St Louis. He then moved several miles down the Mississippi about 1805 and operated Fine's Ferry near the mouth of the Meramec River until his death. His home in St Louis, a 1775 poteaux-sur-sole house, remained standing until about 1865. After the Louisiana Purchase, the house may briefly have been the home of James Wilkinson, the traitorous first territorial governor. It was also briefly the home of the second territorial governor, Meriwether Lewis, in 1808. Lewis turned it over to his friend and former partner in exploration William Clark, who lived there from 1808 to 1811. Clark was the youngest brother of Fine's old captain from the war. The first governor after statehood lived in the house as well.[64]

---

59 Clark, *Memoir of Jane Trimble*, pp.42–43, 60–61.

60 Andrew W. Young, *History of Wayne County, Indiana* (Cincinnati: Robert Clarke & Co., 1872), p.145; Anon. (ed.), *History of Wayne County, Indiana* (Chicago: Inter-State Publishing Co., 1884), vol.2, p.290.

61 Larche, *Pioneers on the Bullskin*, p.157.

62 Chalkley, *Chronicles*, vol.3, p.247.

63 NARA: M804, S36503, Michael Dean pension; Cheri Daniels, 'Is Your Brick Wall Whitewashed?', *Genealogy Literacy*, 11 February 2019, <genealogyliteracy.com/is-your-brick-wall-whitewashed>, accessed 6 December 2024.

64 Grace Lewis, 'The First Home of Governor Lewis in Louisiana Territory: "…the house in which General Clark resides"', *Bulletin of the Missouri Historical Society*, 14:4 (1858), pp.357–368.

James Lamb's house, near Richmond, Indiana. (Author's photo)

Philip Fine lived in this house in St Louis, Missouri in 1804. It was built in 1774 by a French colonist. Later occupants included Meriwether Lewis, William Clark, and the first governor of Missouri. The house was torn down shortly after this daguerreotype image was made ca. 1865. The place where it stood is just a few hundred feet from the southern leg of the Gateway Arch. (Courtesy of the Missouri Historical Society, St Louis)

George Slaughter was not the only veteran reduced to poverty. James Brooks, once one of Slaughter's men, made a fair living as a farmer for many years before incurring 'debts in various stores grog shops & taverns' and declining into destitution.[65] Despite his local prominence, John Chenoweth was also unable to care for himself in his last years. He was 'very inferm and unable to worck to git by living,' he wrote at the age of 74, '& my companion is an ould woman as well as my self not able to wash our clothes. I had a negro gerl but sold her her some years agoo.' He did, he confessed, own 50 acres of land, but it was 'in the woods & veary thin & hilly.' It was enough land to entitle him to vote, but in his estimation, that was not worth the three-cent tax he paid on it each year.[66]

Tommy Miller fell the farthest. Back in 1777, he was one of the 10 ensigns selected by Peter Muhlenberg to fill vacancies. Washington's instructions then were to pick 'such Gentlemen as will not disgrace the Appointment & Commission.'[67] Miller met that standard during the war but disgraced himself when it was over. His son later asserted that he had been a gallant officer, but 'His association in the army had … a ruinous effect upon his morals. When he should have been training up to habits of self-restraint and business, he became addicted to the vices and intemperance, extravagance, gambling and lewdness, seeking his enjoyments in loose company and not applying himself to regular business.' Miller sold his land warrants and opened a grocery store in Richmond, but grew 'so intemperate as, at last, to become partially deranged' and cruel to his wife, Nancy. She 'remained with him until he used personal violence upon her. She had before apprised him, when threatening her with violence, that if he ever so far forgot what was due to her as to assault her, she would leave him.' Nancy left with their children and supported herself '[w]ithout any settled home for many years' as a seamstress.

After losing his grocery, Miller 'so far degraded himself as to enlist as a common soldier' in the Provisional Army raised during the 1798–1801 Quasi-War with France. In a heartbreaking episode, Miller's young son ran away from home to be with his father, but an uncle came to bring him back to his mother.

> I was walking beside my father going down to Main Street, and just around the corner we met Uncle Isham and Mr. Jackson. Some conversation ensued between them, and soon they were engaged in a fight; and as my uncle, being younger, larger and stouter than my father, soon had him down, in terror I ran off, Mr. Jackson merely looking on the fight and not minding me. I ran to the barracks, and, crying, told the soldiers that my uncle was killing my father.[68]

Miller died in 1821.[69]

65 NARA: M804, S36430, James Brooks pension.
66 NARA: J. Chenoweth pension.
67 LOC: George Washington Papers, Ser.4, General Correspondence: George Johnston to Peter Muhlenberg, March 9, 1777
68 Miller, *Life of Miller*, pp.12–17.
69 NARA: T. Miller pension.

17

Old Men

Misfortune continued to follow Leonard Cooper for the rest of his life. He returned to Shenandoah County, married, and became a Methodist. Despite his amputated leg, he got around on a mare that he trained to kneel for him. He routinely rode the horse to court days and militia musters, which were the main community events of the time.[1] Late one spring day in 1821, the horse came home with an empty saddle, dragging the reins behind her in the dust. After a search, Cooper's body was found in the Shenandoah River. His neighbours believed the mare had stumbled in the river's rocky ford, tossing the elderly and disabled veteran who could not save himself from drowning.[2]

Lovely's Purchase

Many 8th Virginia veterans continued to fight Indians after the war, but one of them turned the other way. After teaching school and serving as a sheriff in Tennessee, William Lewis Lovely took a job as a government Indian agent in 1802 at the request of Cherokee tribal leaders.[3] Over time, many Cherokee converted to Christianity, farmed, and bought African slaves. Those who were resistant to such changes moved west, and Major Lovely moved with them. In 1813, he settled with his wife in an abandoned Osage campsite on the east bank of the Illinois Bayou, a mile north of the Arkansas River and just south of the Ozark Mountains.[4] Happy at first, he grew miserable in the same way Martin Carney had at Fort Jefferson in 1781. Lovely had lived with James Madison for a while as a boy and now wrote to the president asking for a new job.[5]

1 NARA: Leonard Cooper pension.

2 LVA: LVA: Revolutionary War Rejected Claims, Leonard Cooper; NARA: L. Cooper pension.

3 James W. Livingood, *Hamilton County* (Memphis: Memphis State University Press, 1981), pp.12–13; Bergherm, 'William Lewis Lovely', p.174.

4 Betty Lovely Smith, 'Lovely County', *Encyclopedia of Arkansas*, <encyclopediaofarkansas.net/entries/lovely-county-2940/>, accessed 30 June 2024.

5 Brent Bergherm, 'William Lewis Lovely', in Nancy A. Williams (ed.), *Arkansas Biography: A Collection of Notable Lives* (Fayetteville: University of Arkansas Press, 2000), pp.173–175.

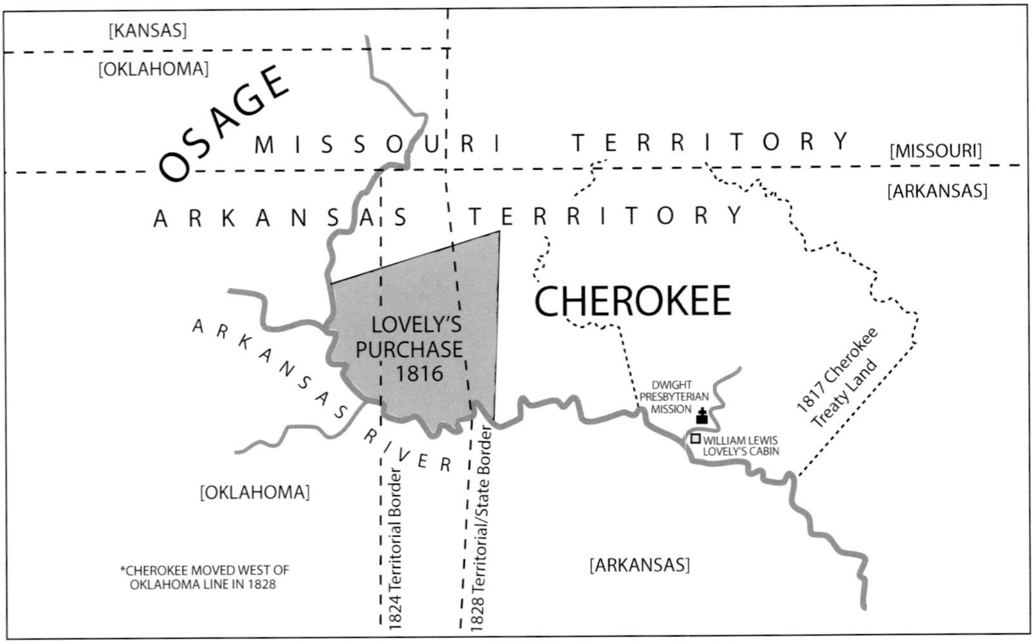

Lovely's Purchase.

> When I took leave of you in the year 1774 You were Sitting on your father's fence little did I expect to write your after nearly half a century had Elapsed my Situation in those days being pricarious as I entered Into the Shawanoe expedition... My Situation is I can assure you disagreable living at upward of three hundred miles from a post office no ways of procuring Information but that which are owing to chances & those Seldom happen. So I may Say with propriety that I am intirely Secluded from the land of the living Surrounded on all Side by Indians togather with the Worst of White Settlers living just below me betwixt whom there are daily disturbances arising & against whom there are No possible means in my power of enforcing any laws.[6]

The Cherokee trusted Lovely and urged him to stay. With that encouragement, and lacking other prospects, the old soldier continued with his work. He played the role of peacemaker when war broke out between the Osage and the Cherokee newcomers.[7] Without authorization from his superiors, he persuaded the Osage to sell him seven million acres of land between the Verdigris River and the Cherokee settlements. The purchase was intended to provide a defined territory for Cherokee settlement but has also been described as a buffer

6 Rutland et al (eds), *Papers of Madison* (Presidential), vol.9, pp.570–573.

7 Thomas Nutall, *A Journal of Travels into the Arkansa Territory, During the Year 1819* (Philadelphia: Thomas H. Palmer, 1821), pp.135–136.

between the warring tribes.[8] Lovely died in 1817, the same year Major General Andrew Jackson negotiated a new treaty that required the people Lovely had called 'the Worst of White Settlers' to vacate the Cherokees' land. A single exception was made for Persis Lovely, the major's widow, who was permitted to keep her home and the site of Major Lovely's grave.

In 1827, land approximating the boundary of Lovely's Purchase was incorporated by the Arkansas territorial government as Lovely County but they then eliminated it in a boundary change the next year. The Cherokee, who addressed Persis as 'Mother', moved west into Oklahoma and left Arkansas open for white settlement. Persis, forgotten in the treaty behind the new arrangements, lost her home. She was, in her own words, 'a woman who is a widow childless and lone in the world.' The old reservation, she told Andrew Jackson, 'included my home: which reservation has since been sold intire, and in consequince i am a houseless wanderer at sixty years of age.'[9] She moved into an empty house near Dwight Mission and begged Andrew Jackson, who was now the president, to be allowed to remain. An act of Congress granted her the land in 1831. She lived there until her death in 1842 when she was buried next to her husband.[10]

The Nation's Guest

'The day will soon arrive,' the *Kentucky Gazette* announced on 12 May 1825, 'when our town is to be honored by the presence of that Hero, who stood in the first rank of the illustrious band that broke the chain of British tyranny.'[11] The announcement was not news; it was a reminder. Lexington had been preparing for months for the arrival of the Marquis de Lafayette. President James Monroe invited the last surviving major general of the war to come as 'the nation's guest' and tour all 24 states of the union as the 50th anniversary of the war approached.[12] Lexington was named for the first battle of the Revolution, and it was the seat of Fayette County, so the town sought to make its celebration the official event for the Commonwealth. The governor denied the request, but that did not stop the community from staging the greatest event possible.[13]

Abraham Bowman had moved to Fayette County after 1784 and was now the county's most celebrated veteran and at the centre of Lexington's two-day program. Because he lived too far from the main road, Bowman hosted Lafayette at the home of his daughter, Mary Keene and her husband John. The general's military escort bivouacked in their yard. In

8 Nutall, *Journal*, pp.135–136; Willard H. Rollings, *The Osage: An Ethnohistorical Study of Hegemony on the Prairie-Plains* (Columbia: University of Missouri Press, 1992), pp.235–244; Lonnie J. White, 'Arkansas Territorial Indian Affairs', *Arkansas Historical Quarterly*, 21:3 (962), pp.193–212; Smith, 'Lovely County'.

9 Sam B. Smith et al (eds), *The Papers of Andrew Jackson*, (Knoxville: University of Tennessee Press, 1980), vol.8, pp.23–24.

10 Brent G. Bergherm, 'Persis Lovely', in Williams (ed.), *Arkansas Biography*, pp.172–173.

11 Edgar Ewing Brandon (ed.), *A Pilgrimage of Liberty: A Contemporary Account of the Triumphal Tour of General Lafayette Through the Southern and Western States in 1825, as Reported by the Local Newspapers* (Athens, Oh.: Lawhead Press, 1944), p.282.

12 Auricchio, *The Marquis*, pp.295–303.

13 Brandon (ed.), *Pilgrimage of Liberty*, p.281, 301.

The grave of Colonel Abraham Bowman in Lexington Cemetery. (Author's photo)

the morning, Bowman rode into town in the hero's green and yellow barouche, pulled by a quartet of bay horses.[14] They were escorted by a grand procession that included the governors of two states, militia, veterans, elected officials, university faculty, students, clergy, and many others. The sidewalks and every window were filled with cheering people. Veterans crowded around them, calling out the names of battles and showing off their scars. One man held up a hand to show the stumps of the fingers he lost at Brandywine, delighted that Lafayette had been wounded in the same fight.[15] Colonel Bowman sat beside The Nation's Guest as he delivered a speech in a chapel so crowded that no one could move, and he sat to the general's right at an outdoor banquet held for 1,400 people.[16]

Lafayette was on a strict schedule and rode away in his carriage after a visit of two days. Bowman, who was 75 years old when Lafayette came, lived long enough to become the last surviving colonel of the Virginia Continental Line in 1831. By then, the Old Dominion's generals had been gone for years. Peter Muhlenberg died in 1807 from the lingering effects of malaria.[17] Bowman himself passed away in 1837 at the age of 88. His descendants preserved the bed Lafayette slept in as a family treasure.[18]

14 Brandon (ed.), *Pilgrimage of Liberty*, p.285; *Boston Commercial Gazette*, 14 Oct. 1824; George Washington Ranck, *History of Lexington Kentucky* (Cincinnati: Robert Clarke & Co., 1872), p.306.

15 Brandon (ed.), *Pilgrimage of Liberty*, p.307; Ranck, *Lexington*, p.307.

16 Brandon (ed.), *Pilgrimage of Liberty*, p.301.

17 Muhlenberg, *General Muhlenberg*, p.69.

18 Wayland, *Bowmans*, p.216.

Woodstock, 1827

One day in January 1827, Jacob Rinker rode from his home into Woodstock to visit his old friend Joachim Fetzer. They were both sons of Swiss immigrants and veterans of the 8th Virginia. Fetzer had tried to desert in the summer of 1777,[19] but that was long forgotten. He was now in his last illness. Rinker was 78 years old, and the 13-mile ride through a cold January rain made him sick as well. Fetzer passed away on 17 January. Rinker died the next day.[20]

Crossing Over the River Styx

In 1828, Congress provided full pensions for veterans who had served to the end of the war. Captain Curry mused about his own mortality when he applied for the support.

> Most of the officers of the Revolution have joined the great majority underground but by the few survivors, the tendered relief will be gratefully received, and will help to smooth the passage of the evening of life. Should this appropriation be thought burthensome, the country will soon be relieved owing to the advanced age of the remains of that army. I am myself 75 years of age, and work hard on my farm for my subsistence – this boon comes late, but on receiving it, we may have enough to pay our passage over the Styx, and prevent any demurrage with old Charon about the use of his Boat.[21]

Peter Muhlenberg is buried next to his wife 'Hannah' (Anna Barbara) at his father's church in Trappe, Pennsylvania. (Author's photo)

19 NARA: M246, f.210, pp.5, 35.
20 Wayland, *Shenandoah County*, p.557
21 NARA: J. Curry pension.

Old Jonathan Grant

Ohio historian Ben Douglass never heard the best parts of Jonathan Grant's story, but it was not for lack of trying. Douglass was thorough as he collected information for a history of Wayne County that was published in 1878. He searched through records and interviewed people of long memory in every corner of the county. Down in the sparsely populated southern end, near the Holmes County line, he interviewed the elderly John Harrison. The octogenarian had settled there in 1816 and remembered how salt was once used for currency. He traded two barrels of it for a two-horse wagon in 1826. He remembered that wheat was worth little until the Ohio and Erie Canal opened. He remembered the handful of Native Americans who remained into the 1820s, including old 'Chief' Dan Lyon, who made wooden ladles and traded them for bacon. And he remembered Grant.

> Old Jonathan Grant lived on the Holmes county side of the line, but in Wayne county then. He was a sort of spy, and an agent to look after the interests of first settlers. The Government had him employed, and donated him one hundred and sixty acres of land where he lived. He lived in true aboriginal style – in an open shanty, between the logs of which dogs could jump; had no floor, and was covered with bark; was a great hunter; bear and deer-skins covered his shanty; prayed and swore in the same breath. The Larwills waited on him in his last sickness; died of cancer, over fifty years ago.[22]

Another local history confirms that Grant was the first settler in Holmes County, could speak the Indians' language, 'knew all about the country,' and had guided surveyors into Indiana after the New Purchase of 1818.[23] John Harrison lived near Grant for more than 15 years but apparently had no idea that his neighbour had crossed the Delaware with George Washington and been wounded at Germantown. Grant, it seems, kept his story to himself.

'Here, sir, the people govern.'[24]

When Peter Helphenstine took his wife and son down the Rhine from the Palatinate and sailed for America in 1754, Maria Theresa was in her ninth year as empress of the Holy Roman Empire. Though she was barred by her gender from ruling in her own name, no one epitomized the Old World better than she. She was the mother of Marie Antoinette and had been the very subject of the War of Austrian Succession. When her husband died in 1765, she remained very much in control as empress dowager. During the American Revolution, she told a British diplomat that she supported the efforts of George III and had 'a hearty

22 Ben Douglass, *History of Wayne County, Ohio* (Indianapolis: Robert Douglass, 1878), pp.609–610.
23 Henry Cring et al, *Caldwell's Atlas of Holmes County, Ohio* (Condit, Ohio: Caldwell Publishing, 1875), p.7.
24 Alexander Hamilton to the New York Ratifying Convention in Harold C. Syrett (ed.), The Papers of Alexander Hamilton (New York: Columbia University Press, 1962), vol. 5, pp.4-104.

desire to see the restoration of obedience and tranquillity in every quarter of his dominions.' Her son, the nominal emperor, was more pointed.

> The cause in which England is engaged is the cause of all sovereigns, who have a joint interest in the maintenance of due subordination and obedience to law in all the surrounding monarchies. I observe with pleasure the vigorous exertions of the national strength, which the king is employing to bring his rebellious subjects to submission, and I sincerely wish success to the measures.[25]

The cause that cost Major Helphenstine his life was, whether he knew it or not, in large measure a redefinition of sovereignty. The process had already begun in Britain, where sovereignty had been taken from the Crown by Parliament in 1689. Parliament still asserts that its sovereignty is 'the most important part of the UK constitution.' [26]

While Parliament defines sovereignty as being 'the supreme legal authority in the UK, which can create or end any law',[27] the word has a different meaning in America. It connotes freedom, independence, and self-sufficiency. This was true from the very beginning. The term does not appear in the Declaration of Independence, but the American understanding of sovereignty is heavily influenced by the Founders' assertions that all people are endowed by God with 'certain unalienable Rights', that governments exist to secure those rights, and that governments derive 'their just powers from the consent of the governed.' Maria Theresa had no time for such notions. She was livid when a Vienna newspaper described the war as a contest between monarchy and popular sovereignty.

When the war ended, Washington said 'the enlarged prospect of happiness, opened by the confirmation of our Independence and Sovereignty, almost exceeds the power of description.'[28] 'We the People, of the United States', began the document that Robert Breckenridge, William Darke, and Jacob Rinker voted to adopt, 'in Order to … secure the Blessings of Liberty to ourselves and our Posterity, do ordain and establish this Constitution for the United States of America.'

The soldiers of the 8th Virginia Regiment (many of whom, or their parents, were born in the Holy Roman Empire) may illustrate better than any other defined group of men the process that transformed the sovereignty of monarchs into self-rule, or popular sovereignty. When Independence was declared, Virginians had enjoyed 169 years of 'benign neglect' and were, for the most part, only concerned with the most local forms of government. When Peter Helphenstine arrived at Winchester in 1755, it was a frontier village far from the centres of even colonial power and an ocean plus a wilderness away from London. Robert Higgins and Ned McCarty grew up still farther out, where the only food, clothing, shelter, and security were those their families provided for themselves. Though it came with

25 William Coxe, *History of the House of Austria*, 3rd edition, 4 vols (London: George Bell and Sons, 1182), vol.3, pp.472–473; Francis Wharton (ed.), *The Revolutionary Diplomatic Correspondence of the United States* (Washington: Government Printing Office,1889), vol. 2, p.476–477.

26 Anon., 'Parliament's Authority,' parliament.uk/about/how/role/sovereignty.

27 Anon., 'Parliament's Authority,' parliament.uk/about/how/role/sovereignty.

28 Fitzpatrick (ed.), *Writings of Washington*, vol.24, p.224.

hardship and danger, Americans continued to cling to the freedom, opportunities, and self-sufficiency of frontier life for more than century.

It is not hard to understand why people living such lives would be prickly about sudden impositions of 'intolerable' laws from 3,500 miles away. John Vance, one of Captain John Stephenson's soldiers from the Youghiogheny Valley, looked back on his life at the age of 67 and declared, 'I served in our Revolutionary War for liberty.'[29]

29 NARA: J. Vance pension.

Appendix I

Company Rosters

Commissions and Enlistments

The original officers had provincial commissions. The regiment was taken into Continental service in the summer of 1776, backdated to 25 May 1776. The officers and men were brought into Continental pay on that date, except for those detached to the 1st Virginia whose retroactive start date was 1 March. Promoted officer commissions were often backdated and do not align with command assignments. Command dates are prioritised in the data below. Command dates after the creation of the 4th-8th-12th Virginia Regiment are not shown. The 1775 enlistment term was one year. The 1776 term was two years. The 1777 term was set at three years, with a bounty land incentive to enlist for the duration of the war. One-year enlistments were revived in 1778 with limited inducements. The regiment began receiving drafted soldiers in 1778, also with one-year terms. Soldiers with one-year terms beginning before 1778 are assessed to be substitutes. Men were encouraged to reenlist at or before the expiration of their terms.

Sources

The primary sources for service data are muster rolls, payrolls, and pensions held by the National Archives, the Wisconsin Historical Society, and the Library of Virginia. Reference was also made to *Compiled Service Records of Soldiers Who Served in the American Army During the Revolutionary War*, a derivative collection of reference cards for each soldier created by the War Department in the 1890s, and to transcriptions posted at *Southern Campaigns Revolutionary War Pension Statements and Rosters*. Other secondary sources are John H. Gwathmey's *Historical Register of Virginians in the Revolution* and E.M. Sanchez Saavedra's *A Guide to Virginia Military Organisations in the American Revolution, 1774-1787*. Suspected errors in transcriptions and secondary sources were checked by referencing the original documents. Any errors are the current author's. Spelling of surnames is inconsistent in original documents but made uniform here for reference purposes with alternates provided only in cases of significant variance.

Service Codes

The following codes are used to indicate elements of each soldier's known service in the most concise manner possible. Codes in parentheses denote uncertainty. Date, unit, or location specificity is provided after a forward slash. The battles of Brandywine, Germantown, Charles Town, Short Hills, Waxhaws, and Eutaw Springs are indicated by their initial letters. Transfer destination units are similarly abbreviated. Promoted officers are listed at both ranks. Sergeants are listed once without reference to dates of appointment. Corporals are not identified. Drummers and fifers are combined as 'D&F.' Battle participation is not usually indicated and cannot be assumed from service dates. Most soldiers still in service on 12 May 1780 were taken prisoner at Charles Town but confirmation for individual enlisted soldiers is rare. Important detached service is noted when documented. Post-consolidation events are not comprehensively shown. Records rarely indicate a reason for early service termination. Soldiers recorded as 'recruited, not joined' are shown as deserters.

C – Croghan Detachment
D – Deserted, not recaptured
DC – Deserted, recaptured
DR – Drafted
E – Exchanged
EC – Escaped from captivity
ED – Early discharge
F – Served to the end of the war
FM – Fort Mifflin detachment
I – Transferred to Invalid Corps
KIA – Killed in action
LG – Washington's Life Guard
LI – Maxwell's Light Infantry
MR – Morgan's Rifles
MIA – Missing in action
O – Elevated from enlistment to cadet or ensign
P – Promoted
POW – Prisoner of war
Q – Officer resigned
R – Reenlisted
S – Left sick and dropped from rolls
SB – Substitute
SN – Supernumerary officer
T – Transferred
U – Status not known
W – Wounded
X – Died in Service
Y – Yorktown Campaign in any capacity

Field Officers

Colonel John Peter Gabriel Muhlenberg (12 Jan. 1776–21 Feb. 1777) P Y F
Colonel Abraham Bowman (22 March 1777–ca. June 1778) SN
Lieutenant Colonel Abraham Bowman (12 Jan. 1776–1777) P
Lieutenant Colonel John Markham (22 March 1777–26 Oct. 1777) *
Major Peter Helphenstine (12 Jan. 1776–ca. 10 Aug. 1776) (Q)
[Major John Stephenson] (ca. Aug. 1776) †
[Major Richard 'Dick' Campbell] (10 Aug. 1776–29 Sept. 1777) ‡
Major William Darke (29 Sept. 1777–29 Nov. 1777) § POW/GT P E Y
Major Jonathan Clark (10 Jan. 1778–ca. June 1778) P POW/C F

*Cashiered. †Brief service claimed in pension and appropriate for seniority but not otherwise recorded. ‡ Promotion reversed. §Promotion retroactive to 4 Jan. 1777.

Staff Officers

Adjutant Francis Swaine (<23 Jan. 1776–ca. 21 Feb. 1777) P
Adjutant Abraham Kirkpatrick (2 April 1777–1 Jan. 1778) *
Adjutant John Smith (1 Jan. 1778–June 1778)
Chaplain Christian Streit (1 Aug. 1776-June 1777)
Surgeon Cornelius Baldwin (20 May 1777–) POW/C F
Surgeon's Mate Frederick Heimberger (19 April 1777–15 March 1778)
Paymaster Hezekiah Stoakes (4 June 1777–June 1778)
Quartermaster Hezekiah Stoakes (1 March 1777–4 June 1777)
Quartermaster Martin Carney (3 June 1777–June 1778)

Warrant Officers

Drum Major Nicholas Neal (9 May 1777–June 1778)
Fife Major William Lipscomb (27 Dec. 1777–June 1778)
Quartermaster Sergeant Martin Carney (3 May 1777–3 June 1778)
Quartermaster Sergeant Ashkenaz Shappee (3 June 1777–ca. April 1778) †
Quartermaster Sergeant Arthur Johnson (ca. May 1778–June 1778)
Sergeant Major John Hoy (16 May 1776–3 December 1776) X
Sergeant Major William Palmer (1 March 1777–17 Feb. 1778)
Sergeant Major John Harding (3 March 1778–ca. 1 May 1778)
Sergeant Major Arthur Johnson (1 May 1778–ca. May 1778)

*Concurrent with commissioned rank as 1st lieutenant in Croghan's Company. †Frequently anglicised to 'Askin Shippey.'

Captain John Stephenson's Company

First in seniority. Completed 10 December 1775 as the Second West Augusta Independent Company of provincial regulars, authorised to recruit 100 enlisted men to perform frontier defence for one year. An early 1776 list of officers survives, but no roll or roster of enlisted men has been found. The enlisted men below have been identified from pension affidavits, deserter advertisements, local histories, and other means. Unconfirmed assessments are in brackets. If the company was at standard strength when regimented, the names of 53 enlisted men are missing.

Captain John Stephenson (10 Dec. 1775–ca. Sept. 1776) (Q)
1st Lieutenant Robert Beall (10 Dec. 1775–ca. Sept. 1776) P/13VA F
[2nd Lieutenant Simon Girty] (10 Dec. 1775–ca. Feb. 1776) (SN) *
2nd Lieutenant Edward Rice (ca. Feb 1776–ca. Sept. 1776)
[3nd Lieutenant Edward Rice] (10 Dec. 1775–ca. Feb. 1776) *
Ensign Simon Morgan (10 Dec. 1775–ca. Sept 1776) P/13VA W/ES F

[Ensign Benjamin Biggs] (ca. Sept. 1776) † P/13VA F
Sergeant Benjamin Biggs † P/13VA
Sergeant Richard Blackston C U
Sergeant John Vance
John Armstrong C U
John Berry ‡
Zephaniah Bryan
Joseph Carter
[Patrick Collins] §
William Davis
John Gardner
John Harrison P/13VA F
John Kirk
[John Knight] §
William Miller D
Samuel Murphy
William Owens
Thomas Ravenscraft ‡
[George Shilling] §
[Isaac Sissell] §
[Wiliam Taylor] §
John Williams ‡

*Weakly sourced and uncertain. Original 100-man independent company was authorised with three lieutenants. C.W. Butterfield identifies Girty as a 2nd lieutenant, but 3rd lieutenant would be more likely to drop as supernumerary. Rice as 3rd lieutenant depends on Butterfield being correct. †Rank assessed from future service. ‡Enlisted but rank not known. §Assessed from service in Stephenson's Company in Dunmore's War and Beall's Company of the 13th Virginia Regiment.

William Darke's Company
Later known as Isaac Israel's Company

Second in Seniority. Built on a company of the Berkeley Minute Battalion. Completed 9 February 1776 in Berkeley County (now West Virginia). Experienced significant attrition during 1776. Darke was promoted to major in 1777 and Isaac Israel then commanded. Combined with Abel Westfall's former company under Captain Abraham Kirkpatrick at Valley Forge, April 1778, with Thomas Miller continuing as ensign. Kirkpatrick's Company continued in the 4th-8th-12th Regiment and the 4th Regiment after the line was consolidated.

Captain William Darke (9 Feb. 1776–29 Sept. 1777) – LI P
Captain Isaac Israel (ca. spring 1778–May 1778)
1st Lieutenant Daniel Culp (9 Feb. 1776–9 May 1777) Q
1st Lieutenant Isaac Israel (3 Aug. 1777–ca. spring 1778) P

2nd Lieutenant Isaac Israel (9 Feb. 1776–3 Aug. 1777) P
2nd Lieutenant Christopher Moyer (9 May 1777–22 Nov. 1777) POW/G EC P
Ensign John Daniel (9 Feb. 1776–5 Aug. 1776) U
Ensign Christopher Moyer (5 Aug. 1776–9 May 1777) P
Ensign Thomas 'Tommy' Miller (18 March 1777–April 1778) P
Cadet Edward McKinney S

Enlistments for 1776:
Sergeant Edward Beason S
Sergeant John Engle C *
Sergeant Daniel Hendricks E
Sergeant Edward McKinney O
Sergeant Leonard Ragar
Sergeant Christian Shryock ED
Sergeant Henry Yeager
D&F John Landers U
Tilman Aldrick S
Jacob Anderson C R S
Robert Avis S
John Baker D
Thomas Beaty S
Francis Bennet ED
Benjamin Blackford U
Manassah Braman S
Isaac Bridgewater T/3SC
Elias Bridgewater T/3SC
Daniel Cameron X/77
John Cartridge R S
John Casa T
John Conelly T
Benjamin Dean T/7VA
William Dean S
John Dowland R
John Duseagh X
William Elice T
William Engle X/76
Robert Ennis
Frederick Falkinbury
Redmond Finley S
David Foulke D †
Moses Gee U
Hugh Griffy ED
Stephen Hacket T
James Hagin T
John Harpendin R X
Jonathan Herrin X/76
Jeremiah Humphreys X/76
Joseph Imfelt ED
David Jackson T
Patrick Kelly C S
William Kelsey T
George Ketcher X/76
Herman Keyser T
Job Lucas U
Mich Mahony T
Alexander McDonald S
Tully McKinny
Francis McRay D
William Moody R F
Abraham Moore D
Joshua Pepper S
William Pingle X/76
Patrick Plunket ED
John Polson X/76
George Pritty X/76
Patrick Punch C
John Purtle U
James Range
James Right
Lewis Ronemus
Joseph Sever T
George Smith X/76
John Smith T
James Still X
Samuel Watson X/76
John Wells S
William Wells T
Thomas West
Nathan Willett POW
John Wimley
William Wright S

Enlistments for 1777

Sergeant Michael Tullis LG
Sergeant John Roberts POW/C
D&F George Johnston
D&F Stephen Vardin
D&F John Williams
Jacob Anderson S
Conrad Casnor D
Hugh Close
John English
Nicholas Ennis S
James Hamilton
John Hewit S
William Hooks
John Hulch U
William Jones
John Kough
Daniel McIntire D

*Left sick in Virginia by Captain Croghan. †Post-certification enlistee.

Richard Campbell's Company

Later known as Matthias Hite's Company and as John Steed's Company.

Third in seniority. Completed 19 February 1776 in Dunmore County (now Shenandoah County). One of two companies from Dunmore County and intended to be the 'English' of the two. The names of one musician and 29 rank-and-file 1776 enlistees, likely casualties, are missing. Captain Campbell was improperly promoted to major in August 1776, and 1st Lieutenant Hite then acted as captain. Campbell's promotion was rescinded in 1777. Campbell was promoted to major in September 1777 and transferred to the 13th Virginia. Lieutenant Hite resigned in October 1777, and Lieutenant Steed assumed command. The company was folded into Captain Kirkpatrick's Company of the provisional 4th-8th-12th Regiment at Valley Forge. Lieutenant Colonel Campbell was killed in action at the Battle of Eutaw Springs on 8 September 1781.

Captain Richard 'Dick' Campbell (19 Feb. 1776–29 Sept. 1777) P/13VA KIA/ES
[Captain Mathias Hite] ca. 10 Aug. 1776–29 Sept. 1777) *
Captain John Steed (30 March 1778–June 1778)
1st Lieutenant Matthias Hite (19 Jan. 19, 1776–7 Oct. 1777) † Q
1st Lieutenant John Steed (ca. Oct. 1777–30 March 1778) P
1st Lieutenant Robert 'Bob' Breckenridge (4 April 1778–June 1778) P POW/C E F
2nd Lieutenant John Steed (19 Feb. 1776–ca. Oct 1777) P
2nd Lieutenant Leonard Cooper (24 May 1776–7 Oct. 1776) P
2nd Lieutenant Robert 'Bob' Brackenridge (10 Aug. 1777–4 April 1778) P
Ensign Leonard Cooper (19 Feb. 1776–24 May 1776) P
Ensign Robert 'Bob' Breckenridge (16 March 1777–10 Aug. 1777) P
Cadet William Dennis (4 Feb. 1777–ca. Sept. 1777)

Enlistments for 1776:

Sergeant Charles Beale U
Sergeant William Combs S
Sergeant John Doyle
Sergeant George Parkerson
Sergeant Anjer Price R Y
D&F John Gesnor R F
D&F William Arrowsmith ED
Jessy Allison MIA
Isaac Anderson
Daniel Arnwine U
George Ashby C LI FM ED
Benjamin Bruce S
Daniel Burner S
Daniel Cloud C
Thomas Cummins S
Henry Davis
John Elsey‡
Peter Emmons C R POW/C F
Nicholas Foster W
David Grate W/B
Benjamin Hawkins C U
Enoch Herrel
Rubin Herrel T/Invalids
Simon Herrel
Abraham Hogman LI
John Jephcoat R (POW/C)
Michael Keller S
Christian Kendrick C
George Lair LI R F
Jessy Lane S
George McGee C W
Collin Mitchum T/5SC R
Daniel Nichols LI R (POW/C)
Peter Parkerson W
Matthew Plumbly
Thomas Price
Robert Rains R POW/C
Jacob Revincom
George Ryan C R POW/C
Vincent Sandy
Solomon Smallin POW
Peter Smith POW/G
George Spickard Y
William Warren
Reuben Washburn
Barton Whitehorn LI W
William Woodford S

Enlistments for 1777:

Sergeant Thomas Byrd R
John Bowman X/79
Samuel Bowman ED
Abraham Burner SB
Peter Collins I F
William Davis X/77
William Eagle
Jacob Forsyth POW/SH E (POW/C)
Benjamin Garvin R (Y)
David Griffith (POW/C)
Frederick Long X/77
Henry Maise U
Henry Minor (W/G)
John Ryder (POW/C)
Thomas Shirley S
William Shovel LI U

Enlistments for 1778:

William George
Rodger McPike R
Mathias Shults
George Stephen
Elias Turner
James Young

*Improper provisional promotion. †Resigned after the Battle of Germantown ‡Taken by Brigadier General Muhlenberg to serve as his waiter.

George Slaughter's Company
Later known as John Graves' Company, Abraham Kirkpatrick's Company, and Isaac Israel's Company.

Fourth in seniority. Possibly built on a company of the Culpeper Minute Battalion. Completed 19 February 1776 in Culpeper County. Slaughter was promoted to major of the 12th Virginia on 4 October 1777. Commanded by Graves at Germantown, by Kirkpatrick and Israel at Valley Forge before the remnant was put in Kirkpatrick's Company of the 4th-8th-12th.

Captain George Slaughter (19 Feb. 1776–4 Oct. 1777) P/12VA Q
(No captain from 4 Oct. to ca. Dec. 1777)
Captain Abraham Kirkpatrick (1 Jan. 1777–April 1778) F
Captain Isaac Israel (ca. April–June 1778) (Q)
1st Lieutenant Henry Field (26 Jan. 1776–3 Aug. 1776) Q
1st Lieutenant James Kirtley (Oct. 7, 1776–10 June 1777) *
1st Lieutenant John Graves (ca. June 10, 1777–22 April 1778) Q
1st Lieutenant Christopher Moyer (June 1778)
2nd Lieutenant James Kirtley (19 Feb. 1776–7 Oct. 1776) P
2nd Lieutenant John Graves (8 Oct. 1776–ca. 10 June 1777) P
2nd Lieutenant Reuben Field (ca. 5 Aug. 1777–) POW/G E P Y F
Ensign John Graves (Feb. 19, 1776–8 Oct. 1776) P
Ensign Reuben Field (March 11, 1777–ca. 5 Aug. 1777) P
Ensign Philip Huffman (ca. May–June 1778) POW/G EC P
Cadet Reuben Field O

Enlistments for 1776:
Sergeant William Field
Sergeant James Newman
Sergeant William Procter W
Sergeant John Rosson LI
Sergeant Lemuel Rucker
Sergeant Robert Spilman
Sergeant Thomas Tillery U
D&F Henry Clatterbuck X/76
D&F Meshack Pearson POW/G EC R T
D&F Samuel West T/Navy
Thomas Abbet X/76
William Abbet X/76
Edward Abbott X/76
John Abbott X/76
Roger Abbott
John Barbee ED
William Cabbage X/76
William Campbell LI
Patrick Carrick T/Navy D
Thomas Chelton S
William Corbin X/76
Charles Creel
Elijah Dawson X/76
Otewell Dawson T/Artillery
Joseph Delaney, Sr. LI W
Abraham Field X/76
Larkin Field P Q
Reuben Field P
William Fincham LI POW/G E
Bozel Freeman X/76
Thomas Freeman DC POW/G E
James Hall
Robert Hanson D
John Henderson ED
Isaac Hiers
Reuben Hollaway X/76

Eppa Hubbard R T/4th Cont. Dragoons
Drury Jackson
Utey Jackson X/76
William Jett
John Jinkins X/77
Jonus Jinkins ED
Jeremiah Johns POW
James Johnston LI
Joseph Jones X/77
Robert Jones X/77
Edward Kennedy X/76
William Kennedy POW
John Mathews
William Mathews
Mason McCarty
Barnett McGinnis X/76
Abraham Mershon
Cornelius Mershon X/76
James Newman X/76
Thomas Newman X/76
John Owen ED
William Payne R POW
James Rains POW/G
Richard Roberts LI
William Robert LI W
Benjamin Ross R (POW/C)
Joseph Rosson
Elzaphan Rucker LI
John Settle X/77
James Shackleford X/77
Lawrence Slaughter
Bryant Sloan ED
James Smith X/77
John Smith X/76
William Smith
James Vowels LI
Aaron Watts
Robert Watts
Francis Weakly S
William Weekly X/76
James Williams X/77
Nehemiah Wood X/76
Lewis Yancy X/76 †

Enlistments for 1777:
Sergeant John Leavel ED
D&F Stephen Rice
Nicholas Arnold D
Richard Bennett POW/W EC Y
James Brooks
John Cage D
Philip Clayton SB
William Courtney MR
Joseph Dean
Joseph Delaney, Jr. SB
James Dowers D
Daniel Farmer DE
Robert Harris
Richard Jenkins DE
John Lee
Robert Metcalf T/1MD
Abner Newman DE
John Sloan W ED
James Smith
William Stone T/13VA O
William Taylor (POW/C)
Thomas West POW/G

Enlistment for 1778:
William Price DR R D

*Cashiered. †Post–certification enlistee.

Jonathan Clark's Company

Later referred to as 'the late Captain Clark's Company', commanded by Lieutenant Cooper.

Fifth in seniority. Completed 4 March 1776 in Dunmore County (now Shenandoah County). One of two companies from Dunmore County and intended to be the 'German' one. Clark was promoted to major on 10 January 1778. Folded into Kirkpatrick's Company of the 4th-8th-12th Regiment.

Captain Jonathan Clark (4 March 1776–10 Jan. 1778) P
1st Lieutenant Jacob Rinker (4 March 1776–10 May 1777) Q Y
(No 1st lieutenant from May 1777 to May 1778)
1st Lieutenant Leonard Cooper (10 May 1777–June 1778) * I F
2nd Lieutenant Adam Dirting (4 March 1776–May 1776)
2nd Lieutenant Taverner Beale (May 1776–March 1777) Q Y
2nd Lieutenant Jacob Parrot (March 1777–May 9, 1777)
2nd Lieutenant Philip Eastin (10 Aug. or 4 Oct. 1777–June 1778) F
Ensign Jacob Parrot (4 March 1776–March 1777)
Ensign Philip Eastin (20 March 1777–June 1778) P

Enlistments for 1776:

Sergeant John Bley C †
Sergeant Griffey Gibbons
Sergeant Thomas Harding C †
Sergeant Jacob Knisely D
Sergeant George Parett X/76
Sergeant Joseph Parett Y
Sergeant Joseph Thomas
D&F Nicholas Neal P
D&F Philip Kibler ED
Volunteer Philip Helphenstine

James Arnwine AKA Erwin
Frederick Bahsdorf ED
James Bartlett T/Navy
Jacob Bauber S
Nicholas Bowder X
Christian Bowman
Jacob Boyer AKA Bowyer
John Branham D
John Breeding D
William Brinkley ED
Nathan Brittain X/76
Thomas Brittain X/76
Henry 'Harry' Brock D
John Brock C X/77
Henry Brock
William Brown ‡ X/77
Michael Buckley R F
William Buddell T/Navy
John Byrd
Adam Cabbage
George Carthey C † R D
George Clower
Christopher Coffelt AKA Kauffelt
Henry Crafton ED
Anthony Cushon R
Isaac Dent X/76
Patrick Duffey T/Navy
Joachim Fetzer DC
Andrew Fine S
Philip Fine
William Flinn D
George French D
Mathias Funk X/76
Griffith 'Griffey' Gibbons R
James Grant ED
Henry Hambleton T/Navy
Martin Honey C X/76
Peter Jordan C †
Michael Keffery D

William Kennedy R D
Philip Kibler ED
Jacob Knisely
Isaac Long T/Navy
William Means R F
William Maunsell T/Navy
John Maxwell X/76
Donald McDonald
Heinrich Meier ED
Philip Mour D
Daniel Norriss T/5SC
George Parrott
Joseph Parrott
Jacob Pereley AKA Berkley
Humphrey Price X/76
Meredith Price C X/77
Jacob Rawber D
William Reader S
John Rinn ‡ T/Navy
Francis Seal D
Christian Shallender D
John Shaver DC
Peter Sink DC
Simon Siron X/76
Thomas Stockdon D
James Strickland ED
Joseph Thompson D
Mathew Toomey X/76 ‡
Jeremiah Wales
George Walker T/SC
Michael Wall X/76
Walter Warner X/76
James White DE
John Williams
Joshua Williams T/SC
Andrew Winebranor T/SC
Christopher Young

Enlistments for 1777:
D&F Henry Redman
D&F John Redman, Jr.
John Dunbar D
Thomas Fine U
Joseph Golliday
Henry Moore X/77
John Nisely
Isaac Pemberton X/78
Henry Redman, Sr. ED
William Redman
Robert Shepperd D
Stephen Smith
John White D

Enlistments for 1778:
Henry Aleshite DR Y
George Chambers DR
William Clark DR Y
Thomas Edghill
John Long DR R
Edward Padget
Jacob Sively DR
Peter Sively DR
Christian Swan S
John Teazle
Andrew Wolfe
John Wyatt POW/C EC Y

*Promotion may have been retroactive †Left sick in Virginia by Captain Croghan. ‡Post-certification enlistee.

Abel Westfall's Company

Later known as Lieutenant Berwick's Company

Sixth in seniority. Completed 12 March 1776 in Hampshire County (now West Virginia). Captain Westfall resigned on November 22, 1777. Combined with William Darke's former company under Captain Abraham Kirkpatrick at Valley Forge, April 1778 with James Berwick continuing as 1st lieutenant (a promotion retroactive to 18 April 1777). Kirkpatrick's Company continued in the 4th-8th-12th Regiment and the 4th Regiment after the line was consolidated.

Captain Abel Westfall (12 March 1776–22 Nov. 1777) Q
1st Lieutenant Robert Higgins (12 March 1776–1 March 1777) P
(No 1st Lieutenant from 1 March to ca. June 1777)
1st Lieutenant James Berwick (April 1778)
2nd Lieutenant Andrew Turk (March 12–ca. Sept. 1776) Q
(No 2nd Lieutenant from ca. Sept. 1776–ca. April 1777)
2nd Lieutenant James Berwick (ca. April 1777–April 1778) * P
Ensign Rees Pritchard (March 12–ca. Sept. 1776) Q
Ensign Laurence Greenholm (7 Oct.–ca. March 1777) Q
Ensign Cornelius Westfall (16 March 1777–21 April 1778)

Enlistments for 1776:

Sergeant Peter Kerns
Sergeant Edward 'Ned' McCarty LI Y
Sergeant Zachariah Pigman LI POW X
Sergeant Strother Settle
Sergeant John Welsh R
Sergeant Cornelius Westfall P
Sergeant Jacob Westfall
Sergeant James Work T/SC
D&F Patrick Callihan X/76
D&F James Christian AKA Christy
D&F Michael Howell

John Allison ED
John Anderson POW/G E
Joseph Baldwin D/77
Edward Barnard ED/77
George Best ‡ SB
Burket Baarer AKA Borer POW
James Brandy POW/G E
Richard Cain LI W
John Chenoweth POW/G E Y
Charles Collins
James Crawley D/876
Edward Dewin U
Terrance Doyle ED/77
Joseph Edwards X/77
Thomas Farrell D/77
James Galloway X/77
John Graham T/5SC
Duncan Graham T/5SC
John Green D/76
Laurence Greenholm ‡ O
Tobias Haut D/76
Henry Hazle D/76
William Henesey POW/G E
John Hicks MR
John Hogg T
Abraham Hornback C MR
James Hornback POW/G
John Huff X/76
Patrick Johnston MR
Joseph Jones D/77
William Kynets X/76
William Kysinger Sub D/77
William Lard T/5SC
Andrew Layton D/76

Francis Lebrown U
Peter Lee D†
Hugh Lewis ‡ X/76
Richard Lowden ED
Edward Martin D/76
William McCormick X/76
John McDermott D/76
James McDonald
Peter McDonald POW/G E
Lawrence McGuire
Michael McKnight (C) F
John Monks
Thomas O'Banion R POW/C X/81
Joseph Pancake MR
Daniel Parks POW/G E R F
Thomas Price D/76
William Price T/SC
Benjamin Russel D
Philip Sanders X/77
Henry Shepler D/76
John Shepler D/76
James Shields
John Stump X/76
James Taff ‡ C MR
William Taylor
Robert Wadsworth LG
Jacob Watson S
Thomas Watson D/76
William Watson T/Invalids
Michael Weese
George Wilfong S
William Winters S
John York D/77

Enlistments for 1777:
Sergeant Thomas Brannan
Sergeant Osburn Flynn MR POW/C
Christy Donally ED
George Faint R FM
Philip Faint § FM
Anthony Fox C R
John Haggen X/78
Moses Johns X/78
Henry Miller MR
Patrick Moore S
Simon Savage D/78
George Villars D
John Williams LI

*Promoted to this position from Croghan's company. Retroactively promoted to 1st lieutenant on unknown date. †Hired Peter Lee as substitute. ‡Post-certification enlistee.

David Stephenson's Company

Seventh in seniority. Completed 25 March 1776 in Augusta County. The names of two sergeants, one musician, and 48 rank-and-file 1776 enlistees, likely casualties, are missing. The company was folded into Captain Croghan's Company of the provisional 4th-8th-12th Regiment at Valley Forge.

Captain David Stephenson (25 March 1776–June 1778) P/5VA F
1st Lieutenant Joseph Dickson (25 March 1776–ca. autumn 1776)
(No 1st lieutenant after Dickson)
2nd Lieutenant John Grattan (25 March 1776–ca. autumn 1776) X
2nd Lieutenant Benjamin Kinley (9 May 1777–June 1778) W/G
Ensign Samuel Coleman (25 March 1776–ca. April 1776) * T F
Ensign Benjamin Kinley (ca. April 1776–9 May 1777) P
Ensign James Hooke (16 March 1777–21 April 1778)

Enlisted for 1776:

Sergeant James Lamb C
Sergeant Johnston Nelson
D&F Thomas Hetherly C U
William Anderson S
Adam Bible
Cornelius Cain C LI
John Campbell
William Donavan LI
Michael Gold R
Joseph Hall
John Ireland C
Michael Kelly C T/Croghan
Robert Leonard R
John Malone R
Thomas Marshall S
George McVey LI
John McWilliams R
William Mills S
John Murray
Charles Sanders ‡ LI MIA/G
Nicholas Sheridan R
David Viah C
Matthew Walker
James Young LI

Enlisted for 1777:

Sergeant Benjamin Crow
Sergeant John Harden P POW/C
Sergeant William McCoy F POW/C
D&F Samuel Henderson
D&F Samuel Jones
William Alford D†
John Bowman
Thomas Clifford
Thomas English R
John Hanks
Edmond Harris U
Joseph Rhea ED
John Sutler
James Walker
James Windon

Enlisted for 1778:

Cornelius Area D
James Blaine DR
James Brownlee DR
Michael Cape DR
John Carr
Nicholas Clark
Jacob Crow
John Fowler
John Hopkins
Michael Mullen DR
Thomas Nichols D
James Patterson POW/C
Joseph Robinet
Thomas Showel
James Squires
James Stunkard
Peter Vanpelt
Theodosius Welch
Thomas Wilson D
Robinson York D

*Transferred to Virginia Navy shortly after the march to Williamsburg. Also served in the 1st Continental Artillery Regiment. †Later enlisted in Robert Higgins' company. ‡Post-certification 1776 enlistment.

Thomas Berry's Company
Later known as Richard Eastin's Company.

Eighth in seniority. Completed 27 March 1776 in Frederick County, Virginia. Captain Berry resigned in April of 1778. The company was folded into Captain Croghan's Company of the provisional 4th-8th-12th Regiment at Valley Forge.

Captain Thomas Berry (27 March 1776–May 1778) SN
1st Lieutenant John Joliffe (27 March 1776–April 6, 1777) X/77
1st Lieutenant Richard Eastin (6 April 1777–7 June 1778) Q
2nd Lieutenant Richard Eastin (16 Feb 1776–6 April 1777) P
2nd Lieutenant Francis Baldwin (10 May 1777–8 May 1778)
Ensign William Meade (27 March–20 Nov. 1776) X/76
Ensign Francis Baldwin (ca. 20 Nov. 1776–10 May 1777) P
Ensign John Kay (16 March 1777–21 April 1778) Q
Cadet John Chapman *
Child volunteer John Kercheval Y

Enlistments for 1776:
Sergeant Rese Bowen X
Sergeant John Chapman LI P
Sergeant John Duncan R
Sergeant Thomas Hampton
Sergeant John Jones
Sergeant John Kay O
Sergeant Benjamin Kercheval MR §
Sergeant Robert McGill LI
Sergeant Jeremiah Redman
D&F Benjamin Carter C
D&F James Oliver

George Albin LG
Abram Anderson ED
Lewis Atkins R F
Francis Baldwin O
Philip Barr
Isaac Beesly D
Joseph Beesly S
Abraham Buckley ED
William Buckley X
Hugh Burns X
James Burns ED
James Chamblin X
Jonathan Chenoweth LG
Isaac Colton T/5SC
Jessy Connell ED†
John Courtney S
Michael Dean
John Donally MIA/B
William Duncan S
Isaac Dunn
Vincent Dunn
Philip Eastin O ‡
Richard Fanshear S
Peter Flecher X/76
Edward Golleyhor POW/G
Peter Gwynne AKA Quinn
Thomas Hankins X/76
Joseph Hickman X/76
Luke Hines X/76
John Hollan D/76
Nicholas Hughes S
Moses Jacobs ED
Richard Johnston ED
James Kay
Denis Kingore X/76
William Laylon R
Charles Love LI
George Loyd
Mathias Martin S
George Mason T/Navy

Neil McDade X/76
Thomas McVay X/76
Thomas Mead U
Barnett Micham ED
Bryan Mooney LI
John Morrison S
William Morrow R D
Joseph Murdock
Gilbert Noriss T/SC5
William Ore
John Rasnor R
Solomon Redman R LI
John Robinson
Jonathan Rose MR
Louis Routt X/76
George Sefres
Jacob Shivertaker D/77
John Simpson FM Y
Thomas Siscoe S
Bean Smallwood R Y
Samuel Sprowl
Joseph Thrasher S
Garett Trotter X/76
Peter Vandevourt X/76
Henry Wysor MR R Y

Enlistments for 1777:
Sergeant Daniel Anderson
Jesse Badders S
John Bradford ED
Perry Chapman D
William Jones R S
William Phillips POW/G E Y
William Pollard Sub
John Sample Sub S
Philip Teboe

Enlistments for 1778:
Abraham Gibbons DR
William McMullin

*Resigned and enlisted. †Superannuated. ‡Promoted to Ensign, Clark's Company. §Listed as 'Scratchwill' in some Morgan musters.

William Croghan's Company

Tenth to be completed but later determined to be ninth in seniority. Completed 19 April 1776 in the West Augusta District. Missed the Suffolk rendezvous. Assigned as a detachment, with stragglers and late recruits from other companies to the 1st Virginia Regiment for the 1776 campaign. 'Parties' under Daniel Culp (Darke's Company), Mathias Hite (Campbell's Company) and Edward Moody (Knox's Company), mostly recruits, were added to Croghan Detachment in August 1776. Continued as Captain Croghan's Company of the 4th-8th-12th regiment.

Captain William Croghan (19 April 1776–June 1778) P Y F
1st Lieutenant Abraham Kirkpatrick (22 March 1776–ca. December 1777) P
(No 1st lieutenant after Kirkpatrick's promotion.)
2nd Lieutenant James Higgins (22 March 1776–June 1777) P SN
2nd Lieutenant Jonathan Smith (16 April 1778–June 1778) F
Ensign James Berwick (19 April 1776–1 October 1776) P *
Ensign Jonathan Smith (17 March 1777–4 October 1777)

(No ensign after Smith's capture at Germantown.)
Cadet Jonathan Smith (ca. 15 December 1776–17 March 1777) P
Child volunteer Adam Dietz W/Waxhaws

Enlistments for 1776:
Sergeant James Cassidy R
Sergeant Henry Marshall ED
Sergeant Thomas McCarty P
Sergeant John McDonald, Jr. POW/G EC
Sergeant John McDoran X/77
Sergeant Edward McGinn
Sergeant Owen Newman † R F
D&F Gabriel Christy †† X
D&F Francis Prush †† X

Ezekiel Abel ††/Hite † LI FM
James Armstrong †
Josiah Arnold W/G
George Askins T/8PA
James Blade † R DE
Barnabas 'Barney' Boner
John Bookmiller ††/Moody U
William Brice ††/Moody U
James Brown †
John Brown ††/Moody X
William Brown R D
Edward Burke ††/Moody KIA/B
Thomas Burns D/77
John Cain †† † ED
Alexander Campbell ††/Hite R
Joseph Carman
John Carter MIA
David Chandler ††/Moody § U
William Cheek ††/Hite
Elihu Chilcott ††/Hite T/3VA
Robert Cochran X/76
Philip Cole X/77
Harmon Commins POW/G E ††/Culp
Jesse Commins ††/Culp
Benjamin Cowen POW/G E
Moses Crawford R LI
Felix Daugherty ††/Hite R D
Archibald Davis ††/Moody U
John Donald
Nicholas Doran X/77
Alexander Drummond R
Adam Duck D/77
Thomas Elwell ††/Culp R F
Richard Evans † R X/G
Philip Faint ††/Hite R FM
William Franks† R
Henry Gaddis
William Gaddis X/77
Patrick Garry † X/76
John Gault R
Thomas Gladden X/77
John Goble D/77
Joseph Gonsley X/77
William Goodman X
James Gorwin †† X/77
Jonathan Grant LI
Hugh Green †† † D/76 W/G
Lewis Greenstaff AKA Grindstaff
Thomas Griffith R FM
John Grimes ††/Culp U
John Gwynn D/77
Patrick Hall † X/77
David Hanson †† X
John Henry † D
Lewis Henry X/76
Christopher Hidner U
Thomas Hills ††/Hite C U
George Hinch R U
John Hinds X/76
Nathaniel Hosier X
John Howard †† †
John James ††/Culp X/77
Enoch Job
Jesse Job X †
James Jones ††/Culp
John Kale ††/Culp U
Benjamin Kelly
Charles Kelly †† D
Aneas Lany LI R
Gregory Lawrence ††/Culp R

Able Levesque ††/Culp X/77
James Lippincott
George Martin X/77
Michael Martin X/77
Moses Martin X/77
James McAnally†
John McCollaster R W/G
John McDonald, Sr. ††/Culp
John McGinty R/3NJ
Paul McGowan W/G MIA/G
Hugh McGrady D/76
Robert Mitchell R U
Alexander Moore † W/B ED
Charles Murphy ††/Hite
James Murray † R
John O'Neal † D
Thomas Owens LI KIA/Clouds
William Penny X
Zachary Price ††/Hite S/77
John Ready ††/Culp †
John Reed, Jr. †† † LI R
James Reagon ††/Moody U
James Riddle ††/Hite †
Thomas Ryan X
Henry Saltsman KIA/G
Michael Shuster X
Henry Skinner † T/Artillery
John Smallman ††/Moody U
James Smyth †† † X/76
Joseph Stuart ††/Culp
Christian Stydner POW/G
William Tomlinson
James Toner ††/Culp † D/77
Richard Tresher ED
James Tucker X/76
John Tucker ††/Hite † X
Daniel Viers X/77
John Vincent ††/Culp R F
Hugh Ward ††/Hite R F
George Watts POW/G
David Williams LI
Daniel Wilson † W/B
John Wooten ††/Moody § U
John Wyndings R

Enlistments for 1777:
D&E Michael Sellers
John Cail S
William Cochran X/78
Jesse Davis LI POW/G
John Donnally X/77
James Echlin T/8PA
Matthew Hannon Sub
John Reed, Sr. LI

Enlistment for 1778:
James McDaniel DR

*Promoted to 2nd lieutenant, Westfall's Company. †Sick and remained in Virginia during time of Croghan's detachment. ††Post–certification enlistee.

James Knox's Company

Raised in Fincastle County. Built on a cadre from the provincial Southwest Independent Company raised for frontier defence in 1775. Ninth to be certified by its county committee but made tenth in seniority for failure to meet enlistment quotas. Musters from 1777 show the company two musicians and 27 rank-and-file men short of a complete roster. Approved by the Fincastle Committee 4 April 1776. First Lieutenant Edward Moody appointed to recruit at Williamsburg. Moody and his recruits were put in Croghan's Detachment. The company was dissolved when Knox, Craig, and Lovely formed a company of the Provisional Rifle Battalion (Morgan's Rifles) in 1777.

Captain James Knox (4 April 1776–July 1777) MR SN
1st Lieutenant Ephraim Drake (4 April 1776) *
1st Lieutenant Edward Moody (ca. 19 June–ca. June 1776) † T/Artillery
1st Lieutenant James Craig (March–July 1777) MR P SN
2nd Lieutenant James Craig (4 April 1776–March 1777)
(No 2nd lieutenant from March to May 1777)
2nd Lieutenant William Lewis Lovely (10 May–July 1777) MR P Y F
Ensign William Ward (4 April 1776) *
Ensign William Lewis Lovely (6 March–10 May 1777) MR Y

Enlistments for 1776:
Sergeant Thomas Boweland S
Sergeant Robert 'Bob' Breckenridge P ‡
Sergeant Martin Carney P
Sergeant Arthur Johnson T/Berry LI P
Sergeant William Scott MR
Sergeant Robert Stuart D/77

John Alexander S
James Carr X/76
Charles Carter X/76
William Cavanagh S
Greenberry Choat D/76
John Collier S
William Cooper D/76
William Ferris D/76
Thomas Firrer ED
William Gillihan T/5SC
Reubin Harris ED
Peter Hendricks D/76
Solomon Hendricks MR
Philip Jones D/77
Peter Kelly T/SC
Ben Keys S
Joseph Lock T/Berry W/G
Timothy Lordon D/76
Martin Maney D/76
John Maroon D/76
Edward Marshall D/76
Samuel McKinney S
John McNeel D/76
John McNinch D/76
John Monroe S
Alexander Moore S
Richard Perkins C § U
Benjamin Pyburn D/76
John Riley D/76
William Scully C § U
Edward Stapleton DC R DC
James Staunton T/SC
John Taylor T/Berry LI
John Vance X/76
Henry Wallis X/76
John Williams D/76
Roland Williams D/76
John Wilson X/76
William Wright T/76

*Drake and Ward only appear in the Fincastle Committee resolution appointing officers. They may have failed to recruit their quotas, refused the appointments, or resigned before the first surviving muster was taken in April 1777. Drake was appointed ensign of Montgomery County militia on 3 March 1777. †Appointed as 'recruiting lieutenant' by the Virginia Committee of Safety after the regiment's departure for the Carolinas. Recruited in Williamsburg and then detached with Croghan. No record of actual service with Knox. ‡Promoted ensign of Captain Westfall's Company.

Robert Higgins' Company

Robert Higgins was elevated to captain by General Washington and instructed to raise a new company to replace John Stephenson's discharged one-year men. After months struggling to recruit, the company was ordered into service at the end of July, joining after the Battle of Brandywine. Surviving men were put in Clark's, Croghan's, and Kirkpatrick's companies of the 4th-8th-12th Regiment in June 1778.

Captain Robert Higgins (March 1, 1777–June 1778) POW/G E Q
1st Lieutenant James Curry (June 24, 1777–June 1778) P POW/C F
2nd Lieutenant John Clark (May 9, 1777–June 1778) POW/G
Ensign Peter Higgins (March 9, 1777–June 1778) P F

Sergeant Robert Chambers FM POW/C
Sergeant James Kelly
Sergeant Jacob Smock

Joseph Ackerman
William Alford D/77
Henry Carrier ED
Hugh Carty S
William Curry D/77
Zachariah Delong POW/G X
Conrad Glanders D/77
James Harper D/77
Michael Keller D/77
Stephen Lewis D/77
Daniel McNaughton POW/G E
Mark Miller U
John Minnis F
John Roberts POW/G
Henry Ruyle POW/G
Jonathan Sandusky
Joshua Shaw S
George Sheets D/77
Peter Sheridan D/77
Michael Sword POW/G E
Christopher Warwick D/78
Benjamin Weeser POW/G
William West D/77

Appendix II

The Remnant

Officers and soldiers still in service in 1783. Officers are listed alphabetically by rank.

Brigadier General Peter Muhlenberg * ❡
Lieutenant Colonel Jonathan Clark ❡ ||
Major David Stephenson ❡
Major William Croghan Major † ❡ ||
Surgeon Cornelius Baldwin
Captain Benjamin Biggs † ❡
Captain Robert Beall † ❡
Captain Leonard Cooper‡ ❡
Captain James Curry ||
Captain Reuben Field ❡
Captain Abraham Kirkpatrick § ❡
Captain William Lewis Lovely
Captain Simon Morgan ❡
Lieutenant Robert Breckenridge § ❡
Lieutenant Samuel Coleman ❡ ||
Lieutenant Philip Eastin ❡
Lieutenant John Harrison † ❡
Lieutenant Peter Higgins
Lieutenant Jonathan Smith

Lewis Atkins § ❡
Michael Buckley § ❡
Peter Collins ‡
Thomas Elwell §
Peter Emmons ❡
George Lair § ❡
William Means *
Michael McKnight § ❡
William Moody § ❡
Owen Newman ❡
Hugh Ward

*Virginia
†Fort Pitt
‡Invalid Corps (New York)
§Posey's Virginia Battalion (Georgia and South Carolina)
❡Belonged to regiment at formation.
||Prisoner on parole.

Appendix III

Deserters

Chronological List of Desertions

Robert Hanson, Slaughter's Co., 11 March 1776
John McNinch, Knox's Co., 7 April 1776
James Crawley, Westfall's Co., April 1776
Benjamin Russel, Westfall's Co., April 1776
Francis McRay, Darke's Co., 20 April 1776
John Maroon, Knox's Co., 20 May 1776
John McNeel, Knox's Co., 20 May 1776
Benjamin Pyburn, Knox's Co., 20 May 1776
John Riley, Knox's Co., 20 May 1776
Greenberry Choat, Knox's Co., 20 May 1776
John Williams, Knox's Co., 20 May 1776
Tobias Haut, Westfall's Co., 23 May 1776
Henry Hazle, Westfall's Co., 23 May 1776
Henry Shepler, Westfall's Co., 23 May 1776
John Shepler, Westfall's Co., 23 May 1776
Edward Martin, Westfall's Co., 23 June 1776
George French, Clark's Co., 24 May 1776
Philip Mour, Clark's Co., 24 May 1776
Peter Sink, Clark's Co., 24 May 1776
Francis Seal, Clark's Co., 9 or 19 July 1776
Hugh McGrady, Croghan's Co., 15 July 1776
John Hollan, Berry's Co., 4 Aug. 1776
John Breeding, Clark's Co., 6 Aug. 1776
William Ferris, Knox's Co., 7 Aug. 1776
Peter Hendricks, Knox's Co., 7 Aug. 1776
Abin Moore, Darke's Co., 7 Aug. 1776
William Flinn, Clarke's Co., 9 Aug. 1776
Edward Marshall, Knox's Co., 9 Aug. 1776
John Green, Westfall's Co., 12 Aug. 1776
John McDermott, Westfall's Co., 12 Aug. 1776
Isaac Beesly, Berry's Co., 20 Oct. 1776

Thomas Price, Westfall's Co., 22 Oct. 1776
Hugh Green, Croghan's Co., 18 Nov. 1776
Nicholas Arnold, Slaughter's Co., Nov. 1776
Edward Stapleton, Knox's Co., 4 Jan. 1777*
Adam Duck, Croghan's Co., Jan. 1777
Philip Jones, Knox's Co., 1 Feb. 1777
William Taylor, Hite's Co., 21 Feb. 1777
Frederick Taylor, Hite's Co., 15 March 1777
John Branham, Clark's Co., March 1777
Joseph Baldwin, Westfall's Co., before April 1777
John O'Neal, Croghan's Co., before 15 April 1777
James Dowers, Slaughter's Co., 25 April 1777 †
Robert Stuart, Knox's Co., 26 April 1777
Thomas Wilson, D. Stephenson's Co., 27 April 1777
John Gwynn, Croghan's Co., April 1777
William Alford, D. Stephenson's Co., 2 May 1777
Thomas Farrell, Westfall's Co., 18 May 1777
John Henry, Croghan's Co., before 18 May 1777
Thomas Burns, Croghan's Co., 19 May 1777
James Toner, Croghan's Co., 19 May 1777
Thomas Watson, Westfall's Co., May 1776
William Cooper, Knox's Co., 1 June 1776
Martin Maney, Knox's Co., 7 June 1776
Michael Keffery, Clark's Co., before June 1777
Thomas Stockdon, Clark's Co., before June 1777
Jacob Knisely, Clark's Co., 2 July 1777
William Kysinger, Westfall's Co., 2 July 1777
Joseph Thompson, Clark's Co., 7 July 1777
Jacob Shivertaker, Berry's Co., 10 July 1777
Conrad Casnor, Darke's Co., 12 July 1777
Daniel McIntire, Darke's Co., 12 July 1777
Andrew Layton, Westfall's Co., 15 July 1777
Peter Sheridan, Higgins' Co., 20 July 1777
Henry Brock, Clark's Co., July 1777
William Curry, Higgins' Co., 20 Aug. 1777
George Sheets, Higgins' Co., 21 Aug. 1777
John Goble, Croghan's Co., 23 Aug. 1777
Joseph Jones, Westfall's Co., before Sept. 1777
Conrad Glanders, Higgins' Co., 3 Sept. 1777
William West, Higgins' Co., 18 Sept. 1777
Jacob Rawber, Clark's Co., Aug. or Sept. 1777
John York, Westfall's Co., 8 Dec. 1777
George Carthey, Clark's Co., winter 1778
John Dunbar, Clark's Co., winter 1778
William Brown, Croghan's Co., winter 1778

William Kennedy, Clark's Co., winter 1778
William Morrow, Berry's Co., 1 March 1778
Enoch Harrel, Campbell's Co., 1 April 1778
Perry Chapman, Berry's Co., 1 April 1778
Vincent Sandy, Campbell's Co., 1 April 1778
Barton Whitehorn, Campbell's Co., 1 April 1778
Cornelius Area, D. Stephenson's Co., 4 April 1778
Robert Shepperd, Clark's Co., 21 April 1778
Felix Daugherty, Campbell's Co., April 1778
Thomas Nichols, D. Stephenson's Co., 24 May 1778
Robinson York, D. Stephenson's Co., 24 May 1778
Simon Savage, Westfall's Co., 25 May 1778

* Deserted twice more, Dec. 1777 and 1 March 1778.
† Joined 9th Pennsylvania Rgt.

Bibliography

Abbreviations

JAR – Journal of the American Revolution
PMHB – Pennsylvania Magazine of History and Biography
VMHB – Virginia Magazine of History and Biography

Archives

American Revolution Institute of the Society of the Cincinnati, Washington
Boston Public Library
    American Revolutionary War Manuscripts Collection
Chicago Historical Society
Collection of Deborah M.S. Brown
College of William & Mary, Williamsburg, Va.
    Archibald Woods Papers
    John Marshall Papers
Federal Bureau of Investigation, Washington
    National Stolen Art File
Filson Historical Society, Louisville, Ky.
    Clark Family Papers
    Temple Bodley Collection
Harlan Crow Library, Dallas, Tex.
Harvard University Library
    Jared Sparks Collection of Miscellanies
Historical Society of Pennsylvania
    Anthony Wayne Papers
    Ferdinand J. Dreer Collection, 1492-1925
    Forges and Furnaces Collection
    Gratz Manuscript Collection
Historical Society of Western Virginia
    Breckenridge Collection 1969.51.001
Jefferson County Museum, Charles Town, W.V.
    William Darke Papers
Kentucky Secretary of State

Virginia and Old Kentucky Patent Series
Library of Congress, Washington
Friedrich Wilhelm Ludolf Gerhard Augustin, Baron von Steuben, papers
George Washington Papers
Geography and Maps Division
Prints and Photographs Division
Thomas Jefferson Papers
Library of Virginia, Richmond
Dunmore County Revolutionary War Papers, 1775-1814
Federal Government Records Collection
Governor's Office
Legislative Petitions of the General Assembly, 1776-1865
Revolutionary War Bounty Land Claims
Revolutionary War Pension Applications
Revolutionary War Rejected Claims
State Government Records Collection
Virginia Land Office, Land Bounty Certificates for French and Indian War Service
Missouri Historical Society Archives
Clark Family Collection, 1766-1991
National Archives and Records Administration, Washington
Case Files of Pension and Bounty Land Warrant Applications Based on Revolutionary War Service
Compiled Service Records of Soldiers who Served in the American Army During the Revolutionary War
General Records of the United States Government
Numbered Record Books Concerning Military Operations and Service, Pay and Settlement Of Accounts, and Supplies
Papers of the Continental Congress
Ratified Indian Treaties
Revolutionary War Rolls
Newport Historical Society, Newport, R.I.
New York Public Library, Manuscripts and Archives Division
George Chalmers Collection
Pennypacker Mills Collection, Schwenksville, Pa.
Princeton University Library
Special Collections – Manuscripts
Rockingham County Clerk of Circuit Court, Harrisonburg, Va.
Minute Books
South Caroliniana Library, University of South Carolina, Columbia
William Tennant Papers
Strasburg Museum, Strasburg, Va.
University of Michigan, William L. Clements Library
Robert Howe orderly book, 1776–1778
Virginia Museum of History & Culture, Richmond, Va.
Marquis de Lafayette Papers

Rare Books Collection
Wisconsin Historical Society, Madison
Draper Manuscript Collection

Period Newspapers

Aurora General Advertiser, Philadelphia
Boston Commercial Gazette
The Columbian Herald, or Southern Star, Charleston
Gazette of the United States and Philadelphia Daily Advertiser, Philadelphia
London Morning Chronicle
The Massachusetts Spy, Or, Thomas's Boston Journal, Boston
New York Gazette and Weekly Mercury
The Pennsylvania Evening Post, Philadelphia
The Virginia Gazette (Dixon and Hunter), Williamsburg
The Virginia Gazette (Pinkney), Williamsburg
The Virginia Gazette (Purdie), Williamsburg
The Virginia Gazette, Or, the American Advertiser (Hayes), Richmond

Published Primary Sources

Abbatt, William (ed.), 'Letters from Virginia, 1774–1781', *The Magazine of History with Notes and Queries*, 3 (1906), pp.151–161

Abbatt, William (ed.), *Memoirs of Major-General William Heath* (New York: W. Abbatt, 1901)

Abbot, W.W. et al (eds), *The Papers of George Washington*, Colonial Series, 10 vols (Charlottesville: University Press of Virginia, 1983–1995)

Agnew, Daniel, 'A Biographical Sketch of Governor Richard Howell, of New Jersey', *PMHB*, 22:2 (1898), pp.221–230

Albion, Robert Greenhalgh and Leonidas Dodson (eds), *Philip Vickers Fithian: Journal, 1775–1776: Written on the Virginia-Pennsylvania Frontier and in the Army Around New York* (Princeton: Princeton University Press, 1934)

Anon., 'Biographical Sketch of Gen. William Darke, of Virginia, by a Citizen of Frederick County, Maryland', *Military and Naval Magazine of the United States* 6:1 (1835), pp.1–9

Anon. (ed.), *Collections of the Connecticut Historical Society*, 31 vols. (Hartford: Connecticut Historical Society, 1860–1967)

Anon., 'Contemporary Account of the Battle of Germantown', *PMHB*, 11:3 (1887), pp.330–332

Anon. (ed.), *Delaware Archives: Military and Naval Records*, 5 vols (Wilmington: Public Archives Commission of Delaware, 1911–1916)

Anon. (ed.), 'The Diary of Captain John Chilton, 3d Virginia Regt', *Tyler's Quarterly Magazine* 12:4 (1931), pp.283–289

Anon. (ed.), 'Diary of Joseph Clark', *Proceedings of the New Jersey Historical Society*, original series, 7:3 (1854), pp.93–110

Anon. (ed.), 'The First Independent Company of Dunmore', *VMHB* 44:2 (1936), pp.102–104

Anon., Fort Henckel Militia musters for June and Sept. 1775, in 'Johann Adam Bible Senior and His Sons, Johann Christian Bible and Adam Bible, Junior', *Greene County Genealogical Society*, <greenecountytngenealogicalsociety.org>, accessed 27 Sept. 2024

Anon., 'Halifax and the Revolution', *North Carolina Historic Sites*, <historicsites.nc.gov/all-sites/historic-halifax/history/halifax-historic-district-importance/halifax-and-revolution>, accessed 8 April 2023

Anon., 'The Journal of Captain Robert Cholmly's Batman', in Charles Hamilton, (ed.), *Braddock's Defeat* (Norman: University of Oklahoma Press, 1959)

Anon (ed.), *Journal of Lieut. William Feltman, of the First Pennsylvania Regiment, 1781–1782* (Philadelphia: Henry Carey Baird, 1853)

Anon. (ed.), *Journal of the House of Delegates of Virginia* (Richmond: various publishers, 1828–)

Anon (ed.), *Journal of the House of Representatives of the United States* (Washington: various publishers, 1826–)

Anon. (ed.), *Journals of Henry Dearborn, 1776–1783* (Cambridge: John Wilson and Son, 1887)

Anon. (ed.), 'The Letters of Col. William Woodford, Col. Robert Howe, and Gen. Charles Lee to Edmund Pendleton', *Richmond College Historical Papers*, 1:1 (1915), pp.96–163

Anon (ed.), 'Letters of Daniel Morgan and Peter Muhlenberg', *PMHB*, 21:4 (1897), pp.488–492

Anon (ed.), 'Mennonite Historians of Eastern Pennsylvania Cemetery Database Report', <mhep.org/files/PDF/CemeteryDatabase/surname-H-report.pdf>, accessed 28 Nov. 2023

Anon. (ed.), *Military Journal of Major Ebenezer Denny* (Philadelphia: J.B. Lippincott & Co., 1859)

Anon. (ed.), 'The Old Virginia Line in the Middle States During the American Revolution', *Tyler's Quarterly Historical and Genealogical Magazine*, 12:1–4 (1931), pp.1–42, 90–141, 198–203, 283–289

Anon (ed.), 'The Papers of General Samuel Smith', *The Historical Magazine*, 7:2 (1870), pp.81–92

Anon., 'The Pioneers of Kentucky', *North American Review*, 62:130 (1846): 71–101

Anon. (ed.), *Proceedings of a General Court-Martial, Held at Brunswick, in the State of New Jersey, By Order of His Excellency Gen. Washington, Commander-in-Chief of the Army of the United States of America, for the Trial of Major-General Lee, July 4th, 1778* (New York: J.M. Bradstreet & Son, 1864)

Anon. (ed.), *The Proceedings of the Convention of Delegates for the Counties and Corporations of Virginia in the Colony of Virginia Held at Richmond Town, in the County of Henrico on the 20th of March, 1775* [2nd Convention] (Richmond: Ritchie, Trueheart & Duval, 1816)

Anon. (ed.), *Proceedings of the Convention of Delegates for the Counties and Corporations in the Colony of Virginia Held at Richmond Town, in the County of Henrico, on Monday the 17th of July, 1775* [3rd Convention] (Richmond: Ritchie, Trueheart & Duval, 1816),

Anon. (ed.), *The Proceedings of the Convention of Delegates Held at the Town of Richmond in the Colony of Virginia on Friday, the 1st of December, 1775 and Afterward by Adjournment in the City of Williamsburg* [4th Convention], (Richmond: Ritchie, Trueheart, & Duval, 1816)

Anon. (ed.), *The Proceedings of the Convention of Delegates Held at the Capitol in the City of Williamsburg in the Colony of Virginia on Monday, the 6th of May, 1776* [5th Convention] (Richmond: Ritchie, Trueheart, & Duval, 1816)

Anon. (ed.), 'Unpublished Papers Relating to the Battle of Germantown', *PMHB*, 1:4 (1877), pp.399–403.

Anon. (ed.), 'Virginia Legislative Papers', *VMHB*, 9:4 (1902) pp.353–368, 12:4 (1905) pp.417–424, 13:1 (1905) pp.36–50, 13:4 (1906) pp.411–424, 14:1 (1906) pp.50–79, 14:2 (1906) pp.126–136, 14:3 (1907) pp.246–259, 14:4 (1907) pp.383–396, 15:1 (1907) pp.14–25, 15:2 (1907) pp.131–147, 15:3 (1908) pp.288–296, 15:4 (1908) pp.406–416, 16:1 (1908) pp.39–55, 16:2 (1908) pp.157–173, 17:1 (1909) pp.52–64, 17:2 (1909) pp.161–177, 17:3 (1909) pp.248–262, 17:4 (1909) pp.364–383, 18:1 (1910) pp.24–44, 18:2 (1910) pp.140–150, 18:3 (1910) pp.255–271, 18:4 (1910) pp.373–393

Aspinwall, Thomas et al (eds), *Collections of the Massachusetts Historical Society*, ser.4, 10 vols (Boston: Massachusetts Historical Society, 1852–1871)

Barber, John W. and Henry Howe (eds), *Historical Collections of New Jersey* (New Haven: J.W. Barber, 1868)

Bartram, William, *Travels Through North and South Carolina, Georgia, East and West Florida, the Cherokee Country, the Extensive Territory of the Muscogulges or Creek Confederacy, and the Country of the Choctaws* (1791; reprinted London: J. Johnson, 1792)

Beatson, Robert (ed.), *Naval and Military Memoirs of Great Britain from 1727 to 1783*, 6 vols (London: Longman, Hurst, Rees, and Orme, 1804)

Beckner, Lucien (ed.), 'Reverend John D. Shane's Notes on an Interview with Elijah Foley of Fayette County', *Filson Club History Quarterly*, 11:4 (1937), pp.252–259

Bellas, Henry Hobart (ed.), *Personal Recollections of Captain Enoch Anderson, an Officer of the Delaware Regiments in the Revolutionary War* (Wilmington: Historical Society of Delaware, 1896)

Biddle, Louis Alexander (ed.), *A Memorial Containing Travels Through Life or Sundry Incidents in the Life of Dr. Benjamin Rush Written by Himself* (Philadelphia: privately published, 1905)

Blake, Thomas, 'Lieutenant Thomas Blake's Journal', in Frederick Kidder, *History of the First New Hampshire Regiment in the War of the Revolution* (Albany: Joel Munsell, 1868), pp.25–56

Boyd, Julian P. et al (eds), *Papers of Thomas Jefferson* (Princeton: Princeton University Press, 1950–)

Boyle, Joseph Lee (ed.) 'The James McMichael Journal, May 27, 1776-October 29, 1776', *JAR*, <allthingsliberty.com/2018/02/james-mcmichael-journal-may-27-1776-october-29-1776/>, accessed 7 Oct. 2024

Boyle, Joseph Lee (ed.) 'The James McMichael Journal, November 1, 1776-June 3, 1777', *JAR*, <allthingsliberty.com/2018/02/james-mcmichael-journal-november-1-1776-june-3-1777/>, accessed 7 Oct. 2024

Boyle, Joseph Lee (ed.) 'The James McMichael Journal, September 12-, 1777-December 23, 1777', *JAR*, <allthingsliberty.com/2018/03/the-james-mcmichael-journal-september-12-1777-december-23-1777/>, accessed 7 Oct. 2024, 4 Oct. 1777.

Boyle, Joseph Lee (ed.), *From Redcoat to Rebel: The Thomas Sullivan Journal* (Bowie, Md.: Heritage Books, 1997)

Brackenridge, Hugh Henry, *Incidents of the Insurrection in the Western Parts of Pennsylvania in the 1794* (Philadelphia: John McCulloch, 1795)

Bradford, S.S. (ed.), 'A British Officer's Revolutionary War Journal', *Maryland History Magazine*, 56:1 (1961), p. 165.

Brandon, Edgar Ewing (ed.), *A Pilgrimage of Liberty: A Contemporary Account of the Triumphal Tour of General Lafayette Through the Southern and Western States in 1825, as Reported by the Local Newspapers* (Athens, Oh.: Lawhead Press, 1944)

Brock, R. A. (ed.), *The Official Letters of Alexander Spotswood, Lieutenant-Governor of the Colony of Virginia, 1710–1722*, 2 vols (Richmond: Virginia Historical Society, 1882–1885)

Brock, Robert Alonzo (ed.), 'Orderly Book of Captain Robert Gamble of the Second Virginia Regiment Commanded by Colonel Christian Febiger, August 21-November16, 1779' in *Collections of the Virginia Historical Society,* New Series, 11 vols. (Richmond: Virginia Historical Society, 1892), vol. 11, pp.219–272

Brock, Robert Alonzo (ed.), 'Orderly Book of the Company of Captain George Stubblefield, Fifth Virginia Regiment, from March 3, 1776 to July 10. 1776, Inclusive', *Collections of the Virginia Historical Society,* New Series, 11 vols. (Richmond: Virginia Historical Society, 1882–1892), vol. 6, pp.141–192

Brymner, Douglas (ed.), *Report on Canadian Archives, 1887* (Ottawa: MacLean, Roger & Co., 1888)

Buell, Rowena (ed.), *The Memoirs of Rufus Putnam and Certain Official Papers and Correspondence* (Boston: Houghton, Mifflin and Co., 1903)

Bunbury, Henry Edward (ed.), *The Lee Papers*, 4 vols (New York: New York Historical Society, 1871–1875)

Butterfield, Lyman H. et al (eds), *The Adams Papers* (Cambridge: Harvard University Press, 1963–)

Butterfield, Lyman H. (ed.), *Letters of Benjamin Rush*, 2 vols (Princeton: Princeton University Press, 1951)

Byars, William Vincent (ed.), *B. and M. Gratz: Merchants in Philadelphia, 1754–1798* (Jefferson City: Hugh Stephens Printing, 1916)

Campbell, Charles (ed.), *The Bland Papers*, 2 vols (Petersburg: Edmund & Julian C. Ruffin, 1840)

Campbell, Charles (ed.), *The Orderly Book of That Portion of the American Army Stationed at or Near Williamsburg, Va., Under the Command of General Andrew Lewis from March 18th, 1776, to August 28th, 1776* (Richmond: privately printed, 1860)

Campbell, Maria Hull, *Revolutionary Services and Civil Life of General William Hull* (New York: D. Appleton & Co., 1848)

Candler, Allen D. (ed.), *The Revolutionary Records of the State of Georgia*, 3 vols. (Atlanta: Franklin-Turner Company, 1908)

Cannon, Jouett Taylor (ed.), 'State Archives – General Expenditures 1792–1798', *Register of Kentucky State Historical Society,* 30:91 (1932), pp.162–172; 30:92 (1932), pp.221–236;

30:93 (1932), pp.297–321; 31:94 (1933), pp.52–70; 31:95 (1933), pp.101–109; 31:96 (1933), pp.201–215; 31:97 (1933), pp.328–340; 32:98 (1934), pp.50–64; 32:99 (1934), pp.125–138.

Chalkley, Lyman, *Chronicles of the Scotch-Irish Settlement of Virginia: Extracted from the Original Court Records of Augusta County, 1745–1800*, 3 vols. (Rosslyn, Va.: DAR, 1912)

Chase, Philander D. et al (eds), *The Papers of George Washington*, Revolutionary War Series (Charlottesville: University Press of Virginia, 1985-)

Chastellux, François-Jean de, *Travels in North-America in the Years 1780-81-82* (New York: White, Gallagher, & White, 1827)

Clark, D.W., *Memoir of Mrs. Jane Trimble: A Tribute of Affection from Her Grandson* (Cincinnati: Methodist Book Concern, 1861)

Clark, William Bell et al (eds), *Naval Documents of the Revolution* (Washington, United States Navy, 1964–)

Collins, Varnum Lansing (ed.), *A Brief Narrative of the Ravages of the British and Hessians at Princeton in 1776–1777* (Princeton: Princeton University Library, 1906)

Commager, Henry Steele and Richard B. Morris (eds), *The Spirit of Seventy-Six: The Story of the American Revolution as Told by its Participants* (1958; reprinted Edison, N.J.: Castle Books, 2002)

Connolly, John, *A Narrative of the Transactions, Imprisonment, and Sufferings of John Connolly, an American Loyalist and Lieutenant-Colonel in his Majesty's Service* (London: 1788; reprinted New York: Charles L. Woodward, 1889)

'Coronation Oath Act 1688', <legislation.gov.uk/aep/WillandMar/1/6/section/III>, accessed 14 Aug. 2022

Crouse, Randy F. McNew (ed.), *The Revolutionary War Diary of Major William Croghan of the Virginia Continental Line, 1779–1780*, 3rd ed., (Huntsville, Ala.: R.F.M. Crouse, 2013)

Crozier, William Armstrong (ed.), *Virginia Colonial Militia: 1651–1776* (1904; reprinted Baltimore: Genealogical Publishing, 2000)

Crumrine, Boyd (ed.), 'Minute Book of the Virginia Court held at Fort Dunmore (Pittsburgh) for the District of West Augusta, 1775–1776', *Annals of the Carnegie Museum* 1(1901–1902), pp.525–568

Crumrine, Boyd (ed.), 'Minute Book of Virginia Court Held for Yohogania County, First at Augusta Town (Now Washington, Pa.), and Afterwards on the Andrew Heath Farm near West Elizabeth; 1776–1780', *Annals of the Carnegie Museum* 2:2 (1903), pp.205–429

Dalcho, Frederich, *Historical Account of the Protestant Episcopal Church in South Carolina* (Charleston: E. Thayer, 1820)

Dann, John C. (ed.), *The Nagle Journal: A Diary of the Life of Jacob Nagle, Sailor, From the Year 1775 to 1841* (New York: Weidenfeld & Nicolson, 1988)

Dann, John C. (ed.), *The Revolution Remembered: Eyewitness Accounts of the War for Independence* (Chicago: University of Chicago Press, 1980)

Davies, K. G. (ed.), *Documents of the American Revolution 1770–1783 (Colonial Office Series)*, 21 vols. (Shannon: Irish University Press, 1972–1981)

Dexter, Franklin Bowditch (ed.), *Diary of David McClure, Doctor of Divinity, 1748–1820* (New York: Knickerbocker Press, 1899)

Dexter, Franklin Bowditch (ed.), *The Literary Diary of Ezra Stiles,* 2 vols. (New York, 1901)

Drayton, John, *Memoirs of the American Revolution From Its Commencement to the Year 1776, Inclusive; As Relating to the State of South-Carolina: And Occasionally Referring to the States of North-Carolina and Georgia*, 2 vols. (Charleston: A.E. Miller, 1821)

Elliott, Bernard, 'Diary of Captain Bernard Elliott', in *Charleston Year Book, 1889* (Charleston: Walker, Evens & Cogswell: 1890), pp.151–262

Ewing, Thomas (ed.), *George Ewing, Gentleman: a Soldier of Valley Forge* (Yonkers, N.Y.: T. Ewing, 1928)

Field v. Slaughter and Others, 22 Oct. 1808, Court of Appeals of Kentucky

Fitzpatrick, John C. (ed.), *The Writings of George Washington*, 39 vols. (Washington: Government Printing Office, 1931–1944)

Flickinger, B. Floyd (ed.), 'The Diary of Lieutenant William Heth while a Prisoner in Quebec, 1776', *Annual Papers of Winchester Virginia Historical Society*, 1 (1933), pp.27–118

Ford, Worthington Chauncey, (ed.), *Journals of the Continental Congress, 1774–1789*, 34 vols. (Washington: Library of Congress, 1904–1937)

Force, Peter (ed.), *American Archives*, 9 vols. (Washington, D.C: U.S. Congress, 1837–1846)

Frazer, Persifor (ed.), *General Persifor Frazer: A Memoir Compiled Principally from His Own Papers by His Great-Grandson* (Philadelphia: privately published, 1907)

Fry, Jacob (ed.), 'Journal of the Rev. Peter Muhlenberg in London, 1772', 4:16 (1885), pp.294–300

Galloway, Joseph, *Historical and Political Reflections on the Rise and Progress of the American Rebellion* (London: G. Wilkie, 1780)

Garden, Alexander, *Anecdotes of the American Revolution*, Second Series (Charleston: A.E. Miller, 1828)

Germann, William, 'The Crisis in the Early Life of General Peter Mühlenberg', *PMHB*, 37:3 (1913), pp.298–329

Gill, Harold B., Jr. and George M. Curtis III (eds), *A Man Apart: The Journal of Nicholas Cresswell, 1774–1781* (Lanham, Md.: Lexington Books, 2009)

Gilreath, Amelia C. (ed.), *Frederick County, Virginia Deed Book Series, Volume 5: Deed Books 15 and 16, 1771–1775, Abstracted* (Nokesville, Va.: A.C. Gilreath, 1992)

Gilreath, Amelia C. (ed.), *Order Book, 1772–1774, Shenandoah County, VA* [abstracts] (Nokesville, Va..: A.C. Gilreath, 1986)

Godwin, Mary R.M., *Clothing and Accoutrements of the Officers and Soldiers of the Virginia Forces: 1775–1778*, Colonial Williamsburg Foundation Library Research Report Series RR0049, Colonial Williamsburg Foundation, June 1962

Graham, Joseph, 'The Battle of King's Mountain', *Southern Literary Messenger*, 11:9 (1845), pp.552–555

Grant, Wiliam, 'Narrative of Sergeant William Grant', in John Romeyn Brodhead and E.B. O'Callaghan (eds), *Documents Relative to the Colonial History of the State of New York Procured in Holland, England and France*, 14 vols. (Albany: Weed, Parsons and Co., 1856–1883)

Gruber, Ira D. (ed.), *John Peebles' American War* (Mechanicsburg, Pa.: Stackpole Books, 1998)

Hadaway, William S. (ed.), *The McDonald Papers*, 2 vols. (White Plains: Westchester County Historical Society, 1926)

Hamer, Philip M. et al (eds), *The Papers of Henry Laurens,* 16 vols (Columbia: University of South Carolina Press, 1968–2003)

Hammon, Neal O. (ed.), *John Floyd: The Life and Letters of a Frontier Surveyor* (Louisville: Butler Books, 2013)

Hammond, Otis G. (ed.), *Letters and Papers of Major-General John Sullivan,* 3 vols (Concord: New Hampshire Historical Society, 1930)

Harris, C. Leon (ed.), 'The Chesterfield Size Roll: Soldiers Who Entered the Continental Line of Virginia at Chesterfield Courthouse After 1 September 1780', *Southern Campaigns American Revolution Pensions and Rosters,* <revwarapps.org/b69.pdf>, accessed 26 Nov. 2024

Harwell, Richard Barksdale (ed.), *The Committees of Safety of Westmoreland and Fincastle: Proceedings of the County Committees, 1774–1776* (Richmond: Virginia State Library, 1956)

Haven, Charles Chauncey, *Thirty Days in New Jersey Ninety Years Ago, An Essay revealing new Facts in Connection with Washington and his Army in 1776 and 1777* (Trenton: State Gazette, 1867)

Hawes, Lilla Mills (ed.), *Lachlan McIntosh Papers in the University of Georgia Libraries* (Athens: University of Georgia Press, 1968)

Hawes, Lilla M. (ed.), *The Papers of Lachlan McIntosh, 1774–1779* (Savannah: Georgia Historical Society, 1957)

Hazard, Samuel (ed.), *Minutes of the Provincial Council of Pennsylvania,* 16 vols (Harrisburg: T. Fenn, 1851–1852)

Hazard, Samuel et al (eds), *Pennsylvania Archives,* 138 vols in 10 ser. [including *Colonial Records*] (Philadelphia: Joseph Severns & Co., 1852–1856)

Heartman, Charles F. (ed.), *Narrative of Johan Carl Buettner in the American Revolution* (New York: C.F. Heartman, 1915)

Heath, Craig L. (ed.), *The George M. Bedinger Papers* (Bowie, Md.: Heritage Books, 2002)

Hemphill, William Edwin et al (eds), *State Records of South Carolina: Journals of the General Assembly and House of Representatives 1776–1780* (Columbia: University of South Carolina Press, 1970)

Hening, William Waller (ed.), *The Statutes at Large, Being a Collection of All the Laws of Virginia from the First Session of the Legislature in the Year 1619,* 13 vols (Richmond, J. & G. Cochran, 1819–1823)

Henry, William Wirt (ed.), *Patrick Henry: Life, Correspondence, and Speeches,* 3 vols (New York: Charles Scribner's Sons, 1891)

Hill, George (ed.), *The Montgomery Manuscripts: 1603–1706 Compiled from Family Papers by William Montgomery of Rosemont, Esquire* (Belfast: Archer and Sons, 1869)

Hough, Franklin B. (ed.), *Journals of Major Robert Rogers* (Albany: Joel Munell's Sons, 1883)

Howard, John Eager, 'Col. John Eager Howard's Account of the Battle of Germantown', *Maryland Historical Magazine,* 4 (1909), pp.314–320.

Hunter, Anne and Elizabeth Bell (eds), *The Journal of Gen. Sir Martin Hunter* (Edinburgh: Edinburgh Press, 1894)

Hutchinson, William T. et al (eds), *Papers of James Madison,* 17 vols (Chicago: University of Chicago Press)

Idzerda, Stanley J. et al (eds), *Lafayette in the Age of the American Revolution: Selected Letters and Papers, 1776–1790*, 5 vols (Ithaca: Cornell University Press, 1977–1983)
Jackson, Donald (ed.), *The Diaries of George Washington*, 6 vols (Charlottesville: University Press of Virginia, 1976–1979)
Jacob, John J., *A Biographical Sketch of the Life of the Late Captain Michael Cresap* (1826, reprinted Cincinnati: William Dodge, 1866)
James, James Alton (ed.), *George Rogers Clark Papers*, 1771–1781 (Springfield: Illinois State Historical Society, 1912)
Jillson, Willard Rouse (ed.), *The Kentucky Land Grants* (Louisville: Filson Club,1925)
Johnson, Joseph, *Traditions and Reminiscences Chiefly of the American Revolution in the South* (Charleston: Walker & James, 1851)
Johnston, Henry P. (ed.) *The Correspondence and Public Papers of John Jay*, 4 vols (New York: G.P. Putnam's Sons, 1890–1893)
Johnston, Hugh Buckner (ed.), 'The Journal of Ebenezer Hazard in North Carolina, 1777 and 1778', *North Carolina Historical Review*, 36:3 (1959), pp.358–381
Jones, David, *A Journal of Two Visits Made to Some Nations of Indians on the West Side of the River Ohio in the Years 1772 and 1773* (Burlington: Isaac Collins, 1774)
Kellogg, Louise Phelps (ed.), *Frontier Advance on the Upper Ohio, 1778–1779* (Madison: Wisconsin Historical Society, 1916)
Kellogg, Louise Phelps (ed.), *Frontier Retreat on the Upper Ohio, 1779–1781* (Madison: Wisconsin Historical Society, 1917)
Kercheval, Samuel, *A History of the Valley of Virginia*, 3rd edition (1902; reprinted Bowie, Md.: Heritage Books, 2001)
Kinkead, Ludie J., (ed.) 'How the Parents of George Rogers Clark Came to Kentucky in 1784–1785', *Filson Club History Quarterly* 3:1 (1928), pp.1–4.
Kipping, Ernst and Samuel Smith (trans. and ed.), *At General Howe's Side, 1776*–1778 [diary of Capt. Friedrich von Muenchhausen] (Monmouth Beach, N.J.: Philip Freneau Press, 1974)
Larabee, Leonard W. et al (eds), *The Papers of Benjamin Franklin* (New Haven: Yale University Press, 1959-)
Lee, Henry, *Memoirs of the War in the Southern Department of the United States*, 2 vols. (Philadelphia: Bradford and Inskeep, 1812)
Lee, Richard H., *Memoir of Richard Henry Lee*, 2 vols (Philadelphia: H.C. Carey and I. Lea, 1825)
Lobdell, Jared C. (ed.), 'The Revolutionary War Journal of Sergeant Thomas McCarty', *Proceedings of the New Jersey Historical Society*, 82:1 (1964), pp.29–46
MacMaster, Richard K. (ed.), 'News of the Yorktown Campaign: The Journal of Dr. Robert Honyman, April 17, 1781-November 25, 1781', *VMHB* 79:4 (1971), pp.387–426
McIlwaine, H.R. (ed.), *Legislative Journals of the Council of Colonial Virginia*, 3 vols (Richmond: Virginia State Library, 1918)
McIlwaine, H.R. (ed.), *Official Letters of the Governors of the State of Virginia* (Richmond: Virginia State Library, 1926)
McIlwaine, H.R. et al (eds), *Executive Journals of the Council of Colonial Virginia*, 6 vols (Richmond: Virginia State Library, 1925–1966)

McIlwaine, H.R. and John Pendleton Kennedy (eds), *Journals of the House of Burgesses of Virginia*, 13 vols (Richmond: Colonial Press, 1905–1915)

McIlwaine, H.R. et al (eds), *Journals of the Council of the State of Virginia*, 5 vols (Richmond: Virginia State Library, 1931–1982)

McRee, Griffith J. (ed.) *Life and Correspondence of James Iredell*, 2 vols. (New York: D. Appleton and Co., 1857)

Martin, Joseph Plumb, *A Narrative of Some of the Adventures, Dangers and Sufferings of a Revolutionary Soldier* (1830, reprinted Eastern Acorn Press, 1991)

Mereness, Newton D. (ed.), *Travels in the American Colonies* (New York: MacMillan, 1916)

Miller, Samuel H. (ed.), *Life of Samuel Thomas* Miller (Lynchburg: J.P. Bell Company, 1911)

Minardi, Lisa et al (eds), Freeman's Auction Catalogue, 2012, *Historic Muhlenberg Property: From a Private Collection Including the Grand Division Color of the 8th Virginia*

Mitchell, James T. and Henry Flanders (eds), *The Statutes at Large of Pennsylvania from 1682 to 1801*, 18 vols (Harrisburg: Clarence M. Busch, 1896–1915)

Mitchell, S. Weir (ed.), 'Historical Notes of Dr. Benjamin Rush, 1777', *PMHB* 27:2 (1903), pp.129–150

Morton, Robert, 'Diary of Robert Morton', *PMHB*, 1:1 (1877), pp.1–39

Moultrie, William, *Memoirs of the American Revolution So Far as It Related to North and South-Carolina, and Georgia*, 2 vols (New York: David Longworth, 1802)

Nickalls, John L. (ed.), *The Journal of George Fox* (Cambridge: Cambridge University Press, 1952)

Nutall, Thomas, *A Journal of Travels into the Arkansa Territory, During the Year 1819* (Philadelphia: Thomas H. Palmer, 1821)

O'Callaghan, F.B. (ed.), *Documents Relative to the Colonial History of the State of New-York*, 15 vols (Albany: Weed, Parsons, & Co., 1853–1887)

Palmer, William P. et al (eds), *Calendar of Virginia State Papers and Other Manuscripts*, 11 vols (Richmond: James E. Good, 1875–1893)

Perry, William Stevens (ed.), *Historical Collections Relating to the American Colonial Church*, 4 vols. (Hartford: by subscription, 1870–1878)

Pickering, Octavius and Charles W. Upham, *Life of Timothy Pickering*, 4 vols (Boston: Little, Brown, and Company, 1867–1873)

Powell, Robert C. (ed.), *A Biographical Sketch of Col. Leven Powell, Including His Correspondence During the Revolutionary War* (Alexandria: G.H. Ramey & Son, 1877)

Powell, William S. (ed.), 'A Connecticut Soldier Under Washington: Elisha Bostwick's Memoirs of the First Years of the Revolution', *William and Mary* Quarterly 6:1 (1949), pp.94–107

Quincy, Josiah (ed.), *The Journals of Major Samuel Shaw, the First American Consul at Canton* (Boston: Wm. Crosby and H.P. Nichols, 1847)

R., [Sergeant], 'The Battle of Princeton', *PMHB*, 20:4 (1896): 515–519

Read, William Thompson (ed.), *Life and Correspondence of George Read, A Signer of the Declaration of Independence With Notices of Some of His Contemporaries* (Philadelphia: J.B. Lippincott, 1870)

Redd, John, 'Reminiscences of Western Virginia, 1770–1790', *VMHB*, 6:4 (1899), pp.337–346, 7:1–4 (1899), pp. 1–16, 7:2 (1899), 113–128, 7:3 (1900), 242–53, 7:4 (1900), 401–405

Rees, John U., *Examples of the Complexity of Continental Army Unit Lineage (The Virginia, Pennsylvania and Massachusetts Continental Lines)*, <scribd.com/doc/307784931/Examples-of-the-Complexity-of-Continental-Army-Unit-Lineage-The-Virginia-Pennsylvania-and-Massachusetts-Continental-Lines>, accessed 30 April 2024.

Rees, John U. (ed.), *'We... wheeled to the Right to form the Line of Battle': Colonel Israel Shreve's Journal, 23 November 1776 to 14 August 1777 (Including Accounts of the Action at the Short Hills)* <scribd.com/document/153790118/We-wheeled-to-the-Right-to-form-the-Line-of-Battle-Colonel-Israel-Shreve-s-Journal-23-November-1776-to-14-August-1777-Including-Accounts-of#>, accessed 2 Sept. 2023

Rees, John U. and Bob McDonald (eds), *'The Action was renew.d with a very warm Canonade': New Jersey Officer's Diary, 21 June 1777 to 31 August 1778*, <academia.edu/36536289/_The_Action_was_renew_d_with_a_very_warm_Canonade_New_Jersey_Officers_Diary_21_June_1777_to_31_August_1778 >, accessed 29 Oct. 2023, 2 Sept. 1777.

Riley, Edward Miles (ed.), *The Journal of John Harrower: An Indentured Servant in the Colony of Virginia, 1773–1776* (Williamsburg: Colonial Williamsburg, 1963)

Robertson, David, *Debates and Other Proceedings of the Convention of Virginia, Convened at Richmond, on Monday the Second Day of June, 1788*, 2nd ed. (Richmond: Ritchie & Worsley and Augustine Davis, 1805)

Rodney, Caesar A. (ed.), *Diary of Captain Thomas Rodney, 1776–1777* (Wilmington: Historical Society of Delaware, 1888)

Rothert, Otto A. (ed.), 'John D. Shane's Interview, in 1841, with Mrs. Wilson of Woodford County', *Filson Club History Quarterly*, 16:4 (1942), pp.227–232

Rutland, Robert A. (ed.), *The Papers of George Mason*, 3 vols (Chapel Hill: University of North Carolina Press, 1970)

Rutland, Robert A. et al (eds), *The Papers of James Madison: Presidential Series*, 11 vols (Charlottesville: University Press of Virginia, 1984–2020)

Ryden, George Herbert (ed.), *Letters To and From Caesar Rodney* (Philadelphia: University of Pennsylvania Press, 1933)

Salley, A. S., Jr. (ed.), *Journal of the Grand Council of South Carolina, April 11, 1692–September 26, 1692* (Columbia: The State Company for the Historical Commission of South Carolina, 1907)

Sandor, Gregory B., *Journal of the Public Store at Williamsburg, 1775–1776* (place unknown: G.B. Sandor, 2015)

Saunders, William L. et al (eds), *The Colonial and State Records of North Carolina*, 30 vols (various publishers, 1886–1914)

Scharf, J. Thomas (ed), *The Chronicles of Baltimore; Being a Complete History of 'Baltimore Town' and Baltimore City From the Earliest Period to the Present Time* (Baltimore: Turnbull Brothers, 1874),

Scull, G. D. (ed.), *The Montresor Journals* (New York: New York Historical Society, 1882)

Sellers, Horace Wells, (ed.) 'Journal by Charles Willson Peale', *PMHB*, 38:3 (1914), pp.271–286

Semple, Robert B., *A History of the Rise and Progress of the Baptists in Virginia* (Richmond: John O'Lynch, 1810)

Sheeder, Frederick, 'East Vincent Township, Chester County, Pennsylvania', *PMHB*, 34:1–3 (1910): pp.74–98, 194–212, 361–380

Showman, Richard K. et al (eds), *The Papers of General Nathanael Greene*, 13 vols (Chapel Hill: University of North Carolina Press, 1976–2005)

Simcoe, John Graves, *Simcoe's Military Journal: A History of the Operations of a Partisan Corps Called The Queen's Rangers* (New York: Bartlett & Welford, 1844)

Slaughter, Thomas, 'Petition of Col. Thomas Slaughter to Lord Dunmore', *VMHB*, 18:1 (1910), pp.60–62

Smith, Paul H. (ed.), *Letters of Delegates to Congress, 1774–1789*, 26 vols (Washington: Library of Congress)

Smith, Sam B. et al (eds), *The Papers of Andrew Jackson*, (Knoxville: University of Tennessee Press, 1980-)

Smith, William Henry (ed.), *The St. Clair Papers: The Life and Public Services of Arthur St. Clair.* 2 vols (Cincinnati, 1882)

Spangler, E.W., (ed.), 'Memoir of Major John Clark, of York County, Pennsylvania', *PMHB*, 20:1 (1896), pp.77–86

Sparks, Jared, ed., *Writings of George Washington*, 12 vols (Boston: American Stationers, 1834–1837)

Stedman, Charles, *The History of the Origin, Progress, and Termination of the American War*, 2 vols (London: P. Wogan, P. Byrne, J Moore, and W. Jones, 1794)

Steedman, W. and Ian Saberton (trans), *Journal of the Hessian Jäger Corps* (Surrey: Grosvenor House Publishing, 2018)

Stone, Edwin Martin (ed.), *The Invasion of Canada in 1775: Including the Journal of Captain Simeon Thayer* (Providence: Knowles, Anthony & Co., 1867)

Strassburger, Ralph Beaver (ed.), *Pennsylvanian German Pioneers: A Publication of the Original Lists of Arrivals In the Port of Philadelphia From 1727 to 1808*, 3 vols (Norristown: Pennsylvania German Society, 1934)

Stryker, William S. (ed.), *Documents Relating to the Revolutionary History of the State of New Jersey*, 5 vols (Trenton: J.L. Murphy, 1901)

Stuart, John, 'Narrative by Captain John Stuart of General Andrew Lewis' Expedition against the Indians in the year 1774, and of the Battle of Point Pleasant, Virginia', *Magazine of American History*, 1:1 (1877), pp.668–679, 740–750

Sullivan, John T.S., *The Public Men of the Revolution* (Philadelphia: Carey and Hart, 1847)

Syrett, Harold C. (ed.), *The Papers of Alexander Hamilton*, 27 vols (New York: Columbia University Press, 1962–1987)

Thacher, James, *A Military Journal During the American Revolutionary War from 1775 to 1783* (Boston: Cottons & Barnard, 1827)

Tait, Liz (ed.), 'The Revolutionary War Diary of Chaplain Andrew Hunter, New Jersey Brigade, Continental Army', RevWar '75, <revwar75.com/library/bob/Hunter17762.htm>, accessed 3 June 2023

Tappert, Theodore G. and John W. Doberstein, (trans), *The Journals of Henry Melchior Muhlenberg*, 3 vols (Philadelphia: Muhlenberg Press, 1942–1945)

Tarter, Brent (ed.), 'The Orderly Book of the Second Virginia Regiment: September 27, 1775-April 15, 1776', *VMHB*, 85:2–3 (1977), pp.156–183, 302–336

Tarleton, Banastre, *A History of the Campaigns of 1780 and 1781 in the Southern Provinces of North America* (London: T. Cadell, 1787)

Tatum, Edward H., Jr. (ed.), *The American Journal of Ambrose Serle, Secretary to Lord Howe, 1776–1778* (San Marino: Huntington Library, 1940)
Thompson, John R. (ed.), 'Selections and Excerpts from the Lee Papers', *Southern Literary Messenger*, 27:5–6 (1858), pp.250–266, 324–332.
Thruston, Buckner, 'Biography of Col. Charles Mynn Thruston', *Southern Literary Messenger*, 6:3 (1840), pp.163–168
Thwaites, Reuben Gold and Louise Phelps Kellogg (eds), *Documentary History of Dunmore's War, 1774* (Madison: State Historical Society of Wisconsin, 1905)
Toner, J.M. (ed.), *Journal of My Journey Over the Mountains; by George Washington, While Surveying for Lord Thomas Fairfax, Baron of Cameron, in the Northern Neck of Virginia, Beyond the Blue Ridge, in 1747–1748* (Albany: Joel Munsell's Sons, 1892)
Tustin, Joseph P. (ed.), *Diary of the American War: A Hessian Journal, Johann Ewald, Field Jäger Corps* (New Haven: Yale University Press, 1979)
Van Schreeven, William J. and Robert L. Scribner (eds), *Revolutionary Virginia: The Road to Independence*, 7 vols (Charlottesville: University Press of Virginia, 1973–1983)
Wainwright, Nicholas B. (ed.), 'A Diary of Trifling Occurrences: Philadelphia, 1776–1778', [Sarah Logan Fischer Diary], *PMHB*, 82:4 (1958), pp.411–465
Wainwright, Nicholas B. (ed.), 'Turmoil at Pittsburgh: Diary of Augustine Prevost, 1774', *PMHB*, 85:2 (1961), pp.111–162
Walker, Felix, 'Felix Walker's Narrative of His Trip With Boone From Long Island to Boonesborough in March, 1775', in George W. Ranck, *Boonesborough* (Louisville: Filson Club, 1901), pp.161–168
Webb, J. Watson (ed.), *Reminiscences of Gen'l Samuel B. Webb of the Revolutionary Army* (New York: Globe Stationery and Printing, 1882)
Wellenreuther, Herman and Carola Wessel (eds), *The Moravian Missionary Diaries of David Zeisberger, 1772–1781* (University Park: Pennsylvania State University Press, 2005)
Wilkin, W.H., *Some British Soldiers in America* (London: Hugh Rees, 1914)
Wilkinson, James, *Memoirs of My Own Times,* 3 vols (Philadelphia: Abraham Small, 1816)
Wilson, John Lyde, *The Code of Honor or Rules for the Government of Principals and Seconds in Duelling* (Charleston: James Phinney, 1858)
Willcock, William B. (ed.), *The American Rebellion: Sir Henry Clinton's Narrative of His Campaigns, 1775–1782, With an Appendix of Original Documents* (New Haven: Yale University Press, 1954)
Williams, Edward G. (ed.), 'A Revolutionary Journal and Orderly Book of General Lachlan McIntosh's Expedition, 1778', *Western Pennsylvania Historical Magazine*, 43:1–3 (1960), pp.1–17, 157–177, 267–288
Withers, Alexander S., *Chronicles of Border Warfare* (1831; reprinted Cincinnati: Robert Clarke, 1895)
Young, Arthur, *A Tour In Ireland, 1776–1779* (New York, Cassell & Company, 1887)
Young, Chester Raymond (ed.), *Westward into Kentucky: The Narrative of Daniel Trabue* (Lexington: University Press of Kentucky, 1981)

Secondary Sources

Albert, George Dallas, *The Frontier Forts of Western Pennsylvania* (Harrisburg: Clarence M. Busch, 1896)

Alden, John Richard, *General Charles Lee: Traitor or Patriot?* (Baton Rouge: Louisiana State University Press, 1951)

Akers, Vince, 'A Detailed History of Painted Stone Station', *Painted Stone Settlers*, <paintedstonesettlers.org/detailedhistory.html>, accessed 23 Nov. 2024

Allison, Wes, 'A Farm of Dreams for Sale', *Washington Post*, 31 Aug. 1996

Ambler, Charles H., *The Life and Diary of John Floyd* (Richmond: Richmond Press, 1918).

Anon. (ed.), '3rd Congress: Virginia 1793', *Mapping Early America Elections*, <earlyamericanelections.org/maps/meae.congressional.congress03.va.county.html>, accessed 23 June 2024

Anon. (ed.), *Ancestral Records and Portraits: a Compilation from the Archives of Chapter I., The Colonial Dames of America*, 2 vols (New York: Grafton Press, 1910)

Anon., 'Bowman's Hill Tower', *Washington Crossing Historic Park*, <washingtoncrossingpark.org/park/bowmans-hill-tower/>, accessed 21 Dec. 2014.

Anon., 'Descendants of John Vance and Elizabeth Glass', Fort Vance Historical Society, <http://fortvance.org/wp-content/uploads/2020/08/Vance_Descendants_of-John-Vance-and-Elizabeth-Glass.pdf>, accessed 15 Oct. 2022

Anon., 'Eastern West Virginia', *North American Forts*, <northamericanforts.com/East/wveast.html>, accessed 12 Sept. 2022

Anon. (ed.), *Field Crops: Usual Planting and Harvesting Dates*, Agricultural Handbook Number 628 (Washington: U.S. Department of Agriculture, 2010)

Anon., 'Historic Moravian Bethlehem: A National Historic Landmark District', <historicbethlehem.org/about-draft/historic-moravian-bethlehem-a-national-historic-landmark-district/>, accessed 20 Aug. 2023

Anon., *History of Bedford, Somerset, and Fulton Counties, Pennsylvania* (Chicago: Waterman and Watkins, 1884)

Anon. (ed.), *The History of Brown County, Ohio* (Chicago: W.H. Beers & Co., 1883)

Anon., 'History of Philadelphia', <britannica.com/place/Philadelphia/History>, accessed 20 Aug. 2023

Anon. (ed.), *History of Franklin and Pickaway Counties, Ohio* (place unknown: Williams Bros., 1880)

Anon., 'History of the Burlington Path', <twp.freehold.nj.us/398/History-of-the-Burlington-Path>, accessed 18 Feb. 2024

Anon., 'A History of Purrysburg, South Carolina', *Carolana*, <carolana.com/SC/Towns/Purrysburg_SC.html>, accessed 7 March 2024

Anon. (ed.), *History of Wayne County, Indiana*, 2 vols (Chicago: Inter-State Publishing Co., 1884)

Anon., 'Life of James Madison', *James Madison's Montpelier*, <www.montpelier.org/learn/the-life-of-james-madison>, accessed 25 Oct. 2022

Anon., *Memoirs of Allegheny County Pennsylvania*, 2 vols (Madison: Northwest Historical Association, 1904)

Anon., 'North River Mills Historic Trace', <historichampshire.org/nrm/memorials/Trace.htm>, accessed 8 Oct. 2022

Anon., *Religion and the Founding of the American Republican* (exhibition), Library of Congress, <loc.gov/exhibits/religion/rel04.html>, accessed 13 Feb. 2024

Anon., 'Revolutionary War in Mount Pleasant', *Mount Pleasant, South Carolina*, <tompsc.com/740/Revolutionary-War-in-Mount-Pleasant>, accessed 29 Nov. 2024

Anon., 'Sheriff History', <vasheriff.org/sheriffs-resources/sheriff-history>, accessed 30 Oct. 2022

Appleton, Thomas H., Jr., 'Lewis Craig', *Dictionary of Virginia Biography, <lva.virginia.gov/public/dvb/bio.php?b=Craig_Lewis>*, accessed 27 Oct. 2022

Armstrong, Zella, *History of Hamilton County and Chattanooga Tennessee*, 2 vols (Chattanooga: Lookout Publishing, 1931)

Ashmead, Henry Graham, *History of Delaware County, Pennsylvania* (Philadelphia: Louis H. Everts, 1884)

Auricchio, Laura, *The Marquis: Lafayette Reconsidered* (New York: Alfred A. Knopf, 2014)

Baker, William S., *Itinerary of General Washington from June 15, 1775 to December 23, 1783* (Philadelphia: J.B. Lippincott, 1892)

Bancroft, George, *History of the United States from the Discovery of the American Continent*, 10 vols (various publishers, 1834–1874)

Barksdale, Kevin T., 'Our Rebellious Neighbors: Virginia's Border Counties During Pennsylvania's Whiskey Rebellion', *VMHB*, 111:1 (2003), pp.5–32

Bell, James B., 'Anglican Clergy in Colonial America Ordained by the Bishops of London', *Proceedings of the American Antiquarian Society*, 83:1 (1973), pp.103–160

Beltzhoover, George M., *James Rumsey, the Inventor of the Steamboat* (West Virginia Historical and Antiquarian Society, 1900)

Bennett, Charles E. and Donald R. Lennon, *A Quest for Glory: Major General Robert Howe and the American Revolution* (Chapel Hill: University of North Carolina Press, 1991)

Berg, Fred Anderson, *Encyclopedia of Continental Army Units* (Harrisburg: Stackpole Books, 1972)

Bigham, Kirk Q., *Major Abraham Kirkpatrick and His Descendants* (Pittsburgh: J.P. Durbin, 1911)

Billias, George Athan, *American Constitutionalism Heard Round the World, 1776–1789: A Global Perspective* (New York: New York University Press, 2009)

Blades, Brook and Wade Catts, '*...The Musket Balls Flew Like Hail Stones...: The Short Hills Battlefield Study*', John Milner Associates, December 2011, <metuchen-edisonhistsoc.org/resources/The+Short+Hills+Battlefield+Study+12-2011+FINAL.pdf>, accessed 23 April 2025

Bonk, David C., *'Men Who Are Determined to be Free:' The Assault on Stony Point, 15 July 1779* (Warwick: Helion & Company, 2018)

Borick, Carl P., *A Gallant Defense: The Siege of Charleston, 1780* (Columbia: University of South Carolina Press, 2012)

Boyle, G.E., 'The 18th (or Royal Irish) Regiment of Foot in North America – 1767–75', *Journal of the Society for Army Historical Research*, 2:8 (1923), pp.63–68

Braund, Kathryn E. Holland, *Deerskins and Duffels: The Creek Indian Trade with Anglo-America, 1685–1815* (Lincoln: University of Nebraska Press, 1993)

Breckenridge, James Malcolm, *William Clark Breckenridge: Historical Research Writer and Bibliographer of Missouriana, His Life, Lineage and Writings* (St. Louis: privately published, 1932)

Breidenbach, Michael D., *Our Dear-Bought Liberty: Catholics and Religious Toleration in Early America* (Cambridge: Harvard University Press, 2021)

Bridwell, Ronald E., 'Wade Hampton I', *South Carolina Encyclopedia*, <scencyclopedia.org/sce/entries/hampton-wade-i/>, accessed 18 May 2024

Brown, Douglas Summers, 'Charles Cummings: The Fighting Parson of Southwest Virginia', *Virginia Cavalcade*, 28:3 (1979), pp.138–143

Brunner, Daniel L., 'Anglican Perceptions of Lutheranism in Early Hanoverian England', *Lutheran Quarterly*, 20:1 (2006), pp.63–82

Buchanan, John, *the Battle of Musgrove's Mill: 1780* (Yardley: Westholme, 2022)

Budd, Richard M., *Serving Two Masters: The Development of American Military Chaplaincy, 1860–1920* (Lincoln: University of Nebraska Press, 2002)

Burk, John, Skelton Jones, and Louis Hue Girardin, *The History of Virginia*, 4 vols (Petersburg: Dickson & Pescud and M.W. Dunnavant, 1804–1816)

Butler, Mann, *A History of the Commonwealth of Kentucky* (Louisville: J.A. James, 1834)

Butler, Nic, 'The Horn Work: Marion Square's Tabby Fortress', *Charleston Time Machine*, Charleston County Public Library, 29 May 2020, <ccpl.org/charleston-time-machine/horn-work-marion-squares-tabby-fortress>, accessed 6 May 2023

Butler, Nic, 'Navigating the Bar of Charleston Harbor: Gateway to the Atlantic', *Charleston Time Machine*, Charleston County Public Library, 17 June 2022, <www.ccpl.org/charleston-time-machine/navigating-bar-charleston-harbor-gateway-atlantic>, accessed 23 April 2023

Butler, Nic, 'Wielding the Sword of State in Early South Carolina', *Charleston Time Machine*, Charleston County Public Library, 5 November 2021, <www.ccpl.org/charleston-time-machine/wielding-sword-state-early-south-carolina>, accessed 21 July 2022

Butterfield, Consul Willshire, *History of the Girtys* (Cincinnati: Robert Clarke & Co., 1890)

Campbell, Alexander V., *The Royal American Regiment: An Atlantic Microcosm, 1755–1772* (Norman: University of Oklahoma Press, 2010)

Candler, Allen D. and Clement A. Evans (eds), *Georgia: Comprising Sketches of Counties, Towns, Events, Institutions, and Persons, Arranged in Cyclopedic Form*, 3 vols (Atlanta: State Historical Association, 1906)

Canny, Nicholas, *Making Ireland British: 1580–1650* (Oxford: Oxford University Press, 2001)

Cartmell, Thomas Kemp, *Shenandoah Valley Pioneers and Their Descendants: A History of Frederick County, Virginia* (Winchester: Eddy Press, 1909)

Carpenter, John S., 'Slaughter Family', *VMHB*, 21:3 (1913), pp.306–310, 21:4 (1913), pp.427–430, 22:1 (1914), pp.99–102, 22:2 (1914), pp.208–211, 22:3 (1914), pp.319–22

Catts, Wade, 'The Battle of Cooch's Bridge', *Cooch's Bridge Chapter, Daughters of the American Revolution*, <coochsbridge.wildapricot.org/Battlefield-History>, accessed 23 Sept. 2023

Cecere, Michael, *A Brave, Active, and Intrepid Soldier: Lieutenant Colonel Richard Campbell of the Virginia Continental Line* (Berwyn Heights, Md.: Heritage Books, 2020)

Cecere, Michael, 'The Fighting Parson's Farewell Sermon', *JAR*, 15 April 2020 <allthingsliberty.com/2020/04/the-fighting-parsons-farewell-sermon>, accessed 21 July 2024

Cecere, Michael, *Second to No Man But the Commander in Chief, Hugh Mercer* (Berwyn Heights, Md.: Heritage Books, 2015)

Chambers, S. Allen, Jr., 'Traveller's Rest', *Society of Architectural Historians Archipedia*, <https://sah-archipedia.org/buildings/WV-01-JE18>, accessed 18 Sept. 2022.

Chandlee, Edward C., *Six Quaker Clockmakers* (Philadelphia: Historical Society of Pennsylvania, 1943)

Clark, Murtie June (ed.), *American Militia in the Frontier Wars, 1790–1796* (Baltimore, Genealogical Publishing, 1990),

Clary, David A. and Joseph W.A. Whitehorne, *The Inspectors General of the United States Army, 1777–1903* (Washington: U.S. Army, 1987)

Coleman, Charles Washington, 'The Virginia County Committees of Safety, 1774-'75', *William and Mary Quarterly*, 5:2 (1896), pp.94–106, and 5:4 (1897), pp.245–255

Collins, Jeffrey, 'S.C.'s Sword of State missing for more than 70 years', *Post and Courier*, 1 Jan. 2014 (updated 2 Nov. 2016), <postandcourier.com/archives/s-c-s-sword-of-state-missing-for-more-than/article_03e6ddab-656c-504b-b0e1-2c0f42c64496.html>, accessed 21 July 2022

Collins, Lewis and Richard H. Collins., *Historical Sketches of Kentucky*, 2 vols (Covington, Ky.: Collins & Co., 1882)

Cring, Henry et al, *Caldwell's Atlas of Holmes County, Ohio* (Condit, Ohio.: Caldwell Publishing, 1875)

Crumrine, Boyd, *History of Washington County, Pennsylvania* (Philadelphia: L.H. Everts, 1882)

Crytzer, Brady J., *Guyasuta and the Fall of Indian America* (Yardley: Westholme, 2013)

Cryzter, Brady J., *The Whiskey Rebellion: A Distilled History of An American Crisis* (Yardley: Westholme, 2023)

Cutten, George Barton, *The Silversmiths of Virginia, Together with Watchmakers and Jewelers, from 1694 to 1850* (Dietz Press, 1952)

Dandridge, Danske, *Historic Shepherdstown* (Charlottesville: Michie Company, 1910)

Daniels, Cheri, 'Is Your Brick Wall Whitewashed?', *Genealogy Literacy*, 11 February 2019, <genealogyliteracy.com/is-your-brick-wall-whitewashed>, accessed 6 December 2024

Dauer, Manning J., *The Adams Federalists* (Baltimore: Johns Hopkins University Press, 1953)

David, James Corbett, *Dunmore's New World* (Charlottesville: University of Virginia Press, 2015)

Devine, Francis E., 'The Pennsylvania Flying Camp, July-November, 1776', *Pennsylvania History* 46:1 (1979)

Dickinson, Al, 'A Leap of Faith in the Historical Record: The Legend of McColloch's Leap', *JAR*, <allthingsliberty.com/2023/11/a-leap-of-faith-in-the-historical-record-the-legend-of-mccollochs-leap>, accessed 20 July 2024

Dixon, David, *Never Come to Peace Again: Pontiac's Uprising and the Fate of the British Empire in North America* (Norman: University of Oklahoma Press, 2005)

Doan, James E., '"An Island in the Virginian Sea": Native Americans and the Irish in English Discourse, 1585–1640', *New Hibernia Review* 1:1 (1997), pp.79–99

Dotterer, Henry S., 'Folk-Names of Places in the Perkiomen Valley', *The Perkiomen Region, Past and Present*, 1:1 (1894), pp.5–6

Dunaway, W.F., Jr., 'The Virginia Conventions of the Revolution', *Virginia Law Register*, 10:7 (1904), pp.568–586

Dunkerly, Robert M., *Decision at Brandywine: The Battle on Birmingham Hill* (Yardley: Westholme, 2021)

Durant, Pliny A., *The History of Union County, Ohio* (Chicago: W.H. Beers, 1883)

Dwyer, William M., *The Day Is Ours! November 1776-January 1777: An Inside View of the Battles of Trenton and Princeton* (New York: Viking Press, 1983)

Ecelbarger, Gary, 'Clement Biddle Partially Clears the "Battle of the Clouds"', *JAR*, 11 March 2021, <allthingsliberty.com/2021/03/clement-biddle-partially-clears-the-battle-of-the-clouds>, accessed 1 Sept. 2024

Ecelbarger, Gary, *George Washington's Momentous Year: Twelve Months that Transformed the Revolution* (Yardley: Westholme, 2024)

Ecelbarger, Gary, 'The Feint That Never Happened: Unheralded Turning Point of the Philadelphia Campaign', *JAR*, 19 Nov. 2020, <allthingsliberty.com/2020/11/the-feint-that-never-happened-unheralded-turning-point-of-the-philadelphia-campaign>, accessed 27 Nov. 2023

Edelson S. Max, *Plantation Enterprise in Colonial South Carolina* (Cambridge: Harvard University Press, 2006

Elliott, Daniel T., *Sunbury Battlefield Survey*, LAMAR Institute Publication Series, Report Number 64 (Box Springs, Ga.: The LAMAR Institute, 2005)

English, William Hayden, *Conquest of the Country North-West of the River Ohio, 1778–1783 and, Life of Gen. George Rogers Clark*, 2 vols (Indianapolis: Bowen-Merrill, 1897)

Faison, Edward K. and David R. Foster, 'Did American Chestnut Really Dominate the Eastern Forest?', *Arnoldia*, 72:2 (2014), pp.18–32

Faris, John T., *Old Roads Out of Philadelphia* (Philadelphia: J.B. Lippincott, 1917)

Farrier, George H. (ed.), *Memorial of the Centennial Celebration of the Battle of Paulus Hook* (Jersey City: M. Mullone, 1879)

Fenn, Elizabeth A., *Pox Americana: The Great Smallpox Epidemic of 1775–1782* (New York: Hill and Wang, 2002)

Fischer, David Hackett, *Washington's Crossing* (Oxford: Oxford University Press, 2004)

Foote, William Henry, *Sketches of Virginia, Historical and Biographical*, ser. 2 (Philadelphia: J.B. Lippincott, 1855)

Foster, John T. and Sarah Whitmer Foster, *Contentment and the Pursuit of Ambition: the Grattans and Their Remarkable Women* (Rose Digital Publishing, 2011)

Friesen, Steven K., 'Martin Mylin, Gunsmith: Fact or Fancy?' *Journal of the Lancaster County Historical Society*, 93:1 (1991), pp.16–24

Futhey, J. Smith and Gilbert Cope, *History of Chester County Pennsylvania* (Philadelphia: Louis H. Everts, 1881)

Gaddis, Jim, 'William Gaddis', <findagrave.com/memorial/63481893/william-gaddis>, accessed 15 Oct. 2022

Gallagher, Jim, 'Virginia Continental Line Reorganisation of 1778 and 1779', *7th Virginia Regiment of the Continental Line*, <7vr.org/single-post/2018/01/07/virginia-continental-line-reorganisation-of-1778-and-1779>, accessed 5 May 2024

Gallay, Allan, 'Jonathan Bryan's Plantation Empire: Land, Politics, and the Formation of a Ruling Class in Colonial Georgia', *William and Mary Quarterly*, 45:2 (1988), pp.253–279

Gallup, Andrew, *A Sketch of the Virginia Soldier in the Revolution* (Westminster, Md.: Heritage Books, 2008)

Garrett, Pamela Hutchison, 'Bio: John Markham', *Markham of Chesterfield*, <markham-chesterfield.com/biographies/markjohn005_bio.pdf>, accessed 30 December 2023

Gatten, Robert E., Jr., 'Clark Land in Virginia and the Birthplace of William Clark', *We Proceeded On*, Lewis & Clark Trail Heritage Foundation, 25:2 (1999), pp.6–10

Gaugler, Nancy K. and Ralph Conner, 'Jost Hite: From the Neckar to the Shenandoah', *Pennsylvania Folklife*, 37:1 (1987), pp.15–32

Gilbreth, Donna, 'Fast Day', *New Hampshire Almanac*, <nh.gov/almanac/fast-day.htm>, accessed 13 Feb. 2024

Gill, Harold B., Jr., 'Wheat Culture in Colonial Virginia', *Agricultural History*, 52:3 (1978), pp.380–393

Glanville, Jim, 'The Fincastle Resolutions', *The Smithfield Review*, 14 (2010), pp.69–119

Glanville, Jim and Ryan Mays, 'William Beverley, James Patton, and the Settling of the Shenandoah Valley', *Essex County Museum and Historical Society Bulletin*, 55 (2010), pp.1–5

Goldstein, Erik, Stuart C. Mowbray, and Brian Hendelson, *The Swords of George Washington* (Woonsocket: Mowbray Publishing, 2016),

Graham, Daniel A., 'The Family of John Potts (1709/10–1768), Ironmaster, and Ruth Savage (1715/16–1786) of Pottstown, Pennsylvania Through the Fourth Generation: A Genealogical Sketch', <montgomerycountypa.gov/DocumentCenter/View/20669/Dan-Graham-Research>, accessed 27 Nov. 2023

Graham, James, *The Life of General Daniel Morgan* (New York: Derby & Jackson, 1856)

Graham, James R., *The Planting of the Presbyterian Church in Northern Virginia Prior to the Organisation of Winchester Presbytery, December 4, 1794* (Winchester: Geo. F. Norton, 1904)

de Grauwe, Luc, 'Emerging Mother-Tongue Awareness: The Special Case of Dutch and German in the Middle Ages and the Early Modern Period', in Andrew R. Linn and Nicola McLelland (eds), *Standardization: Studies from the Germanic Languages* (Amsterdam: John Benjamins Publishing, 2002)

Greene, George Washington, *The Life of Nathanael Greene*, 3 vols (New York: G.P. Putnam and Son and Hurd and Houghton, 1867–1871)

Greene, Jerome A., *The Allies at Yorktown: A Bicentennial History of the Siege of 1781*, Historic Resource Study and Historic Structure report (Denver: National Park Service, 1976)

Greene, W. Jackson, 'Few Traces of Gowen Family Remain at Combahee Ferry', *Gowen Research Foundation Newsletter*, 6:8 (1995)

Gwathmey, John H. (ed.), *Historical Register of Virginians in the Revolution: Soldiers, Sailors, Marines*, 2 vols (1938, reprinted Baltimore: Genealogical Publishing Co., 1973)

Hagist, Don N., *These Distinguished Corps: British Grenadier and Light Infantry Battalions in the American Revolution* (Warwick: Helion & Company, 2021)

de Hass, Wills, *History of the Early Settlement and Indian Wars of Western Virginia* (Wheeling: H. Hoblitzell, 1851)

Hammon, Neal O., *Early Kentucky Land Records, 1773–1780* (Louisville: Filson Club, 1992)

Hammon, Neal O., 'Land Acquisition on the Kentucky Frontier', *Register of the Kentucky Historical Society*, 78:4 (1980), pp.297–321

Hammon, Neal and Richard Taylor, *Virginia's Western War, 1775–1786* (Mechanicsburg, Pa.: Stackpole Books, 2002)

Hanna, William, *History of Greene County, Pa.* (place unknown: W. Hanna, 1882)

Harris, Michael C., *Brandywine: A Military History of the Battle that Lost Philadelphia but Saved America, September 11, 1777* (El Dorado Hills, Ca.: Savas Beatie, 2014)

Harris, Michael C., *Germantown: A Military History of the Battle for Philadelphia, October 4, 1777* (El Dorado Hills, Ca.: Savas Beatie, 2020)

Hayden, Horace Edwin, *Genealogy of the Glassell Family of Scotland and Virginia* (Wilkes-Barre: E.B. Yordy, 1891)

Hays, Samuel, 'A Sketch of Major Joseph Morris', *The Record*, First Presbyterian Church of Morristown, N.J., 5:34–35 (1885), pp.182–184, 186–188

Hendricks, Christopher E., *The Backcountry Towns of Colonial Virginia* (Knoxville: University of Tennessee Press, 2006)

Hodges, Frances Smith Beale, *The Genealogy of the Beale Family, 1399–1956* (Ann Arbor: Edwards Brothers,1956)

Hoffman, Phillip W., *Simon Girty, Turncoat Hero: The Most Hated Man on the Early American Frontier* (Franklin, Tenn.: Flying Camp Press, 2009)

Hofstra, Warren R., *The Planting of New Virginia: Settlement and Landscape in the Shenandoah Valley* (Baltimore: John Hopkins University Press, 2004)

Hofstra, Warren R., 'The Colonial Road', in Warren R. Hofstra and Karl Raitz, (eds), *The Great Valley Road of Virginia: Shenandoah Landscapes from Prehistory to the Present* (Charlottesville: University of Virginia Press, 2010)

Holden, Robert John and Donna Jean Holden, *The Hunting Pioneers, 1720–1840* (Bowie, Maryland: Heritage Press, 2000)

Holton, Woody, *Forced Founders: Indians, Debtors, Slaves, and the Making of the American Revolution in Virginia* (Chapel Hill: University of North Carolina Press, 1999)

Holton, Woody, '"Rebel Against Rebel": Enslaved Virginians and the Coming of the American Revolution', *VMHB*, 105:2 (1997), pp.157–192

Huddle, W.P., *History of Hebron Lutheran Church, Madison County, Virginia, from 1717 to 1907* (New Market, Va.: Henkel & Co, 1908)

Hunter, William A., *Forts of the Pennsylvania Frontier, 1753–1758* (Harrisburg: Pennsylvania Historical and Museum Commission, 1960)

Hurst, Neal Thomas, *'A kind of armour, being peculiar to America:' The American Hunting Shirt* (Bachelors Thesis, College of William and Mary, 2013)

Ingle, Edward, 'Justices of the Peace of Colonial Virginia, 1757–1775', *Bulletin of the Virginia State Library*, 14:2–3 (1921), pp.41–149

Jackson, John W., *Valley Forge: Pinnacle of Courage* (Gettysburg: Thomas Publications, 1992)

Johnston, David E., *A History of Middle New River Settlements and Contiguous Territory* (Huntington, W.V: Standard Printing and Publishing, 1906)

Johnston, Frederick, *Memorials of Old Virginia Clerks* (Lynchburg: J.P. Bell, 1888)

Johnston, George, *History of Cecil County, Maryland* (Elkton: G. Johnston, 1881)

Jolliffe, William, *Historical, Genealogical, and Biographical Account of the Jolliffe Family of Virginia, 1652–1893* (Philadelphia: J.B. Lippincott Co., 1893)

Johnson, William, *Sketches of the Life and Correspondence of Nathanael Greene*, 2 vols (Charleston: A.E. Miller, 1822)

Johnston, Henry P. (ed.), *The Record of Connecticut Men in the Military and Naval Service During the War of the Revolution, 1775–1783* (Hartford: Adjutant General's Office, 1889)

Jones, Ingrid Jewell, 'Edward Snickers, Yeoman', *Proceedings of the Clark County Historical Society*, 17 (1971–1975)

Jones, Virgil Carrington, 'The Sivley Treasure Recovered', in *True Tales of Old Madison County* (Huntsville: Historic Huntsville Foundation, 1992)

Jordan, John W., 'The Military Hospitals at Bethlehem and Lititz During the Revolution', *PMHB*, 22:2 (1889), pp.137–157

Jordan, Terry G. and Matti Kaups, *The American Backwoods Frontier: An Ethnic and Ecological Interpretation* (Baltimore: Johns Hopkins University Press, 1989)

Keller, Kenneth W., 'The Origins of Ulster Scots Emigration to America: A Survey of Recent Research', *American Presbyterians*, 70:2 (1992), pp.71–80

Kelsay, Isabel Thompson, *Joseph Brant, 1743–1807: Man of Two Worlds* (Syracuse: Syracuse University Press, 1984)

Kemper, Charles E., 'The Settlement of the Valley', *VMHB*, 30:2 (1922), pp.169–182

Kidder, William L., *Ten Crucial Days: Washington's Vision for Victory Unfolds* (Lawrence Twp., NJ: Knox Press, 2018)

King, J.W., 'Colonel John Armstrong: His Place in the History of Southwestern Pennsylvania', *Western Pennsylvania Historical Magazine*, 10:3 (1927), pp.129–145

Kline, John Jacob, *The Lutheran Church in New Hanover, Pa.* (New Hanover, Pa.: New Hanover Lutheran Church, 1910)

Klein, Richard S. and Alan H. Cooper, 'Biography of Samuel McCollogh', *Wheeling Intelligencer*, 9 April 1777, <ohiocountylibrary.org/history/biography-samuel-mccolloch/4298>, accessed 17 Oct. 2022

Klotter, James C., *The Breckinridges of Kentucky* (Lexington: University Press of Kentucky, 1986)

Larche, Mignon, *Pioneers on the Bullskin: The Stephenson Story* (Eureka Spring, Ark.: Times-Echo Publishing Co., 1960)

Leiding, Harriette Kershaw, *Historic Houses of South Carolina* (Philadelphia: J.B. Lippincott, 1921)

Lender, Mark Edward and Garry Wheeler Stone, *Fatal Sunday: George Washington, the Monmouth Campaign, and the Politics of Battle* (Norman: University of Oklahoma Press, 2016)

Lender, Mark Edward and James Kirby Martin, 'A Traitor's Epiphany: Benedict Arnold in Virginia and His Quest for Reconciliation', *VMHB* 125:4 (2017), pp.314–357

Lesser, Charles H. (ed.), *The Sinews of Independence: Monthly Strength Reports of the Continental Army* (Chicago: University of Chicago Press, 1976)

Leonard, Cynthia Miller (ed.), *The General Assembly of Virginia, 1930–1619-January 11, 1978,* (Richmond: Virginia State Library, 1978)

Lewis, Grace, 'The First Home of Governor Lewis in Louisiana Territory: "…the house in which General Clark resides"', *Bulletin of the Missouri Historical Society*, 14:4 (1858), pp.357–368

Lipscomb, Terry W., 'The South Carolina Constitution of 1776', *South Carolina Historical Magazine*, 77:2 (1976), pp.138–141

Livingood, James W., *Hamilton County* (Memphis: Memphis State University Press, 1981)

Lockhart, Paul, *The Drillmaster of Valley Forge: The Baron de Steuben and the Making of the American Army* (New York: Harper Collins, 2008)

Lossing, Benson J., *Pictorial Field-Book of the Revolution*, 2 vols (New York: Harper & Bros, 1855)

Loth, Calder (ed.), *Virginia Landmarks Register* (Charlottesville: University Press of Virginia, 1999)

Ludlum, David M., *Early American Winters: 1604–1820* (Boston: American Meteorological Society, 1966)

Luzader, John F., *Saratoga: A Military History of the Decisive Campaign of the American Revolution* (New York: Savas Beatie, 2008)

Lynn, John A., *The Wars of Louis XIV: 1677–1714* (Harlow: Pearson Education, 1999)

MacGregor, Douglas, 'Braddock's Field: "How Brilliant the Morning, How Melancholy the Evening"', *Western Pennsylvania History*, 88:4 (2005), pp.22–29

MacIntyre, Doug, 'Danger at the Breach', *JAR*, 11 May 2023, <allthingsliberty.com/2023/05/danger-at-the-beach>, accessed 3 March 2024

MacMaster, Richard K., *The History of Hardy County, 1786–1986* (Salem, W.Va.: Hardy County Public Library, 1986)

McBurney, Christian, 'Was Richard Stockton a Hero?', *JAR*, 18 July 2016, <allthingsliberty.com/2016/07/was-richard-stockton-a-hero>, accessed 28 July 2023

McCall, Hugh, *The History of Georgia, Containing Brief Sketches of the Most Remarkable Events, Up To the Present Day*, 2 vols (Savannah: William T. Williams,1816)

McCandless, Peter, *Slavery, Disease, and Suffering in the Southern Lowcountry* (Cambridge University Press, 2011, Kindle e-book)

McCrady, Edward, *History of South Carolina in the Revolution, 1775–1780* (New York: MacMillan Company, 1902)

McDonnell, Michael A., *The Politics of War: Race, Class, & Conflict in Revolutionary Virginia* (Chapel Hill: University of North Carolina Press, 2007)

McDonnell, Michael A., 'Popular Mobilization and Political Culture in Revolutionary Virginia: The Failure of the Minutemen and the Revolution from Below', *Journal of American History*, 85:3 (1998), pp.946–981

McGuffey, William Holmes (ed.), *McGuffey's Fifth Eclectic Reader*, revised edition (New York: American Book Company, 1879)

McGuire, Thomas J., *The Philadelphia Campaign*, 2 vols (Mechanicsburg, Pa.: Stackpole Books, 2006)

McNeill, J.R., *Mosquito Empires: Ecology and War in the Greater Caribbean, 1620–1914* (New York: Cambridge University Press, 2010)

Macaulay, Thomas Babington, *The History of England from the Accession of James II*, 5 vols (Philadelphia: E.H. Butler & Co, 1856)

Maas, John R., '"The Greatest Terror Imaginable:" Cornwallis Brings His Campaign to Goochland, June 1781', *Goochland County Historical Magazine*, 41 (2009), pp.12–101

Marshall, Humphrey, *The History of Kentucky*, 2 vols. (Frankfort: George S. Robinson, 1824)

Mattern, David B., *Benjamin Lincoln and the American Revolution* (Columbia: University of South Carolina Press, 1995)

Maxwell, Hu and H.L. Swisher, *History of Hampshire County* (Morgantown: A. Brown Boughner, 1897)

Mazzagetti, Dominick, *Charles Lee: Self Before Country* (New Brunswick: Rutgers University Press, 2013)
Meade, William, *Old Churches, Ministers and Families of Virginia*, 2 vols (Philadelphia: J.B. Lippincott & Co., 1861)
Miller, David W., *Forced Removal of American Indians from the Northeast: A History of Territorial Cessions and Relocations, 1620–1854* (Jefferson, N.C: McFarland & Co., 2011)
Moller, George D., *American Shoulder Arms*, 3 vols (Albuquerque: University of New Mexico Press, 2011)
Montgomery, Robert H., 'Robert Crockett of the Great Calfpasture, Augusta County, Virginia', *VMHB* 63:2 (1955), pp.186–207
Moore, Florence Hendricks, *Descendants of Albert(us) Hendricks(on), 1673–1984* (Charleston, W.Va.: F.H. Moore, 1985)
Moore, George H., *The Treason of Charles Lee* (New York: Charles Scribner, 1859)
Moore, Horatio Newton, *Life and Services of Gen. Anthony Wayne* (Philadelphia: John B. Perry, 1845)
Morgan, Robert, *Daniel Boone: A Biography* (Chapel Hill: Algonquin Books, 2008)
Morton, Oren F., *Annals of Bath County, Virginia* (Staunton: McClure Co., 1917)
Moss, Bobby Gilmer, *Roster of South Carolina Patriots in the American Revolution*, 2 vols. (Baltimore: Genealogical Publishing, 1983)
Mowat, Charles Loch, *East Florida as a British province, 1763–1784* (Berkeley and Los Angeles: University of California Press, 1943)
Muhlenberg, Henry A., *The Life of Major-General Peter Muhlenberg of the Revolutionary Army* (Philadelphia: Carey and Hart, 1849)
Namier, Lewis and John Brooke, *The History of Parliament: The House of Commons, 1754–1790*, 3 vols (London: Secker & Warburg, 1964)
Nelson, John K., *A Blessed Company: Parishes, Parson, and Parishioners in Anglican Virginia, 1690–1776* (Chapel Hill: University of North Carolina Press, 2001)
Nelson, Paul David, *General Horatio Gates: A Biography* (Baton Rouge: Louisiana State University, 1976)
Nelson, Paul David, *The Life of William Alexander, Lord Stirling* (Tuscaloosa: University of Alabama Press, 1987)
Neville, Gabriel, 'A Forty Year Bond: William Darke and George Washington in Politics, Business, and War', *Magazine of the Jefferson County Historical Society*, 84 (2018), pp.23–38
Neville, Gabriel, 'Shenandoah Martyr: Richard Campbell at War', *JAR*, 3 Dec. 2019, <allthingsliberty.com/2019/12/shenandoah-martyr-richard-campbell-at-war>, accessed 27 May 2024
Neville, Gabriel, 'The Stamp Act and Captain Berry', *The 8th Virginia Regiment*, <8thvirginia.com/blog/thomas-berry-and-the-stamp-act>, accessed 4 Nov. 2024.
Neville, Gabriel, 'Virginia's Independent Frontier Companies', *JAR*, 17–18 March, 2021 <allthingsliberty.com/2021/03/virginias-independent-frontier-companies-part-1-of-2/>, accessed 27 Feb. 2023
Norris, J.E. (ed.), *History of the Lower Shenandoah Valley* (Chicago: A. Warner & Co., 1890)
O'Connor, Elizabeth Paschal (Mrs. T.P. O'Connor), *My Beloved South* (New York: G. P. Putnam's Sons, 1913)

Papas, Phillip, *Renegade Revolutionary: The Life of General Charles Lee* (New York: New York University Press, 2014)

Parkinson, Robert G., *Heart of American Darkness: Bewilderment and Horror on the Early Frontier* (New York: W.W. Norton, 2024)

Parry, Guerdon Groves and Lee Kercheval Carr, 'Something About the Kercheval Family', *Register of the Kentucky State Historical Society*, 22:65 (1924), pp.195–202

Paul, James Balfour, *The Scots Peerage* (Edinburgh: David Douglas, 1904–1914)

Pauley, Michael J., 'Beverley', Jefferson Co., W.Va., National Register of Historic Places nomination, 1986, NPS ref. no. 87000486

Pawlett, Nathaniel Mason and Howard H. Newlon, Jr., 'The Route of the Three Notch'd Road: A Preliminary Report', Virginia Highway & Transportation Research Council (1976, 2003), <virginiadot.org/vtrc/main/online_reports/pdf/76-r32.pdf>, accessed 8 Jan. 2023

Pendleton, William Cecil, *History of Tazewell County and Southwest Virginia: 1748–1920* (Richmond: W.C. Hill, 1920)

Pennypacker, Samuel W., 'Bebber's Township and the Dutch Patroons of Pennsylvania', *PMHB*, 31:1 (1907), pp.1–18

Peterson, Dennis G., *Juriaen Westfall Descendants in America* (privately published, 2016)

Peyton, J. Lewis, *History of Augusta County, Virginia* (Staunton: Samuel M. Yost & Son, 1882)

Pierce, Frederick Clifton, *Field Genealogy*, (Chicago: Hammond Press, 1901)

Potts, Gwynne Tuell, *George Rogers Clark and William Croghan* (Lexington: University Press of Kentucky, 2020)

Preston, David, *Braddock's Defeat: The Battle of Monongahela and the Road to Revolution* (Oxford: Oxford University Press, 2015)

Price, David, *John Haslet's World: An Ardent Patriot, The Delaware Blues, and the Spirit of 1776* (New York: Knox Press, 2020)

Price, David, 'When War Came to the Thompson-Neely Farmstead', *JAR*, <allthingsliberty.com/2021/06/when-war-came-to-the-thompson-neely-farmstead>, accessed 23 July 2023

Prown, Jules David, *Art as Evidence: Writings on Art and Material Culture* (New Haven: Yale University Press, 2001)

Ramsay, David, *The History of the American Revolution*, 2 vols (Philadelphia: R. Aitken & Son, 1789)

Ramsay, J.G.M., *Annals of Tennessee* (Charleston: John Russell, 1853)

Ranck, George Washington, *History of Lexington Kentucky* (Cincinnati: Robert Clarke & Co., 1872)

Rankin, Hugh F., *The North Carolina Continentals* (Chapel Hill: University of North Carolina Press, 1971)

Read, Alice, *The Reads and Their Relatives* (Cincinnati: Johnson & Hardin Press, 1930)

Read, Thomas Buchanan, *The Wagoner of the Alleghanies: A Poem of the Days of Seventy-Six* (Philadelphia: J.B. Lippincott, 1863)

Reed, John F., *Campaign to Valley Forge, July 1, 1777-December 19, 1777* (Philadelphia: University of Pennsylvania Press, 1965)

Rees, John U., *Capt. John Paul Schott's Independent Rifle Company, Ottendorff's Corps, Battle of Short Hills, 26 June 1777*, <scribd.com/document/347250413/Capt-John-Paul-Schott-s-Independent-Rifle-Company-Ottendorff-s-Corps-Battle-of-Short-Hills-26-June-1777>, accessed 30 August 2023.

Rees, John U., *Examples of the Complexity of Continental Army Unit Lineage (The Virginia, Pennsylvania and Massachusetts Continental Lines)*, <scribd.com/doc/307784931/Examples-of-the-Complexity-of-Continental-Army-Unit-Lineage-The-Virginia-Pennsylvania-and-Massachusetts-Continental-Lines>, accessed 30 April 2024

Rees, John U., *'We... wheeled to the Right to form the Line of Battle': Colonel Israel Shreve's Journal, 23 November 1776 to 14 August 1777 (Including Accounts of the Action at the Short Hills)*, <scribd.com/document/153790118/We-wheeled-to-the-Right-to-form-the-Line-of-Battle-Colonel-Israel-Shreve-Cars-Journal-23-November-1776-to-14-August-1777-Including-Accounts-of#>, accessed 2 Sept. 2023

Rees, John U. and Bob McDonald (eds), *'The Action was renew.d with a very warm Canonade': New Jersey Officer's Diary, 21 June 1777 to 31 August 1778*, <academia.edu/36536289/_The_Action_was_renew_d_with_a_very_warm_Canonade_New_Jersey_Officers_Diary_21_June_1777_to_31_August_1778>, accessed 29 Oct. 2023, 2 Sept. 1777.

Rife, James Phillip, *'So Calamitous a Situation': The Causes and Course of Dunmore's War, 1744–1774* (master's thesis, Virginia Polytechnic Institute & State University, 1999)

Riffe, Andrew Lewis and Clayton Torrence, 'The Wallers of Endfield, King William County, Virginia', *VMHB* 59:3–4 (1951) pp.337–352, 458–493

Rives, William C., *History of the Life and Times of James Madison*, 2 vols. (Boston: Little, Brown & Co., 1859–1866)

Rodda, Chris, '"Debunk U" Study Guide – Lesson 1', *Huffington Post*, 14 July 2010, revised 6 Dec. 2017, <huffpost.com/entry/debunk-u-study-guide-le_b_645528>, accessed 21 July 2024

Roeber, A.G., *Palatines, Liberty, and Property: German Lutherans in Colonial British America* (Baltimore: Johns Hopkins University Press, 1993)

Rogers, Amelia Clay Lewis Van Meter, 'The Van Meteren's of Holland and America', *Genealogies of Kentucky Families* (Baltimore: Genealogical Publishing, 1981), pp.546–566

Rollings, Willard H., *The Osage: An Ethnohistorical Study of Hegemony on the Prairie-Plains* (Columbia: University of Missouri Press, 1992)

Rossiter, W.S., *A Century of Population Growth* (Washington: Bureau of the Census, 1909)

Rossman, Kenneth R., *Thomas Mifflin and the Politics of the American Revolution* (Chapel Hill: University of North Carolina Press, 1952)

Rouse, Parke, Jr., *The Great Wagon Road: from Philadelphia to the South* (New York: McGraw-Hill, 1973)

Rowland, Lawrence S. et al, *The History of Beaufort County, South Carolina*, 2 vols. (Columbia: University of South Carolina Press, 1996–2015)

Rutkow, Eric, *American Canopy: Trees, Forests, and the Making of a Nation* (New York: Scribner, 2012).

Saguto, Al, 'Shoemaker' [podcast], Past & Present (2 January 2006), *Colonial Williamsburg*, <https://podcast.history.org/2006/01/02/shoemaker/>, accessed 20 July 2022

Saguto, Al, 'Meet the Shoemaker' [podcast], Past & Present (26 March 2012), *Colonial Williamsburg*, <https://podcast.history.org/2012/03/26/meet-the-shoemaker/>, accessed 20 July 2022

Salmon, Emily, 'County Formation During the Colonial Period', *Encyclopedia Virginia*, <encyclopediavirginia.org/entries/county-formation-during-the-colonial-period>, accessed 20 Sept. 2024

Sanchez Saavedra, E.M., *A Guide to Virginia Military Organisations in the American Revolution, 1774–1787* (Richmond: Virginia State Library, 1978)

Schnitzer, Eric and Don Troiani, *Don Troiani's Campaign to Saratoga – 1777* (Guilford, Ct.: Stackpole Books, 2019)

Seaman, Catherine Hawes Coleman, *Tuckahoe and Cohee: The Settlers and Cultures of Amherst and Nelson Counties, 1607–1807* (Sweet Briar, Va..: Sweet Briar College, 1992)

Selby, John E., *The Revolution in Virginia, 1775–1783* (Williamsburg: Colonial Williamsburg, 1988)

Selig, Robert A., Matthew Harris and Wade P. Catts, *Battle of Princeton Mapping Project: Report of Military Terrain Analysis and Battle Narrative* (West Chester, Pa.: John Milner Associates, 2010)

Sibray, David, 'Ancient West Virginia forests once a mosaic of landscapes', *West Virginia Explorer*, 22 January 2022.

Slaughter, Philip, *A History of St. Mark's Parish, Culpeper County, Virginia* (Baltimore: Innes & Co., 1877)

Smith, Betty Lovely, 'Lovely County', *Encyclopedia of Arkansas*, <encyclopediaofarkansas.net/entries/lovely-county-2940/>, accessed 30 June 2024.

Smith, Samuel S., *The Battle of Brandywine* (Monmouth Beach, N.J.: Philip Freneau Press, 1976)

Smith, Scott M., 'Major Robert Rogers and the America Revolution', *JAR*, 23 Nov. 2021 <allthingsliberty.com/2021/11/major-robert-rogers-and-the-american-revolution>, accessed 18 June 2023

Smucker, Isaac, 'A Pioneer of the Alleghanies: Col. Ben. Wilson', *American Historical Record*, 2:18 (1873), pp.263–266

Sosin, Jack M., 'The British Indian Department and Dunmore's War', *VMHB*, 74:1 (1966), pp.34–50

Spangler, Jewel, 'Baptists in Colonial Virginia', (7 December 2020,), *Encyclopedia Virginia*, <encyclopediavirginia.org/entries/baptists-in-colonial-virginia>, accessed 24 Oct. 2022

Sterner, Eric, *The Battle of Upper Sandusky, 1782* (Yardley: Westholme, 2023)

Sterner, Eric, 'Betty Zane and the Siege of Fort Henry, September 1782', *JAR*, <allthingsliberty.com/2020/01/betty-zane-and-the-siege-of-fort-henry-september-1782/>, accessed 17 Oct. 2022

Sterner, Eric, 'The Siege of Fort Laurens, 1778–1779', *JAR*, 17 Dec. 2019

Sterner, Eric, *Till the Extinction of This Rebellion: George Rogers Clark, Frontier Warfare, and the Illinois Campaign of 1778–1779* (Yardley: Westholme, 2024)

Stickle, H.W., 'Monongahela River Navigation', *Professional Memoirs, Corps of Engineers, United States Army, and Engineer Department at* Large, 11:60 (1919), pp.695–713

Strong, Thomas M., *The History of the Town of Flatbush in King's County, Long Island* (New York: Thomas R. Mercein, 1842)

Stryker, William S., *The Battles of Trenton and Princeton* (Boston: Houghton, Mifflin, and Co., 1898)

Sugden, John, *Blue Jacket: Warrior of the Shawnees* (Lincoln: University of Nebraska Press, 2000)

Sweig, Donald M., 'The Virginia Nonimportation Association Broadside of 1770 and Fairfax County: A Study in Local Participation', *VMHB* 87:3 (1979), pp.316–325

Sydnor, Charles S., *American Revolutionaries in the Making: Political Practices in Washington's Virginia* (1952, reprinted New York: Free Press, 1965)

Teeters, Negley K., *They Were in Prison: A History of the Pennsylvania Prison Society, 1787–1937* (Philadelphia: John C. Winston Co., 1937)

Thayer, Theodore, *Nathanael Greene: Strategist of the American Revolution* (New York: Twayne Publishers, 1960)

Thomas, Samuel W., 'William Croghan, Sr. [1752–1822]: A Pioneer Kentucky Gentleman', *Filson Club Quarterly*, 43:2 (1969), pp.30–61

Thorpe, Francis Newton (ed.), *The Federal and State Constitutions Colonial Charters, and Other Organic Laws of the States, Territories, and Colonies Now or Heretofore Forming the United States of America*, 7 vols (Washington, D.C.: Government Printing Office, 1909)

Tillman, S.E., 'A Review of West Point's History', *Quarterly Journal of the New York State Historical Association*, 2:3 (1921), pp.141–155

Todd, John R. and Francis M. Sutton, *Prince William's Parish and Plantations* (Richmond, Garrett and Massie, 1935)

Tracy, Grace L. and John P. Dern, *Pioneers of Old Monocacy: Early Settlement of Frederick County, Maryland, 1721–1743* (Baltimore: Genealogical Publishing, 1987)

Troy, Michael, 'American Revolution' [podcast], interview with William L. Kidder, 18 Feb. 2021, <blog.amrevpodcast.com/2021/02/ar-sp07-larry-kidder-revolutionary.html>, accessed 28 July 2023

Tyler, Lyon Gardiner (ed.), *Encyclopedia of Virginia Biography*, 5 vols (New York: Lewis Historical Publishing, 1915)

Trussell, John. B.B., Jr., *The Pennsylvania Line: Regimental Organisation and Operations, 1776–1783* (Harrisburg: Pennsylvania Historical and Museum Commission, 1977)

Waddell, Joseph Addison (ed.), *Annals of Augusta County, Virginia*, 1st ed. (Richmond: Wm. Ellis Jones, 1886)

Waddell, Joseph Addison (ed.), *Annals of Augusta County*, 2nd ed. (Staunton: C. R. Caldwell, 1902)

Wainwright, Nicholas B., *George Croghan: Wilderness Diplomat* (Chapel Hill: University of North Carolina Press, 1959)

Wallace, Nesbit Willoughby, *A Regimental Chronicle and List of Officers of the 60th, or the King's Royal Rifle Corps, Formerly the 62nd, or the Royal American Regiment of Foot* (London: Harrison and Sons, 1879)

Wallace, Paul A., *The Muhlenbergs of Pennsylvania* (Philadelphia: University of Pennsylvania Press 1950)

Walsh, Martin W., 'May Games and Noble Savages: The Native American in Early Celebrations of the Tammany Society', *Folklore* 108 (1997), pp.83–91

Ward, Christopher L., *The Delaware Continentals* (Wilmington: Delaware Historical Society, 1941)

Ward, George K. (ed.), *Andrew Warde and His Descendants, 1597–1910* (New York: A.T. De La Mare, 1910)

Ward, Harry M., *Adam Stephen and the Cause of American Liberty* (Charlottesville: University Press of Virginia, 1989)

Ward, Harry M., *Charles Scott and the 'Spirit of '76'* (Charlottesville, University Press of Virginia, 1988)

Ward, Harry M., *Duty, Honor or Country: General George Weedon and the American Revolution* (Philadelphia: American Philosophical Society, 1979)

Ward, Townsend, 'The Germantown Road and Its Associations', *PMHB* 6:1–4 (1882), pp.1–20, 129–155, 257–283, 377–401

Watson, John F., *Annals of Philadelphia and Pennsylvania in Olden Time*, 2 vols (Philadelphia: Penington & Hunt, 1844)

Waters, Andrew, *To the End of the World* (Yardley: Westholme, 2022)

Wayland, John W., *The Bowmans: A Pioneering Family of Virginia, Kentucky, and the Northwest Territory* (1943; reprinted Harrisonburg: C.J. Carrier, 1974)

Wayland, John W., *A History of Shenandoah County, Virginia*, second edition (1969; reprinted Baltimore: Genealogical Publishing, 1980)

Wayman, Edith Helphenstine and L. Cleo Mullins, *The Helphinstine Family in America: Major Peter Helphinstine of Winchester, Virginia, 1724–1778* (Richmond: E.H. Wayman and L.C. Mullins, 1988)

Welsh, William M., 'Continental Army Brevets', *JAR*, 3 Nov. 2024, <allthingsliberty.com/2024/11/continental-army-brevets>, accessed 30 Jan. 2025.

White, James Terry (ed.), *National Cyclopedia of American Biography*, 63 vols (New York: James T. White & Co., 1893–)

White, Lonnie J., 'Arkansas Territorial Indian Affairs', *Arkansas Historical Quarterly*, 21:3 (962), pp.193–212

White, Henry Alexander, *Southern Presbyterian Leaders* (New York: Neale Publishing, 1911)

Williams, Flora McDonald, *The Glengarry McDonalds of Virginia* (Louisville: Geo. G. Fetter, 1911)

Williams, Gary S., *'No Man Knows This Country Better': The Frontier Life of John Gibson* (Akron: University of Akron Press, 2022)

Williams, Glenn F., *Dunmore's War: The Last Conflict of America's Colonial Era* (Yardley, Pa.: Westholme, 2012)

Williams, Nancy A. (ed.), *Arkansas Biography: A Collection of Notable Lives* (Fayetteville: University of Arkansas Press, 2000)

Wilson, Howard McKnight, *The Tinkling Spring: Headwater of Freedom* (Fishersville, Va.: Tinkling Spring and Hermitage Presbyterian Churches, 1954)

Winegard, Timothy, *The Mosquito: A Human History of Our Deadliest Predator* (New York: Dutton, 2019)

Winkler, John F., *Peckuwe, 1780: The Revolutionary War on the Ohio River Frontier* (Oxford: Osprey Publishing, 2018)

Winkler, John F., *Wabash 1791* (Oxford: Osprey Publishing, 2011)

Withers, Alexander S., *Chronicles of Border Warfare* (Cincinnati: R. Clarke, 1895)

Wolfe, William W., *History of Keyser, West Virginia, 1737–1913* (Place unknown: Keyprint, 1974), p.3.

Wood, Robert, 'Early Church Schools', *The Goschenhoppen Historians*, <goschenhoppen.org/early-church-schools>, accessed 28 Nov. 2023

Woodman, Henry, *The History of Valley Forge* (Oaks, Pa.: John U. Francis, Sr., 1922)

Woods, Leonora W., 'The Old Northwestern Turnpike', *The Hampshire Review*, 20 Jan. 1937

Wright, Robert K., Jr., *The Continental Army* (Washington: U.S. Army, 1983)

Wust, Klaus, 'Disaffection in the Rear: German Tories in the West Virginia Mountains', *The Report: A Journal of German-American History*, 36 (1975), pp.66–73

Wust, Klaus, *The Virginia Germans* (Charlottesville: University Press of Virginia, 1969)

Young, Andrew W., *History of Wayne County, Indiana* (Cincinnati: Robert Clarke & Co., 1872)

Zambone, Albert Louis, *Daniel Morgan: A Revolutionary Life* (Yardley: Westholme, 2018)

Zielinski, Adam E., 'Robert Morris: The Financier of the Revolution', *American Battlefields Trust*, <battlefields.org/learn/articles/robert-morris-financier-american-revolution>, accessed 19 June 2024

Zimmerman, Colin, 'A Study in Sustainability: The Continental Encampment in Bucks County, December 1776', *JAR*, 20 July 2023, <allthingsliberty.com/2023/07/a-study-in-sustainability-the-continental-encampment-in-bucks-county-december-1776/>, accessed 23 July 2023

Index

From Reason to Revolution – Warfare 1721-1815

http://www.helion.co.uk/series/from-reason-to-revolution-1721-1815.php

The 'From Reason to Revolution' series covers the period of military history 1721–1815, an era in which fortress-based strategy and linear battles gave way to the nation-in-arms and the beginnings of total war.

This era saw the evolution and growth of light troops of all arms, and of increasingly flexible command systems to cope with the growing armies fielded by nations able to mobilise far greater proportions of their manpower than ever before. Many of these developments were fired by the great political upheavals of the era, with revolutions in America and France bringing about social change which in turn fed back into the military sphere as whole nations readied themselves for war. Only in the closing years of the period, as the reactionary powers began to regain the upper hand, did a military synthesis of the best of the old and the new become possible.

The series examines the military and naval history of the period in a greater degree of detail than has hitherto been attempted, and has a very wide brief, with the intention of covering all aspects from the battles, campaigns, logistics, and tactics, to the personalities, armies, uniforms, and equipment.

Submissions

The publishers would be pleased to receive submissions for this series. Please email reasontorevolution@helion.co.uk, or write to Helion & Company Limited, Unit 8 Amherst Business Centre, Budbrooke Road, Warwick, CV34 5WE

You may also be interested in:

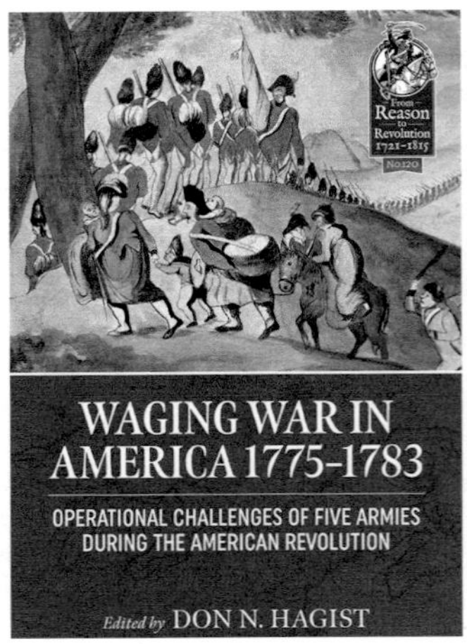

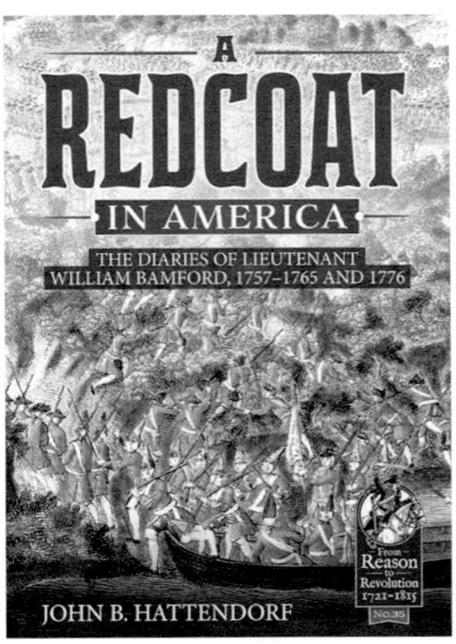

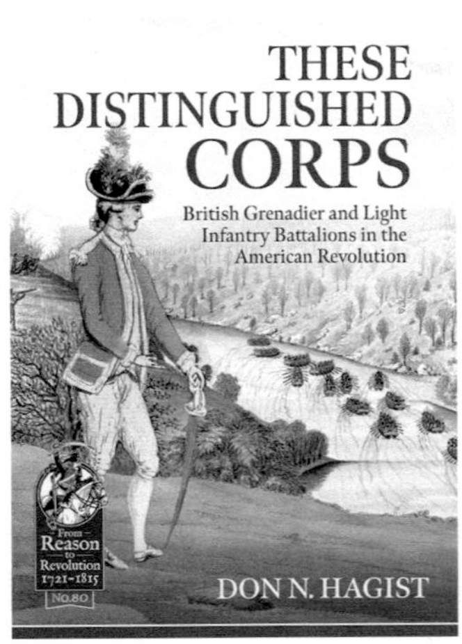